87072
20
MARY IMOGENE BASSETT HOSPITAL
AE038528

THE JOURNAL of PHARMACOLOGY and EXPERIMENTAL THERAPEUTICS

founded by John J. Abel

VOLUME 123

MAY - AUGUST 1958

MARY IMOGENE BASSETT HOSPITAL

Official Publication
of the American Society for Pharmacology and
Experimental Therapeutics Incorporated

Board of Publication Trustees

Chairman: Maurice H. Seevers

Harry Beckman
Louis S. Goodman
Otto Krayer
Lawrence Peters

Editorial Board

Editor: Lawrence Peters

Julius Axelrod
H. L. Borison
Marion de V. Cotten
P. B. Dews
W. W. Douglas
K. P. Dubois
Sydney Ellis
R. F. Furchgott
Avram Goldstein
Harris Isbell
C. J. Kensler
Eva King Killam
Louis Lasagna
N. C. Moran
G. H. Mudge
F. W. Schueler
C. C. Smith
J. L. Strominger
E. W. Sutherland, Jr.
E. Leong Way
T. C. West
L. A. Woods

R. M. Isenberger
Index Editor

BALTIMORE, MARYLAND

REGISTER OF ARTICLES

123:1 May 58

8004 Cardiovascular actions of a bis-isothiourea. L. C. Hendershot.- 1

8005 Effects of vasoconstrictor agents on cardiac irritability. J. L. Gilbert, G. Lange, I. Polevoy, C. McC. Brooks.------------ 9

8006 Pressor effect of histamine in the rabbit.P. Naranjo,E. Banda.- 16

8007 Studies concerning the cardiovascular actions of the central nervous stimulant, methylphenidate.R. A. Maxwell, A. J. Plummer, S. D. Ross, A. I. Daniel.------------------------------ 16 22

8008 Comparative effects of some convulsant drugs on the behavior and electrical activity of the nervous and muscular system of the salamander. J. J. Peters, A. R. Vonderahe, T. H. Powers.- 28

8009 Effects of various phenothiazines on minimal electroshock seizure threshold and spontaneous motor activity of mice. D. H. Tedeschi, J. P. Benigni, C. J. Elder, J. C. Yeager, J. V. Flanigan.-- 35

8010 The effect of reserpine and chlorpromazine on the response of the rat to acute stress. M. Mahfouz, E. A. Ezz.-------------- 39

8011 The binding of d-tubocurarine chloride to plasma proteins. L. Aladjemoff, S. Dikstein, E. Shafrir.------------------------ 43

8012 Comparative pharmacological effects of a number of beta-halogenated pyruvic acids. H. Busch, P. V. Nair, M. Frank, W. R. Martin.-- 48

8013 Effects of certain purines and related compounds on virus propagation. A. C. Hollinshead, P. K. Smith.-------------------- 54

8014 Phenylbutazone metabolites: antirheumatic, sodium-retaining,and uricosuric effects in man. T. F. Yü, J. J. Burns, B. C. Paton, A. B. Gutman, B. B. Brodie.---------------------------------- 63

8015 The passage of thiobarbiturates and their oxygen analogs into brain.L. C. Mark, J. J. Burns, L. Brand, C. I. Campomanes, N. Trousof, E. M. Papper, B. B. Brodie.---------------------- 70

8016 The disulfiram-like activity of animal charcoal. W. C. Clark, H. R. Hulpieu.-- 74

8017 The absorption of drugs from the rat small intestine.L.Schanker, D. J. Tocco, B. B. Brodie, C. A. M. Hogben.----------------- 81

123:2 June 58

8018 Studies on the mechanism of diuretic action of chlorothiazide. R. F. Pitts, F. Kruck, R. Lozano, D. W. Taylor,O. P. A. Heidenreich, R. H. Kessler.------------------------------------ 89

8019 Enzymic and pharmacologic comparison of imidazoleacetylcholine with two related choline esters, murexine and dihydromurexine. I. I. A. Tabachnick, F. E. Roth, J. Mershon, A. A.Rubin, E.T. Eckhardt, W. M. Govier.------------------------------------ 98

8020 The action of pyridylacetylcholine on neuromuscular and ganglionic transmission. A. A. Rubin, J. Mershon, I. I. A. Tabachnick, W. M. Govier.-- 104

8021 A homologous series of soluble n-fatty acid esters(C_2-C_{10}) as substrates for serum cholinesterase. B. H. J. Hofstee.------- 108

MARY IMOGENE BASSETT HOSPITAL

REGISTER OF ARTICLES

123:2 June 58 8022-8039

8022 Differential effects of a quaternary cholinesterase inhibitor, phospholine, and its tertiary analogue, compound 217-AO, on central control of respiration and on neuromuscular transmission. The antagonism by 217-AO of the respiratory arrest caused by morphine. W. Schaumann, C. Job.------------------- 114
8023 An investigation of the structure-activity correlations within a series of ambenonium analogs. A. M. Lands, J. O. Hoppe, A. Arnold, F. K. Kirchner.------------------------------------ 121
8024 Pharmacology of hexahydro-1-azepinepropionamidoxime dihydrochloride (SU-4029). R. A. Maxwell, S. D. Ross, A.J. Plummer.- 128
8025 The pharmacological action of ryanodine on rhythmically contracting mammalian smooth muscle. I. W. Hillyard, L. Procita.- 140
8026 Changes of heart rate caused by direct cardiac action of reserpine. O. Krayer, J. Fuentes.-------------------------------- 145
8027 The release of norepinephrine from the mammalian heart by reserpine. M. K. Paasonen, O. Krayer.------------------------- 153
8028 The effect of temperature upon the positive inotropic action of ouabain. P. R. Saunders, P. N. Sanyal.---------------------- 161
8029 Action of zoxazolamine upon spinal segmental reflexes. L. E. Geiger, P. Cervoni, J. R. Bertino, F. Monteleone.------------ 164

123:3 July 58

8030 Metabolic N- and O-demethylation of morphine- and morphinan-type analgesics. A. E. Takemori, G. J. Mannering.------------ 171
8031 Effects of acrylamide on the central nervous system of the cat. A. S. Kuperman.--- 180
8032 Differential effects on various conditioned responses in cats caused by intraventricular and intramuscular injections of reserpine and other substances. E. R. John, B. M. Wenzel, R. D. Tschirgi.--- 193
8033 Individual differences: I. Correlation between control locomotor activity and sensitivity to stimulant and depressant Dru drugs. S. Irwin, M. Slabok, G. Thomas.---------------------- 206
8034 A study of central nervous system stimulants. G. Chen, B. Bohner. 212
8035 Effects of meprobamate, phenobarbital and dextro-amphetamine on reaction time and learning in man. C. Kornetsky.---------- 216
8036 Comparison of the antipruritic effect of morphine and papaverine in experimental and pathological itch in man. S. G. Macris, G. M. Smith, H. K. Beecher.--------------------------------- 220
8037 Relative hepatotoxicity of seven halogenated hydrocarbons. G. L. Plaa, E. A. Evans, C. H. Hine.------------------------------ 224
8038 Relationship between peripheral cholinolytic potency and tetraethylpyrophosphate antagonism of a series of atropine substitutes. A. G. Karczmar, J. P. Long.-------------------------- 230
8039 Factors affecting the blood pressure response of mammals to the ganglionic blocking agent, chlorisondamine chloride. R. A. Maxwell, A. J. Plummer, S. D. Ross, A. I. Daniel, F. Schneider. 238

MARY IMOGENE BASSETT HOSPITAL

11020

MARY IMOGENE BASSETT HOSPITAL

REGISTER OF ARTICLES

123:4 Aug 58

8040 Reactivation of DFP-inactivated acetylcholinesterase by monoisonitrosoacetone (MINA) and diacetylmonoxime (DAM) in vivo. M. V. Rajapurkar, G. B. Koelle.---------------------------------- 247

8041 The excretion and distribution of meprobamate and its metabolites. S. S. Walkenstein, C. M. Knebel, J. A. Macmullen, J. Seifter.--- 254

8042 Studies on the metabolism of nornicotine in the dog.H.B.Hucker, P. S. Larson.-- 259

8043 Relations between calcium and potassium transfer in human erythrocytes. J. B. Kahn, Jr.--- 263

8044 A statistical evaluation of the relationships among local anesthetic activity, irritancy and systemic toxicity. F. P. Luduena, J. O. Hoppe, J. K. Borland.----------------------------- 269

8045 The cardiovascular and respiratory actions of rauwolscine. B. Levy, G. B. Koelle.--- 278

8046 The mechanism of the hypotensive action of narcotine hydrochloride. L. C. Weaver, W. M. Alexander,B. E. Abreu,A. B. Richards, W. R. Jones, R. W. Begley.------------------------------------ 287

8047 Some pharmacological actions of ryanodine in the mammal. L. Procita.--- 296

8048 Perphenazine, a potent and effective antiemetic. S. C. Wang.--- 306

8049 Carbonic anhydrase inhibition. IX. Augmentation of the renal effect of meralluride by acetazolamide. T. H. Maren.--------- 311

NOTICE

to Subscribers and Readers

Attention is directed to the current method (ACC) of using entry numbers opposite the unit terms and names comprising the Subject and Author sections of the Journal index. These entry numbers coincide with the appropriate accession numbers listed serially at the left of the titles in the Register of Articles. Their purpose is to condense and unify the three parts of the index, and to expedite its use.

For details of the ACC indexing system please see: This Journal, "Index Notices", Vol. 122:2, Jan., and Vol. 122: N1-2, April, 1958.

8004

CARDIOVASCULAR ACTIONS OF A BIS-ISOTHIOUREA

LELAND C. HENDERSHOT

Biochemical Research Laboratory, The Dow Chemical Company, Midland, Michigan

Received for publication January 17, 1958

Bisdiisothioureas elicit both pressor and depressor effects in dogs and cats, the latter effect being due largely to a direct action on vascular smooth muscle (Fastier, 1948), the mechanism of which may be the liberation of histamine (MacIntosh and Paton, 1949).

The potency and availability of one particular

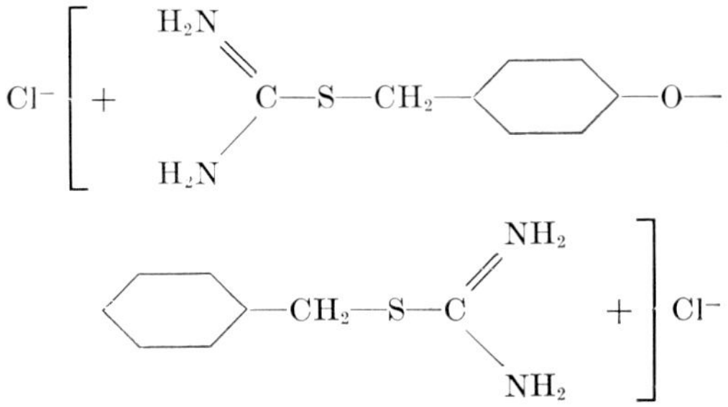

diisothiourea, (2,2′ - oxybis(p - phenylenemethylene)bisisothiourea dihydrochloride), provided a convenient means of gaining further insight into the cardiovascular effects of this type of compound. For convenience, the agent will be referred to as BITU.

METHODS. Mean arterial blood pressure was usually measured from one common carotid artery by means of a conventional mercury manometer recording on smoked kymograph paper. In the leg perfusion experiments and those in which selective injections were made in and about the heart, arterial pressure was recorded from a femoral artery. Unless otherwise noted, anesthesia was produced in dogs by sodium pentobarbital (35 mgm./kgm.) and in cats by Dial-urethane (0.6 ml./kgm.; generously supplied by Ciba Pharmaceutical Products, Inc.). When chloralose anesthesia was employed, 50 to 75 mgm./kgm. of a 10 per cent solution of α-chloralose in warm polyethylene glycol 200 was injected intravenously, being immediately preceded or followed by enough inhaled ether or Fluothane (1,1,1-trifluoro-2-chloro-2-bromothane) vapor to induce sleep. The ganglionic stimulant, DMPP (1,1-dimethyl-4-phenylpiperazinium; generously supplied by Parke-Davis and Co.), was administered in doses of 5 to 10 microgm./kgm.

A Grass stimulator, Model S4B, provided electrical impulses for nerve stimulation. Contractions of the nictitating membrane were obtained by supramaximal stimulation of preganglionic fibers to the superior cervical ganglion (central end of cut vagus in the neck) in cats and dogs and postganglionic fibers in cats. Intraarterial injections were made either by puncturing the common carotid artery close to the superior cervical ganglion with a small gauge needle, through a "T"-cannula placed high in the common carotid artery, or by retrograde injection into the lingual artery after ligation of the occipital, laryngeal and pharyngeal arteries and the external carotid artery cranial to the lingual artery. In these experiments with the nictitating membrane, either chloralose or Dial-urethane anesthesia was employed in the cats and pentobarbital in the dogs.

In the leg perfusion experiments, 2 types of preparations were used: one in which the femoral bed was perfused *via* the carotid artery and external jugular vein of the donor, the other in which the leg was perfused with the dog's own blood (autoperfusion).

In the latter case, the pump (Sigmamator, Model T-6) removed blood from either the femoral or external iliac artery and then returned it to the same vessel. The rate of flow to the leg was thereby kept constant, allowing estimation of vascular resistance in the leg by recording pressure changes from a mercury manometer connected to the pump output tubing. Siliconed tubing was used throughout, being of gum rubber in contact with the pump and polyethylene between pump and blood vessel. The pump was set to deliver 25–50 ml./min. and its tubing volume was 25 ml. Thus, delayed effects were due to direct action on structures in the leg, immediate effects representing reflex actions. Mepesulfate "Roche" (sodium salt of sulfated polygalacturonic acid methyl ester methyl glycoside; Hoffmann-LaRoche, Inc.) was used as an anticoagulant in doses of 40 mgm./kgm. intravenously in these and in the heart-lung experiments.

A continuous record of cardiac output was obtained from the heart lung preparation using the method of Swain (1955) in which a rolling circular manometer (Ueno and Takenaka, 1955) records changes from a differential pressure cannula (Moe, 1949), calibrations being made with the conventional Stolnikov stromuhr connected in series.

Plasma histamine levels were assayed on the guinea pig ileum and the mean arterial pressure of the chloralosed cat (Code and McIntire, 1956). Serial samples of blood were taken with a siliconed syringe and 20-gauge needle containing a small amount of heparin or Mepesulfate. The needle was then removed from the syringe and the blood allowed to run down the wall of a siliconed polyethylene centrifuge tube containing a small amount of anticoagulant. Samples then were centrifuged at 4000 r.p.m. for 15 minutes and the plasma immediately removed from the tube and assayed.

Two per cent stock solutions of BITU were made, using 80 per cent physiological saline—20 per cent propylene glycol as the solvent.

RESULTS. I. *Effect on mean arterial pressure*: In 7 intact anesthetized dogs, intravenous doses of 0.1 mgm./kgm. of BITU produced an average increase in blood pressure of 29.1 (S.E. ± 8.6) mm. of Hg. of 10- to 11-second duration. Doses of 1.0 mgm./kgm. in 17 dogs produced the initial, transient pressor response followed by an average depressor response of 53.8 (S.E. ± 6.4) mm. of Hg. The average duration of the depressor response after 1.0 mgm./kgm. in 6 dogs was 47.8 (S.E. ± 9.3) minutes.

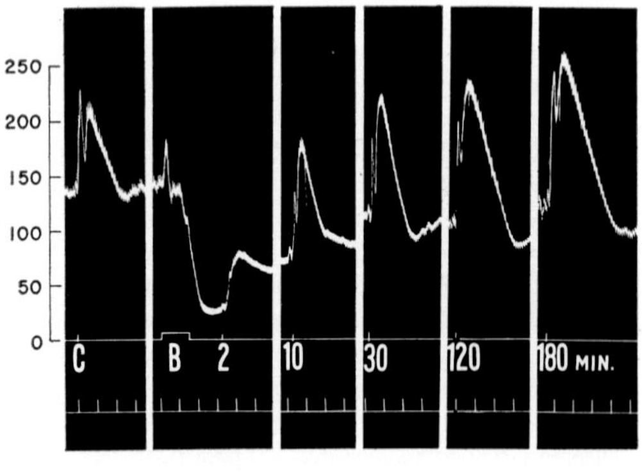

FIG. 1. Potentiation to DMPP induced by BITU.

Dog, pentobarbital anesthesia, carotid arterial blood pressure in mm. Hg, time in minutes. Control intravenous injection of 10 microgm./kgm. of DMPP at "C" followed in 10 min. at "B" by 2.0 mgm./kgm. of BITU intravenously. Successive 10 microgm./kgm. doses of DMPP given at 2, 10, 30, 120 and 180 min. Note early blockade of DMPP followed by progressive development of potentiation.

Neither the hypertensive nor the hypotensive response to intravenously administered BITU in dogs is blocked by vagotomy (6 experiments), alone or in combination with carotid sinus denervation (2 experiments), or by cervical spinal cord section (2 experiments), 2.0 mgm./kgm. of atropine (14 experiments), or 2.0 mgm./kgm. of diphenhydramine (4 experiments). Hexamethonium (2.0 mgm./kgm.; 5 dogs) and chlorisondamine (0.2 mgm./kgm.; 1 dog) block the pressor but not the depressor response. After high spinal anesthesia with procaine (2 dogs) or dorsal root rhizotomy (T_1-T_{11}) (1 dog) both the pressor and depressor components were reduced but nonetheless present.

The hypertensive response occurred sooner after injection of 0.1 to 0.2 mgm./kgm. into the left ventricle of the heart, ascending aorta and descending aorta (2 to 4 seconds), than after injection into the superior vena cava (6 to 8 seconds) in 4 open-chested, lightly pentobarbitalized dogs. The pressor response to these small doses was followed by a depressor response, neither of which were abolished by vagotomy.

Following injection of 0.1 to 0.5 mgm./kgm. into the common carotid or brachiocephalic arteries of 7 dogs, a brief (20 to 25 seconds) hypotensive response occurred 8 to 10 seconds after injection (figure 4). The latter was followed (30 to 40 seconds after injection) by the pressor-depressor complex seen after intravenous administration. Neither the timing nor the quality of these responses illustrated in figure 4 are different when injection is made high in the carotid artery, into the brachiocephalic artery, or into the latter when both carotids are clamped. Tachyphylaxis developed to the immediate hypotensive effect following intracarotid or intrabrachiocephalic injection and also to the pressor component.

II. *Potentiation of the pressor responses to DMPP and norepinephrine (racemic)*. After a single intravenous dose of BITU (1.0 to 2.0 mgm./kgm.) the pressor responses to both DMPP and norepinephrine are enhanced in the dog. The duration of this potentiation is greater for DMPP than for norepinephrine. While significant potentiation to norepinephrine disappears sometime between 31 and 60 minutes, that to DMPP seemingly persists for at least 180 minutes. Figure 1 shows potentiation to DMPP.

The data are presented in 3 ways: mean pressor responses to DMPP and norepinephrine

TABLE 1

*Potentiation of DMPP and norepinephrine by BITU**

Agent	Minutes After BITU	No. Expts.	Mean Arterial Pressure†			
			Basal	S.E.‡	Peak Response	S.E.
			mm. Hg		*mm. Hg*	
DMPP	—	16	128.3	±6.4	175.0	±10.6
	2–10	14	68.4	7.1	136.5	13.7
	11–30	12	92.0	8.2	164.3	16.6
	31–60	6	106.8	12.7	183.3	29.8
	61–90	4	105.0	18.9	179.0	33.8
	91–120	4	120.7	6.7	224.2	13.3
	121–180	4	112.2	5.8	241.7	19.0
Norepinephrine	—	10	114.8	6.9	151.0	9.5
	2–10	8	64.7	9.0	124.2	9.0
	11–30	8	75.0	4.5	118.2	9.8
	31–60	4	91.8	15.0	126.5	24.0

* DMPP (1,1-dimethyl-4-phenylpiperazinium), 5.0 to 10.0 microgm./kgm., dose constant in each experiment. Norepinephrine (racemic), 1.0 to 2.0 microgm./kgm., dose constant in each experiment. BITU (2,2′-oxybis(*p*-phenylenemethylene) bisisothiourea), 1.0 to 2.0 mgm./kgm.

† Basal = mean pressure before DMPP or norepinephrine. Peak response = maximum pressure attained after DMPP or norepinephrine.

‡ Standard error of the mean.

before and after BITU; mean change in pressor responses on a mm. of Hg basis; and mean change in pressor responses on a per cent basis (tables 1 and 2). Mean changes and their significance have been calculated from paired comparison data.

III. *The effect on responses to nerve stimulation.* The effect of BITU on the electrically induced contraction of the nictitating membrane was studied in 6 dogs and 11 cats. Ganglionic blockade was not detected, the response to stimulation of the postganglionic fibers of the superior cervical ganglion being blocked equally as well as that to preganglionic stimulation (cats, figure 2A). When the nictitating membrane and blood pressure both have been depressed, their recoveries are parallel (figure 2B).

The contraction of the nictitating membrane following the injection of acetylcholine (100 microgm. in 0.1 ml.) or DMPP (50 microgm. in 0.1 ml.) into the arterial blood supply of the superior cervical ganglion (3 cats, 1 dog) is also inhibited by BITU.

IV. *Effect on the femoral arterial bed.* Femoral blood flow was recorded continously by means of a Moe differential pressure cannula (Moe, 1949)

TABLE 2

*Potentiation of DMPP and norepinephrine by BITU**

Agent	Minutes After BITU	No. Expts.	Mean Change in Peak Pressor Response (Paired Comparison)†					
			mm. Hg	S.E.‡	P	Per Cent	S.E.	P
DMPP	2–10	14	↑21.6	±5.6	<0.002	↑71.2§	±16.3	<0.001
	11–30	12	↑31.1	8.4	<0.007	↑49.2	15.3	<0.01
	31–60	6	↑37.6	12.9	<0.001	↑36.8	12.2	<0.001
	61–90	4	↑30.2	6.0	<0.02	↑35.0	10.7	>0.05
	91–120	4	↑41.0	12.1	<0.05	↑38.8	14.4	>0.05
	121–180	4	↑40.5	13.1	<0.05	↑57.5	28.0	>0.10
Norepinephrine	2–10	8	↑22.7	7.3	<0.02	↑53.3	6.8	<0.001
	11–30	8	↑13.1	2.9	<0.005	↑29.8	6.4	<0.002
	31–60	4	↓8.8	2.8	>0.05	↓5.0	4.3	>0.3

* DMPP (1,1-dimethyl-4-phenylpiperazinium), 5.0 to 10.0 microgm./kgm., dose constant in each experiment. Norepinephrine (racemic), 1.0 to 2.0 microgm./kgm., dose constant in each experiment. BITU (2,2′-oxybis(*p*-phenylenemethylene)bisisothiourea), 1.0 to 2.0 mgm./kgm.

† The individual blood pressure changes (mm. Hg and per cent) were determined for each injection of DMPP and norepinephrine. The difference (d) between the pressure change before (C_b) and after (C_a) BITU was calculated ($d = C_a - C_b$) and the mean of all the differences in a given time period determined for n experiments ($d_1 + d_2 + d_3 \ldots \div n = \bar{x}$). Fisher's "t" was calculated from the formula (Davies, 1949): $t = \bar{x}\sqrt{\frac{n(n-1)}{Sx^2}}$ where Sx^2 = Sum of the squares of the deviations from the mean difference.

‡ Standard error of the mean.

§ Arrows: upward deflection = increase; downward deflection = decrease.

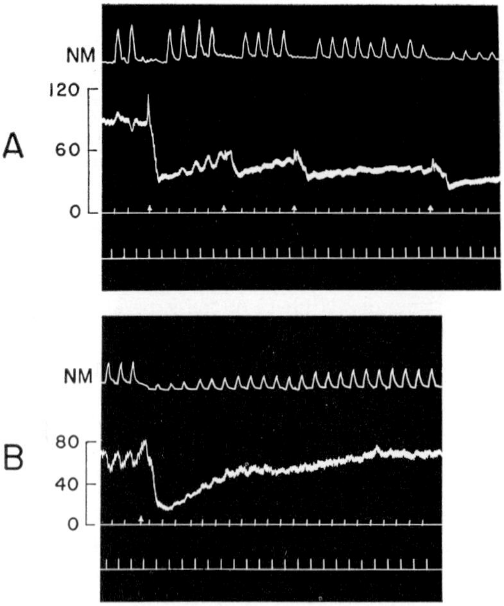

FIG. 2. Contractions of the nictitating membrane (NM) and mean arterial blood pressure in mm. Hg in cats anesthetized with Dial-urethane. Intravenous injections of BITU given at arrows. Times in minutes. A: Alternate preganglionic and postganglionic stimulation of superior cervical ganglion fibers. At arrows, four doses of BITU of 3.0, 1.0, 1.0 and 2.0 mgm./kgm. intravenously in that order. The effects of postganglionic stimulation are blocked equally as well as those of preganglionic stimulation. B: Nictitating membrane contractions elicited by preganglionic stimulation. Single dose of 3.0 mgm./kgm. of BITU intravenously reduced blood pressure and nictitating membrane contractions, both of which show parallel recovery.

connected to a circular manometer (Swain, 1955) in 3 dogs. The rate of flow was increased for about 30 seconds following a dose of 0.1 to 0.2 mgm. of BITU intraarterially. The duration of response was about one minute following a dose of 1.0 mgm. Neither the dilator responses to the intraarterial injection of 0.2 microgm. of epinephrine or 1.0 microgm. of acetylcholine nor the constrictor effect of 5.0 microgm. of epinephrine were altered by the previous administration of BITU.

Further studies on the action of BITU on the femoral vascular bed were conducted on dogs whose legs were perfused through the femoral artery by a pump, either with their own femoral arterial blood (autoperfusion; 5 experiments) or cross circulated *via* the carotid artery and external jugular vein of the donor dog (3 experiments). Prior to perfusion the legs were severed, preserving only the bone, sciatic and femoral nerves and as many of the nerves in the subcutaneous tissue as possible. Resistance in the leg was measured from the output tubing of the pump by means of a mercury manometer. The volume of the tubing was 25 ml. and the pump was set to deliver 25 to 50 ml./min.

Intravenous administration of BITU in an autoperfusion preparation with intact leg innervation results in an immediate drop in arterial pressure with a simultaneous decrease in leg resistance. The simultaneous drop in resistance in the femoral bed, as well as the fact that this response is blocked by hexamethonium, suggest that a reflex mechanism is involved.

After cutting the main trunks of the sciatic and femoral nerves and all of the subcutaneous nerve fibers, the drop in leg resistance following BITU administration occurs after a slight lag period (circulation time thru the pump) rather than simultaneously with the arterial pressure decline. The latter results suggest a direct effect on the femoral bed.

A similar delay occurs when BITU is injected intravenously into the donor animal in a cross-circulation experiment, while intravenous administration to the recipient dog with intact leg innervation results in an immediate response paralleling the arterial pressure response (figure 3). Thus, both a reflex and a direct vasodilation occur following the intravenous administration of BITU.

The magnitude of the response in the perfused leg to a given dose of BITU varies with the condition of the preparation. When vascular tone is high the response is greater than when tone is low. Thus, the relief of tone by denervation results in a diminished absolute response.

Potentiation of the reflex responses to both DMPP and norepinephrine occur parallel with that on the blood pressure. BITU enhanced the reflex vasodilatory phase (reduced leg resistance) of the DMPP response in 3 dogs by an average 21 mm. of Hg (22 per cent). The reflex decrease in leg resistance following intravenously administered norepinephrine was likewise enhanced in 2 of 3 dogs tested (18 mm. of Hg, 20 per cent).

The reflex vasoconstriction which precedes the hypotensive responses was studied in 5 lightly pentobarbitalized dogs with open chests. Autoperfusion of the hind limb was accomplished by cannulation of the external iliac artery. The skin

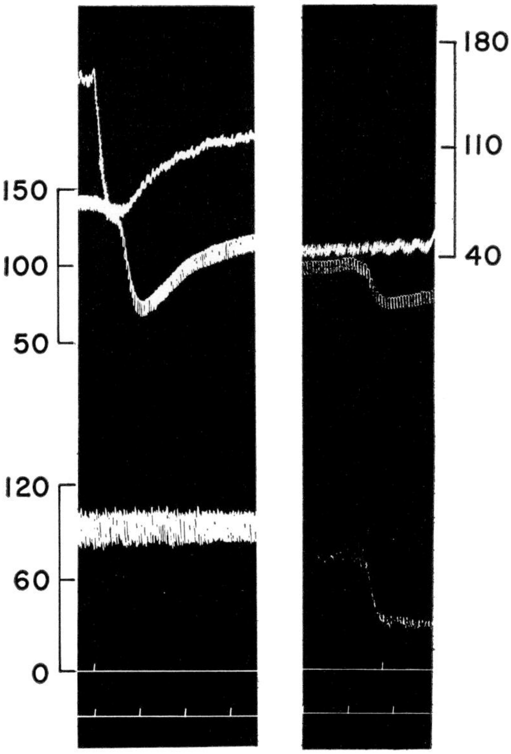

FIG. 3. Direct and reflex vasodilatation caused by BITU in the cross-perfused hind limb of the dog.

Pentobarbital anesthesia. Recording from the top down: mean arterial pressure of donor dog (scale on upper right); vascular resistance in perfused leg of recipient estimated by manometric pressure recording from pump output tubing (scale on upper left); mean arterial pressure of recipient (scale on lower left). Pump delivery: 50 ml./min.; pump tubing volume: 25 ml. Pressures in mm. Hg. Time in minutes. Records are from 2 separate experiments. Left: Intravenous administration of 1.0 mgm./kgm. of BITU into donor dog. Direct vasodilatory effect of BITU on the perfused limb begins after the blood pressure drop in the donor animal. Right: Intravenous administration of 1.0 mgm./kgm. of BITU into recipient dog. Mean arterial blood pressure drop in recipient dog with simultaneous reflex vasodilatation in the innervated perfused leg.

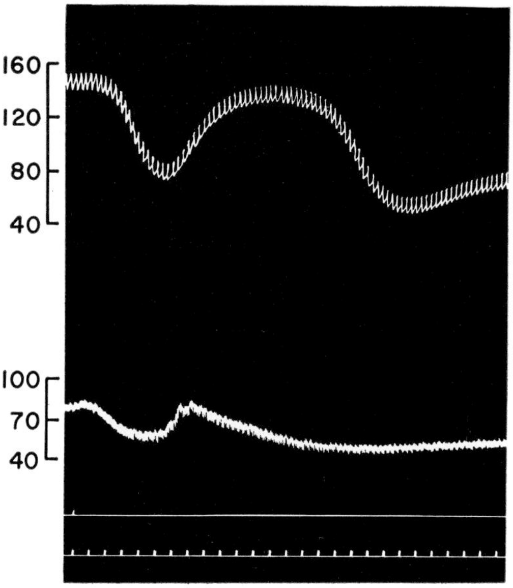

FIG. 4. Central and peripheral effects of BITU. Dog anesthetized lightly with pentobarbital. Above: Vascular resistance in mm. of Hg in hind limb autoperfused through external iliac artery. Below: Mean arterial pressure in mm. of Hg. Time = 5 sec. At signal, 0.5 mgm./kgm. of BITU injected into the carotid artery. Initial hypotension by an action in the head is accompanied by reflex vasodilatation in the leg. The pressor response which follows when BITU reaches the peripheral circulation is accompanied by reflex vasoconstriction in the leg. The mean arterial pressure then drops but leg resistance does not drop until BITU has had time to reach the leg to produce its direct effect, *i.e.* 35 sec. after reaching peripheral circulation. Pump output, 40 ml./min.; tubing capacity of pump, 25 ml.

and leg muscles were not severed. Small doses of BITU (0.1 to 0.2 mgm./kgm.) were injected into the heart, large vessels near the heart, or the carotid artery in the neck. Reflex vasoconstriction in the leg accompanied by hypertension elicited by injection of BITU into the left ventricle, ascending aorta and descending aorta occurred sooner (2 to 4 seconds) than when the injection was into the superior vena cava (6 to 8 seconds). Reflex vasodilatation and hypotension then followed the constrictor effect. Intracarotid injection resulted in hypotension accompanied by reflex vasodilatation in the leg followed by hypertension and reflex vasoconstriction. In any case, when the dose was large enough (0.5 to 1.0 mgm./kgm.) an additional direct vasodilator effect occurred when sufficient time had elapsed for the BITU to reach the leg (figure 4). The reflex vasoconstriction, like the reflex vasodilatation, is blocked by hexamethonium.

The duration of the reflex responses are short: 10 to 20 seconds for vasoconstriction and 2 to 4 minutes for vasodilatation. The direct vasodilator effect is longer, and, in a good preparation, approximates, but does not quite attain, the duration of action on the mean arterial pressure.

Thus, the effect of intravenously administered BITU on the mean arterial pressure is a composite of at least 3 separate actions: reflex vasoconstriction, reflex vasodilatation and direct vasodilatation. The direct effect is of longer duration than the reflex actions. Whether or not the reflex vasodilatation following intravenous injection is due only to an action in the head was not determined, but reflex vasodilatation does occur immediately after intraarterial injection into the head circulation.

V. *Assay of plasma histamine.* In view of the fact that diisothioureas have been reported to produce blood pressure effects suggestive of histamine release in cats (MacIntosh and Paton, 1949), the plasma of 3 dogs treated with BITU was assayed on the guinea pig ileum and that of 3 dogs and 3 cats on the mean arterial pressure of chloralosed cats. No histamine release was detected in the plasma of animals which had received one or more doses of 2.0 to 3.0 mgm./kgm. These doses are quite adequate to produce marked hypotension. It was only when lethal or near lethal doses were administered that histamine was detected in the plasma of the circulating blood. In the latter cases, by cat assay, the plasma of 1 dog (5.0 mgm./kgm. of BITU) contained 0.33 microgm. of histamine base per ml., that of 1 cat (7.0 mgm./kgm. of BITU) 0.08 microgm./ml. Furthermore, hemolysis occurred in both dog and cat blood following such large doses even though physiological saline solutions of BITU were used. Thus, cell wall destruction following large doses of BITU may account for the high histamine levels.

The guinea pig ileum preparations used responded to 0.01 to 0.02 microgm. of histamine base and the chloralosed cats to doses as small as 0.05 microgm. While 0.25-ml. samples of plasma taken from a dog treated with Compound 48/80 gave positive assays in the cat, as much as 3.0 ml. of plasma from dogs or cats receiving 2.0 to 3.0 mgm./kgm. of BITU gave negative or questionable assays. Therefore, it appears unlikely that high plasma histamine levels are significantly responsible for the circulatory effects produced by reasonable doses of BITU.

VI. *Effect on the heart.* Changes in heart rate following intravenous doses of 1.0 mgm./kgm. of BITU are not remarkable. One of 3 dogs developed transient tachycardia immediately after injection (from 138 to 216 beats/min.) and 2 of 3 dogs developed moderate bradycardia 2 minutes after injection (from 198 to 168 and from 168 to 138 beats/min. respectively). Even when the arterial pressure first reaches zero following a lethal dose, heart rate is not seriously impaired (100 to 130 beats/min.).

No abnormalities in the electrocardiogram were seen in 3 animals receiving multiple doses of BITU until lethal levels were reached. Extrasystoles and T-wave depression appeared just before death.

In the dog heart-lung preparation (3 experiments) single doses as high as 20 mgm. injected into the venous inflow to the heart in a volume of 1.0 ml. did not alter cardiac output. The second and third doses of 20 mgm. resulted in a moderately lowered cardiac output, but in one experiment a total of 112 mgm. of BITU was administered without causing a diminution of cardiac output. However, the ability of the heart to compensate to a rise in the height of the venous reservoir of 5 to 10 cm. was decreased by a single dose of 20 mgm. of BITU. After 3 or 4 doses, given 7 to 15 minutes apart, compensation was seriously impaired and irreversible failure occurred. It is unlikely that, with the doses used to produce hypotension in the intact animal, cardiac output was lowered by an action of BITU on the heart. Decreased cardiac output in the intact animal by virtue of decreased venous return remains a possibility.

Discussion. The numerous actions of the isothioureas render them interesting objects of study but collectively comprise a rather complex pharmacological picture. It is fairly clear from previous work, especially by Fastier (1948) and Fastier and Reid (1948), that the structure-activity relationships of the monoisothioureas and the diisothioureas are based mainly on the groupings attached to the isothiourea moiety. Larger groupings (*e.g.* n-hexyl) on the sulfur of the monoisothioureas or separating the two sulfurs of the diisothioureas are likely to make the compound more relaxant and less excitant than smaller groupings (*e.g.* methylene), which produce the opposite effect. Thus, it comes as no surprise that BITU produces mainly depressor effects but also possesses a pressor action.

That the isothioureas possess a direct action on vascular smooth muscle has been unequivocally demonstrated by Fastier (1948), and, in the present study, BITU has been shown to be no exception. But, while it causes direct vasodilator effects in the perfused hind limb of the dog, it also produces reflex vasodilatation. Cutting the sciatic, femoral and remaining cutaneous nerves abolishes this reflex vasodilatation.

In summarizing the data obtained in studying these reflex effects, it is well to keep in mind the following. 1) The hypotension and accompanying reflex vasodilatation always follow the hypertension and simultaneous reflex vasoconstriction when the intravenous route is used. But the sequence of events is reversed when BITU is injected in the carotid or brachiocephalic arteries. Thus, at least part of the reflex vasodilatation arises from the head region. 2) Both the hypertensive spike and reflex vasoconstriction in the leg occur sooner after injection into the left ventricle, ascending aorta or descending aorta (2 to 4 seconds), than after injection into the superior vena cava (6 to 8 seconds). Thus, the receptors for this vasoconstrictor reflex are probably not in the lungs. At least some of them are distal to the aortic arch, but these observations do not preclude the possibility of some being in the coronary bed, ascending aorta or aortic arch. 3) The reflex vasodilatory effects originating in the head do not occur appreciably sooner with injection in the carotid artery high in the neck than into the brachiocephalic artery. Nor are the timing or quality of the response to injection into the brachiocephalic artery altered when both carotids are clamped. Furthermore, denervation of the carotid sinus area does not modify the response to intravenous injection. Thus, the carotid bifurcation likely is not primarily involved. 4) Arterial pressure changes do not correlate well with heart rate; the latter may or may not change following moderate doses of BITU. 5) Since the pressor response is still present after dorsal root rhizotomy or during spinal anesthesia, and since both reflex vasoconstrictor and reflex vasodilator responses are blocked by hexamethonium, it is quite possible that these are ganglionic effects, at least in part.

Thus, the evidence at hand indicates that the reflex vasoconstriction and perhaps some reflex vasodilation caused by intravenously injected BITU are due to actions on peripheral autonomic pathways, probably ganglia, and that some vasodilator receptors for BITU reside in the head. However, the responses to electrical stimulation of pre- and postganglionic fibers of the superior cervical ganglion appear to be blocked equally well by BITU. But, a direct vasodilator mechanism is present also, and brief ganglionic actions would be difficult to detect without more refined techniques.

In the pithed rat hind quarter preparation, Fastier and Reid (1948) have demonstrated sensitization to epinephrine following treatment with a variety of isothioureas. With some of the higher homologues (*e.g.* n-hexylisothiourea; hexamethylene diisothiourea) sensitization was preceded by desensitization in their studies. The sensitization to DMPP in the present study is long lasting and more pronounced than that to norepinephrine. It is possible, nevertheless, that norepinephrine released by DMPP-induced ganglionic stimulation may be the agent to which sensitization occurs rather than to DMPP itself. Interestingly, Page and McCubbin (1956) have demonstrated an enhanced DMPP response following histamine in dogs. Further, small doses of histamine have been shown to potentiate both electrically induced ganglionic transmission (Trendelenburg, 1955) and the stimulating effects of chemical compounds (*e.g.* acetylcholine) on perfused sympathetic ganglia (Konzett, 1952). Since the isothioureas resemble histamine somewhat, both pharmacologically and chemically (Fastier, 1949), the similarity may extend to enhancement of ganglionic transmission.

The question of the significance of histamine being released in detectable quantities by large doses of BITU remains puzzling. If lethal or near lethal doses must administered to produce histamine release, the latter may be merely a manifestation of the toxicity of large doses. However, the localized release of amounts of histamine which are too small to raise significantly the level of histamine in the plasma may well be an important mechanism of action.

SUMMARY

Prolonged hypotension occurs after the intravenous administration of 2,2′-oxybis (*p*-phenylenemethylene)bis-isothiourea (BITU). Brief hypertension precedes the hypotension.

The hypertension is accompanied by reflex vasoconstriction and the hypotension by brief reflex vasodilatation in the perfused hind limb of of the dog. Reflex vasoconstriction is probably due to ganglionic effects; reflex vasodilatation is due, at least in part, to an action in the head. A more persistent vasodilator action is also seen and is attributed to a direct effect on the vasculature.

Cardiac output is not reduced in the dog heart-lung preparation by large doses of BITU but responses to increased right atrial pressure are impaired. In the intact animal, the electrocardiogram remains normal until just before death.

BITU potentiates the actions of norepinephrine and DMP (P1,1′-dimethyl-4-phenylpiperazinium).

A rise in plasma histamine levels was not detected in dogs or cats which had received doses of BITU large enough to cause marked hypotension. Following lethal or near lethal doses, plasma levels of histamine were increased.

REFERENCES

Code, C. F., and McIntire, F. C.: Methods of Biochemical Analysis, pp. 49–96, Vol. III, Interscience Publishers, Inc., New York, 1956.

Davies, O. L.: Statistical Methods in Research and Production, p. 58, Oliver and Boyd, London, 1949.

Fastier, F. N.: Brit. J. Pharmacol., **3:** 198, 1948.

Fastier, F. N.: Brit. J. Pharmacol., **4:** 315, 1949.

Fastier, F. N., and Reid, C. S. W.: Brit. J. Pharmacol., **3:** 205, 1948.

Konzett, H.: J. Mt. Sinai Hosp., **19:** 149, 1952.

MacIntosh, F. C., and Paton, W. D. M.: J. Physiol., **109:** 190, 1949.

Moe, G. K.: Science, **109:** 381, 1949.

Page, I. H., and McCubbin, J. W.: Am. J. Physiol., **184:** 265, 1956.

Swain, H. H.: Univ. Michigan M. Bull., **21:** 411, 1955.

Trendelenburg, U.: J. Physiol., **129:** 337, 1955.

Ueno, A., and Takenaka, F.· Jap. J Pharmacol. **4:** 98, 1955.

8005

EFFECTS OF VASOCONSTRICTOR AGENTS ON CARDIAC IRRITABILITY[1]

J. L. GILBERT, G. LANGE, I. POLEVOY AND C. McC. BROOKS

Department of Physiology, State University of New York, College of Medicine at New York City

Received for publication January 8, 1958

Although epinephrine has been known for about fifty years and, shortly after its discovery, Barger and Dale (1910) reported on the action of 57 adrenergic amines, it was not until the resolution of the racemic form of epinephrine and the resulting availability of levarterenol in 1948 that interest was really stimulated in the use of these amines as vasoconstrictor agents. Since that time there has been a rapid growth in their popularity, chiefly in two specific therapeutic areas: prevention of hypotension in spinal anesthesia, and the treatment of cardiogenic shock resulting from myocardial infarction.

Ideally, for these purposes, it is desirable to have a drug with strong peripheral vasoconstrictor action but with no effect on the excitability of the heart. Probably no such ideal drug exists at the present time although a number of compounds are in popular usage. In spite of the frequent employment of such drugs as levarterenol, methoxamine and mephentermine, and the numerous reports of their actions (reference to these is given later) it seemed to us that basic research on the effects of these drugs on cardiac excitability could be expanded, particularly since they are so often used in situations of the utmost gravity. It was therefore decided to study various vasopressor agents utilizing techniques developed by this department in its previous investigations of cardiac excitability and responsiveness or general irritability (Brooks *et al.*, 1955). The term irritability is used here in the broad sense to include consideration of effects on the threshold to stimulation, conduction time, the speed of recovery after excitation, duration of refractoriness, production of multiple instead of single responses to test stimuli and intrinsic rhythmicity.

METHODS. Mongrel dogs were anesthetized with pentobarbital and the heart exposed by opening the chest under artifical respiration. The sinoauricular node was then crushed and the heart driven by stimuli applied through an auricular electrode at a rate of 172 per minute (350 msec. cycle). When this rate was too slow to prevent action of intrinsic pacemakers, as proved to be the case when epinephrine and mephentermine were infused, a rate of 200 per minute was employed. A stimulating electrode for testing ventricular excitability was attached to the right ventricle. The testing stimulators were triggered with relation to the sweep and the driving stimulator. In the usual experiment, a suction electrode (Wiggers, 1937) was placed on the ventricle together with a standard bipolar pick-up electrode. By use of the latter electrode alone a standard electrogram was obtained and observed by means of an oscilloscope or recorded by a two-channel electrograph. The suction electrode and one pole of the other pick-up electrode were used to obtain a monophasic action potential which was also recorded on the oscilloscope and photographed. A full description of this electrical apparatus is given in the monograph by Brooks *et al.* (1955). Electrocardiographic recordings were also made with bipolar extremity leads. By use of these methods it was possible to determine diastolic threshold from amperage requirements for 3-msec. rectangular pulse stimuli, duration of the absolute and relative refractory periods from the strength interval curves which were obtained, latency of response, time course of the action potential, occurrence of spontaneous beats or multiple responses to test stimuli and changes in atrioventricular conduction. In some experiments additional electrodes were placed on auricle and ventricle to permit determination of conduction time within both chambers. The vagi were cut in all experiments. Blood pressure was recorded from the femoral artery. The effects of drugs on intrinsic (nonsinus) pacemaker action were ascertained by turning off the driving stimulator and observing the rates of ectopic auricular and/or ventricular pacemakers. Determinations of this nature were made before, during and after infusion of the drugs studied.

The drugs, levarterenol,[2] methoxamine,[3]

[1] This work was supported in part by a grant from the Life Insurance Medical Research Fund.

[2] Levarterenol was furnished through the courtesy of the Sterling Winthrop Research Institute.

[3] Methoxamine (Vasoxyl) was furnished through the courtesy of Burroughs Wellcome and Company.

mephentermine[4] and epinephrine were administered by intravenous infusion and in the following concentrations: epinephrine 30 microgm./ml.; levarterenol 2.5 microgm./ml.; mephentermine 500 microgm./ml.; methoxamine 200 microgm./ml. The speed of the infusion was governed solely by the blood pressure response and not by any preconceived estimation of dosage. The blood pressure of the animal usually averaged 80 to 90 mm. Hg at the beginning of the control period, having become somewhat hypotensive as a result of the surgery performed. The drugs were infused at rates which raised the pressure 30 to 50 mm. Hg. In some experiments these pressures were maintained for short periods of about 20 to 30 minutes, then permitted to fall. Infusion was again begun after certain control levels were reached. In other experiments the drug was given continuously for two hours or more, the speed of injection being changed if necessary to maintain the blood pressure at levels between 120 to 140 mm. Hg.

RESULTS. *Effects on arterial pressure.* An interesting corollary of this study of cardiac irritability was the observed difference in the abilities of these drugs to maintain the blood pressure once raised, or to elevate it again after it had been allowed to return to control levels or below. Every one of the four drugs exhibited some degree of tachyphylaxis in effects on arterial pressure, a quality previously noted by others. For example, levarterenol which was made up in a solution containing 2.5 microgm./ml. and injected at rates of 2 to 6 microgm. per minute in dogs weighing between 11 and 16 kgm. showed a slight tachyphylaxis. When a second such dose was given after a period (20 to 60 minutes) of recovery from the first a much smaller rise in arterial pressure resulted. During the long term experiments in which the drug was infused for a period of hours, the blood pressure could not be maintained without gradual increases of dose per unit time. In one experiment an initial rate of 32 drops per minute (about 3.7 microgm./min.) raised the blood pressure from 85 to 130 mm. Hg. After the drug had been stopped and the animal allowed to recover for the second time, the third administration of drug was begun. This was two hours after the beginning of the experiment. At that time a rate of 80 drops per minute or about 6 microgm. per minute was necessary to maintain a blood pressure of 130 mm. Hg.

Epinephrine was given in initial doses of 15 to 30 microgm./min. using a solution of 30 microgm./ml. concentration. In all experiments there was consistent tachyphylaxis, frequently requiring a doubling of the initial rate of drug infusion in order to maintain the desired blood pressure level.

Methoxamine was given at an initial rate varying between 0.5 to 2 mgm./min. Definite tachyphylaxis was noted in 3 out of 4 experiments.

Mephentermine was administered at rates of 1 to 5 mgm./min. This drug exhibited the greatest degree of tachyphylaxis of those tested both in regard to the efficacy of second and third doses and in respect to maintaining pressure over a prolonged period with one continuous administration.

The above observations serve to indicate the procedures which we followed and at the same time call attention to the difficulties encountered in maintaining normotensive or hypertensive blood pressure levels over a long period of time with any of the drugs tested.

Diastolic or resting excitability. Stewart *et al.* (1956) state that voltage thresholds to electrical stimulation of the ventricle were lower in 50 per cent of the animals studied after 3 mgm./kgm. of mephentermine were injected in 1- or 2-ml. volumes into the femoral vein. Siebens *et al.* (1953) noted that epinephrine and levarterenol both produced momentary (3 to 5 min.) decreases in ventricular thresholds. These decreases which were of the order of 10 to 25 per cent were followed by a much more prolonged increase in threshold amounting to between 25 and 50 per cent of the control value. This subnormal excitability lasted up to 30 minutes. In these experiments just mentioned there was no attempt to study effects of continuous administration of drugs.

With our technique the momentary increase in excitability was found with both epinephrine and levarterenol, but the long term effect was a depression. This effect was more clearly demonstrated in the epinephrine experiments (table 1). Methoxamine and mephentermine uniformly produced increases in thresholds. In the case of methoxamine, there was no detectable recovery of excitability while the drug was still being infused, and very little even at the end of its administration. However, the possibility still exists that recovery may occur slowly and only after a

[4] Mephentermine (Wyamine) was furnished through the courtesy of Wyeth Laboratories Inc.

TABLE 1

The effect of vasopressor agents on diastolic threshold, the absolute refractory period (ARP) and atrioventricular conduction (D-R)[1]

Drug	Exp't	Diastolic threshold			ARP (time after QRS complex)			D-R Interval		
		Control	During drug admin. Effects		Control	During drug admin. Effects		Control	During drug admin. Effects	
			Initial	Ultimate		Initial	Ultimate		Initial	Ultimate
		mA	*mA*	*mA*	*msec.*	*msec.*	*msec.*	*msec.*	*msec.*	*msec.*
Epinephrine	#17	0.70	0.65	0.80	145	120		120	110	120
	#18				155	130		180	150	>180
	#19	0.28	0.22	0.38	132	120		120	115	120
Levarterenol	#1	0.16		0.19	130	110		145	120	
	#2	0.28	0.22		150	120		125	95	
	#11	0.25		0.37	170	150				
	#15	0.80		1.50	155	130		150	135	
Mephentermine	#9				150	140	150	160	140	150
	#14	0.32		0.42	155	135		145	135	150
	#23	0.29	0.22	1.10	140	120		150	130	170
	#24	0.48		0.67	130	118	128	150	140	170
	#25	0.36		0.62	145	130	140	116	110	135
Methoxamine	#12	0.21		0.60	160		170	145		190
	#13	0.15		0.30	170	165	170	130		170
	#20	0.27		0.50	135		150	120		170
	#21	0.35		0.85	150	140	155	175		315

[1] The D-R figures are measured from the artefact of the auricular driving stimulus to the beginning of the ventricular R wave of the electrogram.

long drug-free period. Mephentermine produced a similar situation though a partial recovery was observed after the drug was discontinued. In one experiment with mephentermine a second dose produced far less effect on threshold than did the first (a change of threshold of from 0.34 to 0.37 milliamp. as compared to the initial change of from 0.32 to 0.42 milliamp.) indicating the possibility of tachyphylaxis. However the evidence is insufficient to enable conclusions to be drawn with respect to excitability tachyphylaxis.

All the drugs tested can certainly be said to decrease resting excitability, except for the initial momentary opposite effects of epinephrine and levarterenol. For a summary of the data see table 1.

Absolute refractory period. For many years the study of changes in the refractory period has also been considered an extremely important aspect to any investigation of cardiac excitability. In recent years it has been realized that 1) refractoriness can change quite independently of other parameters such as conduction and resting thresholds and 2) that the relationship between changes in refractoriness and susceptibility to arrhythmias is by no means the simple one first supposed and in fact at times there may be none at all (Gilbert *et al.*, 1951).

Stewart *et al.* (1956), by determining the fastest rate of electrical stimulation which the ventricle would follow, found decreases in refractory period with mephentermine. Siebens *et al.* (1953) also found moderate shortening of refractoriness in both auricle and ventricle with epinephrine and levarterenol. Our results were in general confirmatory. Epinephrine shortened the ventricular absolute refractory period (ARP) by 12 to 25 msec. (9 to 17 per cent), though there was some difficulty in maintaining this shortening with continuation of the same dose. Levarterenol shortened the ARP by 20 to 50 msec. (12 to 30

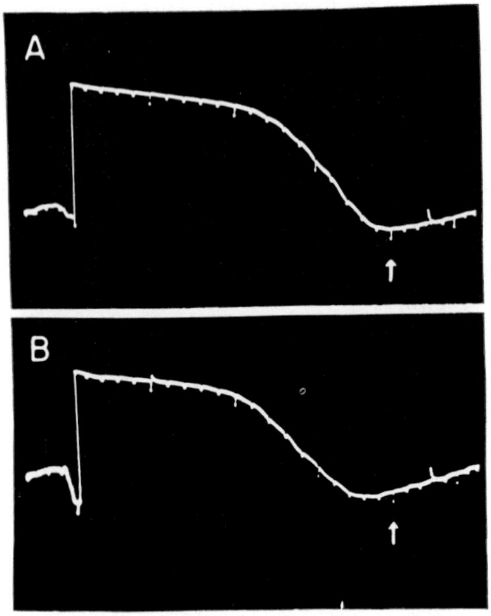

FIG. 1. Shortening in monophasic action potential (B) produced by levarterenol.
Arrows indicate marker at 200 msec. after beginning of potential. A is the control.

per cent). In both cases recovery occurred promptly when the drug was stopped and the shortening could be easily reproduced with readministration. Mephentermine also decreased the ventricular ARP 10 to 20 msec. but only for a short time. There was a return in almost all cases to the control value while the drug was still being administered. Higher infusion rates only speeded up the reversal. This observation casts doubt on any explanation of this drug's salutary action based on its ability to shorten the refractory period. Methoxamine produced the least marked or consistent change in duration of refractoriness, the general tendency being slight lengthening particularly with prolonged or second administration.

Effects on the action potential were somewhat similar qualitatively and even quantitatively to the above. We measured the total action potential as shown (fig. 1). Since the monophasic cardiac action potential shows definite phases, an overshoot, plateau and terminal phase of quick repolarization (Wiggers, 1937; Brooks *et al.*, 1955) it was felt that determination of the effects of the vasoconstrictor agents on these phases would be instructive. However, measurement of the small changes occurring in the various phases of the potential could not be made with sufficient accuracy because of the tendency of the action potential to change somewhat in configuration. Therefore only changes in the duration of the total action potential are reported. Epinephrine shortened the action potential by 10 to 35 msec., levarterenol by 20 to 25 msec., mephentermine by 10 to 20 msec. Second doses of mephentermine caused a reversal of this effect. This accords with the changes in duration of refractoriness referred to above. In contrast to the other drugs methoxamine uniformly caused increases in duration of the action potential by 10 to 38 msec. This likewise corresponds to the effects of this drug on the duration of the absolute refractory period. A summary of the data is shown in table 1.

Conduction. Duration of the interval between application of a stimulus and arrival of an impulse at a ventricular pick-up electrode is determined by both latency of response and speed of conduction but chiefly by the latter. The time between the initiation of an impulse by the driving stimulation of the auricle and its arrival at the ventricular recording electrodes was measured and this, as expected, was shortened by both epinephrine and levarterenol; 5 to 30 msec. (4 to 17 per cent) by the former, and 15 to 50 msec. (10 to 25 per cent) by the latter. The shortening induced by epinephrine was not consistently maintained. No further work was done regarding conduction with these two drugs since ample evidence exists that both increase the rate of conduction in the auricle, A-V node and ventricle.

Very interesting results were obtained however with methoxamine and mephentermine. Though methoxamine produced no significant change in auricular or ventricular conduction, it caused a remarkable increase in A-V conduction time, the increase varying from 0.45 to 140 msec. (30 to 100 per cent) (fig. 2). The degree of slowing seemed to be related quantitatively to the dose rate and there was no tachyphylaxis. Recovery occurred after administration of the drug was stopped. This was not a vagal effect since the vagi had been cut during initial surgery, as previously noted.

In the case of mephentermine, the time from auricular drive to recorded ventricular activation was shortened slightly at first (6 to 20 msec. or 5 to 13 per cent). A second dose or a prolonged administration of the drug reversed this trend and produced a lengthening of A-V conduction time by as much as 20 msec., a 13 per cent increase over the original control value. Gradual return towards the control value took place after the drug was stopped. By measuring conduction times to two separate auricular leads (one adjacent and one distant), it was observed that mephentermine produced no significant change in auricular conduction, but did cause an increase in latency of 8 to 10 msec. This conclusion was reached because there was an equal increase in conduction time to both of the electrodes and no indication of decreased rate of conduction between the two. In the ventricle also, a similar procedure showed that mephentermine produced no change in conduction time. There was however, an increased latency of 9 msec. when the test impulse was placed at a point in the cycle close to the ARP border. This increased latency did not occur when the test stimulus fell in diastole. Thus in summary, the long term effect of mephentermine appears to be 1) moderate increase in latency in the auricle, but no change in auricular conduction, 2) slight slowing of A-V conduction, 3) no change in ventricular conduction and 4) increase in latency in the ventricle for a response to a test stimulus placed close to the ARP. Although our procedures showed no change in ventricular conduction it must be noted here that we found, as did Stewart *et al.* (1956), that a single 10-ml. dose (15 mgm./ml.) of mephentermine speeded ventricular conduction.

Cardiac rhythm. Our final observations have to do with 1) spontaneous ectopic activity in both auricle and ventricle while the heart was being driven, 2) abnormal responses to ventricular test stimuli and 3) changes in natural rhythm produced by the drugs when all extrinsic stimuli were discontinued. The results reported were all obtained following the initial crushing of the S-A node.

Of the four drugs tested methoxamine alone produced no spontaneous extrasystoles of either auricular or ventricular origin. Ventricular responses to test stimuli were always single, and when the artificial drive was shut off it was found that there was no increase in pacemaker activity in either the auricle or ventricle.

On the other hand, all three of the remaining drugs frequently produced spontaneous ectopic activity in both auricle and ventricle, and multiple responses following a ventricular test

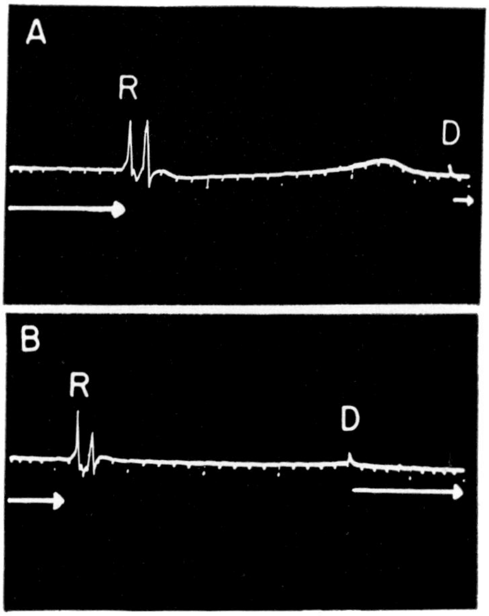

FIG. 2. Records showing A-V conduction time between application of drive stimulus on auricle (artefact at D) to recorded ventricular response (R).

Change in time from control (A) induced by methoxamine is shown in B. Arrows indicate the Drive -R time since D precedes R in time on the continuous sweep. This placement of electrogram (R) at the beginning of the sweep traverse which follows that in which the drive stimulus (D) is shown permitted testing and accurate observation of responses in the entire recovery period following the initial response.

stimulus were not uncommon particularly in the area of the vulnerable period close to the border of the absolute refractory period.

Epinephrine greatly increased ectopic activity in both the auricle and the ventricle. Many spontaneous extrasystoles of ventricular origin were produced. When the drive stimulus was turned off there was pacemaker activity originating in the auricle, though cardiographic evidence indicated that the sino-atrial node had been successfully destroyed. The standard rate of drive (172 per min.) was never enough to dominate the epinephrine-induced pacemaker which appeared to be located in the auricle. In order to artificially drive the heart a rate of 200 per min. was needed. In one experiment removal of epinephrine after a prolonged administration produced auricular fibrillation. This was reversed by the addition of the drug.

Mephentermine at first produced a pacemaker action which exceeded the drive rate of 172 per min. However with prolonged administration or following a second dose of this drug this drive rate was adequate to dominate the heart. A tachyphylactic reaction appears to occur. This drug was found to stimulate ectopic auricular pacemaker activity even though the artificial pacemaker continued to be effective. This effect on pacemaker action was shown by the ECG when the drive was turned off. Spontaneous beats and multiple ventricular responses were noted when testing for changes in the ARP after this drug was administered. Ectopic ventricular activity was frequently seen in association with the abnormal auricular pacemaker activity induced by this drug.

After levarterenol was given, difficulty was occasionally encountered in maintaining auricular drive at the rate of 172 per min. This drug also produced spontaneous extrasystoles in most of the experiments. With the drive shut off there was more of a tendency for a ventricular pacemaker to predominate than with the other drugs. Control gradually reverted to the auricle after the drug was discontinued.

The nature of these experiments does not permit a more precise description of the origins of these abnormal rhythms and their cause. It is certain however, that epinephrine, levarterenol and mephentermine were productive of abnormal spontaneous beats and abnormal responses to test stimuli. Methoxamine had no such effects.

Discussion. It was not the purpose of this work to study the phenomenon of tachyphylaxis but some of our results have bearing on this problem and the interests of others in the changing states of sensitivity to drugs. We observed a tachyphylaxis in terms of blood pressure reactions to these drugs as have others. Hellerstein and Brofman (1951) as well as Eckfeld *et al.* (1954) report progressively decreasing pressor responses and even complete reversal of effect after repeated injections of mephentermine in dogs. Smessaert and Collins (1955) found a moderate degree of tachyphylaxis following repeated administration of the same drug in clinical subjects undergoing spinal anesthesia. deBeer *et al.* (1956) reported similar failure to produce continuous hypertensive effects and they actually obtained depressor responses using doses of 0.4 and 0.8 mgm./kgm. of methoxamine. Lahti *et al.* (1949) found that only very slow infusion rates of methoxamine (0.02 mgm./kgm./min.) could maintain a sustained increase in blood pressure; increases in rate above this level resulted in decreases in pressure. The literature is not so clear with respect to the sustained vasopressor effects of epinephrine and levarterenol, although Wakim and Essex (1952) seem to suspect some cross tachyphylaxis in their experiments with these drugs. They found that the epinephrine effect is smaller than normal if the animal is just treated with norepinephrine and vice versa.

If one thinks of tachyphylaxis in terms of other drug effects the picture is not so clear. No definite conclusions concerning excitability tachyphylaxis can be drawn but a second dose of mephentermine appeared to be less effective. With respect to the effects on the refractory period, duration of the action potential and conduction there was little if any tachyphylaxis or such an action was masked by a reversal of effects. Finally the heart gradually became less sensitive to the tendency of these drugs to augment rate and the generation of ectopic beats. Interpretation of mixed desensitization actions must await further analysis of receptors and modes of action.

Longer latencies after drug administration might be ascribed in part to the suppressed excitability of the tissues. In the A-V conducting system junctional tissue must be crossed and this in association with reduced excitability might account for a selectivity of conduction delay at this point. Mephentermine and methoxamine produced slowing of A-V conduction in association with decreased excitability but epinephrine and levarterenol though having a late depressant action did not slow A-V conduction. The action of these drugs thus is not easily explained.

Methoxamine appears to be an effective vasopressor agent without much influence on pacemaker action and the tendencies toward creation of spontaneous ectopic beats of auricle and ventricle. It does, however, produce heart block more readily than do the other drugs studied.

There are additional peculiarities of these drugs which deserve further attention such as variations in their inotropic actions and in their effects on vulnerability to fibrillation. The studies described here are being continued.

SUMMARY

A study was made of the effects of the vasoconstrictor drugs epinephrine, levarterenol, methoxamine and mephentermine, on excitability, refractory period, rhythmic abnormalities, conduction times and action potential of the heart. The principal observations were as follows:

These drugs with the exception of methoxamine, in doses so graded as to maintain blood pressure levels 30 to 50 mm. Hg above control values, induced ectopic pacemaker action, abnormal spontaneous beats, and abnormal and multiple responses to test stimuli.

The action of methoxamine on the heart can be said to be depressant in that it prolonged the action potential and the absolute refractory period, raised the threshold to stimulation and slowed A-V conduction significantly. This was not due to reflex vagal action.

All four drugs exhibited some degree of tachyphylaxis with respect to blood pressure maintenance and some other actions.

Other details of the comparative effects of these drugs are given in the discussion of results obtained.

REFERENCES

Barger, G., and Dale, H. H.: J. Physiol., **41:** 19, 1910.

Brooks, C. McC., Hoffman, B. F., Suckling, E. E., and Orias, O.: The Excitability of the Heart, Ch. III, Grune and Stratton, N. Y., 1955.

deBeer, E. J., Wnuck, A. L., Fanelli, R. V., Norton, S., and Ellis, C. H.: Arch. Internat. pharmacodyn., **104:** 487, 1956.

Eckfeld, D. K., Abell, L. L., and Seifter, J.: J. Am. Pharm. Assoc. (Scient. Ed.), **43:** 705, 1954.

Gilbert, J. L., Siebens, A. A., Hoffman, B. F., Belford, J., Woske, H. M., and Brooks, C. McC.: Fed. Proc., **10:** 298, 1951.

Hellerstein, H. K., and Brofman, B. L.: Mod. Concepts Cardiovasc. Dis., **20:** 104, 1951.

Lahti, R. E., Brill, I. C., and McCawley, E. L.: This Journal, **115:** 268, 1949.

Siebens, A. A., Hoffman, B. F., Ensen, Y., Farrell, J. E., and Brooks, C. McC.: Am. J. Physiol., **175:** 1, 1953.

Smessaert, A., and Collins, V. S.: Anesthesiology, **16:** 795, 1955.

Stewart, G. H., Lynch, P. R., Barrera, F., and Oppenheimer, M. J.: Am. J. Physiol., **186:** 513, 1956.

Wakim, K. G., and Essex, H. E.: Circulation, **5:** 370, 1952.

Wiggers, H. C.: Am. J. Physiol., **118:** 333, 1937.

8006

PRESSOR EFFECT OF HISTAMINE IN THE RABBIT[1]

PLUTARCO NARANJO[2] AND ENRIQUETA BANDA DE NARANJO

Department of Pharmacology, Universidad Central del Ecuador and Research Department, L. I. F. E. Laboratories, Quito, Ecuador

Received for publication January 20, 1958

The hypotensive effect of histamine upon the arterial blood pressure of the cat and dog has been well known since the first investigations by Barger and Dale (1910) and Dale and Laidlaw (1910). A similar effect has been described in man (Weiss *et al.*, 1932; Katzenstein, 1944; Roth and Kvale, 1954). The problem of the blood pressure effect of histamine in the rabbit has received much less attention. As early as 1927, Feldberg observed that under certain conditions of anesthesia histamine produced a pressor effect, but since then, major interest turned to a more special vascular phenomenon produced by histamine in the rabbit, the constriction of the pulmonary arterioles (Best and MacHenry, 1931; Woodbury and Hamilton, 1941). Only more recently (Naranjo, 1952; Naranjo and de Naranjo, 1953) some attention has been paid to the pressor effect of histamine in the rabbit and to its prevention by antihistamines. The present work was carried out in order to study in this animal species the influence of a) autonomic drugs, b) adrenalectomy and c) anesthesia, on the blood pressure effect of histamine.

METHODS. The experiments were performed with adult rabbits of both sexes, weighing 1.5 to 2 kgm. In the main experiments, they were heparinized and anesthetized with a standard mixture of urethan (700 mgm./kgm.) and pentobarbital sodium (40 mgm./kgm.), administered intraperitoneally. Cannulae were inserted into the right common carotid artery for recording blood pressure, into the external jugular vein for injections, and into the trachea.

Histamine was used as the biphosphate in doses from 0.001 to 0.250 mgm./kgm., and epinephrine HCl in doses from 0.5 to 2.0 microgm./kgm. Successive injections were given after blood pressure had returned to the baseline, histamine being injected 3 to 5 minutes after epinephrine, and epinephrine 5 to 20 minutes after histamine. Both substances, dissolved in 0.9 per cent saline, were administered by rapid intravenous injection (1 to 2 seconds) in a uniform volume of 0.5 ml./kgm.

Other drugs employed were: cocaine HCl, 5 mgm./kgm.; phentolamine methanesulphate (Regitine), 3 mgm./kgm.; dihydroergotamine (DHE), 1 mgm./kgm.; hexamethonium Br, 10 mgm./kgm.; and pendiomide Br, 30 mgm./kgm. They were always administered subcutaneously 15–20 minutes prior to the first subsequent dose of histamine or epinephrine.

In those series of experiments in which dose-effect relationships were studied, the drug was given in progressive doses and no other drug was administered to the animal. In studying the influence of the adrenals on response to histamine, bilateral adrenalectomy was carried out transabdominally after elicitation of control responses in the intact animal.

The influence of anesthesia on the response to histamine was studied with ether, urethan, thiopental Na and the standard urethan-pentobarbital mixture (17:1). The different stages of anesthesia were established with ether by the open drop technique, with the other drugs by varying the dose. Urethan and the mixture of urethan-pentobarbital were administered intraperitoneally and thiopental intravenously.

All numerical data represent averages for groups of 8 to 10 animals.

RESULTS. *Heparinization.* In preliminary experiments it was ascertained that intravenous administration of adequate doses of heparin (50 to 100 units/kgm.) did not modify the blood pressure effect of histamine.

Blood pressure effect of histamine. Doses from 1 to 10 microgm./kgm. failed to cause any change of blood pressure in approximately 75 per cent of animals; in the rest, a slight and transient fall of blood pressure (no more than 5 mm. Hg) was observed. Doses from 10 to 20

[1] Part of this work was carried out in the Department of Pharmacology, Universidad del Valle, Cali, Colombia.

[2] Present address: Department of Pharmacology, University of Utah College of Medicine, Salt Lake City, Utah.

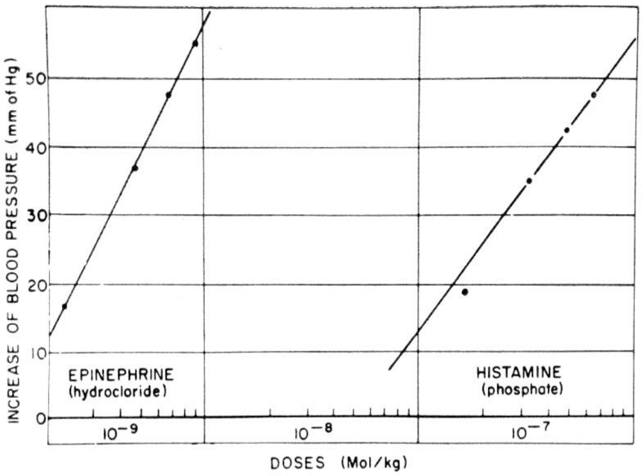

FIG. 1. Dose-pressor effect relationship of epinephrine and histamine in anesthetized rabbits.

microgm./kgm. produced a small rise of blood pressure, varying from 2 to 10 mm. Hg. Higher doses, however, uniformly produced a sharp and marked rise of blood pressure. In the dosage range between 50 and 250 microgm./kgm., the pressor effect of histamine increased (fig. 1) in linear relationship with log dose. Except for a moderate difference in slope, the same relationship prevailed for epinephrine doses approximately 100 times lower than those of histamine.

The pressor phase was followed by a subsequent depressor phase (fig. 3 and 4). In this secondary effect, the two drugs differed in that after doses equieffective in elevating the blood pressure the subsequent drop was greater with histamine. The higher the dose of histamine, the more intense and persistent was the subsequent depression.

Interrelation between histamine and epinephrine. An antagonism between histamine and epinephrine was observed. Depending upon magnitude of dosage, a single epinephrine administration, 3 to 5 minutes prior to histamine, either diminished or reversed the pressor effect of histamine (fig. 2); after repeated doses of epinephrine, (1 to 4 microgm./kgm.) the histamine response was regularly reversed. On the other hand, after a preceding dose of histamine, the pressor effect of epinephrine was diminished but never reversed.

Cocaine by itself did not modify the blood pressure effect of histamine. However the reversal of the histamine pressor effect was obtained with smaller doses of epinephrine in cocainized than in control animals.

Influence of adrenergic blocking agents. Phentolamine (Regitine, 3 mgm./kgm.) and DHE (1 mgm./kgm.), which diminished the pressor effect of 1 microgm./kgm. of epinephrine by 78.0 ± 12 and 81.4 ± 12 per cent, respectively, did not significantly modify the response to histamine (fig. 3). Epinephrine in the same doses as in the former experiments did not reverse the pressor effect of histamine after adrenergic blockade.

Influence of ganglionic blocking agents. Pretreatment with a ganglionic blocking agent increased the pressor response to histamine. The increase amounted to 27 and 32 per cent after 10 mgm./kgm. of hexamethonium and 30 mgm./kgm. of pendiomide, respectively. The subsequent depressor effect of histamine was considerably diminished or abolished after ganglionic blockade.

The mutual antagonism of histamine and epinephrine was not manifest in the presence of ganglionic blockade. Injection of a mixture of histamine and epinephrine resulted in a combined pressor effect which was higher than that of either of the drugs alone. When the dose of one of the substances in the mixture was progressively increased, that of the other substance being kept constant, the increase in pressor effect was proportional to the increased dose.

Influence of adrenalectomy. The pressor effect of histamine was essentially unchanged after

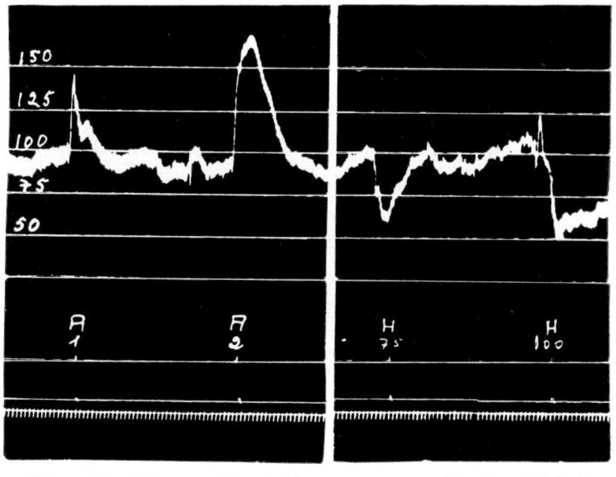

FIG. 2. Reversal of the pressor effect of histamine by epinephrine.

Rabbit, 1.8 kgm., urethan-pentobarbital anesthesia (see text). Blood pressure recorded by means of a mercury manometer. A = epinephrine hydrochloride (successive doses, 1 and 2 microgm./kgm.); H = histamine biphosphate (successive doses, 75 and 100 microgm./kgm.). First dose of histamine 5 minutes after last dose of epinephrine. Time signal: 5 seconds.

adrenalectomy (fig. 4). In six out of ten animals the blood pressure rose to the same peak level before and after adrenalectomy; inasmuch as the removal of the glands produced a deep fall in blood pressure, the histamine-induced rise, in per cent of the baseline value, was even higher after adrenalectomy. In the other four animals even the peak level of blood pressure was 10 to 15 mm. higher after adrenalectomy.

In one group of animals, blocking agents were

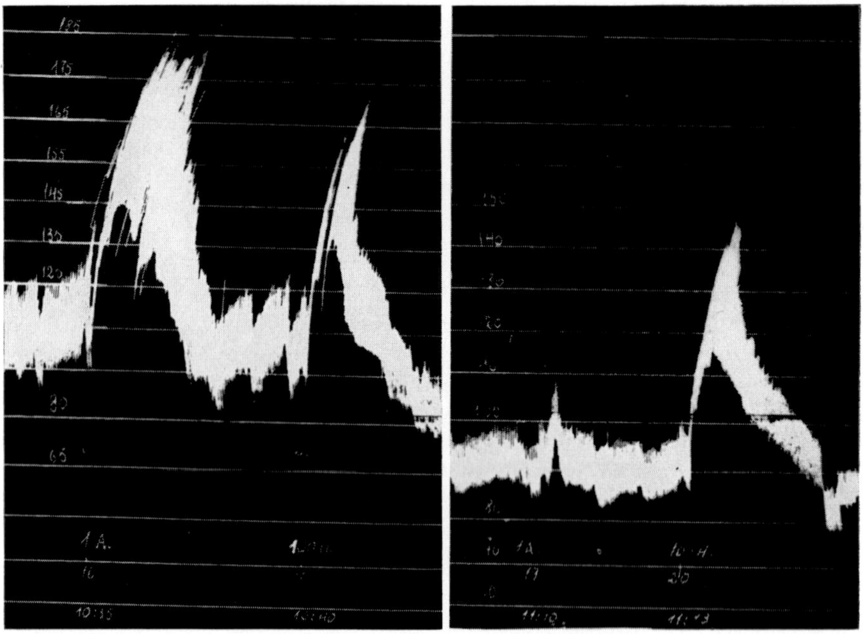

FIG. 3. Influence of adrenergic blockade.

Rabbit, 2.08 kgm., urethan-pentobarbital anesthesia (see text). Recording of the carotid blood pressure by means of a bellows manometer. Left tracing: epinephrine 1 microgm./kgm. and histamine 100 microgm./kgm., respectively. Right tracing: the same drugs and doses, after 20 minutes of subcutaneous administration of 3 mgm./kgm. of Regitine.

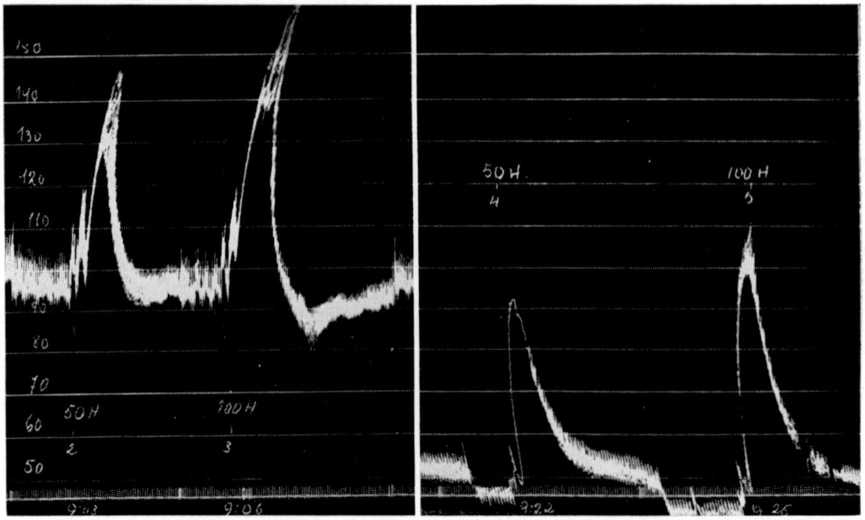

FIG. 4. Pressor effect of histamine before and after bilateral adrenalectomy.

Rabbit, 1.85 kgm., urethan-pentobarbital anesthesia (see text). Recording of the carotid blood pressure by means of a bellows manometer. Left tracing: histamine 50 and 100 microgm./kgm., respectively. Right tracing: the same doses, 10 minutes after adrenalectomy. Time signal: 5 seconds.

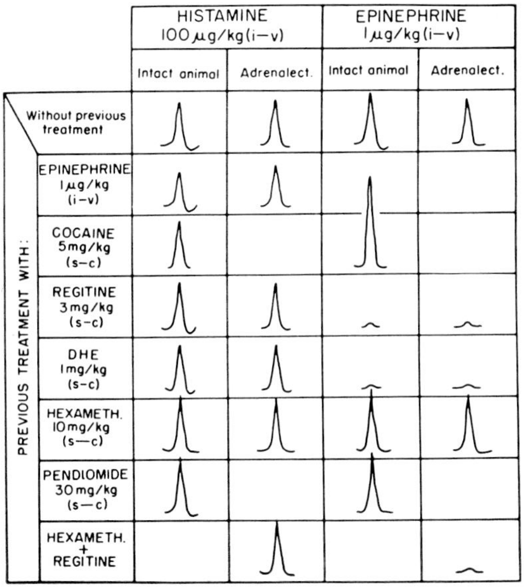

FIG. 5. Pressor effects of histamine and epinephrine after various drugs before and after adrenalectomy.
For explanation see preceding figures and text.

administered immediately before adrenalectomy. Adrenergic blockers, even in a dose capable of abolishing the pressor effect of 1 microgm./kgm. of epinephrine, not only failed to diminish the pressor effect of histamine but rather enhanced it. Ganglionic blockade also enhanced the histamine effect.

Fig. 5 summarizes the major experimental results.

Influence of anesthesia. In unanesthetized animals the blood pressure effect of histamine varied greatly. In some animals a moderate pressor response was observed, followed by a more profound depressor response phase, while in others only a depressor response was produced. Since in the unanesthetized animals histamine elicited very pronounced hypermotility, it was difficult to evaluate to what extent the blood pressure changes were directly induced by histamine and to what extent they were indirect effects due to sequels of histamine action, such as those motor manifestations. Pretreatment with ganglionic blocking agents produced more regularly a pressor response.

Under progressive ether anesthesia it was observed that in the first stage of anesthesia, while the animal still reacted with movements to painful stimuli such as pinching of the skin, the blood pressure effect of histamine was quite the same as in unanesthetized animals. In deeper anesthesia the blood pressure responses were less erratic, and on the third plane of the third stage of surgical anesthesia (Gillespie, 1942) histamine invariably induced a pressor effect.

The results with urethan or the standard urethan-pentobarbital mixture were similar to those described for ether, namely, the deeper the anesthesia, the more prevalent was the pressor response to histamine. With thiopental, although the results were essentially the same, it was not easy to reach an adequate depth of anesthesia; either the anesthesia was too superficial and, consequently, the effect of histamine still variable, or it reached rapidly a toxic and fatal level.

These results suggest that the pressor effect of histamine in the rabbit depends at least in part on the depth of general anesthesia.

DISCUSSION. In rabbits studied under the experimental conditions here reported, histamine produces a rapid and transient rise in arterial blood pressure. Various reports demonstrating that histamine causes depletion of epinephrine from the adrenals in the cat and dog (Elliot, 1912; Houssay and Molinelli, 1925; Burn and Dale, 1926; La Barre, 1927; Szczygielski, 1932), could be interpreted as meaning that, in the rabbit, the histamine pressor effect is mediated by release of endogenous epinephrine. For example, in the spinal cat Burn and Dale (1926) demonstrated that histamine can induce a rise of blood pressure, in contrast to the usual depressor effect seen in the intact animal. However, this pressor effect does not appear after bilateral adrenalectomy. Furthermore, the assumption of release of endogenous epinephrine in the rabbit is eliminated by the present experiments. They demonstrate that the pressor effect of histamine is neither abolished by bilateral adrenalectomy nor diminished or reversed by adrenergic blocking agents in doses capable of diminishing by 80 per cent the effect of 1 microgm./kgm. of epinephrine. These results are most compatible with the interpretation that, in the rabbit, histamine induces a pressor response for which mobilization of epinephrine is not a prerequisite.

Dale and Richards (1918), in one of their earliest studies of histamine found that histamine produced constriction of arterioles in rabbits during artificial limb perfusion. These authors first, and Burn and Dale (1926) later, pointed out that histamine may produce a dual effect: relaxation of the capillary wall and contraction of the smooth muscle of arteries and arterioles. According to Burn and Dale (1926), in the cat, capillary dilatation would be the most manifest response to histamine but normal capillary tone must previously exist. Factors affecting capillary tone, such as the denervation of an organ, may modify the response to histamine. On the other hand, the same workers demonstrated that histamine relaxed both capillaries and arteries both in the dog and monkey and hence did not elicit such dual effects in these species. These findings were later confirmed by Page and Taylor (1947) in the dog. In the rabbit, as it is well known (Best and MacHenry, 1931), histamine produces constriction of the pulmonary arteries, but this phenomenon does not explain the rise of blood pressure in the carotid artery. It could be assumed that the arterial constriction does not occur exclusively in the lungs but may also occur in other organs to such an extent that this factor would be responsible for the rise of blood pressure. In fact, Feldberg (1927) demonstrated in denervated rabbit ears that arterial constriction can be produced by histamine. He concluded that, in the rabbit also, histamine has dual effects: constriction on the arterial branches including the pulmonary arteries, and dilation on the capillaries. Finally, he advanced the hypothesis that capillary tone in the rabbit would be normally weaker than in the cat or dog and easily depressed or abolished by general anesthetics. When the capillary tone is abolished no more dilatation can be produced by histamine and constriction of arteries may become the only visible response, with the consequent rise of blood pressure.

Our findings confirm that under an appropriate depth of surgical anesthesia the dominant response to histamine in the rabbit is the rapid rise of blood pressure, but the hypothesis of a weaker capillary tone in this animal species than in others still requires confirmation.

The results obtained by Slater and Dresel (1952) are particularly interesting in connection with the problem of the mechanism of vasomotor effects of histamine. These authors found that during ganglionic blockade, histamine elicited a pressor response in the cat but not in the dog. During ganglionic blockade, bilateral adrenalectomy in the cat only slightly diminished the pressor response to histamine. This response was, therefore, not primarily due to mobilization of epinephrine from the adrenals. On the other hand, ganglionic blockade of the sympathetic efferent pathways produced decrease of capillary tone secondary to arterial dilatation. Under such experimental conditions, arteriolar constriction produced by histamine becomes prominent. But in the dog, since histamine dilates arteries as well as capillaries, ganglionic blockade does not reverse the depressor effect of histamine.

In the rabbit, as reported here, ganglionic blockade favors the pressor response to histamine in both anesthetized and unanesthetized animals. Our findings demonstrate that the pressor response is not mediated by mobilization of endogenous epinephrine and confirm indirectly Feldberg's (1927) results, *i.e.*, factors causing a decrease in capillary tone enhance the histamine pressor response.

SUMMARY

Contrary to its depressor effect in cat, dog, monkey and man, histamine produced in the anesthetized rabbit a pressor effect qualitatively comparable to that of epinephrine. This effect was favored by general anesthesia. The deeper the anesthesia the more regular was the pressor effect. In unanesthetized animals or under light anesthesia the responses were erratic, there was even a depressor effect.

In the dose range of 50 to 250 microgm./kgm., the relationship between log dose and pressor effect of histamine was linear. A dose approximately one hundred times that of epinephrine was required to produce an equal pressor effect.

Epinephrine and histamine were mutually antagonistic. Epinephrine given before histamine in a single small dose diminished and, given in a single higher dose or repeated small doses reversed, the pressor effect of histamine. Histamine given prior to epinephrine diminished the epinephrine pressor effect but never reversed it. Adrenergic blocking agents did not modify the pressor response of histamine even in doses strongly blocking the epinephrine effect. By ganglionic blockade the pressor effect of histamine was enhanced and the antagonism between epinephrine and histamine was turned into synergism. Adrenalectomy did not decrease the pressor effect of histamine.

In the discussion of these findings it is pointed out that they are all compatible with the conclusion that the pressor effect of histamine was not due to the mobilization of epinephrine.

REFERENCES

Barger. G., and Dale, H. H.: J. Physiol., **40:** 38, 1910.

Best, C. H., and MacHenry, E. W.: Physiol. Rev., **11:** 371, 1931.

Burn, J. H., and Dale, H. H.: J. Physiol., **61:** 185, 1926.

Dale, H. H., and Laidlaw, P. P.: J. Physiol., **41:** 318, 1910.

Dale, H. H., and Richards, A. N.: J. Physiol., **52:** 110, 1918.

Elliott, T. R.: J. Physiol., **44:** 374, 1912.

Feldberg, W.: J. Physiol., **63:** 211, 1927.

Gillespie, N. A.: Anesth. and Analg., **22:** 275, 1942.

Houssay, B. A., y Molinelli, E. A.: Rev. Soc. Argent. Biol., **6:** 547, 1925.

Katzenstein, R.: Yale J. Biol. & Med., **16:** 325, 1944.

La Barre, J.: Arch. Int. Med. Exper., **3:** 42, 1927.

Naranjo, P.: Proc. Soc. Exper. Biol. & Med., **81:** 111, 1952.

Naranjo, P., and de Naranjo, E.: Ann. Allergy, **11:** 699, 1953.

Page, I. H., and Taylor, R. D.: Science, **105:** 622, 1947.

Roth, G. M., and Kvale, W. F.: Am. J. M. Sc., **210:** 653, 1945.

Slater, I. H., and Dresel, P. E.: This Journal, **105:** 101, 1952.

Szczygielski, J.: Arch. exper. Path. u. Pharmakol., **166:** 319, 1932.

Weiss, S., Robb, G. P., and Ellis, L. B.: Arch. Int. Med., **49:** 360, 1932.

Woodbury, R. A., and Hamilton, W. F.: This Journal, **71:** 293, 1941.

8007

STUDIES CONCERNING THE CARDIOVASCULAR ACTIONS OF THE CENTRAL NERVOUS STIMULANT, METHYLPHENIDATE

R. A. MAXWELL, A. J. PLUMMER, S. D. ROSS AND A. I. DANIEL
Research Department, CIBA Pharmaceutical Products Inc., Summit, New Jersey

Received for publication January 29, 1958

The central stimulant properties of methylphenidate were first described by Meier *et al.* (1954). Maxwell *et al.* (1957) have reported that methylphenidate in the dose range of 1 to 6 mgm./kgm. displays a complex of antihypertensive properties. 1) Methylphenidate acts as a potent antagonist to the severe hypertension produced by 0.5 mgm./kgm. of amphetamine sulfate when given before the amphetamine or during the period of amphetamine activity. When given during the amphetamine pressor response methylphenidate lowers the elevated pressure to control levels and not below. 2) Methylphenidate antagonizes the reflex pressor responses elicited by bilateral occlusion of the common carotid arteries for short periods. 3) Methylphenidate lowers, moderately and for a short period, the blood pressure of the unanesthetized renal hypertensive dog. On the basis of the evidence then at hand it was suggested that the site of action of this complex of antihypertensive actions was probably central. We have conducted additional experiments in an attempt to elucidate further the nature and sites of these cardiovascular actions of methylphenidate.

METHODS. All dogs were studied under pentobarbital anesthesia, 30 mgm./kgm. intraperitoneally plus a continuous intravenous infusion of 0.1 mgm./kgm./minute. All cats were studied under the anesthetic effect of 0.75 ml./kgm. of Dial-Urethane (diallylbarbituric acid plus urethan, CIBA) intraperitoneally.

Blood pressures were recorded with an Anderson glass capsule manometer (1941). Spinal preparations were studied under pentobarbital anesthesia and controlled respiration, the cord being severed between the first vertebra and the base of the skull. The cat nictitating membrane preparation was employed, the cervical sympathetic trunk being crushed with a hemostat central to the point of stimulation. Stimulation was at 2 volts, 100-microsecond duration at 20/second. Where denervation of the nictitating membrane was required, the procedure was performed just prior to the experiment by removing one-fourth inch of the vagosympathetic trunk.

The following compounds in aqueous solution were employed in this study: methylphenidate HCl[1], amphetamine sulfate, purified hog renin[2], arterenol HCl (norepinephrine, racemic) and 1,1 - dimethyl - 4 - phenylpiperazinium iodide (DMPP).

RESULTS. *High doses of methylphenidate on blood pressure.* Twenty mgm./kgm. of methylphenidate intravenously—a dose which is 3 to 20 times the dose required to produce the cardiovascular effects described above—produced a sharp, very transient fall in blood pressure but no marked, sustained depressor effects in 4 normotensive dogs (fig. 1). It is clear that methylphenidate is not a hypotensive agent *per se.*

The effect of high doses of methylphenidate on amphetamine-induced hypertension. A typical pressor response of the normotensive dog to 0.5 mgm./kgm. amphetamine is shown in fig. 2. Twenty mgm./kgm. of methylphenidate administered intravenously at the height of the pressor response elicited by 0.5 mgm./kgm. of amphetamine intravenously restored pressure to control levels after an initial transient hypotensive response in 3 dogs tested (fig. 3). Although this dose of methylphenidate was four times that necessary to completely antagonize amphetamine hypertension, it did not produce a *sustained* depression of the blood pressure below normotensive levels. The action of methylphenidate against amphetamine hypertension appears to be, therefore, specifically antihypertensive and not the result of a general hypotensive action.

Methylphenidate-amphetamine interaction in the cat. In order to determine if the antagonistic effect of methylphenidate against amphetamine activity had a peripheral component, the effects of

[1] Ritalin, a trade mark of CIBA Pharmaceutical Products Inc.

[2] Fractions I and J prepared by Princeton Laboratories, Princeton, New Jersey.

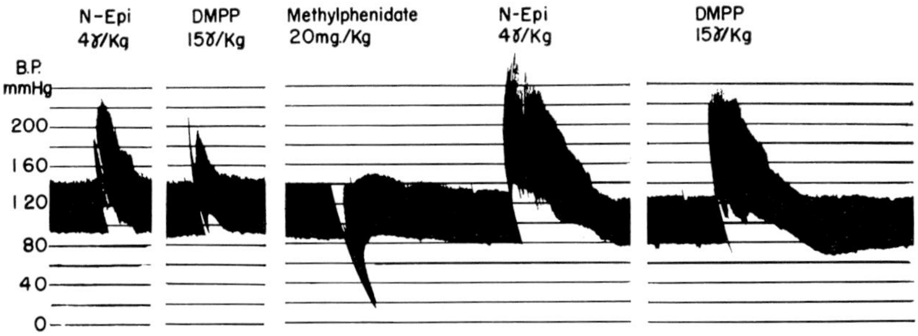

FIG. 1. The effect of a high dose of methylphenidate on the blood pressure of a normotensive dog and its ability to augment the pressor effects of subsequent injections of norepinephrine and DMPP. Pressor responses to norepinephrine and DMPP in the absence of methylphenidate are shown on the left.

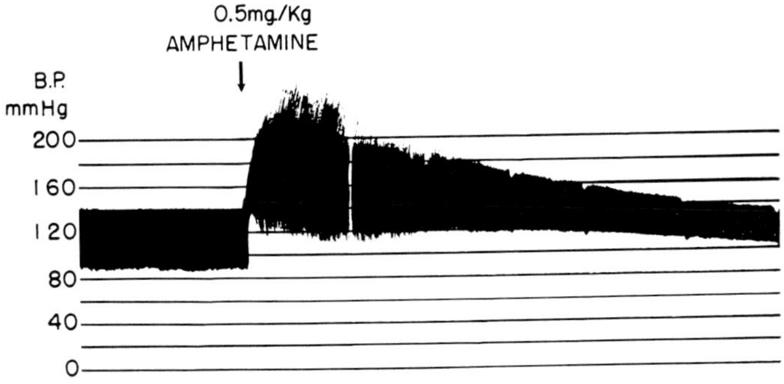

FIG. 2. The pressor response of a normotensive dog to intravenous amphetamine.

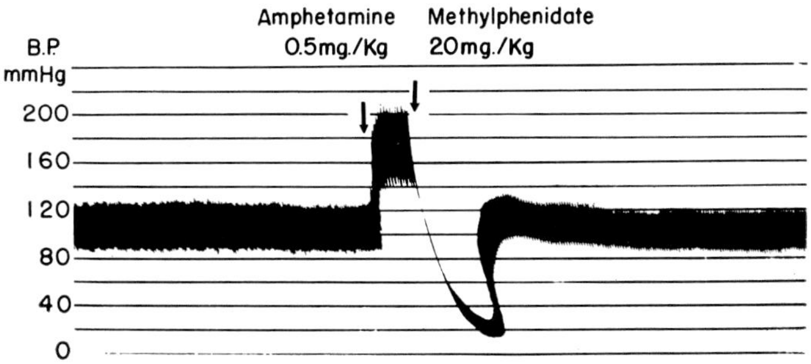

FIG. 3. The effect of a high dose of methylphenidate on the hypertensive response to amphetamine in the normotensive dog.

these agents were studied on the tonus of the cat nictitating membrane and on the blood pressure. One mgm./kgm. of amphetamine intravenously was sufficient to produce a sustained hypertension and also sustained contractions of both the innervated and acutely denervated nictitating membranes. The subsequent intravenous injection of 10 mgm./kgm. of methylphenidate produced marked relaxation of both the innervated and denervated membranes and a return of blood pressure to control levels in the 5 cats studied (fig. 4).

In 3 cats, the administration of 10 mgm./kgm. of methylphenidate was without effect *per se* on the nictitating membranes (fig. 5). This pretreatment with methylphenidate blocked the pressor action and the membrane-contracting effect of 1 mgm./kgm. of amphetamine. However, the administration of 5 and 10 mgm./kgm. produced obvious and sustained contractions of both membranes but did not produce pressor responses (fig. 5). This differential action of amphetamine could possibly have been explained by a difference in the degree of blockade produced by methylphenidate at the smooth muscle of the nictitating membranes and at the arteriolar smooth muscle. The possibility also exists that amphetamine-induced pressor responses were a result of actions more complex and more susceptible to methylphenidate blockade than direct smooth muscle contraction.

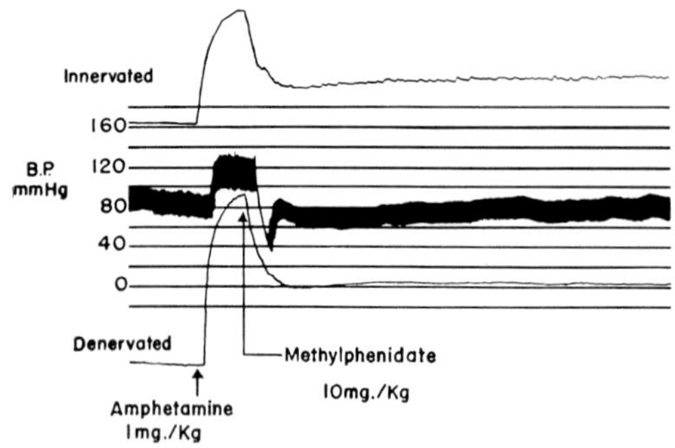

FIG. 4. The ability of methylphenidate to antagonize the sustained contraction of the nictitating membrane and hypertension ordinarily produced by amphetamine.

Amphetamine pressor effect in the spinal dog. The pressor responses induced in 4 spinal dogs by 0.5 mgm./kgm. of amphetamine were markedly less than those induced by the same dose in intact dogs (compare fig. 6 with fig. 2). Generally, pressor responses ranging from 80 to 140 mgm./kgm. were produced in the intact dog by 0.5 mgm./kgm. of amphetamine, while in the 4 spinal dogs the response ranged from 25 to 40 mm. Hg.

Five mgm./kgm. i.v. of methylphenidate completely eliminated the pressor response that was elicited by 0.5 mgm./kgm. of amphetamine in 3 spinal dogs (fig. 6).

Methylphenidate and efferent sympathetic transmission. To determine if a ganglionic or adrenergic blocking component was part of the action of

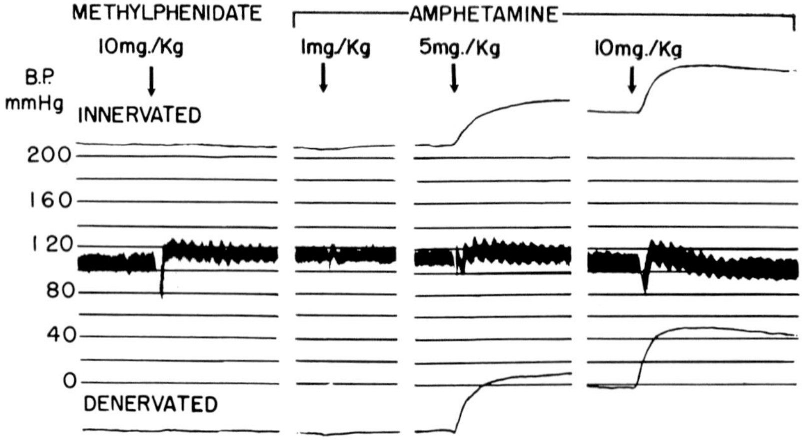

FIG. 5. The effect of pretreatment with methylphenidate on the response of the cat nictitating membrane and the blood pressure to amphetamine.

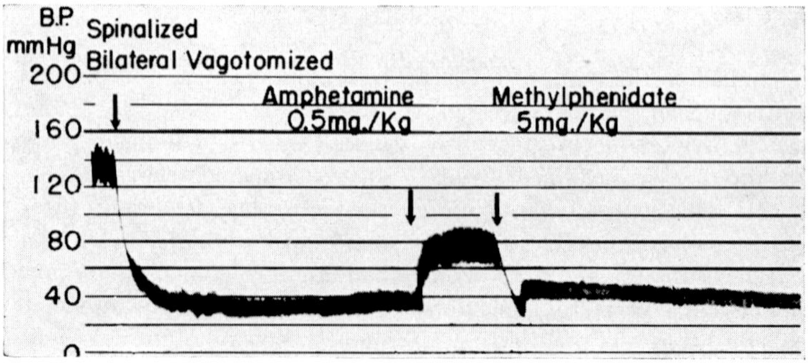

FIG. 6. The effect of methylphenidate on the pressor response to amphetamine in the spinalized dog.

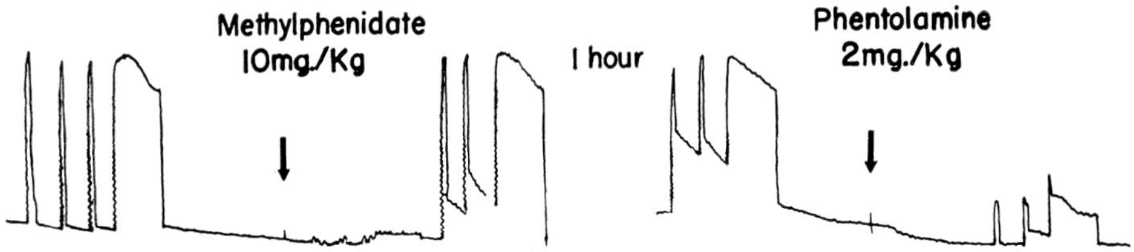

FIG. 7. The inability of 10 mgm./kgm. of methylphenidate to prevent the contractions of the nictitating membrane elicited by preganglionic faradization of the cervical sympathetic nerve.
The ability of phentolamine to prevent the response is also shown, for purposes of contrast.

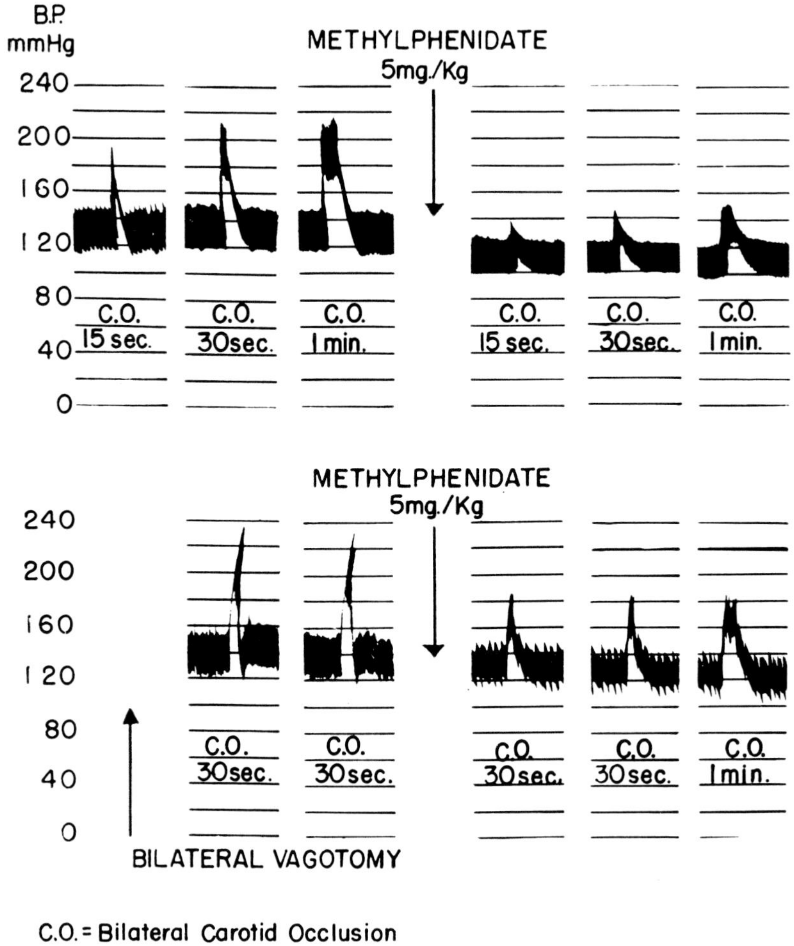

FIG. 8. Effect of methylphenidate on the carotid occlusion pressor responses in intact and bilaterally vagotomized dogs.

methylphenidate, the effect of 20 mgm./kgm. methylphenidate on the pressor responses to the ganglionic stimulant, dimethylphenylpiperazinium iodide (DMPP), and to norepinephrine was studied. This high dose of methylphenidate did not antagonize the pressor effects of DMPP or norepinephrine, on the contrary both were augmented (fig. 1).

To provide more direct evidence that methylphenidate does not affect efferent sympathetic transmission the cervical sympathetic nerve-nictitating membrane preparation was utilized. Five and 10 mgm./kgm. of methylphenidate intravenously did not antagonize the contractions of the nictitating membrane elicited by preganglionic faradization of the cervical sympathetic nerve of two cats studied. In contrast to methylphenidate the administration of 2 mgm./kgm. of phentolamine markedly reduced the height of contraction produced by faradization of the cervical sympathetic trunk (fig. 7).

Methylphenidate and reflex pressor responses. With the knowledge that the efferent sympathetic transmission was unimpaired by methylphenidate, the nature and the site of the antagonizing action of methylphenidate on the reflexly induced pressor responses were studied further. Five and 10 mgm./kgm. of methylphenidate intravenously markedly reduced the pressor response elicited by bilateral common carotid artery occlusion in the intact dog (fig. 8) while not markedly lowering the blood pressure. Control occlusions were applied for 15 seconds, 30 seconds, 1 minute and 2 minutes. Graded responses occurred but a plateau was usually reached within the 2-minute occlusion time. Repetition of the occlusions after methylphenidate administration resulted again in graded responses, but each response was clearly less than its equivalent control. The pressure plateau was lower than that reached before drug administration (fig. 8). These results indicate that the effect of methylphenidate on the carotid reflex pressor response is truly an inhibition and not simply a delaying effect. Since blockade of the efferent sympathetic limb could not be invoked as an explanation for this effect on carotid occlusion responses, it was reasoned that methylphenidate could be acting on cardiovascular centers and/or on cardiovascular afferent receptors. It was decided to test whether methylphenidate affected baroreceptor function.

The infiltration of 0.1 ml. of an aqueous solution containing 2 mgm. of methylphenidate into the tissue surrounding each carotid sinus did not lower blood pressure and did not markedly affect the carotid occlusion reflex pressor response in

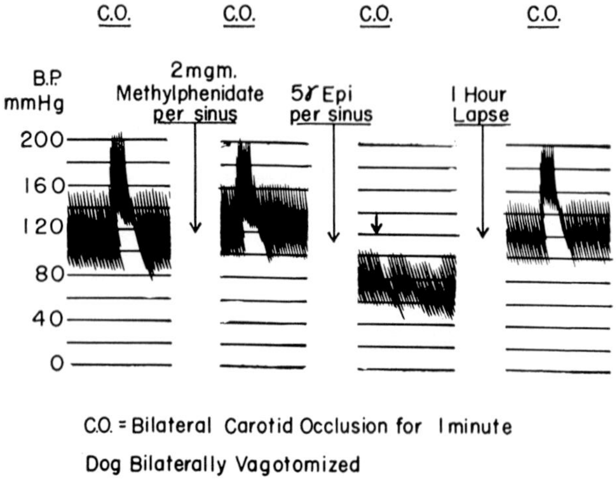

FIG. 9. Lack of effect of methylphenidate infiltration into the carotid sinus area on the carotid occlusion reflex pressor response in a bilaterally vagotomized dog.
Effect of a similar infiltration of epinephrine is shown as a control.

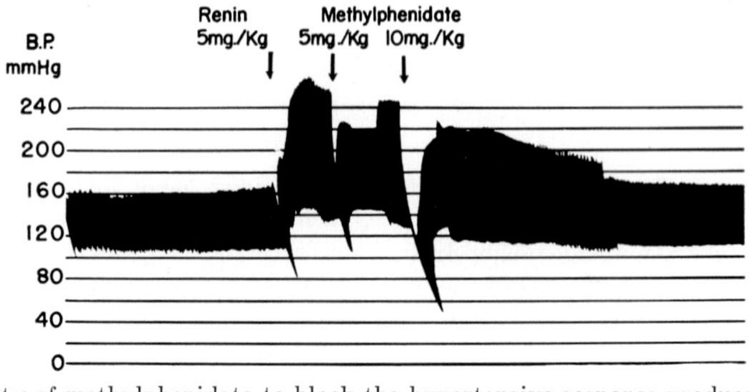

FIG. 10. Inability of methylphenidate to block the hypertensive response produced in a dog by the intravenous injection of renin.

four bilaterally vagotomized dogs (fig. 9). As a control procedure, the subsequent infiltration of 0.1 ml. of an aqueous solution containing 5 microgm. of epinephrine bitartrate into the carotid sinus areas lowered blood pressure and completely eliminated the response to bilateral carotid occlusion (fig. 9) in the four dogs. Apparently methylphenidate did not interfere with the events which normally occur at these afferent structures during induced local hypotension.

Aviado and Schmidt (1955) in a reference to the work of Heymans have reported that the hypertension caused by carotid occlusion is considerably dampened by the concomitant increase in the activity of the aortic pressor receptors, which react to this as to any rise in pressure. It seemed a possibility that the inhibition produced by methylphenidate on carotid occlusion responses might be due to a sensitizing action of methylphenidate on the arch pressor receptors. This "sensitization" was not conceived of as a direct excitation of the pressor receptors since methylphenidate did not generally produce hypotension during the time that it antagonized carotid occlusion pressor responses. Rather, this sensitization was postulated as an increase in the amount of baroreceptor discharge per unit increase in pressure. Such an effect of methylphenidate on these afferent structures was made to appear unlikely by the fact that 5 mgm./kgm. of methylphenidate i.v. produced a clear-cut blockade of the reflex pressor responses even when the function of the arch pressor receptors was ruled out by bilateral section of the vago-aortic nerves (fig. 8).

Methylphenidate and renin hypertension. Because we had reported that methylphenidate would moderately reduce the blood pressure of the renal hypertensive dog we determined the effect of methylphenidate on renin hypertension. Doses of 5 and 10 mgm./kgm. of methylphenidate were ineffective in blocking the hypertension produced by the intravenous administration of 3 to 5 mgm./kgm. (approximately 3 to 5 units/kgm.) of renin in four dogs studied (fig. 10). Methylphenidate had no obvious effect whether given before or during renin hypertension.

Discussion. Methylphenidate in very high doses did not produce sustained hypotension in normotensive dogs. High doses of methylphenidate, administered subsequent to amphetamine, lowered the hypertension elicited by amphetamine to approximately normotensive levels but except for a brief period did not produce marked hypotension. The action of methylphenidate against amphetamine hypertension appears to be therefore specifically antihypertensive and not the result of a general hypotensive action.

At least part of the blocking action of methylphenidate on amphetamine occurs at the periphery. This is indicated by the relaxing action of methylphenidate on the denervated nictitating membrane which had been contracted by amphetamine. Also, the antagonistic effect of methylphenidate on the hypertension elicited by amphetamine in the spinal dog suggests a peripheral site for the antagonism.

In view of the fact that methylphenidate does not possess ganglionic or conventional adrenergic blocking actions and furthermore does not demonstrably affect baroreceptor function, we are forced to the conclusion that the action of this compound against carotid occlusion reflex pressor responses is centrally evoked.

The moderate antihypertensive action of methylphenidate in the renal hypertensive dog, described in an earlier paper (Maxwell *et al.*, 1957), is apparently not elicited by a direct antagonism to the renin pressor system since methylphenidate does not antagonize the hypertension produced by intravenously administered renin.

SUMMARY

The complex of antihypertensive activities exhibited by methylphenidate is explained only in part by effects elicited in the efferent periphery. The blocking effect of methylphenidate on amphetamine hypertension has a distinct efferent peripheral component. The antagonizing effect of methylphenidate on carotid occlusion reflex pressor responses cannot be explained by an obvious afferent or efferent peripheral blockade. The moderate antihypertensive effect of methylphenidate in the renal hypertensive dog cannot be explained by a blocking effect on the renin pressor system.

REFERENCES

Anderson, F. F.: J. Lab. and Clin. Med., **26:** 1520, 1941.

Aviado, D. M., Jr., and Schmidt, C. F.: Physiol. Rev., **35:** 247, 1955.

Maxwell, R. A., Plummer, A. J., Ross, S. D., Paytas, J. J., and Dennis, A. D.: Arch. internat. Pharmacodyn., **CXII:** 26, 1957.

Meier, R., Gross, F., and Tripod, J.: Klin. Wschr., **32:** 450, 1954.

8008

COMPARATIVE EFFECTS OF SOME CONVULSANT DRUGS ON THE BEHAVIOR AND ELECTRICAL ACTIVITY OF THE NERVOUS AND MUSCULAR SYSTEM OF THE SALAMANDER[1]

J. J. PETERS, A. R. VONDERAHE AND T. H. POWERS

Albers Biological Laboratory, Xavier University, and Department of Anatomy, College of Medicine, University of Cincinnati, Cincinnati, Ohio

Received for publication January 15, 1958

Although mammals have been commonly used for experiments investigating convulsant phenomena induced by drugs (Brazier, 1950; Fuhner, 1932; Goodman *et al.*, 1953; Magoun, 1952; Penfield and Jasper, 1954; Toman and Taylor, 1952), the history of biological research indicates that corresponding studies of less complex forms are apt to yield important clues to an understanding of the mechanism of seizures. Since salamanders parallel many of the responses of mammals to convulsive agents (Peters *et al.*, 1956; Peters and Vonderahe, 1954), the underlying physiological and anatomical mechanisms are sufficiently alike to warrant further investigation. In the salamander, the effect of a drug can be studied in a preparation lacking a cerebral cortex naturally, so that the drastic procedures of decortication are unnecessary. The authors realize that in spite of basic similarities between the nervous systems of salamanders and man, there are biological differences, and these differences suggest caution in making broad applications to both forms.

The six convulsant drugs used in this investigation were pentylenetetrazol, picrotoxin, strychnine, nicotine, nikethamide and caffeine.

Materials and methods. In this study 3 principal procedures were employed: 1) behavioral studies of convulsant phenomena, with accompanying neurological tests, to yield information in regard to the time of onset, duration and recovery from the side effects of the 6 drugs; 2) recordings of electrical activity of the central nervous system and associated musculature to reveal differences in the action of various convulsants, especially when behavioral effects were deceptively similar in motionless animals or occur too rapidly for accurate visual observation; and 3) transection of the spinal cord at the second vertebra to expose the effects of a drug on brain and spinal cord after they were separated from each other.

About 200 salamanders, the adult aquatic phase of *Triturus viridescens*, were used. In the final experiments 16 animals were used for each drug: for behavioral tests, 4 animals with intact cord and 4 with a transected cord; for electrical studies, 4 animals with intact cord and 4 with a transected cord. The other animals were used for preliminary experiments in finding an optimum dosage which would consistently produce characteristic effects without being lethal. The drugs were injected into the abdominal cavity at the following dosages per gram of body weight: pentylenetetrazol (Metrazol), 1.0 mgm.; picrotoxin, 0.03 mgm.; strychnine sulphate, 0.075 mgm.; nicotine alkaloid, 0.025 mgm.; nikethamide (Coramine), 2.0 mgm.; and caffeine, 0.2 mgm. If the above dosages are increased by 25 per cent, the effects of picrotoxin and strychnine are usually lethal, while the convulsive effects of the remaining drugs remain essentially unchanged, with more severe side effects and a longer period of recovery.

The following neurological tests were selected to investigate the side effects of drugs on responses which are different phylogenetically and involve various levels of the central nervous system (Peters *et al.*, 1956): 1) withdrawal response to touch, 2) righting on land and 3) in water, 4) corneal and 5) abdominal reflexes, 6) swimming, 7) walking, and 8) optokinetic nystagmus in which eyes or head follow moving objects. These tests were administered at 5, 15, 30, 45, and 60 minutes after injection of the drug, and at longer intervals until the animals returned to normal behavior. For evaluating the responses an arbitrary grading system based on previous experience and comparison with the behavior of untreated salamanders was established. The results are graphically summarized in fig. 3. On the vertical axis are plotted modifications of normal activity, in which 0 is regarded as normal and 6 as an extreme modification, usually reduction in response. The hori-

[1] This investigation was supported by a research grant from the National Institute of Neurological Diseases and Blindness, U. S. Public Health Service.

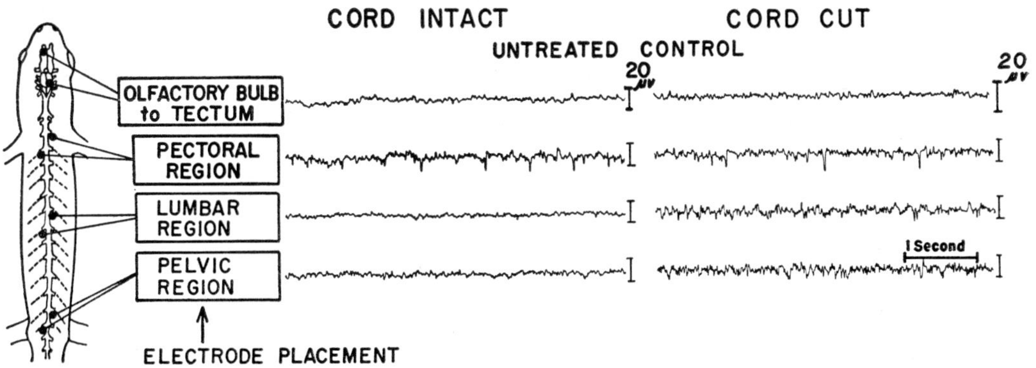

FIG. 1. Dorsal view of the salamander illustrating the placement of electrodes spanning the brain, pectoral, lumbar and pelvic regions of the spinal cord, and a typical recording of electrical activity from a quiet, untreated salamander.
The electrical activity is interpreted as being of neuromuscular origin.

zontal axis indicates time of onset and duration of side effects. In behavioral studies involving a transection of the cord, the salamanders were allowed to recover from shock, and were then observed for 60 minutes after the injection of the drug.

To record the changes in the electrical activity of the nervous and muscular systems during the action of convulsant drugs, pairs of stainless steel needle electrodes, 5 mm. apart, were inserted into the skull to a depth of about one millimeter so as to span the brain from olfactory lobe to the tectum (fig. 1), and into the skin and musculature along the neural spines to span single segments of the pectoral, lumbar, and pelvic regions of the spinal cord. Recordings were made on a Model III D, four-channel Grass electroencephalograph. The electrical activity described in this report is interpreted as being of neuromuscular origin, with the implication that alterations are due fundamentally to changes in the central nervous system. Such electrical changes were not present when the central nervous system was removed from the salamander and the 6 convulsant drugs were applied topically to muscle.

RESULTS. Three general types of seizures were induced by the 6 drugs. Seizures with definite clonic and tonic phases were evoked by Metrazol and picrotoxin: seizures with conspicuously clonic components were produced by strychnine and nicotine: seizures predominantly tonic were produced by Coramine and caffeine. In presenting the data under each heading the following sequence has been observed: behavioral effects with and without transected cord, accompanying changes in electrical activity, time of onset and duration of side effects, and some comparative observations. In a motionless salamander, electrodes spanning various regions of the cord show a dominant rhythm of 30 to 40 per second waves of low amplitude, while those spanning the brain show sequence of 8 to 12, and 18 to 22 waves per second of moderate amplitude (fig. 1). After a transection of the spinal cord this electrical activity remains fundamentally the same.

Metrazol. The onset of the first violent clonic phase is explosively sudden and occurs about 10 minutes after injection. It begins with a repeated lateral lashing of the tail, trunk and head, and is associated with such actions as spinning of the body on its long axis, gasping, rigid extension or flexion of limbs, and secretion of skin glands. During this violent phase, which lasts about 20 seconds, there occurs an electrical discharge of large amplitude and a frequency of 35 to 40 waves per second mingled with brief movement artifacts. After the activity just described the salamander typically assumes an opisthotonoid posture associated with a sustained electrical discharge of very large amplitude and high frequency (fig. 2): this tonic phase lasts from a few seconds to several minutes. Eventually the salamander undergoes relaxation, but this respite is soon interrupted by clonic jerks of trunk and limbs manifested on the electrical record as brief electrical volleys of large amplitude (fig. 2). Gradually the clonic twitches occur less often, so that at the end of 4 hours the salamander is almost motionless. Within 24 hours the animal has recovered normal behavior.

The injection of Metrazol into a salamander with a transected cord is followed by gasping,

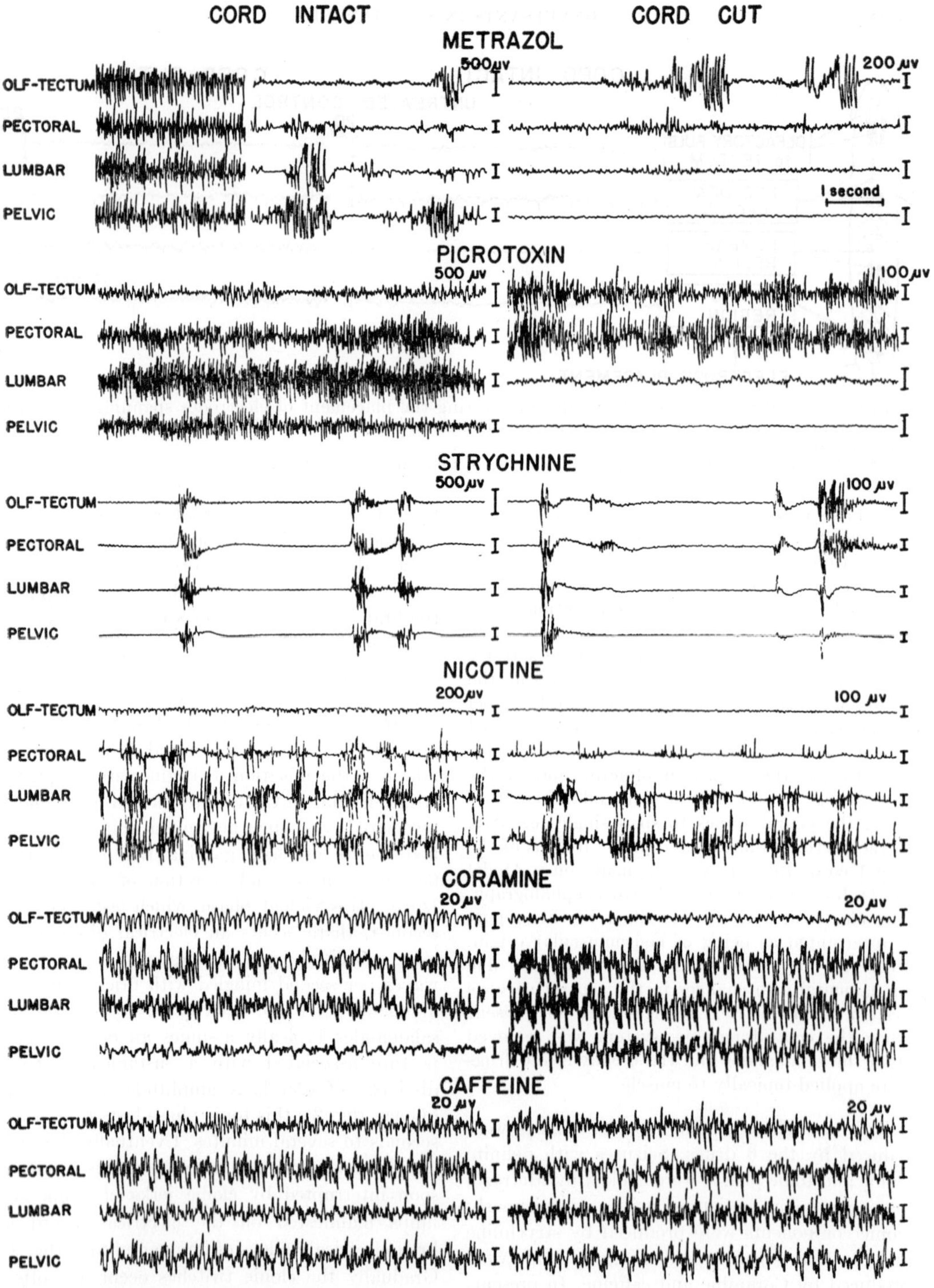

FIG. 2. Changes in electrical activity induced by 6 convulsant drugs, before and after a transection of the spinal cord at the second vertebra.

Sustained electrical discharges of large amplitude are associated with the tonic phases of seizures as illustrated under Metrazol, picrotoxin, nikethamide (Coramine) and caffeine. Clonic phases are associated with brief electrical volleys of large amplitude as illustrated under Metrazol, strychnine and nicotine. After transection of the spinal cord note the electrical activity at the lumbar and pelvic regions, its diminution with Metrazol and picrotoxin, and its persistence with strychnine, nikethamide (Coramine), nicotine and caffeine.

slow writhing movements of the trunk, and erratic placement of limbs. However, the explosively sudden onset of the first clonic phase seen in intact animals is no longer present, there is no definite opisthotonoid posture, and brief spastic jerks and electrical volleys are typically absent in the trunk (fig. 2). Records from the brachial area may show brief bursts of strong electrical activity but these are interpreted as being caused by muscles supplied with nerves anterior to the transection.

In addition to the seizure phenomena described above, Metrazol produces the following side effects (fig. 3). After the major seizure the salamander develops an edema, makes almost no attempt to walk, to right itself in water, or to respond to tactile stimulation. Swimming is vigorous, but aimless and the visual response is slow and inconsistent. The corneal and abdominal reflexes are least affected. Within 24 hours these side effects have disappeared.

Picrotoxin. In regard to behavior and accompanying changes in electrical activity (fig. 2), the seizures induced by picrotoxin bear a striking resemblance to those induced by Metrazol, with the following differences. Under the influence of picrotoxin the edema is more severe, and more time is required for the onset of the violent phase of the seizure (about 30 minutes) and for recovery (about 3 days). After the first clonic-tonic episode similar episodes of less severity may occur within the next few minutes. After a transection of the spinal cord electrical recordings indicate that picrotoxin evokes neither

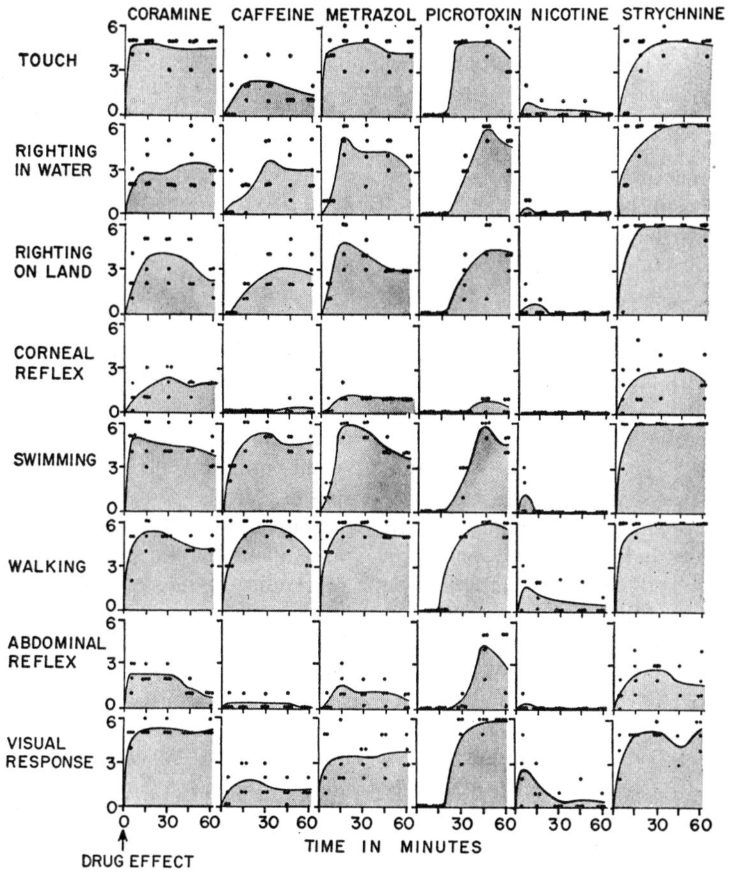

FIG. 3. Graph summarizing various sensory-motor side effects, usually a reduced response to neurological tests, associated with the action of 6 convulsant drugs.

The horizontal axis shows time of onset and duration. The vertical axis shows degree of reduction of response to various stimuli, in which 0 is regarded as normal activity and 6 as a complete absence of response. Each dot represents a single observation; four salamanders were used for each drug.

clonic nor tonic spasms in the region of the cord posterior to the transection (fig. 2).

Strychnine. About 5 minutes after the injection of strychnine the entire body begins twitching about once or twice a minute. During the clonic spasms induced by strychnine electrical activity along the full length of the vertebral axis shows repeated electrical volleys of high frequency and large amplitude, lasting a second or less, and superimposed on a movement artifact (fig. 2). These bodily twitches and associated electrical volleys appear with apparent spontaneity, or can be evoked either by touching the salamander or the support on which it rests. About 30 minutes after injection the apparently spontaneous twitches cease. When a salamander with a transected cord is given strychnine, spastic jerks and accompanying electrical volleys occur on either side of the transection (fig. 2).

When neurological tests are given immediately after the period of strychnine spasticity, they reveal an almost complete extinction of walking, swimming and righting, together with a diminished response in the visual test and the abdominal and corneal reflexes (fig. 3). Several hours after the injection of strychnine the animal shows an improved response to touch and righting. About 2 or 3 days elapse before the side effects disappear.

Nicotine. The effects of nicotine and strychnine are similar in that both drugs produce clonic spasms with accompanying electrical volleys, and that they evoke this effect from the spinal cord even after its separation from the brain (fig. 2). The electrical changes associated with the clonic spasms induced by strychnine and nicotine are definitely different (fig. 2): the electrical volleys induced by strychnine are more wide spread and occur less often, while those induced by nicotine are more local and occur more frequently. In comparison with strychnine, nicotine takes effect more rapidly, produces spasms which are confined mainly to the trunk and which are not evoked by tactile stimulation. The side effects of nicotine are less numerous (fig. 3), less severe, and of briefer duration than those caused by strychnine. Under the influence of nicotine the corneal and abdominal reflexes are almost unaffected.

Nikethamide (Coramine). A few minutes after the injection of nikethamide and during the following one half hour the salamanders undergo athetoid movements of the trunk and limbs, accompanied by gasping, extension of limbs, backward walking, and an occasional arching of the trunk. When not walking the animals adopt a strained S-shaped posture with an exaggerated lateral curvature of the vertebral axis; this posture is associated with a mild tonic phase of a seizure. During this phase the electrical records from the full length of the salamander show a sustained augmentation of amplitude, with unusually regular sequences of waves whose frequency is about 9 to 11 per second (note "olf-tectum" channel in figure 2). With striking uniformity this electrical record persists for about 45 minutes, after which time the S-shaped posture is maintained less often. In a salamander with a transected cord, nikethamide evokes fundamentally the same effects as those described above.

In addition to the tonic-like phase mentioned above, nikethamide produces the following side effects. About 5 minutes after injection the salamander shows labored walking and swimming, and a slower response to touch and to the visual test (fig. 3). In about 15 minutes there is a diminished response to the righting, corneal and abdominal reflexes. A gradual return to normal begins about 3 hours after injection and side effects disappear within 24 hours.

Caffeine. Caffeine and nikethamide are similar in that both drugs induce a relatively mild tonic type of seizure associated with a sustained electrical discharge of increased amplitude which persists in the trunk even after transection of the spinal cord (fig. 2). Neither drug evokes clonic spasms. Both drugs produce a diminished response to most of the neurological tests and require about the same length of time for the disappearance of side effects. In spite of the similarities mentioned above the effects of caffeine differ from those of nikethamide in several obvious respects. The regular sequences of 9 to 11 per second waves described for nikethamide were absent in animals injected with caffeine. Caffeine, unlike nikethamide, leaves the corneal and abdominal reflexes almost normal, but it renders walking and swimming awkward by inducing some rigidity in the trunk and a lateral extension of the limbs. During swimming only the posterior third of the tail is used for propulsion. After transection of the cord, the trunk of a caffeine-treated salamander is less rigid and the animal engages in more frequent writhing movements.

DISCUSSION. In discussing the results special significance should be attached to the fact that drug effects were obtained in an animal lacking a cerebral cortex. A cerebral cortex is not essential for the clonic and tonic phases of a seizure as indicated by the definite clonic and tonic phases produced in the salamander by the action of Metrazol and picrotoxin. However the failure of both of these drugs to evoke the brief electrical volleys characteristic of clonic spasms in the lumbar and pelvic regions of the cord after transection suggests that Metrazol and picrotoxin produce clonus by their action on the brain, probably involving the basal ganglia (Kennard, 1944). Although Metrazol and picrotoxin exhibit numerous similarities as convulsants, the sites and extent of action are not identical. Even after transection, Metrazol provokes sustained electrical discharges of large amplitude characteristic of a tonic phase in both brain and spinal cord. Picrotoxin, on the other hand, failed to evoke seizure phenomena in that region of the spinal cord which is posterior to the transection; consequently in the production of seizures picrotoxin presumably acts through the brain. It should be noted that neither picrotoxin nor Metrazol produced an opisthotonoid posture after transection of the spinal cord: this result suggests that these drugs produce this posture by acting on the brain, which in turn excites long spinal tracts and ventral horn cells of the cord. Such activities as frequent gasping, swallowing and an abundant secretion of skin glands in the salamander indicate that both Metrazol and picrotoxin simulate certain autonomic centers in the medulla.

Although nicotine and strychnine are similar in that both cause spastic jerks of the trunk, even after transection of the spinal cord, conspicuously different behavioral effects and different changes in the electrical recordings suggest different methods and places of action. Unlike strychnine, nicotine produces shallow ripples of skeletal musculature which are local, confined mainly to the trunk, and associated with numerous isolated spike-like electrical discharges. These observations suggest that nicotine probably acts intermittently on anterior horn cells of the spinal cord and associated motor units (Denny-Brown and Pennybacker, 1938; Drill, 1954). Under the influence of strychnine, not of nicotine, even after transection of the cord, spastic twitches and accompanying electrical volleys can be evoked in both head and trunk by a light touch. These results support the view that the action of strychnine tends to be similar throughout the central nervous system and that strychnine lowers inhibition and the threshold to stimulation at reflex arcs (Bradley *et al.*, 1953; Heinbacker and Bartley, 1939).

The slow writhing movements of the salamander after an injection of nikethamide and the rigidity following an injection of caffeine differ considerably from the violent epileptiform convulsions of mammals after a dose of the same drugs (Grau, 1957; Fuhner, 1932; Goodman and Gillman, 1955). These contrasting results may find an explanation in the view that nikethamide and caffeine induce epileptiform convulsions by an excitation of higher motor centers, presumably cortical structures, which are present in mammals but absent in the salamander. Nikethamide, unlike caffeine, produces an electrical record which has a striking regularity in the slower waves, probably because it depresses the first step of neuromuscular transmission (Huidobro and Jordan, 1946), and thus diminishes the magnitude of the muscular contraction and the amplitude of the 30 to 40 per second waves seen in normal records. Caffeine, unlike nikethamide, produces an extreme rigidity of the trunk of the salamander, which is diminished considerably after transection of the cord. It is suggested that this extreme rigidity may be due to the combined effects of caffeine on brain and cord, perhaps on those portions of the reticular formation where inhibition is suppressed. Transection of the cord removes the influence of the brain on long descending spinal tracts and trunk musculature, resulting in a less rigid, more active salamander.

SUMMARY

As indicated by behavior and the electrical activity of the nervous and muscular systems of the salamander, pentylenetetrazol and picrotoxin induce seizures with tonic and clonic phases. These drugs evoke a clonic-tonic type of seizure in the absence of a cerebral cortex. After a transection of the spinal cord neither drug evokes spastic jerks posterior to the transection. Hence lower centers of the brain are required for the combined manifestation of clonic and tonic seizures induced by these two drugs.

Strychnine lowers the threshold to stimulation, and after transection evokes generalized spastic twitches on either side of the cut, suggesting an action of the drug on reflex arcs. Nicotine, before and after transection of the spinal cord, produces only local tremors in the trunk due presumably to its action on the anterior horn cells of the spinal cord.

In the salamander both nikethamide and caffeine produce a tonic type of seizure without clonic components. The extreme rigidity produced by caffeine seems to involve an action of this drug on the brain, since it is diminished considerably after a transection of the cord. Nikethamide does not produce extreme rigidity, but unlike caffeine it produces a striking regularity of slower waves in the electrical record.

Time of onset and duration of side effects as manifested by neurological tests is summarized graphically.

REFERENCES

BRADLEY, K., EASTON, D. M., AND ECCLES, J. C.: J. Physiol., **122**: 474, 1953.

BRAZIER, M. A.: Bibliography of Electroencephalography, International Federation of Electroencephalography and Clinical Neurophysiology, 1950.

DENNY-BROWN, D., AND PENNYBACKER, J. B.: Brain, **61**: 311, 1938.

DRILL, V. A.: Pharmacology in Medicine, McGraw-Hill Book Co., New York, 1954.

FUHNER, H.: Arch. exper. Path. u. Pharmakol., **166**: 437, 1932.

GOODMAN, L. S., AND GILMAN, A.: The Pharmacological Basis of Therapeutics, Macmillan Co., New York, 1955.

GOODMAN, L. S., GREWAL, M. S., GROWN, W. C., AND SWINYARD, E. A.: THIS JOURNAL, **108**: 168, 1953.

GRAU, W. H.: Thesis (Biology), Xavier Univ., Cincinnati, O., 1957.

HEINBECKER, P., AND BARTLEY, S. H.: Am. J. Physiol., **125**: 172, 1939.

HUIDOBRO, F., AND JORDAN, J.: THIS JOURNAL, **86**: 49, 1946.

KENNARD, M. A.: J. Neurophysiol., **7**: 142, 1944.

MAGOUN, H. W.: Epilepsia, third series, **I**: 69, 1952.

PENFIELD, W., AND JASPER, H.: Epilepsy and the Functional Anatomy of the Human Brain, Little, Brown and Co., Boston, 1954.

PETERS, J. J., AND VONDERAHE, A. R.: EEG Clin. Neurophysiol., **6**: 253, 1954.

PETERS, J. J., VONDERAHE, A. R., AND PALMISANO, P. A.: THIS JOURNAL, **118**: 90, 1956.

TOMAN, J. E., AND TAYLOR, J. D.: Epilepsia, third series, **I**: 31, 1952.

8009

EFFECTS OF VARIOUS PHENOTHIAZINES ON MINIMAL ELECTROSHOCK SEIZURE THRESHOLD AND SPONTANEOUS MOTOR ACTIVITY OF MICE[1, 2]

DAVID H. TEDESCHI, JOHN P. BENIGNI, CHARLES J. ELDER, JUANITA C. YEAGER AND JOHN V. FLANIGAN

Research and Development Division, Smith Kline & French Laboratories, Philadelphia, Pennsylvania

Received for publication February 5, 1958

A number of clinical investigators have reported the occurrence of convulsive seizures in nonepileptic patients undergoing intensive therapy with phenothiazine derivatives (Rudy *et al.*, 1956; Feldman, 1957; Voegele and May, 1957). Meszaros and O'Reilly (1956) concluded from their investigations that chlorpromazine has "epileptogenic properties which may lead to manifest fits in susceptible people." These authors have suggested that this effect of phenothiazines in epileptic patients is possibly counterbalanced by a potentiating effect on anticonvulsant drugs and by a reduction in emotional tension. Kalinowsky (1956) has cautioned that chlorpromazine therapy should be discontinued during electroshock therapy because of the "sharp rise in fatalities of patients receiving combined therapy." Goldman (1955), in contrast, reported chlorpromazine as "happily synergistic with electric shock in producing recovery from psychotic states." Reports on the effects of phenothiazines on electroshock seizures elicited in experimental animals are somewhat inconsistent. For example, Heming and coworkers (1956) observed a threshold-lowering effect after chlorpromazine administration. Gujral and co-workers (1956) and Hauschild, as cited by Feller (1955), reported that chlorpromazine possessed anticonvulsant properties. Mercier (1955), in contrast, was unable to demonstrate an effect of chlorpromazine on electroshock seizure threshold. The present report consists of an analysis of the effects of six phenothiazines on minimal electroshock seizure threshold in mice. It is intended to resolve some of the apparently discrepant results reported by previous investigators and to explore a possible relationship between the effects of phenothiazines on electroshock seizure threshold in mice and their tendency to cause seizures in man as reported in the clinical literature.

METHODS. Adult male albino mice obtained from Carworth Farms (CF #1 strain) were used as experimental animals. They were allowed free access to food and water except during the brief experimental test period. The following phenothiazines were tested: 2 - chloro - 10 - (3′ - dimethylamino-propyl)-phenothiazine hydrochloride (chlorpromazine, Thorazine); 10 - (3′ - dimethylamino-propyl)-phenothiazine hydrochloride (promazine, Sparine); 2-chloro-10-[3′(1-methyl-4-piperazinyl)-propyl] - phenothiazine dimaleate (prochlorperazine, Compazine); 2 - trifluoromethyl - 10 - [3′(1 - methyl - 4 - piperazinyl) - propyl] - phenothiazine dihydrochloride (trifluoperazine, Stelazine); 10-(2′ - dimethylamino - isopropyl) - phenothiazine hydrochloride (promethazine, Phenergan); 10-(N - methyl - 3 - piperidylmethyl) - phenothiazine hydrochloride (mepazine, Pacatal). All of the drugs tested were administered by the oral route. With the exception of prochlorperazine and mepazine, all drugs were dissolved in aqueous solution; prochlorperazine and mepazine were suspended in 0.5 per cent tragacanth solution. Doses of drugs are expressed in terms of the base. The minimum current necessary to elicit "threshold seizures" (facial, lower jaw, and/or forelimb clonus without loss of upright posture) or more severe seizures in 50 per cent of mice (CC_{50}) was determined by the method of Swinyard *et al.* (1952, 1957). The apparatus employed for eliciting seizures was similar to that originally described by Woodbury and Davenport (1952). CC_{50}'s were calculated by the method of Litchfield and Wilcoxon (1949). The time of peak drug effect on minimal electroshock seizure threshold (MET) was determined as follows. The drug to be

[1] Presented at the Fall Meetings of the American Society for Pharmacology and Experimental Therapeutics, Baltimore, September, 1957.

[2] The authors are indebted to their colleague Mr. John F. Pauls for assistance in the statistical analysis of the data.

tested was administered orally to 6 groups of 5 mice each. Each group of mice was shocked once with the CC_{50} as previously determined on the same day in saline-treated mice. Groups of drug-treated mice were shocked at 30, 60, 90, 120, 150 and 180 minutes after drug administration and the character of the seizure was recorded. Peak effect was taken as that time after drug administration at which a maximum increase (or decrease in the case of drugs which raise threshold) in the number of threshold seizures or more severe seizures was observed. CC_{50}'s were determined in groups of 30 or more mice for each dose of each drug at its respective time of peak effect. Per cent change in MET was estimated on the basis of control CC_{50}'s determined concomitantly. In general, drugs were tested for their effects on MET in a range of doses which produced equivalent degrees of depression of spontaneous motor activity (SMA) in mice (Winter and Flataker, 1951; Cook *et al.*, 1955). The effect of drugs on SMA was measured as follows. Individual mice were treated with the dose of drug to be tested (8 mice per dose, 8 saline-treated controls per drug, 4 doses per drug). At ten minutes before time of

TABLE 1

Potencies of the depressant effect on spontaneous motor activity of various phenothiazine derivatives

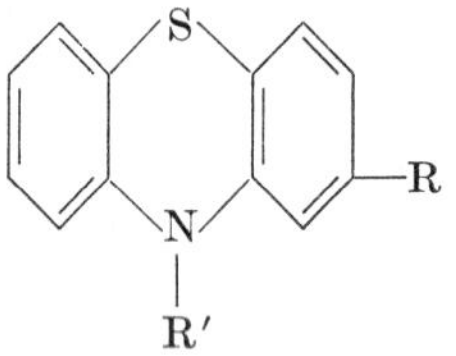

Generic Name	R	R′	Oral DD_{50} (95% Fiducial Limits)
			mgm./kgm.
Trifluoperazine	CF_3	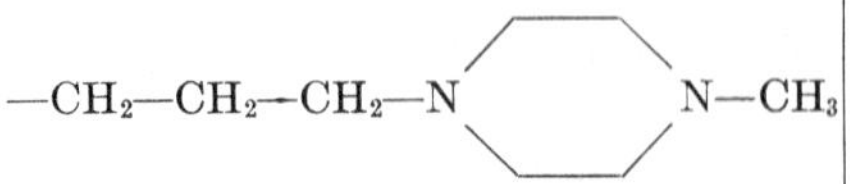	0.85 (0.3–1.4)
Chlorpromazine	Cl	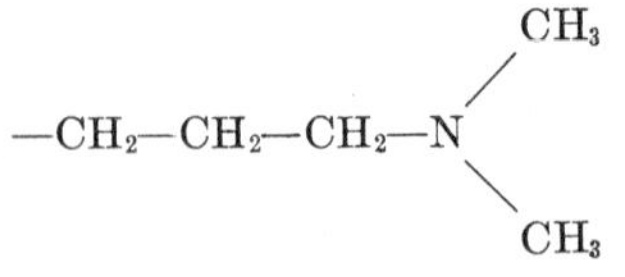	4.7 (3.5–6.5)
Prochlorperazine	Cl	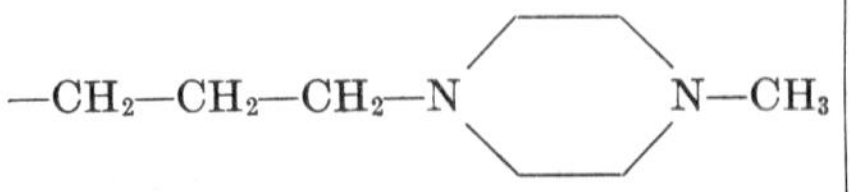	5.8 (4.0–9.8)
Promazine	H	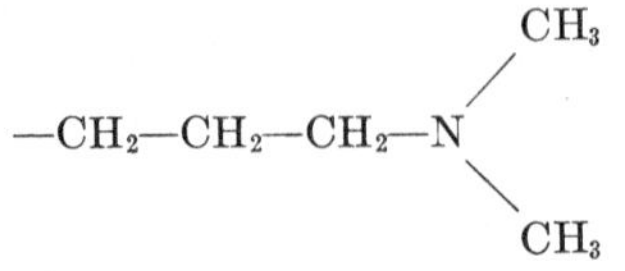	20.8 (14.7–33)
Promethazine	H	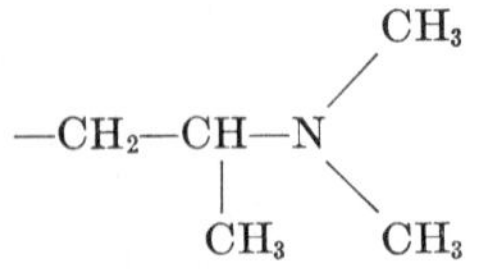	106.1 (68.5–221.4)
Mepazine	H	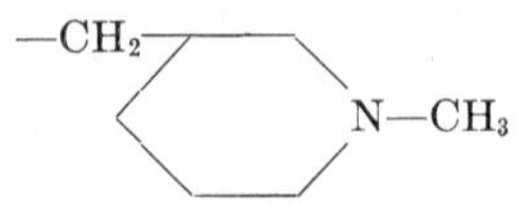	149.1 (116.8–226.2)

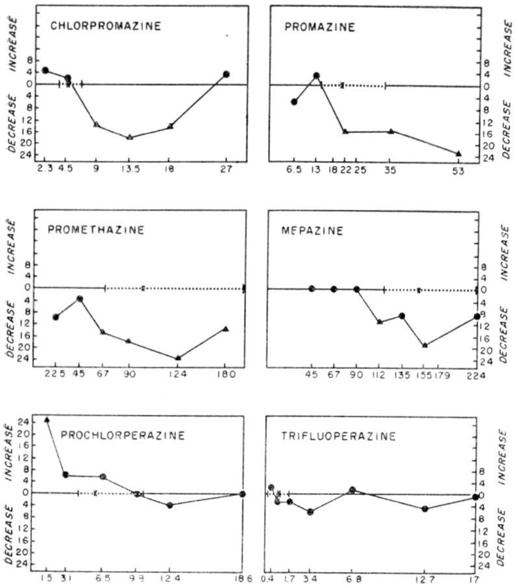

FIG. 1. The effect of various phenothiazines on minimal electroshock seizure threshold and spontaneous motor activity of mice.

The per cent changes in threshold are plotted on the ordinates and the doses tested (mgm./kgm., expressed in terms of free base) are plotted on the abscissae. Per cent changes in threshold are referable to control CC_{50}'s determined concomitantly. Points plotted above zero lines represent increases in threshold, points plotted below the zero lines represent decreases in threshold. Points plotted with a dot are not significantly different from controls. The large X plotted on the horizontal line represents the dose producing a 50 per cent depression of spontaneous motor activity The horizontal bracketed dotted lines represent 95 per cent fiducial limits. See text for discussion.

peak drug effect[3] each mouse was placed in a photo cell counting chamber. The total count was taken after a 10-minute interval for each individual mouse. The data obtained were then analyzed as follows. A dose-response curve was fitted by computing the regression of mean response on logarithm of dose. From this dose-response curve the dose was estimated which would produce a response equal to 50 per cent of the average control response. This dose is referred to as the DD_{50}. The 95 per cent fiducial limits for the estimated curve were computed using Fieller's theorem (Finney, 1952).

RESULTS. Potencies of the depressant effect on SMA of the various phenothiazine derivatives tested are summarized in table 1. The drugs have been arranged in the table in order of descending potency; trifluoperazine is most potent and mepazine least potent. The effects of the drugs on MET are illustrated in figure 1. In general, the doses employed were selected on the basis of the relative potencies of these compounds in producing depression of motor activity. For purposes of comparison, the respective DD_{50}'s and 95 per cent fiducial limits for each drug have been included in the figure. In general, the pattern of seizures evoked in phenothiazine-treated mice was similar to the pattern of seizures elicited in control mice. As shown in the figure, chlorpromazine, promazine, mepazine, and promethazine all significantly decreased MET in one or more of the doses employed. It is interesting to note that doses of chlorpromazine of 4.5 mgm./kgm. or less and of 27 mgm./kgm. failed to alter MET significantly, whereas doses intermediate to these produced significant lowering of MET. Of the six compounds tested, prochlorperazine was the only one which produced a significant increase in threshold; this increase in threshold was observed only at the 1.5 mgm./kgm. dose. Higher doses of this drug failed to alter MET significantly. Trifluoperazine failed to produce a significant change in threshold at any of the doses tested.

DISCUSSION. The data presented indicate that chlorpromazine produces a significant decrease in MET over a narrow range of dosage. Thus, oral doses of 2.3, 4.5 and 27 mgm./kgm. had no significant effect on seizure threshold, whereas doses intermediate to the latter two significantly lowered threshold. These findings are in essential agreement with those reported by previous investigators, some of whom observed a threshold-lowering effect after chlorpromazine (Heming *et al.*, 1956) while others demonstrated an anticonvulsant effect after administration of this compound (Gujral *et al.*, 1956; Tanaka and Kawasaki, 1957). In general, the antielectroshock action of chlorpromazine has been reported only after administration of relatively high doses, whereas a threshold-lowering effect has been reported after administration of comparatively low doses. Four of the six phenothiazines investigated (chlorpromazine, promazine, mepazine and promethazine) produced a significant decrease in MET in doses at or near their respective DD_{50} range of effec-

[3] The time of peak effect employed was the same as that used for the MET test. This time of peak effect coincides with the time of peak depression of SMA as determined by observation of treated mice.

tiveness. It is interesting to note that each of these compounds has been reported to cause seizures in man (Feldman, 1957; Voegele and May, 1957; Rudy *et al.*, 1956; Caruana *et al.*, 1952). In contrast, prochlorperazine and trifluoperazine did not produce a significant decrease in seizure threshold in mice at any of the doses tested. To date, there have been no clinical reports in the literature concerning the production of seizures by either of these compounds. One may speculate, in view of these findings, that *within this chemical series* a correlation may exist between changes in MET produced by these compounds in mice and the tendency of such drugs to cause seizures in man.

Both prochlorperazine and trifluoperazine have been demonstrated to be effective as tranquilizing drugs in man. In view of the fact that the doses of these drugs tested failed to produce a significant decrease in MET it would appear that a minimal seizure threshold-lowering action in mice is not a necessary property of effective, potent tranquilizing agents.

SUMMARY

The effects of chlorpromazine, promazine, prochlorperazine, trifluoperazine, promethazine and mepazine on minimal electroshock seizure threshold and spontaneous motor activity of mice were investigated. All of the drugs tested produced significant depression of motor activity. Ranked in descending order of potency by this test they are trifluoperazine > chlorpromazine > prochlorperazine > promazine > promethazine > mepazine. Chlorpromazine, promazine, mepazine and promethazine all produced significant decreases in minimal electroshock seizure threshold (MET). Chlorpromazine produced a significant decrease in threshold in oral doses of 9 to 18 mgm./kgm., whereas doses of 4.5 and 27 mgm./kgm. failed to produce significant changes in threshold. Trifluoperazine and prochlorperazine did not produce a significant decrease in MET in the doses tested.

The data presented indicate that a minimal electroshock seizure threshold-lowering action is not a necessary property of effective, potent, tranquilizing agents.

REFERENCES

Caruana, H., Hamza, B., and Chileb, H.: Tunisie Med., **40:** 283, 1952.

Cook, L., Weidley, E. F., Morris, R. W., and Mattis, P. A.: This Journal, **113:** 11, 1955.

Feldman, P. E.: J. Clin. Exper. Psychopath., **18:** 1, 1957.

Feller, K.: Arch. exper. Path. u. Pharmakol., **225:** 90, 1955.

Finney, D. J.: Statistical Method in Biological Assay, Haffner Company, New York, 1952.

Goldman, D.: J. A. M. A., **157:** 1274, 1955.

Gujral, M. L., Saxena, P. N., and Kulsreshtha, J. K.: J. Indian M. Profession, **3:** 1141, 1956.

Heming, A. E., Holtkamp, E. E., Huntsman, D. B., Doggett, M. C., and Mansor, L. F.: This Journal, **116:** 28, 1956.

Kalinowsky, L. B.: Am. J. Psychiat., **112:** 745 1956.

Litchfield, J. T., Jr., and Wilcoxon, F.: This Journal, **96:** 99, 1949.

Mercier, J.: Compt. rend. Soc. de Biol., **149:** 379, 1955.

Meszaros, A. F., and O'Reilly, P. O.: Dis. Nerv. System, **17:** 159, 1956.

Rudy, L. H., Himwich, H. E., and Rinaldi, F.: Presented at meeting of American Society for Biological Psychiatry, April 29, 1956.

Swinyard, E. A., Brown, W. C., and Goodman, L. S.: This Journal, **106:** 319, 1952.

Swinyard, E. A., Chin, L., Cole, F. R., and Goodman, L. S.: Proc. Soc. Exper. Biol. & Med., **94:** 12, 1957.

Tanaka, K., and Kawasaki, Y.: Jap. J. Pharmacol., **6:** 115, 1957.

Voegele, G. E., and May, R. H.: Am. J. Psychiat., **113:** 655, 1957.

Winter, C. A., and Flataker, L.: This Journal, **103:** 93, 1951.

Woodbury, L. A., and Davenport, V. D.: Arch. internat. pharmacodyn., **92:** 97, 1952.

8010

THE EFFECT OF RESERPINE AND CHLORPROMAZINE ON THE RESPONSE OF THE RAT TO ACUTE STRESS[1]

MOHAMAD MAHFOUZ AND ESMAT A. EZZ[2]

Department of Pharmacology, Faculty of Medicine, University of Alexandria, Egypt

Received for publication January 23, 1958

It is generally accepted that the suprarenal cortex is activated as a part of the phenomena occurring in response to subjection of an organism to acute stress. This results in depletion of the adrenal ascorbic acid, which occurs within a period less than one hour. This depletion is shown to occur after injection of ACTH (Sayers *et al.*, 1944) as well as after the exposure of an organism to various stressful stimuli such as hemorrhage (Sayers *et al.*, 1945), scalding (Harkins and Long, 1945; Harkins, 1945), exposure to cold (Levin, 1945), ether anesthesia (Bowman and Muntwyler, 1937), ether plus scalding, and ether plus rapid exsanguination (Syndor and Sayers, 1954). The depletion of adrenal ascorbic acid in response to stress does not occur in hypophysectomized rats (Sayers *et al.*, 1945). Depletion of adrenal ascorbic acid also occurs after the injection of normal rats with posterior pituitary hormones; however, this does not occur in hypophysectomized animals (Martini and DePoli, 1956). The effects of injection of epinephrine and surgical trauma on ACTH secretion are blocked by an appropriate hypothalamic lesion (Hume, 1952; Porter, 1953; McCann, 1953).

The aim of this work was to investigate the action of reserpine and chlorpromazine on the response of the rat to acute stress. Chlorpromazine has been reported to inhibit the depletion of adrenal ascorbic acid induced by various stressful stimuli (Hamburger, 1955; Aron *et al.*, 1953; Olling and de Weid, 1956; Sevy *et al.*, 1957). Christy *et al.* (1956) found the stress of insulin hypoglycemia in humans to be inhibited by pretreatment with 100 to 400 mgm. of chlorpromazine. On the other hand, Holzbaur and Vogt (1954) failed to demonstrate such action, and they even found that chlorpromazine itself caused adrenal ascorbic acid depletion in unanesthetized rats. This latter finding was also demonstrated by Olling and de Weid (1956). However, Sevy *et al.* (1957) failed to demonstrate this action.

Sevy *et al.* (1957) found that adrenal ascorbic acid depletion with vasopressin was unaffected by chlorpromazine. This suggests that the drug acts on the prepituitary phase.

The effect of reserpine on the response to stress has not been investigated. Schneider *et al.* (1955) believed that reserpine may facilitate the action of cortical inhibitory centers which depress the hypothalamus.

METHODS. The degree of response to stress and any modification in such a response was assayed by the degree of cortical activity. Cortical activity was assayed by determining the degree of adrenal ascorbic acid depletion since Sayers (1950) found it to be a very reliable index of adrenal cortical activity in acute experiments.

Male albino rats from the same litter were used. All rats were approximately of the same age. The rats were kept under standard conditions with respect to diet, humidity, and room temperature, which was kept constant at 22°C. ± 2°. The day before the experiment, the rats were isolated for 24 hours during which no food was given.

Forms of stressful stimuli. These were selected on the basis of their similarity to forms of stress encountered by humans. The following three were used: 1) Continuous ether anesthesia plus rapid exsanguination: This simulates the stress of surgical operations. Rats were put in a tight glass box designed to standardize the conditions of stress with respect to the concentration of ether and time of exposure. The box has an inlet tube at the bottom and an exit tube at the top. An O_2-CO_2 mixture was passed at a constant pressure through a Wolf bottle containing ether. After 5 minutes, rats were removed from the box and bled from the tail. The site of incision was heparinized to allow

[1] Presented in part at the XX International Physiological Congress, Brussels, Belgium, July 30–August 4, 1956.

[2] Present address: Argonne Cancer Research Hospital, The University of Chicago, Chicago 37, Illinois.

free and rapid bleeding of 8 ml./kgm. b.w. The tail was then tied and the rat returned to the anesthesia box for 30 minutes before decapitation and removal of the adrenals. 2) Heat stress: This was considered to simulate conditions of hyperpyrexia or heat stroke. The rats were put in a wide brass jar closed with a glass cover and possessing an inlet and outlet for aeration. Air was supplied by an aerator at a constant and adequate rate. The jar was immersed in a water bath maintained at a constant temperature of 38°C. The rats were kept at this temperature for one hour, after which they were decapitated immediately and the adrenals removed. 3) Cold stress: This form of stress is becoming more important with the introduction of artificial hibernation and cooling techniques. The rats were put in a refrigerator at a constant temperature of +3°C. for one hour prior to decapitation and adrenalectomy.

Estimation of the adrenal ascorbic acid. After decapitation, the adrenals were dissected, freed from fat and immediately weighed to the nearest 0.1 mgm. Both glands were weighed together. They were ground in a small mortar containing approximately 2 gm. of acid-washed sand and 5 ml. of 4 per cent trichloracetic acid. The contents were transferred to a small bottle, tightly sealed and left over night in a refrigerator. The following morning, the contents of the bottle were transferred to a centrifuge tube and the bottle washed with 5 ml. of 4 per cent trichloracetic acid which was added to the centrifuge tube. After centrifuging for 5 minutes, the supernate was filtered. Analysis for ascorbic acid was then performed by the method of Roe and Keuther (1943).

Drugs and dosage. The drugs were diluted with saline and administered intramuscularly one-half hour before application of acute stress. Half of the dose was injected into each thigh. Twenty rats receiving no drug and not subjected to any stress served as controls. Eight rats received 8.0 microgm. of reserpine/kgm. body weight, were sacrificed one-half hour later without being exposed to stress and their adrenal ascorbic acid was estimated. Another group of eight rats received 2.0 mgm. of chlorpromazine/kgm., were sacrificed one-half hour later without being exposed to stress and their adrenal ascorbic acid was estimated. The rats exposed to stress were divided into three groups: one receiving no drug, another receiving chlorpromazine, and the third receiving reserpine. The rats that received ACTH were divided into three groups: one group received ACTH alone, the second received ACTH one-half hour after the usual dose of chlorpromazine, and the third group received ACTH one-half hour after the usual dose of reserpine. In each case, the rats were sacrificed one-half hour after receiving ACTH.

Results and discussion. The results are shown in table 1. These results indicate that 1) both drugs diminished ascorbic acid depletion in response to stress; 2) neither drug prevented the adrenal ascorbic acid depleting action of ACTH; 3) reserpine was highly effective in the low doses used; and 4) neither drug caused adrenal ascorbic acid depletion when given intramuscularly to unanesthetized rats.

In considering our results, we are assuming that the amount of depletion of adrenal ascorbic acid is proportional to the degree of stress (Sayers and Sayers, 1947). In these experiments, all groups of stressed rats were subjected to stressful stimuli of the same degree and duration whether or not drugs had been given. Therefore, variations in the degree of adrenal ascorbic acid depletion should be due to pretreatment with the drug used.

The action of the drugs used may have been on one or more of the following phases of the response to stress: 1) prepituitary phase of response to stress, 2) pituitary elaboration of ACTH, 3) interference with the action of ACTH on the cortex. The last possibility is eliminated experimentally since neither drug prevents ACTH from causing ascorbic acid depletion. This is supported by the results obtained by Olling and de Weid (1956) and Sevy *et al.* (1957) with chlorpromazine.

Regarding the possibility that the drugs act on the prepituitary phase, consideration must be given to the fact that the nature of this phase is still disputed. According to Sayers (1950), the organism responds normally with reactions mediated by sympathetic nervous receptor (sympathetico-adrenal discharge). This leads to increased tissue metabolism. Corticoids are used up and the pituitary-cortical system is stimulated from the periphery as a result of diminution of the concentration of the corticoids in the tissue fluids. Stimuli may travel as an alternative route via hypothalamic centers to adrenal hypophysis and through it to the adrenal cortex. Against this theory is the work of Bush (1953) which led him to conclude that "a fall in the peripheral concentration of adrenal hormones does not stimulate the release of ACTH directly." Also, severe stress causes adrenocortical stimu-

TABLE I

Inhibition of pituitary adrenocorticotrophic activity by chlorpromazine and reserpine following subjection of rats to various stressful stimuli

Treatment	No. of Rats	Pretreatment with Chlorpromazine, i.m.	Adrenal Ascorbic Acid	No. of Rats	Pretreatment with Reserpine, i.m.	Adrenal Ascorbic Acid
		mgm./kgm.	*mgm./100 gm. fresh tissue*		*μgm./kgm.*	*mgm./100 gm. fresh tissue*
Controls	20	None	337 ± 6.7*	20	None	337 ± 6.7
	8	2	341 ± 10.3	8	8	329 ± 15.5
Heat (exposed to 38°C. for one hour before sacrifice)	9	None	190 ± 15.7	8	None	207 ± 11.3
	16	2	323 ± 9.8	14	8	346 ± 13.3
Cold (exposed to 3°C. for one hour before sacrifice)	6	None	220 ± 19.0	13	None	243 ± 6.7
	14	2	333 ± 10.7	12	8	342 ± 12.1
Ether anesthesia with exsanguination of 8 ml. of blood per kgm.	12	None	270 ± 13.6	8	None	290 ± 9.5
	14	2	345 ± 6.9	12	8	331 ± 11.7
ACTH, i.m., 40 mgm./kgm.	6	None	209 ± 8.6	8	None	233 ± 9.2
	10	2	226 ± 5.5	8	8	225 ± 11.5

* Average ± standard error.

lation even in face of the most intense overdosage of corticoids (Selye, 1953). It was suggested by Schnitzer (1954, 1955) that the first mediator in response to stress is histamine liberated from injured tissues; but the work of Guillemin (1955) showed that epinephrine, norepinephrine, acetylcholine and histamine cannot be sole humoral agents responsible for pituitary stimulation by systemic stress.

In the last few years, the hypothalamic-hypophyseal system has received much attention as the probable pathway by which central neural or neuro-humoral stimuli regulate ACTH secretion. The existing evidence for this is summarized by Harris *et al.* (1954). It points to a humoral rather than a nervous mechanism. The hypothalamus elaborates posterior pituitary hormone that is formed in the neurons of the hypothalamic nuclei (Bargmann *et al.*, 1949, 1951; Hild and Zetler, 1953; Sharrer and Sharrer, 1953). Also, Adams and Sloper (1956) demonstrated the elaboration of the postpituitary principle by the hypothalamus in man, rat and dog. The findings of Martini and DePoli (1956) are consistent with the hypothesis that the posterior pituitary hormones act as a humoral transmitting agent that is released by the hypothalamus in the hypophysial portal system and which activates the anterior pituitary to discharge ACTH.

Considering this and the work of Das *et al.* (1954) and Sevy *et al.* (1957), we can postulate that chlorpromazine and reserpine depress the response of the rat to acute stress by inhibiting the hypothalamic centers.

Another possibility is that these drugs, through their action on the autonomic nervous system, may depress the alarm reaction and thus diminish the response. Whether this action is beneficial or detrimental to welfare of the organism is difficult to determine. However, it was evident that the rats subjected to stress after receiving either of the drugs were in much better condition than rats exposed to the same stress without the benefit of the drugs mentioned.

SUMMARY

Both chlorpromazine and reserpine inhibited the response of the rat to acute stress as measured by the degree of adrenal ascorbic acid depletion. Reserpine was extraordinarily effective in blocking activation in the low doses used. Neither drug prevented the adrenal ascorbic acid depleting action of exogeneous ACTH. The possible mechanisms of action of chlorpromazine and reserpine are discussed. Our results, supported by the results of other authors with chlorpromazine, are suggestive of an action on the prepituitary phase of response to stress, possibly on the hypothalamus.

ACKNOWLEDGMENTS. The authors wish to express their appreciation to Dr. George T. Okita, Mr. Ahmed Mokhtar and Mr. Mohamed Sarya for their kind help; and to Dr. Fouad Bishara, Ciba Company representative, for generous supplies of reserpine.

REFERENCES

ADAMS, C. W., AND SLOPER, J. C.: J. Endocrin., **13:** 221, 1956.

ARON, E., CHAMBON, Y., AND VOISIN. A.: Bull. Acad. Med. (Paris), **137:** 417, 1953.

BARGMANN, W., AND HILD, W.: Acta Anat., **8:** 264, 1949.

BARGMANN, W., AND SHARRER, E.: Am. Scientist, **39:** 255, 1951.

BOWMAN, D. E., AND MUNTWYLER, E.: Proc. Soc. Exper. Biol. & Med., **35:** 557, 1937.

BUSH, I. E.: XIX Cong. Internat. Physiol., 31 Aug.–4 Sept., Montreal, p. 254, 1953.

CHRISTY, N. P., KNIGHT, M., LONGSON, D., AND JAILER, J. W.: J. Clin. Endocrinol. and Metab., **16:** 913, 1956.

DAS, N. N., DASGUPTA, S. R., AND WERNER, G.: Bull. Calcutta Trop. Med., **1:** 566, 1954.

GUILLEMIN, R.: Endocrinology, **56:** 248, 1955.

HAMBURGER, C.: Acta Endocrinol., **20:** 383, 1955.

HARKINS, H. N., AND LONG, C. N. H.: Am. J. Physiol., **144:** 661, 1945.

HARKINS, H. N.: Physiol. Rev., **25:** 531, 1945.

HARRIS, G. W., AND FORTIER, C.: Fourth Annual Report on Stress, Montreal, Canada, p. 106, 1954.

HILD, W., AND ZETLER, G.: Ges. Exptl. Med., **120:** 236, 1953.

HOLZBAUER, M., AND VOGT, M.: Brit. J. Pharmacol., **9:** 402, 1954.

HUME, D. M.: Ciba Foundation Colloquia on Endocrinology, **4:** 87, 1952.

LEVIN, L.: Endocrinology, **37:** 34, 1945.

MARTINI, L., AND DEPOLI, A.: J. Endocrin., **13:** 229, 1956.

MCCANN, S. M.: Am. J. Physiol., **175:** 13, 1953.

OLLING, CH. C. J., AND DE WIED, D.: Acta Endocrinol., **22:** 283, 1956.

PORTER, R. W.: Am. J. Physiol., **172:** 515, 1953.

ROE, J. H., AND KEUTHER, C. A.: J. Biol. Chem., **147:** 399, 1943.

SAYERS, G., SAYERS, M. A., LEWIS, H. L., AND LONG, C. N. H.: Proc. Soc. Exper. Biol. & Med., **55:** 238, 1944.

SAYERS, G., SAYERS, M. A., LIANG, T. Y., AND LONG, C. N. H.: Endocrinology, **37:** 96, 1945.

SAYERS, G., AND SAYERS, M. A.: Endocrinology, **40:** 265, 1947.

SAYERS, G.: Physiol. Rev., **30:** 241, 1950.

SCHNITZER, A.: Internat. Arch. Allerg., **5:** Suppl. 87, 1954.

SCHNITZER, A.: München. med. Wchnschr., **97:** 466, 1955.

SCHNEIDER, J. A., PLUMMER, A. J., EARL, A. E., AND GAUNT, R.: Ann. New York Acad. Sci., **61:** 17, 1955.

SELYE, H.: Annual Report on Stress, **3:** 38, 1953.

SEVY, R. W., OHLER, E. A., AND WEINER, A.: Endocrinology, **61:** 45, 1957.

SHARRER, E., AND SHARRER, B.: Handbuch der Mikroskopischen Anatomie des Menschen. Von Mollendroff und Bargmann eds., Vol. **6**, p. 953, Springer, Berlin, 1953.

SYNDOR, K. L., AND SAYERS, G.: Endocrinology, **55:** 621, 1954.

8011

THE BINDING OF *d*-TUBOCURARINE CHLORIDE TO PLASMA PROTEINS[1]

LEONIE ALADJEMOFF, SHABETAY DIKSTEIN AND ELEAZAR SHAFRIR

Departments of Anesthesiology, Pharmacology and Clinical Biochemistry, Hadassah University Hospital and the Hebrew University-Hadassah Medical School, Jerusalem, Israel

Received for publication February 3, 1958

Muscle relaxants have become an integral part of modern anesthesia since the introduction of curare (Griffith and Johnson, 1942). Responses to relaxant drugs vary considerably from patient to patient. Hypersensitivity to *d*-tubocurarine chloride is known to occur in patients with myasthenia gravis and has also been described in patients not suffering from this pathological condition (Dundee and Gray, 1951; Howell-Jones, 1951; Gray and Halton, 1948). Hyposensitivity or resistance to *d*-tubocurarine chloride is a much rarer phenomenon, observed in patients with liver damage (Dundee and Gray, 1953) and those accustomed to taking large doses of opiates, barbiturates or other sedative and analgetic drugs (Dundee and Gray, 1951).

Plasma levels of *d*-tubocurarine chloride have been determined by Mahfouz (1949) and by Pittinger, Morris and Cullen (1951). A normal reaction to intravenous injection of the drug (muscular relaxation and resulting respiratory depression) was observed by them in all subjects.

In this investigation the levels of *d*-tubocurarine chloride and its distribution in the plasma of normal and refractory subjects were determined.

METHODS. The 9 patients investigated by us were adults in good physical condition. The two refractory patients were males, aged 36 and 47 years respectively. One underwent reamputation and plastic closure after a fresh traumatic amputation of two fingers. On the other, a corrective orthopedic operation of the knee was performed. Both were in good nutritional state. Neither of them was accustomed to taking analgetic drugs and barbiturates, or had received any medication which might have influenced the response to the relaxant drug. Blood counts, plasma protein concentration and electrophoretic pattern, liver and kidney function tests were well within normal limits in both normal and refractory patients. Preanesthetic medication, given after a 5-hour fast, consisted of 0.5 mgm. of atropine sulfate. Morphine and meperidine were omitted in order to avoid their depressant effect on respiration and their possible interference with the chemical determination of *d*-tubocurarine chloride (hereafter called DT). Patients were anesthetized with a 2.5 per cent solution of sodium thiopental and nitrous oxide in oxygen, and the trachea intubated after topical anesthesia with lidocaine. In no instance were ether or cyclopropane used. The plane of anesthesia was kept light, so that patients reacted to the needle prick when a blood sample was taken. A dose of 20 mgm. of DT was injected rapidly. Blood samples were taken into heparinized syringes at varying intervals before and after administration of the relaxant drug. The samples were kept at room temperature (18° to 22° C.) for 15 minutes and then centrifuged for 15 minutes at 1,500 *g*. It was found essential to siphon off the plasma promptly. This was then stored at 4° C. until further processing within 24 hours.

For the determination of total (bound plus free) DT the procedure of Quinn and Woislawski (1950) was used. Determinations were performed on duplicate 3-ml. samples of heparinized plasma and color measurement made in a Coleman spectrophotometer at a 530 mμ wave length. For calibration, various quantities of purified, crystalline DT[2] were added to normal heparinized plasma and the plasma processed according to the method cited. A regression line constructed from the readings obtained, confirmed the validity of Beer's law in the range of 1 to 30 microgm. of *d*-tubocurarine chloride per ml. of plasma. At higher concentrations extraction appeared to be incomplete. From the regression line a value of 0.028 units of optical density per 1 microgm. of DT per ml. of plasma was obtained. Standard deviation of a single determination was 0.023 optical density units.

Paper electrophoresis was performed on What-

[1] This investigation was supported by a grant from the Hadassah Medical Organisation Research Fund and carried out in part in the Laboratory of Clinical Research.

[2] The purified, crystalline *d*-tubocurarine chloride was obtained through the courtesy of Burroughs Wellcome & Co., London, England.

man 3 MM filter paper strips in barbital buffer pH 8.6, ionic strength 0.05. Quantities of 0.05 ml. of heparinized plasma, to which 10 to 20 microgm. of DT had been added, were streaked on several strips and a current of 0.1 milliampere per 1 cm. paper width was applied for 24 hours. The voltage gradient was 12 volts per cm. paper length. The strips were then dried at room temperature and the protein pattern identified by staining with bromphenol blue. Other strips were cut into segments corresponding to the position of the various protein fractions and the cut pieces processed according to the method cited (Quinn and Woislawski, 1950), substituting 3 ml. of distilled water for 3 ml. of heparinized plasma. A special reference graph was constructed relating optical density to concentrations of DT in distilled water.

Healthy mongrel dogs weighing about 8 kgm. were premedicated with 0.5 mgm. of atropine sulfate, anesthetized with 35 mgm. per kgm. of sodium thiopental i.p., and the trachea intubated. A solution of 2 mgm. DT in 10 ml. of 0.9 per cent NaCl was incubated for 1 hour at 37° C. and then rapidly injected into the femoral vein. One week later the same dog received identical anesthesia and then was similarly injected with 2 mgm. of DT in 10 ml. of 4 per cent bovine *gamma*-globulin solution[3] which had been preincubated at 37° C. for one hour. Another week later the same dog, after similar preparation, received 2 mgm. of DT in 10 ml. of 4 per cent human albumin solution[4] preincubated for one hour at 37° C. In all experiments times of onset of curarization and resumption of normal respiration were recorded.

Biological assay of DT was performed with a rat phrenic nerve-diaphragm preparation according to Burn (1950).

Results. The plasma concentration of DT at various time intervals after intravenous administration is given in figure 1. The mean level of DT in 7 normal subjects, 2 minutes after injection was 3.6 microgm. per ml. (range 2.3 to 4.3), while in the two resistant patients the plasma levels at the same time were 10.5 and 8.35 microgm. per ml. Spontaneous respiration was resumed in the normal group on the average after 34 minutes (range 29 to 43), corresponding to an average plasma level of 1.2 microgm. per ml. (range 1 to 1.4). The two resistant patients did not show any signs of curarization whatsoever, and their 34-minute plasma levels of DT were 3.2 and 2.8.

The distribution of DT in electrophoretic plasma fractions is shown in table 1. It is evident

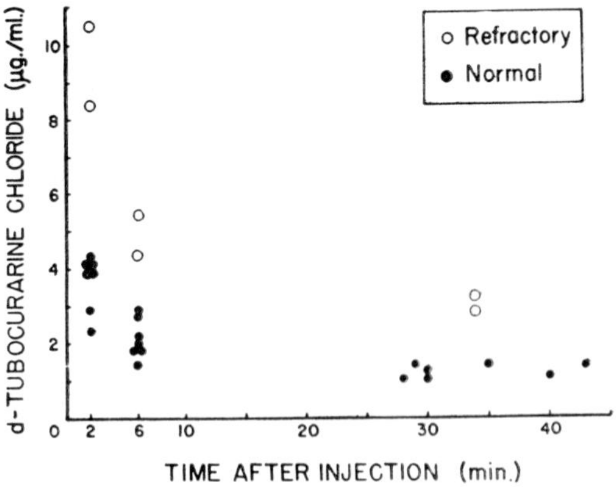

Fig. 1. Plasma levels of *d*-tubocurarine (DT) at various time intervals after intravenous administration.

Twenty mgm. of DT were injected into 9 patients of average weight 60.2 kgm. (range 56 to 68 kgm.).

from the table that in normal plasma the major part of the DT added was found at the point of origin with the *gamma*-globulin fraction, while in refractory plasma the major part of DT added moved with the albumin fraction. In control experiments various quantities of purified DT dissolved in 0.9 per cent NaCl were subjected to paper electrophoresis under conditions similar to those employed for separation of plasma. After a run of 4 hours at a current of 0.1 milliampere per 1 cm. paper width at a voltage gradient of 12 volts per cm. paper length, the paper strips were analyzed for the DT content. It was found that most of the purified DT applied moved towards the cathode, while a small amount of apparently degenerated material remained at the point of application.

In order to test the DT-binding properties of plasma proteins, purified DT was added to a solution of bovine albumin or bovine *gamma*-globulin and subjected to equilibrium dialysis against a constant volume of 0.9 per cent NaCl solution. The distribution of DT between the protein and salt solution as determined by chemical and biological methods is given in table 2. It is evident that considerable amounts of DT were bound to both proteins.

An aliquot of the albumin solution containing bound DT was diluted to a concentration of 2.5 per cent and dialyzed against 0.1 *M* barbital buffer, pH 8.6. A sample of the dialyzed solution was analyzed for DT content and the electrophoretic mobility of albumin determined in a

[3] Armour & Co., Chicago, Ill., U.S.A.
[4] Cutter Laboratories, Berkeley, Calif., U.S.A.

moving boundary Tiselius apparatus. The results presented in table 3 show that the electrophoretic mobility of the DT-containing albumin does not differ significantly from that of a standard albumin solution.

Further, the pharmacological effect of protein-bound DT was investigated. Dogs received 2 mgm. of DT dissolved in various media as summarized in table 4. Following the injection of DT in 0.9 per cent NaCl, a normal response to the drug was observed. When the same dose of DT was injected in a 4 per cent solution of human *gamma*-globulin a reduced response was noted. The administration of DT in a 4 per cent solution

TABLE 1

The distribution of d-tubocurarine chloride among electrophoretic plasma protein fractions

Subject	Amount of DT in 0.05 ml. Plasma	Amount of DT Recovered After Electrophoretic Separation*		
		Albumin	γ-globulin	Other fractions
	μgm.	*μgm.*	*μgm.*	*μgm.*
Normal†	10	4	7	<1
Refractory I‡	10	7	3	<1
Refractory II‡	10	7	5	<1

* Details of electrophoretic separation and determination of DT—see METHODS.

† The figures in the table refer to a representative experiment. In 10 normals 25 to 40 per cent of DT added to plasma was recovered in the albumin fraction.

‡ The electrophoretic pattern of the plasma proteins of the refractory patients was within normal limits.

TABLE 2

*Distribution of d-tubocurarine chloride between protein and salt solution following equilibrium dialysis**

Dialysis Bag Content	Concentration Ratio of DT Inside/Outside†	
	Chemical method	Biological assay
Bovine albumin, 4 per cent in 0.9% NaCl	10:1	9:1
Bovine γ-globulin, 4 per cent in 0.9% NaCl	4.7:1	5:1
NaCl, 0.9%	0.85:1	—

* Ten ml. of protein solution containing 3 mgm. of DT were dialyzed for at least 72 hours at 4° C. against 100 ml. of 0.9 per cent NaCl. In a control experiment 10 ml. of 0.9 per cent NaCl containing 3 mgm. of DT was similarly dialyzed.

† Average recoveries of DT: chemical method, about 90 per cent; biological assay, about 80 per cent.

TABLE 3

Lack of effect of d-tubocurarine chloride on the electrophoretic mobility of human and bovine albumin

	Electrophoretic Mobility $cm.^2 \cdot V^{-1} \cdot sec.^{-1} \cdot 10^{-5}$*	
	Without DT	With DT†
Human albumin	6.65	6.55
Crystallized bovine albumin	6.05	5.95

* The experiment was performed on a 2.5 per cent albumin solution in a 2-ml. cell of Model 38A Perkin-Elmer electrophoresis apparatus. Boundaries were set against 0.1 *M* barbital buffer pH 8.6 used previously for the dialysis of albumin-DT mixture; the mobilities were calculated from the descending boundary patterns. Deviations up to 3 per cent from the standard mobility are within experimental error.

† Concentration of DT in albumin solution was 100 microgm. per ml.

TABLE 4

Onset and duration of curarization in dogs injected with d-tubocurarine chloride*

Dog No.	Dose of DT	Medium in which DT was Injected (10 ml.)	Onset of Curarization (min. after injection)	Duration of Curarization
	mgm.			*min.*
1	2	NaCl, 0.9%	1.5	35.5
2	2		3.0	42.0
3	2		0.5	24.5
1	2	Human *gamma*-globulin, 4% in 0.9% NaCl	4.0	17
2	2		4.0	20
3	2		1.0	30
1	2	Human albumin, 4% in 0.9% NaCl	†	—
2	2		†	—
3	2		†	—
3	4		4.0	25‡
3	11		0.5	45

* Weighing about 8 kgm.

† No effect during 60 minutes of observation.

‡ Shallow respiration and slight cyanosis only.

of human albumin did not elicit any signs of curarization whatsoever. Slight cyanosis was observed on doubling the dose of DT injected into the same animal in the same volume of the medium, while complete curarization resulted when the dose of DT was increased to 11 mgm.

Discussion. In the two cases presented which were refractory to DT, considerably higher plasma levels of the drug than those of the normal controls were demonstrated. This finding suggests that in the plasma of refractory patients DT is bound in excessive quantities and is unable to diffuse out of the vascular system in effective concentration to exert its action at the neuromuscular junction.

Others workers have reported on the ability of various proteins to bind compounds with quaternary and tertiary amine groups, such as morphine (Keleman and Pataky, 1951), atropine (Tonnesen, 1956), *d*-tubocurarine chloride (Karassik, Petrunkina and Petrunkin, 1929) and β-erythroidine (Kirschner and Stone, 1953). In this report the DT-binding properties of plasma proteins were investigated. Paper electrophoresis and equilibrium dialysis experiments showed that plasma proteins are able to bind DT. Remarkable differences in the binding properties of normal and refractory plasma proteins were revealed (table 1). It is difficult to evaluate the results obtained in these experiments, since excessively high concentrations, beyond those reached in the therapeutic administration, of DT were used. However, in contradistinction to normal plasma, the major part of DT added to refractory plasma, moved with the albumin fraction. Therefore it seems probable that the high plasma level of DT in refractory subjects is due to the increased DT-binding capacity of their albumin.

We hesitate to state that the DT found with the *gamma*-globulin fraction is actually bound to this protein, as on electrophoresis of pure DT a small amount of material always remains at the point of application. However, dialysis experiments show that bovine *gamma*-globulin is capable of binding DT. This indicates that the DT in the electrophoretic *gamma*-globulin fraction is at least in part associated with the protein.

The electrophoretic mobility of albumin was not altered significantly by the addition of DT. This is compatible with the low molar ratio of the DT-albumin complex studied (approximately 0.3), which shows that only a negligible portion of the numerous negative charges in the albumin molecule is neutralized.

The absence of curarization upon injection into dogs of DT preincubated with albumin, provides further indication that albumin-bound DT is unable to reach the neuromuscular junction. On the other hand, *gamma*-globulin had only slight effect in reducing the level of curarization.

If the amount of DT, incubated with a fixed amount of albumin, is increased about fivefold, a point is reached at which the amount of free DT is sufficient to effect curarization. It remains to be elucidated, whether only excess of free DT is able to diffuse out of the blood vessels, while albumin-bound DT remains inert. One may assume, however, that the DT-albumin reaction is time dependent. This may explain why DT is inactive when preincubated with relatively small amounts of albumin *in vitro*, as contrasted with its ample effect on relatively brief contact with the large vascular pool of albumin upon direct injection.

SUMMARY

Plasma levels of *d*-tubocurarine chloride were determined in nine patients, who received identical doses of the drug. Exceptionally high plasma levels of the drug were found in two patients refractory to the relaxant.

Paper electrophoresis of plasma to which DT was added *in vitro* showed that in refractory plasma the major part of DT moved with the albumin fraction, while in normal plasma the major part remained with the *gamma*-globulin. The electrophoretic mobility of the albumin was not altered by the addition of DT.

Dialysis experiments showed that both albumin and *gamma*-globulin are able to bind considerable quantities of DT.

Dogs in whom curarization was effected by intravenous injection of DT in 0.9 per cent NaCl did not respond to the same dose of DT after preincubation with albumin. Curarization was effected only after the amount of DT injected relative to albumin was greatly increased.

REFERENCES

Burn, J. H.: Biological Standardization, p. 347, Oxford University Press, 1950.

Dundee, J. W., and Gray, T. C.: Lancet, **2:** 1015, 1951.

Dundee, J. W., and Gray, T. C.: Lancet, **2:** 16, 1953.

Gray, T. C., and Halton, J.: Brit. Med. J., **1:** 784, 1948.

GRIFFITH, H. R., AND JOHNSON, G. E.: Anesthesiology, **3:** 418, 1942.

HOWELL-JONES, H.: Brit. Med. J., **1:** 189, 1951.

KARASSIK, V. M., PETRUNKINA, A., AND PETRUNKIN, M.: Biochem. Ztschr., **70:** 210, 1929, *cf.* Chem. Abstr., **23:** 4956, 1929.

KELEMEN, E., AND PATAKY, S. J.: Acta Med. Hung., **2:** 319, 1951.

KIRSCHNER, L. B., AND STONE, W. E.: THIS JOURNAL, **197:** 188, 1953.

MAHFOUZ, M.: Brit. J. Pharmacol., **4:** 295, 1949.

PITTINGER, C. B., MORRIS, L. E., AND CULLEN, S. C.: J. Lab. & Clin. Med., **38:** 397, 1951.

QUINN, G. P., AND WOISLAWSKI, S.: Proc. Soc. Exper. Biol. & Med., **74:** 365, 1950.

TONNESEN, M.: Acta pharmacol. et toxicol., **12:** 247, 1956.

8012

COMPARATIVE PHARMACOLOGICAL EFFECTS OF A NUMBER OF β-HALOGENATED PYRUVIC ACIDS[1]

HARRIS BUSCH, P. V. NAIR, MICHAEL FRANK AND WILLIAM R. MARTIN

Department of Pharmacology, University of Illinois College of Medicine, Chicago 12

Received for publication November 29, 1957

In an earlier report from this laboratory (Busch *et al.*, 1956) the cholinomimetic effects of some β-substituted pyruvic acids were described. The structural specificity of the type of molecule involved in producing the cholinomimetic effects was interesting, inasmuch as pyruvic acid and a series of two-carbon and four-carbon analogues did not show similar effects. In addition, it became apparent that the mono- and di-substituted pyruvic acids differed markedly in potency and toxicity. However, the methods in the literature for synthesis of these β-substituted compounds yielded mixtures of products. It therefore became necessary in extending these studies to obtain analytically pure compounds by unequivocal methods. The present report describes the chemical synthesis of a number of halopyruvic acids, as well as quantitative data on pharmacological effects, inhibition of cholinesterase and inhibition of oxidation.

MATERIALS AND METHODS. *Synthesis of monohalogenated pyruvic acids.* Monofluoro- and monochloropyruvic acids were obtained by the hydrolytic cleavage of the diethyl esters of fluoro- and chloro-oxaloacetic acids respectively (Nair and Busch, 1958). Monobromopyruvic acid was obtained by a modification of the method of Sprinson and Chargaff (1946) in which pyruvic acid was brominated at room temperature with limiting quantities of bromine. Bromine, dried over concentrated sulfuric acid (25.6 gm., 0.16 mole), was gradually added with stirring to redistilled pyruvic acid (17.6 gm., 0.2 mole) contained in a 100-ml. flask fitted with a calcium chloride tube. The mixture was allowed to stand at room temperature (*ca.* 28° C.) for 48 hours with occasional shaking. Hydrogen bromide and other gaseous products were removed by means of a water pump from the reaction mixture, which became a yellowish-brown syrup. The resultant solution was then fractionated *in vacuo.* The unreacted pyruvic acid distilled off at 41 to 42°/2.5 mm. (identified by its phenylhydrazone, m.p. 193°). Bromopyruvic acid distilled at 94°/0.5 mm. as a pale yellow liquid which immediately solidified in the condenser and receiver[2]. The yield obtained was 16 gm. (61 per cent theory). The product was purified by repeated crystallization from chloroform and obtained as fine white crystals. After drying *in vacuo* over P_2O_5, the product melted at 77 to 78°; it was hygroscopic. Anal. calcd. for $C_3H_3O_3Br$: C, 21.58; H, 1.81; Br, 47.89 per cent. Found: C, 21.52; H, 1.93; Br, 47.7 per cent. The dinitrophenylhydrazone melted at 180 to 181° (Sprinson and Chargaff, 1946, m.p. 180°).

Synthesis of dihalogenated pyruvic acids. Dichloropyruvic acid was prepared according to a modification of the procedure described by Garino and Muzio (1926) for monochloropyruvic acid. Redistilled sulfuryl chloride (135 gm., 1 mole) was gradually dropped from a separatory funnel into redistilled pyruvic acid (44 gm., 0.5 mole) contained in a flask fitted with a calcium chloride tube; a yellowish liquid was obtained at the end of the addition. The mixture was left for 48 hours at room temperature, after which time the flask and contents were warmed on a water bath at a temperature of about 70°, and the removal of the excess of reagent and other gaseous products was completed under reduced pressure. The resultant yellowish-brown syrupy solution was then transferred to a beaker and left in a vacuum desiccator over sodium hydroxide. After a period, varying from 24 to 72 hours, crystals began to appear and finally the contents solidified to a mass. The crude product was washed with benzene, followed by a small quantity of chloroform, and dried. The yield was 39 gm. (about 50 per cent). The product was very soluble in ether and less so in chloroform. It was crystallized from ether-chloroform (also from chloroform alone) and obtained as fine white crystals, which melted at 109 to 110° after drying *in vacuo* over P_2O_5. Anal. calcd. for $C_3H_2O_3Cl_2$: C,

[1] Supported by grants from the U. S. Public Health Service and the Jane Coffin Childs Memorial Fund for Medical Research.

[2] Hot water may be circulated through the condenser to prevent the solidification of the product.

22.96; H, 1.28; Cl, 45.17 per cent. Found: C, 22.63; H, 1.54; Cl, 43.3 per cent. The phenylhydrazone (crystallized from alcohol) melted at 223 to 224°. Dibromopyruvic acid was obtained by a modification of the procedure described by Sprinson and Chargaff (1946) for monobromopyruvic acid. Pyruvic acid, which was purified by distillation (8.8 gm., 0.1 mole), was warmed to 50° in a flask fitted with a separatory funnel and calcium chloride tubes. Bromine (32 gm., 0.2 mole), dried by shaking with concentrated sulfuric acid, was then gradually dropped into the pyruvic acid with stirring. At the end of the addition, a yellowish-brown, fuming, syrupy liquid was obtained. When the initial reaction subsided, the mixture was allowed to cool to room temperature[3]. The remaining hydrogen bromide was removed by means of a water pump. The resultant solution was then fractionally distilled *in vacuo*. A few drops of a colorless liquid distilled over first at 40°/3 mm., which was identified as pyruvic acid by its phenylhydrazone. This was followed by a yellowish liquid which distilled at 119 to 120°/2.5 mm. Warm water was circulated through the condenser to prevent the solidification of the product. The distillate solidified in the receiver to a pale yellow mass, which became white with time in the desiccator containing sodium hydroxide pellets. The yield was 8.8 gm. (*ca.* 53 per cent). The product was purified by crystallization from chloroform and obtained as fine white crystals. After drying *in vacuo*, the product melted at 89 to 90°. Anal. calcd. for $C_3H_2O_3Br_2$: C, 14.66; H, 0.82; Br, 65 per cent. Neutral equivalent, 245.9. Found: C, 14.60; H, 0.82; Br, 62.7 per cent; neutral equivalent, 243.

In vivo assays. Female white mice of the Harlan strain, weighing 18 to 22 gm. were used for the bioassays. Values for the LD_{50} were obtained by observation of the animals for a period of 24 hours following injection of the drugs. The cholinomimetic potency of the compounds was estimated from semiquantitative data on salivation and lacrimation. The endpoint for salivation was either visible formation of droplets of saliva or appearance of 3 wet streaks of saliva when the mouth of the animal was wiped across a shiny, smooth black surface. Control mice did not form droplets of saliva and wiping of the mouth of the animal on the surface did not result in the appearance of more than one wet streak. The endpoint for lacrimation was filling of the lid margin with fluid or filling of the epicanthus. The endpoint for analgesia was the failure of a reactor mouse (Martin *et al.*, to be published) to bite the tail clip applied according to Haffner (1929). The dose of drug producing analgesia in 50 per cent of the animals (AD_{50}) was determined, the data being analyzed according to the method of Litchfield and Wilcoxon (1949). The AD_{50} values in this study represent pooled values for results over a time interval of two to five minutes. Initial studies were performed with rats. These were obtained from the Holtzman Rat Company and ranged in weight from 200 to 350 gm.

In vitro assays. Studies on cholinesterase activity were made by means of the procedure outlined by Nachmansohn and Wilson (1955), utilizing a bicarbonate buffer containing 0.01 *M* $MgCl_2$. Acetylcholinesterase from bovine red cells was obtained from the Winthrop Laboratories and acetylcholine bromide from the Hoffmann-La-Roche Company. Manometric determinations were carried out in a Warburg apparatus. The pH of the buffered system was 7.4.

In experiments in which the effects of halopyruvic acids on oxidations were studied, homogenates of liver, kidney and brain were prepared in Potter-Elvehjem homogenizers. An aliquot of the homogenate containing 40 to 100 mgm. of tissue was added to a solution which contained 0.01 *M* phosphate buffer (pH: 7.4), 0.002 *M* potassium ATP, and the potassium salts of the substrates. The substrates tested were α-ketoglutarate (0.006 *M*), or a mixture of 0.006 *M* pyruvate and 0.003 *M* malate. After an initial period of oxidative activity, the inhibitors were tipped into the main chamber of the Warburg flask from the side arm. The final volume was 3.2 ml. The concentrations of inhibitors which inhibited reaction rate by 50 per cent is expressed as the IC_{50}.

RESULTS. *General effects.* Following intraperitoneal administration of lethal doses of the halogenated pyruvic acids, rats remained quiescent for a period of 2 to 5 minutes, after which they exhibited chewing movements or swallowing, followed by a period of marked salivation for 5 to 20 minutes. At the same time the animals exhibited a variety of signs, including rhinorrhea, marked lacrimation, hyperpnea, wheezing and audible rhonchi.

During this period analgesia was also noted, and the duration was variable but usually brief. The analgesia produced reached a maximum very soon after injection of the halopyruvic acids and then diminished rapidly, long before death, if this occurred. The number of animals exhibiting analgesia did not exceed seventy per cent of the

[3] The mixture was heated at 100° for 24 hours; it was found that heating the mixture at 100° for 24 hours increased the yield from 35 to 40 per cent to 50 to 55 per cent.

TABLE 1

ED_{50}'s for various effects produced by monohalogenated derivatives of pyruvic acids

The experimental data were obtained by studying 10 to 20 animals at each dose. The values were analyzed for $dose_{50}$ and 95 per cent confidence limits, in parentheses, by the method of Litchfield and Wilcoxon (1949).

Derivative	Salivatory $Dose_{50}$	Lacrimatory $Dose_{50}$	AD_{50}	LD_{50}
	mgm./kgm.	*mgm./kgm.*	*mgm./kgm.*	*mgm./kgm.*
Monobromo-				
free acid	—	44 (42–47)	—	72 (62–84)
neutralized	—	97 (89–106)	—	178 (164–193)
Monochloro-				
free acid	95 (63–143)	84 (80–93)	160 (100–256)	153 (139–168)
neutralized	198 (165–237)	183 (172–194)	265 (250–280)	265 (234–299)
Monofluoro-				
free acid	75 (70–80)	53 (47–60)	100 (83–120)	125 (112–163)
neutralized	180 (148–220)	135 (121–149)	225 (197–257)	175 (167–183)

TABLE 2

ED_{50}'s for some pharmacological effects of dihalogenated derivatives of pyruvic acid

Conditions same as table 1.

Derivative	Salivatory $Dose_{50}$	Lacrimatory $Dose_{50}$	AD_{50}	LD_{50}
	mgm./kgm.	*mgm./kgm.*	*mgm./kgm.*	*mgm./kgm.*
Dibromo-				
free acid......	19 (14–25)	11 (7–18)	84 (60–118)	75 (67–84)
neutralized....	20 (15–28)	15 (9–24)	60 (56–64)	84 (72–97)
Dichloro-				
free acid......	40 (32–50)	40 (30–52)	115 (82–161)	280 (248–316)
neutralized....	55 (48–63)	50 (44–57)	98 (78–122)	362 (359–365)

number injected. Thus the increment in the percentage of animals exhibiting analgesia at doses approximating the AD_{50} was small compared to the increment at lower doses, and hence, large confidence limits were found. These and other aspects of the analgesia will be discussed in detail in a subsequent report (Martin *et al.*, to be published).

Miosis was commonly observed and at high doses hemodacryorrhea was occasionally noticed with dichloropyruvic acid. These effects were all readily inhibited by pretreatment of the animals with atropine in doses of 1 to 2 mgm./kgm. After these initial effects subsided, a progressive development of toxic signs was observed. The cholinomimetic effects were followed by lethargy, cyanosis, labored breathing, head drop and occasional clonic movements. Death ensued at times ranging from 30 minutes to 12 or more hours, depending on the dose administered.

Quantitative relationships of pharmacological activity among the halopyruvic acids. The ED_{50}'s for salivation, lacrimation, analgesia and death are presented for the monohalopyruvic acids in table 1 and for the dihalopyruvic acids in table 2. Following injection of monohalopyruvic acids, most, but not all, of the animals exhibited pharmacological responses, even at lethal doses. The intensity of effects produced by monohalopyruvic acids was markedly less than the intensity of effects following treatment with dihalopyruvic acids. The monohalopyruvic acids varied markedly in their toxicity and their potency. Monobromopyruvic acid was the most potent compound of the series in induction of lacrimation, and it was also the most toxic. However, the intensity of lacrimation produced was not as great as that produced by the dihalopyruvic acids and the compound did not produce salivation or analgesia in 50 per cent of the animals at any dose studied. Although it was less potent in producing lacrimation, monochloropyruvic acid induced more pharmacological effects than did monobromopyruvic acid. Following treatment with monochloropyruvic acid, as many as 60 per cent of the animals exhibited analgesia, as compared with 20 per cent with monobromopyruvic acid. Monofluoropyruvic acid was more like the dihalopyruvic acids in the intensity of effects produced, as well as the maximum percentage of animals exhibiting salivation and analgesia. The most potent compounds were the dihalopyruvic acids[4] (Martin *et al.*, to be published), and of these, dibromopyruvic acid was 2 to 3 times more potent and 3 to 4 times more toxic than the corresponding chloro-derivative on a weight basis. Since the molecular weight of dibromopyruvic acid is one and one-half times that of dichloropyruvic acid, dibromopyruvic acid is an even more potent compound considered on a molecular basis. More extensive studies of the central and peripheral pharmacological effects of this compound will be reported in a forthcoming publication (Martin *et al.*, to be published). With the dihalogenated pyruvic acids, salivation and lacrimation were produced in 100 per cent of the animals tested at doses well below the LD_{50}; analgesia was produced in a maximum of only 70 per cent of animals tested, even at

[4] The only trihalopyruvic acid which was synthesized as part of this study was the monohydrate of trichloropyruvic acid (Skraup and Wolfschlag, 1926). On injection into mice, this compound produced no significant pharmacological effects.

LD_{100}. The analgetic $dose_{50}$ was always found to be considerably greater than the corresponding salivatory and lacrimatory $dose_{50}$.

Neutralization of these acids (tables 1 and 2) resulted in a marked decrease in activity of the monohalogenated pyruvic acids, increasing the ED_{50}'s by a factor of approximately 2 for most of the effects studied. In most instances the cholinomimetic and analgetic effects decreased to a greater extent than the toxicity. Neutralization of the dihalopyruvic acids resulted in a much smaller change, inasmuch as increases of 20 per cent were noted in ED_{50}'s for dichloropyruvic acid, while the values of dibromopyruvic acid were essentially unchanged. Since the possibility existed that these compounds might undergo hydrolysis at the site of the halogen group[5], it seemed possible that mesoxalic acid semi-aldehyde

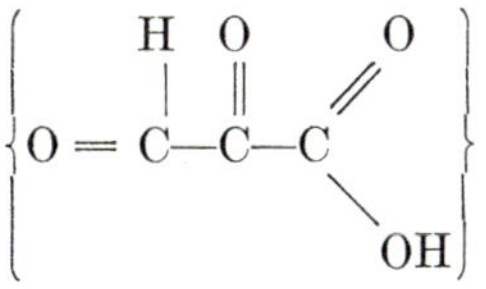

might be formed from the dihalopyruvic acids. Efforts to synthesize this compound did not result in an analytically pure product, but, interestingly, the purest preparations possessed some analgetic activity without cholinomimetic activity.

Inhibition of cholinesterase. The inhibitory effects of these compounds on cholinesterase were investigated (figure 1), and, for the most part, inhibitory activity on this enzyme paralleled the *in vivo* potency of the compound in production of cholinomimetic effects. Monobromopyruvic acid, which produced the weakest pharmacological activity, exhibited no significant anticholinesterase activity. Monochloropyruvic acid, which had a greater *in vivo* activity, exhibited a weak but significant inhibition of cholinesterase activity. The most potent inhibitor of cholinesterase activity was dibromopyruvic acid, which also had the greatest *in vivo* activity. However, the relative anticholinesterase activity of monofluoropyruvic acid and dichloropyruvic acid did not correspond to their respective potencies *in vivo*. Neutralization of these compounds produced a 5 to 10 per cent decrease in their activities. However, the decrease was directly parallel to the decrease in their *in vivo* activities, inasmuch as the activity of dibromopyruvic acid was reduced to an equally significant extent as that of the other compounds tested. At 5 to 10 micromoles per flask, the decrease in anticholinesterase activity of monofluoro- and monochloropyruvic acid was more significant than that for the dihalocompounds.

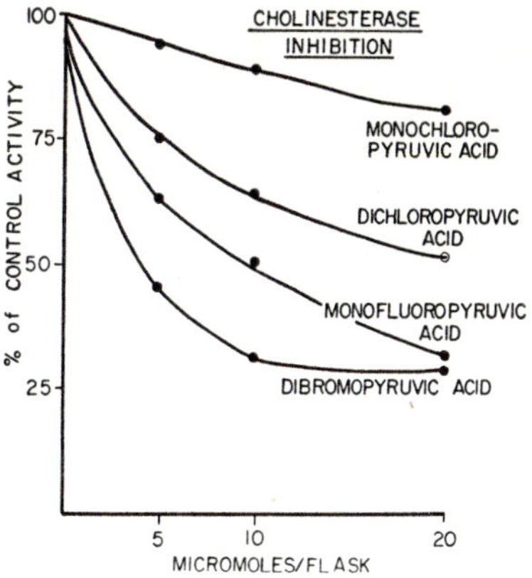

FIG. 1. Inhibition of cholinesterase by halopyruvic acids.

Each flask contained 30 micromol. of acetylcholine in one side arm. The main chamber contained 0.025 M $NaHCO_3$ buffer which was 0.01 M with respect to $MgCl_2$. The concentration of bovine red cell cholinesterase was sufficient to liberate approximately 15 to 20 microliters of CO_2 during each 5-minute interval. After an initial incubation period in which the substrate was demonstrated to be hydrolyzed by the enzyme at a rate equivalent to the control, the inhibitor was added from the side arm to the main reaction chamber. The values indicated are per cent of control activity for a 20-minute linear period 10 minutes after addition of the inhibitor.

Inhibition of oxidations by halopyruvic acids. Figure 2 indicates that each of the halopyruvic acids inhibited oxidation of substrates of the citric acid cycle. The inhibition produced by fluoropyruvic acid has been noted earlier (Busch and Nair, 1957), and it is apparent from the graph that the IC_{50} for oxidations of pyruvate and malate, as well as *alpha*-ketoglutarate, is greater than that of the other compounds tested, *i.e.*, 2.2×10^{-3} M. Each of the other halopyruvic acids was more potent as an inhibitor of oxidative activity. The IC_{50} for dibromopyruvic acid was $1.6 \times 10^{-4} M$, so that dibromopyruvic acid was approximately 14 times as inhibitory to oxidative activity as fluoropyruvic acid. Monochloropy-

[5] Hydroxypyruvic acid was obtained in analytically pure form (Li and K salts) by the hydrolysis of monobromopyruvic acid according to the method of Dickens (F. Dickens, personal communication). This compound did not induce pharmacological effects in animals at doses up to 200 mgm./kgm.

MARY IMOGENE BASSETT HOSPITAL
11020

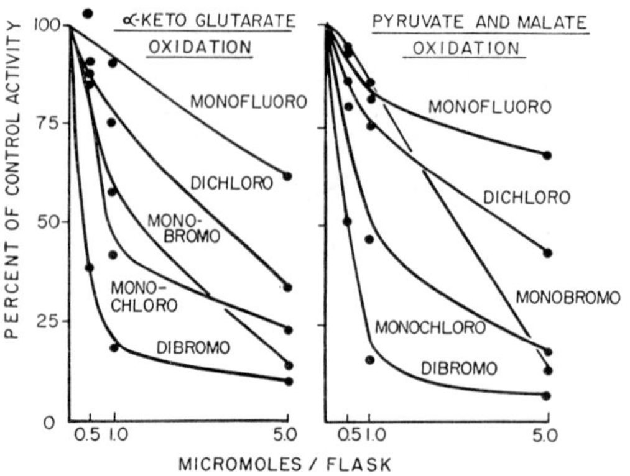

FIG. 2. Inhibition of oxidation of citric acid cycle substrates by halopyruvic acids.

The ordinates are percentages of the oxygen uptake in the absence of halopyruvic acids. Each flask contained 80 mgm. of liver in a 10 per cent KCl homogenate, 10 micromol. of potassium ATP, 10 micromol. of K_2HPO_4 buffered at pH 7.4, and 0.01 *M* $MgCl_2$ in a final volume of 3.2 ml. Substrates and inhibitors were added as the potassium salts. To each flask either 20 micromol. of *alpha*-ketoglutarate or a mixture of 20 micromol. of pyruvate and 10 micromol. of malate were added as the substrates. Results with liver, kidney and brain were essentially the same.

ruvic acid also suppressed oxidative activity strongly; the IC_{50} was 3 x 10^{-4} *M* as compared with 8 x 10^{-4} *M* for monobromopyruvic acid. The inhibitory effects of dichloropyruvic acid were intermediate between those of monofluoro- and monobromopyruvic acids. While these results do not parallel the toxicity of these compounds *in vivo*, they indicate that each of the halopyruvic acids has a significant suppressive effect on the oxidative activity of the citric acid cycle.

DISCUSSION. The effectiveness of the compounds producing the cholinomimetic effects observed in this study seems to be related both to their degree of halogenation and their anticholinesterase activity. Of the wide variety of compounds tested for activity, only the monohalopyruvic acids and the dihalopyruvic acids exhibited significant pharmacological activity (Busch *et al.*, 1956). Even trichloropyruvic acid hydrate did not exhibit similar effects. From the data of this study it is apparent that the dihalopyruvic acids were more potent cholinomimetic agents than the corresponding monohalopyruvic acids. Negative substitution on the *beta* position of pyruvic acid is not the only requisite for activity, inasmuch as hydroxypyruvic acid, trichloropyruvic acid hydrate and oxaloacetic acid did not induce pharmacological effects. It is of interest to compare the relative dose of neostigmine producing cholinergic effects *in vivo* (0.05 to 0.1 mgm./kgm.), with the dose of dibromopyruvic acid producing similar effects (20 mgm./kgm.). The ratio of these doses bears a relationship to the effective concentration producing a 50 per cent inhibition of cholinesterase activity, inasmuch as the effective concentration of neostigmine is 2.3 x 10^{-7} *M* (Smith, Mead and Unna, 1957), as compared with the IC_{50} of 1.3 x 10^{-3} *M* for dibromopyruvic acid. Thus, the ratio of doses producing cholinomimetic effects is 400:1 for dibromopyruvic acid to neostigmine, while the ratio of IC_{50}'s is 4000:1. These considerations and the data relating potency in cholinesterase inhibition and *in vivo* potency suggest that at least part of the activity of these compounds is related to their cholinesterase inhibitory activity. However, along with other evidence, the *in vitro* stimulatory effect of dibromopyruvic acid on contraction of guinea pig ileum (Martin *et al.*, to be published) indicates that these compounds also have a direct cholinomimetic activity. It is not possible to assess from these studies the relative importance of the direct cholinomimetic activity and the anticholinesterase activity of these compounds on the production of the *in vivo* pharmacological effects.

The decrease in the cholinomimetic activity of the monohalopyruvic acids, and to a lesser extent of dichloropyruvic acid, on neutralization may be related in part to the relative activity of a compound which is largely in the form of a carboxylic acid as compared with a compound which is the salt of the acid. However, alkalinization of pyruvic acid and its derivatives also favors enolization and the formation of cis- and trans-enol isomers, as has already been noted for fluoropyruvic acid (Busch and Nair, 1957). In addition, the lability of the halogen-carbon bond in these compounds suggests that they may act, in part, as alkylating agents (Phillips, 1950). In the case of monobromopyruvic acid, the activity of the molecule decreased 2- to 3-fold following neutralization. This result is consistent with the known cleavage of the halogen from the molecule which forms the basis for the preparation of hydroxypyruvic acid (Sprinson and Chargaff, 1946). While this cleavage would be expected to be most marked in the case of the bromo-compound, cleavage of the chlorine can be readily demonstrated from monochloropyruvic acid. The toxicity of these compounds might also be related to alkylation, if the compounds attacked enzymes containing functionally important -SH or -OH groups, with liberation of the halogen and bond formation between the β carbon of the pyruvic acid and the sulfur or oxygen atom.

The lethality of these compounds may be related in part to their inhibitory effects on oxidative activity of the citric acid cycle. The finding that the order of toxicity is not directly related to the order of inhibitory activity on oxidation of the substrates tested suggests that lethality may be the sum of a number of factors of which inhibition of oxidation is one.

SUMMARY

The cholinomimetic and other pharmacological effects of a series of highly purified halopyruvic acids are described and discussed in terms of their inhibitory effects on cholinesterase and their inhibition of oxidations in homogenate systems. The intensity of effects produced by dihalopyruvic acids was greater than that produced by the monohalopyruvic acids. Of the halopyruvic acids studied, dibromopyruvic was the most potent compound in production of salivation, lacrimation and analgesia; in addition, it exhibited the most marked anticholinesterase activity. The toxicity of these compounds was related, in part, to their inhibition of oxidation of substrates of the citric acid cycle.

REFERENCES

Busch, H., Martin, W. R., Nyhan, W. L., and Zaratzian, V.: Science, **124:** 981, 1956.

Busch, H., and Nair, P. V.: J. Biol. Chem., **229:** 377, 1957.

Garino, M., and Muzio, I.: Gazz. Chim. Ital., **52:** 227, 1926.

Haffner, F.: Deut. Med. Wochschr., **55:** 731, 1929.

Litchfield, J. T., and Wilcoxon, F.: This Journal, **96:** 99, 1949.

Nachmansohn, D., and Wilson, I. B.: Methods in Enzymology, Ed. by Colowick, S. P., and Kaplan, N. O., **1:** 642, Acad. Press, N. Y., 1955.

Nair, P. V., and Busch, H.: J. Org. Chem., **23:** 137, 1958.

Phillips, F. S.: Pharm. Rev., **2:** 281, 1950.

Skraup, S., and Wolfschlag, F.: Chem. Zentralblatt, **1:** 229, 1926.

Smith, C. M., Mead, J. C., and Unna, K. R.: This Journal, **120:** 215, 1957.

Sprinson, D. B., and Chargaff, E.: J. Biol. Chem., **164:** 417, 1946.

8013

EFFECTS OF CERTAIN PURINES AND RELATED COMPOUNDS ON VIRUS PROPAGATION[1]

ARIEL C. HOLLINSHEAD[2] AND PAUL K. SMITH

Department of Pharmacology, George Washington University School of Medicine, Washington 5, D. C.

Received for publication February 14, 1958

Only a few of the purine analogues have been found effective against animal viruses (Thompson *et al.*, 1950; Friend, 1951; Moore and Friend, 1951). 2,6-Diamino-purine inhibited multiplication of poliomyelitis virus type 2 (MEF_1) in monkey testicular tissue culture with partial reversal of inhibition by adenine or guanine (Brown, 1952), but it had no effect on poliomyelitis virus infection of HeLa tissue cultures except at concentrations that were inhibitory to cell respiration (Gifford *et al.*, 1954).

Certain benzimidazoles have been studied for their inhibitory effects against influenza virus (Tamm *et al.*, 1954; Tamm, 1954, 1956a, b). Brown (1952) found benzimidazole to have an inhibitory effect upon poliomyelitis virus in tissue culture. It also reduced the mortality produced by poliomyelitis virus in mice (Brown and Craig, 1953).

Some of the benzimidazoles used in the present study interfered with amphibian embryonic development (Liedke *et al.*, 1955) and protracted growth lag phases in cultures of *Tetrahymena gelii* and *Escherichia coli* (Engelman *et al.*, 1953).

MATERIALS AND METHODS. The monkey testicular tissue culture technique was the same as that used previously (Hollinshead and Smith, 1956). The monkey kidney monolayer cell culture technique was adapted from that described by Youngner (1954a, b). The culture medium described by Rappaport (1956) was used. The plaque technique (Dulbecco, 1952) with monkey kidney cells as modified by Hsiung and Melnick (1955) was used. The HeLa cell tissue culture technique was adapted from that described by Syverton *et al.* (1954) and Syverton and Scherer (1954); Eagle's medium (Eagle and Habel, 1956; Eagle, 1955) was used. The chick chorioallantoic membrane tissue culture technique was the same as in the studies of Lum and Smith (1957).

Testicular adapted poliomyelitis virus, Type I (WS strain), was used. Adenovirus (APC type 3) and kidney-adapted influenza A virus (WS-1) were obtained from Dr. K. Takemoto of the National Institutes of Health.

The titration and determination of the specificity of the viruses was performed as previously described (Hollinshead and Smith, 1956, 1956–57; Lum and Smith, 1957). Examination of fresh, stained tissue cultures under high power phase contrast for the absence of foamy virus was included.

Growth curves were determined by the increase of virus concentration in tissue cultures based on yields of virus as detected by periodic transfers to fresh tissue cultures and not on cytopathogenic changes in the original cultures. Tubes collected at each time interval were stored at −18°C. The Dulbecco plaque technique (1952) was used in the case of cultures which "appeared" free of virus because of lack of cytopathogenic effects. In the latter case, such cultures were maintained for a long period of time and tested periodically for possible appearance of latent virus. At the end of the time period, the culture fluid and tissue of each tube were titered separately in serial ten-fold dilutions in fresh tissue cultures or eggs.

Drugs were prepared as described by Kramer *et al.* (1955). Possible fixation of the tissue by the drug was detected by direct microscopic observation in the presence of drug at its highest nontoxic concentration and by respiration studies. Compounds which maintained a therapeutic index of eight or more when tested in preinfected testicular tissue cultures were considered for further study. The therapeutic index is defined as the highest nontoxic concentration of drug divided by the lowest inhibitory concentration.

Twenty-four hours before addition of the drug, 100 ID_{50}'s of virus were added to testicular cultures, six hours before addition of the drug 100 ID_{50}'s were added to chorioallantoic tissue cul-

[1] Aided by grants from the National Institute for Allergy and Infectious Diseases (E 1301), National Institutes of Health, U. S. Public Health Service; the National Foundation for Infantile Paralysis; and G. D. Searle and Co.

[2] This material is, in part, from a dissertation presented by Ariel C. Hollinshead in partial fulfillment of the requirements for the Ph.D. degree.

tures, and 10 ID_{50}'s of virus were added 3 to 5 hours before the drug to the more sensitive HeLa or kidney monolayer cultures. One ID_{50} is defined as the dose of virus which infects the tissue so as to exhibit cytopathogenic effects upon one-half of the tubes inoculated. Four days following inoculation in the case of testicular cultures, two days in the case of kidney cultures (three days as well, for adenovirus infection), 44 hours in the case of chorioallantoic cultures, and 40 to 44 hours in the case of HeLa cultures, the tubes were examined microscopically for drug toxicity and specific virus degeneration. Observations of drug toxicity also were made at the 24-hour interval. All tests were repeated three or more times.

For tests of drugs against infections of mice, MEF_1 type 2 poliomyelitis virus was obtained from Dr. H. M. Powell of Eli Lilly and Co., Indianapolis, Indiana. In order to be peripherally virulent for mice, the virus is passed in suckling hamsters about seven days old. Data were evaluated by the usual Chi-square test using Yate's correction where applicable (Snedecor, 1946).

RESULTS. Nineteen of 75 compounds tested were significantly effective against poliomyelitis virus in testicular tissue culture (table 1). All 12 benzimidazoles exhibited some inhibitory activity in kidney monolayer cultures and 8 of the 12 were partially active in HeLa tissue cultures, the more active being 4-amino-6-ethoxy-benzimidazole and 2-(1-hydroxy-benzyl)-benzimidazole (table 1).

Two nitroquinoxaline compounds were effective against poliomyelitis virus in the three tissue culture systems and a quinoxaline compound was effective in monkey testicular and kidney tissue cultures. 1-Phenyl-4-anilinopyrazolo-(3,4 d) pyrimidine, isoguanine and 2-(*p*-dimethylamino-phenyl)-benzothiazole were effective in all three systems.

Comparison of activity in monkey kidney monolayer tissue cultures using adenovirus, influenza and poliomyelitis virus. Four of the compounds inhibited influenza-infected kidney cultures: 2-(*p*-dimethylaminophenyl)-benzothiazole, 2,3-dimethyl-7-ethoxy-5-nitroquinoxaline, 4-methoxy-6-nitrobenzimidazole and 6-methoxy-4-nitrobenzimidazole. These latter compounds and two others (2-(1-hydroxybenxyl)-benzimidazole and 4-amino-6-ethoxybenzimidazole) inhibited adenovirus-infected kidney cultures.

4-Methoxy-6-nitrobenzimidazole and 2-(1-hydroxybenzyl)-benzimidazole showed more activity against adenovirus and 2,3-dimethyl-7-ethoxy-5-nitro-quinoxaline against both adenovirus and influenza virus than against poliomyelitis virus.

Comparison in two multicellular tissue culture—virus systems. 4-Amino-6-ethoxybenzimidazole, 2-(*p*-dimethylaminophenyl)-benzothiazole, 2-(1-hydroxybenzyl)-benzimidazole, and 4-methoxy-6-nitrobenzimidazole had a ratio of 8 or more in influenza virus-infected chick chorioallantoic membrane tissue cultures. The drugs were four to eight times more toxic for the chorioallantoic membrane tissue culture system than for testicular tissue. It is of interest that 2-(1-hydroxybenzyl)-benzimidazole, one of the compounds most effective against influenza virus-infected chorioallantoic membrane cultures, was ineffective against influenza virus-infected kidney tissue cultures.

Effect of addition of drugs to tissue cultures prior to infection. Twice the minimal effective concentrations of the inhibitory compounds were added to mature cultures of testicular tissue and each tube incubated in roller drums for four days. The cultures then were washed and repeatedly incubated for hourly intervals with fresh wash solution before adding fresh medium and 100 ID_{50}'s of virus. Culture media was replaced from time to time. After microscopic observation on the fourth and eighth days, aliquots of the fluid were transferred to fresh tissue cultures and checked for virus damage. The cultures were run for a longer time interval if virus damage was not perceived in either the older or fresh tissue cultures. In some instances the Dulbecco plaque technique was used for detecting virus particles present in noncytopathogenic twelve-day fluids.

Isoguanine altered the cells in some way to prevent poliomyelitis virus growth. In some cases the benzimidazoles slowed the appearance of virus but in no case did they prevent the eventual appearance of virus on the cultures washed free of the compounds. Two of the quinoxalines and 1-phenyl-4-anilinopyrazolo-(3,4 d) pyrimidine delayed somewhat virus multiplication as well.

Direct virucidal action of drugs in vitro. Twofold concentrations of compounds covering the inhibitory range were incubated at room temperature in a series of tubes each containing 100 ID_{50}'s of poliomyelitis virus. At hourly intervals, aliquots of the mixture were transferred to pairs of tissue culture tubes, incubated and examined

TABLE 1

Inhibitory effect of some purine analogues on poliomyelitis virus in tissue culture

Compound	Therapeutic Indices (Max. nontoxic conc. drug/lowest inhibitory conc.)				Reversing Metabolite (Conc. which reversed inhibition by drug)
	Testes*	Kidney	HeLa	Source†	*mgm./ml.*
4-Amino-6-ethoxybenzimidazole	1.0/0.12=8	0.5/0.06=8	0.5/0.06=8	En	adenine 1.0, 0.5
6-Amino-4-methoxybenzimidazole	4.0/0.25=16	1.0/0.25=4	0.03/0.03=1	En	adenine 1.0, 0.5, 0.25, 0.12 guanine 1.0, 0.5, 0.25, 0.12
4-Amino-6-methoxybenzimidazole	0.06/0.008=8	0.03/0.03=1	0.015/-	En	adenine 1.0
2-Benzimidazolethiol	8.0/0.5=16	2.0/1.0=2	2.0/1.0=2	E	adenine 1.0, 0.5
4-*p*-Chloroanilino-6-methyl-1-phenyl pyrazolo-(3,4 d) pyrimidine	1.0/0.12=8	‡	‡	Ro	
2-*p*-Dimethyl-amino-phenyl-benzothiazole	0.25/0.002=125	0.06/0.002=30	0.06/0.015=4	Du	
2,3-Dimethyl-7-ethoxy-5-nitro-quinoxaline	0.25/0.002=125	0.5/0.25=2	0.25/0.03=8	En	guanine 1.0, 0.5 folic acid 1.0, 0.5
2,3-Dimethyl-7-methoxy-5-nitro-quinoxaline	8.0/0.12=66	2.0/0.5=4	1.0/1.0=1	En	adenine 1.0 folic acid 1.0
2,3-Dimethyl-6-methoxy-quinoxaline	0.25/0.004=62	0.25/0.06=4	0.12/-	En	adenine 1.0 folic acid 1.0, 0.5
6-Ethoxy-4-nitro-benzimidazole	0.5/0.03=16	0.06/0.06=1	0.06/-	En	adenine 1.0
2-(1-Hydroxybenzyl)-benzimidazole	8.0/0.25=32	1.0/0.12=8	0.5/0.12=4	Sc	
2-Hydroxy-4-methoxy-6-nitro-benzimidazole	0.06/0.002=32	0.03/0.03=1	0.015/0.015=1	En	guanine 1.0 cyanocobalamin 0.001 diphosphopyridine nucleotide 1.0
4-Hydroxy-2-methyl-6-nitro-benzimidazole	0.06/0.008=8	0.06/0.06=1	0.06/-	En	guanine 1.0
4-Hydroxy-6-nitrobenzimidazole	1.0/0.12=8	0.5/0.25=2	0.12/-	En	adenine 1.0, 0.5, 0.25, 0.12
Isoguanine	8.0/1.0=8	0.5/0.12=4	0.008/0.004=2	H	guanine 1.0, 0.5, 0.25, 0.12
4-Methoxy-2-methyl-6-nitro-benzimidazole	0.5/0.015=32	0.5/0.25=2	0.12/0.06=2	En	guanine 1.0 guanylic acid 1.0
6-Methoxy-4-nitro-benzimidazole	4.0/0.002=2000	0.5/0.12=4	0.5/0.25=2	En	adenine 1.0 guanine 1.0 adenylic acid 0.12 diphosphopyridine nucleotide 1.0
4-Methoxy-6-nitrobenzimidazole	8.0/0.25=32	2.0/0.12=16	0.12/0.12=1	En	adenine 1.0, 0.5
1-Phenyl-4-anilino-pyrazolo-(3,4 d) pyrimidine	4.0/0.5=8	1.0/0.5=2	1.0/1.0=1	Ro	adenine 0.5, 0.25 guanine 0.5 adenosine-5′-phosphate 0.06, 0.03

* Unsubstituted benzimidazole had a ratio of 2.0/1.0=2 in this system.

† Du—DuPont Research Laboratories, En—Engelmann, M., Columbia University, E—Eastman Kodak Company, H—HM Chemical Company, Ro—Robins, R. K., New Mexico Highlands University, SC—Schmehl, Francis, National Cancer Institute.

‡ Not enough compound available.

for presence of virus. In the case of compounds which appeared to be completely virucidal, fluids were tested by the Dulbecco plaque technique.

4-Hydroxy-6-nitrobenzimidazole appeared to be virucidal but considerable virus was detectable by the Dulbecco plaque technique. 2-(1-Hydroxybenzyl)-benzimidazole inactivated most of the virus although three or four plaques were noted. At higher concentrations, several other compounds reduced the virus concentration.

Reversal of chemical inhibition. This was determined by establishing the final concentration of metabolites which might bring about reversal. In a preliminary test of the effects of the metabolites alone, glycine was found to be inhibitory to to the propagation of poliomyelitis virus at the nontoxic level of 0.25 mgm./ml. and 0.12 mgm./ml. and so was used at 0.06 mgm./ml.

The most consistent antagonists (see table 1) of the benzimidazoles were adenine and/or

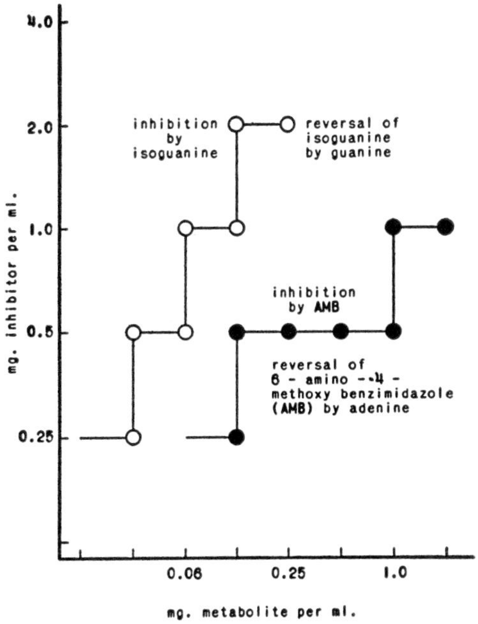

FIG. 1a

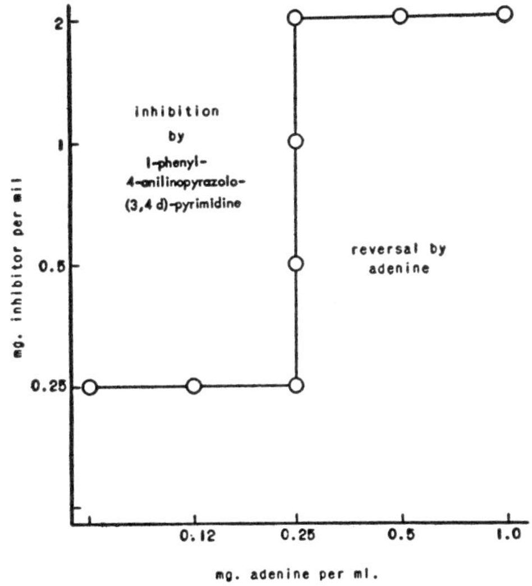

FIG. 1b

FIG. 1. Evidence of the nature of the reversals was obtained.

a) The data illustrated suggest that the relationship between isoguanine and guanine and between 6-amino-4-methoxybenzimidazole and adenine may be competitive. b) Also, the action of 1-phenyl-4-anilinopyrazolo-(3,4 d) pyrimidine appeared to be reversed competitively by adenine but the range of reversal of the latter two compounds was too narrow to give a clearly stepwise result.

guanine. The ribosides guanosine and adenosine did not reverse any of the inhibitory activity of the compounds.

Inhibition by two of the quinoxalines was reversed by adenine and the third by guanine; inhibition by all three was reversed by folic acid indicating that these compounds might possibly be antipteridines.

Three of the reversals probably were competitive (figure 1).

Growth curves. Growth curves of poliomyelitis virus in the presence of some drugs were determined (figure 2.)

Detailed studies of the effects of inhibition on on infected cells. Sterile thin glass rectangles, 30 x 8 mm., were inserted into roller tubes on the day of planting monolayer cultures and the cells

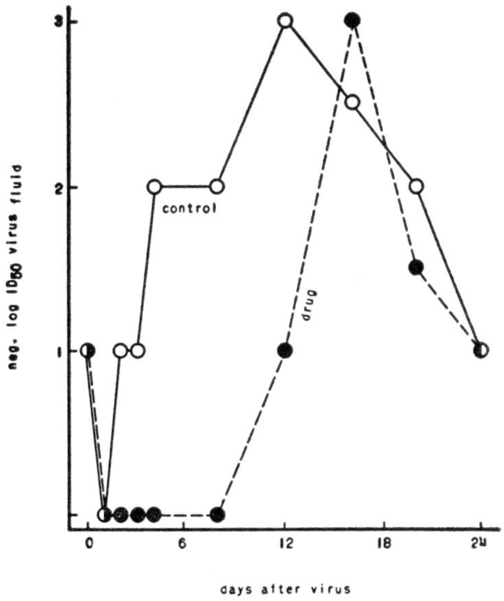

FIG. 2a

FIG. 2. Rate of virus multiplication.

a) 1-Phenyl-4-anilinopyrazolo-(3,4 d) pyrimidine caused a delay of more than 8 days from the time of infection until the appearance of virus in cultures of monkey testicular tissue. b) 6-Methoxy-4-nitrobenzimidazole delayed the appearance of virus and diminished the quantity of virus produced by the cultures. c) A delay of 36 hours in monkey kidney monolayer tissue cultures was produced by the highest concentration of 4-methoxy-6-nitrobenzimidazole as well as by ¼ of that dilution and some delay was evident even in the case of the lowest inhibitory concentration. Although not always the case, in this example titration curves of the infected tissue had a similar shape to those of infected tissue fluids. Most of the benzimidazoles suppressed poliovirus multiplication in kidney cultures for at least 24 hours and in testicular cultures for at least 72 hours.

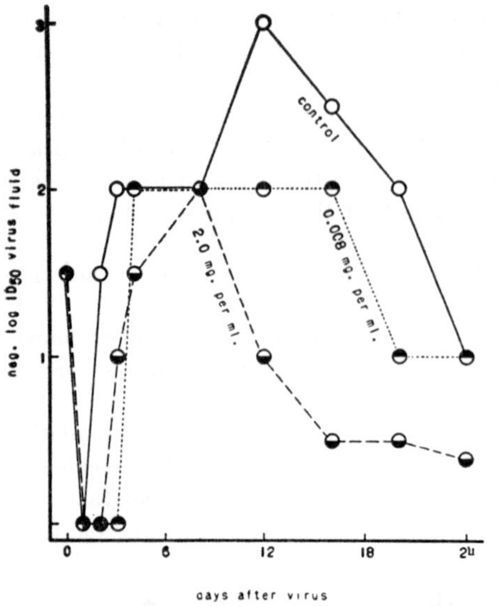

FIG. 2b

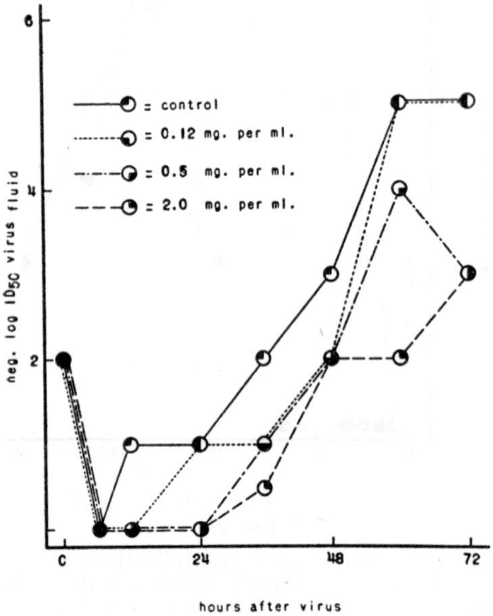

FIG. 2c

grew out on the surfaces. The rectangles were removed at the desired intervals for observation under the phase microscope. Observations of the fresh, unstained tissue were recorded. Others were fixed and stained for further observation of the cells. The method of Long and Taylor (1956) was adapted.

The cytopathic changes in monkey kidney cells after introduction of poliomyelitis virus were compared with normal cells and with infected cells in the presence of an inhibitor. The cytopathic stages in poliomyelitis virus-infected cells were recorded after the manner of Dunnebacke (1956). These results are recorded in table 2. 4-Methoxy-6-nitrobenzimidazole seems to suppress the virus at cytopathic stage II.

Tests of drugs in mice. Drugs were fed in the diet beginning immediately after inoculation of poliomyelitis virus, using the method described by Lum and Smith (1957), and deaths and paral-

TABLE 2

Cytopathic stages of monkey kidney cells infected with type I (WS) poliomyelitis virus in the presence of 4-methoxy-6-nitrobenzimidazole (14 hours after infection)

	Total Cells/ Cover Slip	Inter-phase	Mitotic Cells	Non-spc. Degen.	Cytopathic Stage: I	II	III
		%	%	%	%	%	%
Control	32,000	98	1	1			
Virus infected	29,000	20	—	—	20	15	45
Inhibitor added same time as virus	28,000	41	—	1	37	17	4

TABLE 3

Tests of compounds effective against poliomyelitis virus in tissue culture for their effectiveness against MEF_1 poliomyelitis virus infection of CFW strain albino mice

	Per Cent Drug Tolerated in Diet	No. Deaths/ Drug Group	No. Deaths/ Control Group
Benzimidazolethiol	0.01	7/8	6/8
2-*p*-Dimethylamino-phenyl-benzothiazole	0.06	8/8	6/8
2,3-Dimethyl-7-ethoxy-5-nitroquinoxaline	0.4	6/8	6/8
2-(1-Hydroxybenzyl)-benzimidazole	0.4	1/12	8/11
Isoguanine sulfate	0.2	7/8	6/8
4-Methoxy-6-nitro-benzimidazole	0.4	5/8	6/8
6-Methoxy-4-nitro-benzimidazole	0.4	5/8	6/8

TABLE 4

a. General test of effect of 2-(1-hydroxybenzyl)-benzimidazole when given orally in the diet on the same day as injection of MEF_1 poliomyelitis virus in mice

	10 LD_{50} Virus		Chi-square Test	0.5 LD_{50} Virus		Chi-Square Test	100 LD_{50} Virus		Chi-square Test
	Drug	Control		Drug	Control		Drug	Control	
Total dead per number tested	5/24	15/24	8.57†	0/20	6/20	4.90‡	12/20	14/20*	0.439§
Per cent	20.8	62.5		0.0	30.0		60.0	70.0	
Average days of survival (16-day period)	13.5	8.3		16.0	12.2		10.1	8.7	

b. 2-(1-Hydroxybenzyl)-benzimidazole fed in mouse diet at intervals before inoculation of MEF_1 poliomyelitis virus, i.p.

	Control	Drug, 12 Hr. Before	Chi-Square Test	Drug, 24 Hr. Before	Chi-Square Test	Drug, 48 Hr Before	Chi-square Test
Total dead per number tested	9/20**	2/20	4.51‡	1/20	6.53¶	2/20	4.51‡
Per cent	45.0	10.0		5.0		10.0	
Average days of survival (16-day period)	12.8	15.1		15.4		15.1	

* Partial paralysis of survivors: three out of six.
** Partial paralysis of survivors: four out of eleven.
† $p = <0.01$.
‡ $p = <0.05, >0.02$.
§ $p = >0.05$.
¶ $p = <0.02, >0.01$.

yses were recorded for a period of 16 days. The results appear in table 3.

Further testing of the effects of 2-(1-hydroxybenzyl)-benzimidazole against poliomyelitis virus infections of mice. With 10 LD_{50} inocula of virus survival of drug-treated mice was 79 per cent in comparison with 37 per cent survival of controls. With a mild 0.5 LD_{50} of virus the drug seemed to protect all of the mice. There was little difference in the control and drug groups when overwhelming doses of virus were administered (table 4a).

After overnight fasting, the drug diet was given 48 hours, 24 hours and 12 hours before intraperitoneal inoculation 10 LD_{50}'s of poliomyelitis virus and it was determined that the drug gave protection against virus infection (table 4b). Curves of cumulative mortalities of controls, treated and pretreated mice are presented in figure 3.

Further studies using influenza A (PR'8 strain)-infected chorioallantoic membrane tissue cultures. 2-(1-Hydroxybenzyl)-benzimidazole was the only purine analogue found to be effective in treating mice infected with poliomyelitis virus and also to be effective against influenza infections of the chorioallantoic tissue culture. The compound was not appreciably virucidal nor did it affect the adsorption of influenza virus nor have any effect on the release of influenza virus from the infected cells.

The therapeutic effect of the compound was tested by determining the maximum time which might elapse before prevention of virus multiplication by addition of inhibitory compound would be impossible. Results indicate that the compound is still active at later stages of virus production. 2-(1-Hydroxybenzyl)-benzimidazole prolonged the latent period for two hours in contrast to the controls. It may be seen (figure 4) that there was inhibition during the eclipse and latent periods, and that there was still suppression at later stages.

2-(1-Hydroxybenzyl)-benzimidazole was tested for reversal of inhibition by the same metabolites tried against it in the poliomyelitis virus experi-

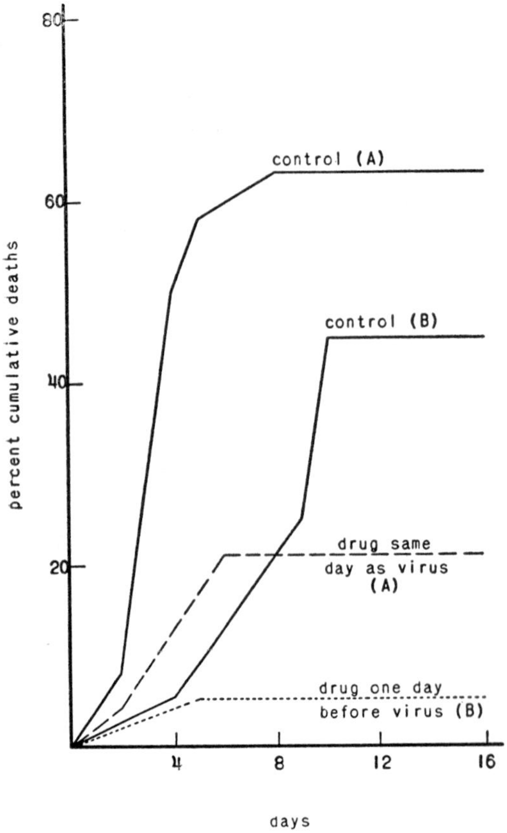

FIG. 3. Cumulative mortality curve of mice infected with poliomyelitis virus and treated with 2-(1-hydroxybenzyl)-benzimidazole.

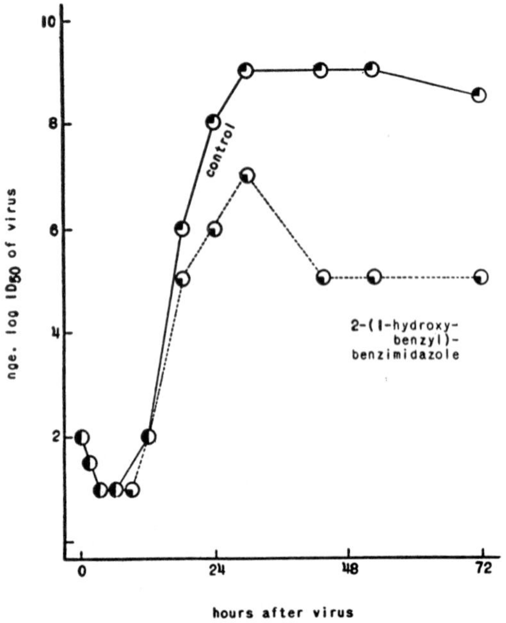

FIG. 4. Effect of 2-(1-hydroxybenzyl)-benzimidazole on the multiplication of influenza A (PR_8) in chick chorioallantoic membrane tissue cultures. Infectivity titer in eggs.

ments but no reversals were evidenced. Therefore, although it was determined that the compound acts by interference with the synthesis of the virus, the nature of this interference was not elucidated.

DISCUSSION. Perhaps the most interesting relation of structure to activity is that, of the 13 more active benzimidazoles and three more active quinoxalines, 11 of the benzimidazoles and all of the quinoxalines were substituted in the positions corresponding to positions 2 and 6 of the purine ring; these positions corresponding to those in guanine and in the effective carcinostatic drug, 2,6-diaminopurine. The two most active pyrazolo-(3,4 d) pyrimidines were substituted in the 1 and 4 positions whereas only one compund was substituted in the 4 and 6 positions, those corresponding to the 6 and 2 positions of purines.

Tamm (1956a, b) found that substitution of chlorine in the 4- and 6- positions greatly enhanced the activity of 5-chlorobenzimidazole against influenza virus, increasing its activity more than tenfold. Unfortunately the 4,5,6-chlorobenzimidazole (TRB) was much more toxic to the chorioallantoic tissue than the unsubstituted benzimidazole so that there was no substantial gain in therapeutic index. Some of the benzimidazoles reported herein have therapeutic ratios several times greater than this when compared to benzimidazole.

Tamm (1956a, b) suggests that inhibition of the formation of influenza virus is at the nucleoside level. Our data also failed to demonstrate reversal of the inhibitory effect of benzimidazoles on influenza but they did demonstrate reversal of their effect on poliomyelitis virus. This suggests that benzimidazoles interfere at an earlier stage in the synthesis of poliomyelitis virus than in the synthesis of influenza virus.

Hurst *et al.* (1953) find that certain quinoxaline-1:4-dioxides are, to date, the most active compounds *in vivo* against the large viruses of the psittacosis-lymphogranuloma group.

In the growth studies with monkey kidney cultures it was observed that the benzimidazoles suppressed multiplication of poliomyelitis virus for about 24 hours. It was found that 2-(1-hydroxybenzyl)-benzimidazole acted to suppress influenza virus growth during the early latent period although it continued to affect virus multiplication at later stages. In the case of kidney cells infected with poliomyelitis virus, 4-methoxy-6-nitrobenzimidazole seems to suppress the virus at the beginning of cytopathic stage II in which the nuclei are becoming irregular and the cytoplasm is beginning to round up. Perhaps this period is equivalent to the early latent period for influenza virus.

It is interesting to observe to what extent effectiveness in one system is of value in predicting effectiveness in another system. Initially, all the compounds were tested in testicular tissue and only those compounds with a therapeutic ratio of eight or more were studied further. Of 18 of of these tested, 14 had a therapeutic ratio of two or more against poliomyelitis virus in kidney tissue and seven had a ratio of two or more against poliomyelitis virus in HeLa cultures. Of ten compounds effective against poliomyelitis virus in testicular tissue four had a ratio of four or more against influenza virus in chorioallantoic explants. This is a much larger proportion of effective compounds than observed by Lum and Smith (1957) who found 12 compounds effective against influenza virus of 568 tested. It would appear from this that there is a somewhat greater probability than that due to chance alone that a drug effective against a virus in one system also will be effective against the same virus in another system or even against another virus in another system.

The results with 2-(1-hydroxbenzyl)-benzimidazole upon the course of poliomyelitis virus infection in mice appear promising. Since the compound probably was not at a maximal concentration in the blood until some time after the virus was administered the fact that the incidence of mortality was reduced seems to warrant further investigation of this or similar compounds.

SUMMARY

Nineteen purines and related compounds were effective in monkey testicular explant tissue cultures against three types of poliomyelitis virus. Of these, 14 were effective in monkey kidney cultures and seven in HeLa cultures. Five compounds were effective against adenovirus, influenza virus and poliomyelitis virus and one inhibited both adenovirus and poliomyelitis virus in this system. Of ten compounds compared in influenza virus-infected chick chorioallantoic membrane tissue cultures and poliomyelitis virus-infected monkey testicular tissue cultures, four compounds were found to be effective in both systems.

Most of the effective drugs were substituted in the same relative positions as guanine.

Virus inhibition was reversed by adenine or guanine or both in most instances. Reversal of inhibition by isoguanine with guanine and by 6-amino-4-methoxy-benzimidazole and adenine appeared to be competitive. Most of the compounds suppressed multiplication of poliomyelitis virus in kidney cultures for at least 24 hours and in testicular cultures for at least 72 hours.

A representative benzimidazole was studied using phase contrast microscopy and found to suppress poliomyelitis virus intracellularly at the beginning of cytopathic stage II.

2-(1-Hydroxybenzyl)-benzimidazole delayed or prevented poliomyelitis virus infection of mice when the compound was given in the diet immediately after inoculation of virus. The compound was found to suppress influenza virus infections of chorioallantoic tissue cultures during the eclipse and latent periods and there was still suppression at later stages.

REFERENCES

Brown, G. C.: J. Immunol., **69:** 441, 1952.
Brown, G. C., and Craig, D. E.: Fed. Proc., **12:** 437, 1953.
Dulbecco, R.: Proc. Nat. Acad. Sci. (U. S.), **38:** 747, 1952.
Dunnebacke, T. H.: Virology, **2:** 399, 1956.
Eagle, H.: J. Exp. Med., **102:** 595, 1955.
Eagle, H., and Habel, K.: J. Exp. Med., **104:** 271, 1956.
Engelman, M., Gillespie, H. B., Greer, S., and Graff, S.: Proc. Am. Assoc. Cancer Res., **1:** 14, 1953.
Friend, C.: Proc. Soc. Exp. Biol. & Med., **78:** 150, 1951.
Gifford, G. E., Robertson, H. E., and Syverton, J. T.: Proc. Soc. Exp. Biol. & Med., **86:** 515, 1954.
Hollinshead, A. C., and Smith, P. K.: This Journal, **117:** 97, 1956.
Hollinshead, A. C., and Smith, P. K.: Antibiotics Ann., 927, 1956–57.
Hsiung, G. D., and Melnick, J. L.: Virology, **1:** 533, 1955.
Hurst, E. W., Landquist, J. K., Melvin, P., Peters, J. M., Senior, N., Silk, J. A., and Stacek, G. J.: Brit. J. Pharmacol., **8:** 297, 1953.
Kramer, P. E., Robbins, M. L., and Smith, P. K.: This Journal, **113:** 262, 1955.
Liedke, K. B., Engelman, M., and Graff, S.: Anat. Record, **123:** 359, 1955.

LONG, M. E., AND TAYLOR, H. C.: Ann. New York Acad. Sci., **63:** 1095, 1956.

LUM, G. S., AND SMITH, P. K.: THIS JOURNAL, **119:** 284, 1957.

MOORE, A. E., AND FRIEND, C.: Proc. Soc. Exp. Biol. & Med., **78:** 153, 1951.

RAPPAPORT, C.: Proc. Soc. Exp. Biol. & Med., **91:** 464, 1956.

SNEDECOR, G. W.: Statistical Methods, 4th ed., The Iowa State College Press, 1946.

SYVERTON, J. T., AND SCHERER, W. F.: Ann. New York Acad. Sci., **58:** 1056, 1954.

SYVERTON, J. T., SCHERER, W. F., AND ELWOOD, P. M.: J. Lab. Clin. Med., **43:** 286, 1954.

TAMM, I.: Science, **120:** 847, 1954.

TAMM, I.: J. Bacteriol., **72:** 42, 1956a.

TAMM, I.: Yale J. Biol. Med., **29:** 33, 1956b.

TAMM, I., FOLKERS, K., SHUNK, C. H., AND HORSFALL, F. L., JR.: J. Exp. Med., **99:** 227, 1954.

THOMPSON, R. L., PRICE, M. L., MINTON, S. A., JR., ELION, G. B., AND HITCHINGS, G. H.: J. Immunol., **65:** 529, 1950.

YOUNGNER, J. S.: Proc. Soc. Exp. Biol. & Med., **85:** 202, 1954a.

YOUNGNER, J. S.: Proc. Soc. Exp. Biol. & Med., **85:** 527, 1954b.

8014

PHENYLBUTAZONE METABOLITES: ANTIRHEUMATIC, SODIUM-RETAINING AND URICOSURIC EFFECTS IN MAN[1]

T. F. YÜ, J. J. BURNS, B. C. PATON, ALEXANDER B. GUTMAN AND BERNARD B. BRODIE

The Departments of Medicine, The Mount Sinai Hospital and Columbia University College of Physicians and Surgeons, New York; The Research Service, Third (New York University) Medical Division, Goldwater Memorial Hospital, New York; and the Laboratory of Chemical Pharmacology, National Heart Institute, National Institutes of Health, Bethesda, Maryland

Received for publication December 23, 1957

A previous report has described the isolation of two metabolites of phenylbutazone (Butazolidin) from the urine of patients receiving the drug (Burns *et al.*, 1955b). One product is formed by the introduction of a phenolic group in the *para* position of a benzene ring (Metabolite I), and the other by the introduction of an alcohol group in the butyl side chain (Metabolite II).[2]

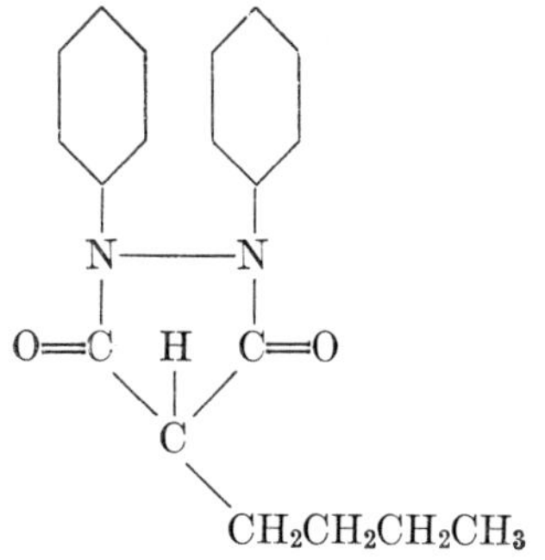

Phenylbutazone

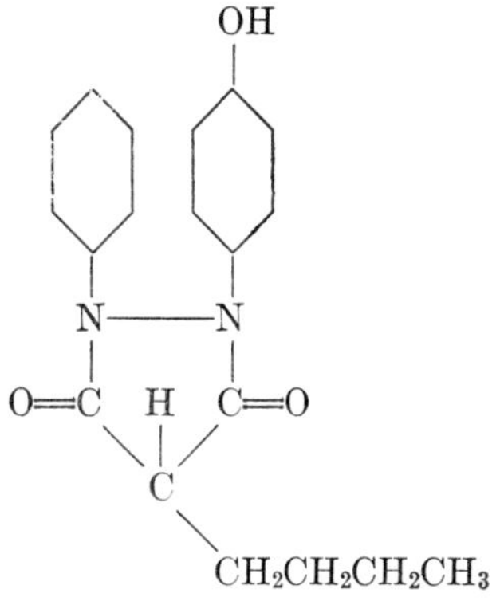

Metabolite I

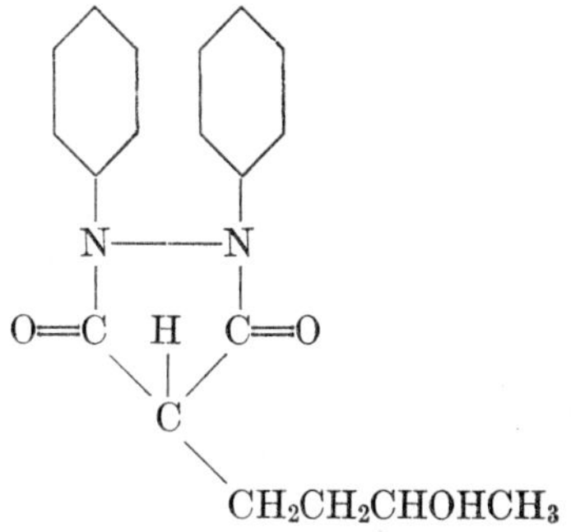

Metabolite II

Phenylbutazone possesses antirheumatic, sodium-retaining and uricosuric properties in man (Brodie *et al.*, 1954; Yü *et al.*, 1953; Yü *et al.*, 1956). The present study indicates that Metabolite I has the potent antirheumatic and sodium effects of the parent drug, whereas Metabolite II possesses enhanced uricosuric activity.

METHODS. Plasma concentrations of phenylbutazone, Metabolite I and Metabolite II were measured by methods previously described (Burns *et al.*, 1953; Burns *et al.*, 1955a). Renal clearance measurements and assays for uric acid and inulin were the same as described previously (Yü *et al.*, 1956).

RESULTS. *Physiological disposition of the metabolite.* Rate of disappearance from plasma: Previous studies have shown that Metabolite I and Metabolite II are extensively metabolized when given intravenously to man (Burns *et al.*, 1955a). The rates of metabolism of the metabolites and of phenylbutazone were compared in three human subjects. The compounds were given intravenously in doses of 600 mgm. and plasma levels were measured at various time intervals. In fig. 1 are given plasma level curves of the three drugs in one of these subjects; these curves are typical of those obtained with the other two subjects.

[1] A preliminary report of these studies has been presented (Burns *et al.*, 1955b; Brodie *et al.*, 1956).

[2] The synthesis of the two metabolites has been recently described (Pfister and Hafliger, 1957; Denes *et al.*, 1957). We are indebted to Dr. F. Hafliger of J. R. Geigy, A. G. Basel, Switzerland, for a generous supply of these compounds.

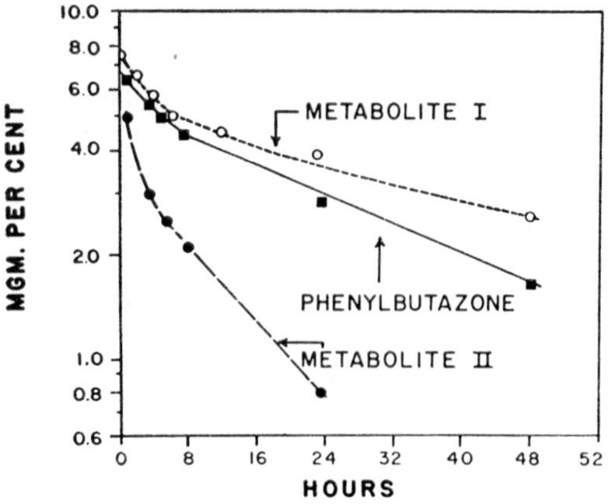

FIG. 1. Plasma levels of Metabolite I, Metabolite II and phenylbutazone after a single 600-mgm. intravenous dose of each compound to the same human subject.

Plasma levels of Metabolite I declined slowly, the biological half-life averaging 3 days, a rate similar to that previously reported for phenylbutazone (Burns *et al.*, 1953). In contrast, Metabolite II disappeared relatively rapidly with a biological half-life averaging 10 hours.

Oral adsorption of metabolites: Information concerning the adsorption of the metabolites from the gastrointestinal tract was obtained by comparing plasma levels of the two compounds in three human subjects following oral and intravenous administration of a single dose of 600 mgm. of each drug. The plasma levels of Metabolite I, which were obtained over a period of from 4 hours to 24 hours after the dose, were approximately the same by either route of administration, indicating that its adsorption was essentially complete. In contrast, no Metabolite II could be detected in plasma at any time after its administration. Because of its poor adsorption, Metabolite II was given intravenously in studies on its pharmacological activities.

Plasma levels of Metabolite I on repeated dosage: Twelve subjects received 800 mgm. of Metabolite I orally, in four divided doses, each day for 8 days or more. Plasma concentrations of Metabolite I were estimated in blood samples obtained just prior to the administration of the morning dose. During the first 3 days plasma levels progressively increased, then reached a plateau and thereafter they were constant from day to day for a given individual. The plateau plasma level varied among the subjects from 8.0 to 16.2 mgm. per cent, a range similar to that obtained with the same dosage schedule of phenylbutazone (Burns *et al.*, 1953).

Plasma binding of Metabolite I and Metabolite II: The extent to which the metabolites were bound to plasma proteins was determined by dialysis at 37° C. for 24 hours through a Visking membrane against isotonic phosphate buffer at pH 7.4. At plasma levels of 5.0 to 15.0 mgm. per cent approximately 98 per cent of Metabolite I and 93 per cent of Metabolite II were bound to plasma protein. A high degree of binding of phenylbutazone to plasma proteins has been reported previously (Burns *et al.*, 1953).

Effect on urinary excretion of electrolytes. Balance studies: The effect of Metabolite I on the urinary excretion of electrolytes was studied in four male subjects. After at least 7 days on a diet in which the intake of sodium was kept constant the subjects received 800 mgm. per day of the drug for a period of 5 days (table 1). The excretion of sodium fell off about 60 per cent from the control values by the third day of medication, followed by a return to the initial values during the remaining period of administration. After discontinuing the drug there was a diuresis with loss of retained sodium. The pattern of chloride excretion was similar to that of sodium and no significant change in potassium excretion was observed. A similar retention of sodium was observed when three of these subjects (E. K., J. L., A. S.) were given equivalent doses of phenylbutazone.

To determine the effect of Metabolite II, the compound was administered intravenously to three normal subjects in doses of 800 mgm. daily for 3 days. Metabolite II produced less sodium and water retention than that obtained with the same dose of phenylbutazone (table 2, data in one subject).

Renal clearance studies: The effect of the two phenylbutazone metabolites on the excretion of sodium and chloride was studied further by renal clearance techniques. Slow, sustained intravenous infusion of Metabolite I elicited distinct retention of sodium and chloride at plasma drug levels as low as 2.0 mgm. per cent (table 3), with increasing salt retention as the plasma levels rose. Inulin clearance was unchanged in two subjects (M. R., I. S.) and declined about 15 per cent in the two others. The results obtained with Metabolite I are similar to those previously found for phenylbutazone (Yü *et al.*, 1956). Intravenous

TABLE 1

Effect of Metabolite I on urinary excretion of electrolytes in human subjects

Day	Dose of drug*	E. K.			J. L.			A. S.**		O. G.		
		Na	K	Cl	Na	K	Cl	Na	K	Na	K	Cl
	mgm.	*mEq./day*			*mEq./day*			*mEq./day*		*mEq./day*		
1	0.0	118	48.5	133	82.3	59.4	83.8	87.2	49.2	44.7	72.8	51.4
2	0.0	112	47.0	124	86.5	73.1	86.3	77.6	63.9	50.8	67.2	50.1
3	800	78.9	42.3	73.9	78.4	66.1	79.0	35.9	52.4	14.7	54.5	22.7
4	800	61.2	58.1	84.0	44.1	64.4	44.5	43.2	55.1	16.8	54.1	17.5
5	800	45.8	53.6	64.7	39.4	50.9	65.1	32.1	48.3	20.2	57.4	22.7
6	800	50.9	37.6	61.3	64.5	65.3	68.1	104	43.4	42.3	61.9	40.7
7	800	73.7	61.0	96.1	50.2	52.1	75.2	78.7	60.2	64.8	69.9	58.4
8	0.0	286	52.2	335.4	92.4	69.7	94.3	91.2	40.0	49.0	57.4	48.1
9	0.0	39.1	38.2	35.0	106	68.4	97.0	102	52.2	42.4	63.3	48.0
10	0.0	52.2	38.4	59.1	127	71.9	124.5	144	62.5			
11	0.0	53.0	56.4	73.2	145	71.4	141.6	135	58.7			

* Metabolite I was administered orally, divided in four equal doses throughout the day.
** Chloride excretion was not measured in this patient.

TABLE 2

*Effect of Metabolite II and phenylbutazone on electrolyte and water excretion in the same subject**

Day	Metabolite II					Phenylbutazone				
	Dose	Urine volume	Na	K	Cl	Dose	Urine volume	Na	K	Cl
	mgm.	*ml.*	*mEq./24 hours*			*mgm.*	*ml.*	*mEq./24 hours*		
1	0.0	1520	68.4	52.1	61.8	0.0	1220	74.9	47.1	63.5
2	0.0	1320	61.3	49.0	56.0	0.0	1270	75.3	52.7	69.5
3	0.0	1380	65.6	51.3	60.3	0.0	1210	70.8	45.8	64.6
4	0.0	1420	67.0	54.8	63.1	0.0	1170	81.9	49.1	63.8
5	800	1340	51.7	46.9	51.7	800	950	41.4	45.6	41.2
6	800	1360	66.1	48.6	60.6	800	710	21.3	36.4	22.4
7	800	1360	61.2	48.1	58.9	800**	670	14.4	34.0	16.3
8	0.0	1380	74.4	46.0	67.9	800	590	11.0	29.5	11.6
9	0.0	1280	75.0	46.1	60.5	0.0	710	14.7	47.7	19.5
10	0.0	1220	75.8	41.5	65.3	0.0	770	25.3	39.5	23.1
11	0.0	1360	85.5	47.2	76.3	0.0	970	41.6	44.6	35.1

* Metabolite II was administered by intravenous injection and phenylbutazone was given orally.
** On this day of phenylbutazone medication patient developed clinical edema.

infusion of Metabolite II was also followed by retention of sodium and chloride (table 4), but to a lesser extent than that observed with Metabolite I.

Effect on urinary excretion of uric acid. Oral administration: Metabolite I was administered orally to four patients for 3 days and the serum concentration and daily urinary excretion of uric acid were measured. Two patients received 1200 mgm. per day of the drug, one patient 800 mgm. per day and one patient 400 mgm. per day. One of the patients receiving 1200 mgm. per day showed a 28 per cent increase in urinary urate excretion the first day and a 45 per cent increase the second day; correspondingly the serum urate declined from a control level of 9.6 mgm. per cent to 6.2 mgm. per cent by the end of 3 days. The other patients showed no detectable uricosuria.

Renal clearance studies: The effects of slow intravenous infusion of Metabolite I were ob-

TABLE 3

Effect of slow, sustained intravenous infusion of Metabolite I on renal clearance of inulin, urate, sodium and chloride

Subject (Body Surface Area)	Period	Drug Infused*	Plasma Metabolite I	C_{inulin}	C_{urate}	$\frac{C_{urate}}{C_{inulin}}$	C_{Na}	C_{Cl}
	min.	*mgm.*	*mgm. per cent*	*ml./min.*	*ml./min.*	*per cent*	*ml./min.*	*ml./min.*
M. R. (1.98 m.²)	Control**	0		106	7.06	6.66	1.34	1.43
	0–22	28	0.3	102	6.38	6.25	1.33	1.42
	22–43	69	0.7	100	6.69	6.72	1.28	1.36
	43–63	132	1.6	111	7.75	6.98	1.26	1.29
	63–83	144	2.6	107	6.61	5.96	1.03	0.82
	83–104	291	4.1	98.5	6.28	6.38	0.83	0.61
	104–125	468	5.9	115	5.93	5.15	0.65	0.47
J. Z. (2.00 m.²)	Control**			136	6.41	4.72	2.16	2.13
	0–23	30	1.8	129	5.16	4.00	2.14	2.04
	23–44	90	5.9	118	4.63	3.92	1.05	1.46
	44–65	210		118	3.80	3.22	0.83	1.01
	65–87	360		116	4.32	3.72	0.70	0.76
	87–108	545	8.4	116	4.32	3.72	0.70	0.76
	108–128	770	10.2	115	6.20	5.40	0.53	0.48
	128–161	1140	14.0	115	9.03	7.85	0.53	0.48
I. S. (1.79 m.²)	Control**			128	8.94	6.98	3.48	4.20
	0–19	30	0.4	128	9.05	7.08	3.32	4.16
	19–38	80	0.9	136	11.0	8.09	3.54	4.40
	38–59	230	1.8	127	10.3	8.12	2.98	3.35
	59–80	400	3.2	135	12.1	8.97	2.38	2.44
	80–104	635	5.2	123	11.1	9.02	1.88	1.78
	104–122	830	8.2	131	15.8	12.1	2.69	1.34
	122–160	1230	13.0	127	20.3	16.0	1.40	1.03
J. B. (1.66 m.²)	Control**			93.5	8.37	8.94	2.16	2.82
	0–28	45	1.3	78.6	5.50	6.99	1.62	2.17
	28–50	115		76.5	5.36	7.01	1.45	1.84
	50–76	230	5.7	74.5	5.85	7.85	1.39	1.74
	76–98	370		71.1	6.26	8.18	1.19	1.39
	98–119	535	10.5	76.4	6.18	8.09	1.16	1.27
	119–155	910	13.1	80.3	10.4	13.0	1.08	1.09
	155–170	1065	15.3	81.4	15.6	19.2	1.30	1.12

* Metabolite I was administered in 5 per cent glucose solution.

** Mean of three 20-minute periods.

served in four subjects (table 3). In order to demonstrate a distinct uricosuric effect it was necessary to inject about 1.0 gm. of the drug, which produced plasma levels of about 10 mgm. per cent (J. Z., I. S., J. B.). C_{urate}/C_{inulin} increased to about the same extent noted with phenylbutazone in equivalent dosage (Yü *et al.*, 1953; Yü *et al.*, 1956).

The uricosuric properties of Metabolite II were found to be much more pronounced than those of the parent drug or of Metabolite I. C_{urate}/C_{inulin} increased at plasma drug levels as low as 2.0 mgm. per cent (table 4). A distinct uricosuric effect was noted when as little as 200 to 400 mgm. of Metabolite II had been given. When Metabolite II was given intravenously by a rapid infusion at a dosage of about 15 mgm. per kgm. body weight, the mean C_{urate}/C_{inulin} rose from a control value of 9.75 per cent to a mean peak of 43.4 per cent (table 5). The uricosuria induced by Metabolite II was associated with a progressive decrease in the serum urate concentration, the mean control

TABLE 4

Effect of slow, sustained intravenous infusion of Metabolite II on renal clearance of inulin, urate, sodium and chloride

Subject (Body Surface Area)	Period	Drug Infused*	Plasma Metabolite II	C_{inulin}	C_{urate}	$\frac{C_{urate}}{C_{inulin}}$	C_{Na}	C_{Cl}
	min.	*mgm.*	*mgm. per cent*	*ml./min.*	*ml./min.*	*per cent*	*ml./min.*	*ml./min.*
C. V. (1.86 m.²)	Control**	0		87.6	4.97	5.67	1.58	2.42
	0–22	30	trace	74.5	4.27	5.73	1.44	2.21
	22–44	60	trace	81.0	4.27	5.28	1.31	2.11
	44–66	115	0.6	89.0	5.83	6.54	1.64	2.62
	66–88	175	1.3	88.0	7.64	8.68	1.49	2.45
	88–109	260	2.2	95.4	10.5	11.0	1.58	2.50
	109–128	385	3.2	75.3	11.9	15.8	1.05	1.64
	128–155	620	4.9	73.8	12.1	16.4	1.01	1.56
L. S. (2.07 m.²)	Control**			104	6.55	6.30	0.60	1.03
	0–21	30	0.5	91.2	6.29	6.89	0.68	1.04
	21–46	95	0.9	84.3	6.08	7.21	0.47	0.83
	46–70	190	1.5	93.8	6.12	6.55	0.47	0.75
	70–101	360	4.2	84.7	7.99	9.43	0.36	0.66
	101–124	515	5.2	114	22.2	19.5	0.48	0.75
	124–165	830	8.9	100	27.8	27.8	0.47	0.50

* Metabolite II was administered in 5 per cent glucose solution.

** Mean of three 20-minute periods.

serum urate falling from 9.1 mgm. per cent to a mean minimum value of 6.4 mgm. per cent in about 5 hours.

Antirheumatic effects. Metabolite I was administered orally to 45 patients with acute gouty arthritis in doses of 200 mgm. 3 to 5 times daily. In 35 patients the symptoms of acute inflammation remitted completely within 24 to 48 hours, and in four patients within a week; two patients showed only a partial response at the end of one week and four patients did not respond favorably. These results correspond closely with those obtained with phenylbutazone (table 6).

Metabolite I was administered orally to ten patients with active rheumatoid arthritis. Five of these patients who received 600 to 800 mgm. per day of the drug for periods of from 3 to 10 days showed marked relief of joint pain and stiffness comparable to that obtained with phenylbutazone; three patients who received 400 mgm. per day had an equivical response; in two patients receiving 200 mgm. daily the drug was ineffective.

Two patients with acute gouty arthritis were given intravenously 1200 mgm. of Metabolite II, the compound was administered in two equal doses spaced 12 hours apart. No improvement was observed in either patient, but a good response was subsequently obtained when they were treated with phenylbutazone in a dosage of 600 mgm. daily for 2 days.

Side reactions: Of the 65 patients who received Metabolite I, five had side reactions. One patient, who had previously exhibited skin allergy to both phenylbutazone and one of its analogues, G-25671, (Yü *et al.*, 1956), developed a macular rash after a single 200-mgm. dose of Metabolite I. Another patient developed a maculopapular rash after taking the drug for 6 weeks. One patient who was known to have duodenal ulcer developed recurrence of ulcer pain after taking 800 mgm. per day of Metabolite I for 3 days. One patient gained 6 pounds in weight, with noticeable pitting edema of both legs, after taking 600 mgm. of Metabolite I daily for 10 days. Another patient developed abdominal cramps after taking a single dose of 200 mgm. of the drug. In incidence and types of side reactions, our experience with Metabolite I is similar to that we have observed in the short term use of phenylbutazone.

Discussion. The results obtained in this study indicate that introduction of a hydroxyl group in the *para* position of a benzene ring of phenylbutazone results in a compound with properties similar to those of the parent drug. Like phenylbuta-

TABLE 5

Effect of intravenous injection of Metabolite II on renal clearance of inulin and urate

Subject (Body Surface Area)	Period	Plasma Metabolite II	C_{inulin}	Plasma Urate	C_{urate}	$\frac{C_{urate}}{C_{inulin}}$
	min.	*mgm./per cent*	*ml./min.*	*mgm./per cent*	*ml./min.*	*per cent*
M. S. (1.94 m.^{2})	Control*		89.2	9.1	7.60	8.52
	Metabolite II 1.3 gm.** (16 mgm./kgm.)					
	0–20	13.0	79.3	8.9	33.9	42.7
	20–43	12.1	82.5	8.7	35.5	43.0
	43–64		66.9		22.4	33.5
	64–84		65.3		23.3	35.7
	84–108	10.2	97.0	8.2	31.6	32.6
	108–126		97.5		30.5	31.3
	126–186	9.1	74.1	8.0	21.3	28.8
	186–251	7.9	67.9	7.4	16.3	24.0
	251–312	8.6	60.4	6.9	14.0	23.2
J. Z. (2.00 m.^{2})	Control*		122	8.8	5.65	5.43
	Metabolite II 1.3 gm.** (15 mgm./kgm.)					
	0–21	16.0	116	8.6	25.0	21.6
	21–49	14.6	108	8.6	46.1	42.7
	49–72		117		38.6	33.0
	72–96		112		32.6	29.1
	96–118	11.3	112	7.6	32.5	29.0
	118–173	10.2	130	7.5	33.7	25.8
	173–233	10.1	111	6.0	25.7	23.1
	233–322	8.8	114	6.0	27.4	24.0
M. F. (1.73 m.^{2})	Control*		57.1	9.4	8.77	15.3
	Metabolite II 1.0 gm.** (15 mgm./kgm.)					
	0–26	12.4	67.3	9.2	18.9	28.1
	26–59	12.2	84.8	9.2	37.7	44.5
	59–119		53.7		14.3	26.6
	119–167		69.5		16.4	23.6
	167–240		68.0		17.2	25.3
	240–300	11.0	55.5	7.2	16.0	28.9
	300–359	10.7	68.5	6.4	21.7	31.7

* Mean of three 20-minute periods.

** Metabolite II was given in 100 ml. of 5 per cent dextrose.

zone, Metabolite I is well absorbed when given orally and is metabolized slowly in man. The drug has the potent antirheumatic and sodium-retaining effects of phenylbutazone. On the other hand, introduction of a hydroxyl group in the butyl side chain (Metabolite II) results in a compound that is not absorbed when given orally. After intravenous injection, Metabolite II is metabolized in man at a considerably faster rate than the parent drug. The drug possesses little sodium-retaining and antirheumatic properties, but it is considerably more potent as a uricosuric agent than phenylbutazone.

It is of interest that two metabolites of phenylbutazone, formed by introduction of hydroxyl groups at different positions in the phenylbuta-

TABLE 6

Comparative response to Metabolite I and phenylbutazone in patients with acute gouty arthritis

Response to Drug	Metabolite I		Phenylbutazone	
	No. of patients	Per cent of total	No. of patients	Per cent of total
Complete remission within 24-48 hours	35	78	150	79
Complete remission within a week	4	9	8	4
Partial response	2	4	21	11
Unsatisfactory response	4	7	12	3

zone molecule, have such contrasting pharmacological activities. This finding has suggested the synthesis of other analogues of phenylbutazone which have various substitutions in the benzene ring or the butyl side chain. For instance, substitutions of a chloro, methyl or nitro group in the *para* position of the benzene ring leads to compounds possessing potent antirheumatic and sodium-retaining activity.[3] In contrast, substitutions of various groups in the butyl side chain result in compounds which have potent uricosuric activity but only mild antirheumatic and sodium-retaining properties. In fact, two of these compounds, thio derivatives of phenylbutazone, appear to offer considerable promise as uricosuric agents for the treatment of gout (Yü *et al.*, 1956; Burns *et al.*, 1957).

Metabolite II has no clinical usefulness since it is not absorbed when given orally. However, finding that Metabolite I has potent antirheumatic activity in acute gout and rheumatoid arthritis has encouraged its further clinical evaluation.

[3] Unpublished observations.

SUMMARY

Two metabolites of phenylbutazone which were isolated from human urine possess some of the pharmacological activities of the parent drug. Metabolite I, formed by the introduction of a phenolic group in a benzene ring, has the potent antirheumatic and sodium-retaining effects of phenylbutazone. Metabolite II, formed by the introduction of an alcohol group in the butyl side chain, possesses reduced sodium-retaining and antirheumatic properties, but it is a considerably more potent uricosuric agent than phenylbutazone.

REFERENCES

Brodie, B. B., Lowman, E., Burns, J. J., Lee, P., Chenkin, T., Goldman, A., Weiner, M., and Steele, J.: Am. J. Med., **16:** 181, 1954.
Brodie, B. B., Burns, J. J., Paton, B., Steele, J. M., Yü, T. F., and Gutman, A. B.: Abs., Contemporary Rheumatology, Elsevier Publishing Co., 1956.
Burns, J. J., Rose, R. K., Chenkin, T., Goldman, A., Schulert, A., and Brodie, B. B.: This Journal, **109:** 346, 1953.
Burns, J. J., Gutman, A. B., Yü, T. F., Paton, B., Perel, J., Steele, J. M., and Brodie, B. B.: Fed. Proc., **14:** 323, 1955a.
Burns, J. J., Rose, R. K., Goodwin, S., Reichenthal, J., Horning, E. C., and Brodie, B. B.: This Journal, Abs., **113:** 9, 1955b.
Burns, J. J., Yü, T. F., Ritterband, A., Perel, J., Gutman, A. B., and Brodie, B. B.: This Journal, **119:** 418, 1957.
Denes, R., Hafliger, F., and Goodwin, S.: Helv. Chim. Acta, **40:** 402, 1957.
Pfister, R., and Hafliger, F.: Helv. Chim. Acta, **40:** 396, 1957.
Yü, T. F., Sirota, J. H., and Gutman, A. B.: J. Clin. Invest., **32:** 1121, 1953.
Yü, T. F., Paton, B. C., Chenkin, T., Burns, J. J., Brodie, B. B., and Gutman, A. B.: J. Clin. Invest., **35:** 374, 1956.

8015

THE PASSAGE OF THIOBARBITURATES AND THEIR OXYGEN ANALOGS INTO BRAIN[1]

LESTER C. MARK, J. J. BURNS, LEONARD BRAND, C. INES CAMPOMANES, NATALIE TROUSOF, E. M. PAPPER AND BERNARD B. BRODIE

Department of Anesthesiology, Columbia-Presbyterian Medical Center, and New York University Research Service, Goldwater Memorial Hospital, New York City and the Laboratory of Chemical Pharmacology, National Heart Institute, National Institutes of Health, Bethesda, Maryland

Received for publication December 16, 1957

Previous studies have shown that there is no demonstrable barrier to the passage of thiopental into the brain (Mark *et al.*, 1957). It has been shown that concentrations of thiopental in dog brain are maximal almost instantaneously after intravenous administration of the drug. In man the same phenomenon was inferred from the prompt onset of sleep and the prompt appearance of electroencephalographic changes after thiopental injection.

The present study began as a comparison of the rate of penetration into brain of thiopental and its oxygen analog, pentobarbital. The animal data verified the clinical impression of a somewhat slower onset of action with pentobarbital, but the difference between the two drugs was not sharply delineated. Accordingly, it was decided to extend the study to two other barbiturate pairs, barbital-thiobarbital and phenobarbital-thiophenobarbital.

METHODS AND MATERIALS. Thiopental and pentobarbital were determined by methods previously described (Brodie *et al.*, 1950; Brodie *et al.*, 1953). Phenobarbital was determined by the procedure used for pentobarbital except that ethylene dichloride was used as the solvent. Thiobarbital and thiophenobarbital were determined by the procedure used for thiopental except that ethylene dichloride was used as the solvent and the ultraviolet absorption was measured in 0.5 *N* NaOH. Barbital was determined by a previously described method (Giotti and Maynert, 1951). For analysis of barbital in brain, 2 ml. of a homogenate, containing 0.5 gm. of tissue, was used. This method gave negligible blank values and the recoveries averaged 95 per cent.

The oil to water partition ratios of the various barbiturates were determined by distributing 4.0 mgm. of each compound between peanut oil (5 ml.) and pH 7.4 phosphate buffer (20 ml.).

Each dose of barbiturate was given intravenously to dogs over a period of 5 seconds. After suitable time intervals, the animals were killed by the rapid intravenous injection of 4 to 6 ml. of a saturated solution of potassium chloride, which produced cardiac standstill within 5 seconds. Heart blood was immediately obtained by cardiac puncture. The cranium was then opened to permit removal of the brain for analysis of its barbiturate content.

RESULTS. *Comparison between thiopental and pentobarbital.* Two groups of 10 dogs each received thiopental or pentobarbital in doses of 20 mgm. per kgm. and the animals were killed in 30 seconds, 1 minute or 3 minutes. The ratios of brain to plasma concentration for thiopental were the same at 30 seconds as they were at 3 minutes. With pentobarbital the early ratios were somewhat less than the later ones, but the differences were not marked (table 1).

Comparison between thiobarbital and barbital. Thiobarbital and barbital were each administered to 8 dogs in doses of 100 mgm. per kgm. Thiobarbital produced unconsciousness within 2 to 3 minutes. In contrast, barbital induced no obvious effects for about 20 minutes, at which time there appeared a mild incoordination of the hind limbs and a staggering gait as though the dog were intoxicated. The ataxia increased with repeated falling to the floor until the animal was no longer able to rise. Attempts at movement then ceased. Finally, about 30 to 40 minutes after the barbital injection, the dog became unconscious. Parallel to the effects of the drugs the brain to plasma concentration ratios for thio-

[1] This work was supported in part by the Research and Development Division, Office of the Surgeon General, Department of the Army, under Contract No. DA-49-007-MD-629, in part by a research grant No. B-1288 from the National Institute of Neurological Diseases and Blindness, Public Health Service, and in part by Abbott Laboratories, North Chicago, Illinois.

barbital rose to a maximum value in 3 minutes, whereas the ratios for barbital rose steadily from low values at 3 minutes to intermediate values at 9 minutes and finally reached a maximal value in 30 to 60 minutes.

Comparison between thiophenobarbital and phenobarbital. Six dogs were given thiophenobarbital and six dogs received phenobarbital in doses of 100 mgm. per kgm. The animals given thiophenobarbital were asleep within 2 minutes. With phenobarbital there was a similar gradual progression of symptoms as described for barbital, except that the onset was slightly more rapid, about 10 to 15 minutes, and the dogs were fully asleep by 20 to 30 minutes. The brain to plasma concentration ratios for thiophenobarbital reached a maximum in 3 minutes while with phenobarbital the ratios rose steadily over a period of one hour.

Relative oil to water partition coefficients of the various barbiturates. The relative lipid solubility of each drug was expressed as the ratio of the concentration of drug in the oil phase to that in the water phase. The value of the ratio for each thiobarbiturate was found to be 10 to 11 times greater than the value for the corresponding oxygen analog (table 3).

Discussion. While the blood-brain barrier is almost totally impermeable to certain substances, for example, sodium ferricyanide, arsenicals and protein, it is ordinarily manifested as a *relative* impedance to the free passage of substances from the general circulation into the central nervous system. All the barbiturates cross into the brain, but they differ in the rates at which the passage occurs and thus vary in time of onset of anesthetic action. Butler first formulated the hypothesis relating lipid solubility of the barbiturates and their rate of entry into brain; the more highly soluble drugs penetrating more rapidly (Butler, 1942). He subsequently demonstrated in mice, using the representative oxybarbiturates, barbital and hexethal, that there is a delay in the passage of barbital into the brain, in contrast to the rapid penetration by hexethal (Butler, 1950).

The portions of this report dealing with barbital, phenobarbital and pentobarbital confirm Butler's observations with barbital and hexethal. After the intravenous administration of barbital or phenobarbital the onset of action is delayed and is followed by a further slow progression to full development of hypnotic effects. Associated with this sequence of events there is a gradual rise in drug concentration in the brain as compared with plasma (table 2). With pentobarbital there is rapid onset of sleep and a correspondingly prompt rise in brain to plasma concentration ratio (table 1).

TABLE 1

Thiopental and pentobarbital in dog brain after intravenous doses of 20 mgm. per kgm.

Time	Plasma	Brain	Brain to Plasma Ratio
Thiopental			
	mgm./l.	*mgm./kgm.*	
30 seconds	42	31	0.74
30 seconds	56	45	0.80
30 seconds	26	23	0.89
30 seconds	38	42	1.1
30 seconds	29	42	1.4
30 seconds	26	36	1.4
3 minutes	30	25	0.83
3 minutes	21	19	0.89
3 minutes	33	37	1.1
3 minutes	62*	79	1.3
Pentobarbital			
30 seconds	41	18	0.44
30 seconds	51	28	0.55
30 seconds	29	24	0.83
30 seconds	39	34	0.87
30 seconds	27	25	0.94
30 seconds	31	30	0.97
1 minute	28	25	0.89
1 minute	36	34	0.95
3 minutes	45*	55	1.2
3 minutes	23	32	1.4

* Dose 40 mgm. per kgm.

The anticipated explanation appears in table 3. The slowly acting barbital and phenobarbital have relatively low oil to water partition ratios and so should pass more slowly into brain than pentobarbital, which has a higher degree of lipid solubility.

The present study extends Butler's observations to the thiobarbiturates, the data indicating that these compounds pass into the brain more readily than do their oxygen analogs. Maximum

TABLE 2

Barbiturates in dog brain after intravenous doses of 100 mgm. per kgm.

Time	Plasma	Brain	Brain to Plasma Ratio
Thiobarbital			
	mgm./l.	*mgm./kgm.*	
1 minute	348	132	0.38
1 minute	249	101	0.41
3 minutes	200	129	0.65
3 minutes	186	143	0.77
9 minutes	174	131	0.75
9 minutes	159	126	0.79
60 minutes	133	94	0.71
60 minutes	116	92	0.79
Barbital			
3 minutes	73*	15	0.21
3 minutes	147	39	0.26
9 minutes	154	61	0.40
9 minutes	163	70	0.43
30 minutes	126	80	0.63
30 minutes	102	69	0.68
60 minutes	78†	53	0.68
60 minutes	156	123	0.79
Thiophenobarbital			
3 minutes	171	95	0.56
3 minutes	111‡	77	0.69
3 minutes	133‡	108	0.81
3 minutes	80§	68	0.85
60 minutes	44†	29	0.66
60 minutes	99	80	0.81
Phenobarbital			
3 minutes	215	76	0.35
3 minutes	174	73	0.42
30 minutes	138	98	0.71
30 minutes	143	103	0.72
60 minutes	122	131	1.1
60 minutes	113	136	1.1

* Dose 40 mgm. per kgm.
† Dose 60 mgm. per kgm.
‡ Dose 75 mgm. per kgm.
§ Dose 50 mgm. per kgm.

TABLE 3

Oil to water partition ratios

Barbital	0.26	Thiobarbital	2.3
Phenobarbital	1.0	Thiophenobarbital	11.
Pentobarbital	5.8	Thiopental	63.

brain to plasma concentration ratios are achieved more rapidly with thiobarbital and thiophenobarbital than with barbital and phenobarbital (table 2); and so also are the hypnotic effects. These findings can be correlated with a tenfold difference in relative lipid solubilities between the thio- and the oxybarbiturates (table 3).

It is tempting to speculate that sulfur-substitution in the barbiturate molecule permits the compound to cross the blood-brain barrier rapidly by some specialized mechanism. Such a concept is dispelled, however, by the finding that while the brain to plasma ratios with thiobarbital reach equilibrium by 3 minutes, the value at 1 minute is considerably lower, indicating a brief delay in crossing the barrier (table 2). Thus the fact that thiobarbiturates enter brain more rapidly than do the corresponding oxybarbiturates is probably due to a generic effect of the sulfur atom in increasing lipid solubility rather than a specific sulfur effect *per se*.

On this basis, an oxybarbiturate which is sufficiently lipid soluble should pass into brain as rapidly as a thiobarbiturate. Such is indeed the case, since pentobarbital, an oxybarbiturate with a high degree of lipid solubility (table 3), passes into brain at a somewhat more rapid rate than thiobarbital (table 1, table 2). In fact, the passage of pentobarbital into brain is sufficiently rapid so that it is difficult to demonstrate a difference between this oxybarbiturate and its thio analog, thiopental (table 1). Thus, while the range of brain to plasma concentration ratios with pentobarbital at 30 seconds is at a somewhat lower level than the corresponding values with thiopental, the upper figures with pentobarbital are well within the lower limits of the range with thiopental (table 1).

The rapidity with which pentobarbital passes into brain is also borne out from preliminary results of electroencephalographic studies in man. Characteristic changes in the electrical activity of the brain were detected within 15 to 30 seconds following administration of either pentobarbital or thiopental. However, the maximum change in electrical activity following pentobarbital was delayed 1 to 2 minutes from the onset while following thiopental, both onset and peak effect were simultaneous.

SUMMARY

Thiobarbiturates pass into brain more rapidly than do their oxygen analogs. This is probably due to their higher lipid solubility, rather than to any specific effect of the sulfur-substitution in the molecule.

REFERENCES

BRODIE, B. B., MARK, L. C., PAPPER, E. M., LIEF, P. A., BERNSTEIN, E., AND ROVENSTINE, E. A.: THIS JOURNAL, **98:** 85, 1950.

BRODIE, B. B., BURNS, J. J., MARK, L. C., BERNSTEIN, E., AND PAPPER, E. M.: THIS JOURNAL, **109:** 26, 1953.

BUTLER, T. C.: THIS JOURNAL, **74:** 118, 1942.

BUTLER, T. C.: THIS JOURNAL, **100:** 219, 1950.

GIOTTI, A., AND MAYNERT, E. W.: THIS JOURNAL, **101:** 296, 1951.

MARK, L. C., BURNS, J. J., CAMPOMANES, C. I., NGAI, S. H., TROUSOF, N., PAPPER, E. M., AND BRODIE, B. B.: THIS JOURNAL, **119:** 35, 1957.

8016

THE DISULFIRAM-LIKE ACTIVITY OF ANIMAL CHARCOAL[1]

W. C. CLARK AND H. R. HULPIEU

Department of Biochemistry and Pharmacology, Indiana University Medical Center, Indianapolis

Received for publication November 14, 1957

Moench (1950) observed that patients who were given animal charcoal for several days became ill if they drank alcoholic beverages. The major symptoms of this illness were cutaneous flushing, dyspnea, increased pulse and a fall in blood pressure but no nausea or vomiting. This symptom complex is similar to the well known disulfiram-alcohol reaction (Hald *et al.*, 1948, 1949: Hald and Jacobsen, 1948; Jacobsen and Martensen-Larsen, 1949; Jacobsen, 1952). Moench suggested that animal charcoal might be useful as a substitute for tetraethylthiuram disulfide (TETD, disulfiram, Antabuse). He did not follow changes in blood acetaldehyde. The present communication reports a study of the pharmacology of animal charcoal in relation to that of ethanol. Animal charcoal was studied with respect to toxicity, dosage, onset and duration of its disulfiram-like action, comparative activity with disulfiram and cyanamide, and its effect on the rate of disappearance of ethanol from the body. Attempts were made to identify the compound in animal charcoal responsible for its disulfiram-like action.

MATERIALS AND METHODS. *Materials.* Animal charcoal is the residue that remains after destructive distillation of blood and bones in the absence of air. Its complex composition and low carbon content are shown in table 1. The animal charcoal used was bone charcoal obtained from Mallinckrodt Chemical Works. The vegetable charcoals employed were: 6 of the Nuchar series and a special synthetic charcoal supplied by the West Virginia Pulp and Paper Company, 2 Norits made by the American Norit Company, and Darco 60 obtained indirectly through the courtesy of Eli Lilly Company. These vegetable charcoals are about 95 per cent carbon and contain at most only traces of the other substances found in animal charcoal. The disulfiram was that supplied by the Ayerst Laboratories.

Methods. Single and repeated oral doses of animal charcoal were administered to dogs. These animals were then observed for toxic symptoms and tested at various intervals for sensitivity to ethanol. An animal was considered to be sensitized if ethanol produced a greater increase in blood acetaldehyde after animal charcoal administration than that from ethanol only. In order to be certain that such an increase was not an artifact, a blood acetaldehyde of less than 100 micrograms per cent was considered as a normal reaction to the standard dose of ethanol. An increase in blood acetaldehyde was chosen as the criterion for sensitization because dogs do not exhibit the symptoms of the disulfiram-alcohol reaction observed in man. They do respond with characteristic increases in blood acetaldehyde. The ethanol was given by intravenous infusion over a 10-minute period and the animal charcoal was mixed with food or administered as a slurry by stomach tube. The standard dose of ethanol was 1 gm./kgm. diluted with 4 volumes of 0.9 per cent solution of sodium chloride. Blood acetaldehyde was followed (method of Stotz, 1943) for 2½ hours after the injection of ethanol. The dichromate method of Harger *et al.* (1950) was used to determine the concentrations of ethanol in the blood. Similar studies were made with dogs given vegetable charcoals, other adsorbents or calcium cyanamide. The residues left after heat treatment or extraction of animal charcoal with common solvents were tested for their ability to sensitize the animals to ethanol.

Disulfiram, animal charcoal and a vegetable charcoal (Norit A) were compared for the production of sensitivity to ethanol in 9 human subjects. In man sensitivity to ethanol is characterized by an increase in blood acetaldehyde accompanied by flushing, lowering of blood pressure, increased heart rate and frequently nausea.

RESULTS. *Toxicity, single doses.* Groups of five or more dogs were given single doses of animal charcoal ranging from 0.5 to 5.0 gm./kgm. These animals were observed for at least seven days in comparison with stock dogs and with dogs which had received vegetable or acid-washed animal charcoal. The dogs treated with charcoal could be

[1] This investigation was supported in part by a grant from the Committee on Problems of Alcohol, National Academy of Sciences-National Research Council.

distinguished from the stock dogs only by the blackness and dryness of their stools. The stools passed following administration of animal charcoal were blacker than those after equal doses of vegetable or acid-washed animal charcoal.

Toxicity, repeated doses. Daily doses of 0.5, 1.0 and 2.0 gm./kgm. of animal charcoal were fed to dogs for from 7 to 154 days. This dosage produced no symptoms except a variable degree of loss of appetite, which was most evident during the first few days of a feeding period. Mild weight losses accompanied the reduced food intake. The over-all effect appeared to be the same as feeding an unsavory diet. Initial and final weights of the dogs for different feeding periods are shown in table 2. One of the 56 dogs used in this study did poorly and continued to lose weight. This dog exhibited symptoms characteristic of distemper and was sacrificed three weeks after removal of the animal charcoal from the diet. He had received 2 gm./kgm. of animal charcoal for 154 days. Comparable weight losses occurred in 8 dogs fed animal charcoal which had been treated with strong hydrochloric acid and thoroughly washed.

Nine human subjects who each took 9 gm. of animal charcoal per day for 3 weeks experienced no untoward effects unless ethanol was ingested.

Onset and duration of action, single doses. One-half, 1.0, 2.0, 3.0 and 5.0 gm./kgm. doses of animal charcoal were administered to groups of five or more dogs by stomach tube. The animals were challenged with ethanol from 1 to 72 hours later. Ethanol after the 0.5 and the 1.0 gm./kgm. doses of animal charcoal produced no increase in blood acetaldehyde above that found after ethanol only. In only an occasional instance was there a definite increase in blood acetaldehyde in the dogs receiving the 2.0-gm. and the 3.0-gm. doses of animal charcoal, while all animals exhibited an increase after 5.0 gm./kgm. The 5.0-gm. dose was chosen to study in detail the onset and duration of action. The data are summarized in table 3 and show that an effect developed within 1 hour, persisted at least 24 hours and had disappeared in 48 hours.

Onset and duration of action, repeated doses. Ineffective single doses of animal charcoal, if repeated daily, sensitized dogs to ethanol. The criterion for sensitization was the same as that described under MATERIALS AND METHODS. The time necessary to produce sensitization varied with the dose and the dog. Doses of 0.5 and 1.0 gm./kgm. became effective in 5 to 7 days, while 2.0 gm./kgm. required 3 to 4 days. Persistence of sensitivity was studied in dogs by challenging with ethanol at weekly intervals following the last dose of animal charcoal. One of 6 dogs that had received a daily dose of 2.0 gm./kgm. for 21 days lost its sensitivity at the first test, while 2 of the six responded with small increases in blood acetaldehyde at the third test. Two dogs fed 0.5 gm./kgm. for 112 days; two fed the 1.0 gm. dose for 154 days, and two fed 2.0 gm. for 154 days, all exhibited sensitivity to ethanol at the third test. No typical increases in blood acetaldehyde were observed at the fourth challenge.

Animal charcoal vs. disulfiram and cyanamide. The sensitizing action of animal charcoal, di-

TABLE 1

*Analyses of animal charcoal**

Ingredient	Per Cent
A	
Loss on drying	2–4
Volatile material	16.5
Fe_2O and Al_2O_3	0.6
CaO	45.8
MgO	0.6
P_2O_5	34.2
SiO_2	0.9–1.0
Sulfur (as SO_3)	0.5
CO_2	3.5
Carbon	8.0–10.0
Specific gravity	2.6
B	
Sulfide sulfur	0.016
Total nitrogen (Kjeldahl)	1.0
Cyanamide	none
Ash	80.4
Acid-insol. residue, sample I (Ash 15.3%)	25.0
Acid-insol. residue, sample II (ash 18.2%)	28.0
Alcohol-extractable material	0.17
Ether-extractable material	0.11

* The data in list A were supplied by A. Q. Butler of Mallinckrodt Chemical Works, and those in list B were obtained in our laboratory. The sulfide sulfur was determined by the method of Dietz *et al.* (1948) and cyanamide by the method of Pinck (1925).

TABLE 2

The effect of oral administration of animal charcoal on weight in dogs

Days Fed	Dose	No. of Dogs	Mean Weight of Dogs	
			Initial	Final
Animal charcoal				
	gm./kgm.		*kgm.*	*kgm.*
7	1.0	8	12.6	12.2
7	2.0	20	12.0	11.7
21	2.0	14	12.9	12.1
112	0.5	2	16.0	15.8
154	1.0	2	17.2	16.1
154	2.0	2	17.3	17.0
Acid-washed animal charcoal				
7	2.0	4	15.5	14.9
21	2.0	4	14.4	13.6

sulfiram and cyanamide to ethanol was compared in dogs. The test dose of alcohol was given the morning after the last daily dose of animal charcoal or disulfiram and 30 minutes after a single dose of cyanamide. The several experiments are summarized in table 4. These data indicate that the administration of 3 daily doses of 35 mgm./kgm. of disulfiram or a single dose of 2 mgm./kgm. of cyanamide (3.8 mgm. calcium cyanamide) have about the same sensitizing effect

TABLE 3

Onset and duration of the disulfiram-like action in dogs of single 5 gm./kgm. doses of animal charcoal, administered orally

A test dose of 1 gm./kgm. of ethanol was given i.v. at varying times after the animal charcoal. An increase in blood acetaldehyde is indicative of a positive reaction (see text). Variation is expressed as a range in place of standard deviation where the number of observations was three or less.

No. Dogs	Interval Between Charcoal and Ethanol	Blood Acetaldehyde After Ethanol			
		0 min.	45 min.	90 min.	150 min.
	hr.	*μgm.%*	*μgm.%*	*μgm.%*	*μgm %*
18	0	28 ± 30	86 ± 41	83 ± 48	63 ± 34
3	1	23	139	132	94
	Range	(0.0–50)	(92–165)	(123–127)	(37–123)
3	3	12	118	126	160
	Range	(12–12)	(62–177)	(75–165)	(123–220)
3	15	21	145	150	92
	Range	(12–25)	(92–177)	(110–190)	(62–110)
6	24	30 ± 24	138 ± 144	101 ± 73	101 ± 59
6	48	11 ± 15	29 ± 26	54 ± 42	71 ± 39
5	72	31 ± 11	71 ± 25	66 ± 35	66 ± 20

as 2 gm./kgm. of animal charcoal for seven days. The large individual variations and the time-dose effect reported in the previous section enjoins caution in projecting these ratios to conditions other than those of the present experiments.

Human subjects became sensitized to ethanol when they received 9 gm. animal charcoal daily from 1 to 3 weeks. The daily administration of 0.5 to 1.0 gm. of disulfiram has been shown to sensitize patients (Jacobsen and Martensen-Larsen, 1949; Raby, 1954). Doses of 50 to 100 mgm. have been recommended for calcium cyanamide (Ferguson, 1956). Comparative doses in mgm./kgm., estimated from these figures and the weights of our subjects, would be: animal charcoal 100 to 125; disulfiram 5 to 10; and calcium cyanamide 0.5 to 1.0 (cyanamide 0.25 to 0.50) mgm./kgm.

Animal charcoal and the disappearance rate of ethanol. The effect of animal charcoal on the first stage of the metabolism of ethanol was studied by comparing the rate of disappearance of ethanol from the blood of animals treated with animal charcoal with that of untreated dogs. The fall in blood alcohol was followed for 6 hours and the mean rate of disappearance calculated for each dog. The data shown in table 5 indicate that the rate of disappearance of ethanol was not changed by the administration of animal charcoal.

The active ingredient, comparison with other adsorbents. The possibility that the disulfiram-like action of animal charcoal is associated with its adsorptive properties was investigated by comparing its action with that of other adsorbent agents. The agents studied were: purified animal charcoal; the vegetable charcoals, Darco G-60, Norit SG, Nuchar, Nuchar C-1000, Nuchar CN, Nuchar C-115-N, Nuchar N-1000, and Nuchar WA unground; aluminum hydroxide (Amphogel); bentonite; kaolin; and hydrated silicic acid. These substances were fed in daily doses of 2 gm./kgm. for 1 week before the dogs were challenged with ethanol. In no instance was there a characteristic elevation of blood acetaldehyde.

Extraction of animal charcoal. Animal charcoal was extracted by repeated washings with ethanol, diethyl ether, chloroform, ethyl acetate, distilled water, and various concentrations of acetic acid, hydrochloric acid and ammonium hydroxide. Ethanol, ether, chloroform or ethyl acetate removed about 0.1 per cent of the animal charcoal as an oily material. The water and ammonium hydroxide extracts consisted of small amounts of inorganic materials. About 75 per cent of the animal charcoal was removed by the hydrochloric acid as inorganic salts. Hydrochloric acid also rapidly liberated hydrogen sulfide (see table 1). With acetic acid the amount of solids removed was smaller and hydrogen sulfide was more slowly and less completely liberated. All of the residues and the extracted materials were tested for disulfiram-like activity. None of the extracted materials produced a sensitivity to ethanol. Each of the carbonaceous residues, except those after acid extraction, had disulfiram-like activity comparable to that of the original animal charcoal. The material remaining after washing with 4.7 per cent hydrochloric acid was largely carbon and was devoid of activity. Treatment with 25 per cent acetic acid slowly diminished the activity of the residue.

Heat stability. Thin layers of animal charcoal were heated in a dry oven at temperatures sufficiently high to cause slight ashing and in an autoclave at 15 pounds pressure. Such treatment continued for as long as 1 week failed to destroy the disulfiram-like activity. Animal charcoal was ashed and the residue tested for activity by feeding dogs 2.0 gm./kgm. per day for 1 week and then challenging with the standard dose of ethanol. Equivocal increases in blood acetaldhyde were obtained. These increases were greater than those observed in the same animals from ethanol only, but not sufficient to be considered as definite sensitivity.

Synthetic charcoals. The presence of 1 per cent of nitrogen in animal charcoal (table 1) suggested that cyanamide might have been formed during the manufacturing process. We were unable to detect the presence of cyanamide in such charcoal by the method of Pinck (1925), using an acetate buffer for extraction of the animal charcoal as suggested to us by Dr. De Lapp of the American Cyanamid Company. This method was sufficiently sensitive to permit the detection of 1 mgm. of calcium cyanamide added to 50 gm. of animal charcoal. Charcoals with no disulfiram-like activity developed such activity when calcium cyanamide was added to them.

The possible role of sulfide was studied by feeding vegetable charcoals to which ferrous sulfide had been added, and by the use of a special synthetic charcoal, prepared by heating under reducing conditions Indulin C, tricalcium phosphate, ferrous sulfate and cane sugar. Neither ferrous sulfide by itself nor the synthetic charcoals sensitized the dogs to ethanol.

TABLE 4

Mean concentration of blood acetaldehyde in dogs given ethanol i.v. after treatment with animal charcoal, cyanamide or disulfiram, administered orally

The test dose of ethanol was 1 gm./kgm. for all experiments. Variation is given as a range in place of standard deviation where the number of observations was three or less (in parentheses).

Dose Per Kgm.	Days Given	No. of Dogs	Blood Acetaldehyde After Ethanol			
			0 min.	45 min.	90 min.	150 min.
Ethanol only						
			μgm.%	*μgm.%*	*μgm.%*	*μgm.%*
	1	18	28 ± 30	86 ± 41	83 ± 48	63 ± 34
Animal charcoal						
2.0 gm.	3	5	23 ± 18	182 ± 87	200 ± 79	189 ± 103
2 gm.	7	14	24 ± 14	277 ± 231	280 ± 229	220 ± 152
2 gm.	21	12	23 ± 15	425 ± 401	418 ± 340	325 ± 247
Disulfiram						
35 mgm.	3	2	61 (55–67)	400 (230–570)	325 (210–440)	265 (150–380)
250, 200, 150 mgm.	3	2	31 (25–37)	1202 (1004–1400)	1384 (1293–1475)	1153 (1030–1275)
Cyanamide						
2 mgm.	1	2	59 (56–63)	260 (248–272)	263 (227–300)	129 (122–137)
10 mgm.	1	2	34 (31–37)	730 (420–1505)	600 (235–1450)	417 (196–995)
20 mgm.	1	3	43 (37–50)	1665 (1245–2250)	1523 (820–1750)	871 (640–1395)

Calcium phosphate, when fed at a dose of 2 gm./kgm. daily for 3 weeks, was inactive either alone or when mixed with vegetable charcoals and heated.

Human subjects. Normal: Two normal subjects drank 0.33 gm./kgm. of ethanol before and during treatment with animal charcoal or with Norit A. The charcoals were taken daily in three doses of 3 gm. each, during the week before receiving the test dose of ethanol. The amount of ethanol and the maximum changes of blood acetaldehyde in the blood of these subjects are shown in table 6. The administration of ethanol after animal charcoal was followed by a typical disulfiram-like reaction. The main symptoms were flushing of the face, neck and chest, air hunger, nausea and headache. Blood pressures fell and the heart rates increased. The blood pressure of one subject fell to 88/44 and his heart rate increased from

TABLE 5

The effect of animal charcoal on the first stage of ethanol metabolism as measured by the rate of disappearance of blood alcohol over a 6-hour period following alcohol administration

Experiment	No. of Dogs	Average Disappearance Rate
		mgm. %/hr.
Ethanol only, 1 gm./kgm., i.v.	15	14.5 ± 2.7
Animal charcoal, 2 gm./kgm. for 7 days before administration of ethanol	14	13.5 ± 1.4
Animal charcoal, 2 gm./kgm. for 14 days before administration of ethanol	12	13.8 ± 3.5

70 to 106. No such reaction occurred when Norit A was given.

Alcoholics: The sensitizing action of animal charcoal and disulfiram was compared in 7 patients at the LaRue D. Carter Memorial Hospital. These patients were chronic alcoholics brought to the hospital while intoxicated. On admission both blood ethanol and blood acetaldehyde were determined. The lowest blood alcohol was 75 mgm. per cent and the highest was 375 with blood concentrations of acetaldehyde of 750 and 1420 microgm. per cent respectively. The patients exhibited only the usual signs of prolonged intoxication. After these patients had been "dried out" they were given either disulfiram or animal charcoal and challenged with a test dose of ethanol. The dosage of animal charcoal was 3 gm. three times per day for 1 week. The disulfiram was administered for from 3 to 7 days. The dosage regime was 2.0 gm. the first day, 1.5 gm. the second, 1.0 gm. the third, and then a maintenance dose of 0.5 gm. per day. The test dose of ethanol was 0.17 or 0.33 mgm./kgm., taken as whiskey. Three of the patients were given a test dose of whiskey both after disulfiram and after animal charcoal premedication. Clinically the reaction of the patients given animal charcoal could not be distinguished from that of the patients given disulfiram. The concentration of blood acetaldehyde during these reactions varied greatly, the highest after disulfiram was 910 micrograms per cent and after animal charcoal, 880 micrograms per cent. The maximum concentration of blood alcohol ranged from 17 to 31 mgm. per cent. None of the patients vomited

TABLE 6

Maximum blood alcohol and acetaldehyde concentrations in two normal human subjects challenged with ethanol before and after treatment with animal and with vegetable charcoal.

The dose of ethanol was 0.33 gm./kgm. taken as whiskey. Variation is expressed as a range, in parentheses. Blood alcohol and acetaldehyde was determined at 45, 75 and 195 minutes after the alcohol. Maximum values occurred at the 45- and 75-minute periods.

	Blood Concentration		Disulfiram-like Reaction
	Acetaldehyde	Ethanol	
	μgm.%	*mgm.%*	
Ethanol only (8 observations)	340 (70–628)	42 (24–65)	absent
Animal charcoal plus ethanol	889 (628–1150)	49 (47–51)	present
Norit A plus ethanol	412 (312–512)	46 (44–48)	absent

but both the disulfiram- and the animal charcoal-treated patients complained of nausea.

Discussion. Jacobsen and his co-workers (1948–49) introduced disulfiram as an aid in the rehabilitation of chronic alcoholics. Repeated daily doses of disulfiram which produce no symptoms, sensitize patients so that disagreeable effects follow the consumption of even small amounts of ethanol. These effects are collectively known as the disulfiram- or Antabuse-alcohol reaction. This reaction is characterized by cutaneous flushing, conjunctival edema, fall in blood pressure, tachycardia, headache, nausea and vomiting. The disulfiram-alcohol reaction is a symptom complex which is variable in degree for each of its components, *i.e.* the fall in blood pressure may be small or vomiting may not occur. This fact, we believe, accounts for the conflicting claims that one method or agent is superior to another for producing sensitivity to ethanol.

The disulfiram-alcohol reaction is associated with increases in the concentrations of blood acetaldehyde above those occurring from ethanol only. This increase in blood acetaldehyde is quite variable even in the same subject given the same doses of disulfiram and alcohol. This variation in blood acetaldehyde is greater for man than for the dog (tables 4 and 6). However, even in man there is a rough correlation of the dosage for both disulfiram and ethanol with the increase in blood acetaldehyde and the severity of symptoms. Inhibition, by disulfiram, of the enzymes necessary for the metabolism of acetaldehyde accounts for its accumulation in the blood (Kjeldgaard, 1949). Oxidation of ethanol to acetaldehyde, the first step in the metabolism of alcohol, is not inhibited by disulfiram (Jacobsen, 1952; Westerfeld, 1955).

Recently cyanamide (calcium carbimide, Temposil; see Smith *et al.*, 1957 for refs.) has been recommended as a substitute for disulfiram. Disulfiram has a slow onset of sensitization, is cumulative, and has a prolonged action, while cyanamide rapidly produces sensitization which is of short duration. Advantages are claimed for each type of action. The effective daily dose of cyanamide is smaller than that for disulfiram. The reaction is the same for both agents in regards to symptoms and increased blood acetaldehyde.

A third useful agent for sensitization to alcohol was suggested by Moench (1950). He observed that a symptom complex similar to the disulfiram-alcohol reaction followed the drinking of alcoholic beverages during administration of animal charcoal. Animal charcoal is an innocuous agent that has long been used as a decolorizing agent for food and drug products, as an adsorbent type of antidote in poisoning and for the relief of dysentery. The sensitization to ethanol resulting from animal charcoal administration appears to be the same as that produced by disulfiram. The present investigation establishes this similarity for symptoms, increases in blood acetaldehyde and the time-dose relationship for both production and persistence of the sensitivity. Both agents may be given daily to animals for long periods without toxic effects.

Human subjects who took animal charcoal, exhibited no symptoms and did not complain of the subtle side effects of disulfiram such as drowsiness, lethargy, abdominal discomfort or impotence. However, our clinical series was limited and the administration of the animal charcoal was discontinued after 21 days. In our experiments the daily administration of 9 gm. of animal charcoal produced sensitization to ethanol equivalent to that resulting from 0.5 gm. of disulfiram. Clinical studies over longer periods of time should be made to establish minimal dosage and to confirm or disprove the lack of side reactions. Animal charcoal appears to have all the advantages of disulfiram except for larger dosage and the possible psychic effect of black stools.

Some active substance must be absorbed from the charcoal because activated vegetable charcoals and other adsorbents do not produce sensitization to ethanol. The active substance in animal charcoal is not destroyed by prolonged moist or dry heat and is insoluble in most common laboratory solvents. The sensitizing activity of animal charcoal is destroyed by treatment with strong acids.

SUMMARY

Animal charcoal contains about 10 per cent carbon. The remainder is a mixture of calcium phosphate and calcium carbonate plus small amounts of nitrogen, iron, sulfur, magnesium and silicon. Animal charcoal contains about 16 per cent volatile materials and yields 80 per cent ash. Strong acids rapidly liberate hydrogen sulfide from animal charcoal.

Animal charcoal is not toxic when fed to dogs in single doses as large as 5 gm./kgm., or in daily doses of 2 gm./kgm. for as long as 154 days. It produced no symptoms when 9 gm. were taken daily by human subjects for 21 days.

The action of animal charcoal is identical with that of disulfiram with respect to the production of sensitivity to ethanol, as determined by onset, duration of action and changes in blood acetaldehyde. A disulfiram-like reaction can be evoked in dogs by ethanol administration as soon as one hour and as long as 24 hours after a single large dose of animal charcoal. Repeated daily doses of 0.5 to 2 gm./kgm. of animal charcoal resulted in a sensitivity to ethanol which persisted for as long as three weeks. Clinically the sensitization to ethanol resulting from animal charcoal is indistinguishable from that produced by disulfiram. Human subjects became sensitive to ethanol after 7 daily doses of 9 gm. of animal charcoal.

Animal charcoal does not influence the metabolism of alcohol as measured by its rate of disappearance from the body.

The ingredient in animal charcoal responsible for its disulfiram-like activity is extremely heat stable and is insoluble in water, ammonium hydroxide solutions and organic solvents. This disulfiram-like activity of animal charcoal is destroyed by treatment with strong acid. Evidence is presented which indicates that the disulfiram-like activity of animal charcoal is not due to cyanamide or to a labile sulfide compound.

Animal charcoal can be substituted for disulfiram in the treatment of alcoholics.

ACKNOWLEDGMENT. We thank the entire staff of the LaRue D. Carter Memorial Hospital for their cooperation in the clinical tests, also Catharine Wakely and John E. Preston for valuable technical assistance.

REFERENCES

DIETZ, R. F., HIGGINSON, H. R., AND PARKER, C.: J. Research Nat. Bur. Standards, Research Paper RP1871, **40**: 263, 1948.
FERGUSON, J. K. W.: Canad. M. A. J., **74**: 793, 1956.
HALD, J., JACOBSEN, E., AND LARSEN, V.: Acta pharmacol. et toxicol., **4**: 285, 1948.
JACOBSEN, E.: Pharmacol. Rev., **4**: 107, 1952.
HALD, J., AND JACOBSEN, E.: Acta pharmacol. et toxicol., **4**: 305, 1948.
HALD, J., JACOBSEN, E., AND LARSEN, V.: Acta pharmacol. et toxicol., **5**: 179, 1949.
HARGER, R. N., RANEY, B. B., BRIDWELL, E. G., AND KITCHELL, M. F.: J. BIOL. Chem., **183**: 197, 1950.
JACOBSEN, E., AND MARTENSEN-LARSEN, O.: J. A. M. A., **139**: 918, 1949.
KJELDGAARD, N. O.: Acta pharmacol. et toxicol., **5**: 397, 1949.
MOENCH, G. L.: New York J. Med., **50**: 308, 1950.
PINCK, L. A.: Industr. Engineer. Chem., **17**: 459, 1925.
RABY, K.: Quart. J. Stud. Alcohol, **15**: 21, 1954.
SMITH, J. A., WOLFORD, J. A., WEBER, M., AND MCLEAN, D.: J. A. M. A., **165**: 2181, 1957.
STOTZ, E. A.: J. Biol. Chem., **148**: 585, 1943.
WESTERFELD, W. W.: Texas Rep. Biol. & Med., **13**: 559, 1955.

8017

ABSORPTION OF DRUGS FROM THE RAT SMALL INTESTINE[1]

LEWIS S. SCHANKER, DOMINICK J. TOCCO, BERNARD B. BRODIE AND C. ADRIAN M. HOGBEN[2]

Laboratory of Chemical Pharmacology and Laboratory of Kidney and Electrolyte Metabolism, National Heart Institute, National Institutes of Health, Public Health Service, U. S. Department of Health, Education and Welfare, Bethesda, Maryland

Received for publication January 15, 1958

An understanding of the factors that govern the intestinal absorption of foreign compounds would furnish a useful guideline for predicting the rapidity and degree of absorption of a new drug. While the literature abounds with reports of the absorption of drugs, the nature of the experiments is such that a clear pattern of how drugs are absorbed is not discernible. Many of the studies involve indirect measurements, appraising intestinal absorption by the rate of appearance of drug in plasma, the excretion in urine, or by the speed of onset or degree of pharmacologic action. This information, though valuable in judging the absorption of a particular drug, has not yielded a generalized picture because of the variables of drug distribution, metabolism and urinary excretion. In more direct studies, absorption has been measured by the disappearance of a drug from the gut. In general, these are concerned with absorption from an intestinal loop *in situ*. Occasionally they deal with the absorption of several closely related compounds but more often with only a single compound, for example, choline (Rohse and Searle, 1955), Dromoran (Fisher and Long, 1953), mecamylamine (Zawoiski *et al.*, 1956) and salicylic and acetylsalicylic acids (Bradley *et al.*, 1936). The widely different experimental conditions used in the various studies make it difficult to recognize the properties of drugs that govern their absorption.

Previous studies in our laboratory have shown that the boundary between plasma and the gastric lumen allows the passage of drugs in their lipid-soluble unionized form but is resistant to the penetration of the ionic form. Accordingly the dissociation constant of a drug is one of the most important characteristics which determines its passage across the gastric mucosa. The concept of a lipoid membrane between plasma and gastric lumen permits the prediction of the extent to which basic drugs are concentrated in the gastric juice after their intravenous administration and also the prediction that acidic drugs are absorbed directly from the stomach (Shore *et al.*, 1957; Schanker *et al.*, 1957; Hogben *et al.*, 1957b).

The present report describes the absorption of a large number of acidic and basic compounds by the rat small intestine. The results, which indicate that the dissociation constant is an important factor in determining the intestinal absorption of drugs, are compatible with the concept that drugs are passively absorbed in the unionized form, possibly across a lipoid barrier.

METHODS AND MATERIALS. *Experimental procedure.* Male Sprague-Dawley rats weighing 120 to 200 gm. were fasted for about 20 hours prior to the experiments but water was allowed *ad libitum.* During the fasting period, the animals were kept in cages having wide-mesh floors to prevent coprophagy. The animals were anesthetized with pentobarbital and the small intestine exposed by a midline abdominal incision. The intestine was cannulated at the duodenal and ileal ends with polyethylene cannulae having inside diameters of 2.5 mm. and outside diameters of 3.5 mm. The stomach and cecum were closed off by ligatures, care being taken not to occlude major blood vessels. In most of the experiments, the bile duct was ligated. The intestine was replaced in the abdomen, the incision closed and perfusion, from pylorus to ileocecal junction, started immediately.

The perfusion solution (pH 7.2) consisted of 1 *mM* per l. of drug together with the following salts in *mM* per l.: NaCl 145, KCl 4.56, $CaCl_2$ 1.25, Na_2HPO_4 1.33, and NaH_2PO_4 0.33. The solution was maintained at 37° C. and was perfused with a Bowman infusion pump at a rate of 1.5 ml.per

[1] A preliminary account of this work has appeared previously, Fed. Proc., **15:** 480, 1956.

[2] Present address: Department of Physiology, The George Washington University School of Medicine, Washington, D. C.

minute. A 1-ml. graduated pipette, placed vertically in the perfusion system by means of a T-tube, indicated changes in intralumenal pressure. After passage of the fluid through the intestine, the pH of the outflow, collected under oil, was 6.6.

A. Single perfusion technique: The small intestine was first cleared of particulate matter by perfusion with a drug-free solution for 30 minutes. The solution containing drug was then perfused for 30 minutes to displace the previous wash, after which four 10-minute samples were collected from the ileal outflow. The concentration of drug was measured in each of the collected samples and the relative rate of absorption was calculated from the difference in the concentration entering and leaving the intestine.

The necessity for perfusing the intestine with drug solution for 30 minutes before measuring drug absorption was established by showing that the outflowing concentration of inulin-C^{14}, a substance which was not absorbed, did not become constant until after 25 minutes of perfusion. This steady state concentration of inulin was 1.03 ± 0.02 times the concentration in the inflowing solution indicating a small decrease in the volume of the perfusion fluid. This volume change, due to the absorption of water, was determined in a large number of experiments by actual measurement of the rates of inflow and outflow. The mean decrease in volume was 3 per cent which agreed with the inulin concentration ratio of 1.03. Consequently, the mean values of the relative change in drug concentration were corrected by 3 per cent. As indicated below, the absorption of inulin is insignificant.

B. Recirculation technique: Drugs whose absorption rates were slow when measured by the above procedure were also studied by a recirculation technique which exaggerated the decrease in drug concentration. The intestine was first perfused for 30 minutes with drug solution containing either inulin-C^{14} or phenol red. The tubings attached to the inflow and outflow cannulae were then transferred to a flask containing 30 ml. of drug solution. This volume was then continuously circulated through the small intestine for 3 hours. The relative rate of absorption was calculated from the decrease in drug concentration, corrected for the volume change as follows:

$$\text{Per cent absorbed} = 100 - 100\left(\frac{C_{\text{drug final}}}{C_{\text{drug initial}}} \times \frac{C_{\text{indicator initial}}}{C_{\text{indicator final}}}\right).$$

After recirculation for 3 hours, the mean concentration of the volume change indicator, inulin or phenol red, was 1.20 ± 0.11 times the initial concentration. When known quantities of these same substances were circulated through the intestine for 3 hours and the intestine then thoroughly washed with saline, 97 ± 2 per cent of the inulin and 98 ± 2 per cent of the phenol red were recovered. Thus the negligible absorption of inulin and phenol red permits their use as indicators of volume change.

Unless otherwise specified, ± will refer to the range of values.

Analytical methods. The analytical methods have been described or cited in a previous publication (Schanker *et al.*, 1957)[3] except for the following. A. Tensilon (3-hydroxyphenyldimethylethyl ammonium chloride): Samples were diluted with 0.1 *N* NaOH to give a final concentration of 5 to 80 microgm. per ml. Optical densities were measured at 295 mμ. B. *m*-Nitrobenzoic acid: Samples were diluted with 1 *N* HCl to give a final concentration of 3 to 40 microgm. per ml. of the drug. Optical densities were measured at 265 mμ. C. *o*-Nitrobenzoic acid: Samples were diluted with 3 *N* HCl so that the final concentration of drug was 3 to 50 microgm. per ml. Optical densities were measured at 270 mμ. D. Bromphenol blue (tetrabromophenolsulfonphthalein): Samples containing bromphenol blue were diluted with 1.7 *M* K_2HPO_4 and the optical densities measured at 600 mμ. E. Isotopes: Acetic acid-1-C^{14}, phenol-1-C^{14}, urea-C^{14} and inulin-C^{14} were measured by the liquid counting technique of Cotlove (1955). F. Tromexan (ethyl biscoumacetate) was estimated according to Brodie *et al.* (1952a), phenylbutazone according to Burns *et al.* (1953) and theophylline according to Brodie *et al.* (1952b).

Dissociation constants. The dissociation constant for Tromexan was determined by distribution of the drug between heptane and various 0.1 *M* aqueous buffers as described by Butler (1953). The dissociation constants of theophylline and phenylbutazone have been reported by Shore *et al.* (1957), and those of *p*-nitroaniline, *o*-nitrobenzoic acid and *m*-nitrobenzoic acid by Vandenbelt *et al.* (1954). The dissociation constants of other compounds studied were cited in a previous publication (Schanker *et al.*, 1957).

Drug Binding. The binding of drugs to nondialyzable substances in the intestinal perfusates was measured by the ultrafiltration technique of Rehberg (1943).

RESULTS. The reproducibility of the values obtained with the single perfusion technique was investigated by measuring the absorption of a

[3] The authors wish to express their appreciation to Dr. Herbert Broida and Mrs. Margaret W. Chapman of the National Bureau of Standards for their invaluable help in the analysis of deuterium oxide.

typical acid and base. Salicylic acid was absorbed to the extent of 60 per cent (standard deviation ± 10 per cent) in 30 animals; aniline was absorbed 54 per cent (standard deviation ± 10 per cent) in 43 animals.

Absorption from various segments of the small intestine. The absorption of salicylic acid and aniline from different segments of the small intestine was measured and compared with that of the entire small intestine. The intestine was divided into various segments and each was perfused simultaneously with the drug solution. The results are presented in table 1. The absorption from each segment was proportional to its length and the summated absorption of the segments equaled that of the entire small intestine. Thus, in spite of anatomical and physiological differences in various parts of the small intestine, absorption was similar in the upper, middle and lower one-thirds.

Failure to find evidence for specific transport mechanisms. In looking for evidence that drugs might be absorbed by specific processes, the absorption of salicylic acid and aniline was measured at various concentrations. The proportion of salicylic acid and aniline absorbed was found to be constant over a wide concentration range; that is, the amount absorbed was directly proportional to the concentration (table 2). The failure to find evidence of saturation of the absorption process over a wide concentration range suggests, but does not prove, that salicylic acid and aniline are absorbed by a physical process.

Further indirect evidence of a physical process was seen in the failure of one drug to alter the absorption of another. When solutions of the following pairs of acids or bases were perfused, each drug was absorbed as though it were present alone: salicylic acid and acetylsalicylic acid, quinine and aniline, aminopyrine and aniline, *p*-toluidine and Tensilon, and *p*-hydroxypropiophenone and quinine.

It is also noteworthy that the presence of aniline did not modify the absorption of any of the acidic drugs studied nor did salicylic acid modify the absorption of any basic drug. Consequently these two compounds were selected as "internal standards." When the absorption of an acidic drug was being measured, aniline absorption was measured simultaneously; when a basic drug was studied, salicylic acid absorption was simultaneously measured. The observed rates of absorption of a given drug could then be corrected for variation among individual animals on the basis of the deviation from the mean rate of absorption of the reference material, aniline or salicylic acid.

TABLE 1

Absorption of drugs from various segments of the rat small intestine

Absorption was initially determined for the entire length of small intestine. The intestine was then divided into 2 portions and absorption measured in each simultaneously. The results are the mean values from 6 experiments.

Intestinal Segment	Per Cent Absorbed	
	Salicylic acid	Aniline
Entire length	55	51
Upper one-third	20	19
Lower two-thirds	33	30
Entire length	61	55
Upper two-thirds	40	37
Lower one-third	18	16

TABLE 2

Effect of concentration on intestinal absorption

The per cent absorbed is expressed as the mean ± the range followed by the number of experiments in parentheses.

Drug	Perfusion Solution Initial Concentration	Per Cent Absorbed
	mM per l.	
Salicylic acid	0.5	53 ± 4 (4)
	1.0	60*
	10.0	54 ± 5 (4)
Aniline	0.1	58 ± 5 (4)
	1.0	54†
	10.0	59 ± 4 (4)
	20.0	54 ± 5 (3)

* Standard deviation, ±10 per cent for 30 experiments.

† Standard deviation, ±10 per cent for 43 experiments.

Absorption of drugs after a single perfusion through the small intestine. The relative rates of absorption of a considerable number of acidic and basic drugs were determined. A relation between the dissociation constant and the degree of absorption was evident (tables 3 and 4). Most

TABLE 3

Absorption of organic acids from the rat small intestine

The per cent absorbed is expressed as the mean ± the range followed by the number of experiments in parentheses.

Acid	pK_a	Per Cent Absorbed	
		Actual	Relative to aniline
5-Sulfosalicylic	(strong)	<2 (2)	<2
Phenol red	(strong)	<2 (4)	<2
Bromphenol blue	(strong)	<2 (2)	<2
o-Nitrobenzoic	2.2	5 ± 2 (2)	5
5-Nitrosalicylic	2.3	9 ± 2 (3)	9
Tromexan	2.9	35 ± 7 (3)	37
Salicylic	3.0	60*	—
m-Nitrobenzoic	3.4	53 ± 0 (2)	50
Acetylsalicylic	3.5	20 ± 4 (6)	21
Benzoic	4.2	51 ± 5 (2)	54
Phenylbutazone	4.4	65 ± 7 (3)	54
Acetic	4.7	42 ± 1 (3)	40
Thiopental	7.6	55 ± 6 (3)	67
Barbital	7.8	30 ± 4 (2)	25
p-Hydroxypropiophenone	7.8	61 ± 9 (5)	61
Phenol	9.9	51 ± 8 (3)	60

* Standard deviation, ±10 per cent for 30 experiments.

TABLE 4

Absorption of organic bases from the rat small intestine

The per cent absorbed is expressed as the mean ± the range followed by the number of experiments in parentheses.

Base	pK_a	Per Cent Absorbed	
		Actual	Relative to salicylic acid
Acetanilide	0.3	42 ± 5 (2)	43
Theophylline	0.7	29 ± 1 (3)	30
p-Nitroaniline	1.0	68 ± 7 (2)	61
Antipyrine	1.4	32 ± 6 (3)	30
m-Nitroaniline	2.5	77 ± 2 (2)	63
Aniline	4.6	54*	—
Aminopyrine	5.0	33 ± 4 (4)	27
p-Toluidine	5.3	59 ± 3 (3)	56
Quinine	8.4	15 ± 2 (6)	15
Ephedrine	9.6	7 ± 3 (2)	6
Tolazoline	10.3	6 ± 1 (2)	5
Mecamylamine	11.2	<2 (2)	<2
Darstine	(strong)	<2 (2)	<2
Procaine amide ethobromide	(strong)	<2 (2)	<2
Tetraethylammonium	(strong)	<2 (2)	<2
Tensilon	(strong)	<2 (2)	<2

* Standard deviation, ±10 per cent for 43 experiments.

of the drugs were readily absorbed except for the stronger acids and bases. The stronger acids with a pK_a below 2.9 were slowly absorbed (less than 9 per cent), while the weaker acids with a pK_a greater than 2.9 were generally rapidly absorbed (21 to 67 per cent). The weaker bases with a pK_a less than 8 were rapidly absorbed (27 to 63 per cent), while the stronger bases with a pK_a greater than 9 were slowly absorbed (less than 7 per cent).

Absorption of drugs after 3 hours of continuous intestinal perfusion. The single perfusion technique permitted the study of the absorption of drugs which have rapid absorption rates. This technique, however, did not reveal with accuracy the considerable difference known to exist between the rates of absorption of ephedrine and of a quaternary ammonium compound because the decrease in concentration of these drugs was too small for valid comparison. Accordingly a number of the drugs that were relatively slowly absorbed by the single perfusion method were re-examined by the recirculation technique in order to magnify the differences in the concentration changes.

Definite absorption of the stronger acids, 5-nitrosalicylic and *o*-nitrobenzoic, and the stronger bases, quinine, ephedrine, tolazoline and mecamylamine, was now observed (table 5). However, no significant absorption was evident for the very strong sulfonic acid, phenol red, or for the very strong quaternary ammonium bases, Darstine (mepiperphenidol) and procaine amide ethobromide.

The possibility that the apparent rates of absorption might be due to chemical transformation was excluded in the following manner. Thirty ml. of saline were recirculated through the small intestine for 3 hours. Drugs were then dissolved in the resultant solution and incubated in a water bath at 37° C. for 3 hours. No destruction was demonstrated for *o*-nitrobenzoic acid, 5-nitrosalicylic acid, quinine, ephedrine, tolazoline or mecamylamine.

Absorption and drug binding. The possibility that the absorption of certain drugs might be affected by their binding to nondialyzable material in the intestinal perfusate was investigated by measuring the ultrafiltrability of drugs in the solution that had been recirculated for 3 hours as well as in the ileal outflow samples in the single perfusion experiments. For these experimental conditions, the binding was negligible (< 4 per cent) for quinine, ephedrine, tolazoline, mecamylamine, Darstine, procaine amide ethobromide, Tensilon, antipyrine, aminopyrine, aniline, phenol red, *o*-nitrobenzoic acid, 5-nitrosalicylic acid, acetylsalicylic acid and salicylic acid.

Absorption in the presence and absence of bile. While bile was excluded in the majority of experiments, the absorption of all drugs listed in tables 3 and 4 except acetanilide and *p*-nitroaniline was also studied when the bile duct had not been ligated. The continuous secretion of bile, as confirmed by a detectable color in the outflowing perfusate, had no measurable effect on the rates of absorption of any of the drugs.

Isotopic exchange of water, sodium, chloride and urea. While the absorption of the isotope is not synonymous with the net absorption of the unlabeled material, the exchange rates do indicate the extent to which these small polar materials can move across the intestinal wall. The concentrations in the perfusion fluid were: deuterium oxide, 5 per cent by volume; Na^{22} and Cl^{36}, tracer amounts; and 1 *mM* of C^{14}-labeled urea per l. Absorption was studied by the single perfusion technique. Deuterium oxide was absorbed to the extent of 41 ± 6 per cent in seven animals; radiosodium, 14 ± 3 per cent and radiochloride, 8 ± 3 per cent in the same four animals; urea-C^{14}, 11 ± 2 per cent in three animals. The apparent degree of absorption of urea-C^{14} should be considered a maximal value. Urea is split to some extent by bacterial urease in the intestine permitting the absorption of some C^{14} as $C^{14}O_2$. But even if the absorption of urea were as rapid as indicated by the value of 11 per cent, it is clear that urea is absorbed substantially less rapidly than many weak organic electrolytes.

DISCUSSION. In considering the various ways in which substances might be absorbed from the intestine, it is helpful to have in mind a general picture of cell membranes. A widely accepted concept is that cells are bounded by a lipoid membrane interspersed with small pores and that lipid-soluble substances can easily penetrate cells by dissolving in the lipid-like phase (Collander 1937; Höber, 1945). In contrast, polar substances may penetrate if they are small enough to pass through the pores. The total area of these pores is considered to be much less than that of the lipoid area. This picture of the membrane is based on experiments showing that a number of foreign compounds permeate plant cells, erythrocytes and sea-urchin eggs at rates proportional to their solubility in fat-like solvents, while certain lipid-insoluble molecules of small molecular weight appear to penetrate through pores. In addition to purely physical processes of penetration, it is recognized that specialized mechanisms are required to transport certain polar substrates across the cell boundary.

TABLE 5

Absorption of drugs after 3 hours of continuous circulation through the rat small intestine

The per cent absorbed is expressed as the mean ± the range followed by the number of experiments in parentheses.

Drug	pK_a	Per Cent Absorbed	
		Observed	*Relative to quinine*
Acid			
Phenol red	(strong)	<2 (4)	<2
o-Nitrobenzoic	2.2	11 ± 4 (3)	10
5-Nitrosalicylic	2.3	36 ± 3 (7)	38
			Relative to 5-nitrosalicylic acid
Base			
Quinine	8.4	55 ± 3 (4)	53
Ephedrine	9.6	29 ± 4 (2)	29
Tolazoline	10.3	9 ± 2 (4)	9
Mecamylamine	11.2	26 ± 2 (3)	27
Darstine	(strong)	<2 (3)	<2
Procaine amide ethobromide	(strong)	<2 (2)	<2

The question arises whether drugs are absorbed by simple diffusion or by means of specialized transport mechanisms. If a substance is absorbed by a specific transport mechanism, there should be evidence of saturation at high concentrations of substrate. The lowered proportion of glucose absorbed with increased concentration is a familiar feature of an active transport system (Höber, 1945). In contrast, the proportion of salicylic acid and aniline absorbed by the rat intestine is unchanged over a wide range of concentrations suggesting, but not proving, that these drugs are absorbed by physical processes. As further evidence of a passive process, the rates of absorption of a large number of drugs are not affected by the presence of a second drug. In contrast, glucose and galactose show mutual interference when both are present in the gut (Cori, 1926).

A clue to the nature of drug absorption is the relationship between the dissociation constant and the degree of absorption of drugs of widely diverse chemical structures. Most drugs are weak organic acids or bases which are present in the body partly in the dissociated and partly in the undissociated form.[4] The concentration of each form depends on the dissociation constant of the organic electrolyte and on the pH of the solution in which it is dissolved. As seen in tables 3 and 4, the absorption of a large number of drugs is related to the dissociation constant. Thus most of the drugs are readily absorbed but there is a distinct reduction in the degree of absorption for strong acids with a pK_a less than 2.9 and for strong bases with a pK_a greater than 8.4. This suggests that only the unionized form of a drug readily crosses the intestinal barrier and that ions cross with difficulty. Even among highly ionized drugs, there is a distinct difference between the degree of absorption of a partially ionized compound and that of a completely ionized one (table 5).

Closer examination of the data would suggest that the simple model of a barrier selectively permeable to the unionized moiety must be qualified since there is a rapid absorption of moderately strong acids like salicylic acid. At pH 6.6, the pH of the fluid leaving the intestine, the ratio of unionized to ionized salicylic acid is about 1 to 4000. This seems too small a proportion of unionized drug to explain the rapid absorption of the compound. However this apparent inconsistency is based on the premise that the pH at the absorbing surface is also 6.6. Studies, which have been presented in preliminary form (Hogben *et al.*, 1957a), suggest that absorption may be governed by an effective pH at the epithelial boundary which is lower than 6.6.

In considering passive diffusion through pores, Höber and Höber (1937) concluded that urea, a lipid-insoluble material, was absorbed by passively penetrating through small pores in an otherwise predominantly lipoidal membrane. Our studies of the absorption of urea and D_2O suggest that molecular size may not be a major factor in determining the absorption of most drugs. Thus the polar molecule, D_2O is absorbed to the extent of only 41 per cent and the absorption of a slightly larger species, urea, is less than 11 per cent. These rates should be contrasted with rates of 50 per cent or more for the much larger lipid-soluble drugs like phenylbutazone and thiopental. Furthermore, *m*-nitrobenzoic acid is absorbed much more rapidly than *o*-nitrobenzoic acid, though both compounds have the same molecular weights; acetanilide, nitroaniline and tetraethylammonium have similar molecular weights but are absorbed at substantially different rates. It would appear that diffusion through pores may be a factor only in the absorption of compounds of very small molecular weight.

It seems reasonable to suggest accordingly that, in general, drugs of widely different chemical structures cross the intestinal barrier by diffusing through a boundary which is selectively permeable to the unionized form. This becomes comprehensible on the assumption that the boundary, like that described by Collander (1937) for cells in general, is lipoid in nature. Compounds having the same pK_a values would not necessarily penetrate a lipoid barrier at the same rates since other factors such as solubility in the membrane might be important. For example, barbital is absorbed much less rapidly than thiopental despite the similar pK_a values of the two compounds. Similarly *p*-nitroaniline is absorbed much more rapidly than antipyrine, yet both have similar pK_a values. These differences in absorption may be explained when more is known about the chemical constituents that define the physicochemical properties of the lipoid boundary.

It is noteworthy that there is an apparent upper limit to the extent of absorption, about 50 to 60 per cent, with the single perfusion technique. One of the following factors must impose this upper limit: the permeability of the intestinal mucosa, the rate of intestinal blood flow, or diffusion from the center of the stream flowing through the intestine. Since many drugs with a diversity of chemical and physical properties are absorbed at this rate, it is not likely that the permeability of the mucosa is the limiting factor under these experimental conditions. If absorption were limited by the rate of intestinal mucosal

[4] The dissociation constant of both acids and bases is expressed as a pK_a which is the negative logarithm of the acidic dissociation constant. The pK_a is defined by the Henderson-Hasselbalch equation:

$$\text{for acids} \ldots\ldots \ pK_a = pH + \log \frac{[\text{unionized acid}]}{[\text{ionized acid}]},$$

$$\text{for bases} \ldots\ldots \ pK_a = pH + \log \frac{[\text{ionized base}]}{[\text{unionized base}]}.$$

An acidic drug with a small pK_a is a very strong acid and one with a large pK_a a very weak acid. A base with a small pK_a is a very weak base.

blood flow, the binding of drugs to plasma proteins should have a substantial effect on the degree of absorption. But the plasma binding of aniline, salicylic acid, phenylbutazone, *p*-hydroxypropiophenone and thiopental ranges from 20 to 90 per cent while the compounds are all absorbed to the extent of about 60 per cent. It is possible that the upper limit of absorption of these drugs is determined by the rate at which a drug can diffuse through the intestinal solution to reach the wall. In any event, it is clear that absorption from the small intestine of the rat is a very rapid process, the half-time for many drugs being approximately five minutes.[5]

It should be made clear that the experiments we have described were designed to delineate the general characteristics of the barrier between the intestinal lumen and plasma and not to yield absolute values for the absorption of drugs as administered therapeutically. Nevertheless, it is possible to consider a number of tentative predictions. Organic electrolytes should be readily absorbed from solution if the unionized form is lipid-soluble and if the pK_a for an acid is greater than 2, and for a base is less than 11. The poor absorption of certain water-soluble drugs, formerly considered somewhat of a mystery, now becomes logical because their unionized forms are not lipid-soluble or because they are completely ionized in the gut. For example, the poor absorption of unionized substances such as mannitol and inositol (Höber and Höber, 1937) is explainable on the basis of lipid-insolubility. The absorption of quaternary ammonium compounds and sulfonic acids would be expected to be poor since they are completely ionized at physiologic hydrogen ion concentrations Levine *et al.* (1955) have suggested that the poor absorption of quaternary ammonium compounds is due to their binding to intestinal mucin, forming nonabsorbable complexes. Since we have shown that three quaternary ammonium compounds are poorly absorbed even though they are not bound to nondialyzable substances in the intestinal perfusate, it is probable that the poor absorption of quaternary ammonium compounds is due to the impermeability of the intestinal mucosa to these ions.

[5] This rapid rate of absorption is obtained in spite of a moderate distension of the gut by about eight ml. of solution and conditions that largely suspend intestinal motility. It is conceivable that under normal conditions where the intestinal contents are well mixed by the motility of the intestine, diffusion of drug to the intestinal wall would be less significant and absorption could become blood flow-limited.

In actual practice, factors other than the dissociation constant and lipid solubility of a drug may limit its intestinal absorption. For example, some drugs are poorly absorbed because of their low solubility in the intestinal contents; and others because they are unstable in the gastrointestinal tract.

SUMMARY

The relative rates of absorption of a large number of drugs have been measured by perfusing solutions of drugs through the entire small intestine of the anesthetized rat. A single perfusion of the small intestine differentiated very rapid absorption from less rapid absorption. A continuous recirculation of the drug solution through the intestine separated less rapid absorption from very slow absorption.

The degree of ionization of an organic electrolyte in solution appears to be one of the most important factors determining its absorption from the rat small intestine. Acidic drugs were rapidly absorbed if their pK_a's were greater than 3. Basic drugs were rapidly absorbed if their pK_a's were less than 8. The stronger acids and bases were relatively slowly absorbed and the absorption of very strong acids and bases was imperceptible.

Absorption of drugs from the rat small intestine can be best explained by assuming simple diffusion of unionized drug across a barrier which may be lipoidal in nature.

REFERENCES

Bradley, W. B., Schnedorf, J. G., and Ivy, A. C.: Am. J. Digest. Dis., **3**: 415, 1936.

Brodie, B. B., Axelrod, J., and Reichenthal, J.: J. Biol. Chem., **194**: 215, 1952a.

Brodie, B. B., Weiner, M., Burns, J. J., Simson, G., and Yale, E. K.: This Journal, **106**: 453, 1952b.

Burns, J. J., Rose, R. K., Chenkin, T., Goldman, A., Schulert, A., and Brodie, B. B.: This Journal, **109**: 346, 1953.

Butler, T. C.: This Journal, **108**: 474, 1953.

Collander, R.: Trans. Faraday Soc., **33**: 985, 1937.

Cori, C. F.: Proc. Soc. Exp. Biol. & Med., **23**: 290, 1926.

Cotlove, E.: Fed. Proc., **14**: 32, 1955.

Fisher, A. L., and Long, J. P.: This Journal, **107**: 241, 1953.

Höber, R.: Physical Chemistry of Cells and Tissues, Blakiston, Philadelphia, 1945.

Höber, R., and Höber, J.: J. Cell. and Comp. Physiol., **10:** 401, 1937.
Hogben, C. A. M., Schanker, L. S., and Brodie, B. B.: Fed. Proc., **16:** 307, 1957a.
Hogben, C. A. M., Schanker, L. S., Tocco, D. J., and Brodie, B. B.: This Journal, **120:** 540, 1957b.
Levine, R. M., Blair, M. R., and Clark, B. B.: This Journal, **114:** 78, 1955.
Rehberg, P. B.: Acta Physiol. Scand., **5:** 305, 1943.
Rohse, W. G., and Searle, G. W.: Am. J. Physiol., **181:** 207, 1955.
Schanker, L. S., Shore, P. A., Brodie, B. B., and Hogben, C. A. M.: This Journal, **120:** 528, 1957.
Shore, P. A., Brodie, B. B., and Hogben, C. A. M.: This Journal, **119:** 361, 1957.
Vandenbelt, J. M., Henrich, C., and Vandenberg, S. G.: Anal. Chem., **25:** 726, 1954.
Zawoiski, E. J., Baer, J. E., Braunschweig, L. W., Paulson, S. F., and Shermer, A.: Fed. Proc., **15:** 205, 1956.

ERRATUM

There is an error in an abstract by Martin Lubin and Peter B. Schneider, entitled "The Exchange of Potassium for Cesium and Rubidium in Frog Muscle", which appeared on pages 45A to 46A in Vol. *122*, No. 1, of the Journal (January, 1958). The expression "10 micromol./l." in the first sentence of the text of the abstract should read "10 millimol./l."

8018

STUDIES ON THE MECHANISM OF DIURETIC ACTION OF CHLOROTHIAZIDE[1]

R. F. PITTS, F. KRÜCK[2], R. LOZANO[3], D. W. TAYLOR, O. P. A. HEIDENREICH[4] AND R. H. KESSLER

Department of Physiology, Cornell University Medical College, New York

Received for publication January 9, 1958

Chlorothiazide (Diuril), a heterocyclic sulfonamyl compound synthesized by Novello and Sprague (1957), shows promise of being a clinically useful diuretic in the treatment of the edema of congestive heart failure (Ford, 1958; Bayliss *et al.*, 1958), chronic liver disease (Laragh, 1958) and chronic renal disease (Schreiner, 1958). In addition it exhibits a primary antihypertensive action and potentiates the antihypertensive actions of a variety of agents currently employed in the treatment of essential hypertension (Fries *et al.*, 1958; Heider *et al.*, 1958; Wilkins *et al.*, 1958). Because it is effective orally and to date has exhibited minimal signs of toxicity, it may well find a place in diuretic therapy and in the treatment of hypertension.

Beyer *et al.* (1957, 1958) have shown that chlorothiazide exhibits properties both of carbonic anhydrase inhibitors and of mercurial diuretics. Due to the fact that the molecule contains a free sulfonamyl group, it inhibits carbonic anhydrase *in vitro* and in large dosage *in vivo*, alkalinizes the urine and increases the urinary excretion of potassium. In addition it causes natriuresis and chloruresis, actions similar to those of mercurial diuretics. In fact in the usual orally effective dose, the major response is chloruresis and natriuresis. The urine may fail to become alkaline, although potassium excretion is usually enhanced.

Because of its possible clinical use and its interesting pharmacological properties, we have attempted to learn more about the mechanism of its diuretic action. We have administered chlorothiazide to dogs in doses sufficient to produce a maximal renal response. At the peak of the diuretic action of the drug, we have administered either acetazoleamide (Diamox) or chlormerodrin (Neohydrin) in a dose sufficient to produce the maximal renal response. The order of drug administration has then been reversed, *i.e.* either acetazoleamide or chlormerodrin has been given in maximal dosage and at the peak of diuretic action we have administered chlorothiazide. From such studies we conclude that chlorothiazide blocks the same mechanism for exchange of sodium and hydrogen ions and thus facilitates the same mechanism for exchange of sodium and potassium ions, blocked and facilitated respectively, by acetazoleamide. Chlorothiazide, however, is somewhat less potent than acetazoleamide in both of these actions. Chlorothiazide also blocks the reabsorption of sodium and chloride ions, though less effectively than does chlormerodrin when one compares maximally effective doses of the two agents. Because their respective blocking actions are additive when each is given in maximal dosage, we conclude that chlorothiazide and chlormerodrin either block different reabsorptive mechanisms or, more probably, interfere with different enzymatic reactions supplying energy to a single reabsorptive mechanism (Pitts, 1958). It follows that there are not less than three biochemically distinct mechanisms or sources of energy concerned with the reabsorption of sodium and chloride ions: one sensitive to mercurials, one sensitive to chlorothiazide and one or more resistant to both drugs. The mechanisms responsible for bicarbonate reabsorption including the mechanisms for sodium, hydrogen and potassium exchange, are all affected in a qualitatively similar fashion by chlorothiazide and acetazoleamide, presumably as a consequence of their anti-carbonic anhydrase activities. In these latter actions acetazoleamide is the more potent.

[1] Aided by grants from the National Heart Institute, National Institutes of Health and the Life Insurance Medical Research Fund.

[2] Lederle Fellow.

[3] Fellow of the Rockefeller Foundation.

[4] Fellow of the New York Community Trust.

METHODS. This report is based on 29 experiments performed on female mongrel dogs anesthetized with 30 mgm. per kgm. of pentobarbital. The anesthetic was administered intravenously and supplemented as necessary with small additional doses. Each of the 9 types of experiments summarized in the tables has been repeated 2 or more times on different dogs with essentially identical results.

In each experiment 0.85 per cent saline was infused intravenously at a rate of 10 ml. per min. for 2½ hours prior to and throughout the course of the experiment. This procedure was adopted to expand extracellular stores of sodium and chloride ions in order that the profound diureses induced would not unduly deplete reserves. Creatinine was incorporated in the saline in amounts sufficient to ensure maintenance of plasma levels optimum for the measurement of glomerular filtration rate.

At the end of 2½ hours, urine collections were begun. Clearance periods were 10 min. in length and arterial blood samples were drawn at the midpoint of each clearance period through a retention needle in the femoral artery. After two control periods with relatively constant urine flow, a priming dose of the diuretic was given and the drug was added to the infusion. The standard dosages for maximal diuretic action were as follows: chlorothiazide and acetazoleamide, 10 mgm. per kgm. prime, 15 mgm. per kgm. per hr. infusion; chlormerodrin, 2 mgm. per kgm. prime, 2 mgm. per kgm. per hr. infusion. The dosages of chlorothiazide and acetazoleamide were not necessarily the minimal ones which would produce maximal renal responses; the dosage of chlormerodrin probably approximated that value. When diuresis had reached its peak, the second drug was given in a priming dose and added to the infusion. Each experiment was continued for a sufficiently long period to demonstrate the maximal effect of the second drug.

In all experiments in which either chlorothiazide or acetazoleamide was given, both blood and urine were collected and handled anaerobically in order to insure validity of pH and bicarbonate measurements. In those experiments in which chlormerodrin alone was given, this precaution was not taken, for the urines were uniformly acid. Blood and urine pH were measured with a Cambridge pH meter, using a water jacketed condenser-type glass electrode maintained at 38°C. Blood samples were centrifuged under oil in paraffin capped tubes and total CO_2 of plasma and urine were measured by the method of Van Slyke and Neill (1924). Bicarbonate was calculated using the Henderson-Hasselbalch equation.

Chlormerodrin was synthesized in our laboratory with radioactive mercury (Hg^{203}, Kessler, Lozano and Pitts, 1957), to facilitate the determination of plasma concentration and rate of excretion of the diuretic. Aliquots of plasma and urine were counted in a well-type scintillation counter. Chlorothiazide was determined by the Bratton and Marshall (1939) method following alkaline hydrolysis of *p*-toluenesulfonic acid filtrates of plasma and urine according to the procedure of Beyer *et al.* (1957). Other analytical methods were those commonly employed in our laboratory (Dorman, Sullivan and Pitts, 1954).

RESULTS. The experiments summarized in table 1 illustrate the basic elements of the diuretic actions of chlorothiazide, acetazoleamide and chlormerodrin. Experiments 6 and 16 clearly demonstrate that either chlorothiazide or acetazoleamide, given in a priming dose of 10 mgm. per kgm. and infused at a rate of 15 mgm. per kgm. per hr., produces a maximal renal response not enhanced by a second priming dose of the same drug and doubling the rate of infusion. Both chlorothiazide and acetazoleamide markedly enhance the excretion of sodium, potassium and bicarbonate. Chlorothiazide in addition enhances the excretion of chloride, an action which acetazoleamide exhibits to only an insignificant degree. The four columns to the right of this table illustrate the fact that these actions may be nominally assigned to depression of tubular reabsorption, with the reservation that kaluresis no doubt represents increased potassium secretion (Berliner, Kennedy and Orloff, 1954). The effect of acetazoleamide on potassium secretion is somewhat greater than is that of chlorothiazide, the former causing net secretion in some periods (*i.e.* negative reabsorption values). Both drugs depress bicarbonate reabsorption and alkalinize the urine, the effect of acetazoleamide exceeding that of chlorothiazide. Both act promptly, exerting their effects within the first 10 min. after administration. Both, in admittedly high intravenous dosage, depress glomerular filtration rate. However it is interesting that the second dose caused no additional depression of filtration rate. As Beyer *et al.* (1957, 1958) have shown, the renal clearance of chlorothiazide is high, approximating effective renal plasma flow.

Experiments 7 and 8 illustrate some of the difficulties experienced in selecting a dose of chlormerodrin which produces a maximal renal reresponse. Actually some 7 experiments were performed before selecting a dose of 2.0 mgm. per kgm. prime and 2.0 mgm. per kgm. per hr.

TABLE 1

Effects of chlorothiazide, acetazoleamide and chlormerodrin on renal excretion and reabsorption of electrolytes by the dog, when each drug is administered alone in dosage sufficient to produce its maximal renal response and when administered in twice that dosage

Total Elapsed Time	Urine Flow	Glom. Filt. Rate	Plasma Concentration						Clearance		pH		Rate of Excretion				Per Cent of Filtered Reabsorbed			
			Na	K	Cl	HCO_3	Chlorothz.	Hg	Chlorothz.	Hg	Plasma	Urine	Na	K	Cl	HCO_3	Na	K	Cl	HCO_3
Experiment 6, dog 3, weight 23 kgm.																				
min.	*ml. per min.*		*milliequivalents per liter*				*mgm. %*	*micro-gm./ml.*	*ml. per min.*				*microequivalents per minute*							
0–10	6.3	132	151	3.63	128	18.8					7.42	5.56	335	78	502	2	98.0	82.9	97.1	99.9
10–20	6.0	136	151	3.65	129	18.8					7.42	5.45	292	80	452	1	98.5	82.9	97.3	99.9
20	Chlorothiazide: 10 mgm. per kgm., prime in 3 min.; 15 mgm. per kgm. per hr., infusion																			
20–30	11.2	127	148	3.49	132	18.4	3.08		267		7.44	7.27	488	223	1090	288	97.3	47.2	94.0	88.2
30–40	12.0	109	148	3.38	128	17.9	1.92		380		7.44	7.41	1380	287	1380	297	90.9	15.9	90.5	85.5
40–50	11.6	112	152	3.32	131	17.5	1.71		365		7.44	7.42	1350	233	1360	284	91.7	34.0	91.1	86.2
50–60	10.6	111	148	3.40	130	16.8	1.62		363		7.42	7.42	1350	202	1310	260	91.3	43.6	91.4	86.7
60	Chlorothiazide: 10 mgm. per kgm., prime in 3 min.; 30 mgm. per kgm. per hr., infusion																			
60–70	10.2	108	148	3.35	129	17.0	5.38		256		7.43	7.40	1440	195	1380	273	90.6	41.2	90.5	85.8
70–80	9.8	107	148	3.32	131	16.6	3.60		341		7.43	7.37	1440	195	1340	275	90.3	42.3	90.7	85.2
80–90	9.0	112	148	3.24	132	16.4	3.22		349		7.42	7.43	1380	207	1310	265	91.2	40.0	91.6	86.3
90–100	8.0	115	145	3.12	129	16.0	3.10		341		7.42	7.37	1290	195	1220	244	92.1	40.7	92.2	87.4
Experiment 16, dog 8, weight 21 kgm.																				
0–10	3.4	96.8	149	3.36	123	22.9					7.23	6.11	393	38	442	7	97.2	87.7	96.0	99.6
10–20	3.8	98.3	149	3.46	121	22.7					7.22	6.23	448	40	475	12	96.8	87.7	96.0	99.6
20	Acetazoleamide: 10 mgm. per kgm., prime; 15 mgm. per kgm. per hr., infusion																			
20–30	6.8	85.3	149	3.49	121	22.2					7.21	7.33	766	174	626	301	93.0	38.5	94.2	85.0
30–40	7.7	73.1	149	3.22	121	22.5					7.20	7.51	820	250	593	460	92.0	−11.6	93.6	73.3
40–50	7.5	76.1	149	3.09	122	22.4					7.18	7.47	750	228	540	411	93.1	−1.8	94.4	77.0
50–60	7.7	75.8	149	3.09	121	21.2					7.18	7.46	781	208	547	422	92.8	6.7	94.4	75.2
60	Acetazoleamide: 10 mgm. per kgm., prime; 30 mgm. per kgm. per hr., infusion																			
60–70	8.2	76.6	149	2.81	123	21.1					7.19	7.45	815	204	550	461	92.5	0.5	94.5	72.8
70–80	8.0	74.1	148	2.92	123	20.5					7.19	7.46	850	212	527	481	91.8	−3.4	94.5	70.0
80–90	7.5	73.8	149	2.96	123	20.4					7.19	7.45	850	205	517	472	91.9	1.0	94.5	70.2
90–100	6.9	72.9	149	2.96	124	20.1					7.21	7.45	798	178	490	443	92.1	13.2	95.0	71.3
Experiment 7, dog 2, weight 16.5 kgm.																				
0–10	4.2	77.6	147	2.64	130							5.47	210	19	257		98.0	90.4	97.6	
10–20	4.6	85.1	150	2.78	130							5.53	230	21	278		98.2	90.7	97.6	
20	Chlormerodrin: 2.0 mgm. Hg per kgm., prime in 3 min.; 1.0 mgm. Hg per kgm. per hr., infusion																			
20–30	4.8	79.9	150	2.92	132			15.2		10.8		5.50	240	22	299		97.8	90.4	97.4	
30–40	7.8	86.0	150	2.78	132			8.67		37.0		5.30	626	31	744		94.9	86.2	93.8	
40–50	13.0	84.8	150	3.06	130			6.12		39.1		5.30	1260	52	1640		88.8	78.8	85.8	
50–60	18.2	85.0	150	2.92	135			5.94		38.3		5.38	2060	73	2280		83.1	69.2	81.1	
60–70	20.7	83.1	153	3.06	130			5.85		37.9		5.48	2490	52	2730		79.4	78.6	75.9	
70–80	18.3	79.8	155	3.06	131			5.68		36.4		5.37	2330	46	2580		80.2	80.2	76.4	

TABLE 1—*Continued*

Total Elapsed Time	Urine Flow	Glom. Filt. Rate	Plasma Concentration						Clearance		pH		Rate of Excretion				Per Cent of Filtered Reabsorbed			
			Na	K	Cl	HCO_3	Chlor-othz.	Hg	Chlor-othz.	Hg	Plasma	Urine	Na	K	Cl	HCO_3	Na	K	Cl	HCO_3
Experiment 7, dog 2, weight 16.5 kgm.—*Continued*																				
min.	*ml. per min.*		*milliequivalents per liter*				*mgm. %*	*micro-gm./ml.*	*ml. per min.*				*microequivalents per minute*							
80	Chlormerodrin: 2.0 mgm. Hg per kgm., prime in 3 min.; 2.0 mgm. Hg per kgm. per hr., infusion																			
80–90	20.8	80.8	155	3.19	130			29.4		17.8		5.51	2700	52	3000		77.2	78.8	71.1	
90–100	20.7	77.2	155	3.19	131			16.1		38.6		5.55	2500	52	3000		77.9	77.8	71.7	
100–110	18.6	76.4	155	3.34	126			14.0		36.8		5.53	2550	47	2700		77.3	80.8	73.3	
110–120	16.9	72.5	155	3.34	126			13.4		36.0		5.49	2320	43	2550		78.2	81.5	73.5	
120–130	15.4	70.2	155	2.61	126			12.9		35.4		5.47	2110	39	2260		79.6	77.9	75.7	
130–140	14.0	67.2	155	2.60	124			12.6		35.1		5.44	1920	39	2090		80.6	79.0	76.2	
Experiment 8, dog 4, weight 19 kgm.																				
0–10	14.2	124	149	3.64	121							7.25	1710	138	1790		90.4	67.8	88.6	
10–20	12.2	119	149	3.52	124							7.27	1570	136	1670		90.6	65.8	89.2	
20	Chlormerodrin: 2.0 mgm. Hg per kgm., prime in 3 min.; 2.0 mgm. Hg per kgm. per hr., infusion																			
20–30	10.7	120	149	3.52	123			20.9		24.4		7.27	1510	104	1600		91.1	74.0	89.8	
30–40	18.2	116	149	3.41	126			10.9		54.1		6.95	2530	75	2690		84.6	80.0	82.5	
40–50	19.7	106	149	3.52	119			9.68		51.1		6.47	2820	85	3070		81.2	76.2	76.8	
50–60	20.6	96.5	150	3.41	122			9.13		50.3		6.15	2840	87	3170		79.4	72.4	74.3	
60–70	19.0	92.4	150	3.64	119			9.68		48.0		6.34	2660	91	2930		79.8	71.4	74.6	
70	Chlormerodrin: 2.0 mgm. Hg per kgm., prime in 3 min.; 4.0 mgm. Hg per kgm. per hr., infusion																			
70–80	10.4	79.3	149	3.52	122			32.1		22.8		6.39	1410	89	1620		87.4	66.3	84.1	
80–90	16.6	83.2	150	3.30	119			24.9		36.8		6.18	2110	90	2370		82.1	65.6	77.2	
90–100	14.7	72.8	150	3.75	120			24.1		34.2		6.48	1880	84	2180		82.1	67.6	76.2	
100–110	14.2	60.4	149	3.30	119			24.5		29.4		6.65	1880	74	2020		78.1	60.1	73.3	
110–120	13.6	62.6	149	2.84	123			26.6		29.0		6.95	2000	70	2120		77.5	58.7	73.7	

infusion. It is evident from experiment 7 that 2.0 mgm. per kgm. prime and a rate of infusion of 1.0 mgm. per kgm. per hr. is not adequate, for an additional prime and double the rate of infusion caused significantly greater natriuresis and chloruresis. On the other hand when the initial prime and rate of infusion were 2.0 mgm. per kgm. and 2.0 mgm. per kgm. per hr. respectively, repeating the prime and doubling the rate of infusion so depressed glomerular filtration rate as to render this regimen suspect. Depression of filtration rate was equally evident when chlormerodrin was infused at a rate of 4.0 mgm. per kgm. per hr., even though the second priming dose was omitted. On the basis of these and other experiments, we have accepted as the standard regimen a priming dose of 2.0 mgm. per kgm. and a rate of infusion of 2.0 mgm. per kgm. per hr. This dose of chlormerodrin causes marked natriuresis and chloruresis as a consequence of reduction in tubular reabsorption, with no very significant or consistent effect on the renal handling of potassium. If the urine is acid initially, it remains so (experiment 7). If it is initially alkaline, it becomes more acid (experiment 8). Because of this fact and to reduce the analytical load, bicarbonate was not analyzed in those experiments in which chlormerodrin alone was given.

Experiments 19 and 17 in table 2 illustrate the fact that chlorothiazide and acetazoleamide exert qualitatively similar actions on the renal tubular reabsorption of bicarbonate and on the renal handling of potassium. Acetazoleamide is obviously the more potent of the two drugs in these

TABLE 2

Effects of chlorothiazide and acetazoleamide on renal excretion and reabsorption of electrolytes by the dog, when the two drugs are administered successively, each in dosage sufficient to produce its maximal renal response

Total Elapsed Time	Urine Flow	Glom. Filt. Rate	Plasma Concentration					UV/P	pH		Rate of Excretion				Per Cent of Filtered Reabsorbed			
			Na	K	Cl	HCO_3	Chlor-othz.	Chlor-othz.	Plas-ma	Urine	Na	K	Cl	HCO_3	Na	K	Cl	HCO_3
Experiment 19, dog 8, weight 21 kgm.																		
min.	*ml. per min.*		*milliequivalents per liter*				*mgm. %*	*ml./min.*			*microequivalents per minute*							
0–10	2.6	97.3	143	3.23	119	24.9			7.38	6.87	440	24	480	30	96.5	92.0	96.0	98.8
10–20	3.0	91.1	145	3.18	118	25.5			7.37	6.92	490	28	450	40	96.1	89.8	96.0	98.5
20 Chlorothiazide: 10 mgm. per kgm., prime; 15 mgm. per kgm. per hr., infusion																		
20–30	6.9	85.4	147	3.23	119	24.6	3.10	181	7.35	7.24	1170	85	900	220	90.2	67.5	92.5	90.0
30–40	6.8	75.2	147	3.13	120	24.1	1.62	402	7.31	7.28	1050	153	840	260	90.0	31.7	88.8	86.3
40–50	7.5	77.0	143	3.09	121	23.4	1.36	491	7.31	7.26	1060	163	900	270	89.8	27.9	90.8	85.8
50–60	8.0	78.5	145	3.14	122	24.0	1.48	449	7.29	7.22	1140	154	950	270	89.3	34.1	90.4	86.3
60 Acetazoleamide: 10 mgm. per kgm., prime; 15 mgm. per kgm. per hr., infusion. Chlorothiazide: 15 mgm. per kgm. per hr., infusion																		
60–70	7.8	66.9	147	3.07	122	22.1	1.58	260	7.27	7.33	1150	203	890	350	87.6	−4.1	89.7	77.5
70–80	6.8	64.1	144	2.66	121	22.9	1.54	277	7.28	7.35	960	219	780	350	89.0	−35.2	90.4	77.4
80–90	7.5	63.3	146	2.71	123	22.1	1.56	261	7.27	7.35	1040	205	860	330	88.3	−25.8	89.5	77.5
90–100	9.3	69.0	147	2.75	123	21.3	1.54	281	7.28	7.34	1300	208	1040	380	86.5	−14.9	88.4	75.5
100–110	9.6	67.1	145	2.81	123	21.8	1.64	257	7.26	7.37	1350	208	1100	400	85.4	−16.2	92.1	73.9
Experiment 17, dog 3, weight 21 kgm.																		
0–10	3.9	109	149	3.50	123	18.5			7.30	6.76	882	23	843	32	94.3	93.8	94.0	98.7
10–20	4.2	98.4	150	3.66	124	18.1			7.32	6.50	808	29	731	17	94.3	91.5	94.3	99.0
20 Acetazoleamide: 10 mgm. per kgm., prime; 15 mgm. per kgm. per hr., infusion																		
20–30	5.0	82.9	150	3.39	122	16.0			7.20	7.58	980	230	720	445	91.8	18.1	93.1	68.0
30–40	5.5	86.0	150	3.22	122	15.2			7.22	7.59	1150	142	736	488	90.7	46.0	93.3	64.3
40–50	5.2	76.4	148	3.24	125	16.3			7.21	7.56	1060	130	655	468	90.0	44.7	93.4	64.2
50–60	4.2	78.7	147	3.04	123	16.0			7.22	7.61	800	160	479	434	92.6	29.5	92.3	67.1
60 Chlorothiazide: 10 mgm. per kgm., prime; 15 mgm. per kgm. per hr., infusion. Acetazoleamide: 15 mgm. per kgm. per hr., infusion																		
60–70	7.0	81.6	147	3.08	124	16.2	3.48	256	7.24	7.43	1390	206	1150	432	87.8	13.8	89.2	68.9
70–80	7.4	75.0	149	3.17	125	16.3	1.88	343	7.24	7.37	1450	201	1180	414	86.3	11.1	88.7	67.8
80–90	7.0	75.0	149	3.36	124	16.2	1.66	304	7.22	7.36	1370	209	1120	397	87.1	12.5	88.6	68.9
90–100	7.2	76.6	148	3.36	125	16.1	1.60	297	7.20	7.34	1370	233	1120	414	87.3	4.9	88.9	68.1

respects. Thus it is evident in experiment 19 that the administration of acetazoleamide following chlorothiazide, increased the excretion of bicarbonate and potassium significantly, whereas in experiment 17, acetazoleamide initially produced maximal depression of bicarbonate reabsorption which was not enhanced by chlorothiazide. It is also evident from these 2 experiments that chlorothiazide depresses the reabsorption of chloride much more significantly than does acetazoleamide.

Experiments 15 and 14 in table 3 illustrate the fact that although chlorothiazide and chlormerodrin are both natriuretic and chloruretic, their

TABLE 3

*Effects of chlorothiazide and chlormerodrin on renal excretion and reabsorption of electrolytes by the dog, when the two drugs are administered successively, each in dosage sufficient to produce its maximal renal response**

Total Elapsed Time	Urine Flow	Glom. Filt. Rate	Plasma Concentration						Clearance		pH		Rate of Excretion				Per Cent of Filtered Reabsorbed			
			Na	K	Cl	HCO_3	Chlorothz.	Hg	Chlorothz.	Hg	Plasma	Urine	Na	K	Cl	HCO_3	Na	K	Cl	HCO_3
Experiment 15, dog 4, weight 18 kgm.																				
min.	*ml. per min.*		*milliequivalents per liter*				*mgm. %*	*microgm./ml.*	*ml. per min.*				*microequivalents per minute*							
0–10	4.7	91.7	146	3.75	122	19.2					7.30	6.06	560	25	590	5	95.5	92.5	95.0	99.8
10–20	3.9	92.1	147	3.64	120	18.4					7.33	5.98	550	26	560	3	95.8	91.8	95.0	99.9
20	Chlorothiazide: 10 mgm. per kgm., prime; 15 mgm. per kgm. per hr., infusion																			
20–30	7.1	84.2	147	3.75	121	17.9	2.71		195		7.33	7.04	1120	68	1020	160	90.5	77.3	90.4	90.0
30–40	8.2	82.6	147	3.64	120	17.8	1.39		425		7.33	7.27	1290	147	1150	204	88.8	49.3	88.9	86.8
40–50	7.2	75.9	147	3.63	124	17.7	1.18		360		7.32	7.26	1090	126	1010	160	89.6	51.9	89.8	88.7
50–60	6.7	75.5	148	3.63	122	17.9	1.20		298		7.30	7.23	1070	111	1010	143	89.9	57.4	89.5	90.0
60	Chlormerodrin: 2.0 mgm. per kgm., prime; 2.0 mgm. per kgm. per hr., infusion. Chlorothiazide: 15 mgm. per kgm. per hr., infusion																			
60–70	6.2	76.5	146	3.75	122	17.1	1.23	14.5	294	18.8	7.32	7.22	1060	72	980	131	90.0	73.2	90.0	90.5
70–80	4.9	73.6	147	3.63	122	16.9	1.24	10.6	287	35.0	7.30	7.18	940	33	880	95	90.8	87.0	90.6	92.8
80–90	6.5	72.1	146	3.37	122	17.2	1.28	9.50	255	37.1	7.29	6.84	1140	17	1120	58	88.6	92.6	87.9	95.7
90–110	11.6	74.6	145	3.51	123	17.0	1.37	9.95	259	39.3	7.30	6.46	1850	19	1850	41	81.9	92.6	80.8	97.0
110–130	16.0	73.7	144	3.75	122	16.8	1.37	10.4	269	41.7	7.31	6.48	2450	27	2460	53	75.8	89.7	74.0	96.1
130–150	17.2	70.1	144	3.57	121	16.4	1.42	10.7	247	42.9	7.33	6.47	2530	44	2615	48	73.7	81.5	70.5	96.1
Experiment 14, dog 5, weight 14 kgm.																				
0–10	6.7	52.2	151	3.59	131	17.5					7.31	6.26	390	21	440	9	94.7	88.3	94.3	99.0
10–20	7.2	51.5	152	3.64	128	17.5					7.31	6.35	420	37	480	13	94.5	79.5	92.5	98.5
20	Chlormerodrin: 2.0 mgm. Hg per kgm., prime; 2.0 mgm. Hg per kgm. per hr., infusion																			
20–30	7.3	48.6	152	3.70	131	16.9		37.2		4.12	7.32	6.35	460	35	690	12	93.5	79.5	89.6	98.5
30–40	10.2	49.4	153	3.70	132	16.8		22.0		12.2	7.32	6.01	880	35	960	8	87.8	80.0	85.9	99.0
40–50	14.2	49.4	155	3.82	134	16.7		20.6		12.1	7.32	5.88	1520	41	1659	7	79.2	77.2	76.2	99.1
50–60	15.7	46.1	155	3.87	133	17.3		19.5		13.6	7.32	5.79	1850	41	1980	6	73.0	75.5	69.6	99.2
60–70	14.8	41.1	155	4.12	134	17.3		20.8		11.8	7.32	5.67	1830	42	1950	4	69.8	74.0	66.5	99.3
70	Chlorothiazide: 10 mgm. per kgm., prime; 15 mgm. per kgm. per hr., infusion. Chlormerodrin: 2.0 mgm. Hg per kgm. per hr., infusion																			
70–80	16.9	37.7	156	4.02	133	16.9	5.10	19.8	86.5	13.7	7.34	6.86	2280	46	2330	97	59.0	68.0	55.6	84.0
80–90	15.8	35.8	157	4.05	133	15.7	2.55	17.4	163	16.2	7.34	6.86	2200	41	2230	92	58.9	70.3	55.4	82.6
90–100	13.0	30.8	157	3.95	133	16.2	2.23	15.0	132	16.4	7.36	6.61	1790	38	1880	42	61.1	67.0	56.3	91.2
100–110	12.8	31.4	157	3.93	132	15.1	2.17	14.7	130	18.4	7.39	6.49	1770	48	1880	28	62.2	59.0	56.8	93.8

* In almost every case, the results are given as values for each individual 10-minute period. In a few instances, the values for 2 successive periods were averaged since they were virtually the same.

TABLE 4

*Effects of acetazoleamide and chlormerodrin on renal excretion and reabsorption of electrolytes by the dog, when the two drugs are administered successively, each in dosage sufficient to produce its maximal renal response**

Total Elapsed Time	Urine Flow	Glom. Filt. Rate	Plasma Concentration					UV/P	pH		Rate of Excretion				Per Cent of Filtered Reabsorbed			
			Na	K	Cl	HCO_3	Hg	Hg	Plasma	Urine	Na	K	Cl	HCO_3	Na	K	Cl	HCO_3
Experiment 21, dog 9, weight 25 kgm.																		
min.	*ml. per min.*		*milliequivalents per liter*				*micro-gm./ml.*	*ml./min.*			*microequivalents per minute*							
0–10	4.7	104	143	3.26	118	19.8			7.33	7.53	770	92	738	142	94.4	71.3	94.2	93.3
10–20	4.7	99.4	144	3.38	119	19.9			7.33	7.43	780	92	728	128	94.3	71.2	94.3	91.0
20	Acetazoleamide: 10 mgm. per kgm., prime; 15 mgm. per kgm. per hr., infusion																	
20–30	6.3	90.4	144	3.26	119	19.5			7.33	7.72	935	185	712	415	91.7	69.8	93.7	77.5
30–40	6.9	79.3	143	3.15	120	18.8			7.30	7.78	1050	278	614	708	89.4	−17.3	93.9	54.8
40–50	7.0	79.1	143	3.04	122	18.4			7.28	7.81	1000	243	572	630	89.6	−6.1	94.4	56.9
50–60	6.6	75.9	143	3.09	121	18.3			7.23	7.73	876	212	515	578	91.5	4.8	94.9	60.1
60	Chlormerodrin: 2.0 mgm. Hg per kgm., prime; 2.0 mgm. Hg per kgm. per hr., infusion. Acetazoleamide: 15 mgm. per kgm. per hr., infusion																	
60–70	5.4	74.5	143	3.16	123	17.2	20.9	4.18	7.24	7.73	738	170	376	507	92.7	24.1	96.1	62.2
70–80	5.2	72.4	144	3.20	123	17.1	10.8	29.8	7.26	7.75	790	71	347	504	92.0	67.6	96.2	60.1
80–90	6.8	68.6	144	3.16	124	16.5	9.94	29.5	7.25	7.63	1010	78	632	594	89.3	61.9	93.0	50.0
90–110	11.5	66.1	144	3.16	124	16.2	10.5	29.3	7.25	7.43	1660	91	1310	398	81.7	54.1	84.9	64.4
110–130	14.4	58.4	145	3.33	125	15.8	12.0	26.7	7.25	7.21	1900	106	1800	318	75.2	45.4	76.4	65.5
130–150	14.0	52.1	145	3.26	125	15.4	13.5	24.9	7.24	7.20	1910	113	1810	150	73.7	29.7	73.6	82.2
Experiment 26, dog 10, weight 28 kgm.																		
0–10	3.9	93.9	146	3.78	127	18.6			7.34	6.87	50	55	88	14.7	99.5	83.3	99.4	99.2
10–20	4.2	90.6	148	3.82	127	18.2			7.37	6.86	50	79	97	21.2	99.5	76.0	99.4	99.0
20	Chlormerodrin: 2.0 mgm. Hg per kgm, prime; 2.0 mgm. Hg per kgm. per hr., infusion																	
20–30	3.7	81.6	148	3.87	128	17.7	17.7	9.90	7.34	6.98	46	72	86	24.0	99.7	76.0	99.3	98.5
30–40	3.2	80.0	149	4.22	127	17.9	9.80	41.0	7.34	6.62	91	62	114	12.1	99.5	80.6	99.0	99.2
40–50	5.0	82.6	149	4.21	130	17.3	8.90	43.5	7.38	6.56	329	37	380	9.5	97.2	88.8	96.5	99.3
50–70	10.5	83.4	149	3.84	128	17.5	8.21	48.1	7.40	6.14	1090	65	1240	7.8	89.2	78.9	89.0	99.4
70–90	14.4	77.1	150	3.87	129	17.8	8.30	48.6	7.35	6.19	1730	73	1890	10.7	84.1	74.9	82.1	99.3
90	Acetazoleamide: 10 mgm. per kgm., prime; 15 mgm. per kgm. per hr., infusion. Chlormerodrin: 2.0 mgm. Hg per kgm. per hr., infusion																	
90–100	17.8	60.3	152	4.21	127	18.3	9.30	41.7	7.36	7.15	2360	89	2270	226	72.8	63.3	73.4	80.5
100–110	15.3	49.8	150	4.35	128	18.6	9.92	35.7	7.33	7.33	2060	90	1880	326	71.0	56.8	72.0	66.5
110–120	14.6	49.4	150	3.71	128	18.4	10.7	36.2	7.34	7.26	2010	82	1820	264	71.5	52.9	72.5	72.4
120–130	16.8	52.5	150	3.47	129	17.2	11.3	36.5	7.34	7.14	2350	88	2160	302	68.7	49.1	69.8	68.3

* In almost every case, the results are given as values for each individual 10-minute period. In a few instances, the values for 2 successive periods were averaged since they were virtually the same.

mechanisms of action are probably different. Our argument derives from the following facts: chlorothiazide in experiment 15 depressed chloride reabsorption from the control level of 95.0 per cent to 88.9 per cent; from experiment 6 in table 1, it is evident that doubling this dose of chlorothiazide does not enhance chloruresis; however, as shown in experiment 15, the administration of chlormerodrin further depressed chloride reabsorption to 70.5 per cent. Furthermore in experiment 14, chlormerodrin depressed chloride reabsorption from 92.5 to 66.5 per cent. The subsequent administration of chlorothiazide further decreased chloride reabsorption to 55.4 per cent. It is evident that chlorothiazide can block an additional fraction of chloride reabsorption following maximal blockade by chlormerodrin.

Although in the paragraph above we have emphasized chloruresis, it is evident that the same statements apply to natriuresis. Furthermore, it is interesting that the kaluresis produced by chlorothiazide is partially reversed by chlormerodrin (experiment 15), in line with the observation of Berliner, Kennedy and Orloff (1951) that mercurial diuretics interfere with potassium secretion. In addition, in experiment 15 it is evident that the usual depression of urine pH observed when chlormerodrin is given alone (experiment 8) is likewise seen when the urine is alkalinized by the infusion of chlorothiazide. Chlormerodrin thus has the effect of enhancing bicarbonate reabsorption (see extreme right column of experiment 15). Acidification, enhanced bicarbonate reabsorption and depressed potassium secretion are no doubt all causally interrelated.

Experiments 21 and 26 in table 4 complete our diuretic comparisons. It is evident that the natriureses induced by acetazoleamide and chlormerodrin are of different origins and are additive. Acetazoleamide enhances the excretion of sodium and bicarbonate; chlormerodrin enhances the excretion of sodium and chloride. Independent of which drug is given first, each exerts its characteristic effect on the reabsorption of these ions. Since acetazoleamide is more potent than chlorothiazide in promoting the secretion of potassium, the blocking action of chlormerodrin is even more evident. Acetazoleamide is also more potent in blocking bicarbonate reabsorption than is chlorothiazide. Therefore, urine pH, although it falls after chlormerodrin, still remains on the alkaline side of neutrality in the presence of acetazoleamide. There seems to be little if any depression of the diuretic activity of chlormerodrin by acetazoleamide. This is in line with other observations on the dog (Berliner, Kennedy and Orloff, 1951) but in opposition to findings in man (Orloff and Walser, 1956). Whether this constitutes a species difference or is merely related to the much higher mercurial dosage in the dog experiments is uncertain, although we are inclined to the latter view.

Discussion. Our experiments confirm the description by Beyer *et al.* (1957, 1958) of the diuretic action of chlorothiazide, namely that it depresses the renal tubular reabsorption of sodium, chloride and bicarbonate and facilitates the secretion of potassium. The latter action is the cause of potassium depletion, now recognized as a potential but easily correctable hazard when the drug is administered repeatedly over long periods of time. The depression of reabsorption of bicarbonate and alkalinization of the urine are expressions of the activity of chlorothiazide as an inhibitor of carbonic anhydrase (Pitts and Alexander, 1945; Pitts and Lotspeich, 1946; Pitts, Ayer and Scheiss, 1949). Stimulation of potassium secretion is likewise an expression of the inhibition of carbonic anhydrase (Berliner, Kennedy and Orloff, 1954). This enzyme is concerned with the provision of hydrogen ions in ready supply to a distal tubular mechanism which exchanges them for sodium ions in the tubular urine (Pitts *et al.*, 1958). If the cellular supply of hydrogen ions is reduced by virtue of inhibition of carbonic anhydrase, cellular potassium ions are substituted for hydrogen ions in the exchange mechanism. There is no reason to believe that there are any qualitative differences in the actions of sulfanilamide, chlorothiazide and acetazoleamide on these renal mechanisms. However, marked quantitative differences are evident with potency increasing in the order listed above.

Chlorothiazide induces a significant chloruresis, a property shared with mercurial diuretics but not exhibited in any significant degree by the other carbonic anhydrase inhibitors. The chloruresis induced does not *per se* indicate that the diuretic specifically blocks a mechanism for the active transport of chloride. It is possible that all chloruretic diuretics interfere specifically with a single active transport mechanism for sodium and that chloruresis is merely a passive consequence of the increased rate of excretion of sodium (Pitts, 1958). If this is true, it follows that chlorothiazide blocks one moiety of this mechanism, *i.e.* it inhibits one chain of reactions which supply energy to the system; chlormerodrin inhibits another. In fact we feel that there are not less than 3 and possibly more systems which supply energy to the sodium reabsorbing mechanism, one inhibited by chlorothiazide, one inhibited by mercurials and one or more resistant to both drugs. This view derives from the following observations: a) chlorothiazide when given in a priming dose of 10 mgm. per kgm. and infused at a rate of 15 mgm. per kgm. per hr. blocks the reabsorption of 5 to 10 per cent of the chloride normally reabsorbed; b) doubling the dose does not increase tubular blockade; c) chlormerodrin, when given in a priming dose of 2.0 mgm. per kgm. and infused at a rate of 2.0 mgm. per kgm. per hr. blocks the reabsorption of 15 to 20 per cent of the chloride normally reabsorbed; d) doubling the dose does not increase tubular blockade; and e) the administration of chlormerodrin following chlorothiazide or of chlorothiazide following chlormerodrin blocks the same fraction of reabsorption which is blocked when the drug is given alone. Since chlorothiazide and chlormerodrin together block less than 50 per cent of total sodium chloride reabsorption, there must be still a third system sensitive to neither inhibitor. Chlorothiazide in addition blocks that moiety of sodium reabsorption dependent on carbonic anyhdrase activity.

SUMMARY

The intravenous administration of chlorothiazide, acetazoleamide and chlormerodrin to dogs in various combinations and in doses capable individually of producing maximal renal responses, has led to the following conclusions concerning the mechanism of action of chlorothiazide.

Chlorothiazide, by virtue of its activity as an inhibitor of carbonic anhydrase, induces natriuresis and kaluresis and causes the excretion of alkaline urine containing bicarbonate. Since these actions are qualitatively similar to those produced by acetazoleamide, and since the prior administration of acetazoleamide reduces the response to chlorothiazide, these two drugs probably act on the same renal mechanisms. However, acetazoleamide is significantly more potent than is chlorothiazide in its action as a carbonic anhydrase inhibitor.

Chlorothiazide also induces natriuresis and chloruresis in a manner analogous to that of mercurial diuretics. However, when chlorothiazide and chlormerodrin are administered in combination in doses sufficient individually to produce maximal effects, the responses are additive. We interpret these results as indicating that chlorothiazide and chlormerodrin either block different mechanisms for reabsorption of sodium and chloride ions or more probably interfere with different enzymatic reactions supplying energy to a single reabsorptive mechanism.

REFERENCES

Bayliss, R. I. S., Marrack, D., Pirkis, J., Rees, J. R., and Zilva, J. F.: Ann. New York Acad. Sci., **71:** 442, 1958.

Berliner, R. W., Kennedy, T. J., Jr., and Orloff, J.: Am. J. Med., **11:** 274, 1951.

Berliner, R. W., Kennedy, T. J., Jr., and Orloff, J.: Arch. int. pharmacodyn., **97:** 299, 1954.

Beyer, K. H.: Ann. New York Acad. Sci., **71:** 363, 1958.

Beyer, K. H., Baer, J. H., Russo, H. F., and Haimbach, A.: Fed. Proc., **16:** 282, 1957.

Bratton, A. C., and Marshall, E. K., Jr.: J. Biol. Chem., **128:** 537, 1939.

Dorman, P. J., Sullivan, W. J., and Pitts, R. F.: J. Clin. Invest., **33:** 82, 1954.

Ford, R. V.: Ann. New York Acad. Sci., **71:** 397, 1958.

Freis, E. D., Wanko, A., Wilson, I. M., and Parrish, A. E.: Ann. New York Acad. Sci., **71:** 450, 1958.

Heider, C., Dennis, E., and Moyer, J. H.: Ann. New York Acad. Sci., **71:** 456, 1958.

Wilkins, R. W., Hollander, W., and Chobanian, A. V.: Ann. New York Acad. Sci., **71:** 465, 1958.

Kessler, R. H., Lozano, R., and Pitts, R. F.: J. Clin. Invest., **36:** 656, 1957.

Laragh, J.: Ann. New York Acad. Sci., **71:** 409, 1958.

Novello, F. C., and Sprague, J. M.: J. Am. Chem. Soc., **79:** 2028, 1957.

Orloff, J., and Walser, M.: quoted by Berliner, R. W.: Pharm. Rev., **8:** 137, 1956.

Pitts, R. F.: Am. J. Med., in press, 1958.

Pitts, R. F., and Alexander, R. S.: Am. J. Physiol., **144:** 239, 1945.

Pitts, R. F., Ayer, J. L., and Schiess, W. A.: J. Clin. Invest., **28:** 35, 1949.

Pitts, R. F., Gurd, R. S., Kessler, R. H., and Hierholzer, K.: Am. J. Physiol., in press, 1958.

Pitts, R. F., and Lotspeich, W. D.: Am. J. Physiol., **147:** 138, 1946.

Schreiner, G.: Ann. New York Acad. Sci., **71:** 420, 1958.

Van Slyke, D. D., and Neill, J. V.: J. Biol. Chem., **61:** 523, 1924.

8019

ENZYMIC AND PHARMACOLOGIC COMPARISON OF IMIDAZOLE-ACETYLCHOLINE WITH TWO RELATED CHOLINE ESTERS, MUREXINE AND DIHYDROMUREXINE[1]

I. I. A. TABACHNICK, F. E. ROTH, J. MERSHON, A. A. RUBIN, E. T. ECKHARDT AND W. M. GOVIER

Department of Pharmacology, Research Division, Schering Corporation, Bloomfield, New Jersey

Received for publication December 11, 1957

Erspamer and Benati (1953) and Whittaker and Michaelson (1954) have isolated a choline ester containing the imidazole nucleus, β-[imidazolyl-4-(5)]-acrylcholine (murexine, imidazoleacrylcholine or ImAcrCh), from several invertebrate tissues. The pharmacological evaluation of this ester, as well as its reduced analogue imidazolepropionylcholine (dihydromurexine or ImPrCh), has revealed properties which are both similar to and different from the effects of acetylcholine (ACh) (Erspamer and Dordoni, 1947; Kewitz, 1955; Conroy *et al.*, 1956; Tabachnick and Roth, 1957; Winbury *et al.*, 1958; Erspamer and Glässer, 1957). The choline esters that contain imidazole are hydrolyzed by nonspecific cholinesterase[2] (ChE) and not by the specific ChE (Foldes *et al.*, 1957; Grelis and Tabachnick, 1957).

Grunert and Kewitz (1955) apparently isolated imidazoleacetylcholine (ImACh) from mammalian brain. Since ImACh may serve as a neurotransmitter, it seemed of interest to investigate some aspects of the pharmacology and enzymology of this compound and to compare it with other imidazole-containing choline esters.

METHODS. *Cholinesterase substrate.* A modification of the method of Ammon (1933) was employed to study ImACh as a substrate for various cholinesterases (Grelis and Tabachnick, 1957). Specific ChE was prepared from bovine red blood cells (Winthrop-Stearns, Inc.). Nonspecific ChE was obtained as a concentrate of human plasma (Cholase). The buffer was 0.07 *M* $NaHCO_3$, pH 8.0. Rat brain ChE was prepared by the method of Bayliss and Todrick (1956) with one exception, the $CaCl_2$ concentration was reduced to 0.0012 *M*. The vessel contents were equilibrated with the CO_2 and N_2 gas mixture to a final pH of 7.6. In all instances, the final volume of contents per flask was 2.0 ml.

Anticholinesterase activity. This parameter was studied employing a spectrophotometric method which measures the change in absorbance (at 250 mμ) due to enzymic hydrolysis of acetylthiocholine or butyrylthiocholine by specific or nonspecific ChE respectively (Tabachnick, 1956; Rubin *et al.*, 1957; Tabachnick *et al.*, 1958).

Amine oxidase. Inhibition of diamine oxidase (DAO) and monoamine oxidase (MAO) was studied manometrically (Tabachnick and Roth, 1957). The activity of a compound was expressed in terms of the pI_{50}, the negative logarithm of the molar drug concentration which inhibited the enzyme activity 50 per cent. The pI_{50} was interpolated from a log concentration-per cent graph.

Guinea pig tracheal chain. A modification of the preparation of Castillo and de Beer (1947) was employed. The chain was suspended in a 50-ml. bath containing Krebs-Henseleit (1932) solution aerated with 95 per cent O_2 plus 5 per cent CO_2 and maintained at 37°C. Responses of the chain to the drugs were recorded kymographically through a frontal-writing lever.

Frog rectus abdominis muscle. A rectus muscle of a frog (*Rana pipiens*) was suspended in a 5-ml. bath containing frog-Ringer solution (Burn, 1952). The drugs were added to the bath and allowed to remain in contact with the muscle exactly 90 seconds, at which time the drug was washed out. Five minutes after the wash, the muscle was again challenged. The design of the experiment required the testing of two concentrations of the unknown and two concentrations of an ACh standard. The responses were recorded kymographically, and the results analyzed by the method of Finney (1952) to obtain a potency ratio.

[1] Presented in part at the Fall Meetings of the American Society for Pharmacology and Experimental Therapeutics, Baltimore, Maryland, September 4–7, 1957 by two of the authors (I.I.A. Tabachnick and F. E. Roth).

[2] Cholinesterases may be classified into two types (Koelle, 1955); specific (true, acetyl-, red cell) and nonspecific (pseudo-, plasma, serum, butyro-).

Mouse inclined screen. Freshly prepared solutions were injected into a lateral tail vein of CF #1 mice (18 to 22 gm.). The mice were then placed on a screen inclined 60° from the horizontal (Smith *et al.*, 1953). A mouse was considered paralyzed if it dropped off the screen. The dose that caused 50 per cent of the mice to drop off (DO_{50}) and its confidence limits were determined by the method of Litchfield and Wilcoxon (1949). Four different doses with 5 or 6 mice per dose were employed.

Cat gastrocnemius musle-sciatic nerve. Six cats were anesthetized with Dial (diallylbarbituric acid) solution (0.7 ml./kgm., intraperitoneally) and the femoral vein was cannulated for injection of the test drugs. Contraction of the gastrocnemius was induced by supramaximal stimulation (10-second intervals; 150 cycles/second; 8 volts) of the sciatic nerve through shielded platinum electrodes. The response was recorded by means of a spring loaded lever counterbalanced with rubber bands.

Autonomic activity. Seven dogs were anesthetized with sodium pentobarbital (35 mgm./kgm., intraperitoneally) and arranged for kymographic recording of blood pressure and respiration. In some experiments the dogs were maintained under artificial respiration. The imidazole-containing choline esters were evaluated as to their effects on respiration and blood pressure as well as on their ability to modify the blood pressure responses induced by ACh (5 microgm./kgm.), epinephrine (2 microgm./kgm.), histamine (5 microgm./kgm.), serotonin (25 microgm./kgm.) and 1,1-dimethylphenylpiperazinium iodide (DMPP, 10 to 20 microgm./kgm.).

Ganglionic stimulation was studied in six cats anesthetized with Dial (Ciba) solution (0.7 ml./kgm., intraperitoneally). The cats were arranged for kymographic recording of blood pressure, respiration and the responses of the nictitating membrane. Drugs were administered into the common carotid artery, with the external carotid artery occluded.

Mouse acute toxicity. Each agent was administered intravenously at four dosage levels to CF #1 mice (18 to 22 gm.). The log dose-per cent effect curve was plotted to determine the LD_{50} and its 95 per cent confidence limits (Litchfield and Wilcoxon, 1949). A minimum of 20 mice was used for each assay.

Drugs. The following were used in this study: imidazoleacrylcholine bromide; imidazolepropionylcholine bromide; imidazoleacetylcholine bromide hydrobromide[3]; butyrylcholine iodide; acetyl-β-methylcholine bromide; BW 284C51 or 1:5 bis(4-allyldimethylammoniumphenyl) pentan-3-one diiodide; succinyldicholine chloride; eserine sulfate; aminoguanidine bicarbonate; acetylthiocholine iodide; butyrylthiocholine iodide; edrophonium bromide; *d*-tubocurarine chloride; epinephrine bitartrate; histamine phosphate; serotonin creatinine sulfate; 1,1-dimethylphenylpiperazinium iodide; hexamethonium chloride, atropine sulfate. The authors are grateful to Dr. L. O. Randall (Hoffmann-La Roche), Dr. H. Fevold (Baxter Laboratories) and Dr. K. I. Colville (Burroughs-Wellcome) for generous supplies of some of the agents used in this study.

[3] Imidazoleacetylcholine was synthesized in the chemical laboratories of Schering Corporation by Dr. F. H. Clarke, Jr.

RESULTS. *Cholinesterase substrate studies.* The hydrolysis by nonspecific ChE of ImACh, ImAcrCh, ImPrCh, and butyrylcholine (BuCh), expressed as microliters of CO_2 evolved per hour (initial velocities) was 209, 40, 980 and 990, respectively. The substrate concentration was $10^{-2}M$, final. Eserine ($10^{-5}M$) inhibited the enzymic hydrolysis of BuCh as well as the imidazole-containing choline esters by approximately 80 per cent. The non-enzymic hydrolysis of ImACh was greater than that of other choline esters tested. ImACh was not metabolized significantly by rat brain homogenates whereas BuCh was metabolized by this preparation (table 1). BW 284C51, a selective inhibitor of specific cholinesterase (Austin and Berry, 1953), inhibited only the hydrolysis of acetyl-β-methylcholine.

Anticholinesterase activity. The imidazole-containing esters or succinyldicholine (SDC) were approximately 10^3 to 10^4 times less potent than eserine in inhibiting specific or nonspecific ChE (table 2).

Amine oxidase. ImAcrCh and ImPrCh (pI_{50} = 3.3 and 3.6, respectively) were at least 100 times more potent than ImACh (pI_{50} = 1.7) in inhibiting DAO. Aminoguanidine (pI_{50} = 7.2), a potent inhibitor of DAO (Schuler, 1952), was approximately 10^5 times more potent than ImACh. ImACh ($10^{-2}M$ final concentration) inhibited MAO less than 10 per cent. Tabachnick and Roth (1957) demonstrated that the inhibition of MAO by ImAcrCh and ImPrCh was weak.

Guinea pig tracheal chain. ImACh (4 and 10 microgm./ml. of bath solution) potentiated the contraction induced by histamine (2 microgm./ml. of bath solution). ImACh was approximately one-tenth or one-twentieth as potent as ImAcrCh or ImPrCh, respectively in potentiating the effects of histamine. The potentiation of

TABLE 1

Hydrolysis of choline esters by rat brain homogenates

Contents of Warburg flasks: 0.2 ml. of substrate in side arm #1; 0.2 ml. of $10^{-4}M$ BW 284C51 in side arm #2; 1 ml. of 20 per cent homogenate of rat brain and buffer in main compartment. Incubated for 30 minutes, t = 37°. Each value represents the mean of 4 to 12 determinations. (+) and (−) indicate the presence or absence of BW 284C51, respectively.

Substrate	Final Concentration	μl. CO_2 Evolved/Flask/30′	
		−	+
	M		
Acetyl-β-methylcholine	$10^{-1.5}$	321.7	9.6
Imidazoleacetylcholine	$10^{-2.0}$	3.5	0
Butyrylcholine	$10^{-2.0}$	104.6	98.7

TABLE 2

Inhibition of cholinesterases by various substances

Each cuvette contained 1 ml. of enzyme (1:500 dilution of cholase or 40 units of Winthrop-Stearns bovine red cell acetylcholinesterase), 1 ml. of inhibitor (in 0.1 *M* NaH_2PO_4-Na_2HPO_4 buffer, pH 6.4), and either 1 ml. of buffer or 1 ml. of substrate (final concentration $6.7 \times 10^{-4}M$).

Inhibitor	pI_{50} Obtained with Cholinesterase from	
	Human plasma	Bovine red cells
Imidazoleacetylcholine	2.2	2.6
Imidazoleacrylcholine	3.2	—
Imidazolepropionylcholine	2.7	—
Succinyldicholine	3.1	3.0
Eserine	6.6	6.7

histamine by ImPrCh and ImAcrCh was not affected by atropine but was prevented by chlorpheniramine (Tabachnick and Roth, 1957). A similar pattern was obtained when ImACh was employed.

Frog rectus abdominis muscle. In the non-eserinized muscle, with ACh assigned an activity value of 100, ImAcrCh, ImACh and ImPrCh demonstrated values (95 per cent confidence limits) of 14 (12 to 15), 24 (14 to 26) and 131 (81 to 154), respectively. ImAcrCh, was the only ester not potentiated by eserine (0.001 per cent). The potentiation of the choline ester effect by eserine appeared to be directly related to the rate of enzymic hydrolysis of the esters. *d*-Tubocurarine chloride (0.001 per cent) effectively antagonized the actions of the choline esters.

TABLE 3

The effect of some intravenously administered choline esters on neuromuscular function using the inclined screen technique (DO_{50}) and on lethality (LD_{50}) in mice

Agent	DO_{50}*	LD_{50}*
Imidazoleacetyl-choline	0.54 (0.50–0.59)	2.08 (1.65–2.60)
Imidazolepropionyl-choline	2.35 (1.74–3.17)	16.3 (13.7–19.4)
Succinyldicholine	0.17 (0.14–0.21)	0.32 (0.26–0.38)

* Results expressed in terms of mgm./kgm. of base with 95 per cent confidence limits.

Mouse inclined screen technique. It was demonstrated that ImACh was more potent than ImPrCh but less potent than SDC (table 3). The DO_{50}'s for these esters were 0.54, 2.4 and 0.17 mgm./kgm., respectively.

Cat gastrocnemius-sciatic preparation. The doses of ImPrCh, ImACh, ImAcrCh and SDC necessary to produce a 50 per cent blockade of transmission were 14, 286, 135 and 20 microgm./kgm., respectively. Edrophonium, at doses which did not influence the preparation (0.1 mgm./kgm., intravenously), enhanced the blockade induced by ImACh.

Autonomic activity. Intravenous ImPrCh (0.1 to 0.3 mgm./kgm.) and ImACh (1 to 4 mgm./kgm.) produced slight bradycardia and hypotension which was rapidly followed by a period of tachycardia and hypertension (fig. 1A). Hexamethonium (2 mgm./kgm.) abolished the hypertensive effect but enhanced the hypotensive action produced by both esters whereas atropine (1.0 mgm./kgm.) effectively blocked the hypotensive phase (fig. 1B). ImACh or ImPrCh did not affect the blood pressure response of anesthetized dogs to intravenous ACh, epinephrine, histamine or serotonin, but they slightly reduced the pressor effect of DMPP. The pressor response of DMPP (10 microgm./kgm.) was blocked by hexamethonium (fig. 1A, 1B).

Preliminary results indicated that ImPrCh and ACh, at doses of 50 microgm. (total, injected into the common carotid), were approxi-

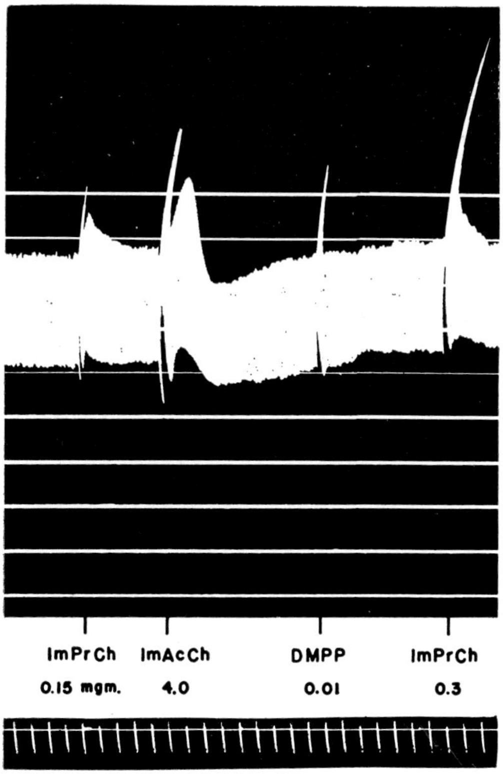

FIG. 1. A. The effects of ImPrCh, ImAcCh (imidazoleacetylcholine) and DMPP on the blood pressure of the anesthetized dog.

Doses are in terms of mgm./kgm. administered intravenously. Horizontal lines represent mm. of Hg with the first line 0 and increments of 20 mm. per line. Time marker divisions represent 1 minute.

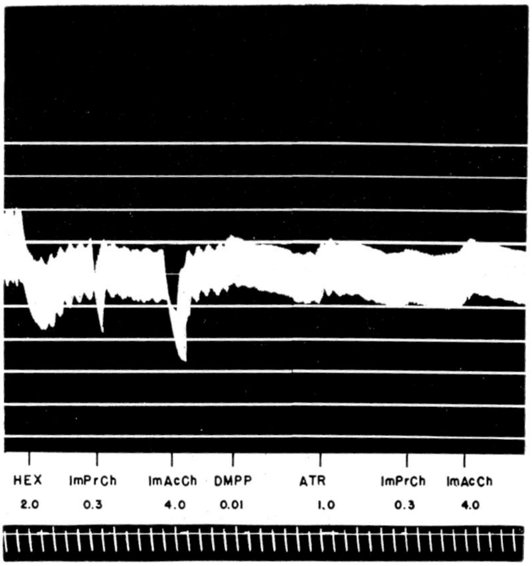

1. B. The effects of hexamethonium (Hex) and atropine (ATR) on the response of blood pressure to agents depicted in fig. 1A.

Remainder of legend and explanation of parameters as in fig. 1A.

mately equipotent in stimulating ganglia, as measured by retraction of the nictitating membrane. ImACh was less potent than ImPrCh or ImAcrCh. Hexamethonium and atropine (3 mgm./kgm. and 1 mgm./kgm., respectively) abolished the response of the nictitating membrane to acetylcholine and the imidazole-containing choline esters.

Mouse acute toxicity. The LD_{50}'s of ImACh, ImPrCh and SDC were 2.1, 16.8 and 0.32 mgm./kgm., respectively. The order of toxicity paralleled the potency of the agents in the mouse inclined screen studies (table 3).

DISCUSSION. The stimulation of autonomic ganglia by the imidazoleacylcholine esters may be assumed since these esters elicited a hypertensive phase upon intravenous administration and retraction of the nictitating membrane upon close arterial (carotid) administration. This assumption was confirmed since hexamethonium blocked the hypertensive action of the imidazole-containing choline esters as well as that of the ganglionic stimulant, DMPP.

d-Tubocurarine abolished the contracture of the frog rectus muscle and edrophonium enhanced the neuromuscular block induced in the cat by ImAcrCh, ImPrCh and ImACh. These results indicate that the imidazole-acylcholine esters may be classified as "depolarizing-type" agents. Indeed, Erspamer and Glässer (1957) have suggested this mechanism of action and Quilliam (1957) has confirmed a "depolarizing-type" blockade by ImAcrCh employing electrical methods to measure potentials at the end-plate region.

The imidazoleacylcholine esters demonstrated peripheral cholinergic stimulation. This was clearly seen after hexamethonium blockade of ganglionic stimulation which resulted in the abolition of the hypertensive phase and enhancement of the hypotensive phase. Atropine blocked the hypotensive response induced by either ACh or the imidazole-containing choline esters, confirming the existence of a peripheral cholinergic effector site of action for ImACh, ImPrCh and ImAcrCh, as observed by Winbury *et al.* (1958). These results are in contrast to those of Erspamer and Glässer (1957) who concluded that these esters display little or no cholinergic action.

The potentiation of histamine and the inhibition of diamine oxidase by ImPrCh and ImAcrCh was demonstrated previously (Tabachnick and Roth, 1957). The present studies showed that ImACh also potentiated the effects of histamine on guinea pig smooth muscle and inhibited diamine oxidase. In both respects, ImACh was considerably less potent than ImPrCh or ImAcrCh.

Grelis and Tabachnick (1957) and Foldes *et al.* (1957) have reported that ImPrCh is rapidly and ImAcrCh is slowly metabolized by human plasma (nonspecific) ChE. Neither ester was metabolized by bovine red cell (specific) ChE. The present study indicates a qualitatively similar pattern for ImACh, *i.e.*, this ester was metabolized at approximately one-fifth the rate of ImPrCh or BuCh in the presence of human plasma (nonspecific) ChE and was not hydrolyzed by the specific enzyme.

We have previously suggested that ImPrCh showed some specificity for nonspecific ChE (Grelis and Tabachnick, 1957). However, rat brain homogenates, which contain nonspecific ChE and metabolize BuCh (Bayliss and Todrick, 1956) do not metabolize ImACh. The specificity of imidazoleacylcholine esters will be investigated further, employing other species since Ord and Thompson (1952) have indicated that rat brain nonspecific ChE is unusual in that it shows greatest selectivity towards propionylcholine as a substrate.

In general, the order of activity obtained in the present studies was ImPrCh > ImAcrCh > ImACh. This would suggest that the alkyl side-chain of the imidazole-containing choline ester plays an important role in the activity obtained. The three-carbon, saturated lateral chain compound (ImPrCh) was the most potent of the structures investigated. Modification of this structure, *e.g.*, ImAcrCh or ImACh, diminished activity. These conclusions are in agreement with those expressed by Winbury *et al.* (1958) and Erspamer and Glässer (1957). In one species (mouse), however, the order of activity was ImACh > ImPrCh > ImAcrCh. The increased activity of ImAch in the mouse as compared to that in other species may be related to differences in cholinesterase specificity noted with various species (Augustinsson, 1948).

It remains of interest that ImACh, as well as other choline esters containing the imidazole nucleus, are hydrolyzed by nonspecific and not specific ChE (Foldes *et al.*, 1957; Grelis and Tabachnick, 1957). If ImACh or an analogous imidazole-containing choline ester functions as either a neurotransmitter or humoral agent, one might expect that its actions would be associated with tissues that possess high concentrations of the enzyme which will metabolize this ester. It is suggested that the function and locus of action of an imidazoleacylcholine ester might be sought employing structures of high nonspecific cholinesterase concentration as a frame of reference.

SUMMARY

Imidazoleacetylcholine (ImACh) has been compared with imidazoleacrylcholine (ImAcrCh) and imidazolepropionylcholine (ImPrCh) in some enzymic and pharmacologic studies. As with ImAcrCh and ImPrCh, ImACh causes neuromuscular blockade, stimulates ganglia, weakly stimulates the peripheral cholinergic effector sites, potentiates histamine, causes contracture of the frog *rectus abdominis* muscle, inhibits cholinesterases and diamine oxidase and is hydrolyzed by some nonspecific cholinesterases. *In general*, the order of activity is ImPrCh > ImAcrCh > ImACh.

The ganglionic stimulation, peripheral cholinergic stimulation and frog rectus actions are blocked by hexamethonium, atropine and *d*-tubocurarine, respectively.

Acknowledgment. The authors are indebted to Mr. S. Tozzi and Miss Marilyn Larson for their contributions to this study. We are grateful to Mr. Gordon B. Thomas for the statistical analyses in this paper.

REFERENCES

Ammon, R.: Arch. ges. Physiol., **233:** 486, 1933.
Augustinsson, K.-B.: Acta Physiol. Scand. **15:** Supplem. 52, 1948.
Austin, L., and Berry, W. K.: Biochem. J., **54:** 695, 1953.
Bayliss, B. J., and Todrick, A.: Biochem. J., **62:** 62, 1956.
Burn, J. H.: Practical Pharmacology, Blackwell Scientific Publications, Oxford, 1952.
Castillo, J. C., and de Beer, E. J.: This Journal, **90:** 104, 1947.
Conroy, C., Kappell, B., Ferruggia, T., and Randall, L. O.: Fed. Proc., **15:** 412, 1956.
Erspamer, V., and Benati, O.: Science, **117:** 161, 1953.
Erspamer, V., and Dordoni, F.: Arch. int. Pharmacodyn., **74:** 263, 1947.
Erspamer, V., and Glässer, A.: Brit. J. Pharmacol., **12:** 176, 1957.

FINNEY, D. J.: Statistical Method in Biological Assay, Hafner Publishing Co., New York, 1952.
FOLDES, F. F., ERDOS, E. G., BAART, N., AND SHANOR, S. P.: Proc. Soc. Exper. Biol. & Med., **94**: 500, 1957.
GRELIS, M. E., AND TABACHNICK, I. I. A.: Brit. J. Pharmacol., **12**: 320, 1957.
GRUNERT, G., AND KEWITZ, H.: Naturwiss., **42**: 628, 1955.
KEWITZ, H.: Arch. exper. Path. u. Pharmakol., **225**: 111, 1955.
KOELLE, G. B.: J. Neuropath. Exper. Neurol., **14**: 23, 1955.
KREBS, H. A., AND HENSELEIT, K.: Zeit. f. physiol. chem., **210**: 33, 1932.
LITCHFIELD, J. T., AND WILCOXON, F. W.: THIS JOURNAL, **96**: 99, 1949.
ORD, M. G., AND THOMPSON, R. H. S.: Biochem. J., **51**: 245, 1952.
QUILLIAM, J. P.: Brit. J. Pharmacol., **12**: 388, 1957.
RUBIN, A. A., MERSHON, J., GRELIS, M. E., AND TABACHNICK, I. I. A.: Fed. Proc., **16**: 333, 1957.
SCHULER, W.: Experientia, **8**: 230, 1952.
SMITH, C. M., PELIKAN, E. W., MARAMBA, L., AND UNNA, K. R.: THIS JOURNAL, **108**: 317, 1953.
TABACHNICK, I. I. A.: Biochim. Biophys. Acta, **21**: 580, 1956.
TABACHNICK, I. I. A., MERSHON, J., GRELIS, M. E., AND RUBIN, A. A.: Arch. Internat. Pharmacodynam., in press, 1958.
TABACHNICK, I. I. A., AND ROTH, F. E.: THIS JOURNAL, **121**: 191, 1957.
WHITTAKER, V. P., AND MICHAELSON, I. A.: Biol. Bull., **107**: 304, 1954.
WINBURY, M. M., WOLF, J. K., AND TABACHNICK, I. I. A.: THIS JOURNAL, **122**: 207, 1958.

THE ACTION OF PYRIDYLACETYLCHOLINE[1] ON NEUROMUSCULAR AND GANGLIONIC TRANSMISSION

A. A. RUBIN, J. MERSHON, I. I. A. TABACHNICK AND W. M. GOVIER

Department of Pharmacology, Research Division, Schering Corporation, Bloomfield, New Jersey

Received for publication December 16, 1957

Imidazoleacrylcholine (murexine, ImAcrCh) and imidazoleacetylcholine (ImACh) have been isolated from natural sources (Erspamer and Benati, 1953; Grunert and Kewitz, 1955). Both substances are similar to but less potent than acetylcholine in their ability to stimulate autonomic ganglia and peripheral cholinergic effector sites (Tabachnick *et al.*, 1958; Winbury *et al.*, 1958; Erspamer and Glässer, 1957).

In preliminary pharmacologic experiments, Pasini, Vercellone and Erspamer (1956) found pyridylacrylcholine (PAcrCh) to be the most potent member of a series of heterocyclic analogues of ImAcrCh. It was therefore considered of interest to investigate certain excitatory and metabolic aspects of the pyridyl analogue of of ImACh, pyridylacetylcholine (PACh), the chemical structure of which may be written as follows:

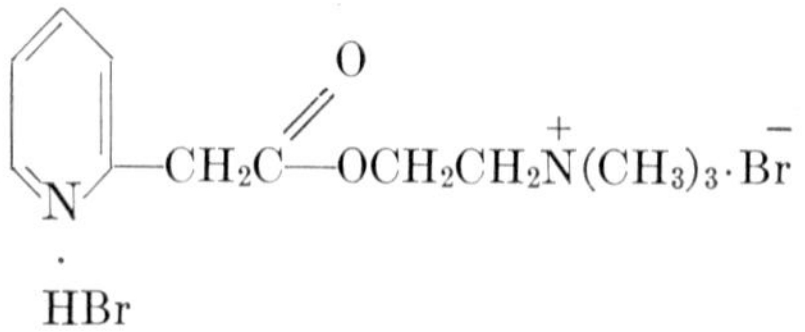

METHODS. *Gastrocnemius.* The sciatic nerve of the anesthetized cat (Dial (diallylbarbituric acid) 70 mgm./kgm.) was stimulated with supramaximal shocks delivered every 10 seconds by a Grass stimulator at a frequency of 130 cycles per second (8 volts, 0.2-millisecond duration). Contractions of the muscle were recorded on a kymograph by a spring-loaded lever. Injections were made into the femoral vein.

Nictitating membrane. Injections were made into the common carotid artery of the anesthetized cat (Dial, 70 mgm./kgm.) following occlusion of the external carotid artery. Contractions of the membrane were recorded on a kymograph by a sensitive frontal writing lever.

[1] Pyridylacetylcholine was synthesized in the chemical laboratories of Schering Corp. by Dr. F. H. Clarke, Jr.

Frog rectus abdominis. This muscle was suspended in a 5-ml. bath containing frog Ringer solution at room temperature. Drugs were in contact with the muscle for 1.5 minutes, washed out and added again 3.5 minutes later. The experimental design required the use of two concentrations of both PACh and the standard, acetylcholine. A potency ratio was obtained by

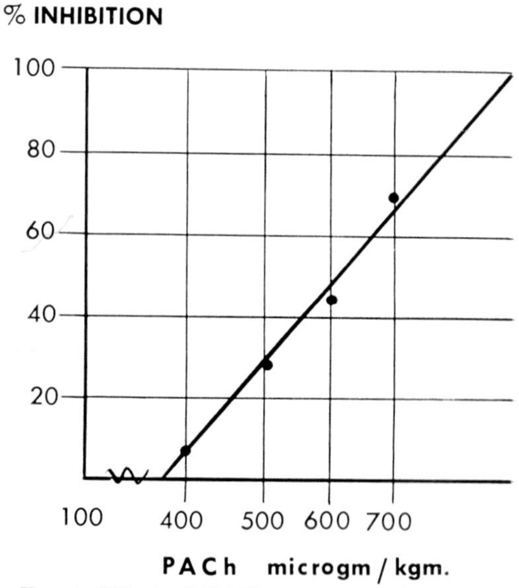

FIG. 1. Effect of PACh on contractions of the cat gastrocnemius muscle.
Abscissa: doses of PACh on log scale. Ordinate: per cent inhibition of muscle stimulated by supramaximal electrical shocks.

analyzing the data according to the method of Finney (1952).

Enzymic studies. PACh was investigated as a potential cholinesterase substrate by conventional manometric techniques (Ammon, 1933). Substrate and inhibitor, when used, were placed in the sidearms of Warburg flasks. The main compartment contained 0.07 *M* $NaHCO_3$ and either bovine red blood cell acetylcholinesterase (15 units per flask) or human plasma cholinesterase (0.2 ml. of a 1:375 dilution of Cholase per flask). The final

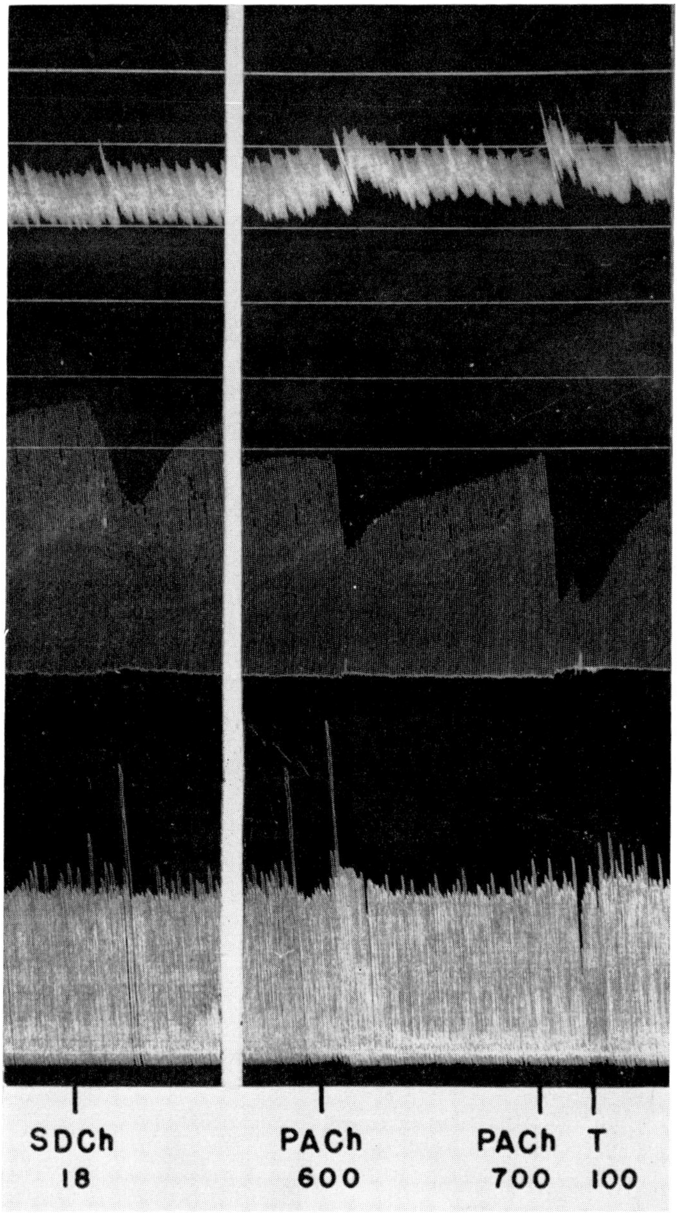

FIG. 2. Effect of PACh, succinyldicholine (SDCh) and Tensilon (T) on contractions of the cat gastrocnemius muscle.

Supramaximal stimuli were applied to the sciatic nerve at 10-second intervals. The upper tracing represents blood pressure; the middle, gastrocnemius contractions; and the lower, respiration. Doses are expressed as microgm./kgm.

volume was 2.0 ml., the temperature 37°C. The system was gassed for 15 minutes with a mixture of 95 per cent N_2 and 5 per cent CO_2. The final pH was 8.0. After equilibration, the substrate and inhibitor were tipped into the main compartment, and readings were taken at 3- to 6-minute intervals. Initial reaction rates were expressed as microliters of CO_2 evolved in one hour.

RESULTS. *Gastrocnemius.* Intravenous injections of PACh transiently inhibited neuromuscular transmission in the cat. Data from 6 experiments show that the ED_{50} of PACh (630 microgm./kgm.) was considerably higher than that of succinyldicholine (20 microgm./kgm.), and somewhat higher than that of ImACh (286 microgm./kgm.). A typical dose-response curve for PACh is shown in fig. 1. Doses of PACh below 300 microgm./kgm. had no apparent effect on neuromuscular transmission. Edrophonium (100 microgm./kgm.), a cholinesterase inhibitor, enhanced the neuromuscular blockade initiated by PACh (fig. 2).

Nictitating membrane. PACh was 28 per cent as potent as acetylcholine in eliciting a contraction of the nictitating membrane (6 experiments). ImACh, on the other hand, induced membrane contractions only at very high doses (*e.g.*, 500 microgm.). Since hexamethonium (3.0 mgm./kgm.) completely inhibited the contractions otherwise produced by PACh in atropinized animals, it is evident that the superior cervical ganglion was the primary site of drug action.

Frog rectus abdominis. An evaluation of the responses of the rectus abdominis muscle to rnjections of PACh and acetylcholine (5 experiments) revealed essentially the same relative potency value as that obtained with the nictitating membrane preparation. PACh was 25 per cent as potent as acetylcholine. On the same relative basis, ImACh was somewhat less potent than PACh, possessing 14 per cent of the activity of acetylcholine. Muscle responses to both PACh and ImACh were antagonized by *d*-tubocurarine chloride (0.001 per cent).

Enzymic studies. PACh and ImACh were hydrolyzed by human plasma cholinesterase. At a final concentration of 10^{-2} M, the rates of hydrolysis for PACh, ImACh and butyrylcholine were 155, 209 and 990 microliters of CO_2 per hour, respectively. At the same final substrate concentrations, 10^{-5} M eserine inhibited the hydrolysis of PACh (89 per cent), ImACh (79 per cent) and butyrylcholine (82 per cent). Of these three choline esters, only ImACh underwent nonenzymic hydrolysis to any significant extent. Neither PACh nor ImACh was appreciably hydrolyzed by acetylcholinesterase.

DISCUSSION. Recently, Pasini *et al.* (1946) found that substitution of a pyridyl group for the imidazolyl nucleus of ImAcrCh resulted in an eightfold increase in the response of the frog rectus abdominis muscle. Results obtained from the same preparation and reported in this paper show that the pyridyl analogue of ImACh is only two times more potent than its parent compound. Apparently, pyridyl substitution in either choline ester results in enhanced activity. The extent of this activity, however, is determined by the nonheterocyclic portion of the molecule. Additional evidence in support of this assumption was reported by Tabachnick *et al.* (1958) who found that ImAcrCh and its reduced analogue imidazolepropionylcholine were, respectively, two and nine times as potent as ImACh.

Studies in the cat revealed that PACh is a more potent ganglionic stimulant than ImACh but a less potent neuromuscular depressant. That this latter phenomenon is probably not due to decreased availability of the drug at the target organ was demonstrated by enzymic studies. PACh was hydrolyzed less rapidly than ImAch in the presence of nonspecific cholinesterase; moreover, only ImACh was hydrolyzed nonenzymically to any significant extent. It would appear, therefore, that in this species the PACh molecule has a weaker affinity for neuromuscular end plate receptors than does the ImACh molecule. Paton and Zaimis (1951) suggested that there may be spatial differences in the arrangement of ganglionic and neuromuscular receptors. Consequently, the presence of a second nitrogen in the imidazole nucleus may favorably influence an ImACh receptor association at the neuromuscular end plate but not at the ganglion.

SUMMARY

Pyridylacetylcholine (PACh) is less active than its analogue imidazoleacetylcholine (ImACh) in inhibiting neuromuscular transmission, but is much more active in stimulating autonomic ganglia.

PACh is hydrolyzed less rapidly than ImACh by plasma cholinesterase. Neither PACh nor ImACh is hydrolyzed by acetylcholinesterase.

ACKNOWLEDGMENT. We wish to acknowledge the help of Mr. Gordon Thomas, Schering Corporation, Bloomfield, New Jersey for the statistical analysis.

REFERENCES

AMMON, R.: Arch. ges. Physiol.. **233:** 486. 1933.
ERSPAMER, V., AND BENATI, O.: Science, **117:** 161, 1953.
ERSPAMER, V., AND GLÄSSER, A.: Brit. J. Pharmacol., **12:** 176, 1957.
FINNEY, D. J.: Statistical Methods in Biological Assay. Hafner Publishing Co., New York, 1952.
GRUNERT, G., AND KEWITZ, H.: Naturwiss., **42:** 628, 1955.
PASINI, C., VERCELLONE, A., AND ERSPAMER, V.: Gazz. Chim. Ital., **86:** 266, 1956.
PATON, W. D. M., and ZAIMIS. E. J.: Brit. J. Pharmacol., **6:** 155, 1951.
TABACHNICK, I. I. A., ROTH, F. E., MERSHON, J., RUBIN, A. A., ECKHARDT, E. T., AND GOVIER, W. M.: THIS JOURNAL, **123:** 98, 1958.
WINBURY, M. M., WOLF, J. K., AND TABACHNICK, I. I. A.: THIS JOURNAL **122:** 207, 1958.

8021

A HOMOLOGOUS SERIES OF SOLUBLE n-FATTY ACID ESTERS (C_2-C_{10}) AS SUBSTRATES FOR SERUM CHOLINESTERASE[1,2]

B. H. J. HOFSTEE

Palo Alto Medical Research Foundation, Palo Alto, California

Received for publication December 9, 1957

The activity patterns of two pancreatic esterases (Hofstee, 1952b) and two liver esterases (Hofstee, 1954) with respect to varying carbon chain length of the acyl moiety of the substrates have been found to be characteristic for each enzyme. In these investigations, the sodium salts of n-fatty acid esters of hydroxybenzoic acids provided soluble substrates, the hydrolysis of which could be followed continuously by direct spectrophotometric measurement (Hofstee, 1951, 1952a).

The present investigation was undertaken to establish such patterns for esterases in human blood serum. Results by others, reviewed by Whittaker (1951), indicate that the optimal number of n-acyl C atoms for serum cholinesterase is at least four and is independent of the rest of the substrate molecule. Another enzyme, "A-esterase" (Aldridge, 1953), present in serum, attacks certain esters at rates decreasing in the order of C_2, C_3, C_4.

It was found that serum cholinesterase attacks the present series of substrates (esters of *m*-hydroxybenzoic acid) at a rate that increases with the increasing length of the carbon chain of the ester up to at least 10 C atoms. The lower members of the series (C_2, C_3) are also hydrolyzed by a noncholinesterase enzyme similar to "A-esterase."

Materials and methods. The following *enzyme preparations* were used: a) pooled fresh undialyzed human blood serum, b) centrifuged, pooled serum, dialyzed for three to four days in running distilled water, and c) a purified preparation of human serum cholinesterase, kindly furnished by Dr. Avram Goldstein of Stanford University. The precipitate of preparation b, having no activity, was discarded. The supernatant was kept frozen in small lots. The ultraviolet light absorption of this preparation was considerably less than that of undialyzed serum. With respect to acetylcholine as the substrate, preparation c (Sp-IV-6-3, see Goldstein and Doherty, 1951) was roughly 50 times as active as whole dried plasma. It contains approximately 0.5 per cent cholinesterase.

The *substrates*, n-fatty acid esters of *m*-hydroxybenzoic acid, were the same as used previously for liver esterase (Hofstee, 1954). In the absence of enzyme these *meta* esters are more stable than the corresponding *ortho* compounds while the reverse is true with respect to enzymatic hydrolysis by serum. The substrates will be referred to as C_2, C_3, *etc.* according to the acyl carbon chain length. Because of the ionized carboxyl group they are soluble at pH > 7. They were used at concentrations below the critical concentration of micelle formation (Hofstee, 1955a).

Activities (velocity, initial rates) were determined spectrophotometrically (Hofstee, 1951, 1952a) at 300 mμ in pH 8 Veronal buffer at 30°C. The substrates were dissolved in buffer by dropwise addition of *N* NaOH and constant agitation, keeping the pH below 8.

At 300 mμ the n-fatty acid esters of *m*-hydroxybenzoic acid do not absorb, but the hydrolysis of 1 micromol. of ester in a volume of 3 ml. results in an increase in $E_{1\ cm.}$ of 0.37 due to the absorption of free hydroxybenzoic acid. This allows initial rates to be determined over a 1-cm. light path at substrate concentrations slightly lower than $10^{-3}M$. The nonenzymatic hydrolysis of the substrates, less than 1 per cent per 30 min., was automatically subtracted from the total hydrolysis by the presence of substrate in the reference cell in the same concentration as in the reaction mixture. Extensive use was made of a cuvette[3] with seven compartments, allowing 6 rate determinations to be carried out simultaneously.

The absorption of light by serum itself does not interfere with determinations up to amounts of 0.5 ml. of dialyzed serum in the reaction mixture (3 ml.). However, with the proper substrate and in the presence of sufficient Ca^{++} which effects as much as a 25-fold activation (see below) less

[1] Supported by grant number C-2289(C3) from the National Cancer Institute, National Institutes of Health, U. S. Public Health Service.

[2] Presented, in part at the Pacific Slope Biochemical Conference in Seattle, Washington, June 1956.

[3] Made by the Pyrocell Company, New York.

TABLE 1

Influence of time and enzyme concentration on the enzymatic hydrolysis of 0.01 M m-butyryloxybenzoic acid by dialyzed human blood serum expressed as $\Delta E^{1\ cm.}_{300\ m\mu}$

	0.033 *M* Ca^{++}			No Ca^{++}		
Amount of serum (λ) per 3 ml	3.125	6.25	12.5	31.25	62.5	125
0–15 min	0.030	0.057	0.113	0.045	0.087	0.163
15–30 min	0.024	0.053	0.108	0.042	0.080	0.151
30–45 min	0.033	0.055	0.115	0.043	0.085	0.159
45–60 min	0.030	0.054	0.115	0.042	0.080	0.156
Total	0.117	0.219	0.451	0.172	0.332	0.629
x Dilution* (specific activity)	0.468	0.438	0.451	0.688	0.664	0.629
% Deviation from average specific activity	+3.5	−3.1	−0.2	+4.2	+0.6	−4.7

* Based on the highest enzyme concentration used.

than 10 microl. (λ) of serum are needed for an activity determination.

Provided ΔE values of at least 0.1 are measured, the inherent error of the method is not greater than a few per cent as is indicated by a series of rates determined simultaneously at the same enzyme and substrate concentrations, temperature and pH. However, as has been pointed out previously (Hofstee, 1952a), the maximum over-all experimental error is higher. On the basis of our experience with this assay method, differences in rates of less than 5 to 10 per cent are not considered significant unless a series of determinations indicates a trend. In this connection it should be noted that in the tables and figures given below, each column or point represents a single rate determination.

Table 1 gives the results of some experiments on the constancy of the rate and proportionality between rate and enzyme concentration. It can be seen that within "experimental error", and in the presence as well as in the absence of Ca^{++}, the rate is constant for at least one hour after temperature equilibration, while the observed increase in ΔE during this period is proportional to the enzyme concentration.

RESULTS. Figure 1 shows the influence of the carbon chain length on the total esterolytic activity of the three enzyme preparations without activators added. Data of this kind have meaning only when the substrates that are compared are in solution and at a concentration below the critical

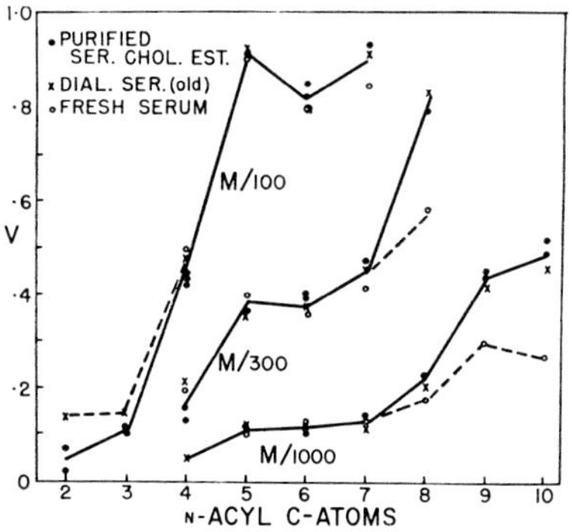

FIG. 1. Influence of the number of C atoms in the n-fatty acid moiety of the substrates (esters of *m*-hydroxybenzoic acid at different concentrations) on the total esterolytic activity (v, micromol./15 min.) of approximately 0.6 mgm. purified human serum cholinesterase and of 0.1 to 0.2 ml. of serum.

concentration of micelle formation (CMC).[4] For this reason the curves are less extended at high than at low concentrations.

Identification of cholinesterase. The following evidence is presented to show a) that the hydrolysis of all the substrates by the purified preparation is entirely due to cholinesterase and b) that 90 to 100 per cent of the hydrolysis by the dialyzed or by the untreated serum, at least with C_4

[4] The CMC of the C_{10} ester is about $2.5 \times 10^{-3}M$. With a decreasing number of C atoms it increases by a factor of 3 for each successive member of the series (to be published).

TABLE 2

Inhibition (per cent) of the esterolytic activity of whole human serum (50 microl.) and of purified serum cholinesterase (4 mgm.) by 2×10^{-6} M physostigmine with n-fatty acid esters of m-hydroxybenzoic acid as the substrates

Substrate	C_2	C_3	C_4	C_5	C_6	C_7	C_8	C_9	C_{10}
Concentration	0.01 *M*	0.01 *M*	0.01 *M*	0.01 *M*	0.01 *M*	0.01 *M*	0.001 *M*	0.001 *M*	0.001 *M*
Whole serum	19	72	92	99	98	96	90	90	93
Purified cholinesterase	100	100	99	97	99	100	99	99	99

through C_7 as the substrates, is also caused by the action of this enzyme. 1. Regardless of the substrate that is used, the activity of the purified enzyme preparation is practically completely inhibited by 2×10^{-6} *M* physostigmine (table 2). Inhibition by such low concentrations of this inhibitor is considered to be specific for the cholinesterases (Richter and Croft, 1942). Inhibition to the extent of 90 to 100 per cent also occurs with whole serum as the enzyme source, with the exception of the cases when C_2 or C_3 is used as the substrate (see below). Similar results were obtained with 10^{-6} *M* prostigmine or 3.3×10^{-5} *M* Diparcol (diethazine, diethylaminoethyl-N-dibenzoparathiazine) as the inhibitor (*e.g.*, Todrick, 1954). In our experience aliesterases such as those in liver and pancreas, are not inhibited by Diparcol or other phenothiazines in this low concentration (unpublished observations). It has been shown previously (Hofstee, 1951) that with acetylsalicylic acid as the substrate the activity of serum is inhibited by Parathion (diethyl-*p*-nitrophenyl thiophosphate) and by tri-*o*-cresyl phosphate, at least in the presence of Ca^{++} (see below). 2. The relative activity with respect to different members of the present series of substrates (C_4 through C_7) does not change with purification (figure 1). 3. If the enzyme that hydrolyzes the present substrates were not cholinesterase, one might expect that it was partly or completely removed during the purification. Instead, similar to cholinesterase, it is concentrated several hundredfold in the purified preparation as compared to serum (figure 1). 4. Inactivation of dialyzed serum by heat treatment is independent of the substrate from C_3 through C_8 (table 3) indicating that the same enzyme hydrolyzes all these esters. 5. The same extent of activation by calcium ion is observed regardless of whether the purified enzyme or whole serum is used as the enzyme source (see below).

TABLE 3

Decrease (per cent) of the esterolytic activity of human blood serum by heat with respect to different substrates in 0.0033 M concentration

	0.033 *M* Ca^{++}, 25 λ serum					No Ca^{++}, 62.5 λ serum		
Substrate	C_3	C_4	C_5	C_6	C_7	C_7	C_8	C_9
4 Minutes at 55°C.	25	23	26	25	25	27	25	17.5
8 Minutes at 55°C.	48	44	48	47	46	48	46	38

Other esterases. The physostigmine resistant fraction of the activity of whole serum (table 2) would indicate a noncholinesterase enzyme of the "A-esterase" type (Aldridge, 1953) that attacks C_2 and C_3 in decreasing order. The possibility cannot be excluded, however, that all or part of this activity is of a nonspecific kind such as that of pure serum albumin with acetyl esters as substrates (Dirks and Boyer, 1951). In any event, the results indicate that this fraction was removed during the purification.

The results with substrates of carbon chain longer than C_8 were somewhat inconsistent. The behavior of the dialyzed serum with respect to C_4 through C_{10} (figure 1) seems identical with that of the purified enzyme. However this preparation was kept frozen for more than one year during which time its activity, relative to the longer chain esters, apparently had increased. It can be seen (figure 1) that for these substrates the relative activity of a sample of fresh serum is lower than that of the old dialyzed serum and of the purified enzyme.

It was also observed that the inhibition by 10^{-5} *M* Diparcol and by 10^{-6} *M* Prostigmine (neostigmine), at least of the original dialyzed serum, decreased with increasing carbon chain length above C_8. Furthermore, the heat stability of this preparation with respect to C_9 was greater than in the case of the other substrates (table 3). Although these last results might indicate the presence of an inhibitor-resistant and more heat stable enzyme that preferentially attacks the longer chain esters, this would not be consistent with the observation that the relative activity of fresh serum with these substrates is lower instead of higher than that of purified cholinesterase. These matters will be further investigated.

The data of table 2 that indicate physostigmine inhibition of the order of 90 per cent or more are less accurate than usual because they are based on determinations of small residual activities. The fact, however, that especially with whole serum the inhibition is consistently less than 100 per cent would indicate a small noncholinesterase fraction even with respect to the substrates C_4 through C_8. However, when the cholinesterase is specifically activated several fold, as was the case in subsequent experiments, this fraction becomes even more insignificant.

On the basis of these considerations and the over-all results of this section it would appear that, at least with C_4, C_5, C_6 or C_7 as the substrate, whole serum can be used for studies of serum cholinesterase.

Influence of the substrate concentration. The data of figure 1 represent reaction rates (v) at varying substrate concentrations (S) from which, theoretically, V_m(v, for $S \rightarrow \infty$) and K_M (S when $v = V_m/2$) could be determined by the usual procedures. However, for accurate determination of these constants more experimental points are needed. Nevertheless, from $K_M = \Delta v/\Delta(v/S)$ it is found that the Michaelis constants, for all the substrates, are considerably larger than 10^{-2} *M*. This would mean that even at the highest substrate concentration (10^{-2} *M*) used the enzyme is less than one-half saturated, while saturation of the order of 90 per cent would require substrate concentrations $> 10^{-1}$ *M*. The use of such high concentrations, through which unambiguous estimation of the constants could be made (*e.g.* Hofstee, 1956) is impractical[5] in the present assay procedure.

In any event, the Michaelis constants are much larger in our series than with acetylcholine as the substrate (Augustinsson, 1950). Evidence will be presented elsewhere that the high K_M values are a consequence of the negative charge of the present substrates due to ionization of the free carboxyl group. It is thereby assumed that the active center of the enzyme also possesses a negative charge (Bergmann and Wurzel, 1954) which repels that of the substrate. The presence of certain bivalent metal ions, *eg.* Ca^{++}, that would neutralize these charges, results in a decrease of K_M to the extent of one-twentieth to one-thirtieth of its original value but has only little influence on V_m (to be published).

Activation of cholinesterase by bivalent metal ions. The esterolytic activity of the serum enzyme with the present negatively charged substrates, in contrast to neutral or positively charged substrates (Vander Meer, 1953), is spectacularly increased by certain bivalent metal ions, especially Mn^{++} and the alkaline earth metals as shown in table 4. Even Ni^{++} activates the enzyme, but Cd^{++} inhibits (see below).

The contribution of "noncholinesterase" enzymes to the activity with C_4 through C_7 as the substrates, less than 10 per cent in the absence of metal (see above), might become appreciable in the presence of activating metallic ions, because the extent of their activation could be higher than that of cholinesterase. However, the following evidence indicates that the activation with these substrates, and even with C_2 and C_3, is mainly or entirely due to cholinesterase. 1. The decrease in activity after heat treatment is about the same whether determined in the absence or in the presence of Ca^{++} (see C_7 in table 3). The metal does not reveal a difference in heat stability of the activity with respect to the substrates C_3 through C_7 (table 3). 2. With 10^{-2} *M* C_5 as the substrate, an activation of approximately fivefold was obtained by 10^{-1} *M* Ca^{++} in the case of either the purified enzyme or whole serum. In both cases the increased activity was abolished by 2×10^{-6} *M* physostigmine to the extent of more than 90 per cent. Although with C_2 as the substrate the inhibition of the activity of serum by 10^{-6} *M* Prostigmine is less than 50 per cent in the absence of metal ions, here the inhibition is about 90 per cent in the presence of 0.0033 *M* Ca^{++}. This would indicate that cholinesterase is activated while the "A-enzyme" is not. In the interpretation of the quantitative aspects of these results, consideration must be given to the possibility that Ca^{++}

[5] Although substrate concentrations $> 10^{-2}M$ could be used, at concentrations of the order of $10^{-1}M$ nonenzymatic hydrolysis to the extent of a fraction of 1 per cent would result in a "background density" that might interfere with spectrophotometric measurements (Mehler, 1954).

TABLE 4

The influence of metal ions on the activity of serum cholinesterase in 25 microl. of dialyzed serum with 0.0066M m-butyryloxybenzoic acid as the substrate*

Salt, 0.0033 *M*	None	NaCl	$MgCl_2$	$CaCl_2$	$SrCl_2$	$BaCl_2$	$CdCl_2$	$MnSO_4$	$NiSO_4$
Relative activity	100	96	271	508	420	421	23	540	182

* Be^{++}, Co^{++}, Al^{+++}, Fe^{++}, Zn^{++} and Cu^{++} form precipitates in the reaction mixture.

partly reverses the effect of the inhibitor (to be published).

The results of experiments on the influence of the carbon chain length of the substrate on the activation by Ca^{++} are presented in figures 2A and 2B. The experiments have not been carried out beyond C_7 because $CaCl_2$ forms a precipitate with substrates of longer carbon chain. It may be observed that the activation is less with the longer chain substrates than with C_4 and C_3 where, with 0.1 *M* Ca^{++}, it is of the order of 25-fold. This might contradict the evidence given above that only one enzyme is involved in the activation. However, as suggested above, Ca^{++} might facilitate the approach of these negatively charged substrates to the active center of the enzyme. Steric or other factors influenced by the carbon chain length may hereby play a role.

Despite high activation, the presence of metal ions does not appear to be essential for activity

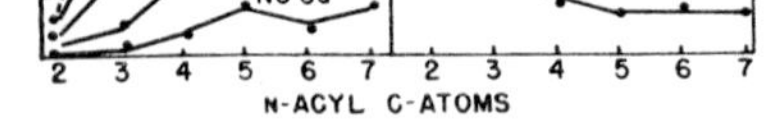

Fig. 2. A. Influence of the number of C atoms in the n-acyl moiety of the substrate (0.0033 *M*) on the increase in esterolytic activity of serum by Ca^{++} in different concentrations. The values for $Ca^{++} \to \infty$ were obtained by a graphical procedure based on a linear relationship between the activation (Δv) and $\sqrt{(\Delta v)/[Ca^{++}]}$ (to be published).

B. The data of part A expressed as the ratio of the activity in the presence (v_a) and in the absence (v_0) of Ca^{++}. Since v_0 of C_3 is low and inaccurate and v_0 of C_2 almost nil (fig. 2A) at the enzyme concentration used, the v_a/v_0 ratio cannot be determined accurately for these substrates.

as is shown by the following observations. 1. The activity did not disappear upon several days' dialysis of serum in running distilled water. The purified enzyme is active without metal ions added. 2. The activity of dialyzed serum was not influenced by an equal amount of the same preparation heated for several minutes at 100°. 3. The activity of dialyzed serum was not or was only slightly affected by adding 10^{-3} *M* ethylenediaminetetraacetic acid (Versene) to the reaction mixture even when the enzyme was pretreated with this compound for several hours at room temperature in the absence of substrate.

These data do not exclude the possibility of the presence of an essential metal having a much higher affinity for the enzyme than for Versene (*e.g.*, Hofstee, 1955b). On this basis inhibition by another metal (*e.g.* Cd^{++}, table 4) with comparable affinity could then occur through competition.

Discussion. The results show that cholinesterase in serum is clearly characterized by the present procedure. Its activity pattern with respect to the acyl carbon chain length of the substrate is entirely different from that of two esterases in hog pancreas (Hofstee, 1952b) and two esterases in horse liver (Hofstee, 1954). The evidence suggests that the "A-esterase" present in serum (Aldridge, 1953) attacks the lower members of this series of substrates. One of the liver esterases, similar to "A-esterase", was also detected in this manner even in the presence of the other esterase (Hofstee, 1954). These observations suggest that many more as yet unknown nonlipase esterases (Hofstee, 1952a) may be identified and characterized by the present method, even in crude extracts from natural tissues and in body fluids.

The present results provide an improvement of the spectrophotometric method for assay of serum cholinesterase described previously (Hofstee, 1951). It is indicated that with C_4, C_5, C_6 or C_7 as the substrate. even in whole serum and especially in the presence of Ca^{++}, practically all activity is due to cholinesterase. Under optimum conditions the rate compares favorably with that of the hydrolysis of other substrates (see Augustinsson, 1948) and not more than 10 microl. of serum are needed for an activity determination.

SUMMARY

The activity of "cholinesterase" in human blood serum with the sodium salts of a homologous series of n-fatty acid esters of *m*-hydroxybenzoic acid as the substrates increases in a characteristic manner with increasing acyl carbon chain length up to at least 10 C atoms.

Depending on the substrate and its concentration, the enzymic hydrolysis of these anionic esters is increased up to the order of 20- to 30-fold by certain bivalent metal ions, notably Mg^{++}, Ca^{++}, Sr^{++}, Ba^{++} and Mn^{++}, but these ions are not essential for activity.

The results provide an improvement of a direct and continuous spectrophotometric method for the assay of serum cholinesterase presented previously.

ACKNOWLEDGMENT. The author is indebted to Dr. Avram Goldstein of Stanford University for valuable comment on the manuscript of this paper.

REFERENCES

ALDRIDGE, W. N.: Biochem. J., **53:** 110, 1953.
AUGUSTINSSON, K-B.: Acta Physiol. Scand., **15:** Suppl. 52, 1948.
AUGUSTINSSON, K-B.: The Enzymes, Sumner, J. B., and Myrbäck, K., editors, Vol. **I:** part 1, p. 460, Academic Press Inc., New York, 1950.
BERGMANN, F., AND WURZEL, M.: Biochim. et biophys. acta, **13:** 251, 1954.
DIRKS, B. M., AND BOYER, P. D.: Cereal Chem., **28:** 483, 1951.
GOLDSTEIN, A., AND DOHERTY, M. E.: Arch. Biochem., **33:** 22, 1951.
HOFSTEE, B. H. J.: Science, **114:** 128, 1951.
HOFSTEE, B. H. J.: J. Biol. Chem., **199:** 357, 1952a.
HOFSTEE, B. H. J.: J. Biol. Chem., **199:** 365, 1952b.
HOFSTEE, B. H. J.: J. Biol. Chem., **207:** 219, 1954.
HOFSTEE, B. H. J.: Abstr. 3rd Internat. Bioch. Congr.: 4–7, 1955a.
HOFSTEE, B. H. J.: Arch. Biochem., **59:** 352, 1955b.
HOFSTEE, B. H. J.: Enzymologia, **XVII:** 273, 1956.
MEHLER, A. H.: Science, **120:** 1043, 1954.
RICHTER, D., AND CROFT, P. G.: J. Biol. Chem., **36:** 746, 1942.
TODRICK, A.: Brit. J. Pharmacol., **9:** 76, 1954.
VANDER MEER, C.: Nature, **171:** 78, 1953.
WHITTAKER, V. P.: Physiol. Rev., **31:** 312, 1951.

8022

DIFFERENTIAL EFFECTS OF A QUATERNARY CHOLINESTERASE INHIBITOR, PHOSPHOLINE, AND ITS TERTIARY ANALOGUE, COMPOUND 217-AO, ON CENTRAL CONTROL OF RESPIRATION AND ON NEUROMUSCULAR TRANSMISSION. THE ANTAGONISM BY 217-AO OF THE RESPIRATORY ARREST CAUSED BY MORPHINE[1]

W. SCHAUMANN[2] AND C. JOB[3]

Department of Pharmacology, University of Frankfurt and Department of Pharmacology, University of Innsbruck

Received for publication January 2, 1958

It has been reported that in rats and mice eserine antagonizes the respiratory arrest which follows a large dose of morphine. Neostigmine, which does not pass the blood-brain barrier, was found to be effective as an antagonist only when injected intracisternally (Schaumann, 1958a). These results were surprising, because an *inhibition* of respiration was observed with the cholinesterase inhibitors in the absence of morphine. However, since the anticholinesterases impaired neuromuscular transmission, their central actions were difficult to evaluate in these experiments from the records of respiratory movements. In the following investigations, a method described by Job and Schaumann (1958) was used to discriminate between the central and the peripheral effects. The left phrenic nerve was cut and action potentials were recorded from the central end. The contractions of the right, innervated half of the diaphragm were also recorded. Changes in strength of the muscular contractions which were not accompanied by comparable variations in the central activity were attributed to an action on the neuromuscular junction.

With this method we investigated the effects of two cholinesterase inhibitors on the central control of respiration, their actions on the neuromuscular junction, and the antagonism of compound 217-AO against the respiratory arrest produced by morphine. The compounds 217-AO and 217-MI (Phospholine) were used; these are two potent irreversible anticholinesterases recently investigated by Koelle and Steiner (1956). The only chemical difference between them is that 217-AO contains a tertiary nitrogen atom and is therefore much more soluble in lipoids then Phospholine, which has a quarternary nitrogen atom. Koelle and Steiner gave lethal doses of both substances to rabbits and found that the cholinesterase activity of the brain was normal after Phospholine had been injected, whereas it was reduced to an average of 9 per cent of its normal value by 217-AO.

This difference in distribution made the two compounds particularly suitable for the present study of the central and peripheral effects of cholinesterase inhibitors on respiration. Central actions of irreversible cholinesterase inhibitors are known to be accompanied by a considerable reduction in cholinesterase activity. The findings of Koelle and Steiner therefore exclude the possibility that the effects of Phospholine are of central origin. In unpublished experiments it was found that Phospholine is 2.5 to 3 times more active than 217-AO in potentiating the fall in blood pressure on electrical stimulation of the vagus nerve. A difference in action between doses of both compounds which are equipotent peripherally must be attributed to the central effects of 217-AO.

MATERIALS AND METHODS. The experiments were done on rats anesthetized with urethane. The blood pressure in the carotid artery was measured with a membrane manometer and was recorded on a kymograph. All injections were given into a jugular vein through a polyethylene tube. Both vagi were cut to prevent afferent impulses from the heart and the lungs from obscuring any central effects produced by the anti-

[1] This investigation was supported in part by the Deutsche Forschungsgemeinschaft.

[2] Present address: Frankfurt/M, Pharmakologisches Institut der Universität, Ludwig Rehnstr. 14, Germany.

[3] Present address: Innsbruck, Pharmakologisches Institut der Universität, Peter Mayrstr. 1, Austria.

cholinesterases and to abolish efferent parasympathetic discharges. The diaphragm was split along the midline. A thread was tied to the middle of the right half and connected with a mechano-electrical transducer. Its contractions were recorded isometrically and displayed on a cathode ray oscilloscope. The animals were artificially ventilated, the minute-volume being so adjusted that spontaneous respiratory movements were present.

The left phrenic nerve was freed in the neck from the surrounding tissues, cut peripherally and placed on electrodes in a warm paraffin bath. The action potentials in the nerve were recorded on the second beam of the oscilloscope. The electrical activity in the phrenic nerve was fed into an electronic integrator in order to facilitate the evaluation of central activity during each breath. The integrator was a simple device where the negative part only of the more or less diphasic action potentials were used to charge a condenser. Across the condenser was a resistance which was adjusted to allow the charge on the condenser to leak away between inspirations. The voltage across the condenser was amplified and displayed on a second cathode ray oscilloscope, the size of the deflection being greater, the greater the electrical activity in the nerve. The contractions of the diaphragm, the action potentials of the phrenic nerve and the excursions of the integrator were photographed simultaneously on the same film. The details of the experimental setup have been described by Job and Schaumann (1958).

At the beginning of each experiment, the animals were first hyperventilated to abolish respiratory activity and then underventilated until respiration came back and slowly increased in intensity. The relationship between the excursions of the integrator and those of the transducer was thus established; it was linear except for severe degrees of hyperpnea, when the latter increased somewhat more slowly (Job and Schaumann, 1958, fig. 2). In those preceding experiments it was found unsuitable to assay the action of anticholinesterases on neuromuscular transmission by recording the contractions of the diaphragm on indirect electrical stimulation. The result depended on the frequency of stimulation rather than on the dose of the cholinesterase inhibitor given. This method has therefore not been used during the present investigations.

The compounds used were 2-diethoxyphosphinylthioethyldimethylamine acid oxalate (217-AO), 2-diethoxyphosphinylthioethyltrimethyl ammonium iodide (217-MI, Phospholine)[4], morphine hydrochloride, atropine sulfate and phentolamine (Regitine).

RESULTS. Phospholine was given in nine experiments. Although it does not pass the blood-brain barrier, there was usually a slight enhancement of central activity as measured by the phrenic nerve discharges after 0.05 mgm./kgm. of Phospholine, and this was accompanied by an increase in the contractions of the diaphragm (fig. 1b). For one reason already mentioned, this effect of Phospholine cannot have been brought about by a direct central action. Besides, the most prominent central effect of anticholinesterases in the rat is a large rise in blood pressure (Dirnhuber and Cullumbine, 1955; Hornykiewicz and Kobinger, 1956; Schaumann, 1958a). However, the blood pressure remained constant at 75 mm. Hg while the tracings illustrated in fig. 1 were taken. The increase in central activity may have been due to peripheral effects like bronchorrhea or a stimulation of the carotid bodies. When the total dose of Phospholine amounted to 0.1 mgm./kgm., there was still an increase in the central respiratory activity (fig. 1c), but the contractions of the diaphragm were greatly diminished. It is clear that the higher dose of Phospholine inhibited neuromuscular transmission. A comparison of the small contractions in fig. 1c with the normal contractions in fig. 1a shows that in the treated animals there was, after a normal onset of the contractions, a more rapid decline in their strength. This sequence of events is explained by a Wedensky type of block which is brought about by accumulation of acetylcholine at the motor end plates during the contractions (Douglas and Paton, 1954). The onset of neuromuscular inhibition was accompanied by muscular fibrillation and fasciculation which caused the unsteady base line of the mechanical records seen at the end of fig. 1b.

Fig. 2 shows the effects of a single high dose of Phospholine. Within 10 seconds, 2 mgm./kgm. of Phospholine almost completely blocked the neuromuscular transmission. While the records of fig. 2a were taken, the blood pressure rose from 85 to 125 mm. Hg. This suggests that the

[4] The compounds 217-AO and 217-MI were kindly provided by Dr. Robert A. Lehman, Campbell Pharmaceutical Co., New York 1, N. Y.

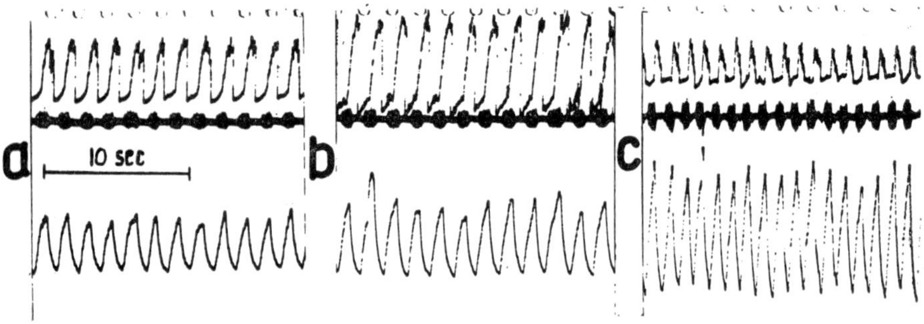

FIG. 1. Inhibition of neuromuscular transmission by Phospholine.

Rat, 220 gm. In this and the following figures the tracings from above down are: 1) contractions of the innervated half of the diaphragm, 2) action potentials of the phrenic nerve, 3) integrated action potentials. Record (a) is the control. Records (b) and (c) were each taken 4 minutes after injection of successive doses of 0.05 mgm./kgm. of Phospholine.

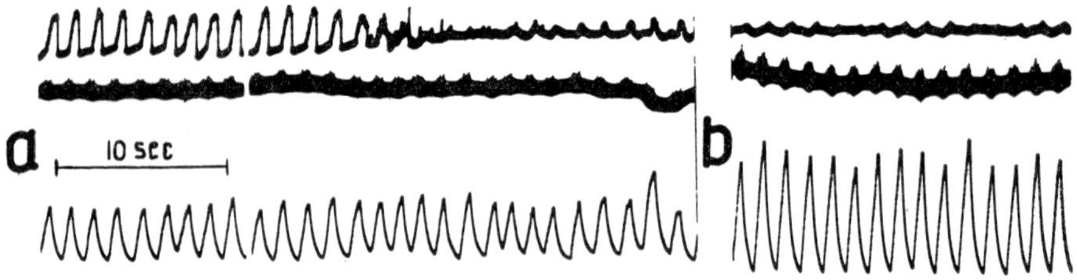

FIG. 2. Effects of a large dose of Phospholine.

Rat, 300 gm. Tracings as in fig. 1. The interruption of the tracings in (a) indicates the injection of 2 mgm./kgm. of Phospholine. Record (b) was taken 7 minutes later.

enormous dose given had a weak central action, although at first there was no change in the central respiratory activity. After seven minutes there was an increase in the electrical activity of the phrenic nerve. But this increase, shown in fig. 2b, is unlikely to have been caused by a central effect of Phospholine, because the blood pressure had by then fallen to 30 mm. Hg—and such a fall in blood pressure by itself usually produced similar changes in respiration.

According to the results demonstrated in fig. 1 and 2, Phospholine paralyzed respiration only by blocking the neuromuscular junction. This agrees with the finding of Koelle and Steiner (1956) that only the intracarotid injection of a large dose of Phospholine produced a significant inhibition of the brain cholinesterase.

The compound 217-AO (twelve experiments) had quite different effects both on blood pressure and respiration. A dose of 0.2 mgm./kgm. raised the blood pressure by 90 to 130 mm. Hg, *i.e.* to values of about 200 mm. Hg. This was undesirable in experiments where the respiratory effects were to be analyzed, because alterations in cerebral blood flow, together with the stimulation of the baroreceptors in the carotid sinus might have interfered with the evaluation of the action of 217-AO on the central control of respiration. Therefore in some of the experiments the animals were premedicated with phentolamine, an adrenolytic agent which prevented the rise in blood pressure caused by eserine (Schaumann, 1958a) and 217-AO without interfering with their effects on respiration. In animals treated with phentolamine, the injection of 0.1 mgm./kgm. of 217-AO was followed by a slight increase in the frequency of respiration and in central activity as measured by the integrator (fig. 3b). Since this stimulation also occurred after doses of Phospholine which do not penetrate into the central nervous system, it is unlikely that it is due to a direct central action. After 0.2 mgm./kgm. (fig. 3c) and particularly after 0.3 mgm./kgm. of 217-AO (fig. 3d), there was a considerable decrease in central activity. Usually there was also a decrease in the frequency of respiration. In experiments where the animals had not been pretreated with phentolamine, the same inhibition was observed during the rise in blood pressure following the injection of 217-AO. All the evidence thus suggests that it is a specific central action of this substance.

It is noteworthy that in fig. 3c and d the con-

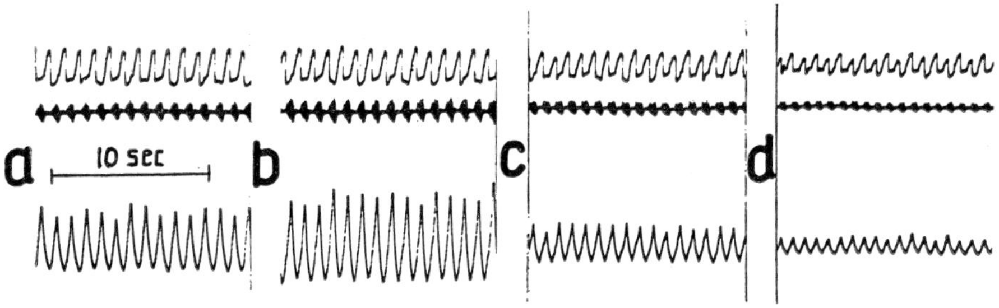

FIG. 3. Central inhibition of respiration by 217-AO.
Rat, 300 gm. Tracings as in fig. 1. Phentolamine (3.5 mgm./kgm.) had been given 10 minutes before the first injection of 217-AO. (a) Control after injection of phentolamine. Records (b), (c) and (d) were taken 3 minutes after the injection of 0.1 mgm./kgm. of 217-AO each.

tractions of the diaphragm were stronger than would be expected from the decrease in central activity. Obviously, there was no inhibition of neuromuscular transmission as after injection of Phospholine. This is the more remarkable since 217-AO would be expected to affect neuromuscular transmission in the same way as this substance; the doses of 0.1 mgm./kgm. of Phospholine and 0.3 mgm./kgm. of 217-AO used in the experiments illustrated by fig. 1 and 3 are roughly equipotent in regard to their peripheral effects. The next two figures will bring further evidence on this point.

In previous experiments it was found that eserine restarted respiration when it had been arrested by morphine (Schaumann, 1958a). The same result was obtained with 217-AO. In the experiment of fig. 4 respiration was stopped by giving 25 mgm./kgm. of morphine (fig. 4a). A subsequent injection of 217-AO slowly brought back the central respiratory activity (fig. 4b), as can be seen from the reappearance of the discharges in the phrenic nerve and of the diaphragmatic contractions. Thus respiration was here stimulated by 217-AO, although the dose given in this and other similar experiments would have produced a strong central inhibition in a normal animal.

In the experiment of fig. 4, phentolamine had been given to prevent the rise in blood pressure otherwise produced by 217-AO. Without previous administration of phentolamine, the same antagonism between 217-AO and morphine was observed. Respiration then came back shortly after the blood pressure started rising.

A comparison of fig. 4b with the control record before the injection of morphine shows that after 217-AO the contractions of the diaphragm soon exceeded their previous strength, although at first the central activity remained comparatively low.

So far, only central effects of 217-AO have been mentioned: the rise in blood pressure, the central inhibition of normal respiration and the excitation after respiratory arrest by morphine. However, when these central effects were prevented by a previous injection of atropine, 217-AO acted like Phospholine. This is illustrated in fig. 5. After 5 mgm./kgm. of atropine, a dose of 0.2 mgm./kgm. of 217-AO caused a slight increase in central activity, and at the same time reduced the contractions of the diaphragm to less than 20 per cent of their control value. This corresponds to the effect of Phospholine shown in fig. 1. Without atropine, the same dose of 217-AO would have inhibited the respiratory center without causing a visible inhibition of neuromuscular transmission.

DISCUSSION. The respiratory failure produced by cholinesterase inhibitors is brought about mainly by their action on the central nervous system, but they also act by blocking the neuromuscular junction (Douglas and Matthews, 1952; de Candole *et al.*, 1953). de Candole *et al.* found that the respective importance of central and peripheral actions varies with the animal species and with the cholinesterase inhibitor used.

The present experiments emphasize the significance of the physico-chemical properties of the anticholinesterases. Phospholine, which is very poorly soluble in lipoids, inhibited neuromuscular transmission without showing much central effect. The compound 217-AO, on the other hand, has an oil-water partition coefficient which is more than two hundred times higher, and it easily passes the blood-brain barrier (Koelle and Steiner, 1956). Thus it has the same peripheral actions as

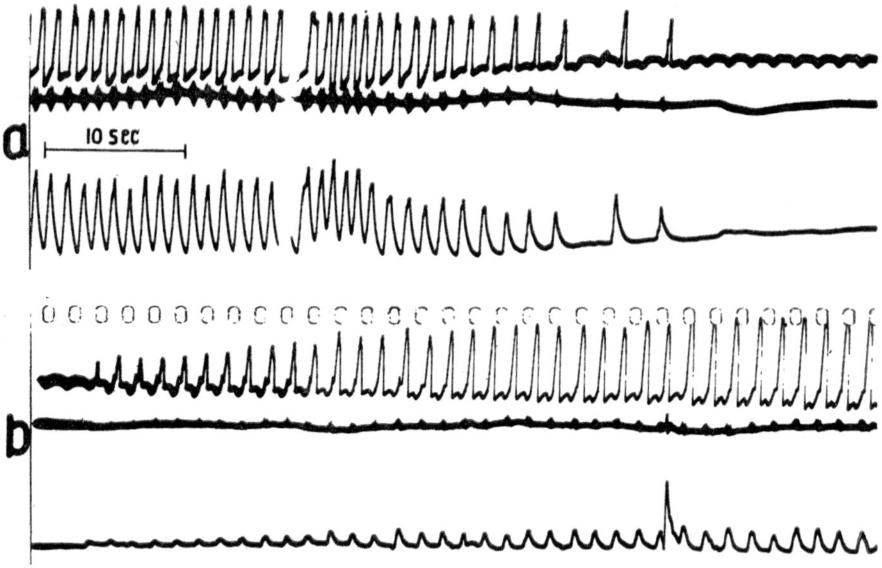

FIG. 4. Antagonism by 217-AO of respiratory arrest caused by morphine.
Rat, 200 gm. Tracings as in fig. 1. Five mgm./kgm. of phentolamine had been given 8 minutes before morphine. In (a) 25 mgm./kgm. of morphine were given during the interruption of the tracings. Record (b) was taken 3 minutes after the injection of 0.3 mgm./kgm. of 217-AO.

Phospholine, but in addition moderate doses affect the central mechanisms controlling respiration.

With 217-AO, two quite different effects were observed on neuromuscular transmission. When the respiration had been stopped by morphine, the contractions of the diaphragm were restored to normal by 217-AO, although the central activity was low. In other words, there was a potentiation of the nervous activity at the neuromuscular junction. Fig. 3 pointed in the same direction: 217-AO reduced the central activity much more than it diminished the strength of the diaphragmatic contractions. On the other hand, when atropine was given and the respiratory center was protected to some extent from the effect of the anticholinesterase, 217-AO strongly inhibited neuromuscular transmission. This seeming discrepancy is explained by the mechanism of the neuromuscular block which occurs after inactivation of the cholinesterase. The acetylcholine liberated from the motor nerve endings is only slowly destroyed. During *weak activity* of the nerve, the accumulation of suboptimal quantities of acetylcholine *potentiates* neuromuscular transmission; during *strong activity* of the nerve, the accumulation of paralyzing amounts of acetylcholine *inhibits* it. This confirms the conclusions drawn by Douglas and Matthews (1952) from their experiments with TEPP. Obviously, the neuromuscular block depends not only on the dose of the cholinesterase inhibitor, but also on the nervous activity. In other words, the more active the respiratory center is, the more favorable will be the conditions for a Wedensky inhibition at the neuromuscular junction. This may lead to a vicious circle, because the impaired respiratory movements will reduce ventilation which in turns stimulates the respiratory center by accumulation of carbon dioxide.

This interrelation between central activity and neuromusuclar block should be taken into account in the treatment of anticholinesterase poisoning. If atropine prevents or abolishes a central respiratory paralysis, a neuromuscular block may still occur and may cause a failure of respiration. This may partly explain why atropine has little effect against lethal doses of various anticholinesterases (Askew, 1957; Erdmann and Lendle, 1957; Hobbiger, 1957). Relief of the neuromuscular block, which can be achieved with pyridine-2-aldoxime-methiodide (PAM), is by itself also ineffective in restoring respiration (Bethe *et al.*, 1957; Brown *et al.*, 1957), because PAM does not penetrate into the central nervous system and therefore does not reactivate the cholinesterase of the brain (Kewitz and Nachmansohn, 1957). A

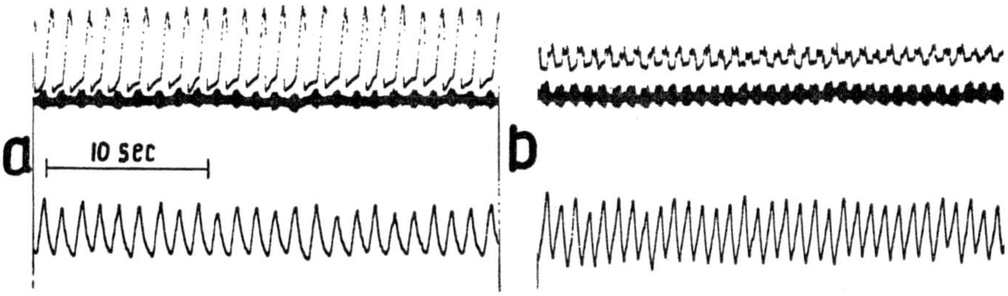

FIG. 5. Inhibition of neuromuscular transmission by 217-AO.
Rat, 250 gm. Tracings as in fig. 1. Five mgm./kgm. of atropine had been given 5 minutes before 217-AO. (a) Control after atropine, (b) 3 minutes after the injection of 0.2 mgm./kgm. of 217-AO.

combination of atropine and PAM, however, restores respiration very effectively (Brown *et al.*, 1957) and potentiates the protection against lethal doses of alkylphosphates offered by either drug alone (Askew, 1957; Hobbiger, 1957).

As in previous experiments with eserine, 217-AO antagonized the respiratory arrest caused by morphine, although it inhibited respiration centrally if given alone. An explanation of this phenomenon has been offered by Schaumann (1958a) and shall be briefly summarized here. On the guinea pig ileum, morphine prevents contractions produced by cholinesterase inhibitors by reducing the release of acetylcholine from the intestinal wall (Paton, 1957; Schaumann, 1957, 1958b). The action of morphine on the guinea pig intestine and on respiration are specific for all potent analgesics. It is suggested that morphine stops respiration in the same way, namely by reducing the liberation of acetylcholine, in this case at cholinergic synapses in the central nervous system; and that eserine and 217-AO antagonize this paralysis by preserving the reduced amounts of acetylcholine liberated in the presence of morphine.

Morphine and other potent analgesics have repeatedly been reported to inhibit cholinesterase (for ref. see Schaumann, 1958a). However, this effect is not related to the analgesic potencies of the various compounds studied (Knoll, Komlós and Porszasz, 1951; Randall *et al.*, 1953; Tonini, 1955; Young *et al.*, 1955; Herken, Maibauer and Müller, 1957) and cannot be regarded as specific for the action of these drugs. In the normal rat, morphine causes a fall in blood pressure, in the vagotomized rat a small rise (Evans, Nasmyth and Stewart, 1952) which is insignificant compared to the dramatic central effect of cholinesterase inhibitors (Schaumann, 1958a). The respiratory arrest produced by morphine is certainly not due to an inhibition of cholinesterase.

SUMMARY

In experiments on rats, the action potentials in the left cut phrenic nerve and the contractions of the innervated right half of the diaphragm were recorded. With this method we investigated the effects of Phospholine and compound 217-AO, two anticholinesterases of similar chemical structure, on the central control of respiration and on the neuromuscular junction.

Low doses of Phospholine, which do not penetrate into the central nervous system, inhibited the neuromuscular transmission, whereas even large amounts had no central effect on respiration.

Because of its better lipoid solubility, 217-AO easily penetrates the blood-brain barrier. It inhibited respiration by a direct central action without visibly impairing neuromuscular transmission. However, neuromuscular block was observed when the central effects were prevented by atropine.

It was found that when the activity of the motor nerve was weak, the cholinesterase inhibitors enhanced neuromuscular transmission; but when nervous activity was strong, they blocked it.

Although 217-AO inhibited the respiratory center, it antagonized the respiratory arrest produced by morphine.

ACKNOWLEDGMENT. We wish to thank Drs. J. M. Ritchie and W. W. Douglas for their help in preparing the manuscript and in reading the proofs.

REFERENCES

ASKEW, B. M.: Brit. J. Pharmacol., **12:** 340, 1957.
BETHE, K., ERDMANN, W. D., LENDLE, L., AND

SCHMIDT, G.: Arch. exper. Path. u. Pharmakol., **231:** 3, 1957.
BROWN, R. V., KUNKEL, A. M., SOMERS, L. M., AND WILLS, J. H.: THIS JOURNAL, **120:** 276, 1957.
DE CANDOLE, C. A., DOUGLAS, W. W., LOVATT EVANS, C., HOLMES, R., SPENCER, K. E. V., TORRANCE, R. W., AND WILSON, K. M.: Brit. J. Pharmacol., **8:** 466, 1953.
DIRNHUBER, P., AND CULLUMBINE, H.: Brit. J. Pharmacol., **10:** 12, 1955.
DOUGLAS, W. W., AND MATTHEWS, P. B. C.: J. Physiol., **116:** 202, 1952.
DOUGLAS, W. W., AND PATON, W. D. M.: J. Physiol., **124:** 325, 1954.
ERDMANN, W. D., AND LENDLE, L.: Arch. exper. Path. u. Pharmakol., **230:** 208, 1957.
EVANS, A. G. J., NASMYTH, P. A., AND STEWART, H. C.: Brit. J. Pharmacol., **7:** 542, 1952.
HERKEN, H., MAIBAUER, D., AND MÜLLER, S.: Arch. exper. Path. u. Pharmakol., **230:** 313, 1957.
HOBBIGER, F.: Brit. J. Pharmacol., **12:** 438, 1957.
HORNYKIEWICZ, O., AND KOBINGER, W.: Arch. exper. Path. u. Pharmakol., **228:** 493, 1956.
JOB, C., AND SCHAUMANN, W.: Arch. exper. Path. u. Pharmakol., **233:** 255, 1958.
KEWITZ, H., AND NACHMANSOHN, D.: Arch. Biochem., **66:** 271, 1957.
KNOLL, J., KOMLÓS, E., AND PORSZASZ, J.: Acta physiol. Hung., **2:** 479, 1951.
KOELLE, G. B., AND STEINER, E. C.: THIS JOURNAL, **118:** 420, 1956.
PATON, W. D. M.: Brit. J. Pharmacol., **12:** 119, 1957.
RANDALL, L. O., KRUGER, J., CONROY, C., KAPPELL, B., AND BENSON, W. M.: Arch. exper. Path. u. Pharmakol., **220:** 26, 1953.
SCHAUMANN, W.: Brit. J. Pharmacol., **12:** 115, 1957.
SCHAUMANN, W.: Arch. exper. Path. u. Pharmakol., **233:** 98, 1958a.
SCHAUMANN, W.: Arch. exper. Path. u. Pharmakol., **233:** 112, 1958b.
TONINI, G.: Boll. Soc. ital. Biol. sper., **31:** 771, 1955.
YOUNG, D. C., VANDER PLOEG, R. A., FEATHERSTONE, R. M., AND GROSS, E. G.: THIS JOURNAL, **114:** 33, 1955.

8023

AN INVESTIGATION OF THE STRUCTURE-ACTIVITY CORRELATIONS WITHIN A SERIES OF AMBENONIUM ANALOGS

A. M. LANDS, J. O. HOPPE, AARON ARNOLD AND FRED. K. KIRCHNER

Pharmacology Section, Sterling-Winthrop Research Institute, Rensselaer, New York

Received for publication January 4, 1958

Previous communications have described the anticholinesterase and pharmacologic activities of ambenonium (Mytelase, Win 8077) and some of its analogs (Arnold *et al.*, 1954; Lands *et al.*, 1955; Karczmar, 1957; Lands *et al.*, 1957). These compounds have interesting effects on the excitability of voluntary muscle and the autonomic nervous system. In an extension of these investigations, we have examined a large number of ambenonium analogs in an effort to obtain more knowledge of the nature of the acetylcholine-sensitive receptors and the structural optima of synthetic compounds which react with them. The results obtained are described in this communication.

METHODS. Acetylcholinesterase (AChE) inhibition by various compounds was determined by the electrometric titration procedure of Michel (1949) as modified by Arnold, Soria and Kirchner (1954). With this modified method, the hemolyzed red cells were added in 0.5-ml. volume rather than 1.0 ml., as originally suggested. The point of 50 per cent inhibition was estimated by plotting on log-probit paper the amount of inhibitor used against the amount of inhibition observed.

Acute toxicity was determined in male Swiss (Webster strain) albino mice weighing 22 ± 2 gm. by the method previously described (Hoppe *et al.*, 1949). The 24-hour $LD_{50} \pm$ s.e. was calculated for all determinations.

Motor paralysis has been determined by the mouse inclined screen procedure (Hoppe, 1950). In the potentiation studies, neostigmine was administered subcutaneously at a dose of 0.1 mgm./kgm. (ED_{50} is 0.28 ± 0.03 mgm./kgm.) ten minutes before administration of the paralyzing drug (Hoppe *et al.*, 1955). Groups of ten mice were used for each dose level; four or more doses were used for the determination of the ED_{50} value.

Antidotal action against tetraethylpyrophosphate (TEPP) toxicity was determined in male Swiss mice by the method described by Lewis *et al.* (1955). Two LD_{50} doses of TEPP were injected intraperitoneally 15 minutes after medication with the test compound in combination with atropine sulfate, 10 mgm./kgm. Ten mice were used at each dose level of antidote compound, as in the toxicity tests previously described. The amount of antidote that would reduce 2 LD_{50}'s to an LD_{50} was designated the PD_{50}.

The measurement of molecular lengths was made with Fisher-Hirschfelder-Taylor models. With these models, the sizes, shapes, faces and angles are based on the published results of Pauling and Brockway (1937). All measurements were made in the maximally extended position, one centimeter in the model representing one angstrom unit in the natural atom. Schueler (1953a, b) has attempted to develop formulae whereby the mean square distances between charged portions of simple molecules can be computed. However, this method does not seem to be suitable for application in the present instance. The *bis*-quaternary molecules used in this investigation include a fairly rigid dicarbonyl group and contain quaternary ammonium groups which provide hindrance to free mobility. Because of the manifold difficulties of determining the exact configuration, either in solution or upon near approach to the receptor surface, we have arbitrarily chosen to use the maximally extended lengths, measured as indicated above.

RESULTS. *1. The effect of ortho-substitution in the benzyl group.* Substitution in the benzene ring at the *ortho* position increases the inhibitory action against AChE (table 1). This is greatest when the substituent is bromine (No. 3) and least with the fluoro (No. 2) and methoxy (No. 5) analogs. It is interesting to note that chloro substitution in one ammonium center (No. 6) provides a compound with inhibitory action less than that of the *bis*-2-chlorobenzyl compound (ambenonium) but more potent than the corresponding *bis*-benzyl analog (No. 1), in which there is no chloro substitution.

Voluntary muscle paralysis (mouse, inclined screen) is greatest with those compounds most

TABLE 1

The pharmacologic actions of a series of N,N'-bis(diethylaminoethyl)-oxamide-bis-benzylhalide quaternary salts

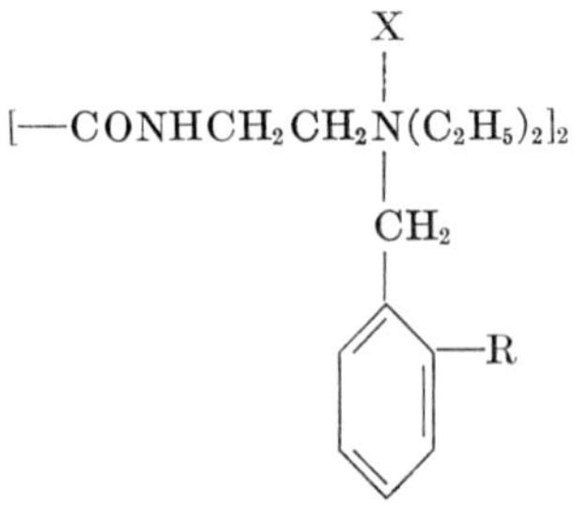

Compound No.	Structure R	Structure X	a* Muscle Relaxation ED_{50}	b† Toxicity LD_{50}	Ratio a/b	c‡ Neostigmine Potentiation ED_{50}	d§ Synergism with Neostig.	e¶ TEPP Antag. PD_{50}	f‖ Anticholinesterase Activity (Neostig. = 100)
			mgm./kgm.	*mgm./kgm.*		*mgm./kgm.*		*mgm./kgm.*	
1	H	Cl	6.4 ± 0.45	19.4 ± 1.6	0.33	0.64 ± 0.23	6.4	0.54 ± 0.15	3.6
2	F	I	3.7 ± 0.3	18.8 ± 1.3	0.18	0.18 ± 0.03	13.7	0.315 ± 0.13	5.1
Ambenonium	Cl	Cl	0.13 ± 0.01	5.0 ± 0.4	0.026	0.023 ± 0.002	3.6	0.01 ± 0.00	580.0
3	Br	Br	0.08 ± 0.02	5.0 ± 0.8	0.016	0.022 ± 0.001	3.2	0.025 ± 0.005	4100.0
4	I	Br	0.12 ± 0.02	4.6 ± 0.4	0.026	0.025 ± 0.004	3.0	none††	770.0
5	OCH_3	Cl	2.3 ± 0.1	6.5 ± 0.2	0.35	1.1 ± 0.06	1.3	0.415 ± 0.09	14.0
6	Cl/2**	Cl	0.31 ± 0.04	7.2 ± 0.6	0.044	0.04 ± 0.006	5.0	0.028 ± 0.01	430.0
7	CH_3	Br	2.4 ± 0.35	8.8 ± 0.4	0.27	0.17 ± 0.03	9.0	0.160 ± 0.04	80.0
Neostigmine			0.28 ± 0.03	0.55 ± 0.06	0.51	0.14 ± 0.03	1.3	none	100.0
Eserine			0.73 ± 0.06	0.74 ± 0.09	1.0	0.30 ± 0.03	1.5	0.27	58.0
Edrophonium			22.0 ± 3.0	52.0 ± 4.0	0.42	7.9 ± 0.37	1.8	7.6 ± 1.7	<1.0
d-Tubocurarine			0.37 ± 0.02	0.6 ± 0.02	0.61	0.67 ± 0.05	0.4	0.29	<1.0

* Mouse, inclined screen, s.c. ED_{50} ± s.e.

† Mouse, s.c. LD_{50} ± s.e.

†† Mouse, inclined screen, s.c. ED_{50} ± s.e. following the s.c. administration of 0.1 mgm./kgm. of neostigmine 10 minutes before the paralyzing drug.

§ Increase in potency beyond that expected, calculated on the assumption that the Win compound acts additively with neostigmine. Example, ambenonium:

$$\frac{\text{Win } ED_{50}}{\text{pretreat. } ED_{50} \times 100/64} = \frac{0.13}{0.023 \times 100/64} = 3.6.$$

¶ Dose of drug protecting 50 per cent of treated mice (PD_{50} ± s.e.) against the lethal action of tetraethylpyrophosphate.

‖ Anticholinesterase activity *in vitro* (Arnold *et al.*, 1954) expressed in terms of neostigmine activity.

** Chloro-substitution of one benzene ring only.

†† No dose-response relationship. A 30 to 40 per cent effect at doses of 0.01 to 0.2 mgm./kgm.

effective in blocking AChE activity (table 1). A comparison of the subcutaneous ED_{50} with the corresponding LD_{50} doses (column a *vs.* column b) shows that the paralyzing action of the most potent compounds is greater than would have been expected from a comparison with neostigmine or *d*-tubocurarine with which are obtained ratios of 0.5 to 0.6. Ratios of this order are obtained with many curare-like agents and must represent a direct action of the agent at the receptor surface (Chase *et al.*, 1944; Marsh, 1951; Hoppe 1951). The more potent oxamides may paralyze through some indirect mechanism. Pretreatment of the mice with small amounts (0.1

mgm./kgm. s.c.) of neostigmine can markedly reduce the amount of certain compounds required for voluntary muscle paralysis (Hoppe *et al.*, 1955; Lands *et al.*, 1957). In the present experiments, ambenonium (*ortho*-chloro compound) and the bromo- and iodo- analogs are less potentiated than the weaker anticholinesterase compounds (No. 1, 2 and 7). It seems probable from the recent findings of Koelle (1957a, b) that the figures in column f (table 1) do not represent the true AChE inhibitory potency of these compounds. The figures in column c may represent the additional inhibitory action required to provide a critical concentration of ACh at the post junctional membrane. This would indicate that the relative activity of ambenonium and No. 1 is 1:28 rather than 1:161 as indicated by the AChE values given in column f.

Protection of atropinized mice against the toxic actions of tetraethylpyrophosphate (TEPP) are shown also in table 1 (column e). Although the potent AChE inhibitors, ambenonium and No. 3 and 6, are very effective antagonists of TEPP, this action is weak in the case of No. 4 in which AChE inhibitory action exceeds that of ambenonium. Neostigmine does not protect the mouse against TEPP although *d*-tubocurarine is effective. In general, the most effective oxamide antagonists of TEPP were also most effective in causing voluntary muscle paralysis and were most potentiated by neostigmine pretreatment.

The position as well as the number of the chlorine substituents may influence activity (table 2). The *ortho*-chloro compound (ambenonium) is distinctly more potent than the *meta*-chloro (No. 8), the *para*-chloro (No. 9) or the *meta, para*-dichloro (No. 10) analogs.

2. The effect of distance between ammonium centers. Results obtained with a series of ambenonium homologs in which the distance between the terminal N centers has been varied between about 11.5 Å and 20 Å are shown in table 3. Lengthening the chain by adding methylene groups between the ammonium centers and the amido groups provides compounds of high AChE inhibiting potency at connecting lengths of 11.5 Å, and at

TABLE 2

The effect on pharmacologic action resulting from substitution in the benzene ring of N,N′-bis(2-diethylaminoethyl)oxamide-bis-benzylhalide

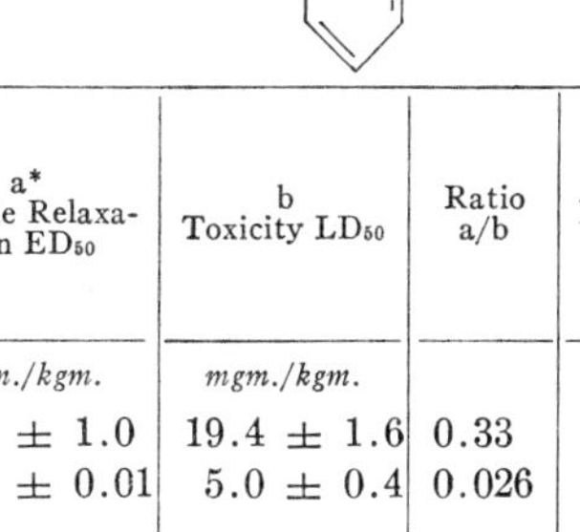

Compound No.	Structure R	Structure X	a* Muscle Relaxation ED_{50}	b Toxicity LD_{50}	Ratio a/b	c Neostigmine Potentiation ED_{50}	d Synergism	f Anticholinesterase Activity (Neostig. = 100)
			mgm./kgm.	*mgm./kgm.*		*mgm./kgm.*		
1	H	Cl	6.4 ± 1.0	19.4 ± 1.6	0.33	0.64 ± 0.23	6.4	3.6
Ambenonium	2-Cl	Cl	0.13 ± 0.01	5.0 ± 0.4	0.026	0.023 ± 0.002	3.6	580.0
8	3-Cl	Cl	3.6 ± 0.4	8.2 ± 0.8	0.44			55.0
9	4-Cl	Cl	4.2 ± 0.5	16.0 ± 1.1	0.38	2.0 ± 0.25	1.3	14.0
10	3,4-diCl	Cl	10.0 ± 3.0	22.4 ± 1.3	0.45	9.5 ± 0.6	0.67	2.4
5	2-methoxy	Cl	2.3 ± 0.1	6.5 ± 0.2	0.35	1.1 ± 0.6	1.3	14.0
11	4-methoxy	Cl	4.0 ± 0.34	8.7 ± 0.7	0.46	4.0 ± 0.3	0.64	<0.1

* See footnotes, table 1.

TABLE 3

The effect on pharmacologic action resulting from changes in length of the hydrocarbon chain between the nitrogen centers of N,N'-bis(2-diethylaminoethyl)oxamide-bis(2-chloro)-benzylhalide

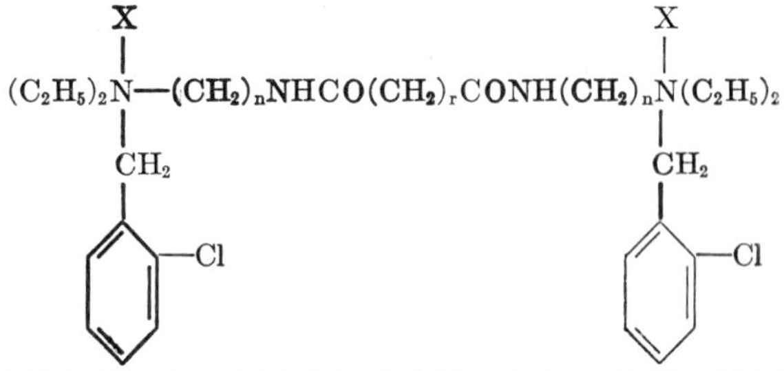

Compound No.	Structure			Approx. N - N Distance	a* Muscle relaxation ED_{50}	b Toxicity LD_{50}	Ratio a/b	c Neostigmine Potentiation ED_{50}	d Synergism	f Anticholinesterase Activity (Neostig. = 100)
	n	r	X							
				Å	*mgm./kgm.*	*mgm./kgm.*		*mgm./kgm.*		
Ambenonium	2	0	Cl	11.5–12.0	0.13 ± 0.01	5.0 ± 0.4	0.026	0.023 ± 0.002	3.6	580.0
12	2	2	Cl	14.1–14.6	2.7 ± 0.8	6.1 ± 0.5	0.44	0.64 ± 0.11	2.7	23.0
13	2	4	Cl	16.7–17.2	2.0 ± 0.1	6.0 ± 0.7	0.33	1.57 ± 0.15	0.8	9.0
14	2	6	Cl	19.3–19.8	1.8 ± 0.2	6.4 ± 0.4	0.28	0.46 ± 0.11	2.5	53.0
15	3	0	Cl	14.1–14.6	1.7 ± 0.12	7.2 ± 0.5	0.27	0.27 ± 0.08	4.0	20.0
16	4	0	I	16.7–17.2	0.22 ± 0.01	2.05 ± 0.14	0.01	0.025 ± 0.005	5.6	340.0
17	5	0	I	19.3–19.8	0.12 ± 0.01	2.1 ± 0.2	0.057	0.031 ± 0.003	2.5	650.0

* See footnotes, table 1.

17 to 20 Å, (ambenonium, No. 16 and 17). The least effective compound in this structural group has a distance of about 14 Å (No. 15). If the molecule is lengthened by introducing methylene groups between the carbonyls, activity is diminished (No. 12, 13 and 14) suggesting that both carbonyl groups play some role, probably by serving to attach the molecule to the active site.

The most potent AChE inhibitors are most effective in causing voluntary muscle paralysis in the mouse. As discussed above, the relationship to neostigmine potentiation is less obvious. The potent AChE inhibitor (No. 17) shows a synergism ratio (2.5, table 3, column d) not greater than that for the much less effective compounds No. 12 (2.7) and No. 14 (2.5).

The subcutaneous LD_{50} dose does not appear to be related closely to either the AChE inhibitory potency or the dose causing mice to drop from the inclined screen in the test for muscle paralysis.

3. Effects resulting from changes in the structure of the ammonium group. Changes in the structure of the groups substituted in the ammonium centers, in the presence of the *ortho*-chlorobenzyl quaternizing group, can bring about significant alterations in potency (table 4). Ethyl substitution provides the most effective AChE inhibition. It is particularly interesting to note that methyl substitution is not favorable for this action. Replacement of the *ortho*-chlorobenzyl group by methyl abolishes this characteristic effect on AChE. Thus, N,N'-*bis*(3-diethylaminopropyl)-oxamide-*bis*(methobromide) has little or no inhibitory action on AChE, produces paralysis (inclined screen) in mice only at large doses (ED_{50} 7.0 ± 0.5 mgm./kgm., s.c.) and has a corresponding low toxicity (LD_{50} 30 mgm./kgm., s.c.). This should be compared with compound No. 15 which is a potent AChE inhibitor (20 per cent neostigmine) but with comparatively low paralyzing and toxic actions. The ED_{50}/LD_{50} ratio is about 0.25 for each.

These relatively weak inhibitors of AChE cause muscle paralysis (inclined screen) in the mouse at about one-fourth to one-half of the toxic

TABLE 4

The effect of pharmacologic action resulting from changes in the substitutions in the nitrogen center of ambenonium analogs

A.

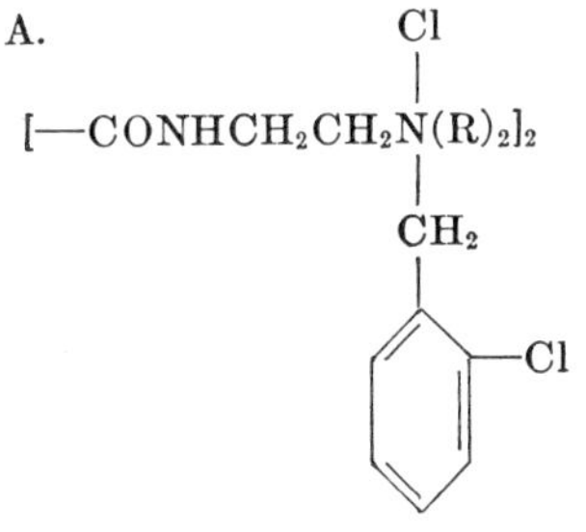

B.

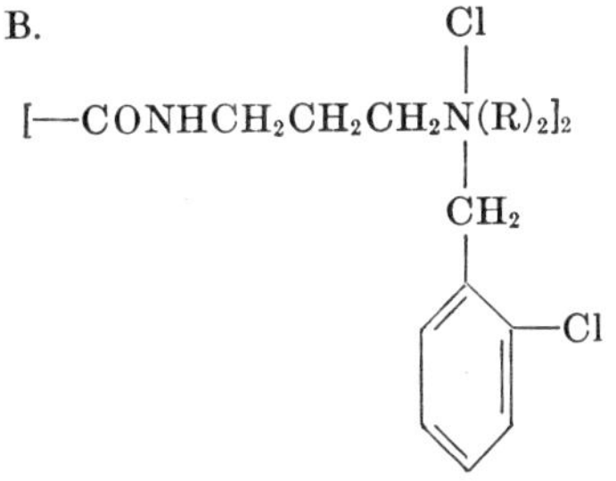

Compound No.	Structure R	a* Muscle Relaxation ED_{50}	b Toxicity LD_{50}	Ratio a/b	Acetylcholinesterase Activity (Neostig. = 100)
		mgm./kgm.	*mgm./kgm.*		
A.					
Ambenonium	ethyl	0.13 ± 0.01	5.0 ± 0.4	0.026	580
18	methyl	4.5 ± 0.2	8.15 ± 0.3	0.55	3
19	propyl	2.6 ± 0.1	4.8 ± 0.13	0.54	17
20	pyrrolidyl	2.2 ± 0.1	4.2 ± 0.3	0.52	8
21	piperidyl	3.0 ± 0.2	6.4 ± 0.5	0.47	4
B.					
15	ethyl	2.0 ± 0.2	7.2 ± 0.5	0.28	20
22	methyl	2.4 ± 0.4	5.5 ± 0.4	0.44	1
23	pyrrolidyl	2.0 ± 0.18	4.1 ± 0.5	0.49	8
24	piperidyl	1.6 ± 0.14	3.4 ± 0.17	0.47	1.5
25	morpholino	11.0 ± 2.0	30 ± 2.5	0.37	7.6

* See footnotes, table 1.

dose (LD_{50}, s.c.). Comparison with the data shown in previous tables indicates that significant differences in this ratio are obtained in most instances when the AChE inhibitory action exceeds that value represented by a neostigmine ratio of about 300 per cent.

4. Effects obtained when the molecule contains only one quaternary group. When only one *ortho*-chlorobenzyl quaternary group is present, there is a distinct reduction in AChE inhibitory potency (table 5). This is illustrated by compound No. 31, an analog of ambenonium, in which only one of the two basic nitrogen atoms is quaternized, *viz.*, as the *ortho*-chlorobenzo chloride. As with the less potent compounds previously described, the motor paralysis which this compound produces is markedly potentiated by neostigmine. Total length is critical, as indicated by the reduction in potency when the distance between the nitrogen centers is increased by one methylene group (No. 32). If the symmetrical ambenonium molecule is reduced to the half molecule (No. 26) activity is greatly reduced.

Discussion. A careful evaluation of the inhibitory action of a homologous series of compounds may provide knowledge with regard to the dimensions of the active site in enzyme systems (Sizer, 1957). In the present series, greatest AChE inhibitory activity was obtained when two of the substituents in the nitrogen center are ethyl and the third is an *ortho*-halogen substituted benzyl group. In this respect, these compounds resemble the benzoquinonium series described by Hoppe *et al.* (1955) in which anti-ChE potency is weak in the triethyl analog but most potent in the corresponding diethyl *ortho*-chloro-benzyl compound. The importance of dissimilar groups substituted in the nitrogen center of various effective AChE inhibitory agents has been pointed out by Blaschko *et al.* (1949).

The *bis*-ammonium structure favors high activity, as is indicated by a comparison of ambenonium, the potent inhibitor, with the half molecule with which little inhibitory action is obtained. The distance between terminal N centers is optimal at about 12 Å and again at 17 Å to 20 Å. This appears to be in agreement with the recent observations of Barlow (1955) who found AChE inhibition at C8 but greatest at C11 to C12 in a series of choline analogs in which the distance between nitrogen centers was increased by inserting methylene groups. He reports that with the corresponding acetates, hydrolysis by AChE occurred most readily when the N-N distance is C8.

In ambenonium and its analogs, the position of the carbonyl group of the potent AChE inhibitors is in the optimal position described by Wilson and Bergmann (1950) and by Fries, Baldridge and their associates (1954a, b, 1955). The oxamide carbonyls cannot be separated (by inserting methylene groups) without a marked loss of potency. This suggests that the diameter of the esteratic site is not less than 3 Å nor larger than about 6 Å. If we measure from the center of this

TABLE 5

The inhibition of AChE by monoquaternary compounds related to ambenonium

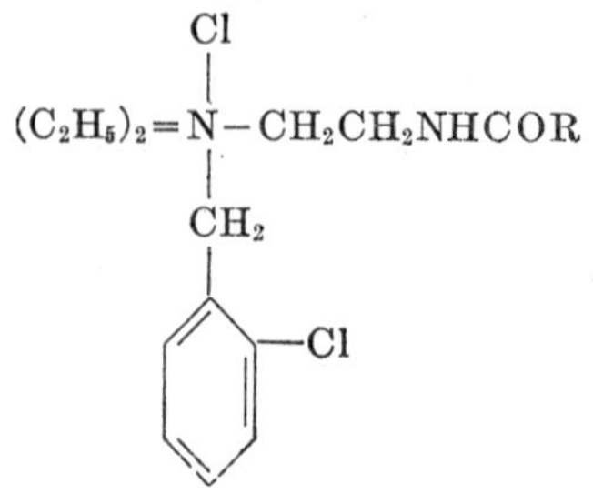

Compound No.	Structure	Approx. N-N Distance	Anticholinesterase Activity (Neostig. = 100)
		Å	
26	H	5.5**	0.2
27	CH_3	7.0	<0.1
28	$COOC_2H_5$	9.5–10.0	6.4
29	$CONHC_3H_7$	10.5–11.0	6.6
30	$(CH_2)_4COOC_2H_5$	16.0–16.5	0.2
31*	$CONH(CH_2)_2N(C_2H_5)_2$	11.5–12.0	31.0
32	$CONH(CH_2)_3N(C_2H_5)_2$	12.8–13.3	6.2

* Mouse s.c. ED_{50}, 4.0 ± 0.6 mgm./kgm.; s.c. LD_{50}, 28.3 ± 1.5 mgm./kgm. Neostigmine potentiation is marked, the activity ratio being 5.7.

** Measured from N centers to CO center. Other compounds measured to center of the terminal group. Compounds No. 31 and 32 are measured between terminal nitrogen centers.

double carbonyl group and make the further assumption that the molecule reacts in a maximally extended state, the position of the cationic heads of potent molecules would indicate anionic receptor sites at approximately 6 Å and 9 Å. The space between these distances is strangely unreactive. It should be noted that the carbonyl-N distance of ACh is 5.5 Å when measured as indicated above. Decamethonium (C10), with an extended length of about 15 Å is not an AChE inhibitor. Model measurements of neostigmine, pyridostigmine and physostigmine also indicate carbonyl-N distances of about 6 Å whereas the potent inhibitor described by Funke *et al.* (1953) and Jacob (1954, 1955) has a half-length of about 9 Å. Possibly, there is a mosaic of active sites so that *bis*-ammonium compounds would bridge over more than one enzyme center. Optimal lengths of these *bis*-compounds could be expected at distances of about 12 Å and 18 Å.

The receptor site/or sites at the neuromyal junction appears to have structural requirements different from those of AChE. There appears to be a 6 Å and a 9 Å area, each of which plays some role in the excitation process. Amyltrimethylammonium and *d*-tubocurarine show reciprocal antagonism as do decamethonium and *d*-tubocurarine (Dallemagne and Philippot, 1952a, b). The gallamine analog, 2-diethylaminoethoxybenzene ethiodide (9 Å) may either excite or block, depending upon dosage (Bülbring and Depierre, 1949). Similar findings have been reported for gallamine by Bülbring and Depierre (1949) and Riker and Wescoe (1951), and for *d*-tubocurarine by McIntyre and King (1943). We also have observed in our studies that small doses of *d*-tubocurarine may increase the twitch amplitude to indirect motor stimulation in cats. In the light of Koelle's (1957a, b) recent findings, excitation may result from some previously unsuspected AChE inhibitory action. However in these cases, it is replaced rapidly by blockade. Whereas methyl substitution favors excitation at the shorter site, the ethyl substituted compounds are weak blocking agents (Barlow *et al.*, 1953; Thesleff, 1955). Ethyl substitution favors blockade with the longer compounds (Riker and Wescoe, 1951; Hoppe *et al.*, 1955). Hoppe *et al.* (1955) have demonstrated marked facilitatory properties, similar to those noted here for ambenonium, with the potent AChE inhibitor, the *bis*-diethyl-*ortho*-chlorobenzylamino quaternary analog of benzoquinonium, whereas the corresponding triethyl analog was reported to have properties similar to those of *d*-tubocurarine.

Previous results reported from this laboratory (Lands *et al.*, 1957) have shown that mouse red cell AChE is blocked by neostigmine. Further, this compound may act with ambenonium to potentiate a muscle paralysis (inclined screen) which is antagonizable by *d*-tubocurarine and which presumably results from ACh accumulation at the postjunctional membrane of the motor endplate. However, comparison of toxicity data with the dose required to produce paralysis with ambenonium and related oxamide compounds discloses paralyzing effects much greater than would be anticipated from the corresponding toxicity values. Possibly neostigmine and edrophonium (ratios of 0.51 and 0.42) do not block mouse AChE at the motor endplate inasmuch as similar ratios are obtained with many quaternary alkylammonium compounds (Lands *et al.*, 1957. Alternatively, the oxamide compounds may influence some other component of action which plays an important role in the transmission process. This is also suggested by the marked synergism resulting from combined treatment with neostigmine and some members of the ambenonium series. This synergism indicates some neostigmine effect at the motor endplate other than that which will protect against the toxic actions of TEPP but at the same time one which which facilitates the transmission process.

SUMMARY

Inhibition of AChE has been demonstrated with ambenonium and related compounds. The structure of the ammonium group shows highly specific requirements for optimum activity. Effective blocking agents are obtained with *bis*-ammoium quaternary compounds at extended lengths of about 12 Å and again at about 17 Å to 20 Å.

An extensive investigation in the albino mouse has shown that ambenonium and related compounds may cause voluntary muscle paralysis at lower doses than would be expected from a comparison with known curarizing drugs, evaluated in terms of their respective toxicities. Facilitation as well as motor paralysis (inclined screen) is most marked with compounds having distances between the terminal N centers of 12 Å or 17 Å to 20 Å.

Effective facilitatory compounds are also effective antagonists of tetraethylpyrophosphate toxicity in mice. Inasmuch as this is not observed with the potent anticholinesterase, neostigmine, it is suggested that this protection involves more than protective binding of AChE.

ACKNOWLEDGMENT. The authors wish to acknowledge with gratitude the technical assistance provided by Miss Nancy Harvey, Mr. Leon Duprey and Mr. Kenard Turner, Jr. Grateful appreciation is expressed to the Wellcome Research Laboratories, Tuckahoe, N. Y. for decamethonium bromide (Syncurine) and to Hoffmann-La Roche, Inc., Nutley, New Jersey for edrophonium (Tensilon Chloride) and neostigmine (Prostigmin).

REFERENCES

ARNOLD, A., SORIA, A. E., AND KIRCHNER, F. K.: Proc. Soc. Exper. Biol. & Med., **87:** 393, 1954.
BALDRIDGE, H. D., JR., MCCARVILLE, W. J., AND FRIESS, S. L.: J. Am. Chem. Soc., **77:** 739, 1955.
BARLOW, R. B.: Brit. J. Pharmacol., **10:** 168, 1955.
BARLOW, R. B., ROBERTS, T. D. M., AND REID, D. A.: J. Pharm. and Pharmacol., **5:** 35, 1953.
BLASCHKO, H., BÜLBRING, E., AND CHOU, T. C.: Brit. J. Pharmacol., **4:** 29, 1949.
BÜLBRING, E., AND DEPIERRE, F.: Brit. J. Pharmacol., **4:** 22, 1949.
CHASE, H. F., LEHMAN, A. J., AND RICKARDS, E. E.: THIS JOURNAL, **82:** 266, 1944.
DALLEMAGNE, M. J., AND PHILIPPOT, E.: Experientia, **8:** 273, 1952a.
DALLEMAGNE, M. J., AND PHILIPPOT, E.: Brit. J. Pharmacol., **7:** 601, 1952b.
FRIESS, S. L., AND MCCARVILLE, W. J.: J. Am. Chem. Soc., **76:** 1363, 1954a.
FRIESS, S. L., AND MCCARVILLE, W. J.: J. Am. Chem. Soc. **76:** 2260, 1954b.
FUNKE, A., JACOB, J., AND DANIKEN, K. VON: Compt. rend. Acad. Sci. (Paris), **237:** 1809, 1953.
HOPPE, J. O.: THIS JOURNAL, **100:** 333, 1950.
HOPPE, J. O.: Ann. New York Acad. Sci., **54:** 395, 1951.
HOPPE, J. O., SEPPELIN, D. K., AND LANDS, A. M.: THIS JOURNAL, **95:** 502, 1949.
HOPPE, J. O., FUNNELL, J. E., AND LAPE, H.: THIS JOURNAL, **115:** 106, 1955.
JACOB, J.: Experientia, **10:** 33, 1954.
JACOB, J., AND DECHAVASSINE, M.: Experientia, **11:** 235, 1955.
JACOB, J.: Arch. internat. pharmacodyn. et de therap., **101:** 446, 1955.
KOELLE, G. B.: Fed. Proc., **16:** 313, 1957a.
KOELLE, G. B.: THIS JOURNAL, **120:** 488, 1957b.
KARCZMAR, A. G.: THIS JOURNAL, **119:** 39, 1957.
LANDS, A. M., KARCZMAR, A. G., HOWARD, J. W., AND ARNOLD, A.: THIS JOURNAL, **115:** 185, 1955.
LANDS, A. M., HOPPE, J. O., KARCZMAR, A. G., AND ARNOLD, A.: THIS JOURNAL, **119:** 541, 1957.
LEWIS, J. R., MCKEON, W. B., JR., AND LANDS, A. M.: Arch. internat. pharmacodyn. et de therap.: **102:** 371, 1955.
MARSH, D. F.: Ann. New York Acad. Sci., **54:** 307, 1951.
MCINTYRE, A. R., AND KING, R. E.: Science, **97:** 516, 1943.
MICHEL, H. O.: J. Lab. Clin. Med., **34:** 1564, 1949.
PAULING L., AND BROCKWAY, L. O.: J. Am. Chem. Soc., **59:** 1223, 1937.
RIKER, W. F., AND WESCOE, W. C.: Ann. New York Acad. Sci., **54:** 373, 1951.
SCHUELER, F. W.: Arch. internat. pharmacodyn. et de therap., **93:** 417, 1953a.
SCHUELER, F. W.: Arch. internat. pharmacodyn. et de therap., **95:** 376, 1953b.
SIZER, I. W.: Science, **125:** 54, 1957.
THESLEFF, S.: Acta pharmacol. et toxicologica, **11:** 179, 1955.
WILSON, I. B., AND BERGMANN, F.: J. Biol. Chem., **185:** 479, 1950.

8024

PHARMACOLOGY OF HEXAHYDRO-1-AZEPINEPROPIONAMIDOXIME DIHYDROCHLORIDE (SU-4029)

R. A. MAXWELL, S. D. ROSS AND A. J. PLUMMER

Research Department, CIBA Pharmaceutical Products Inc., Summit, New Jersey

Received for publication January 22, 1958

In a recent study (Maxwell *et al.*, 1957) it was demonstrated that the central nervous stimulant, methylphenidate, possessed the capacity to antagonize carotid occlusion pressor responses, to eliminate the severe pressor effects of amphetamine and ephedrine, and to lower moderately the arterial pressure of the renal hypertensive dog. In conjunction with this study, the pharmacological activities of another compound, Su-4029, were elucidated. Although chemically different from methylphenidate and not a motor stimulant, Su-4029 possesses many of the same cardiovascular properties exhibited by methylphenidate. In contrast to the relatively short duration of action of methylphenidate, however, Su-4029 has a duration of action after single intravenous dosage which is measured in weeks.[1]

Su-4029, prepared by Mull *et al.* (to be published) is hexahydro-1-azepinepropionamidoxime dihydrochloride:

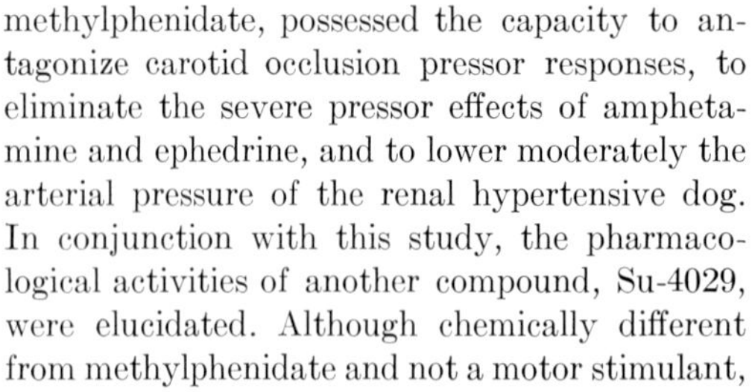

METHODS. Su-4029 is a white crystalline powder with a melting point of 183 to 185°C., with decomposition, and a molecular weight of 258. It is readily soluble in water. The activity of Su-4029 described in the text was detected by giving a single intravenous injection of 30 mgm./kgm. of the compound to be studied, and then, after three days, testing for the carotid occlusion reflex pressor responses and for the pressor response elicited by intravenous amphetamine. The anesthetic used was sodium pentobarbital, 30 mgm./kgm. i.p., plus a continuous intravenous infusion of 0.1 mgm./kgm./minute. Blood pressures were measured with an Anderson glass-capsule manometer (1941). In the long-term experiments periods up to ten weeks were allowed to elapse between drug administration and testing.

Unanesthetized normotensive and hypertensive dogs were trained to lie quietly and calmly in the supine position. Blood pressures were taken by femoral arterial needle puncture and were recorded through a Sanborn electromanometer and polyviso. Drugs were given through a 19-gauge needle inserted in the jugular vein. Chronic renal hypertension was produced by the method of Goldblatt *et al.* (1933). Neurogenic hypertension was produced by the method of Grimson (1941). Annoying stimulation was applied to the neurogenic hypertensive animals by shaking their heads vigorously, but not roughly, for periods of 10 to 30 seconds.

The preparation of a dog for study of the carotid occlusion response in the unanesthetized state was modified from the method of McCubbin *et al.* (1956). The right carotid sinus was removed and the medial one-third of the right vago-sympathetic trunk cut. One inch of the complete left vago-sympathetic trunk was resected and the left common carotid artery explanted into a fold of skin. Occlusion of this artery was carried out by completely clamping a 9½-inch long serrated, rubber-tipped, sponge forceps on the shaven loop.

Cats were studied under 0.8 ml./kgm. of Dial-Urethane (Ciba) anesthesia. Arterial pressures were recorded with the Anderson manometer and isotonic lever systems were used for study of the nictitating membrane response. Acute denervation of the membrane was performed by removing one-fourth inch of the vago-sympathetic trunk in the cervical region. The preganglionic cervical sympathetic trunk was stimulated at 2 volts, 100 microseconds duration, 20/sec.

Electrocardiograms were taken on unanesthetized dogs using standard leads and plate electrodes.

Aqueous solutions of amphetamine sulfate (racemic), ephedrine HCl, arterenol (norepinephrine, racemic) and chlorisondamine chloride were used in these studies.

Isolated tissue and organ studies. Isolated tissues

[1] A preliminary announcement of this work has been submitted to Nature.

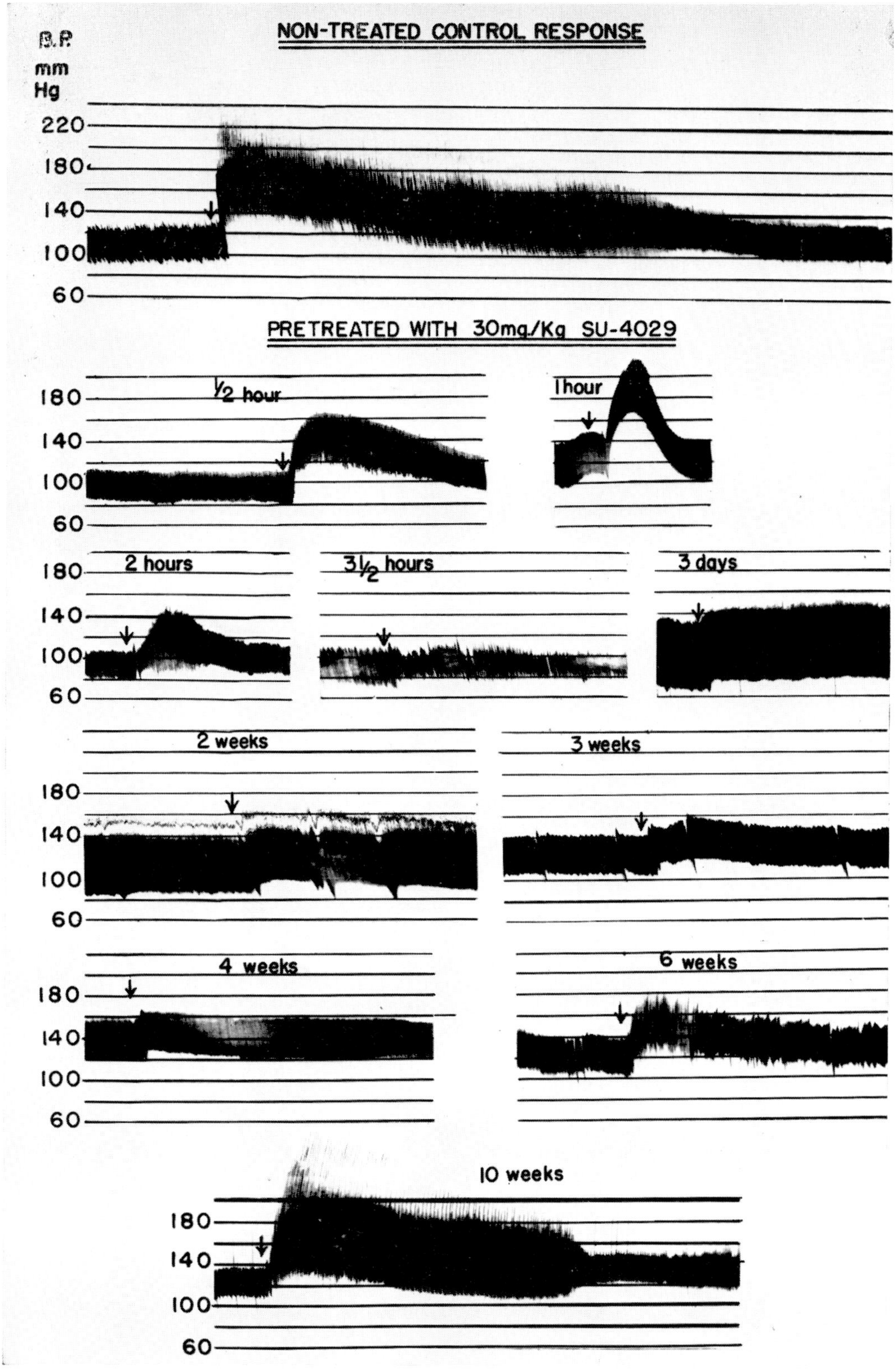

FIG. 1. Time course of inhibition of amphetamine-induced hypertension by Su-4029 in the normotensive anesthetized dog.

Time notations refer to time elapsed after a single intravenous injection of Su-4029. Five-tenths mgm./kgm. of amphetamine administered intravenously at arrows.

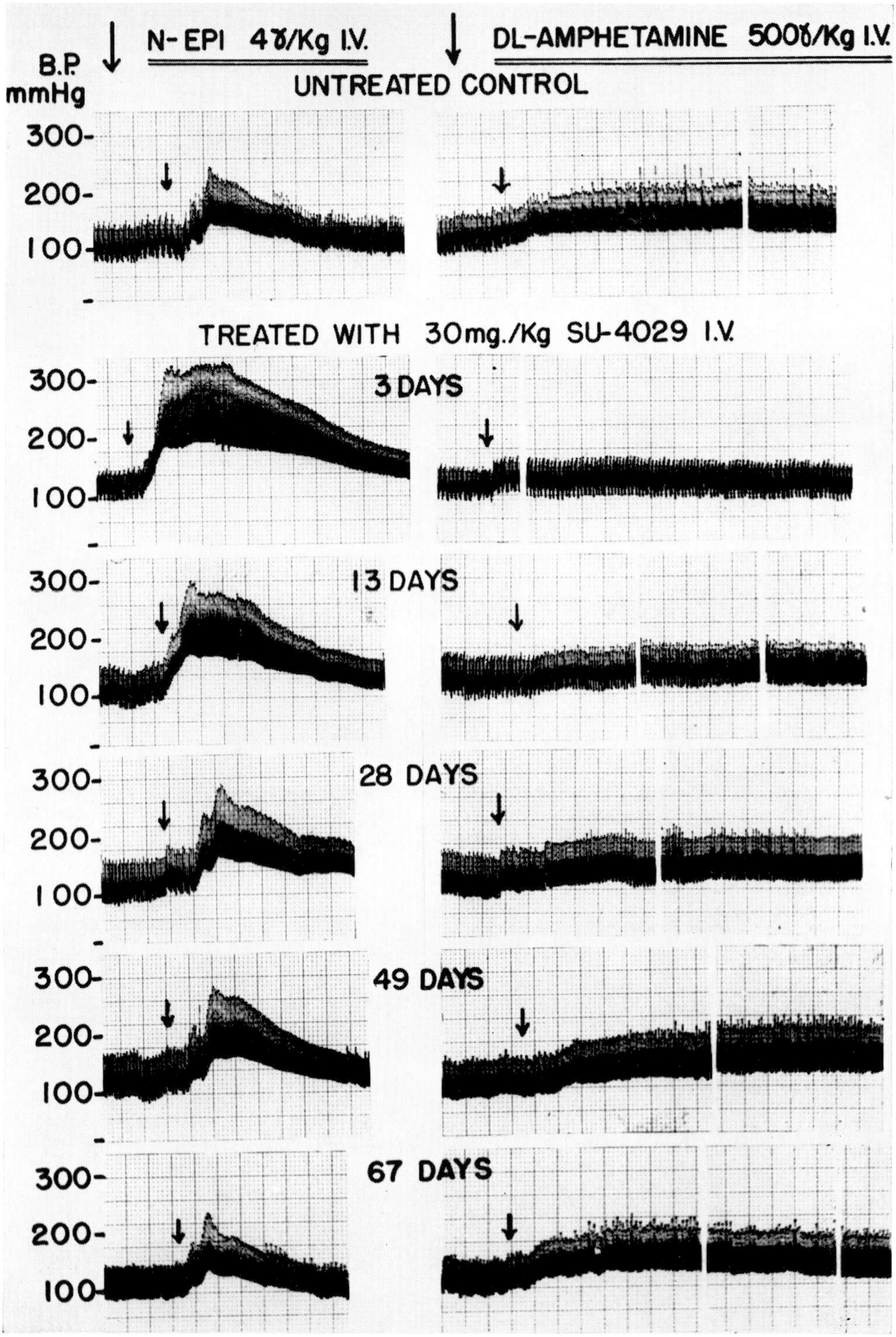

FIG. 2. Effect of Su-4029 on the blood pressure response of the unanesthetized normotensive dog to norepinephrine and amphetamine.

Time notations refer to time elapsed after a single intravenous injection of Su-4029. All tracings are from the same animal.

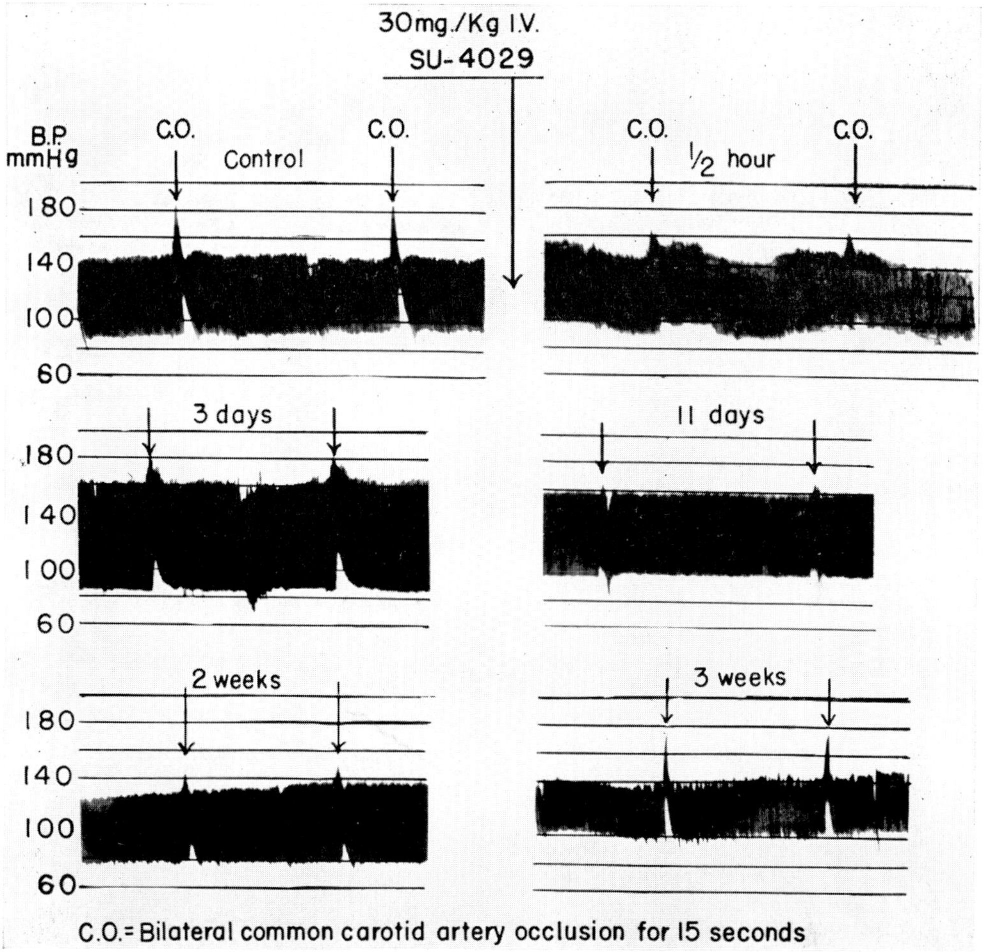

FIG. 3. Effect of Su-4029 on carotid occlusion pressor response in the normotensive anesthetized dog. Time notations refer to time elapsed after a single intravenous injection of Su-4029.

were suspended in the apparatus of Anderson *et al.* (1949) which was filled with the aerated modified Locke's solution of Cantoni and Eastman (1946). Recordings were made using an isotonic lever system and smoked drum kymograph. The isolated heart was studied in the apparatus of Anderson and Craver (1948).

RESULTS. *Effects of Su-4029 on normotensive canine arterial blood pressure.* Intravenous administration of 30 mgm./kgm of Su-4029 to seven normotensive anesthetized dogs did not result in marked or consistent alterations in arterial pressure over a 3-hour period. In two of the seven animals initial transient pressor responses of 15 and 20 mm.Hg were noted. In five animals a very gradual decline of 15 to 30 mm. Hg in mean pressure was observed during the 3-hour period. In 30 dogs studied over a period of 3 days to 10 weeks after Su-4029 injection, there were no marked deviations in the blood pressures from control values (fig. 1 and 3).

In three unanesthetized dogs, at 22 to 24 hours after an intravenous dose of 30 mgm./kgm. of Su-4029, there occurred a narrowing of pulse pressure which returned to normal within two to four days (fig. 5). Mean blood pressures were not significantly changed during the 20 to 67 days of study (fig. 2 and 5).

Inhibition of amphetamine- and ephedrine-induced hypertension. Su-4029 in a single intravenous dose of 30 mgm./kgm. markedly antagonized the severe hypertension elicited by the intravenous administration of 0.5 mgm./kgm. of amphetamine. Partial antagonism was observed

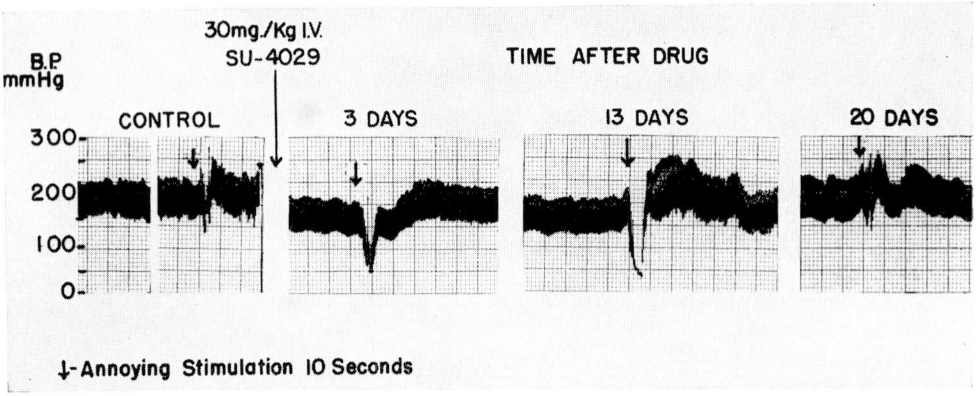

FIG. 4. Effect of Su-4029 on the blood pressure and pressor spikes elicited by annoying stimulation in the unanesthetized neurogenic hypertensive dog.
Time notations refer to time elapsed after a single intravenous injection of Su-4029.

at one-half hour after Su-4029 administration and was complete by three and one-half to five hours. The antagonism continued beyond 6 weeks after a single injection but was not present at 10 weeks (fig. 1). Intravenous administration of doses of amphetamine up to 10 mgm./kgm. were without pressor effect when tested on dogs which had been pretreated with 30 mgm./kgm. of Su-4029 three days earlier. The antagonistic action of Su-4029 against amphetamine has also been demonstrated in two unanesthetized dogs (fig. 2). Su-4029 exerted no obvious antagonism on the motor stimulating effect of amphetamine in the unanesthetized dog.

An intravenous dose of 30 mgm./kgm. of Su-4029 similarly inhibited the hypertensive reponse produced by the intravenous administration of 0.6 mgm./kgm. of ephedrine in 4 dogs studied. This inhibiting effect on ephedrine hypertension was still present 11 days after a single injection of Su-4029. On the third day after Su-4029 administration, a 10-fold dose of ephedrine, *i.e.* 6 mgm./kgm., was required to produce the pressor response that had been evoked by 0.6 mgm./kgm. prior to Su-4029 administration.

Su-4029 did not antagonize the sustained pressor response of 60 mm.Hg produced by an intravenous dose of 100 microgm./kgm. of naphazoline in six dogs.

Potentiation of the pressor response to norepinephrine. Intravenous administration of 30 mgm./kgm. of Su-4029 profoundly enhanced the pressor response evoked by the intravenous injection of 4 microgm./kgm. of norepinephrine to two unanesthetized dogs. This effect lasted for approximately seven weeks (fig. 2). In eight anesthetized dogs, three days after pretreatment with 30 mgm./kgm. of Su-4029, the pressor responses to norepinephrine were double those generally observed before pretreatment.

Inhibition of reflex pressor responses. The reflex pressor spikes caused by bilateral common carotid artery occlusion for 15 and 30 seconds in the anesthetized dog were markedly suppressed by the intravenous administration of Su-4029. This blockade, which in all fifteen cases was practically a comple obliteration of pressor effects, lasted for approximately two to three weeks after a single injection (fig. 3).

In one unanesthetized dog 30 mgm./kgm. of Su-4029 antagonized carotid occlusion pressor responses for a 2-week period.[2]

Antihypertensive effects in neurogenic and renal hypertensive dogs. Thirty mgm./kgm., i.v., of Su-4029 produced a moderate lowering of the blood pressure of two unanesthetized neurogenic hypertensive dogs and reversed the pressor spikes induced by annoying stimulation (fig. 4). The reversal of pressor spikes was followed by a secondary, transient rise in pressure. These antihypertensive effects lasted for approximately two weeks (fig. 4).

Su-4029 in the same dose markedly lowered the blood pressure of two unanesthetized dogs

[2] Since submission of this manuscript we have studied the effect of infiltration of Su-4029 into the carotid sinus areas on the carotid occlusion reflex pressor response. In all cases the animals were studied after bilateral section of the vago-aortic nerves. Infiltration of 2.5 mgm. of Su-4029 in 0.1 ml. of saline into each sinus did not affect

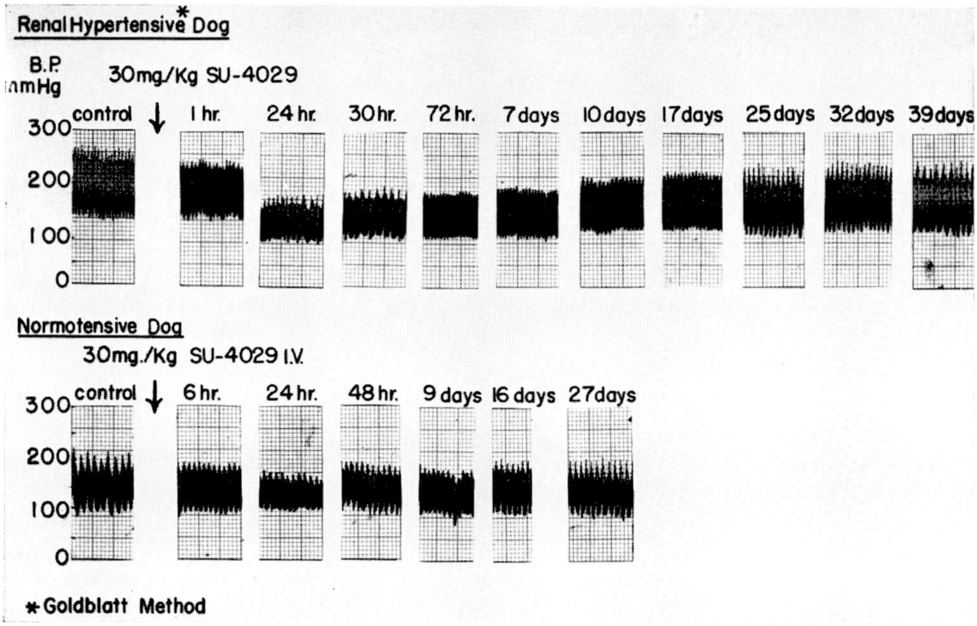

FIG. 5. Effect of Su-4029 on the blood pressure of unanesthetized renal hypertensive and normotensive dogs.

Time notations refer to time elapsed after a single intravenous injection of Su-4029.

with renal hypertension for a period of one to three weeks (fig. 5).[3]

Pretreatment with 30 mgm./kgm. of Su-4029 three days prior to testing did not antagonize the pressor action of 1 to 3 mgm./kgm. (approximately 1 to 3 units) of purified renin extract in four dogs tested.

Central nervous activity. Su-4029 had no obvious sedative or stimulating properties in the unanesthetized dog in intravenous doses up to 30 mgm./kgm. One hundred mgm./kgm. subcutaneously produced no effect on the activity of mice as measured in 6 animals in the Anderson jiggle cage over a 2-hour period.

Pretreatment of 5 cats with intravenous doses of 10 mgm./kgm. of Su-4029 was not effective in inhibiting behavioral aberrations produced by 15 mgm./kgm. of morphine sulfate subcutaneously.

Pretreatment of 2 dogs with 30 mgm./kgm. of Su-4029 three days prior to the administration of 0.5 mgm./kgm. of reserpine phosphate intravenously did not obviously alter the sedation and side effects produced by the reserpine.

Effects of Su-4029 on isolated organs and tissues. These studies were of a screening type and usually involved only one experiment per observation reported. Su-4029 had no effect on the isolated guinea pig jejunum with a concentration of 100 microgm. of drug per ml. of bath fluid. The isolated guinea pig uterus did not respond to a

---

the carotid occlusion pressor responses in 5 dogs studied. Infiltration of 5 mgm. in 0.1 ml. of saline into each sinus antagonized the reflex pressor responses in 4 of the 7 dogs studied. Ten mgm. in 0.1 ml. of saline infiltrated into each sinus markedly reduced the carotid occlusion reflex pressor responses in 8 out of 9 dogs within one-half hour following administration. However, 3 days after the infiltration of 10 mgm. into each sinus in 6 dogs and 20 mgm. into each sinus of 2 dogs, no marked antagonism to the reflex pressor responses could be observed in any of these animals. We conclude that this afferent action of Su-4029 is not sufficient to explain the prolonged antagonism of this compound on the carotid occlusion reflex pressor response. Since we have also not been able to demonstrate blockade of the efferent sympathetic limb it would seem that this protracted antagonism to carotid occlusion pressor responses following intravenous Su-4029 is centrally evoked.

[3] Bein and coworkers (personal communication) have confirmed the long-acting antihypertensive effect of Su-4029 by demonstrating this action in renal hypertensive rats. Similar results have been obtained by Chart and coworkers (personal communication) in rats with adrenal regeneration hypertension.

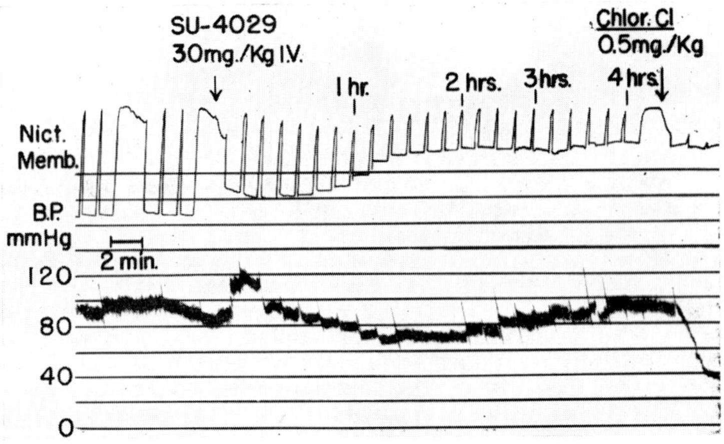

FIG. 6. Effect of Su-4029 on the contractions of the cat nictitating membrane produced by preganglionic stimulation of the cervical sympathetic trunk.
Faradization given for 10-second and 2-minute intervals. Blood pressure also shown.

concentration of 10 microgm. of Su-4029 per ml. of bath fluid; 100 microgm./ml. produced stimulation after one minute. Ten microgm. of Su-4029 per ml. of bath fluid did not antagonize acetylcholine stimulation of the isolated guinea pig ileum; 100 microgm./ml. produced a slight antagonism. One microgm. of Su-4029 per ml. of bath fluid demonstrated slight antihistaminic activity in the guinea pig ileum preparation. This activity was not enhanced by increasing the concentration to 10 or 100 microgm./ml. Su-4029 was without effect on the amplitude of contraction, heart rate or coronary flow of the isolated cat heart when 1 microgm. to 320 microgm. were injected into the coronary perfusion fluid over the course of a minute. Perfusion of the heart with 30 microgm. of Su-4029 per ml. of perfusion fluid for a 30-minute period also had no effect. Only a very slight increase in the tonus of an isolated spiral segment of dog carotid artery was produced during its suspension in a 30 microgm./ml. solution of Su-4029 for 4 hours. Responsiveness of the arterial segment to epinephrine and norepinephrine was unaltered by this prolonged exposure to Su-4029.

Cumulative effect and oral activity in the dog. Intravenous administration to 3 dogs of 5 mgm./kgm. of Su-4029 for 5 days caused a blockade of both the carotid occlusion pressor responses and amphetamine hypertension comparable to that produced by the intravenous administration of one single dose of 30 mgm./kgm. One single intravenous dose of 5 mgm./kgm. had only negligible activity in blocking these responses.

The oral admininstration of doses of 5 and 10 mgm./kgm./day over a period of 5 to 10 days evoked significant blockade of pressor effects caused by carotid occlusion and amphetamine in 6 dogs. This indicated a cumulative effect of repeated low oral doses, since a single oral dose of 10 mgm./kgm. produced no blockade of pressor responses.

Su-4029 was active orally in lowering the blood pressure of two renal hypertensive dogs mentioned above when given in doses of 5 and 10 mgm./kgm./day over a period of 5 to 10 days.

Side effects. Intravenous administration of 30 mgm./kgm. of Su-4029 produced a short period of moderate vomiting and diarrhea after a lapse of 2 to 4 hours. For 1 to 2 days the dogs were quiet and anorexic. By the third day after injection the behavior of the animals appeared normal. Dogs treated with one 30 mgm./kgm. injection of Su-4029 have been observed over periods as long as 10 weeks and no gross behavioral differences between these animals and untreated dogs have been observed. Su-4029 produced a transient period of bradycardia after 3 to 6 hours; however, it did not markedly relax the nictitating membranes and did not cause mydriasis or myosis.

The oral administration of 5 to 10 mgm./kgm./day to six dogs for periods of five to ten days did not produce vomiting or anorexia and the behavior of the animals was normal both during drug administration and after.

Thirty mgm./kgm., i.v., of Su-4029 produced, after a 5-hour lapse, intermittent and brief periods of ventricular extrasystoles in one dog and inverted T waves in lead II in a second dog. These effects lasted for not more than 24 hours and 4 days respectively. The electrocardiograms then returned to normal. Five mgm./kgm./day of Su-4029 orally for ten days did not affect the electrocardiogram in one dog and produced heightened T waves four hours after the first oral 5 mgm./kgm. dose of Su-4029 in the second dog. During the rest of the course of drug administration the electrocardiogram was normal.

Toxicity. The acute intravenous LD_{50} of Su-4029 in rats was 123 mgm./kgm. All deaths were delayed and occurred within 24 hours. The 100 per cent survival dose by the intravenous route was 100 mgm./kgm. and the "LD_{100}" was 150 mgm./kgm. The oral LD_{50} in rats was 500 to 750 mgm./kgm. Three dogs have been treated with two doses of 30 mgm./kgm. of Su-4029 i.v. spaced approximately one month apart. These animals have been observed over a 4-month period and do not differ behaviorally from normal animals in any grossly observable way.

Two dogs were sacrificed after treatment with 20 mgm./kgm./day of Su-4029 orally for 30 days. There was no gross anatomical or histological evidence of damage to the major organs and glands of these two animals.

Studies concerning mechanism of action. Ganglionic blockade: Since Su-4029 was not an adrenolytic agent, it was studied for possible ganglionic blocking activity. Thirty mgm./kgm. failed to block the contractions of the cat nictitating membrane which were evoked by preganglionic faradization of the cervical sympathetic trunk (fig. 6). Injection of Su-4029 produced a sustained increase in the tonus of the membrane. Subsequent administration of 320 microgm./kgm. of the ganglionic blocking agent, chlorisondamine chloride, produced a marked antagonism to the membrane contractions produced by faradization of the cervical sympathetic trunk but did not affect the tonus of the membrane (fig. 6). Furthermore, in dogs which had been pretreated 3 days earlier with intravenous Su-4029, there could not be demonstrated obvious inhibition of the pressor spikes elicited by the administration of 15 microgm./kgm. of the ganglionic stimulant DMPP (1:1-dimethyl-4-phenylpiperazinium iodide).

In 6 anesthetized cats 30 mgm./kgm. of Su-4029 retracted both denervated and innervated nicititating membranes and potentiated the contracting action of epinephrine, norepinephrine and serotonin (fig. 7). Three mgm./kgm. of phentolamine relaxed the cat nictitating membranes which had been contracted following Su-4029 administration (fig. 7).

Acute administration of 30 mgm./kgm. of Su-4029 intravenously caused a partial retraction of denervated nictitating membrane of the unanesthetized dog over a 6-hour period.

Administration of amphetamine to 8 anesthetized cats which had been given 30 mgm./kgm. of Su-4029 three to six hours before, produced in all cases a clear-cut contraction of both innervated and denervated membranes. In four of these animals the response of the blood pressure to amphetamine was much reduced or negated as compared to untreated controls.

Interaction of amphetamine, norepinephrine and Su-4029 pretreatment in spinalized dogs: Total cord transection between the base of the skull and the atlas reduced the over-all magnitude

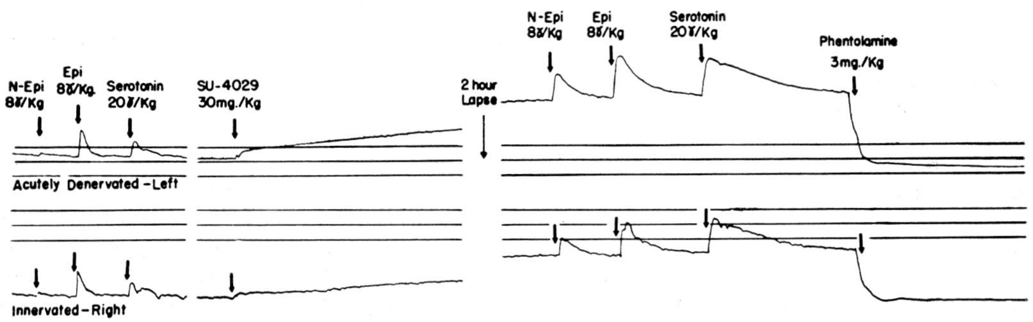

FIG. 7. Effect of intravenous Su-4029 on the response of the cat nictitating membrane to intravenous norepinephrine, epinephrine and serotonin.

Also shown is the effect of intravenous phentolamine on the increased tonus of the membrane that occurs following Su-4029 injection.

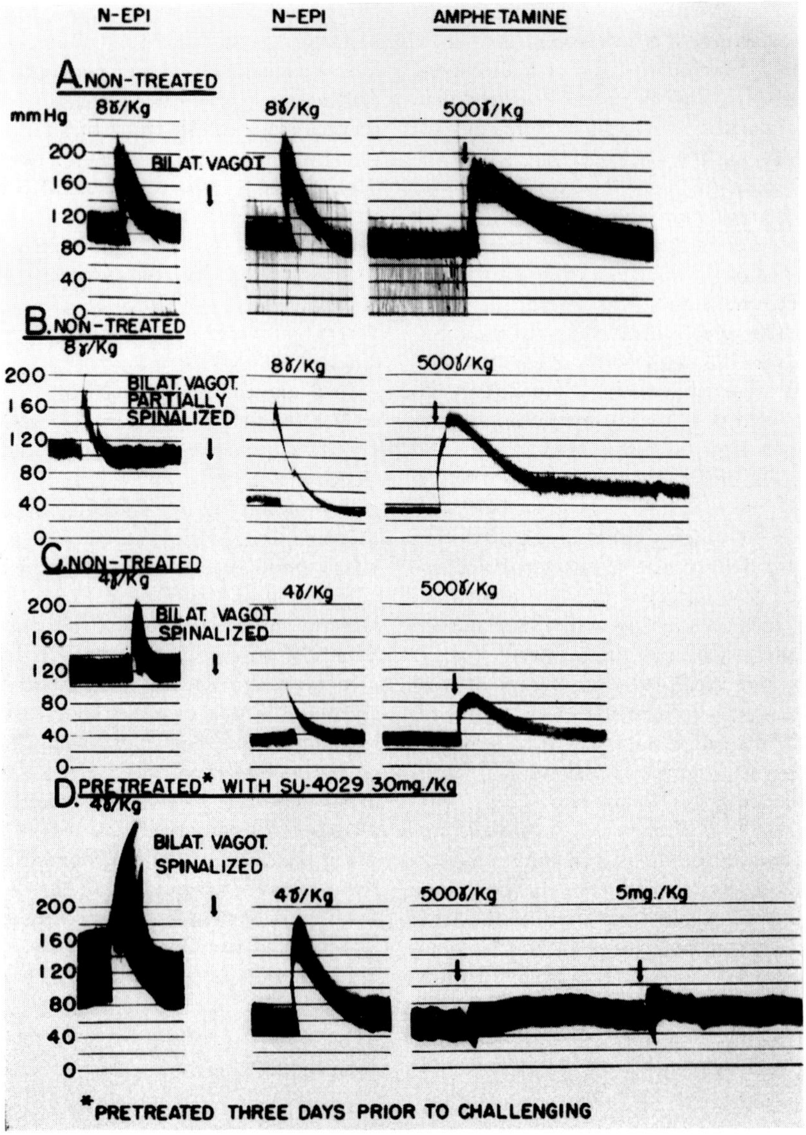

FIG. 8. Effects of partial and complete high spinal cord transection on the pressor responses of the dog to norepinephrine and amphetamine (tracings A, B, C).

Also shown is the lack of effect of high cord transection on the norepinephrine-augmenting and amphetamine-antagonizing actions of Su-4029 (tracing D).

of the pressor responses of four dogs to amphetamine and norepinephrine (compare fig. 8a and c) although the percentage rise in blood pressure was approximately the same as that seen in the intact dog. In one animal in which spinalization was incomplete as judged by the presence of clearly defined respiratory motions, the pressor responses to amphetamine and norepinephrine were much greater than those seen after complete spinalization (fig. 8b). In four dogs pretreated with 30 mgm./kgm. of Su-4029 three days prior to spinalization no pressor response was produced by amphetamine administration after spinalization (fig. 8d). The potentiation of the norepinephrine-induced pressor response generally seen after Su-4209 pretreatment in normal dogs was not markedly inhibited by cord transection (fig. 8d).

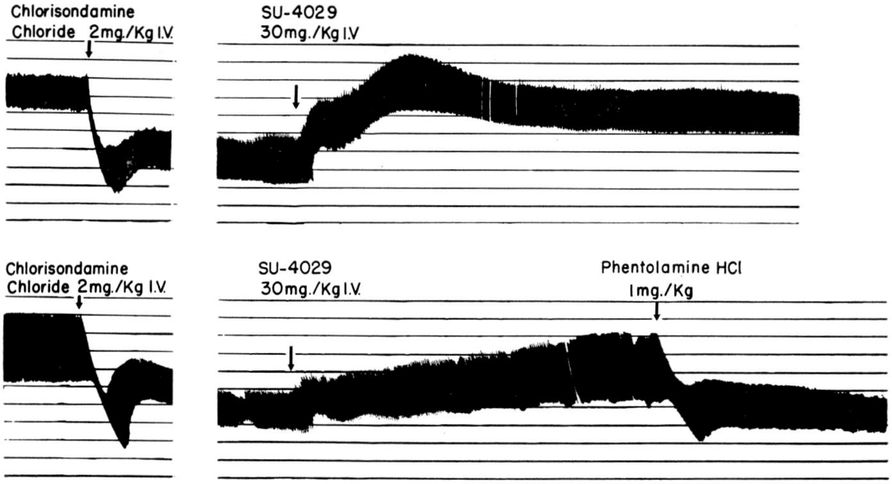

FIG. 9. Pressor responses elicited by administration of Su-4029 during the hypotension produced by the ganglionic blocking agent, chlorisondamine chloride.
Also shown is the antagonistic action of intravenous phentolamine on this pressor response.

Acute Su-4029 in spinalized dogs and dogs under ganglionic blockade: In 2 out of 3 dogs spinalized at the base of the skull and 3 dogs given 2 mgm./kgm. intravenously of the ganglionic blocking agent, chlorisondamine chloride, the subsequent administration of 30 mgm./kgm. of Su-4029 produced rapid pressor responses of 40 to 60 mm. Hg (fig. 9) which were sustained for approximately one-half to two hours. One to three mgm./kgm. of phentolamine given intravenously negated the pressor responses elicited by Su-4029 in these animals.

Specificity of chemical structure for pharmacological activity. Twenty-eight analogues of Su-4029, prepared by Mull and coworkers (to be published), have been studied at 3 days after administration to determine their ability to antagonize carotid occlusion reflex pressor responses and the pressor responses induced by amphetamine (table 1). From these studies it was determined that analogues with the pyrrolidino or piperidino ring systems (Su-4549, Su-3857) were inactive. Analogues with an 8- or 9-membered ring system (Su-4852, Su-4975) possessed Su-4029-like activity. Su-4029 containing methyl substitution in the 4-position of the ring (Su-4923) was active. Introduction of oxygen into the Su-4029 ring in the 2-position markedly reduced activity (Su-4355). Shortening or lengthening of the Su-4029 carbon chain resulted in diminution of activity (Su-4607, -4662, -4661). Alteration of the oximido group resulted in diminution of activity except in the case of Su-5176.

DISCUSSION. Certain responses to Su-4029 which are most likely attributable to action in the efferent periphery are: 1) the contraction of the acutely denervated nictitating membrane, 2) the pressor responses in the spinal dog and the dog under ganglionic blockade, 3) the blockade of the pressor response which can be elicited by amphetamine following high cord transection, 4) potentiation of the norepinephrine-induced pressor response in the spinalized dog and 5) augmentation of the response of the cat nictitating membrane to norepinephrine, epinephrine and serotonin. However, the anti-hypertensive effects of Su-4029 seem not to be limited to one site of action. The fact that we could not demonstrate ganglionic blockade or adrenolytic properties for Su-4029 would suggest that the suppressing action of this compound on the carotid occlusion pressor response originated at sites other than the efferent periphery.

The mechanism underlying Su-4029 activity is not completely understood. The dramatic pressor response obtained in spinal dogs and in dogs under ganglionic blockade, and the contracting effect on the denervated nictitating membrane of the dog and cat produced by acute administration of Su-4029, attest to a peripheral sympathetic-like action of rapid onset and several hours duration. It is possible that this is a direct action of

TABLE 1

Analogues of Su-4029 arranged according to their capacity to antagonize carotid occlusion reflex pressor responses and the pressor responses induced by amphetamine

Tests performed three days after administration of the drug.

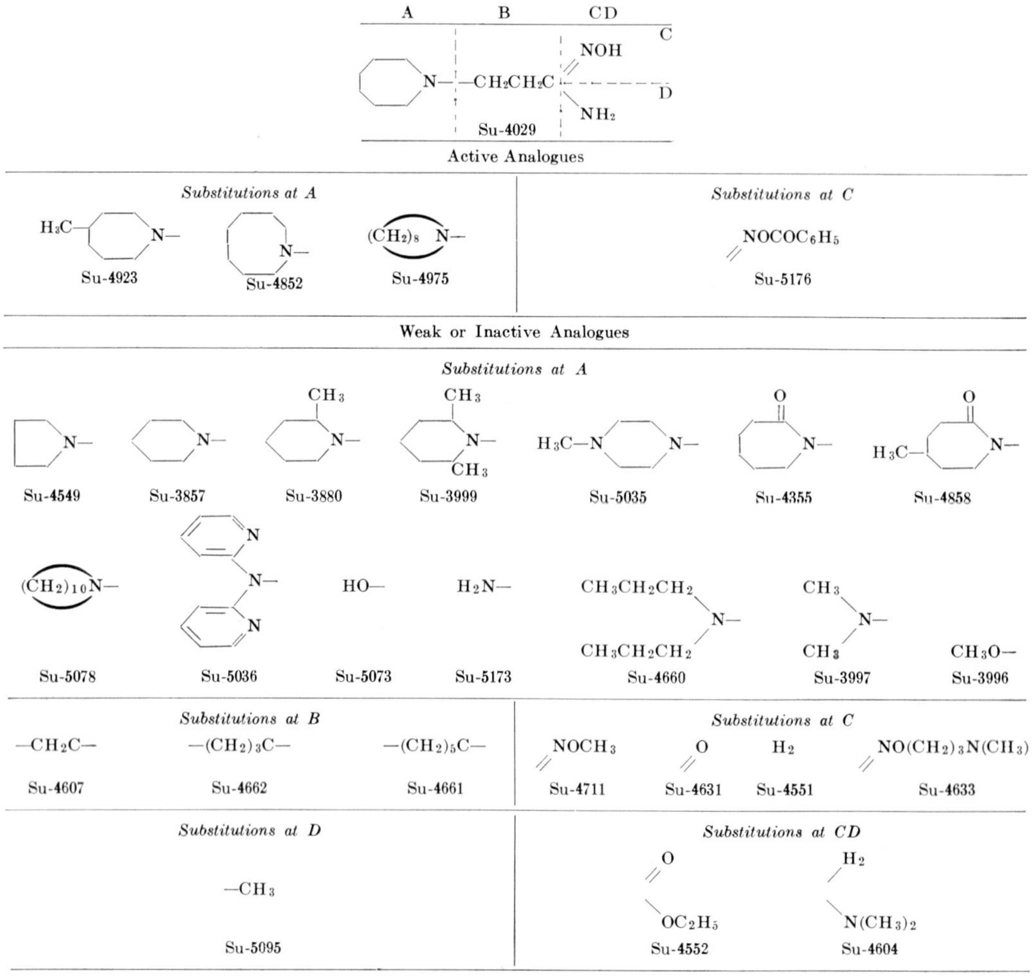

Su-4029 on the peripheral receptors. However, the absence of obvious sympathetic-like effects of Su-4029 on isolated tissues and organs would make the *in vivo* effects seem to be of indirect origin *e.g.*, possibly due to a release of sympathetic neurohumoral agents. The blocking action of phentolamine on the pressor responses produced by Su-4029 after spinalization or ganglionic blocking agents in dogs and on the contracted cat membranes lends some support to this thesis. Whether indirect or direct, these early sympathetic-like actions may well be a reflection of changes that account for the protracted antihypertensive effects of Su-4029.

SUMMARY

Hexahydro-1-azepinepropionamidoxime dihydrochloride (Su-4029) has been studied for its effects on the cardiovascular system of the dog. A single intravenous dose of 30 mgm./kgm. of this compound lowered the arterial pressure of neurogenic and renal hypertensive dogs while not notably affecting the blood pressure of normotensive dogs. However, in normotensive animals

30 mgm./kgm. of Su-4029, given intravenously, eliminated the severe hypertension elicited by doses of amphetamine and ephedrine and also markedly antagonized carotid occlusion reflex pressor responses. These antihypertensive effects were slow in onset and lasted for approximately 2 to 6 weeks following single injections. Su-4029 was orally active and had a cumulative action when given in small daily doses. Su-4029 is neither an adrenergic nor a ganglionic blocking agent. One site of action of Su-4029 is the sympathetic efferent periphery although this will not explain all the actions of this compound. Su-4029 produces marked sympathetic-like effects of rapid onset and relatively short duration and it is suggested that these effects may reflect the onset of the primary alterations which are responsible for the protracted antihypertension seen after Su-4029 administration.

REFERENCES

ANDERSON, F. F.: J. Lab. & Clin. Med., **26:** 1520, 1941.

ANDERSON, F. F., AND CRAVER, B. N.: THIS JOURNAL, **93:** 135, 1948.

ANDERSON, F. F., BARRETT, W. E., AND CRAVER, B. N.: Arch. int. Pharmacodyn., **78:** 544, 1949.

CANTONI, G. L., AND EASTMAN, G.: THIS JOURNAL, **87:** 392, 1946

GOLDBLATT, H., LYNCH, J., HOUZAL, R. F., AND SOMMERVILLE, W. W.: Am. J. Path., **9:** 942, 1933.

GRIMSON, K. S.: Arch. Surg., **43:** 1, 1941.

MAXWELL, R. A., PLUMMER, A. J., ROSS, S. D., PAYTAS, J. J., AND DENNIS, A. D.: Arch. internat. Pharmacodyn., **CXII:** 26, 1957.

MCCUBBIN, J. W., GREEN, J. H., AND PAGE, I. H.: Circ. Res., **4:** 205, 1956.

8025

THE PHARMACOLOGICAL ACTION OF RYANODINE[1] ON RHYTHMICALLY CONTRACTING MAMMALIAN SMOOTH MUSCLE[2]

IRA W. HILLYARD[3] AND LEONARD PROCITA[4]

Department of Pharmacology, St. Louis University School of Medicine, St. Louis 4, Missouri

Received for publication February 13, 1958

Investigations concerned with the pharmacologic action of ryanodine on mammalian skeletal muscle (Procita, 1956) and cardiac (atrial) muscle (Furchgott and De Gubareff, 1956; Hillyard and Procita, 1956) have demonstrated the high degree of specificity which this purified alkaloid, derived from the South American plant *Ryania speciosa Vahl,* possesses for activated striated muscle. In the skeletal muscle the end result is an irreversible contracture, and in cardiac muscle complete inability of the atria to contract.

The present paper is concerned with results of experiments in which the action of ryanodine on rhythmically contracting smooth muscle of the isolated rabbit intestine was studied.

METHODS. Albino hutch rabbits weighing 1 to 2 kgm., fed *ad libitum* and in a postabsorptive state, were sacrificed by a blow on the head followed by jugular vein exsanguination. A 10- to 15-cm. segment of duodenum, distal to the pylorus, was removed, cleaned and placed in oxygenated Tyrode's solution at room temperature. Test strips, approximately 2 to 2.5 cm. in length, were suspended from a glass holder in a 50-ml capacity pyrex organ bath, the latter being mounted in turn in a larger constant temperature water bath maintained, for most experiments, at 37.5°C. The Tyrode's solution was saturated with a gas mixture of 95 per cent oxygen and 5 per cent carbon dioxide and had a pH of 7.5. Its composition per liter was as follows: NaCl 120 *mM*, KCl 5.6 *mM*, $CaCl_2$ 2.2 *mM*, $MgCl_2$ 2.8 *mM*, $NaHCO_3$ 36.2 *mM*; dextrose 10 *mM* was the substrate. The organ bath was so constructed that the Tyrode's solution could enter from an inlet near the bottom after having passed through glass heat exchange coils, the latter situated in the water bath, and then when desired could be removed, with the aid of suction, through an overflow outlet near the top of the chamber. Only longitudinal muscle changes, recorded with an ink-writing cardiac lever under a weight of approximately 3 gm., were measured in the following experiments. All drugs used were prepared in fresh Tyrode's solution and pH adjustments made when necessary. Solutions were so prepared that no more than 0.5 ml. of any drug was required to effect the desired final concentration in the bath. In this communication all concentrations of drugs are expressed in terms of either the total amount per 50 ml., or in final molar concentration in the Tyrode's solution bathing the test strip of muscle. The molecular weight of ryanodine was taken as 500.

RESULTS. Ryanodine, in concentrations as low as $10^{-7}M$, produces a gradual increase in the longitudinal muscle tonus of well oxygenated isolated rabbit intestinal segments in Tyrode's solution. Usually the effect of this agent on the intestinal segment is directly dependent on its concentration. A concentration of $10^{-4}M$, for example, produces a rather rapid effect, with maximal rise in tone being reached in 5 to 10 minutes. This action of ryanodine is illustrated in figure 1. This same figure also illustrates that thorough changing of the Tyrode's solution in the muscle bath is without beneficial effect on the intestinal strip as the muscle tonus continues to increase. Even extended periods of washing are of no avail in reverting the muscle tonus to its original level. The irreversibility of the action of ryanodine on isolated intestinal strips is comparable to that observed in isolated auricle preparations from kittens, rabbits and rats.

Effect of variation in activity on ryanodine-induced tonus changes. Previous observations of the effect of ryanodine on cat skeletal muscle

[1] The ryanodine used in this work was generously supplied by Dr. E. F. Rogers of Merck and Co.

[2] Supported in part by a grant from the St. Louis Heart Association.

[3] Present address: Research Laboratories, Mead Johnson and Company, Evansville 21, Indiana.

[4] Present address: Department of Pharmacology, State University of New York, Downstate Medical Center, Brooklyn 3, New York.

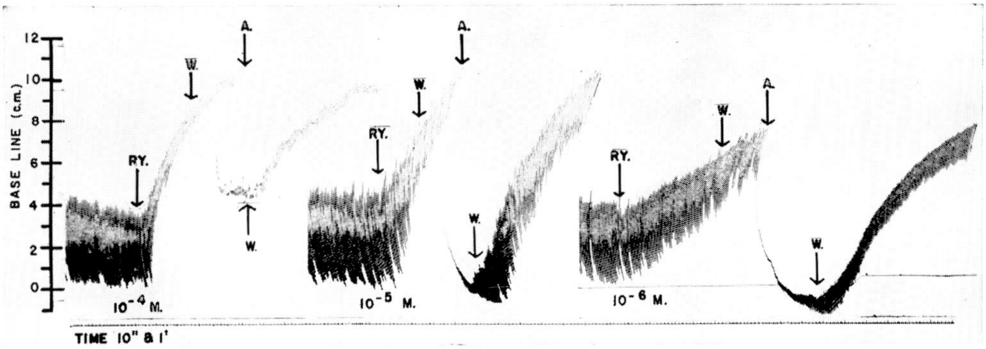

FIG. 1. The effect of ryanodine on the spontaneous activity and longitudinal muscle tonus of isolated rabbit duodenal strips.

RY, ryanodine; W, 2-minute wash; A, epinephrine, 1 microgm. per ml. Time in 10 seconds and 1 minute. Ordinate shows base line changes in cm.

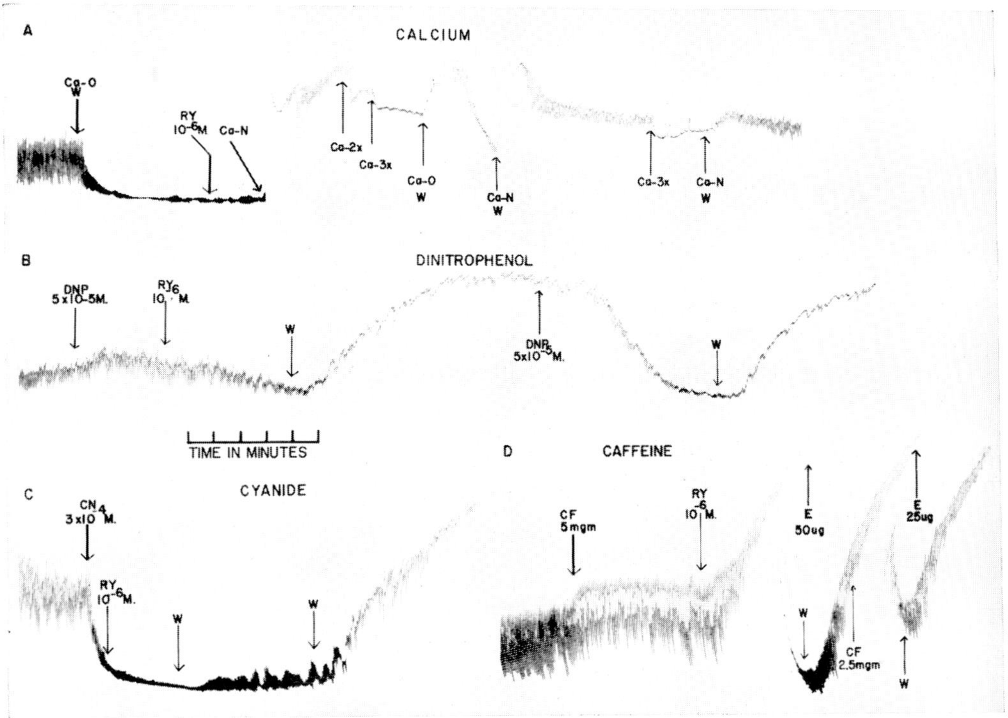

FIG. 2. Modification and antagonism of the ryanodine (RY) contracture of isolated rabbit duodenum.

A. Ca-O, calcium-free Tyrode's; Ca-N, normal calcium concentration (2.2 *mM*); Ca-2x, two times the normal Tyrode's calcium concentration (4.4 *mM*); Ca-3x, three times the normal Tyrode's calcium concentration (6.6 *mM*). B. DNP, dinitrophenol. C. CN, sodium cyanide. D. CF, caffeine; E, epinephrine; W, 2-minute wash. See text for discussion.

(Procita, 1956) and mammalian auricle preparations (Hillyard and Procita, to be published) indicated that the activity or tone of the particular type of muscle being studied determined, to a degree, the rate of onset and over-all effectiveness of ryanodine. In the experiments described below conditions were chosen which would diminish or enhance the activity of the muscle segment. The effectiveness of ryanodine on these altered states of activity was then studied.

Effect of 2,4-dinitrophenol (DNP): The addition, in terms of final concentration, of $5 \times 10^{-5} M$

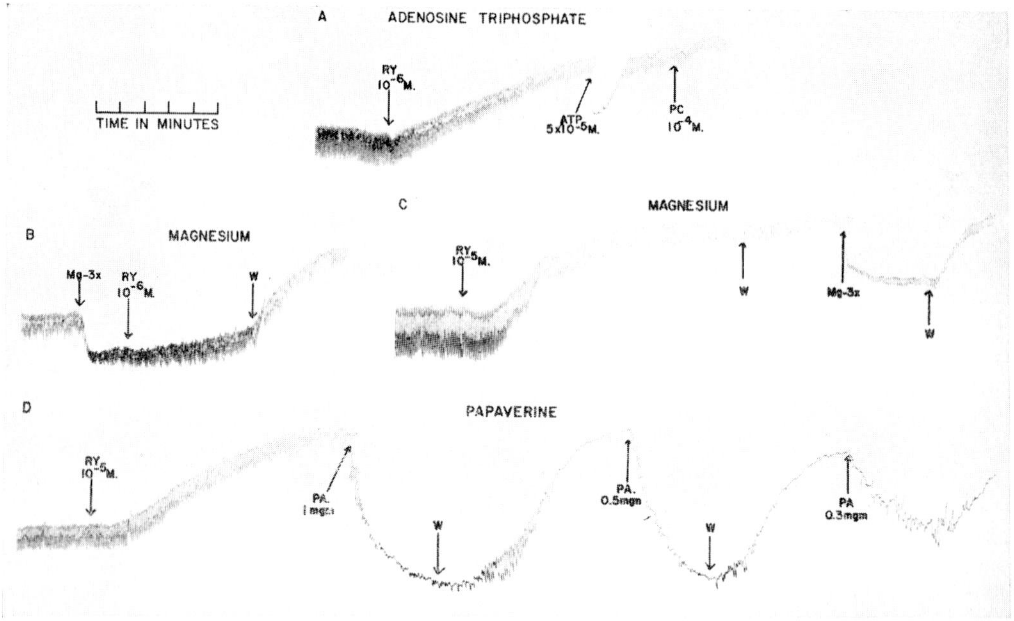

FIG. 3. Modification and antagonism of ryanodine-(RY) induced contracture of isolated rabbit duodenal strips.

A. Adenosine triphosphate (ATP), creatine phosphate (CP). B. and C. Mg-3x, 3 times the normal Tyrode's concentration of magnesium (8.4 *mM*). D. Papaverine (Pa); W, 2-minute wash. See text for discussion.

DNP, as illustrated in figure 2B, had very little initial effect on the intestinal segment. The addition of $10^{-6}M$ ryanodine approximately four minutes later did not produce the usual relatively prompt action which generally occurred over a five-minute period. Within a minute, however, following a change of the Tyrode's solution the usual effect of ryanodine appeared. At the height of the ryanodine effect a second addition of $5 \times 10^{-5}M$ DNP effected a relaxation of the contracted intestinal segment, but again a change of Tyrode's solution revealed the persistence of the ryanodine effect.

Effect of sodium cyanide: As is illustrated in figure 2C, cyanide, in a concentration of $3 \times 10^{-4}M$, produced a profound depression of rhythmic contractility in the intestinal segment. When this was followed by the addition of $10^{-6}M$ ryanodine, here also, there was no noticeable action of the ryanodine until the Tyrode's solution had been thoroughly changed. Then the usual ryanodine-induced contracture became apparent readily. Although not shown in figure 2C, the readdition of cyanide effected a relaxation of the intestinal segment, and then washing with fresh Tyrode's solution brought about a reappearance of the contracture similar to that described above for DNP.

Effect of decreased and increased calcium environment: The replacement of normal Tyrode's solution by a calcium deficient Tyrode's solution produced a marked diminution in rhythmical activity of the intestinal segment as shown in figure 2A. The addition of $10^{-6}M$ ryanodine during this period of time, with no calcium present, produced no apparent effect on the mechanical response of the muscle strip. When calcium was added back to the Tyrode's solution, or the latter was replaced by a normal Tyrode's solution, a pronounced augmentation in tone appeared, followed by rhythmical activity and the usual ryanodine effect as shown in figure 2A. In the same segment, increasing the calcium concentration from 0.0022 to 0.0044 *M* and 0.0066 *M* brought about a slight relaxation of the contracted muscle, while replacement by a calcium-free Tyrode's solution effected a greater relaxation, which, in turn, was reversed by a normal Tyrode's solution. Here, as in previously described situations and subsequent ones, the effect of ryanodine persisted.

Effect of increased magnesium: As shown in

figure 3B a threefold increase of the magnesium (to 0.0084 M) reduced the rhythmical activity of the strip slightly and slowed the time of onset of the effect of $10^{-6}M$ ryanodine. After washing, however, the tone of the segment increased fairly rapidly. In figure 3C is shown the effect of 3 times the normal magnesium content on the increased tonus produced by $10^{-5}M$ ryanodine. A partial relaxation is evident, as in the reversal when the solution was replaced by a normal Tyrode's solution.

Effect of caffeine: In an attempt to determine what effect an increase in activity of the intestinal strip would have on the ryanodine-induced contracture, caffeine was added to the muscle bath prior to the addition of ryanodine. The effect of caffeine itself in a total amount of 5 mgm. had no significant action other than to effect a slight elevation of the tone. Ryanodine, however, in a final concentration of $10^{-6}M$, with the caffeine still present, induced the contracture somewhat more rapidly. This is evident by comparing figure 1 with figure 2D, in which a similar concentration of ryanodine was utilized.

Effect of some agents which relax intestinal smooth muscle on the ryanodine contracture. Epinephrine: As illustrated in figure 1 epinephrine, in doses of 50 microgm., induced an excellent relaxation of the ryanodine-contracted intestinal segment. The relaxation, however, was transient in nature as removal of the epinephrine from the muscle chamber caused a return of the ryanodine-contracted state.

Papaverine: This agent, which is very effective in relaxing most smooth muscle, proved to be, as illustrated in figure 3D, as effective as epinephrine in relaxing the ryanodine-contracted duodenal segment. As observed with other agents previously described, the intestinal segment remained relaxed only as long as the papaverine was present in the bath. Removal by washing brought about an immediate return to the contracted state.

Other agents: Procyclidine hydrochloride (Kemadrin), an antispasmodic related to trihexyphenidyl, and the antihistaminic pyrilamine (Neo-antergan) were also found to be effective in relaxing the ryanodine-contracted intestinal strip. In the case of the latter named agent less than 2-mgm. amounts were ineffective. With either agent, however, removal of it from the muscle chamber resulted in a return of the intestine to the contracted state. In other experiments atropine was partially effective, in doses much greater than those required to block the action of acetylcholine.

Finally, as illustrated in figure 3A adenosine triphosphate (ATP) and creatine phosphate (PC) were also utilized. In the former instance the relaxation effected was transitory in nature and reversal to the contracted state occurred without washing. Creatine phosphate was not at all effective. Sodium pyrophosphate, in a final concentration of $10^{-4}M$ was also found to be ineffective.

Discussion. The foregoing experiments clearly demonstrate that ryanodine, in addition to having a profound effect on skeletal and cardiac muscle as previously reported (Procita, 1956; Hillyard and Procita, 1956; Furchgott and De Gubareff, 1956), is pharmacologically active also on rhythmically contracting smooth muscle. The irreversible contracture produced in smooth muscle is qualitatively similar to the effect produced in skeletal muscle by ryanodine. On the other hand, in cardiac (atrial) muscle the course of events after ryanodine is a rapid and progressive loss of contractility. There are two features of the ryanodine effect which are, however, common to all three types of muscle: a) the speed of onset and magnitude of the effect appear to be directly related to the degree of activity of the muscle, and b) thus far the ryanodine effect has been found to be persistent once initiated.

The importance of some degree of existing activity in the muscle preparation is evident from the experiments described in this communication. Variations of the calcium concentration, and also of the environmental temperature (unpublished experiments) of the bath, which chiefly influence the existing rhythmical activity, have a decided effect in slowing the time of onset of the ryanodine-induced contracture. In addition, such agents as DNP and sodium cyanide, both of which depress the muscle through their effect on metabolic activity, inhibit the action of ryanodine so long as they are concurrently present with the ryanodine. This also appears to be the case for any agent which depresses the rhythmical activity of the muscle. On the other hand, caffeine, which presumably stimulates activity in the muscle (metabolic or otherwise) appears to hasten the onset of the ryanodine effect. The importance of activity in the muscle is further substantiated from observations on the considerably less active isolated duodenal or ileal strips from guinea pigs, rats or kittens, on which ryanodine produced no observable effect. All of the experimental evidence to date would suggest then that while activity of the muscle is required for the action of ryanodine to occur, it is not required for penetration and attachment of the ryanodine molecule to its particular site of action.

The irreversibility of the action of ryanodine is indicated by the demonstration that following the thorough washing of the muscle bath the contracture persisted. The irreversibility is further emphasized by those experiments in which a ryanodine-contracted muscle, when relaxed by such smooth muscle relaxants as epinephrine and papaverine, returned to the contracted state following the removal of the relaxing agents from the muscle bath. The persistence of the ryanodine effect, utilizing relatively small concentrations of the drug, would suggest a remarkable degree of specificity for interference with some important step in the relaxation mechanism of smooth muscle.

SUMMARY

The purified South American plant alkaloid, ryanodine, in concentrations extending to $10^{-7}M$, produces a progressive increase in the longitudinal muscle tonus of rhythmically active isolated duodenal strips from the rabbit.

The rate of onset and the degree of the ryanodine effect is dependent on the degree of existing activity in the muscle. Alteration of the environment by such methods as decreasing the ionic calcium strength, increasing the ionic magnesium strength, the addition of such metabolic inhibitors as DNP or cyanide, all changes which decrease the activity of the muscle, will either slow the rate of onset of the ryanodine contracture or inhibit it.

The ryanodine-induced contracture of intestinal smooth muscle is irreversible. Temporary antagonism or prevention is possible with agents capable of producing a relaxation of smooth muscle. Removal of the antagonist, however, brings about a prompt return of the contracted state.

REFERENCES

FURCHGOTT, R. F., AND DE GUBAREFF, T.: Fed. Proc., **15**: 425, 1956.
HILLYARD, I. W., AND PROCITA, L.: Fed. Proc., **15**: 438, 1956.
PROCITA, L.: THIS JOURNAL, **117**: 363, 1956.

8026

CHANGES OF HEART RATE CAUSED BY DIRECT CARDIAC ACTION OF RESERPINE[1, 2]

OTTO KRAYER AND JAIME FUENTES[3]

Department of Pharmacology, Harvard Medical School, Boston, Massachusetts

Received for publication February 13, 1958

In the previous investigations dealing with the chronotropic cardiac action of the *Rauwolfia* alkaloids (Bein, 1956) emphasis is placed predominantly on the primary sites of action outside the heart. The present study was started in 1955 to examine, in the isolated heart of the dog, three effects of reserpine due to direct cardiac action, *i.e.*, the rate-increasing effect, previously observed by Plummer *et al.* (1954) in the heart-lung preparation; the rate-decreasing effect in the heart with normal sino-atrial (S-A) rhythm; and the rate-decreasing effect in the heart under the influence of epinephrine or ephedrine, to which Salva (1955) and Chatterjee and Häusler (1955) have already drawn attention.

METHODS. More than 60 heart-lung preparations of the dog (HLP) were used throughout these studies, according to the technique described by Krayer (1931). Care was taken to keep the general conditions of the HLP as uniform as possible. The arterial blood pressure ranged between 96 and 111 mm. Hg. The systemic output at the start of the experiments averaged 600 ml./min. (range 450 to 750 ml.). Total blood volume averaged 1100 ml. (range 900 to 1200 ml.). The lungs were ventilated with a mixture of 95 per cent oxygen and 5 per cent carbon dioxide, except in three experiments in which room air was used. The blood temperature ranged from 38° to 39°C. between experiments. In an individual experiment it did not vary, as a rule, by more than ±0.2°C.; only in an occasional experiment was the change as much as ±0.5°C.

In order to examine the action of reserpine upon the activity of the atrioventricular (A-V) node, A-V nodal rhythm was evoked in 5 experiments, as described earlier (Krayer *et al.*, 1955).

The reserpine used in these experiments was from two batches; one consisted of reserpine base,[4] the other was a lyophilized preparation of reserpine phosphate[5] containing 2 mgm. of ascorbic acid and 12 mgm. of lactose for 1 mgm. reserpine phosphate. The reserpine base was brought into solution with acetic acid. If large doses were to be given, 5 per cent glucose solution was used as a solvent. The lyophilized preparation was dissolved in distilled water. The injections were made into the venous blood supply close to the heart. The time taken for an individual injection of reserpine was usually 1 to 2 minutes for doses up to 2 mgm., and up to 4 minutes for larger doses. In several experiments in which large doses of reserpine acetate were given, continual determinations of the blood pH were made (see fig. 3); no changes were detectable. The blood samples were drawn anaerobically and the pH measured in a Beckman Model G pH meter. All samples were read at room temperature and corrected back to 38°C. using the factor described by Rosenthal (1948). For most determinations a hypodermic type glass electrode (Beckman 290-78) in combination with a fiber type reference electrode (Beckman 270) was utilized. The accuracy of this electrode system is ±0.03 pH unit.

Two sets of controls (5 experiments each) were run. In one, nothing was administered; in the other, the material used for lyophilizing,[5] put up in an identical way but without reserpine, was injected in amounts corresponding to the dose of 3 mgm. of reserpine base (in table 1 this is indicated by the symbol P3).

To increase the heart rate, *l*-epinephrine or *l*-ephedrine were used. Epinephrine in the form of the bitartrate was given by continuous infusion using a motor-driven syringe. The solution of about 1:10,000 (w/v) of the base in distilled water

[1] Some of the results of this study were briefly reported at the Federation meeting in Atlantic City, April 1956 (Krayer and Fuentes, 1956).

[2] This work was supported by grants from the American Heart Association, the U.S. Public Health Service (H-2205) and the Eugene Higgins Trust.

[3] Rockefeller Travelling Fellow. Present address: Department of Pharmacology, Medical School of Leon, Mexico.

[4] Generously supplied by Dr. Norbert Neuss, Eli Lilly and Company, Indianapolis, Indiana.

[5] Generously donated by Dr. F. Yonkman, Ciba Pharmaceutical Products, Inc., Summit, New Jersey.

TABLE 1

The rate-increasing effect of reserpine in the dog heart-lung preparation with regular S-A rhythm

Exp. No.	Reserpine	Initial Rate	Increase in % of Initial Rate	Time to Maximal Effect*	Duration of Maximal Action†
	mgm.	*beats/min.*		*min.*	*min.*
19a	—	150	8	60	
42a	—	145	0	60	
42b	—	143	−1	60	
42d	—	146	1	60	
63	—	159	12	60	
			Ave. 4 (S.D. 5.7)‡		
43	P3§	147	3	40	
51	P3	112	7	60	
64	P3	160	−5	60	
65	P3	125	0	60	
66	P3	140	2	60	
			Ave. 1 (S.D. 4.4)		
14	0.01	125	9	50	
21a	0.01	133	8	50	
21i	0.01	143	6	30	
22i	0.01	177	1	50	
			Ave. 6 (S.D. 3.6)	Ave. 45 (S.D. 10.0)	
28i	0.03	152	7	25	>13
31i	0.03	149	11	60	30
33i	0.03	139	15	65	35
			Ave. 11 (S.D. 4.0)	Ave. 50 (S.D. 21.8)	
9	0.1	187	12	35	22
36	0.1	183	11	30	17
37	0.1	176	14	35	22
38	0.1	146	23	30	24
			Ave. 15 (S.D. 5.5)	Ave. 33 (S.D. 2.9)	
8	0.3	140	29	45	>17
35	0.3	160	27	25	18
10	0.6	127	18	30	>10
11	1	170	24	20	19
12	1	121	38	35	15
27	1	160	28	25	7
28	1	136	65	25	10
29	1	159	23	12	11
			Ave. 36 (S.D. 17.5)	Ave. 23 (S.D. 8.4)	

TABLE 1—*Continued*

Exp. No.	Reserpine	Initial Rate	Increase in % of Initial Rate	Time to Maximal Effect*	Duration of Maximal Action†
	mgm.	*beats/min.*		*min.*	*min.*
39	3	135	39	20	11
41	3	142	49	15	8
42	3	168	36	18	9
48	3	116	38	15	—
49	3	165	31	20	—
50	3	126	59	25	13
52	3	148	50	25	16
56	3	126	54	20	13
62	3	156	24	20	13
8i	3	130	48	13	10
23i	3	152	26	15	8
			Ave. 41 (S.D. 11.6)	Ave. 19 (S.D. 4.0)	
4	5	195	16	12	>2
13	5	130	64	20	—
19	5	163	31	20	9
20	5	160	49	25	>5
22	5	162	17	10	10
			Ave. 35 (S.D. 20.8)	Ave. 17 (S.D. 6.2)	
21	10	162	28	15	5

* In the control experiment without reserpine and with P3 the time indicates the period of observation *after* establishment of initial rate which usually required 20 to 30 min.

† No data are given with 0.01 mgm. reserpine, because the effect was uncertain; (>) means that some other observation was made after the time indicated; (—) means that a slight drop in temperature precluded accurate determination.

‡ S.D. = standard deviation.

§ P3 indicates lyophilizing material without reserpine, corresponding to 3 mgm. of the alkaloid.

was administered at the rate of approximately 5 microgm./min. for 3 to 5 minutes to bring the concentration in the blood of the HLP near the desired level. This was then established and maintained by shifting the rate of infusion to 3 microgm./min. Ephedrine was given as sulfate in two or three divided doses of 1 mgm. each as described by Krayer and Ourisson (1954).

The doses of the drugs refer to the bases, except in the case of atropine, the doses of which refer to the sulfate.

RESULTS. 1. *The rate-increasing effect of reserpine.* The rate-increasing action was studied in 36 experiments in the normal heart using doses from 0.01 mgm. to 10 mgm. of reserpine. The results, together with the corresponding heart rate data of two sets of five control experiments each, are given in table 1. The time course of the effect is illustrated in the representative experiments of fig. 1.

The rate-increasing effect becomes distinctly noticeable at a dosage level of 0.03 mgm., and rises proportional to the dose up to the level of 1 to 5 mgm. Higher doses do not appear to cause a greater increase in rate, but this has not been adequately explored. The effect develops gradually. The maximum is attained within 10 to 50 minutes; the higher the dose, the more rapidly the maximum develops. However, even in the range of 3 to 10 mgm., 10 to 25 minutes are required to reach the maximal heart rate. The duration of the maximal effect is in the order of 10 to 25 minutes and tends to be shorter with

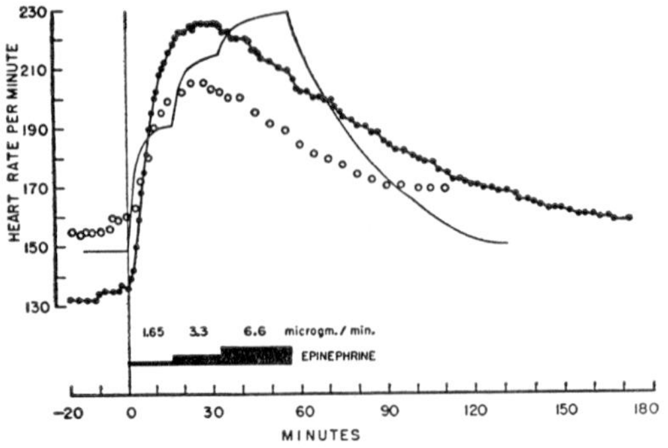

FIG. 1. The effect of reserpine and of continuous infusion of epinephrine upon heart rate.

Dog heart-lung preparations. Open circles: Dog 10.9 kgm. female. Mean art. pressure 104 mm. Hg. Temp. 38.8 ± 0.1° C. Full circles: Dog 10.1 kgm. female. Mean art. pressure 99 mm. Hg. Temp. 38.5 ± 0.2° C. Continuous line without individual experimental points: Dog 13.2 kgm. female. Mean art. pressure 112 mm. Hg. Temp. 37.2 ± 0.5. In all three experiments the total blood volume was approximately 1000 ml. and the systemic output about 450 ml./min. In the first and second experiments 1 mgm. reserpine was given at zero time; in the third experiment, starting at zero time, *l*-epinephrine bitartrate was administered by continuous infusion at 1.65, 3.3 and 6.6 microgm./min. (of the base), as indicated by the black bar. For further explanation see text.

the higher doses. As a rule, more than 3 hours are required for the return to the initial rate.

In the heart with A-V rhythm (see table 2) the rate-increasing effect is similar, except that the development of the maximal effect proceeds faster than with S-A rhythm. Only in one of the five experiments (exp. 30) did the rate rise conspicuously above the initial rate prior to the exclusion of the S-A node. In the representative experiment of fig. 2 (exp. 33) the time intervals between atrial and ventricular activation are recorded. They were obtained by measuring the time interval between an auricular complex, recorded directly throughout the experiment from the same point in the auricle, and the corresponding ventricular complex. Changes in these measurements indicate either changes in V-A conduction or shifts of the pacemaker. It is to be remembered that the clamp, used to exclude the S-A node, was left in place, and no reversion to S-A rhythm with consequent increase in rate was possible in these experiments.

2. *The rate-decreasing effect of reserpine.* After a total dose of 1 mgm. reserpine, or more, has exerted its maximal cardioaccelerator effect, no further increase in heart rate can be obtained by the same or even a larger additional dose; rather, the effect is a decrease in heart rate. In ten experiments, the heart rate decrease could be pushed to the initial rate, or below, by a total dose of 15 mgm. reserpine. Higher doses lowered the rate still further. In two of the experiments (*e.g.*, see fig. 3), a change in the sequence of atrial and ventricular activation eventually appeared. In all the others, regular S-A rhythm was maintained throughout. The phenomenon of the biphasic action of reserpine is illustrated in the representative experiment of fig. 3. The rate-decreasing effect develops fast; the new level of rate is nearly reached within one to two minutes after the end of the injection and is well established within ten minutes. Increments of 5 mgm. of reserpine are best suited for a step-wise increase of the effect.

The secondary rate-decreasing action of large doses of reserpine is also apparent when the heart is under A-V rhythm (see fig. 2).

3. *The antiaccelerator action of reserpine.* In the 10 experiments just described an attempt was made to antagonize the rate-decreasing effect of large doses of reserpine by ephedrine or epinephrine. Both substances proved effective. However, the maximal heart rate obtained with 2 to 3 mgm. of ephedrine in 6 experiments averaged only 176 (range 128 to 200) beats/min. after pretreatment with 20 mgm. reserpine or more (for comparison with the response of the normal HLP see below). Likewise, in 3 experiments, the continuous infusion of 3 microgm./min. of epinephrine increased the rate relatively little. In the experiment of fig. 3, even the continuous

TABLE 2

The rate-increasing effect of reserpine in the dog heart-lung preparation with A-V rhythm

Exp. No.	Initial Rate (S-A rhythm)	Reserpine Dose	A-V Nodal Rhythm: Rate before reserpine	A-V Nodal Rhythm: Maximal rate after reserpine	Time to Reach Maximal Rate
	beats/min.	*mgm.*	*beats/min.*	*beats/min.*	*min.*
34	152	0.3	80	125	20
31	145	1.0	79	119	7
32	166	1.0	60	178	10
30	125	3.0	70	168	5
33	168	3.0	99	170	10

infusion of 32 microgm./min. failed to restore the initial rate.

When acceleration was produced in the normal heart (two experiments) by continuous infusion of 3 microgm. of epinephrine/min., complete inhibition of acceleration was achieved by successive doses of reserpine. In both experiments (initial rates: 140 and 191/min.) the maximal rate level established by epinephrine (219 and 248/min.) was further increased (to 230 and 259/min.) by 1 mgm. reserpine, given as the first dose. Increasing the total dose of reserpine in the HLP by increments of 5 mgm. or 10 mgm. reduced the rate in step-wise fashion, as seen with antiaccelerator substances of the veratramine type. As in the case of veratramine, the new rate level, as a rule, was established within a few minutes and was maintained. The dose causing 50 per cent inhibition of acceleration in both cases was about 10 mgm. Further increase

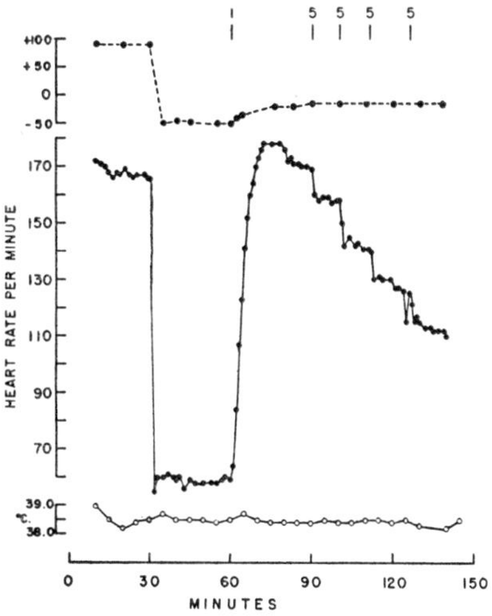

FIG. 2. The effect of reserpine upon A-V nodal activity.

Dog 12.2 kgm. female. Heart-lung preparation. Total blood volume 1200 ml. Mean arterial pressure 96 mm. Hg. Systemic output 620 ml. before, 340 ml. after clamping off S-A nodal region, and 570 ml. after 1 mgm. of reserpine (between time 70 and 90 min.). Successive doses of 5 mgm. of reserpine gradually decreased output to 400 ml. at time 140. Curves from top to bottom: sequence of atrial and ventricular activation in msec., (+) indicates normal sequence, (−) ventricular activation precedes atrial activation, zero indicates simultaneous activation; heart rate per minute; temperature of blood. At time 30, the S-A nodal region was clamped off; at time 60, 90, 100, 111 and 126, reserpine was administered as indicated by the figures (mgm.) at the top. For further explanation see text.

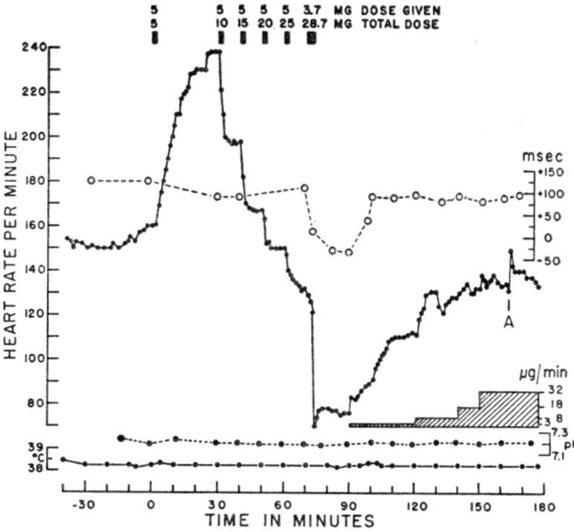

FIG. 3. The effect of cumulative doses of reserpine upon heart rate.

Dog 9 kgm. female. Total blood volume 1180 ml. Mean arterial pressure 111 mm. Hg. From top to bottom: sequence of atrial and ventricular activation, calibration at right in msec., (+) indicates normal sequence, (−) ventricular activation precedes atrial activation, zero indicates simultaneous activation; heart rate per minute; pH of blood; temperature. At the times indicated at the top and in doses (of the base) in mgm. indicated by the figures, reserpine was administered in the form of reserpine acetate. During the time indicated by the shaded area (bottom right), epinephrine was infused. At A, 10 mgm. of atropine sulfate was injected. For further explanation see text.

in the total dose to 37.5 mgm. and 30 mgm. reserpine, respectively, caused further slowing concomitant with the appearance of irregularities of rate and rhythm.

In order to compare this effect quantitatively with the antiaccelerator action of veratramine, six experiments were made using ephedrine. After the heart rate (initial rate: 140 to 184, average 160/min.) had been increased to the maximal value (246 to 280, average 266/min.), doses, usually of 5 mgm., of reserpine were given at intervals of 10 to 15 minutes until inhibition of acceleration was complete. The results are plotted in fig. 4 on the right. In the absence of atropine in one of the experiments, the dose-response curve was not altered. The dose of reserpine causing 50 per cent inhibition of acceleration (I_{50}) in the six experiments averaged 16.5 mgm. (range 8 to 21 mgm.). For comparison, the effect of veratramine determined under comparable conditions (7 experiments, taken from Krayer and Ourisson, 1954) is plotted on the left; the I_{50} averaged 0.28 mgm. (range 0.24 to 0.33 mgm.).

4. *The effect of reserpine upon cardiac output.* Unless the competence of the heart was reduced at the start of the experiment, rate-increasing doses of reserpine had no distinct effect upon systemic output. Often, however, a very slight decrease in right atrial pressure became noticeable. With reduced competence there was an increase in systemic output concomitant with the increase in rate.

Rate-decreasing doses of reserpine led to reduction of cardiac output. This became marked when the dose increased beyond 20 mgm., and severe heart failure ensued when doses of 25 mgm. or more were given. The failure was not strictly proportional to the degree of slowing of the heart rate.

Epinephrine, norepinephrine and ephedrine increased the systemic output in this heart failure, even when they did not appreciably increase the heart rate. Similarly, in an HLP, pretreated with epinephrine (continuous infusion) or ephedrine, large doses of reserpine caused less impairment of competence than in the absence of the sympathomimetic amine, even if there was a strong rate-decreasing action. In fact, with appropriate doses of reserpine, it was possible to abolish, largely or completely, the rate-increasing effect of ephedrine in a failing heart and yet

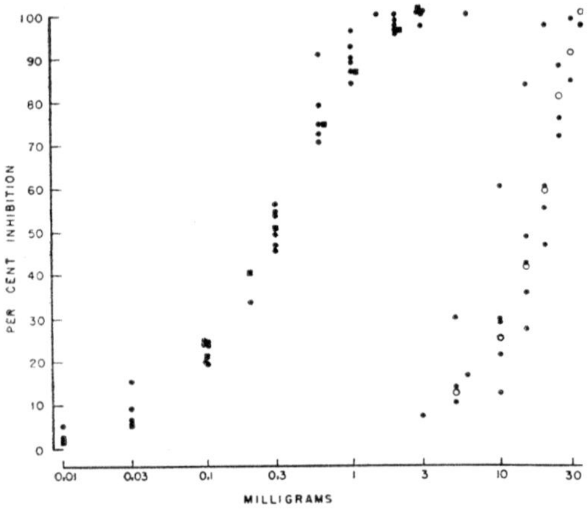

FIG. 4. Comparison of the antiaccelerator potency of reserpine with that of veratramine.

Seven dog heart-lung preparations (on the left) with veratramine (taken from Krayer and Ourisson, 1954) and six with reserpine (on the right). All experiments with reserpine except one (open circles) were made in the presence of atropine sulfate about 1:100,000 (w/v). For further explanation see text.

TABLE 3

Absolute heart rate increase in the dog heart-lung preparation by a single initial dose of 1, 3 or 5 mgm. of reserpine and by continuous infusion of 3 microgm. of l-epinephrine/min.

Heart Rate Increase	Number of Hearts	Reserpine	Epinephrine* Number of Hearts
beats/min.		*mgm.*	
20–29	2	5, 5	1
30–39	2	1, 3	
40–49	5	1, 1, 1, 3, 3	5
50–59	3	3, 3, 5	10
60–69	4	3, 3, 3, 3	22
70–79	4	3, 3, 5, 5	18
80–89	1	1	13
90–99			8
100–109			2
110–119			1
Total number of hearts	21†		80

* These data are taken from Krayer and Benforado, 1955, table 3. Temperature range 37.5 to 39°C., average 38.3°C.

† Temperature range 37.5 to 39°C., average 38.5° C.

retain a considerable degree of its positive inotropic action.

DISCUSSION. The evidence presented indicates that, in the dog, reserpine exerts an action upon the heart in the absence of connections with the central nervous system.

The rate-increasing effect of reserpine in the HLP, first observed by Plummer *et al.* (1954), has been confirmed. This effect has the characteristics of a continuous infusion of epinephrine or norepinephrine as can be seen from a comparison of the present results with earlier studies of the two catechol amines using the same experimental technique (Krayer, 1949a, b). Comparing the absolute rate increase and taking into account the variability of the epinephrine response (Krayer and Benforado, 1955), the intensity of the rate-increasing action of 1 to 5 mgm. reserpine, as shown in table 3, is somewhat less than that of the continuous infusion of 3 microgm. of epinephrine/min. In both cases, epinephrine infusion and reserpine administration by a single dose, a period of time of the same order, *i.e.* 10 to 25 minutes, is required to obtain the maximal effect. Discontinuation of epinephrine infusion results in an immediate decrease in heart rate; the decay curve, at first, is steep and becomes progressively flatter as the heart rate approaches the level of the initial rate. To reach this level, as a rule, requires 60 minutes, sometimes longer, but at the most, 90 minutes. The decay curve of the reserpine effect invariably is less steep than that after stopping epinephrine infusion. Furthermore, after doses between 1 and 5 mgm. of reserpine, initial rate is not reestablished even two hours after the heart rate began to decline. The difference is illustrated in fig. 1 (see also Paasonen and Krayer, 1958, fig. 1). Our information on norepinephrine, although less extensive, indicates no difference in action upon the HLP between the two catechol amines.

These observations can best be explained by assuming a rather rapidly rising and then fairly steady release of epinephrine and/or norepinephrine from their stores as soon as reserpine reaches its site of action. As the concentration of free catechol amine rises, the rate of "loss"[6] also increases until rate of release and rate of "loss" are equal. The beginning of heart rate decrease indicates that release becomes smaller than "loss." However, there continues to be some release for two hours or longer. This latter assumption is supported by the more rapid decline of the heart rate curve after discontinuation of epinephrine (or norepinephrine) infusion, which shows exclusively the influence of "loss" (see fig. 1).

There is no evidence to indicate what concentration of epinephrine or norepinephrine is maintained at the site of the pacemaker of the heart when the level of increased heart rate is reached which corresponds to a continuous infusion of 3 microgm./min. of either of the two catechol amines. Consequently, the experiments give no quantitative information on the amounts of epinephrine or norepinephrine which have to be released by about 3 mgm. (1 to 5 mgm.) reserpine in order to achieve a comparable rate increase. However, since the release very probably takes place in close proximity to the pacemaker, the amounts per minute involved may be relatively small.

The increase in A-V nodal activity and the influence upon right atrial pressure and output in the normal HLP and in the HLP with reduced competence agree well with the assumed release of catechol amine by reserpine. Further evidence supporting this explanation, as well as a discussion of the relevant literature referring to the release of catechol amines by reserpine in the central nervous system and in other systems, will be presented in a subsequent publication (Paasonen and Krayer, 1958).

The rate-decreasing effect of reserpine in the HLP of a normal dog only becomes apparent if, after the heart rate increase by an initial dose of reserpine, adequate amounts are administered. To bring the heart rate to or below the initial rate, total doses of 10 to 20 mgm. are required, either in a single dose or in fractional doses. Contrary to what is seen with veratramine, further increase in the total dose may lead in some hearts to a change in the sequence of atrial and ventricular activation. As with veratramine, atropine administration is without influence on the rate decrease caused by reserpine.

When the heart rate has been increased to, and is maintained at, a high level by symphathomimetic amines, initial doses of 5 mgm. of reserpine cause the rate to decrease. That doses between 1 and 5 mgm. reserpine occasionally raise the rate above the level due to the administration of sympathomimetic amine indicates that reserpine still exerts its rate-increasing, *i.e.* catechol amine-releasing, activity. Therefore, our attempts to compare quantitatively the antagonistic action of reserpine to the chronotropic effect of ephedrine with that of veratramine do not give accurate information, because, with the former, the activity of the pacemaker is increased not only by ephedrine but also by the release of the intrinsic catechol amine. Consequently, the relative potency of reserpine is probably greater than 1/40 that of veratramine (on a molar basis), as the I_{50} values of 16.5 mgm. for reserpine (M. W. 608.67) and 0.28 mgm. for veratramine (M. W. 409.59) would indicate.

Inspection of the dose-response curves of fig. 4 shows a difference in their shape. While the veratramine curve has a fairly symmetrical S-shape, the reserpine curve gives the appearance of a straight-line relationship between per cent inhibition (above 30 per cent) and log dose. This is an expression of the fact that, in the straight-line part of the curves, equal increments in effect are obtained by logarithmic increases of the total veratramine dose, while with reserpine

[6] The term "loss" is here used in the sense introduced by Veldstra (1956).

the same increment in effect is obtained by about the same increment in the total dose. It is perhaps of interest in this connection that, in the HLP with S-A rhythm, veratramine antagonizes the acceleration caused by the sympathomimetic amine but does not alter the sequence of A-V activation. The cases in which this sequence was clearly altered by large doses of reserpine indicate a factor not present in the action of veratramine.

Salva (1955) based his assumption that reserpine has antiaccelerator activity on experiments in the spinal cat. In this preparation, the rate-increasing action of epinephrine and norepinephrine upon the heart was antagonized, while there was no decrease in the vasopressor effect of the two catechol amines. Our experiments on the HLP show the effect to be atropine-resistant. In regard to the selectivity of the cardiac action, reserpine antagonizes the positive chronotropic effect of the sympathomimetic amines much more than their positive inotropic action. However, while veratramine is devoid of negative inotropic action (in doses which completely inhibit the positive chronotropic effect of 3 mgm. ephedrine), reserpine, in the larger doses required for the same effect, impairs the force of contraction and, in this regard, resembles sparteine (Fuentes, 1957) more than veratramine. Other earlier experiments in which the selectivity of this antagonistic action of *Rauwolfia* alkaloids was noticed (see, for example, Chatterjee and Häusler, 1955) do not contribute to the clarification of the reserpine activity because they were made with preparations containing, in addition, other alkaloids. Although further studies on the antagonism of reserpine to sympathomimetic effects are required to ascertain, in general, the degree of the selectivity of its action upon autonomic effectors, innervated by adrenergic nerve fibers, Salva's classification of reserpine as an antiaccelerator cardiac agent appears justified.

SUMMARY

Reserpine in single doses of 0.03 mgm. and above, when given to the isolated dog heart-lung preparation, causes a heart-rate increasing effect. The effect has the appearance of a continuous infusion of epinephrine or norepinephrine and in the dosage range of 1 to 5 mgm. is similar to the effect of approximately 3 microgm./min. of either of the two catechol amines given over a period of about 50 minutes. Long lasting release of epinephrine and/or norepinephrine best explains the phenomenon. Reserpine, in doses of 5 mgm. or larger, given to the heart under the chronotropic influence of sympathomimetic amines, has a rate-decreasing action which resembles the antiaccelerator action of veratramine in that it is atropine-resistant and antagonizes the positive chronotropic effects of extraneously supplied sympathomimetic amines. Such doses also antagonize the rate-increasing effect of initial doses of reserpine. Measured against ephedrine, the antiaccelerator potency of reserpine in the dog heart-lung preparation is about 1/40 that of veratramine (on a molar basis). Doses of 20 mgm. of reserpine and above have a negative inotropic effect upon the isolated dog heart in the heart-lung preparation.

ACKNOWLEDGMENT. The authors take pleasure in acknowledging the expert technical help given to them in the course of this investigation by Mr. Werner Mosimann, Mr. Douglas Ruane, Miss Brigitte Hofheinz and Mrs. Shirley Ruane. The pH determinations were carried out by Mr. Louis S. Harris.

REFERENCES

BEIN, H. J.: Pharmacol. Rev., **8:** 435, 1956.
CHATTERJEE, M. L., AND HÄUSLER, H. F.: Bull. Calcutta School Trop. Med., **3:** 70, 1955.
FUENTES, J.: THIS JOURNAL, **119:** 427, 1957.
KRAYER, O.: Arch. exper. Path. u. Pharmakol., **162:** 1, 1931.
KRAYER, O.: THIS JOURNAL, **96:** 422, 1949a.
KRAYER, O.: THIS JOURNAL, **97:** 256, 1949b.
KRAYER, O., ARORA, R. B., AND MEILMAN, E.: THIS JOURNAL, **113:** 446, 1955.
KRAYER, O., AND BENFORADO, J. M.: Arch. ges. Physiol., **260:** 177, 1955.
KRAYER, O., AND FUENTES, J.: Fed. Proc., **15:** 709, 1956.
KRAYER, O., AND OURISSON, P.: THIS JOURNAL, **112:** 341, 1954.
PAASONEN, M., AND KRAYER, O.: THIS JOURNAL, **123:** 153, 1958.
PLUMMER, A. J., EARL, A., SCHNEIDER, J. A., TRAPOLD, J., AND BARRETT, W.: Ann. New York Acad. Sci., **59:** 8, 1954.
ROSENTHAL, T. B.: J. Biol. Chem., **173:** 25, 1948.
SALVA, J. A.: Actualités pharmacologiques, Ed. R. Hazard, 8ième ser. pp. 153–176, Masson et Cie, Paris, 1955.
VELDSTRA, H.: Pharmacol. Rev., **8:** 339, 1956.

8027

THE RELEASE OF NOREPINEPHRINE FROM THE MAMMALIAN HEART BY RESERPINE[1, 2]

MATTI K. PAASONEN[3] AND OTTO KRAYER

Department of Pharmacology, Harvard Medical School, Boston, Massachusetts

Received for publication February 13, 1958

It has been shown (Plummer *et al.*, 1954, Krayer and Fuentes, 1956, 1958) that reserpine increases the heart rate in the dog heart-lung preparation (HLP). Krayer and Fuentes (1958) found 0.03 mgm. of reserpine capable of producing a detectable response when injected into the blood volume of about one liter of the HLP. Within the range of 0.03 to 5 mgm. the rate-increasing action was roughly proportional to the dose and, initially, resembled that produced by continuous infusion of epinephrine (E) or norepinephrine (NE). Holzbauer and Vogt (1956) and Carlsson and Hillarp (1956) found that reserpine releases catechol amines, in addition to 5-hydroxytryptamine, from brain tissue and adrenal glands. Evidence, obtained in the dog heart and in the rat heart, is presented in this publication which supports the assumption that the reserpine-induced heart rate increase may, in fact, be the consequence of NE release from the heart.

METHODS. The technique used for the HLP was the same as described in earlier studies (Krayer and Fuentes, 1958). The conditions were kept as uniform as possible regarding mean arterial pressure (about 100 mm. Hg), systemic output (500 to 700 ml. per min.) and total blood volume (about 1000 ml.). A mixture of 95 per cent oxygen and 5 per cent carbon dioxide was used for artificial ventilation. The work capacity of the heart was tested in the customary way (Krayer, 1931) by increasing the volume load in measured steps. The temperature of the blood was between 38 and 39°C. and in an individual experiment remained constant within about 0.5°C. Heart rate was read usually every minute from electrocardiographic records taken with a Grass ink-writing oscillograph. In order to preclude damage and save the right atrial tissue of the heart for the estimation of the catechol amine content, the right atrial pressure (RA pressure) was usually recorded by a water manometer through a cannula inserted via the vena cava inferior. In a few experiments pulmonary arterial pressure was recorded from one of the arterial branches of the right upper pulmonary lobe using a bromoform manometer. All injections were made close to the right atrium into the rubber tubing carrying the blood supply to the vena cava superior. Defibrinated blood was used in most experiments; in a few, clotting of the blood was prevented by giving heparin (3 mgm./kgm.) to the bleeder dog, as well as to the HLP dog prior to the isolation of heart and lungs.

Catechol amines were estimated in tissue taken from the right atrium (RA) and left ventricle (LV) of the dog heart and in the rat heart and lungs. The weight of the dog RA tissue was from 1.2 to 3 gm. (and up to 5.7 gm. in bleeder dogs); a piece weighing 6 gm. was taken from the apex of the LV of the dog. As a rule, two rat hearts and two pairs of rat lungs respectively were used for each determination. The tissues were ground with sand and 5 per cent trichloroacetic acid and extracted with the trichloroacetic acid for one hour at room temperature.

The simplified method using aluminum oxide[4] directly for adsorbtion of catechol amines (von Euler and Orwén, 1955) was first tried. For unexplained reasons our heart extracts, prepared according to this method from dogs, rats and cats, always had a strong blood pressure-decreasing component in the cat. The pressure fell within a few seconds after the injection and the depression

[1] The results of this study were reported at the Federation meeting in Chicago, April, 1957 (Paasonen and Krayer, 1957).

[2] This work was supported by grants from the U.S. Public Health Service (H-2205), the American Heart Association and the Eugene Higgins Trust.

[3] Research Fellow in Pharmacology. Present address: Department of Pharmacology, University of Helsinki, Finland.

[4] Aluminum oxide from the following sources was used: Woelm, Eschwege, Germany (non-alkaline, activity grade 1); Merck and Company, Inc., Rahway, N. J. (for chromatographic adsorbtion); E. Merck A. G., Darmstadt, Germany (for chromatographic adsorbtion according to Brockmann).

lasted from one-half minute to two minutes. It was not due to histamine or acetylcholine (the cat was treated with antagonists) and the response was different from that produced by isoproterenol or ATP. The cocaine pretreatment of the cat was not responsible for the reaction. In view of this interference, we followed the procedure suggested earlier by von Euler (p. 64, 1956).

After filtration, the catechol amines were adsorbed on aluminum hydroxide *in statu nascendi*. Provided, instead of water, 0.9 per cent sodium chloride solution (saline) was used for washing the aluminum hydroxide precipitate, separation by centrifugation was easy; one minute at about 3500 revolutions per minute proved to be sufficient. After washing twice with 20 ml. of saline, 0.25 *N* sulfuric acid was added to the residue to attain pH 3 to 4. This was then taken up with four volumes of an acetone-ethanol mixture (equal parts) and left overnight in the refrigerator at about 4°C. After filtration the acetone-ethanol mixture was removed by concentration *in vacuo*. Finally, the volume was adjusted to 1.2 to 2.5 ml., and the solution was used for bioassay usually within three days. Except in the case of the E assay, the storage period was very seldom longer. However, if a longer period was necessary the samples were kept in a deep freeze refrigerator (at −15°C.). Recoveries of NE and E, added to the tissue and acid mixture prior to grinding, were from 70 to 90 per cent of the calculated amounts. All concentrations of NE and E refer to wet weight of tissue.

Samples of coronary blood of 150 to 200 ml. were taken from the coronary sinus outflow diverted outside the heart by means of a Morawitz cannula. The samples were cooled in ice and centrifuged for 30 minutes in a refrigerated centrifuge at 2700 revolutions per minute. Under vigorous shaking, 5 ml. of 100 per cent (w/v) trichloroacetic acid were added to 100 ml. of plasma. The subsequent procedure was identical with that applied to the other tissues. The recoveries of catechol amines added to the plasma were about 20 per cent in one experiment with defibrinated blood, and about 55 per cent in another with heparinized blood. The values presented in the text are not corrected according to the recoveries.

The assays for NE and E were made biologically using the cat blood pressure and the isolated rectal cecum of the hen according to the procedure of von Euler (1948). Most cats were anesthetized with pentobarbital sodium given intraperitoneally; in some, chloralose was used by intravenous administration. Respiration was artificial. The injections of the test solutions were made into a femoral vein. Blood pressure was recorded from a carotid artery by a mercury manometer. Before starting the assay, the cat was pretreated by the combination of substances used by Kärki (1956): atropine sulfate, 2 mgm./kgm., subcutaneously; cocaine hydrochloride, 8 mgm./kgm., ergotamine tartrate, 0.15 mgm./kgm., and mepyramine maleate, 3 mgm./kgm., intramuscularly. The threshold dose for NE was about 0.005 microgm.; the preparation was 3 to 8 times more sensitive for NE than for E.

A piece of hen rectal cecum was suspended in an 8-ml. bath volume at 38°C. The bath fluid was Tyrode solution containing one-half the usual concentration of potassium chloride. To insure proper oxygenation, air was bubbled through the solution. (Oxygen with 5 per cent carbon dioxide gave less constant results.) The sensitivity of this method was 16 to 50 times higher for E than for NE.

The reserpine used was a lyophilized preparation of reserpine phosphate[5] containing for every 10 mgm. of the base 20 mgm. of ascorbic acid and 120 mgm. of lactose. The alkaloid was brought into solution with 5 ml. of distilled water for 10 mgm. of the base. Control experiments with the vehicle containing no reserpine[5] were found to have no effect. Stock solutions of *l*-epinephrine bitartrate,[6] *l*-norepinephrine bitartrate monohydrate[6] and 5-hydroxytryptamine creatinine sulfate[7] were made up in 0.01 *N* hydrochloric acid and were used for about three weeks. Unless otherwise indicated, all doses mentioned in the text refer to the bases.

RESULTS. 1. *Effect of reserpine upon the dog HLP.* a. Change in catechol amine content of the heart: If the reserpine-induced heart rate increase is due to the liberation of catechol amines from the heart tissue, as suggested by Krayer and Fuentes (1958), a decline in the content of E and NE of the heart tissue might be expected. In seven control HLP experiments, the normal content of the two catechol amines was determined. It was compared with the catechol amine content of 8 hearts taken from HLP experiments between 60 and 180 minutes after the administration of reserpine. The dose of reserpine was 3 mgm. in each of the experiments. The injection was made over a period of 2 minutes. The time course of the rate-increasing effect is shown in fig. 1 (upper curves).

The results of the two series of experiments are given in table 1. When reserpine was left

[5] Generously prepared for us by Ciba Pharmaceutical Products, Inc., Summit, N. J.

[6] Donated by Sterling-Winthrop Research Laboratories, Rensselaer, N. Y.

[7] Donated by The Upjohn Company, Kalamazoo, Mich.

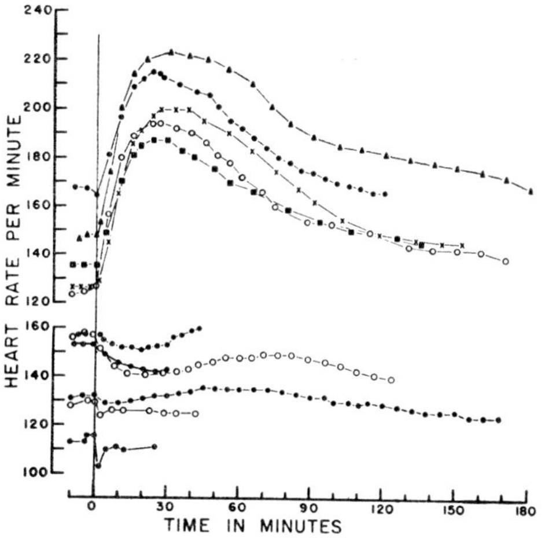

FIG. 1. The effect of reserpine upon the rate of the isolated dog heart.

Heart-lung preparations. Five upper curves: HLP from normal dogs. Six lower curves: HLP from dogs pretreated with reserpine (0.5 mgm./kgm. body weight intraperitoneally) 3 and 2 days previous to isolation of the heart. At zero time: injection of 3 mgm. reserpine. For further explanation see text.

acting for less than two hours there was no clear-cut difference in the NE content between reserpine-treated and control hearts. However, a marked difference became obvious if the hearts were exposed to reserpine for two hours or more. The mean NE content of RA in the reserpine-treated hearts of this latter group (0.31 microgm./gm.) was 27 per cent of the control mean (1.17 microgm./gm.); and the mean NE content of LV was 13 per cent of the control (0.048 as compared to 0.37 microgm./gm.).

The E content of the two types of heart tissue amounts to about 5 per cent of the NE content (table 1). No consistent decline occurred in the course of the experiments as a result of the administration of reserpine to the HLP. Low values were sometimes found in the controls as well as in the reserpine-treated hearts.

b. Effect upon heart rate after pretreatment with reserpine: If the tachycardia produced by reserpine in the HLP is the result of catechol amine release from the heart tissue, depletion of the heart in catechol amines prior to setting up the HLP should prevent the rate-increasing effect.

Two dogs were treated with 0.5 mgm. of reserpine per kgm., intraperitoneally, on two consecutive days. They were bled to death under ether anesthesia 48 hours after the last injection,

TABLE 1

Content of norepinephrine and epinephrine in right auricle (RA) and left ventricle (LV) of dog heart-lung preparations

Above, controls; below, after injection of 3 mgm. reserpine.

Experiment Date	Norepinephrine		Epinephrine		Time*
	RA	LV	RA	LV	
	micro-gm./gm.	*micro-gm./gm.*	*micro-gm./gm.*	*micro-gm./gm.*	*min.*
1/7/57	0.89	0.28	0.017	0.013	120
1/11/57	0.94	0.24	0.13	0.018	195
1/16/57	1.35	0.45	0†	0.014	83
2/7/57	1.40	0.53	0.034	0.026	120
3/21/57	1.62	0.28	0.032	0†	180
4/3/57	1.34	0.60	0.025	0.009	180
5/22/57	0.86	0.27	0.06	0.065	180
Mean....	1.20	0.38	0.043	0.022	
S.D......	0.299	0.146	0.043	0.021	
1/23/57	0.65	0.14	0.026	0.021	60
1/28/57	0.93	0.21	0.086	0.013	105
2/4/57	0.93	0.18	0.04	0.016	90
3/11/57	0.25	0.05	0.027	0.013	120
3/18/57	0.33	0.047	0.033	0.017	150
3/22/57	0.49	0.07	0.002	0.003	180
4/4/57	0.37	0.07	0.028	0.005	170
5/21/57	0.10	0.005†	0.028	0.01	180
Mean....	0.51‡	0.096‡	0.034	0.012	
S.D......	0.307	0.072	0.024	0.007	

* Approximately 20 minutes were allowed to elapse in all experiments to establish the initial rate. Time in the reserpine experiments refers to the beginning of the injection of 3 mgm. of the alkaloid as zero time. In the controls it refers to a comparable zero time.

† Not detectable.

‡ Significantly lower than control group in this table ($P < 0.01$).

and the NE and E content of the hearts was determined. The following results were obtained. *NE content:* RA, 0.019 microgm./gm. and <0.014 microgm./gm. (not detectable); LV, 0.01 microgm./gm. and 0.012 microgm./gm. Comparison of these figures with those of the normal controls for the HLP dogs in table 1 indicates that reserpine pretreatment reduced the NE content to only about 2 per cent of the control values. *E content:* the values for E in all the tissue samples of the hearts from the two dogs ranged between 0.008 and 0.011 microgm./gm., which represents about one-fourth of the averages found in the hearts of normal dogs used for the HLP.

Six dogs were pretreated with reserpine as indicated, three and two days prior to using them for setting up the HLP. When 3 mgm. of reserpine was administered to the HLP no heart rate increase occurred; if anything, there was a slight and transient decrease in rate, as shown in fig. 1. (lower curves). The hearts were analyzed for NE and E in four of these experiments 30 to 40 minutes after the administration of 3 mgm. reserpine, *i.e.*, at a time when, in the HLP from a normal dog, the rate-increasing effect was maximal or had begun to decline (see fig. 1). No NE was detectable (RA: <0.012 – <0.037 microgm./gm.; LV: <0.004 – <0.008 microgm./gm.). The E values likewise were low in these hearts (RA: <0.002, 0.005, 0.006, 0.013 microgm./gm.; LV: 0.002, 0.003, 0.003, 0.008 microgm./gm. respectively).

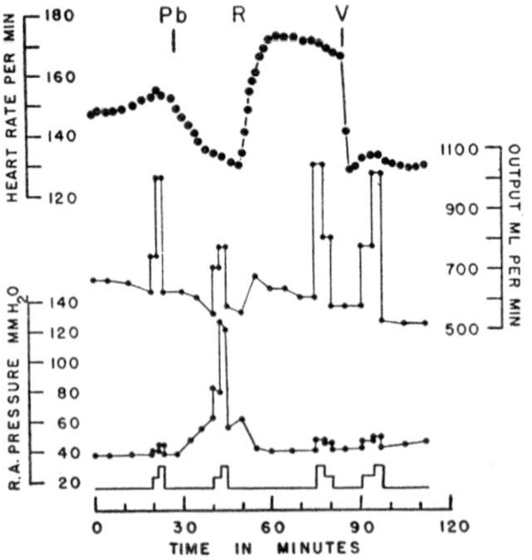

FIG. 2. The effect of reserpine upon heart rate and competence of the isolated dog heart.

Dog 8.7 kgm., male. Heart-lung preparation. Mean arterial pressure 104 mm. Hg. Total blood volume 1020 ml. Temperature 38.6 ± 0.1° C. From top to bottom: heart rate, calibration at left in beats per minute; systemic output, calibration at right in ml. per minute; right atrial pressure (water manometer attached to auricular appendage), calibration at left in mm. water; level of blood in supply vessel, the baseline corresponds to a height of 120 mm. above the zero line of the right atrial pressure. For each of the 4 competence tests the blood level was raised in either two steps of 50 mm. each or in one step of 100 mm. and was subsequently decreased to the basal level in one or two steps. Abscissa: time in minutes. Starting at Pb: sodium pentobarbital 175 mgm. was administered in five divided doses. At R: 3 mgm. reserpine were injected within two minutes starting at time 50. At V: veratramine, 0.7 mgm., was given within two minutes. For further explanation see text.

The response of the HLP to NE was not abolished by the pretreatment of the dog with reserpine. In two HLP from such animals (initial rate 102 and 123/min., respectively), the continuous infusion of 3 microgm. of NE/min. led to a maximal rate of 156 and 200/min., respectively.

c. The catechol amine content of plasma after reserpine administration: Attempts to demonstrate that depletion of NE leads to an increase in the NE concentration of the coronary sinus outflow failed. In one experiment in which defibrinated blood was used, no NE (<0.24 microgm./l. of plasma) was found prior to reserpine administration; and approximately 15 and 30 minutes after the injection of reserpine it was barely detectable (about 0.24 microgm./l. of plasma). In the first and second of these plasma samples E was found in a concentration of 0.42 microgm./l.; in the sample obtained 30 minutes after reserpine the value for E was 0.8 microgm./l. In a second experiment with heparinized blood, no NE (<0.3 microgm./l. of plasma) was found, while the following concentrations of E were present in the same three plasma samples taken before, 25 and 45 minutes after the administration of reserpine: 0.9, 1.0 and 1.2 microgm./l., respectively. When control blood of this experiment was incubated at 37°C. for 25 minutes with 3 mgm. of reserpine/l., there was no change in the content of the two catechol amines.

d. Influence of reserpine administration upon the work capacity of the heart: It was pointed out previously (Krayer and Fuentes, 1958) that the decrease in right atrial pressure after reserpine administration in the HLP suggested an influence upon contractility concomitant with the rate-increasing effect. This assumption was subjected to a more rigorous test during the present investigation. When failure had occurred in an HLP either spontaneously or as the result of the negative inotropic effect of administered sodium pentobarbital prompt reversal of the failure and improvement of competence was caused by the injection of 3 mgm. of reserpine, as shown in the representative experiment of fig. 2. Moreover, this experiment demonstrates that the rate-increasing effect could be abolished by veratramine, while the heart retained its ability to adjust its output to increase in blood supply, thus providing a further argument in favor of

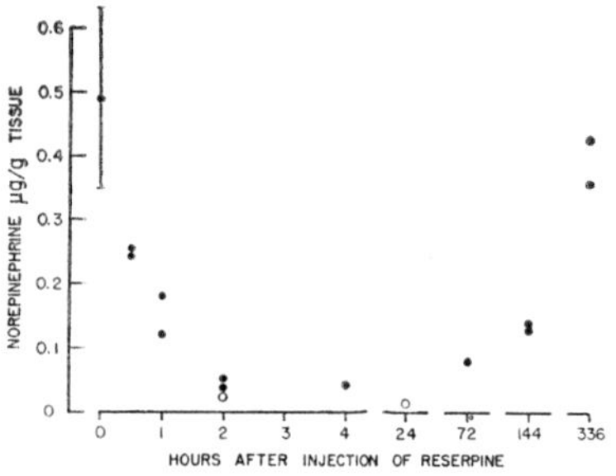

FIG. 3. The effect of reserpine upon the norepinephrine content of the rat heart *in situ*.

Rats 180 to 220 gm. body weight, male. Reserpine, 5 mgm./kgm. body weight, intraperitoneally, was given at zero time. The mean of the normal value ±S.D. was obtained from 26 rats in 13 experiments. Otherwise each circle represents the result from two combined hearts. The open circles represent experiments in which the NE content was too low to be detectable. For further information see text.

the role of sympathomimetic amines in the positive chronotropic action. No signs of positive inotropic action of reserpine occurred in the HLP of dogs whose hearts, prior to isolation, had been depleted of catechol amines.

e. Effect of 5-hydroxytryptamine on the heart rate: In two HLP experiments, 5-hydroxytryptamine, which is known to be released from tissues by reserpine, was given by continuous infusion. In one of the experiments, doses of 0.1, 1, 10 and 100 microgm./min. were administered, each for periods of 20 to 30 minutes; in the other, 3 microgm./min. was infused for 60 minutes. Little or no effect upon heart rate was observed. (Infusions between 10 and 100 microgm./min. markedly increased pulmonary arterial pressure. No such pressure increase in the pulmonary artery was noticed in several experiments after the administration of 3 to 5 mgm. of reserpine.)

In three experiments, single doses of 5-hydroxytryptamine up to 1 mgm. were given. Although in two of these experiments an immediate heart rate increase occurred with the 1-mgm. dose (19 per cent and 7 per cent of initial rate, respectively), the effect subsided within 10 minutes. In the third experiment, the rate did not change.

2. *Effect of reserpine upon the catechol amine content in the heart and lungs of the rat in situ.* As was pointed out above, the heart of the dog can be largely depleted of NE by treatment with reserpine. In order to obtain information on the character of the time course of this phenomenon the rat was used as experimental animal. The results are given in fig. 3. Two hours after a dose of 5 mgm. of reserpine/kgm., injected intraperitoneally, 10 per cent or less (<0.023, 0.033, 0.051 microgm./gm.) of the control NE value (0.491 ± 0.141, S.D.) was found in the heart. After six days, recovery was obvious, although the NE content remained far below the control values. A period of about two weeks was required to replenish the NE stores.

The E content of the rat heart was about 5 per cent of the NE content. There was no indication of a depletion of E along with that of NE. In fact, if there was any change, the values of E obtained 5 and 14 days after reserpine administration were higher than expected.

Reserpine also depleted the rat lungs of NE. The mean concentration in this tissue was 0.043 microgm. of NE/gm. and 0.027 microgm. of E/gm. in three experiments on the combined lung tissue of two animals each (NE: 0.038, 0.043, 0.048 microgm./gm.; E: 0.026, 0.024, 0.031 microgm./gm. respectively). In three experiments, two hours after 5 mgm. of reserpine/kgm., intraperitoneally, no NE (<0.009 microgm./gm.) was found; while there was no definite decrease in E content, the values being 0.02, 0.02, 0.024 microgm./gm.

3. *The content of catechol amines in the "normal" dog heart.* The data given in the first part of table 1 refer to dogs of the size usually used for the HLP. Since, as a rule, the dogs which serve as a source of blood for this preparation are considerably larger (and possibly older) the hearts of such animals were examined to see whether or not there is a correlation between body weight and catechol amine content of the heart. The values obtained from the hearts of nine bleeder dogs are assembled in table 2. The first 6 animals were anesthetized with sodium pentobarbital, 35 mgm./kgm. body weight, given intraperitoneally; for the other three, ether served as the general anesthetic agent.

The mean body weight of these nine dogs was 22 kgm. (range 17 to 26 kgm.); and the mean weight of the heart was 178 ± 38.2 (S.D.) gm. The corresponding values of the HLP dogs were: body weight 9.8 (8.7 to 13 kgm.), and heart weight 82 ± 12.3 (S.D.) gm.

As a rule, the sino-auricular node was included with the RA. From two bleeder dogs, the area containing sino-auricular nodal tissue (0.9 gm.) was separately analyzed. The NE content (see

TABLE 2

*Content of norepinephrine and epinephrine in right auricle (RA) and left ventricle (LV) of the heart of large dogs**

Figures in brackets represent values found in tissue containing S-A nodal area.

Experiment Date	Norepinephrine		Epinephrine	
	RA	LV	RA	LV
	micro-gm./gm.	*micro-gm./gm.*	*microgm./gm.*	*microgm./gm.*
1/7/57	1.03	0.093	0.045	0†
1/11/57	0.65	0.028	0.054	0.024
1/16/57	0.39	0.18	0.007	0.01
1/23/57	0.62	0.15	0.016	0.027
1/28/57	0.99	0.051	0.10	0†
2/4/57	0.70	0.23	0†	0.016
2/7/57	0.97	0.29	0†	0.034
	(0.94)		(0.042)	
2/13/57	0.81	0.065	0.007	0.008
2/15/57	0.67	0.11	0.006	0.009
	0.38		0.025	
Mean.....	0.76	0.13	0.026	0.014
S.D.......	0.210	0.087	0.033	0.011

* Mean body weight 22 (17 to 26) kgm.; used as bleeders for heart-lung preparations.

† Not detectable.

table 2) was of the same order as, or less than, that found in the other part of RA.

Using Student's t-test (Fisher, 1950) the difference between the NE contents (but not between the E contents) in RA and LV of the larger and smaller dogs were found to be statistically significant ($P < 0.01$).

DISCUSSION. The results of the present investigation strengthen the assumption (Krayer and Fuentes, 1958) that the rate-increasing effect of reserpine in the HLP is due to the release of catechol amine. They point to NE as the substance most probably involved. The positive inotropic action concomitant with the heart rate increase in the failing heart thus is satisfactorily explained, as is the selective abolition of the rate-increase by veratramine.

The direct action of reserpine in the dose of 3 mgm./1000 ml. of blood in the HLP, if anything, is a slight and transient negative chronotropic effect. This is masked by the indirect action and becomes apparent if the heart has been depleted of NE prior to setting up the HLP.

In favor of NE as the responsible agent is the fact that, in the HLP, the NE content of the heart is about 20 times that of E, and it is only the former which, under the influence of reserpine, shows a marked decrease while E content in the HLP (and in the rat heart) is not significantly changed. A decrease in E content was found in the HLP of dogs pretreated with reserpine, but because of the great variability of the E values even these figures are not significantly below normal. On the other hand, no NE was found in these hearts, in agreement with the complete absence of the rate-increasing effect of 3 mgm. of reserpine.

The situation in the dog heart and in the rat heart is comparable to degeneration of the adrenergic nerves, a process which causes NE to disappear, but influences the E content much less, as was shown by Goodall (1951) in the sheep heart. If NE is located predominantly in the adrenergic nerves and E in different structures, the preferential release of NE by reserpine would appear to indicate a differential action upon the tissue elements in which the two catechol amines are physiologically held. Although the NE content was decreased both in the RA and LV of the HLP, there is evidence that the depletion in LV proceeded faster. The ratio RA concentration divided by LV concentration in the reserpine-treated groups was twice that in the control group. Whether or not this has any bearing on the relatively rapid rate increase in the HLP with A-V nodal rhythm (Krayer and Fuentes, 1958) cannot be decided.

That during the early part of the experiment in the HLP the concentration of NE does not change while the positive chronotropic action is most pronounced, emphasizes the well recognized difficulty of correlating concentrations or changes of concentrations with rates of release and intensity of action. For this reason, definitive statements on the relative importance of NE and E in the phenomenon described here must await the availability of better techniques for their determinations and for following their course in the tissue of the heart.

We assume that, as a result of the reserpine action, NE is released in proximity to the pacemaker tissue, thus increasing the rate of the heart, and in the vicinity of the contractile tissue, thus increasing the force of contraction. The same holds for the conduction tissue, since A-V conduction, likewise, is characteristically changed (Innes and Krayer, 1957).

Presumably the release occurs at or near the

sites where the conditions for inactivation of catechol amines are best. Hence, contrary to the situation when NE is infused, concentration decreases towards the bloodstream in the capillaries and relatively little escapes into the blood flow of the coronary veins. This would agree with our failure to detect NE in the coronary sinus outflow; however, our methods of determination are neither sensitive nor accurate enough to give validity to this observation. Why, in one experiment, there was an indication of the appearance of E in the coronary sinus outflow cannot be explained. It calls to mind that, on perfusion of the isolated rabbit heart, Day (1956) found more E than NE liberated.

We do not believe that the lungs in the HLP play any role in the reserpine-induced tachycardia, although, as was shown in the rat, NE can undoubtedly be released from this tissue. The amount of NE in the lungs is very much smaller than in the heart (von Euler, p. 141, 1956). Moreover, after the release the heart could only be reached via the circulation. To achieve in this way an adequate concentration of NE at the sites of action in the heart appears improbable.

The catechol amine content of defibrinated blood is negligible. Any significant role of NE or E from this source in the reserpine-induced tachycardia is ruled out by the experiments in the HLP from dogs pretreated with reserpine. The blood used in these experiments was obtained from normal bleeder dogs.

Reserpine liberates catechol amines from different parts of the central nervous system and from the adrenal glands (Holzbauer and Vogt, 1956; Carlsson and Hillarp, 1956; Bertler *et al.*, 1956; Brodie *et al.*, 1957) producing a state comparable to total sympathectomy. The release of NE from the heart in the HLP is of interest, because it emphasizes the ability of reserpine to cause an effect without the participation of the central nervous system. Denervation greatly reduces the release of catechol amines from the adrenal glands (Kroneberg and Schümann, 1957). It is possible that the somewhat lower rate of NE disappearance from the heart in the HLP as compared to the intact rat was due more to the absence of the central nervous system than to species differences.

In the whole animal the signs of catechol amine liberation after reserpine are recognizable only under special circumstances. Probably due to extracardiac action of reserpine, its rate-increasing cardiac effect remains masked when the heart is *in situ*. The discovery of the NE-releasing ability of reserpine probably explains why it increases the blood pressure after iproniazid (Chessin *et al.*, 1956) and after chlorisondamine (Maxwell *et al.*, 1957). The same explanation can probably be applied to the reserpine-induced contraction of denervated vessels of the rabbit (McQueen *et al.*, 1955) and of the denervated relaxed nictitating membrane (Maxwell *et al.*, 1957).

In view of the fact that Krayer and Fuentes (1958) found a heart rate increase in the HLP with concentrations as low as 30 microgm./l. of blood (compared to 1 mgm./l. as found by Plummer *et al.*, 1954) direct effects upon the heart of his kind may well participate in the over-all circulatory action of the drug in intact animals and man. The possibility of a slowly developing NE depletion, for example, in the heart, and its consequences requires examination.

SUMMARY

Experiments were conducted in the heart-lung preparation of the dog (HLP), in intact dogs, and in intact rats in order to examine further the effect of reserpine upon the content of norepinephrine (NE) and epinephrine (E) of the heart. The analyses of the catechol amine content of the tissues (right atrium and left ventricle of the dog heart, total heart and total lungs of the rat) were made biologically using the blood pressure of the cat and the rectal cecum of the hen.

The heart rate increase in the HLP after reserpine administration is the result of NE release from the heart tissue. In the HLP in a state of myocardial failure there is a concomitant positive inotropic effect. Veratramine antagonizes the reserpine-induced tachycardia but not the improvement of the work capacity of the heart.

Administration of reserpine (about 3 mgm./l. of blood) to the HLP leads to a marked decrease of the NE content of the heart after two hours or more; the E content, which normally is 5 per cent that of NE, shows no clear-cut decrease. There is no increase in the NE or E content of the plasma taken from the coronary sinus outflow during the maximal heart rate increase following administration of 3 mgm. reserpine to the HLP.

Dogs treated with reserpine (0.5 mgm./kgm.

body weight, intraperitoneally) 3 and 2 days prior to removal of the heart for analysis do not have NE in their hearts, the cardiac stores of E, though apparently lower, are not depleted. In the HLP, prepared from dogs pretreated in this manner, reserpine does not increase the heart rate.

In the rat heart *in situ*, reserpine (5 mgm./kgm. body weight, intraperitoneally) causes the disappearance of 90 per cent or more of NE within two hours. Replenishment requires about two weeks. There is no indication of E depletion along with the disappearance of NE. Likewise, in the rat lungs *in situ*, a depletion of NE, but not of E, follows the administration of reserpine.

5-Hydroxytryptamine, when given to the HLP by continuous infusion at rates between 0.1 and 100 microgm./min. does not increase the heart rate.

The contents of NE and E in the hearts of large sized (17 to 26, average 22 kgm.) dogs are significantly lower than those of small sized (8.7 to 13, average 9.8 kgm.) dogs.

ACKNOWLEDGMENT. The authors take pleasure in expressing their thanks to Miss B. Hofheinz and Mr. W. Mosimann for their expert technical help.

REFERENCES

BERTLER, Å., CARLSSON, A., AND ROSENGREN, E.: Naturwissenschaften, **43:** 521, 1956.

BRODIE, B. B., OLIN, J. S., KUNTZMAN, R. G., AND SHORE, P. A.: Science, **125:** 1293, 1957.

CARLSSON, A., AND HILLARP, N.-Å.: Kungl. Fysiograf. Sällrk. Lund Förh., **26:** Nr. 8, 1956.

CHESSIN, M., DUBNICK, B., KRAMER, E. B., AND SCOTT, C. C.: Fed. Proc., **15:** 409, 1956.

DAY, M.: J. Physiol., **134:** 558, 1956.

FISHER, R. A.: Statistical methods for research workers, Oliver and Boyd, Edinburgh, 1950.

GOODALL, McC.: Acta physiol. scandinav., **24:** Suppl. 85, 1951.

HOLZBAUER, M., AND VOGT, M.: J. Neurochemistry, **1:** 8, 1956.

INNES, I. R., AND KRAYER, O.: J. Physiol., **139:** 18P, 1957.

KÄRKI, N. T.: Acta physiol. scandinav., **39:** Suppl. 132, 1956.

KRAYER, O.: Arch. exper. Path. u. Pharmakol., **162:** 1, 1931.

KRAYER, O., AND FUENTES, J.: Fed. Proc., **15:** 709, 1956.

KRAYER, O., AND FUENTES, J.: THIS JOURNAL, **123:** 145, 1958.

KRONEBERG, G., AND SCHÜMANN, H. J.: Arzneimittel-Forsch., **7:** 279, 1957.

MAXWELL, R. A., ROSS, S. D., PLUMMER, A. J., AND SIGG, E. B.: THIS JOURNAL, **119:** 69, 1957.

MCQUEEN, E. G., DOYLE, A. E., AND SMIRK, F. H.: Circulation, **11:** 161, 1955.

PAASONEN, M. K., AND KRAYER, O.: Fed. Proc., **16:** 326, 1957.

PLUMMER, A. J., EARL, A., SCHNEIDER, J. A., TRAPOLD, J., AND BARRETT, W.: Ann. New York Acad. Sci., **59:** 8, 1954.

VON EULER, U. S.: Arch. internat. pharmacodyn., **77:** 477, 1948.

VON EULER, U. S.: Noradrenaline, C. C. Thomas, Springfield, Ill., 1956.

VON EULER, U. S., AND ORWÉN, I.: Acta physiol. scandinav., **33:** Suppl. 118, 1, 1955.

8028

EFFECT OF TEMPERATURE UPON THE POSITIVE INOTROPIC ACTION OF OUABAIN[1]

PAUL R. SAUNDERS AND PULAK N. SANYAL

Department of Pharmacology, School of Medicine, University of Southern California, Los Angeles

Received for publication January 23, 1958

Various aspects of the effects of temperature upon the response of myocardium to cardiac glycosides have been investigated. The toxic dose has been found to decrease with increasing temperature (Fuhrman, 1946). Several studies (Fischer, 1928; Sollmann *et al.*, 1915) on frog hearts have indicated that the rate of onset of action of these drugs is also accelerated by an increase in temperature. Gutman (1944) has found a similar relationship for the loss of excitability produced by digitoxin in frog skeletal muscle. Adequate studies on the effect of temperature upon the kinetics of the onset of action of ouabain in mammalian myocardium are lacking, however. We have studied this relationship in isolated ventricle strips contracting at a constant rate, since previous work (Sanyal and Saunders, 1958) has indicated that the rate of onset of action of ouabain is dependent upon the frequency of contraction. Our results differ from those reported previously with amphibian hearts and indicate that the rate-limiting step in the onset of action is independent of temperature and may therefore be of a physical rather than chemical nature.

METHODS. Strips were prepared from the right ventricular wall of hearts of male guinea pigs (150 to 200 gm.), mounted and stimulated at a frequency of 50 or 100 per minute in a bicarbonate-buffered medium gassed with a 1 per cent carbon dioxide—99 per cent oxygen mixture (pH 7.4), as described previously (Sanyal and Saunders, 1957). Force of contraction was measured by recording the deflection of a light beam reflected from a mirror attached to a spring lever (previously calibrated by addition of known weights to the lever arm at the point of attachment of the muscle strip). Five and one-half millimolar glucose was present in the medium. The concentration of ouabain (U.S.P.) used was 2.3×10^{-7} M (1:6,000,000).

The force of contraction of control strips in the presence of glucose at the temperatures and frequencies used remained constant for at least five hours after the conclusion of the initial equilibration period of an hour or more at both frequencies, except at 17°C. and 50 per minute, in which case the force declined slightly to 88 per cent of the initial value in 5 hours. The strips were equally stable in the absence of glucose at 100 per minute at 37°C., but the force decreased slowly at 27°C. to about seventy per cent of the initial value 5 hours after the equilibration period.

Six control experiments (no drug added) were performed at each temperature and frequency studied.

RESULTS. *Relation between temperature and force of contraction.* Strips were set up at temperatures of 17, 27, 32 and 37°C. with a frequency of 50 per minute, and at 27, 32 and 37°C. with a frequency of 100 per minute (the strip would not follow the latter frequency at 17°C.). The steady force of contraction at the end of the initial equilibration period ("initial force") under these conditions is given in table 1. It is seen that the force decreased with increasing temperature at both frequencies. Hollander and Webb (1955) found a similar relationship in rat atrium, as did Katzung and Farah (1956) in turtle myocardium at low frequencies.

Effect of temperature upon magnitude of positive inotropic action of ouabain. Ouabain was added at the end of the equilibration period to strips contracting at various temperatures with a frequency of 50 or 100 per minute. The data in table 2 indicate that the positive inotropic response increased steadily with increasing temperature.

Effect of temperature upon rate of onset of positive inotropic action of ouabain. The rates of onset of response to ouabain in the experiments described above were compared. The relation between re-

[1] This investigation was supported (in part) by research grant H-94 from the National Heart Institute, Public Health Service.

TABLE 1

Force of contraction of ventricle strips at various temperatures

Temp.	Force of Contraction*	
	Frequency (per min.)	
	50	100
°C.	*mgm.*	*mgm.*
17	250 ± 6	
27	225 ± 8	150 ± 7
32	150 ± 5	125 ± 8
37	90 ± 6	110 ± 10

* Mean values ± S.E. (6 experiments at each temperature, at both frequencies).

TABLE 2

Effect of temperature upon magnitude of positive inotropic action of ouabain

Temp.	Maximum Per Cent Increase in Force of Contraction*	
	Frequency (per min.)	
	50	100
°C.		
17	0 (6)†	—
27	15 ± 1 (6)	5 ± 1 (4)†
32	44 ± 5 (6)	27 ± 2 (6)
37	85 ± 6 (7)	48 ± 3 (8)

* Mean values ± S.E. expressed as per cent of "initial force" at temperature and frequency indicated.

† No. of experiments (in parentheses).

sponse and time can be expressed as follows:

$$-\frac{d(F_m - F)}{dt} = k(F_m - F),$$

where F_m = maximum increase in force in the presence of the drug (expressed as per cent of "initial force" at temperature and frequency indicated), F = increase in force at time t after addition of drug, and k = rate constant (Sanyal and Saunders, 1958). The equation may also be expressed in the integrated form: $-ln(F_m - F) = Kt +$ constant. Plots gf $(F_m - F)$ vs. t (figure 1) on semilogarithmic coordinates gave straight lines, indicating that the rate-determining step at the temperatures and frequencies used was first-order. A first-order relationship over a wide range of frequencies at 37°C. has been reported previously (Sanyal and Saunders, 1958).

The slope was measured for each experiment at all temperatures and frequencies and the mean values are given in table 3. The value could not be calculated accurately for the experiments at 27°C. at a frequency of 100 per minute, due to the very small effect of the drug. The slopes at 50 per minute did not differ significantly (P > 0.3, "t" test); the difference at 100 per minute was also not significant (0.2 > P > 0.1). It is evident that the effect of temperature upon the rate of onset of action of ouabain is negligible by comparison with the marked effect upon the ultimate magnitude of the action.

Discussion. Our observation that the onset of action of ouabain is not affected significantly by an increase in temperature suggests that the rate-determining step is probably a physical process. It was suggested previously (Sanyal and Saunders, 1958), on the basis of the effect of activity upon onset, that the rate was not determined by

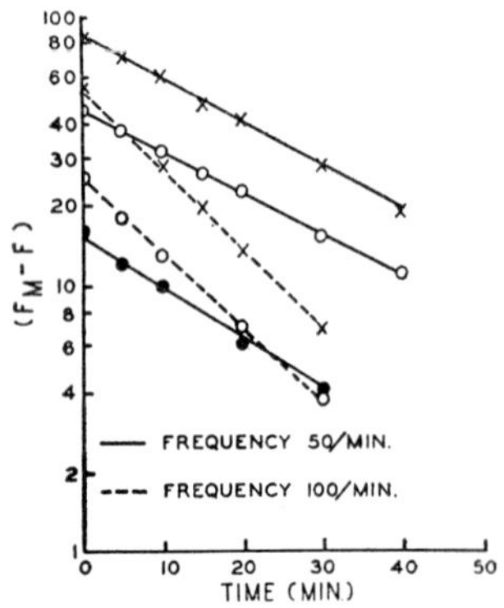

Fig. 1. Typical experiments showing $(F_m - F)$ plotted as a function of time after addition of ouabain (see text), at various temperatures. ●——●, 27°C.; ○——○, 32°C.; ×——×, 37°C.

TABLE 3

Slope of $(F_m - F)$ vs. time curves as function of temperature

Temp.	Slope of $(F_m - F)$ vs. "t"*	
	Frequency (per min.)	
	50	100
°C.		
27	−0.56 ± 0.03	—
32	−0.57 ± 0.04	−0.99 ± 0.03
37	−0.61 ± 0.04	−1.17 ± 0.09

* Mean values ± S.E. Slopes determined from semilogarithmic plots of $(F_m - F)$ vs. "t", as in figure 1.

diffusion or combination of the drug with receptors in the cell; rather, it appeared more likely that some step between combination with the cell and the observed biological response (increased force of contraction) was rate-limiting. Assuming the correctness of this view, the present work indicates that this step is highly insensitive to temperature, as is generally true of physical rather than chemical processes. Speculation as to its nature would be premature, but it might be noted that such temperature-insensitive processes are not unknown in muscular contraction; *e.g.*, Sandow (1952) found that the rate of action of the spike-activation link of excitation-contraction coupling is independent of temperature.

The lack of effect of temperature upon the onset of action is in contrast to the marked effect upon the magnitude of the positive inotropic response, indicating that different factors are involved in these two aspects of the action of the drug. The decreased effect at lower temperature may be related to some change in the ionic state of the heart. A decrease in intracellular potassium at lower temperature has been found in heart (Gollan *et al.*, 1957) and skeletal muscle (Shaw and Simon, 1955; Calkins *et al.*, 1954). Ionic changes are indicated by the results of Trautwein and Dudel (1954) and Hollander and Webb (1955), who have found an increased duration of the action potential of myocardium at lower temperatures. Recent studies on the mechanism of action of cardiac glycosides have emphasized the loss of potassium from heart (Schreiber, 1956; Holland and Dunn, 1954) and the inhibition of potassium uptake by skeletal muscle (Johnson, 1956) and red blood cells (Solomon *et al.*, 1956) which occurs in the presence of these drugs. It may be that the relative effect of cardiac glycosides is less when the intracellular concentration of potassium has been decreased previously by low temperature. Hadju (1953) found a decreased effect when the intracellular concentration of potassium was decreased by rapid rates of stimulation. However, it might be pointed out that although a loss of this ion from the myocardium does occur in the presence of toxic concentrations of cardiac glycosides (Hagen, 1939; Wood and Moe, 1942), there is evidence that this is not the case with lower doses; *e.g.*, it has been shown that therapeutic doses in humans do not affect the potassium balance of the heart (Gonlubol *et al.*, 1956).

SUMMARY

The effect of temperature upon the rate and magnitude of the positive inotropic action of ouabain upon isolated guinea pig ventricle strips has been studied at frequencies of contraction of 50 and 100 per minute.

The magnitude of the positive inotropic action of a fixed concentration of ouabain increased markedly with increase in temperature. At a frequency of 50 per minute, the per cent increase in force of contraction ranged from zero at 17°C. to 85 at 37°C.

The rate of onset of action of ouabain, however, was not affected significantly by increase in temperature, and it was suggested that the rate-determining process may be of a physical rather than chemical nature.

ACKNOWLEDGMENT. We wish to thank the Allan Hancock Foundation for the use of facilities during this investigation.

REFERENCES

CALKINS, E., TAYLOR, I. M., AND HASTINGS, A. B.: Am. J. Physiol., **177**: 211, 1954.
FISCHER, H.: Arch. exper. Path. u. Pharmakol., **135**: 39, 1928.
FUHRMAN, F. A.: Physiol. Rev., **26**: 247, 1946.
GOLLAN, F., RUDOLPH, G. G., AND OLSON, N. S.: Am. J. Physiol., **189**: 277, 1957.
GONLUBOL, F., SIEGEL, A., AND BING, R. J.: Circulation Res., **4**: 298, 1956.
GUTMAN, S. A.: THIS JOURNAL, **80**: 126, 1944.
HAGEN, P. S.: THIS JOURNAL, **67**: 50, 1939.
HAJDU, S.: Am. J Physiol., **174**: 371, 1953.
HOLLAND, W. C., AND DUNN, C. E.: Am. J. Physiol., **179**: 486, 1954.
HOLLANDER, P. B., AND WEBB, J. L.: Circulation Res., **3**: 604, 1955.
JOHNSON, J. A.: Am. J. Physiol., **187**: 328, 1956.
KATZUNG, B., AND FARAH, A.: Am. J. Physiol., **184**: 557, 1956.
SANDOW, A.: Yale J. Biol. Med., **25**: 176, 1952.
SANYAL, P. N., AND SAUNDERS, P. R.: Proc. Soc. Exp. Biol. & Med., **95**: 156, 1957.
SANYAL, P. N., AND SAUNDERS, P. R.: THIS JOURNAL, **122**: 499, 1958.
SCHREIBER, S. S.: Am. J. Physiol., **185**: 337, 1956.
SHAW, F. H., AND SIMON, S. E.: Aust. J. Exp. Biol. Med. Sci., **33**: 153, 1955.
SOLLMANN, T., MENDENHALL, W. L., AND STINGEL, J. L.: THIS JOURNAL, **6**: 533, 1915.
SOLOMON, A. K., GILL, T. J., 3RD, AND GOLD, G. L.: J. Gen. Physiol., **40**: 327, 1956.
TRAUTWEIN, W., AND DUDEL, J.: Arch. ges. Physiol., **260**: 104, 1954.
WOOD, E. H., AND MOE, G. K.: Am. J. Physiol., **136**: 515, 1942.

8029

ACTION OF ZOXAZOLAMINE UPON SPINAL SEGMENTAL REFLEXES

LESLIE E. GEIGER, PETER CERVONI, JOSEPH R. BERTINO AND FRANK MONTELEONE

Clinical Research Division, U. S. Army Chemical Warfare Laboratories, Army Chemical Center, Maryland

Received for publication January 23, 1958

Zoxazolamine (Flexin[1], 2-amino-5-chlorobenzoxazole) produces skeletal muscular relaxation by inhibition of reflex pathways within the spinal cord (Funderburk and Woodcock, 1955; Kamijo and Koelle, 1955). In this respect zoxazolamine resembles its structural analogues, benzazole and benzimidazole (Funderburk *et al.*, 1953; Goodman *et al.*, 1943) and the glycerol ether, mephenesin (Henneman *et al.*, 1949; Kaada, 1950). The therapeutic use of the latter compounds has been restricted by a combination of brief duration of action, low potency or high toxicity. Zoxazolamine, however, has been reported to be an orally effective, relatively nontoxic skeletal muscle relaxant in humans (Abrahamsen and Baird, 1956; Amols, 1956; Millichap and Hadra, 1956; Rodriguez-Gomez *et al.*, 1956; Smith *et al.*, 1956).

In comparison with mephenesin, Marsh (1955) found zoxazolamine to be approximately twice as effective in producing flaccidity in mice and cats at similar doses, orally or intraperitoneally. Comparing the effects of these two drugs upon spinal segmental reflexes of unanesthetized spinal cats, Kamijo and Koelle (1955) found zoxazolamine approximately ten times as effective in the inhibition of polysynaptic pathways. It was also found that the drug was inactive at the neuromuscular junction at doses below 60 mgm./kgm. i.v. in spinal cats, a level at which the flexor reflex is totally inhibited. At higher doses neuromuscular block occurred, resulting in flaccidity at 150 to 180 mgm./kgm. i.v. The lack of modification of this block by previous administration of neostigmine and the absence of fasciculations and twitching prior to the onset of block suggested that there was no resemblance either to the action of curare or of depolarizing agents. Marsh (1955) found that zoxazolamine produced no significant cardiovascular effects in the dosage range sufficient for production of flaccidity.

In this study the influence of zoxazolamine upon the activity of the cat's lumbosacral spinal cord is reported. Internuncial cell activity was evaluated by electrical recording from ventral roots and by examination of the variation in the frequency of motor unit discharges observed in thin ventral root filaments. In this manner the mechanism of diminution of the withdrawal reflex by zoxazolamine was examined using modifications of the electrophysiological techniques of Lloyd (1943) and Holmstedt and Skoglund (1953).

METHODS. Cats (2 to 3 kgm.) were used in all experiments. Ether anesthesia was maintained during tracheal cannulation, common carotid ligation and vertebral artery clamping. The spinal cord was then sectioned through the atlanto-occipital membrane. Anesthesia was discontinued and the animal was respired with room air at 25 strokes per minute through a variable port cannula. At least three hours were allowed to elapse before recording in order to eliminate possible influence of the anesthetic. In animals whose blood pressure was monitored, a carotid artery was cannulated. A polyethylene cannula, inserted via the femoral artery to a length sufficient to reach the thoracic or superior abdominal aorta, was used for intraarterial injections. A cephalic vein was also cannulated for injection. Body temperature was maintained by use of heating pads and/or infrared lamps.

Following transection of the cord, the animal was rigidly fixed by means of spine clamps and pins through the iliac crests. The cord and roots were exposed through lumbosacral laminectomy and a midline dural incision. All exposed nervous structures were immersed in a pool of heavy mineral oil the temperature of which was monitored. Platinum or silver electrode hooks were used for both stimulation and recording. All responses were recorded monophasically and displayed on an oscilloscope.

In one group of experiments, the response of the seventh lumbar ventral root in response to stimulation of the corresponding dorsal root was recorded. In a second series of experiments, the

[1] Flexin is the trademark of McNeil Laboratories.

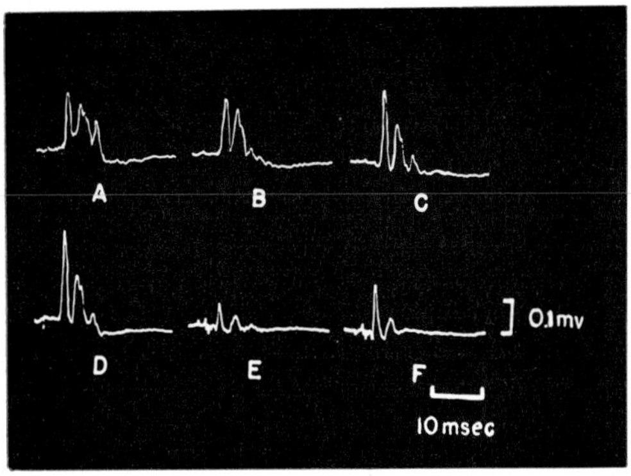

FIG. 1. Responses in L7 ventral root to deep peroneal nerve stimulation.

A, Control; B, 2 min. following intravenous injection of 30 mgm./kgm. of zoxazolamine; C, 10 min. following injection; D, 150 min. following injection; E, 10 min. following intravenous injection of 42 mgm./kgm. of zoxazolamine; F, 30 min. following second injection. Stimulus frequency, 0.3 per sec.; intensity, 0.65 V increased at D to 0.71 V; duration, 0.1 msec.

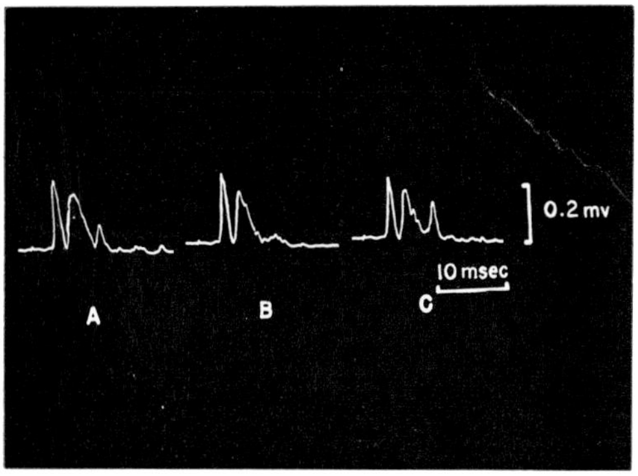

FIG. 2. Responses in L7 ventral root to deep peroneal nerve stimulation.

A, Control; B, 2 min. following intravenous injection of 16 mgm./kgm. of zoxazolamine; C, 34 min. following injection. Stimulus frequency, 0.5/sec.; intensity, 0.75 V; duration, 0.1 msec.

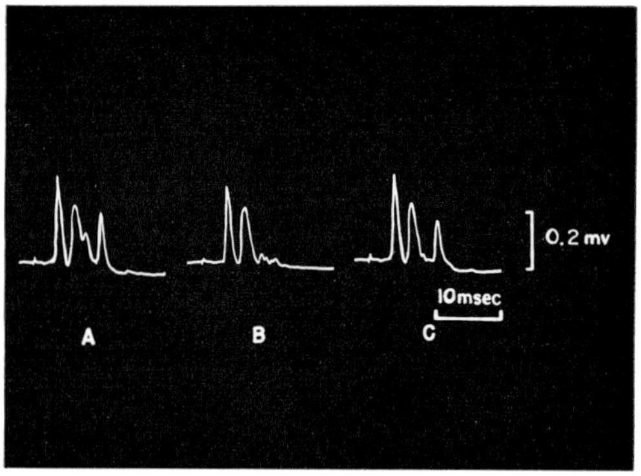

FIG. 3. Responses in L7 ventral root to deep peroneal nerve stimulation.

A, Control; B, 2 min. following intravenous injection of 32 mgm./kgm.; C, 25 min. following injection. Stimulus frequency, 0.5/sec.; intensity, 1.4 V; duration, 0.2 msec.

common or deep peroneal nerve was stimulated in order to disperse temporally the motoneurone responses recorded in the ipsilateral sixth or seventh lumbar ventral root. In these, the corresponding dorsal root was kept intact. The dorsal and ventral roots of several superior and inferior ipsilateral segments were sectioned intradurally and all nerves to the leg, with the exception of the sciatic, were cut.

In a third series of experiments, dorsal roots were stimulated with shocks of high intensity in order to activate repetitive single unit discharges which were recorded from thin ventral root filaments. When high voltage or tetanic stimuli were employed, a minimal paralytic dose of succinylcholine was injected intravenously (0.25 mgm./kgm./10 min.) in order to control twitching caused by contralateral and suprasegmental diffusion of the stimulus.

Due to the relative insolubility of zoxazolamine in water, the compound was administered as a 10 per cent solution in polyethylene glycol. This solvent was found to be without effect on any of the responses studied.

RESULTS. *Whole ventral root recording.* The series of experiments in which potential changes were recorded from whole ventral root in response to dorsal root or peripheral nerve stimulation have been grouped together for consideration. A total of 37 intravenous (i.v.) and 12 intraarterial (i.a.) injections of zoxazolamine were given to 13 animals. The dose per injection varied from 0.5 to 42 mgm./kgm. Injections were given over a 2- to 10-second interval. At least 50 per cent recovery was allowed before repetition of the same or larger concentrations. The maximum total dose given to any one animal was 120 mgm./kgm. over a period of several hours. No deaths were observed.

The monosynaptic spike was found to be unchanged in amplitude or width by any i.v. injection containing less than 20 mgm./kgm. of zoxazolamine. Following 1 of 4 injections between 20 and 30 mgm./kgm. the amplitude of the spike was depressed by 40 per cent for 5 minutes. In

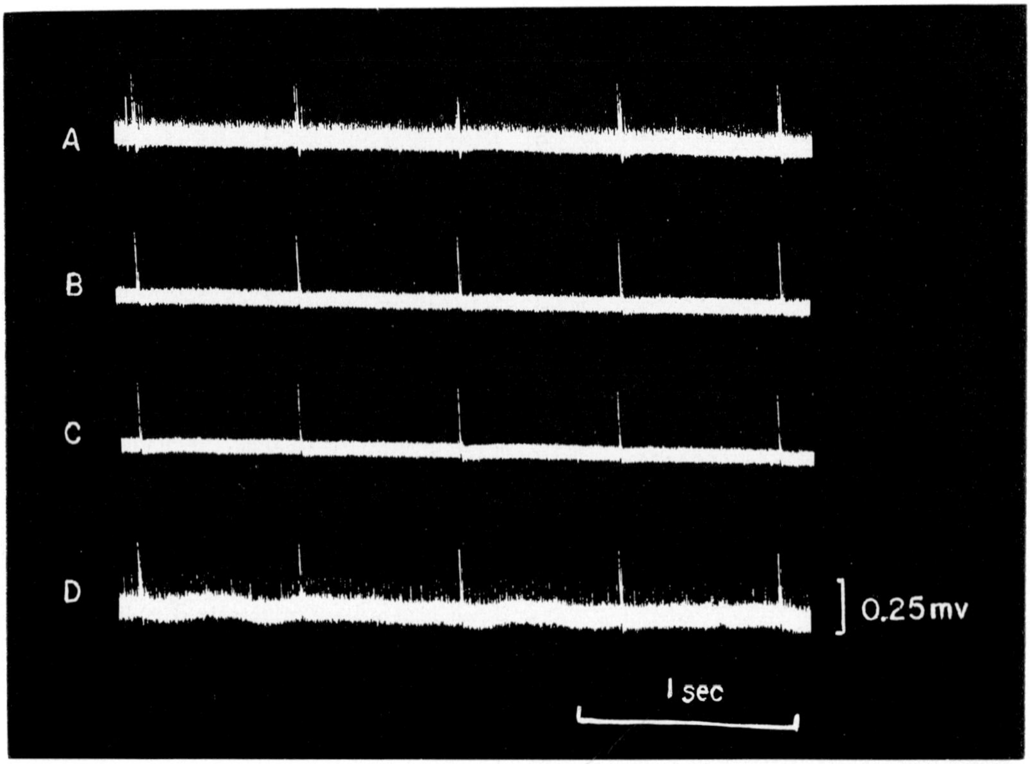

FIG. 4. Responses in L7 ventral root filament to L7 dorsal root stimulation.

A, Control; B, 2 min. following intravenous injection of 30 mgm./kgm. of zoxazolamine; C, 30 min following injection; D, 60 min. following injection. Stimulus frequency, 0.3/sec.; intensity, 11 V; duration, 0.9 msec.

the other 3, a 25 per cent increase in amplitude lasting approximately one hour was found. In all injections of between 30 and 40 mgm./kgm. i.v., the amplitude of this complex was diminished by 50 to 75 per cent for 5 to 15 minutes. Figure 1 is an oscillographic tracing demonstrating this effect. With i.a. injection, 50 per cent depression or greater was found if the dosage was more than 20 mgm./kgm. Depression lasted 5 to 45 minutes.

The 3-neurone arc represented by the first spike in the polysynaptic complex, that commencing 2.5 msec. after onset of the monosynaptic deflection, exhibited a similar degree of sensitivity to the drug as the 2-neurone, monosynaptic pathway (see figure 1).

The most striking effect of zoxazolamine was upon the polysynaptic reflexes which appeared 4.5 and 7 msec. after commencement of the monosynaptic spike. Injections of less than 15 mgm./kgm. i.v. or 8 mgm./kgm. i.a. were ineffective. In the dosage range of 15 to 30 mgm./kgm. i.v., a consistent amplitude depression of at least 50 per cent within 15 seconds after administration was found. Above this level a 90 to 100 per cent decrease was seen. Recovery occurred in each case but varied roughly with the dosage from 15 to 120 minutes. Figures 1, 2 and 3 are oscillographic recordings showing these effects.

Ventral root filament recording. In the experiments in which dorsal roots were stimulated with intense shocks in order to activate repetitive single unit discharges which were recorded from thin ventral root filaments, 28 injections of zoxazolamine were given in 9 preparations. The i.v. dosage ranged from 10 to 40 mgm./kgm. and the i.a. dosage from 2 to 30 mgm./kgm. Both the frequency of discharge evoked by the stimulus and the background activity were markedly diminished upon injection of sufficient quantity of drug (figures 4, 5, 6, table 1). To obtain the estimate for degree of inhibition given in table 1 and figure 6, the spikes falling within the first

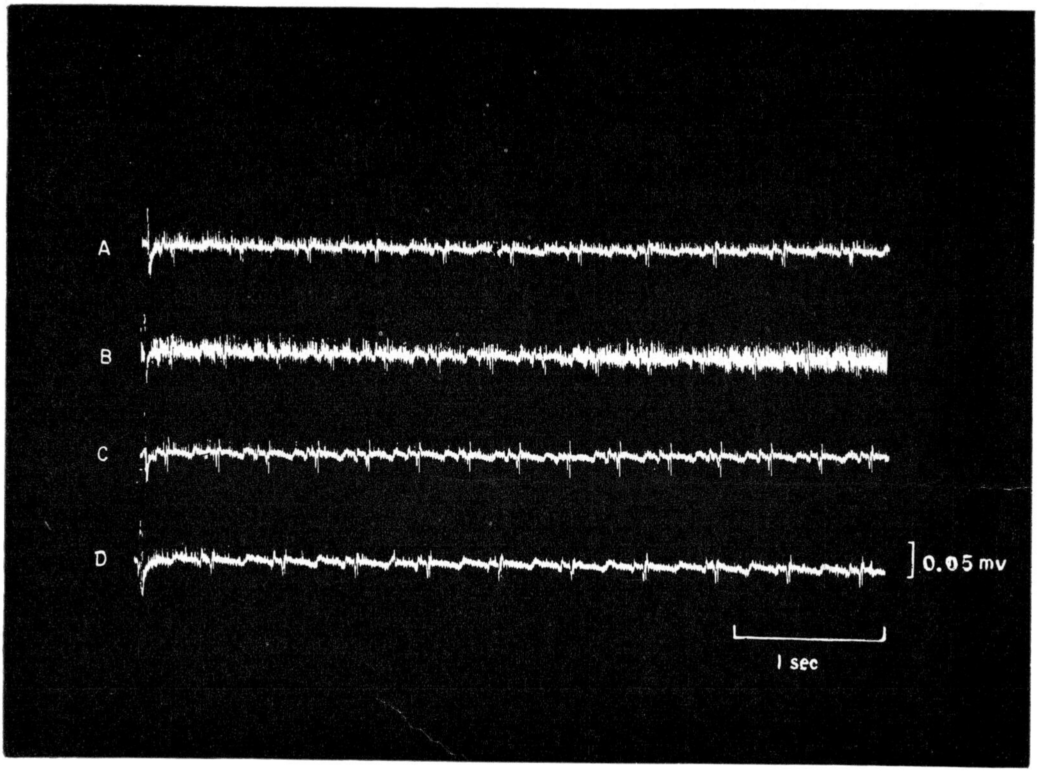

FIG. 5. Responses in L7 ventral root filament to L7 dorsal root stimulation.
A, Control; B, 10 sec. following intraarterial injection of 20 mgm./kgm. of zoxazolamine; C, 2 min. following injection; D, 45 min. following injection. Stimulus intensity, 1.4 V; duration, 0.1 msec.

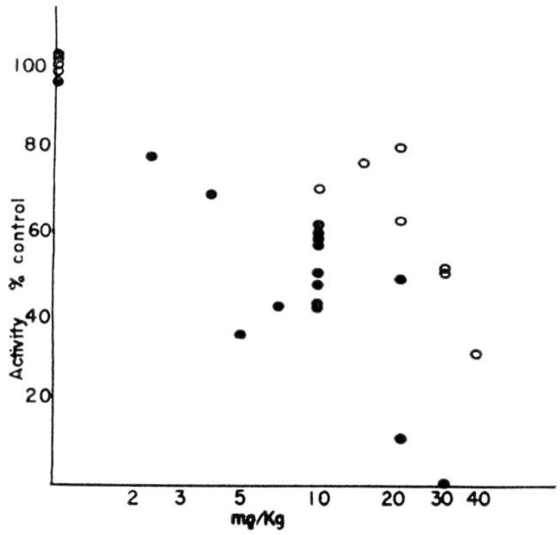

FIG. 6. Depression of motoneurone activity by zoxazolamine.
● Intraarterial injection; ○ intravenous injection. Abscissa: Amount of zoxazolamine injected. Ordinate: Per cent reduction of arithmetic mean of spike counts for ten successive stimuli after injection as compared to preinjection control.

second following the stimulus for 10 successive traces were counted within the control, postinjection and recovery periods. Per cent depression was calculated from the arithmetic means of the spike counts within these periods.[2] The time of maximum inhibition, occurring within 2 to 12 minutes following injection, was selected in each case. The limits given in table 1 represent the comparison between maximum and minimum counts in the control and treated groups. Also in

[2] The following is a sample calculation using raw data from animal No. 31. The number of spikes falling during the first second following stimulus for 10 successive stimuli (control) were: 10, 10, 12, 13, 9, 11, 12, 11, 10 and 12 with a mean value of 11. After the third injection of 10 mgm./kgm. of zoxazolamine, i.a., the number of spikes falling during the first second following stimulus for 10 successive stimuli (10 min. postinjection) were: 4, 6, 3, 5, 3, 6, 4, 7, 4 and 4 with a mean value of 5. Therefore, the per cent depression of activity was 45 per cent with limits of 30 to 54 per cent.

TABLE 1

Degree and duration of depression of motoneurone activity by zoxazolamine

Animal	Dose		Per Cent Inhibition		Recovery Time
	Single	Cumulative	Mean	Limits	
	mgm./kgm.	*mgm./kgm.*			*min.*
33	2 i.a.				
	4 i.a.	6	75	74–77	60
	10 i.a.	16	61	60–62	45
	10 i.a.	36	61	60–61	37
	20 i.a.	56			
	20 i.a.	76	46	45–46	
44	7 i.a.		42	30–47	180*
31	5 i.a.				
	10 i.a.				
	10 i.a.	25	45	30–54	
	10 i.a.	35			
	10 i.a.	45	50	43–54	50
	10 i.a.	55	43	36–50	45
32	10 i.a.		60	56–63	80
	10 i.a.	20	47	44–52	85
	5 i.a.	25	36	21–40	30
	2.5 i.a.	27.5	78	73–79	20
40	20 i.a.		10	0–20	30
41	20 i.a.				
	30 i.v.	50	50	33–60	180
43	10 i.v.		71	66–74	15*
	15 i.v.	25	77	72–80	20*
	30 i.a.	55	0		120†
25	20 i.v.		62	61–63	40
	20 i.v.	40	81	80–88	35
	30 i.v.	70			
	40 i.v.	110	27	20–31	90
39	30 i.v.		51	46–60	100

* Degree of recovery 25 to 50 per cent.

† No recovery.

table 1, the effect of previous drug administration on the preparation is seen. Each injection is, however, considered independently in figure 6. This graph is a plot of per cent inhibition as a function of dosage. The values at zero dosage level represent control injections of the vehicle.

Figure 5 illustrates that following i.a. injection, rapid firing of motoneurones lasting 4 to 7 seconds occurs. This was a consistent finding following each i.a. injection containing zoxazolamine but not of those containing the vehicle alone.

The minimal paralytic doses of succinylcholine used in the second series were found to be without effect upon the responses studied. This is in agreement with the findings of other investigators who have used this agent to obtain paralysis during central recording (Purpura and Grundfest, 1956).

Blood pressure was monitored in 8 animals. Sixty-seven injections of polyethylene glycol or 10 per cent zoxazolamine in polyethylene glycol in dosages from 5 to 50 mgm./kgm. were given during manometric recording. On i.v. injection of 30 mgm./kgm. a maximum drop of 10 mm. Hg with a duration of 3 minutes was found. Intra-arterial injection at doses up to 50 mgm./kgm. produced only minor and transient pressure changes.

Discussion. The electrophysiological techniques employed in this series of experiments have provided an analysis of the mode of action of zoxazolamine upon spinal reflexes, free from interference by the unavoidable variables of mechanical recording. The complication of possible block at the neuromuscular junction was automatically excluded. Interaction of afferent proprioceptive impulses with the reflex under consideration was minimized by denervation of the extremity, section of adjacent roots and by use of the neuromuscular blocking agent, succinylcholine. For these reasons the results reported are not directly comparable to those of Kamijo and Koelle (1955). These investigators demonstrated that the withdrawal reflex of spinal cats was abolished often by as little as 5 mgm./kgm. of zoxazolamine i.v. In most preparations 4 to 16 mgm./kgm. caused a 32 per cent to total inhibition. The facilitation of the knee jerk by contralateral sciatic nerve stimulation and its inhibition by ipsilateral sciatic nerve stimulation were also reduced at these doses. The monosynaptic knee jerk was less sensitive, being inhibited only at higher doses. Thus, the most susceptible pathways were polysynaptic. It was expected, therefore, that in the present experiments the amplitude and duration of the polysynaptic complexes in ventral roots would be inhibited by comparable concentrations of zoxazolamine. It was found, however, that the first polysynaptic complex, the three-neurone arc, exhibited a degree of sensitivity to the drug which was not greater than that of the monosynaptic reflex. Only the later polysynaptic complexes were consistently depressed by intravenous injection of zoxazolamine in dosages comparable to those reported by Kamijo and Koelle (1955). These late complexes represent reflex arcs subserved by nerve fibers of slower conduction velocities or arcs with more than three interposed synapses.

Two interpretations are consistent with these results. The first being that the drug acts upon all synapses of reflex pathways, the degree of depression being proportional to the number of synapses interposed. The action of mephenesin was interpreted in this manner by Kaada (1950). The second is that certain cells within internuncial systems may be specifically sensitive to zoxazolamine. Henneman *et al.* (1949) considered mephenesin to act in this manner. Synapses or cells sensitive to zoxazolamine are necessarily present in those polysynaptic reflexes containing more than three neurones or containing afferent fibers of slow conduction velocity on the basis of the present work. The depression of the two- and three-neurone reflexes by higher doses of the drug is then due to a facilitatory effect of zoxazolamine upon internuncial systems which act to depress the excitatory state of motoneurones. Conversely, inhibitory systems may be facilitated. The present studies do not distinguish between these interpretations.

In the experiments discussed above, reflex discharges in ventral roots are recordable only within the first 25 to 30 msec. following stimulation. Splitting of the ventral root into thin filaments allows the recording of asynchronous repetitive discharges. If the stimulus is of sufficient intensity to excite C fibers, activity persists for more then one second in appropriately chosen filaments (Henneman, 1957). The frequency of such repetitive discharges was decreased by zoxazolamine at doses comparable to those which diminish the withdrawal reflex. Quantitative analysis of dose-response and dose-duration of response relations was difficult since the number of experimental animals utilized was limited by the complexity of the preparation. Thus, one animal was used for several injections of zoxazolamine. It should be emphasized, however, that in most instances full recovery was awaited before subsequent injection. The spike counts and per cent inhibitions presented in table 1 and figure 6 are also complicated by the variation of the number of spikes which could be evoked from preparation to preparation. In spite of these drawbacks, a dose-response curve was obtained for both intravenous and intraarterial injection. Administration of zoxazolamine by these two routes differed in that lower doses were required to produce inhibition by the i.a. route and following i.a. injection a brief period of rapid motoneurone discharge was seen. Possibly the high local concentration of zoxazolamine when given i.a. caused depolarization of the motoneuronal membrane or stimulation of excitatory internuncial systems. After cessation of the rapid activity, the characteristics of the recorded discharges and the duration of depression were dependent on dosage, rather than route of injection.

If it is assumed that the origins of the repetitive montoneurone discharges are in reverberating internuncial circuits, these experiments furnish further evidence that the site of action of zoxazolamine is upon synapses contained within the internuncial systems or upon the internuncial cells themselves.

The existence of various types of motoneurone impulses were not taken into consideration in the present report. *Gamma* motoneurones innervate the intrafusal fibers of muscle spindle organs. Increased frequency of discharge accompanies reflex contraction and accelerates the rate of discharge of muscle spindle organs leading in turn to a state of residual temporal facilitation of the motoneurone pool (Kuffler and Hunt, 1952; Granit, 1956). The lack of effect of zoxazolamine at usual doses upon the stretch reflex (Kamijo and Koelle, 1955) indicates that the *gamma* motoneurone is not exceptionally sensitive to the drug. *Alpha* tonic motoneurone discharges, and interneurones which sustain stretch reflexes (Granit *et al.*, 1957) may, however, be specifically sensitive. In future studies we hope to separate the effects of centrally acting skeletal muscle relaxants upon the various motoneurone systems.

SUMMARY

The effects of zoxazolamine upon reflex discharges in ventral roots of spinal cats were examined.

Two- and three-neurone arcs were inhibited by intravenous injection of 30 to 40 mgm./kgm. zoxazolamine.

Complexes in ventral roots representing 4- and 5-neurone reflexes or reflexes mediated by slowly conducting fibers were inhibited by intravenous injection of 15–30 mgm./kgm. zoxazolamine.

Prolonged repetitive activity in ventral root filaments in response to intense dorsal root stimulation was also decreased at these doses.

The amount of zoxazolamine which is sufficient

to depress the withdrawal reflex also inhibits the rate of repetitive discharge of motoneurones.

The possible sites of action of zoxazolamine are discussed.

ACKNOWLEDGMENT. The authors wish to thank Dr. Vernon B. Mountcastle for his guidance. Zoxazolamine used in these studies was supplied by McNeil Laboratories.

REFERENCES

ABRAHAMSEN, E. H., AND BAIRD, H. W.: J.A.M.A., **160:** 749, 1956.
AMOLS, W.: J.A.M.A., **160:** 742, 1956.
FUNDERBURK, W. H., KING, E. E., DOMINO, E. F., AND UNNA, K. R.: THIS JOURNAL, **107:** 356, 1953.
FUNDERBURK, W. H., AND WOODCOCK, R. T.: Fed. Proc., **14:** 341, 1955.
GOODMAN, L. S., GILMAN, A., AND HART, N.: Fed. Proc., **2:** 80, 1943.
GRANIT, R. J.: J. Physiol., **131:** 32, 1956.
GRANIT, R. J., PHILLIPS, C. G., SKOGLUND, S., AND STEG, G.: J. Neurophysiol., **20:** 470, 1957.
HENNEMAN, E., KAPLAN, A., AND UNNA, K.: THIS JOURNAL, **97:** 331, 1949.
HENNEMAN, E.: Science, **126:** 1345, 1957.
HOLMSTEDT, B., AND SKOGLUND, C. R.: Acta Physiol. Scand., **29** (Suppl. 106): 410, 1953.
KAADA, B. R.: J. Neurophysiol., **13:** 89, 1950.
KAMIJO, K., AND KOELLE, G. B.: Proc. Soc. Exper. Biol. & Med., **88:** 565, 1955.
KUFFLER, S. W., AND HUNT, C. C.: A. Res. Nerv. & Ment. Dis. Proc., **30:** 24, 1952.
LLOYD, D. P. C.: J. Neurophysiol., **6:** 111, 1943.
MARSH, D. F.: Fed. Proc., **14:** 366, 1955.
MILLICHAP, J. G., AND HADRA, R.: Neurology, **6:** 843, 1956.
PURPURA, D. P., AND GRUNDFEST, H.: J. Neurophysiol., **19:** 573, 1956.
RODRIGUEZ-GOMEZ, M., VALDEZ-RODRIGUEZ, A., AND DREW, A. L.: J.A.M.A., **160:** 752, 1956.
SMITH, R. T., KRON, K. M., PEAK, W. P., AND HERMANN, I. F.: J.A.M.A., **160:** 745, 1956.

8030

METABOLIC N- AND O-DEMETHYLATION OF MORPHINE- AND MORPHINAN-TYPE ANALGESICS[1,2,3]

A. E. TAKEMORI[4] AND G. J. MANNERING

Department of Pharmacology and Toxicology, The University of Wisconsin, Service Memorial Institutes' Madison 6

Received for publication February 24, 1958

The metabolic demethylation of morphine and several of its congeners is known to occur both in whole animals and in isolated systems employing liver slices or fractions of liver homogenates. In *in vivo* studies the following morphine-type analgesics have been shown to be N-demethylated: morphine (March and Elliott, 1952; Elliott *et al.*, 1954), codeine (Adler *et al.*, 1952, 1955) and meperidine (Plotnikoff *et al.*, 1952, 1955a, 1955b). Using rat liver slices, Plotnikoff *et al.* (1952) demonstrated the demethylation of meperidine. Axelrod (1956a) showed that a liver microsome system could demethylate a number of N-methyl compounds, including morphine, dihydromorphinone (Dilaudid), meperidine (Demerol), methyldihydromorphinone (Metopon), 3-hydroxy-N-methylmorphinan (Dromoran) and methadone. The O-demethylation of codeine is known to occur in the intact rat (Adler and Latham, 1950), monkey (Mellett *et al.*, 1954) and man (Mannering *et al.*, 1954a; Adler *et al.*, 1955). Evidence for both N- and O-demethylation of 3-methoxy-N-methylmorphinan by the dog was provided by Brossi *et al.* (1955). The transformation of codeine to morphine was also shown to be effected by liver slices (Adler *et al.*, 1950, 1952) and by a microsome system from liver (Axelrod, 1955b).

While studying the metabolic fate of methylated aminoazo dyes, Mueller and Miller (1953) observed a demethylating system in liver homogenates, later localized in the microsomes (Conney *et al.*, 1957), which required diphosphopyridine nucleotide (DPN), triphosphopyridine nucleotide (TPN), hexosephosphate and oxygen for maximal activity. They showed that N-demethylation was accomplished by an oxidative process rather than by methyl transference or hydrolysis, and that the quantity of formaldehyde formed during the reaction bore a stoichiometric relationship to the amount of demethylated dye formed. Axelrod (1955a, b, 1956a, b) described a similar oxidative mechanism occurring in microsome preparations which was responsible for the N- and O-demethylation of a number of drugs and other foreign substances, including morphine-type analgesics. The microsome system requiring TPNH and oxygen appears to find general application in the oxidation of compounds foreign to the body, for it has been shown to perform not only in demethylation and other dealkylation processes, but also in side-chain oxidation (Cooper and Brodie, 1955), deamination (Axelrod, 1955c) and hydroxylation (Mitoma and Udenfriend, 1955). The seeming paradox of a system requiring both oxygen and reduced TPN may find some explanation in the recent evidence presented by Gillette *et al.* (1957) who showed that in a microsome system, an enzyme, termed TPNH oxidase, catalyzes the interaction of TPNH and oxygen to form TPN and hydrogen peroxide. The rate of demethylation of monomethyl-4-aminoantipyrine paralleled the rate of peroxide generation by TPNH oxidation. The authors suggest that this system may act in other metabolic pathways of drug oxidation.

The N-demethylation of narcotic drugs has taken on new interest because of views expressed recently by Axelrod (1956c) and by Beckett *et al.*

[1] A preliminary report of this work was presented at the Meeting of the American Society for Pharmacology and Experimental Therapeutics in Baltimore, Maryland, September, 1957.
[2] Supported in part by the Research Committee of the Graduate School from funds supplied by the Wisconsin Alumni Research Foundation and by Hoffmann-LaRoche, Inc., Nutley, New Jersey.
[3] The material in this investigation will appear in a thesis in partial fulfillment of the requirements for the degree of Doctor of Philosophy in the Department of Pharmacology and Toxicology, University of Wisconsin, Madison, Wisconsin.
[4] Present address: Institute for Enzyme Research, University of Wisconsin, Madison, Wisconsin.

TABLE 1

N- and O-demethylation of morphine- and morphinan-type analgesics by livers of various species

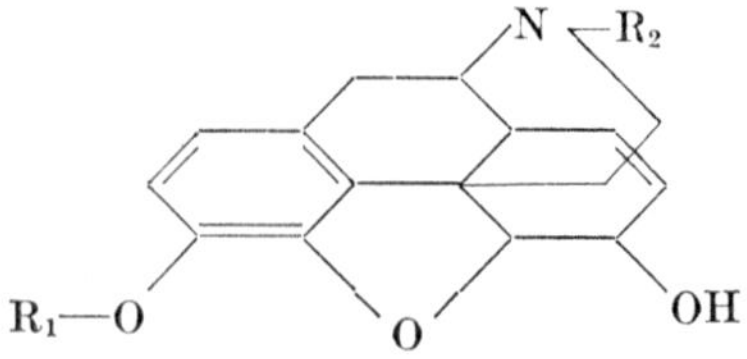

Morphine series

Compound	Substitutions		Micromoles Formaldehyde Formed/Gm. Tissue/Hr.					
	R_1	R_2	Rat	Mouse	Guinea pig	Rabbit	Cat	Dog
l-Normorphine	—H	—H	0.00	0.00	0.00	0.00	0.00	0.00
l-Morphine	—H	$—CH_3$	0.32	0.78	0.12	0.22	—*	—*
l-Norcodeine	$—CH_3$	—H	0.48	0.48	0.18	0.78	0.05	—*
l-Codeine	$—CH_3$	$—CH_3$	1.24	2.82	1.42	1.44	0.14	0.12
Morphinan series								
l-3-Hydroxymorphinan	—H	—H	0.00	0.00	0.00	0.00	0.00	0.00
l-3-Hydroxy-N-methylmorphinan (Dromoran)	—H	$—CH_3$	0.34	0.66	0.46	0.52	0.03	—*
l-3-Methoxymorphinan	$—CH_3$	—H	0.66	1.36	0.76	0.80	—†	—†
l-3-Methoxy-N-methylmorphinan (levomethorphan)	$—CH_3$	$—CH_3$	1.38	4.16	1.86	2.16	0.46	0.34

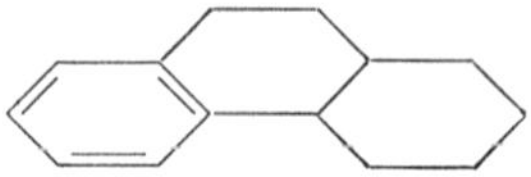

Morphinan series

* Values too low for accurate measurement.

† Compound not available at time of experiment.

(1956c). Axelrod has pointed out the similarity between the receptors for narcotic drugs and the enzymes that N-demethylate these drugs. The receptors and enzymes have been reported to be alike with respect to substrates with which they interact, stereospecificity and antagonism by N-allylnormorphine. On the basis of these similarities, it was suggested that any changes occurring in demethylating enzyme activity during the development of tolerance might reflect changes taking place on the drug receptor, and experimental evidence was presented which strongly supported this thesis (Axelrod, 1956c). Beckett *et al.* (1956c) offer the interesting idea that oxidative demethylation (dealkylation) to produce nor-compounds may be the first step in the reaction sequence leading to analgesia.

The present paper is an attempt to define the enzymatic kinetics for N- and O-demethylation of morphine- and morphinan-type analgesics and to point out certain dissimilarities between receptors for narcotic drugs and the enzymes that N-demethylate these drugs. It will also be shown that the system responsible for the demethylation of these compounds differs from that required for the demethylation of aminoazo dyes, and that N- and O-demethylating systems may also differ.

MATERIALS AND METHODS. *Materials.* Compounds were so selected that N- and O-demethylation could be studied separately in individual compounds and in combination in a single compound. The following morphine- and morphinan-type compounds were studied (table 1): *l*-normorphine hydrochloride[5] and *l*-3-hydroxymorphinan

[5] These compounds were kindly supplied by the National Institutes of Health, Bethesda, Maryland.

hydrobromide[6] (no methyl groups); *l*-morphine sulfate and *l*-3-hydroxy-N-methylmorphinan tartrate[6] (N-methyl groups); *l*-norcodeine hydrochloride[5] and *l*-3-methoxymorphinan hydrochloride (O-methyl groups); *l*-codeine phosphate and *l*-3-methoxy-N-methylmorphinan hydrobromide[6] (N- and O-methyl groups). The alkaloids were prepared as aqueous solutions containing 4 micromole per ml. The methylated aminoazo dye used was 3-methyl-4-monomethylaminoazobenzene (3-methyl-MAB) dissolved in 95 per cent ethanol (10 micromole per ml.).

Tissue preparation. Male mice (Swiss-Webster) weighing 25 ± 5 gm. were used. Livers from mice of this weight were shown to possess the highest demethylating capacity. Animals were decapitated and bled, the livers were removed and immediately placed in ice cold isotonic KCl. Livers from at least five mice were pooled and a 12 per cent homogenate was prepared in cold isotonic KCl using a teflon pestle-pyrex tube tissue grinder. The homogenate was centrifuged at 9000 × g with refrigeration (0 ± 2°C.) for 10 minutes. The residues were washed with isotonic KCl and recentrifuged as described above. The supernatants and washings, containing microsomes and soluble fractions, were combined so that each 5 ml. contained an equivalent of 500 mgm. of liver tissue. Liver preparations from rats, guinea pigs, rabbits, dogs and cats were prepared in a similar manner.

Measurement of enzyme activity. The complete reaction mixture (10 ml.) contained the following constituents adjusted to pH 7.4: substrate (4 micromol., except in the case of 3-methyl-MAB where 1 micromol. was used), TPN (0.5 micromol.), glucose-6-phosphate (5 micromol.), nicotinamide (40 micromol.), magnesium chloride (20 micromol.), semicarbazide (75 micromol.), 2 ml. of 0.2 *M* KH_2PO_4-Na_2HPO_4 buffer (pH 7.4), and 5 ml. of liver preparation. The mixture was incubated with shaking (120 oscillations per minute) at 37°C. under air in a Dubnoff metabolic shaker. At appropriate time intervals, 2-ml. aliquots of the reaction mixture were transferred to a distilling flask containing 4 ml. of a 30 per cent trichloroacetic acid solution (Mueller and Miller, 1953; Axelrod, 1955a). Four ml. of distillate were collected and analyzed for formaldehyde content by the chromotropic acid procedure of MacFadyen (1945). All values were corrected for a predetermined distillation loss of 10 per cent.

PROCEDURES AND RESULTS. *Kinetics.* Mice were used in this study because of the high demethylating capacity of their livers as compared with those of other species studied.[7] The results are shown in figure 1. Each point on the curve represents an average of three to five determinations. The reaction was linear for only 15 to 20 minutes for both N- and O-demethylations. There was a sharp departure from zero order kinetics after 30 minutes. In accordance with this observation, incubation periods of 15 minutes were chosen for routine assays of the enzyme. The departure from linearity could not be attributed to limiting amounts of substrate or known cofactors, to product inhibition (either formaldehyde or the resulting nor-compounds), or to formaldehyde disappearance. Conney *et al.* (1956, 1957) demonstrated similar kinetics in the enzymatic demethylation of 3-methyl-MAB.

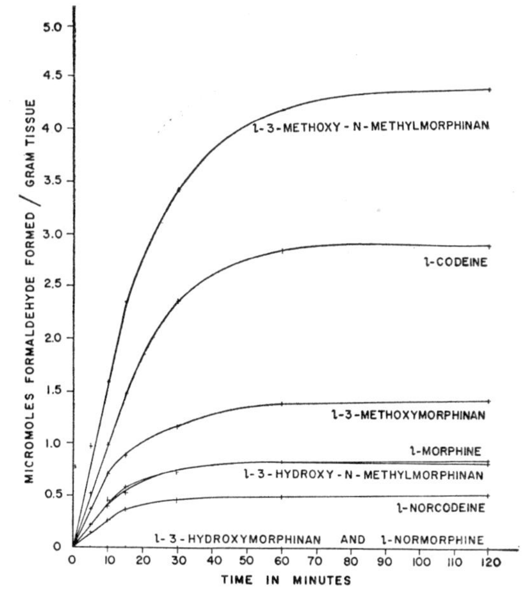

FIG. 1. Curves showing the rates of N- and O-demethylation of morphine- and morphinan-type compounds by mouse livers.

When analogs of the two series are compared, it is seen that the morphinan compounds are more readily demethylated than are corresponding members of the morphine series. It is also to be noted that when a single compound possesses both N- and O-methyl groups, the amount of

[6] These compounds were kindly supplied by Hoffmann-LaRoche, Inc., Nutley, New Jersey.

[7] This is in disagreement with the reports of Axelrod (1955b, 1956a) that microsomal preparations from mouse livers are completely lacking in their capacity to O- or N-demethylate narcotic drugs. Since these publications, Axelrod (private communication) has found considerable strain difference in the demethylating capacity of mouse livers. Some strains were found to have high enzyme activity while others had negligible activity.

demethylation occurring is greater than the sum of that obtained with its two analogs bearing only the N-methyl or O-methyl group. Thus, the rate of *l*-codeine demethylation was greater than the combined demethylation rates of *l*-morphine and *l*-norcodeine, and that of *l*-3-methoxy-N-methylmorphinan greater than the added demethylation rates of *l*-3-hydroxy-N-methylmorphinan and *l*-3-methoxymorphinan. The question that arises here is whether the increased demethylation results from ether cleavage or from N-demethylation.

Effect of 3-position substitution on N-demethylation. Indirect evidence that the augmented rate of demethylation resulting from substitution of a methoxyl for a hydroxyl group in the 3-position is a result of increased N- rather than O-demethylation was obtained by studying ethylmorphine (Dionin), a compound with an ethoxyl rather than a methoxyl group in the 3-position. The chromotropic acid procedure is highly specific for formaldehyde, hence any acetaldehyde formed through oxidative dealkylation of the ethoxyl group does not interfere with the measurement of N-demethylation. *dl*-N-methylmorphinan, which has no substituent in the 3-position, was also studied. The previously described procedure was followed with the reaction being stopped after 15 minutes of incubation. The results are given in table 2. It is seen that N-demethylation of ethylmorphine and of *dl*-N-methylmorphinan is greatly increased over that of their 3-hydroxy analogs.

TABLE 2

Influence of etherification of the 3-hydroxyl group on the rate of N-demethylation by livers of mice

Compound	Micromoles Formaldehyde Formed/Gm. Tissue/15 Min.
l-Morphine	0.50
l-Norcodeine	0.34
l-Codeine	1.60
l-3-Hydroxy-N-methylmorphinan (Dromoran)	0.50
l-3-Methoxymorphinan	0.84
l-3-Methoxy-N-methylmorphinan (levomethorphan)	2.36
dl-N-methylmorphinan	1.30
Ethylmorphine (Dionin)	2.22
Thebaine	2.10

Direct proof of increased N-demethylation was obtained by quantitative analysis of the end-products of codeine metabolism. Eight micromol. of codeine phosphate were incubated for 15 minutes as described previously with a quantity of microsomal plus soluble fractions equivalent to 1 gm. of mouse liver. Codeine and its metabolites were isolated from the reaction mixture using differential solvent extraction and chromatography on pH 7.0 phosphate-buffered paper developed with neutral isoamyl alcohol as described by Mannering *et al.* (1954b). The spots were identified by spraying with an iodoplatinate reagent, cut from the paper, wetted with concentrated ammonium hydroxide, and extracted with 10 per cent ethanol in chloroform. The extracts were evaporated to dryness and the residues thus obtained were analyzed using the methyl orange procedure of Brodie *et al.* (1947). When the procedure was applied to control mixtures containing known quantities of codeine, norcodeine and morphine, 95 per cent recoveries were obtained. From the original 8 micromol. of codeine incubated, 2.05 micromol. of norcodeine and 0.30 micromol. of morphine were recovered. The quantity of formaldehyde liberated in the process (2.17 micromol.) approximates stoichiometric expectations. This sevenfold greater production of norcodeine than of morphine clearly demonstrates that the augmented rate of demethylation which occurs when the 3-hydroxyl group is muzzled is a result of N- rather than O-demethylation.

Stereospecificity of demethylating enzymes. Axelrod (1956a) has shown that the pharmacologically active *levo* isomers of certain narcotic drugs are much more readily demethylated by a liver microsome system than are the inactive or relatively inactive *dextro* forms. These data were obtained from systems which had been incubated for two hours. If stereospecificity is to be related to the fit of the drug to the enzyme surface, the measure of enzyme activity must be made when the enzyme is completely saturated with substrate and hence, is catalyzing the reaction at maximum velocity. Interpretations on observations made at a time when the reaction has stopped or is proceeding at less than an optimal rate cannot be properly evaluated. It was therefore desired to determine whether stereospecificity

TABLE 3

Demethylation of l- and d-isomers of morphinan-type drugs by livers of mice and rats

Compound	Micromoles Formaldehyde Formed/Gm. Tissue			
	Mouse		Rat	
	Minutes		Minutes	
	15	120	15	120
l-3-Hydroxy-N-methylmorphinan (Dromoran)	0.58	0.64	0.28	0.40
d-3-Hydroxy-N-methylmorphinan (dextrorphan)	0.50	0.58	0.28	0.32
l-3-Methoxymorphinan	0.80	0.92	0.68	0.96
d-3-Methoxymorphinan	0.62	0.86	0.48	0.76
l-3-Methoxy-N-methylmorphinan (levomethorphan)	2.06	2.60	2.16	2.98
d-3-Methoxy-N-methylmorphinan (dextromethorphan)	1.46	1.82	1.02	1.64

could still be shown during the first 15 minutes when the reaction is proceeding linearly.

Liver preparations from male albino mice weighing 25 to 30 gm. and rats (Holtzman strain) weighing 60 to 80 gm. were incubated with *d*- and *l*-isomers of morphinan-type compounds and the amounts of formaldehyde liberated at 15- and 120-minute intervals were measured. The results are recorded in table 3. During the 15-minute period both mouse and rat liver preparations demethylated *d*- and *l*-3-hydroxy-N-methylmorphinan with equal facility. After two hours of incubation there was no increase in the capacity to demethylate the *levo* isomer. Demethylation of the *levo* isomer of 3-methoxy-N-methylmorphinan was markedly greater than that of the *dextro* isomer during both incubation periods and with both species. Stereospecificity was much less pronounced when 3-methoxymorphinan was employed as the substrate.

N-allylnormorphine is known to inhibit microsomal N- and O-demethylation of narcotic drugs (Axelrod and Cochin, 1956, 1957). Since it is believed that N-allyl derivatives of morphine and morphinan analgesics exert their antagonistic effects because they possess the same configuration as the compounds they antagonize, and that stereoisomerism is an essential part of the similarity necessary for this antagonism (Beckett *et al.*, 1956c), the stereospecificity studies were extended to include an investigation of the inhibitory effects of *l*- and *d*-isomers of 3-hydroxy-N-allylmorphinan on the demethylation of morphinan compounds by livers of mice. Demethylating capacities were measured after 15 minutes of incubation with 1 micromol. of allyl derivative being employed to antagonize 4 micromol. of morphinan substrate in each mixture. The results are given in table 4. It is

TABLE 4

Inhibitory effect of l- and d-3-hydroxy-N-allylmorphinan on the demethylation of l- and d-isomers of morphinan-type drugs by livers of mice

Compound	Micromoles Formaldehyde Formed/Gm. Tissue/15 Min.	Per Cent Inhibition
l-3-Hydroxy-N-methylmorphinan	0.58	
l-3-Hydroxy-N-methylmorphinan + *l*-3-hydroxy-N-allylmorphinan	0.36	38
l-3-Hydroxy-N-methylmorphinan + *d*-3-hydroxy-N-allylmorphinan	0.36	38
d-3-Hydroxy-N-methylmorphinan	0.54	
d-3-Hydroxy-N-methylmorphinan + *l*-3-hydroxy-N-allylmorphinan	0.32	41
d-3-Hydroxy-N-methylmorphinan + *d*-3-hydroxy-N-allylmorphinan	0.30	44
l-3-Methoxy-N-methylmorphinan	2.50	
l-3-Methoxy-N-methylmorphinan + *l*-3-hydroxy-N-allylmorphinan	1.66	34
l-3-Methoxy-N-methylmorphinan + *d*-3-hydroxy-N-allylmorphinan	1.76	30
d-3-Methoxy-N-methylmorphinan	1.72	
d-3-Methoxy-N-methylmorphinan + *l*-3-hydroxy-N-allylmorphinan	1.06	38
d-3-Methoxy-N-methylmorphinan + *d*-3-hydroxy-N-allylmorphinan	1.06	38

seen that stereospecificity does not play a role in the inhibition of the demethylation of morphinan drugs by their allyl antagonists.

Demethylating capacity of livers from different species. Demethylation studies similar to those described for the mouse were performed on rats, guinea pigs, rabbits, dogs and cats. Male animals were used in all cases. The same experimental procedure was employed except that the period of incubation was extended from 15 to 60 minutes to obtain measurable metabolism in those species where the demethylating capacities of the livers were very low, *e.g.*, in the dog and cat.

Examination of table 1 reveals a disproportion in the comparative N- and O-demethylating capacities of livers from different species. For example, in mice, N-demethylation was greater than O-demethylation when morphine-type substrates were used, whereas O-demethylation was greater than N-demethylation when the morphinan series was employed. However, in rabbits, O-demethylation predominated regardless of the type of substrate utilized. Axelrod (1955b) has studied the O-demethylation of codeine in the rabbit and observes a strict stoichiometric relationship between codeine disappearance, morphine formation and formaldehyde generation. These results would insist that microsome systems derived from rabbit livers do not N-demethylate codeine, a view incompatible with the present evidence. The livers of guinea pigs and rats also possessed O-demethylating activity in predominance. This disproportion in the N- and O-demethylating capacities of different species suggests that different enzymes may be responsible for the two types of demethylation. The increased N-demethylation which results when the 3-position is methoxylated, previously noted in mouse liver experiments, was also observed with livers from all species studied.

Inhibition of demethylating activity by SKF 525-A[8]. It has been demonstrated that SKF 525-A inhibits the biotransformation of a number of drugs and other foreign substances *in vivo* (Cook *et al.*, 1954a,b; Axelrod *et al.*, 1954) as well as *in vitro* (Cooper *et al.*, 1954). Axelrod (1956b) has shown that the enzymatic O-demethylation of codeine is markedly inhibited by SKF 525-A while that of acetophenetidin is only slightly affected by this compound, thus indicating that more than one enzyme system is involved in the cleavage of aromatic ethers. It was sought in this experiment to determine whether the enzymes responsible for the N-demethylation of narcotic compounds and of aminoazo dyes might be differentiated by selective inhibition with SKF 525-A.

[8] SKF 525-A (β-diethylaminoethyldiphenylpropylacetate HCl) was generously supplied by Smith, Kline & French Laboratories, Philadelphia, Pa.

TABLE 5

Effect of SKF 525-A ($10^{-5}M$) on the demethylating activity of livers of mice

Compound	Per Cent Inhibition*
l-Morphine	52
l-Norcodeine	37
l-Codeine	50
l-3-Hydroxy-N-methylmorphinan (Dromoran)	43
l-3-Methoxymorphinan	55
l-3-Methoxy-N-methylmorphinan (levomethorphan)	50
dl-N-methylmorphinan	51
3-Methyl-MAB	0

* Average of three determinations.

Fractions of mouse liver, prepared as described previously, were incubated with the morphine and morphinan series of compounds and with 3-methyl-MAB. SKF 525-A was added to the reaction mixture in final concentrations of 10^{-3} to 10^{-5} *M*. Concentrations above 10^{-5} *M* almost completely inhibited the demethylation of the narcotic compounds, while concentrations as high as 10^{-3} *M* had no effect on the demethylation of 3-methyl-MAB, thus strongly indicating that different enzymes are responsible for the demethylation of 3-methyl-MAB and the narcotic compounds. The effect of SKF 525-A (10^{-5} *M*) on demethylation is shown in table 5.

Effects of 3-methylcholanthrene on enzyme synthesis. Using 3-methyl-MAB as the substrate, Conney *et al.* (1956) recently reported a marked increase in the demethylating capacity of rat livers after a single intraperitoneal injection of 3-methylcholanthrene. They also presented evidence favoring the view that the increase in activity was due to the induction of enzyme synthesis rather than to enzyme activation. It was of interest to see whether 3-methylcholanthrene could also induce increased demethylation of the morphine- and morphinan-type compounds.

Male albino rats (Holtzman strain) weighing 50 ± 10 gm. were used for this study. Rats were used in preference to mice because their livers were shown to be more susceptible to the induction of synthesis of the 3-methyl-MAB demethylating enzyme. The exact feeding regimen of Conney *et al.* (1956) was followed. The rats were injected intraperitoneally with 10 mgm./kgm. of 3-methylcholanthrene in corn oil 24 hours preceding assay of demethylating activity. Groups of control rats were given corn oil injections. The livers were assayed as described previously.

No change in either N- or O-demethylation of the morphine or morphinan compounds occurred as a result of pretreatment with 3-methylcholanthrene. There was also no increase in the rate of demethylation of methadone and meperidine. However, in agreement with the results of Conney *et al.* (1956), nearly a threefold increase in the capacity to demethylate 3-methyl-MAB occurred. The above data provide further evidence for the lack of similarity of the enzymes responsible for the demethylation of narcotic compounds and methylated aminoazo dyes.

The pH optima of 3-methyl-MAB and narcotic demethylating systems. The demethylating activity of mouse livers was measured at various pH values utilizing 15-minute incubation periods. The following buffer systems were employed in a final concentration of 0.1 *M*: potassium acid phthalate—NaOH, pH 5.0; sodium succinate—HCl, pH 6.0; KH_2PO_4—Na_2HPO_4, pH 7.0 and pH 7.5; trishydroxymethylaminomethane—HCl, pH 8.0 and pH 8.5; boric acid—NaOH, pH 9.0; and $NaHCO_3$—Na_2CO_3, pH 10.0.

Maximum demethylation of the narcotic compounds occurred in the pH range of 7.9 to 8.1, while optimal demethylation of 3-methyl-MAB was seen at about pH 7.4. The optimum pH for methadone and meperidine demethylation was the same as that observed for the morphine- and morphinan-type narcotics. These observations give additional support to the view that different enzymatic pathways are required for demethylation of narcotic compounds and methylated aminoazo dyes.

Discussion. Of the theories proposed to explain the attachment of narcotic drugs to the biologic receptors responsible for narcotic activity, those of Beckett and co-workers (1954, 1956a,b,c) would seem to best fit the experimental facts. The steric and chemical features of the drug conferring analgesic activity are thought to be 1) a basic center, which associates at physiological pH with an anionic site on the receptor surface, 2) a flat aromatic structure allowing strong collective van der Waals' force bonding to a flat portion of the receptor (thus re-enforcing the ionic bond), 3) a rigid molecule restricting the basic group and flat structure to almost the same plane, and finally 4) a suitably orientated projecting hydrocarbon moiety to form with the basic center and flat structure, a three-dimensional pattern.

Accepting this concept, one would expect hydroxylation in the 3-position of morphine and morphinan compounds to further assist the formation of the drug-receptor complex through hydrogen bonding, and conversely, any masking of this hydroxyl group would result in reduced narcotic activity. Indeed, the great loss of narcotic activity that results when the phenolic hydroxyl group is substituted suggests that hydrogen bonding may be essential for high potency. If the receptors for narcotic activity strongly resemble those found on the N-demethylating enzyme surface, as has been stated by Axelrod (1956a,c), it follows that blocking or obliterating the 3-hydroxyl group should result in decreased N-demethylation. That N-demethylation is actually increased raises some question as to the strong similarity of narcotic drug receptors and enzyme receptors for narcotic drug demethylation. It is possible, however, that narcotic drugs are N-demethylated through the actions of more than one enzyme, in which case the above argument would not necessarily apply. One might conceive of one enzyme with a strong affinity for morphine but with a relatively low affinity for codeine, and a second demethylating enzyme where the relative affinities for the two compounds are reversed. Axelrod (1956a) has already suggested that the liver contains more than one demethylating enzyme for narcotic drugs. This suggestion is based largely on the observation that the microsomal preparations from livers of a variety of species do not demethylate different narcotic drugs at the same relative rates. While this kind of evidence is suggestive, it cannot be accepted as proof of the existence of more than a single enzyme for the N-demethylation of narcotic drugs. It may merely mean that the enzymes for the N-demethylation of narcotic drugs differ somewhat in different species, not that more than one are present in the same species.

A further possibility exists that the increased N-demethylation seen with the codeine-type molecule relates not so much to improved attachment to the demethylating enzyme as it does to improved transport of the drug to the enzyme surface. The reduced polarity which results when the 3-hydroxyl group is blocked by substitution may allow more ready passage of the drug across the microsome "membrane." If a free hydroxyl group in the 3-position tends to impede transport into the microsome, treatment of microsome preparations with surface-active agents should improve the accessibility of such compounds to the demethylating enzyme. Desoxycholate is a surface-active agent which has been used for the solubilization of microsomal hemochromogen (Strittmatter and Ball, 1952, 1954) and glucose-6-phosphatase (Beaufay and de Duve, 1954; Ashmore and Nesbett, 1955). Preliminary studies in this laboratory show that desoxycholate does not improve the N-demethylating capacity of liver microsomes when morphine is used as the substrate. Desoxycholate concentrations below 1×10^{-4} *M* had no effect on the demethylation of morphine and concentrations above 2×10^{-4} *M* rapidly decreased enzyme activity until complete inactivation occurred at 1×10^{-3} *M*. While not conclusive, this would suggest that the augmentation of N-demethylation that results when the 3-hydroxyl group is substituted is not due to improved availability of the drug to the enzyme.

A more serious objection to the view that the receptors for narcotic action and those for the demethylation of narcotic drugs are similar is seen in the lack of stereospecificity shown by the demethylating system in its actions on the *levo* and *dextro* isomers of 3-hydroxy-N-methylmorphinan and in the lack of specificity of the inhibitory action of the *d*- and *l*-isomers of 3-hydroxy-N-allylmorphinan.

While the *dextro* isomer of 3-hydroxy-N-methylmorphinan (Dextrorphan) is capable of producing certain toxic manifestations in man and other animals, it is generally agreed that it does not possess the morphine-like properties of its *levo* enantiomorph (Randall and Lehmann, 1950; Fromherz, 1951; Benson *et al.*, 1952a; Isbell and Fraser, 1953). Similar stereospecificity for this compound was not shown by the demethylating system. This is not in agreement with the previous observation of Axelrod (1956a) that the *levo* isomer is demethylated three times more readily than the *dextro* form. On the other hand, in agreement with Axelrod, considerable stereospecificity was shown for the *levo* form of 3-methoxy-N-methylmorphinan.

The N-allyl derivatives of morphine and morphinan analgesics exert their antagonistic effects largely because they possess the same configuration as the compounds they antagonize (Beckett *et al.*, 1956c). That stereoisomerism is an essential part of the similarity necessary for antagonism is shown by the fact that *d*-3-hydroxy-N-allylmorphinan fails to antagonize *l*-3-hydroxy-N-methylmorphinan (Dromoran) (Benson *et al.*, 1952b). Accordingly, if the receptors for demethylation and narcotic action are similar, then the N-allyl isomers should show stereospecificity in antagonizing demethylation. This did not prove to be the case. *Levo* and *dextro* isomers of 3-hydroxy-N-allylmorphinan were equally effective in antagonizing the demethylation of morphinan compounds, and conversely, *dextro*- and *levo*-rotatory morphinan derivatives were inhibited equally well by the allyl antagonists (table 4).

Axelrod (1956c) has shown that when morphine is injected into rats repeatedly in amounts calculated to induce tolerance, the capacity of the livers of these animals to demethylate narcotic drugs is markedly reduced. It is suggested that there is a great similarity between the receptors for narcotic drugs and the enzymes that N-demethylate these drugs and that the continuous interaction of narcotic drugs with these receptors leads to their inactivation. Thus, in one instance, tolerance develops, and in the other, a loss of demethylating capacity occurs. In this manner the demethylating process can serve as a model for the phenomenon of tolerance. The strength of this concept lies in the degree of similarity between the receptors for narcotic action and the receptors for demethylating enzyme activity. The present studies would indicate that this similarity is not as great as has been proposed.

At first glance, the finding that stereospecificity is not a requirement for N-demethylation would seem to contradict the view of Beckett *et al.*

(1956c) that N-dealkylation may be the first step in the reaction sequence leading to analgesia. This need not be the case. It may merely mean that if such a sequence does exist, then stereospecificity is not a requirement for the first step, but is a requirement in a subsequent reaction or reactions. Further, while N-demethylation has not been shown to occur in the central nervous system, if it does, as Beckett and co-workers suggest, there is no justification for assuming that it occurs in the same manner as in the liver.

SUMMARY

The kinetics of the enzyme reaction(s) found in a mouse liver microsome system responsible for the N- and O-demethylations of morphine- and morphinan-type compounds have been studied. The demethylating capacities of the livers of several species have been investigated.

Evidence has been presented to show that the system responsible for the demethylation of narcotic compounds differs from that required for the demethylation of aminoazo dyes, and that N- and O-demethylating systems may also differ.

The presence of a free hydroxyl group in the 3-position of both morphine and morphinan compounds retards N-demethylation.

The presented studies show that the similarity between the receptors for narcotic action of morphine and morphinan compounds and the receptors for the enzymes that demethylate these compounds is not as great as has been proposed.

These observations are discussed as they relate to theories which have been offered picturing the demethylation reaction as a model for the development of tolerance and theories which involve the participation of N-demethylation in the events leading to analgesia.

REFERENCES

Adler, T. K., and Latham, M. E.: Proc. Soc. Exp. Biol. & Med., **73:** 401, 1950.
Adler, T. K.: This Journal, **106:** 371, 1952.
Adler, T. K., Fujimoto, J. M., and Way, E. L.: This Journal, **113:** 1, 1955.
Ashmore, J., and Nesbett, F. B.: Proc. Soc. Exper. Biol. & Med., **89:** 78, 1955.
Axelrod, J., Reichenthal, J., and Brodie, B. B.: This Journal, **112:** 49, 1954.
Axelrod, J.: This Journal, **114:** 430, 1955a.
Axelrod, J.: This Journal, **115:** 259, 1955b.
Axelrod, J.: J. Biol. Chem., **214:** 753, 1955c.
Axelrod, J.: This Journal, **117:** 322, 1956a.
Axelrod, J.: Biochem. J., **63:** 634, 1956b.
Axelrod, J.: Science, **124:** 263, 1956c.
Axelrod, J., and Cochin, J.: Fed. Proc., **15:** 395, 1956.
Axelrod, J., and Cochin, J.: This Journal, **121:** 107, 1957.
Beaufay, H., and de Duve, C.: Bull. Soc. Chim. Biol., **36:** 1551, 1954.
Beckett, A. H., and Casy, A. F.: J. Pharm. Pharmacol., **6:** 986, 1954.
Beckett, A. H., Casy, A. F., and Harper, N. J.: J. Pharm. Pharmacol., **8:** 848, 1956a.
Beckett, A. H., Casy, A. F., and Harper, N. J.: J. Pharm. Pharmacol., **8:** 860, 1956b.
Beckett, A. H., Casy, A. F., and Harper, N. J.: J. Pharm. Pharmacol., **8:** 847, 1956c.
Benson, W. M., Stefko, P. L., and Randall, L. O.: Fed. Proc., **11:** 322, 1952a.
Benson, W. M., O'Gara, E., and Van Winkle, S.: This Journal, **106:** 373, 1952b.
Brodie, B. B., Udenfriend, S., and Dill, W.: J. Biol. Chem., **168:** 335, 1947.
Brossi, A., Häfliger, O., and Schnider, O.: Arzneim.-Forsch., **5:** 62, 1955.
Conney, A. H., Miller, E. C., and Miller, J. A.: Cancer Res., **16:** 450, 1956.
Conney, A. H., Brown, R. R., Miller, J. A., and Miller, E. C.: Cancer Res., **17:** 628, 1957.
Cooper, J. R., Axelrod, J., and Brodie, B. B.: This Journal, **112:** 55, 1954.
Cooper, J. R., and Brodie, B. B.: This Journal, **114:** 409, 1955.
Cook, L., Navis, G., and Fellows, E. J.: This Journal, **112:** 473, 1954a.
Cook, L., Toner, J. J., and Fellows, E. J.: This Journal, **111:** 131, 1954b.
Elliott, H. W., Tolbert, B. M., Adler, T. K., and Anderson, H. H.: Proc. Soc. Exp. Biol. & Med., **85:** 77, 1954.
Fromherz, K.: Arch. internat. pharmacodyn., **85:** 387, 1951.
Gillette, J. R., Brodie, B. B., and La Du, B. N.: This Journal, **119:** 532, 1957.
Isbell, H., and Fraser, H. F.: This Journal, **107:** 524, 1953.
MacFadyen, D. A.: J. Biol. Chem., **158:** 107, 1945.
Mannering, G. J., Dixon, A. C., Baker, E. M., III, and Asami, T.: This Journal, **111:** 142, 1954a.
Mannering, G. J., Dixon, A. C., Carroll, N. V., and Cope, O. B.: J. Lab. and Clin. Med., **44:** 292, 1954b.
March, C. H., and Elliott, H. W.: Fed. Proc., **11:** 373, 1952.
Mellett, L. B., Muehlenbeck, H., and Woods, L. A.: Fed. Proc., **13:** 386, 1954.
Mitoma, C., and Udenfriend, S.: This Journal, **113:** 40, 1955.
Mueller, G. C., and Miller, J. A.: J. Biol. Chem, **202:** 579, 1953.
Plotnikoff, N. P., Elliott, H. W., and Way, E. L.: This Journal, **104:** 377, 1952.
Plotnikoff, N. P.: This Journal, **113:** 44, 1955a.
Plotnikoff, N. P.: Fed. Proc., **14:** 379, 1955b.
Randall, L. O., and Lehmann, G.: This Journal, **99:** 163, 1950.
Strittmatter, C. R., and Ball, E. G.: Proc. Nat. Acad. Sc., **38:** 19, 1952.
Strittmatter, C. F., and Ball, E. G.: J. Cell. & Comp. Physiol., **43:** 57, 1954.

8031

EFFECTS OF ACRYLAMIDE ON THE CENTRAL NERVOUS SYSTEM OF THE CAT[1]

ALBERT S. KUPERMAN[2]

Department of Pharmacology, Cornell University Medical College, New York 21

Received for publication March 10, 1958

Acrylamide ($CH_2{=}CHCONH_2$) is a reactive vinyl monomer that possesses extensive industrial applications. Because of its widespread use, toxicologic tests have been made. It has been found that the chronic administration of acrylamide to a wide variety of animal species produces unusual and similar neurotoxic manifestations, the nature of which depend on rate of administration and the magnitude of dosage (Hazleton, unpublished observations; Chenoweth, personal communication; Kuperman, 1957). A chronic syndrome not unlike that of cerebellar deficit results from the repeated administration of a small dose. On the other hand, a large single dose produces an acute effect characterized by severe tonic-clonic convulsions.

The impetus for the pharmacologic studies undertaken in this and other laboratories was a series of accidental cases of human acrylamide poisoning. The manifestations of this poisoning are similar to those observed in animals and are predominantly neurologic. The present report, therefore, is primarily concerned with efforts to localize the action of acrylamide in the central nervous system.

METHODS. All experiments were performed with cats. Acrylamide[3] was administered intravenously or intraperitoneally in freshly prepared aqueous solution, unless otherwise specified. The purity of the acrylamide used in these studies was not less than 99.2 per cent. It is a white crystalline solid; melting point 84.5 ± 0.3°C.; water solubility 2.04 gm./ml.

Spinal cord transection. The spinal cord was transected acutely under ether anesthesia at C1 and respiration was thereafter maintained artificially. Chronic spinal cats were prepared aseptically under pentobarbital anesthesia by cutting at T12 or L1. A chronic spinal cat was not used for an experiment until several days after the operative procedure.

Decerebellation. Total ablation of the cerebellum was achieved aseptically under pentobarbital anesthesia. After removal of the occipital bone, the cerebellum was aspirated by the posterior approach. Periods of several months were permitted to elapse before any experiments were conducted on these animals so that the more severe disturbances of equilibrium had time to disappear completely or to become attenuated.

Decortication. Chronic decorticate cats were prepared aseptically under thiopental sodium (Pentothal) anesthesia. After extensive craniotomy and a longitudinal dural incision on each side of the midline, the cerebral cortex was undercut with a dull blade. Although complete removal of the cortical tissue was attempted in some cases, areas of the hippocampal cortex and uncus were sometimes left intact. In other cases, only the removal of somatic motor and sensory areas on each side of the cruciate sulcus was accomplished. These decorticate preparations were not used for experiments until at least ten days after surgery.

Decerebration. Supracollicular decerebrations were performed under ether anesthesia. The brain stem was exposed after removal of the posterior pole of the occipital lobe and a 2-mm. wedge of tissue was then aspirated in a plane passing from the rostral border of the superior colliculi to the mammillary body. The common carotid arteries were clamped during the aspiration procedure. Infracollicular decerebrations were also performed under ether anesthesia. Following the removal of the posterior two-thirds of the cerebellum, the brain stem was transected with a dull blade in a plane extending from about 3 mm. behind the inferior colliculi to the rostral border of the pons. Pressure was exerted on the vertebral arteries during this transection. At the conclusion of an experiment, 10 per cent formalin was infused via the carotid artery, the brain removed *in toto*, and the position of the brain stem transection verified.

[1] This work was supported by a grant from the American Cyanamid Company.

[2] Taken from a thesis submitted in partial fulfillment of requirements for the degree of Doctor of Philosophy at the Graduate School of Medical Sciences, Cornell University.

[3] Generously supplied by the American Cyanamid Company.

Spontaneous electrical activity. Electrical activity of the central nervous system was recorded with a Grass model 11A 4-channel electroencephalograph. The cat was secured on its abdomen, intubated with an endotracheal tube for artificial respiration and paralyzed with 1.5 to 2.0 mgm./kgm. of gallamine triethiodide (Flaxedil) intravenously.

The EEG effects of convulsive doses of acrylamide were observed by taking continuous recordings from the scalp with bipolar stainless steel electrodes. EEG changes were observed in the chronically poisoned cat after control tracings were obtained for two or three consecutive days; tracings were taken 24 to 48 hours after each succeeding dose. Upon the termination of each recording, the paralysis was relieved by the cautious administration of edrophonium chloride (Tensilon). In this way, the gross signs of poisoning in an animal were noted between recordings and correlated with EEG changes. Tracings were again obtained with stainless steel scalp electrodes.

For the cortical localization of chronic EEG effects, unipolar silver screw electrodes were inserted aseptically through several areas of the calvarium onto the dural surface. Silver screw electrodes were also utilized to record electrospinograms (ESG) from the chronically intoxicated cat; these were bipolar and were inserted aseptically into the appropriate vertebrae.

In many acute experiments and in those which were performed on decerebrate cats, EEG tracings were obtained directly from the pial surface of the cerebral cortex with silver ball electrodes. These were separated by 2 mm. on the cortex of the middle suprasylvian or lateral gyrus. In some cases the ESG was simultaneously recorded with bipolar electrodes inserted into the spinal gray matter. These spinal electrodes were made from 0.0035-inch enameled silver wire. Craniotomies, laminectomies, and dural incisions were performed under ether and several hours were allowed following anesthesia before recording experimental data or dosing. Skin edges surrounding exposed neural tissue were elevated to form a pool which was filled with mineral oil equilibrated with 95 per cent O_2–5 per cent CO_2. The oil pool was maintained at a temperature of 37 to 39°C. by a heat lamp. Cut and exposed skin and muscle tissues were periodically infiltrated with procaine.

RESULTS. *Effects of nonconvulsive doses on intact unanesthetized cats.* Acrylamide in doses of 1 to 50 mgm./kgm. a day produced postural and motor incoordination. This disturbance was strikingly similar to the asynergia caused by ablation of the nonvestibular cerebellum. An ataxia associated with decomposition of movement and dysmetria was a constant and prominent sign of poisoning. During the maintenance of a fixed position, synchronous postural tremors of the head and neck musculature were also apparent. A more irregular type of tremor was noted in the limbs during locomotion; this latter type was designated ataxic tremor since it never appeared prior to the development of simple ataxia (Carrea and Mettler, 1947). Locomotion was frequently complicated by forelimb crossing and the occurrence of all of these deficits in an animal caused falling. In addition to postural and motor dysfunction, acrylamide usually produced signs of behavioral disturbances ranging from fearful apprehension to viciousness.

TABLE 1

Development of ataxia after repeated doses of acrylamide

Daily Dose	No. Cats	Cumulative Dose*	Time*
mgm./kgm.		*mgm./kgm.*	*days*
1	5	101 ± 30	125 ± 26
2	7	132 ± 24	91 ± 18
5	3	78 ± 5	22 ± 3
10	8	126 ± 29	19 ± 6
15	5	102 ± 10	9 ± 11
25	11	102 ± 20	6 ± 2
40	6	73 ± 21	3 ± 1
50	3	100 ± 0	2 ± 0

* Mean ± per cent S. D.

Acrylamide was administered by a variety of routes. However, whether the route was intravenous, intraperitoneal, subcutaneous, intramuscular or oral, the characteristic effects of chronic poisoning appeared at identical dose levels and after equivalent latencies.

The inverse relationship between the dose injected per day and the time to appearance of ataxia is indicated in table 1. A more interesting and unusual fact is the relative constancy of the cumulated dose at the onset of poisoning regardless of the amount injected daily. Inspection of the data given in table 1 shows that the variations in cumulative dose required to produce ataxia are distributed around a central mean of 102 mgm./kgm. To determine the normalcy of this distribution, all of the determined cumulative doses required to produce ataxia in 48 cats were divided into 15 groups; this procedure facilitated

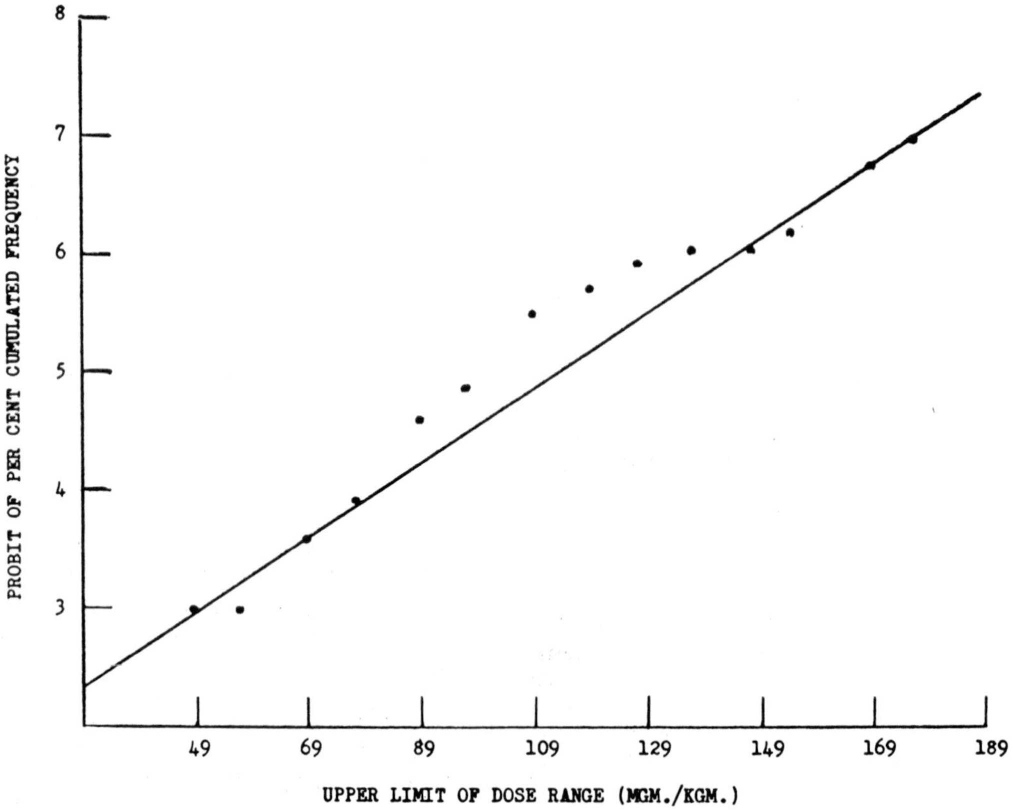

FIG. 1. Normal distribution of cumulative doses required for development of ataxia. Daily doses varied from 1 to 50 mgm./kgm. Method taken from Bliss (1938).

handling of the large amount of data. In accordance with the method of Bliss (1938), the per cent cumulated frequency of each dose range was calculated and converted to the corresponding probit. Plotting each probit against the respective dose range resulted in a number of points through which a linear regression line was drawn (figure 1). The closeness of fit is sufficient evidence for the existence of a normal distribution.

The continued daily administration of acrylamide after the appearance of the postural, motor and behavioral disturbances resulted not only in a progressive worsening of these effects, but also in the gradual development of a generalized and profound weakness which culminated in death. This general lassitude was associated with a gradual decrease in blood pressure which eventually reached shock levels. If dosage was halted before these effects became too severe, the animal recovered completely. The recovery period varied from a few weeks to several months depending on the severity of intoxication. The average cumulative dose required in 8 cats for the moribund stage of poisoning was 320 mgm./kgm., more than 3 times the mean cumulated dose needed for ataxia.

Post-mortem examination of cats dead from severe acrylamide poisoning or of cats sacrificed during initial stages revealed no characteristic morphologic changes. Extensive microscopic examination of brains and spinal cords from such animals were negative[4]. Microscopic examinations of other organs, blood and urine chemistry tests, and liver function studies likewise have uncovered no information on the nature of the poisoning (Hazleton, unpublished observations).

Effects of convulsive doses on intact unanesthetized cats. The single injection of 75 to 1000 mgm./kgm. of acrylamide resulted in a disturbance characteristic of generalized central excitation. The most constant effects in their usual order of

[4] Histopathological studies were performed by Dr. Charles Berry and Dr. Louis D. Stevenson at Cornell University Medical College.

appearance in any one cat were ataxia, tremors, weakness, emesis, defecation, signs of mass sympathetic discharge, behavior suggestive of hallucinations, and periodic tonic-clonic convulsions. An animal rarely survived the consequences of the repeated seizures.

In the acute poisoning, a considerable latent period always existed between the time of intravenous administration and the onset of effects. This latency was inversely related to dose and varied from 7 to 12 hours at 75 mgm./kgm. to 1 hour at the 1000 mgm./kgm. level. Even the excessive dose of 5 gm./kgm. required at least 15 minutes before effects appeared.

Spinal cats. In 6 chronic spinal cats, daily administration of 25 mgm./kgm. of acrylamide had no visible effect on reflex activity in the hind limbs. Characteristic signs of toxicity did appear, however, in those body segments above the transection level.

In 6 chronic spinal cats, single doses of 400 to 700 mgm./kgm. failed to evoke seizures of the lower limbs although the forelegs exhibited the typical tonic-clonic movements. In 4 of these cats the knee jerk became clonic many minutes after the appearance of foreleg convulsions. Since a possible explanation for the absence of hind limb convulsions in these cats was the relatively small number of internuncial circuits in the severed cord, acrylamide was next administered to acute high spinal preparations in 500 mgm./kgm. doses. Again knee jerk clonus was the only indication of heightened spinal cord excitability.

Decerebellate cats. The disturbance in the chronically poisoned cat resembled cerebellar asynergia so closely that a primary locus of action within the nonvestibular cerebellum was postulated. If this was the case, then acrylamide in nonconvulsive doses would have had little or no effect on the chronic decerebellate cat. However, the complete syndrome of chronic toxicity appeared in 3 such cats after 4 to 6 daily injections of 25 mgm./kgm. The moderate ataxia and postural tremors of the chronic decerebellate cat became progressively more severe during the repeated administrations; correspondingly, the ataxic tremors became more pronounced.

Each decerebellate cat was also given an acute convulsive dose of 500 mgm./kgm. subsequent to full recovery from chronic poisoning. In each instance the effects normally associated with this dose were observed.

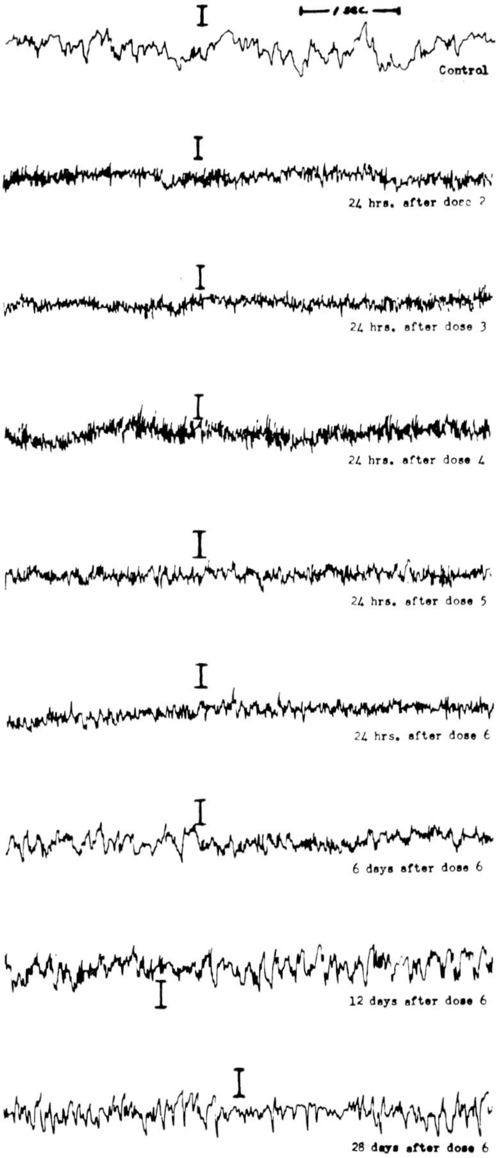

FIG. 2. Effect of daily intravenous administration of 25 mgm./kgm. of acrylamide on EEG.
A total of 6 doses was injected. Signs of intoxication appeared within 24 hours after the fourth dose. Recovery was well under way by the 28th day after the last injection and was complete on the 36th day. Note pronounced change in EEG even before the appearance of overt neurologic deficit. Scalp electrodes, cat paralyzed with Flaxedil, calibration: 20 microV.

Decorticate cats. Daily acrylamide injections of 25 mgm./kgm. were given to 2 chronic decorticate preparations. Before drug administration, the cats walked slowly and deliberately with hind limbs flexed at the hip and knee joints. They exhibited catatonic behavior. Ataxia was just perceptible. After 4 doses of acrylamide, the ataxia in both animals was obviously increased. It is important to note that neither the postural nor ataxic tremors were observed.

A dose of 500 mgm./kgm. was administered to each of 2 decorticate cats. In both, repetitive tonic-clonic convulsions appeared in addition to ataxia, tremors and signs of mass activity of the sympathetic nervous system.

Decerebrate cats. Doses of acrylamide from 400 to 700 mgm./kgm. were administered to 3 cats previously decerebrated at the supracollicular level. Repetitive tonic-clonic seizures of moderate intensity were produced in each cat but signs associated with excessive sympathetic discharge were not seen. In two cats previously decerebrated at the infracollicular level, these doses resulted in only brief periods of myoclonic movements.

Influence of nonconvulsive doses on spontaneous electrical activity of the cerebral cortex and spinal cord. A characteristic and unequivocal EEG change was produced by repeated administration of 15 to 40 mgm./kgm. or a single dose of 65 mgm./kgm. of acrylamide. This change involved a pronounced increase in wave frequency, complete abolition of large voltage slow waves, and desynchronization (figure 2). This activity was recorded from all areas of the cerebral cortex and did not originate from a circumscribed cortical focus insofar as could be determined.

Wave frequency was obtained by randomly choosing at least ten 1-second intervals from an EEG record, counting every blip for each interval and averaging the counts. The greatest drug-induced frequency changes ranged from 40 to 80 per cent above controls. A 25 per cent increase was chosen as a minimum indication of pharmacologic effect. This response was highly significant compared with the mean daily frequency variations observed in 15 different control cats. According to this criterion, an EEG alteration was exhibited by 80 per cent of the acrylamide-treated animals. The probability of appearance of this EEG effect, as well as its intensity, was not dependent upon the initial control frequency. In this connection, it should be emphasized that self-contained controls were used in all these experiments (see METHODS).

The typical curve of action of this electrocortical response to acrylamide is shown in figure 2. Note the gradual rise to peak change and the subsequent slowing despite continued drug administration. Reversibility of the effect, after cessation of dosage, is also apparent.

There existed significant variation in the dose-response relationships of the EEG effect (table 2). Table 2 also reveals the difficulty of establishing definite correlation between EEG change and gross disturbances, especially in view of the fact that 20 per cent of the poisoned cats did not show the EEG effect. On the assumption that such a correlation did actually exist, experiments were performed which had as their purpose the localization of the electrocortical response. Presumably, this was equivalent to localizing the site of that action of acrylamide which was responsible for the overt neurotoxic disturbance. The experiments with decorticate, decerebellate and spinal cats suggested that an action on the brain stem might be responsible for the syndrome of chronic acrylamide intoxi-

TABLE 2

Effect of acrylamide on EEG frequency; relationship between EEG change and signs of intoxication

Daily Dose	No. Cats	No. Showing 25% Frequency Increase	Days to 25% Increase*	Cumulative Dose Resulting In:			
				25% Increase (range)	Maximum increase*	Ataxia*	First neurologic deficit (range)
mgm./kgm.				*mgm./kgm.*	*mgm./kgm.*	*mgm./kgm.*	*mgm./kgm.*
15	5	4	4.5 ± 2	60–75	86 ± 11	95 ± 4	75–105
25	9	6	3.3 ± 25	25–75	71 ± 11	104 ± 15	50–100
40	6	6	2.8 ± 29	40–80	80 ± 0	80 ± 0	40– 80
65	5	4	1.3 ± 7	65	65 ± 0	65 ± 0	65
Total.....	25	20					

* Mean ± per cent S.D.

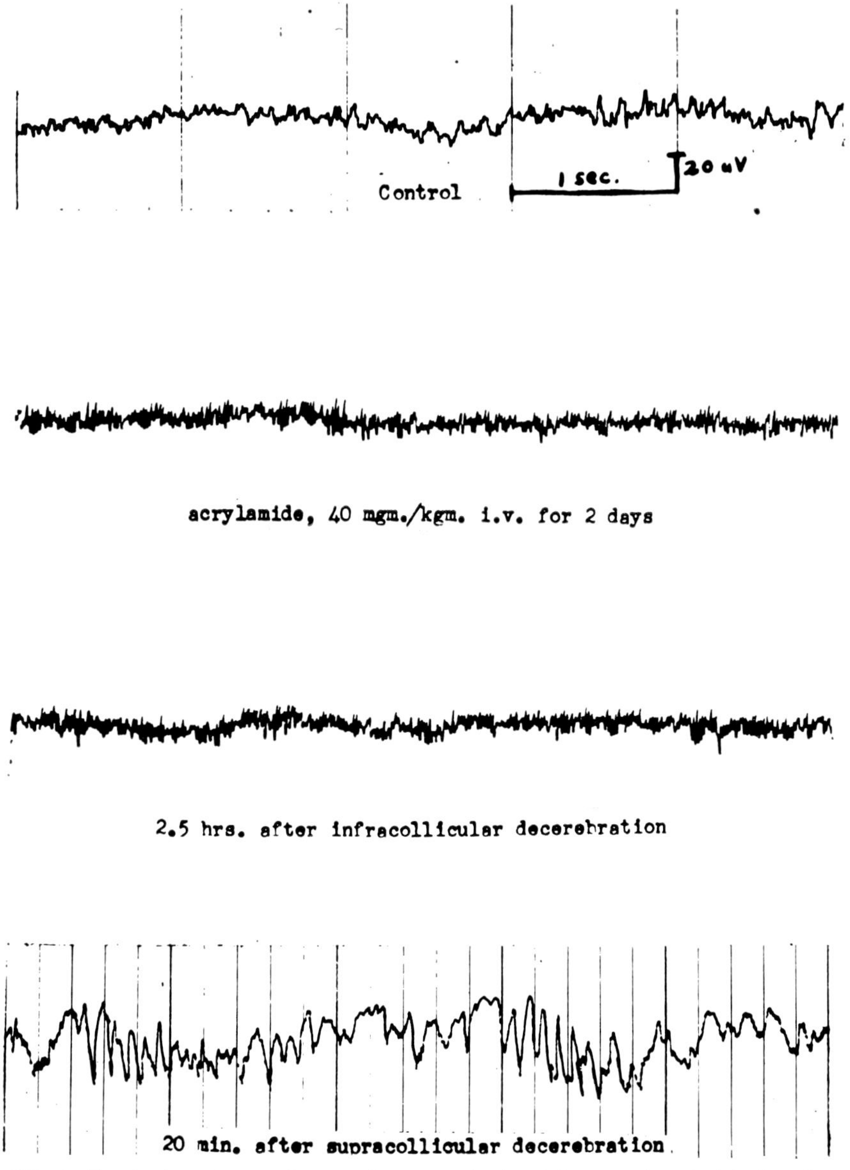

FIG. 3. Effect of brain stem transections on electrocortical activity associated with chronic acrylamide poisoning.

Infracollicular decerebration performed about 24 hours after second dose. Supracollicular transection achieved 3 hours later. Recordings taken directly from pial surface.

cation. If this is the case, then the appearance or nonappearance of the abnormal EEG pattern may depend on a cortical-subcortical interaction.

Three high spinal transections and 3 infracollicular decerebrations were performed on cats poisoned by two consecutive daily doses of 40 mgm./kgm. acrylamide. The abnormal EEG pattern presented by each of them was not affected by the surgical procedure. In each of 3 decerebellate cats the daily administration of 25 mgm./kgm. produced the characteristic EEG effect. The electrocortical activity of the nonpoisoned infracollicular decerebrate cat is slow and exhibits periodic spindle bursts (Lindsley *et al.*, 1949). This fact is noted because it is important to recognize that acrylamide can

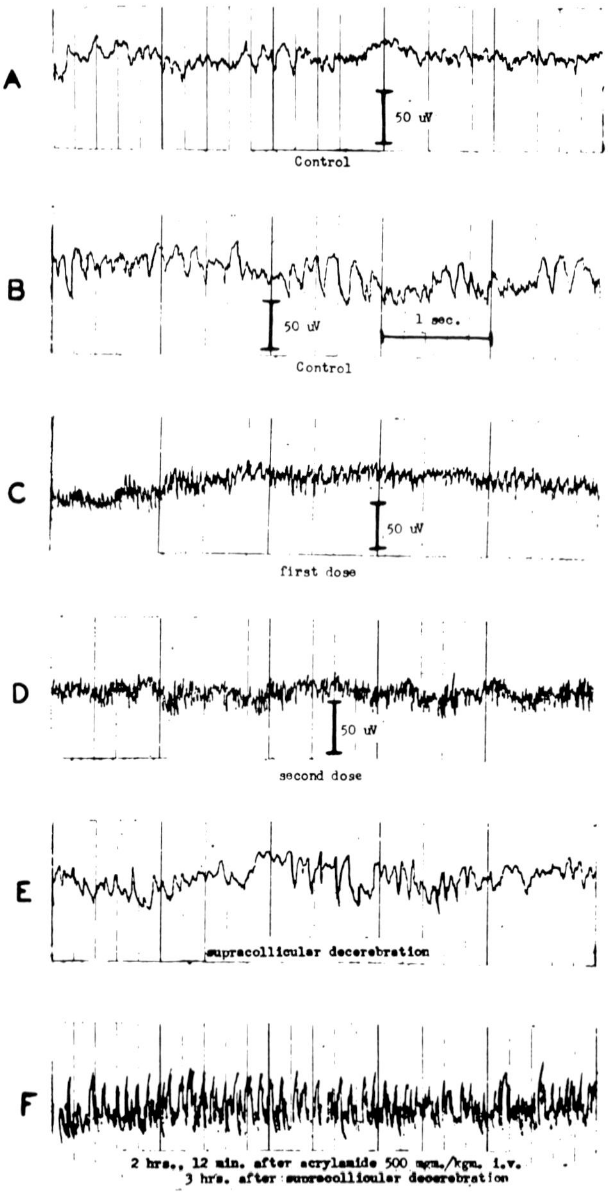

FIG. 4. Effect of supracollicular transection on EEG pattern produced by injections of 40 mgm./kgm. of acrylamide on two consecutive days.

A and B taken on two different but consecutive days. Transection performed about 24 hours after second dose. Note seizure EEG pattern in F produced by convulsive dose of acrylamide. Recordings taken directly from pial surface.

produce its EEG effect against a background of EEG abnormality.

Two daily injections of 40 mgm./kgm. of acrylamide produced the typical EEG change in each of 5 cats. Two of them were subjected to infracollicular transection, a procedure which had no effect on EEG disturbance. Subsequently, these same two cats were transected at the supracollicular level; complete abolition of the acrylamide EEG pattern was effected in both (figure 3). In its place there appeared a synchronous, high voltage, low frequency activity with periodic

8- to 12-cycle per second spindling, activity equivalent to that obtained from the *cerveau isolé* preparation described by Bremer (1935). The 3 remaining cats were transected at the supracollicular level only and in each of them the acrylamide-induced EEG disturbance also disappeared. To determine whether the isolated cerebrum possessed any pharmacologic reactivity to acrylamide, a convulsive dose was injected into each of 3 supracollicular decerebrate cats. Typical seizure activity resulted in each case (figure 4).

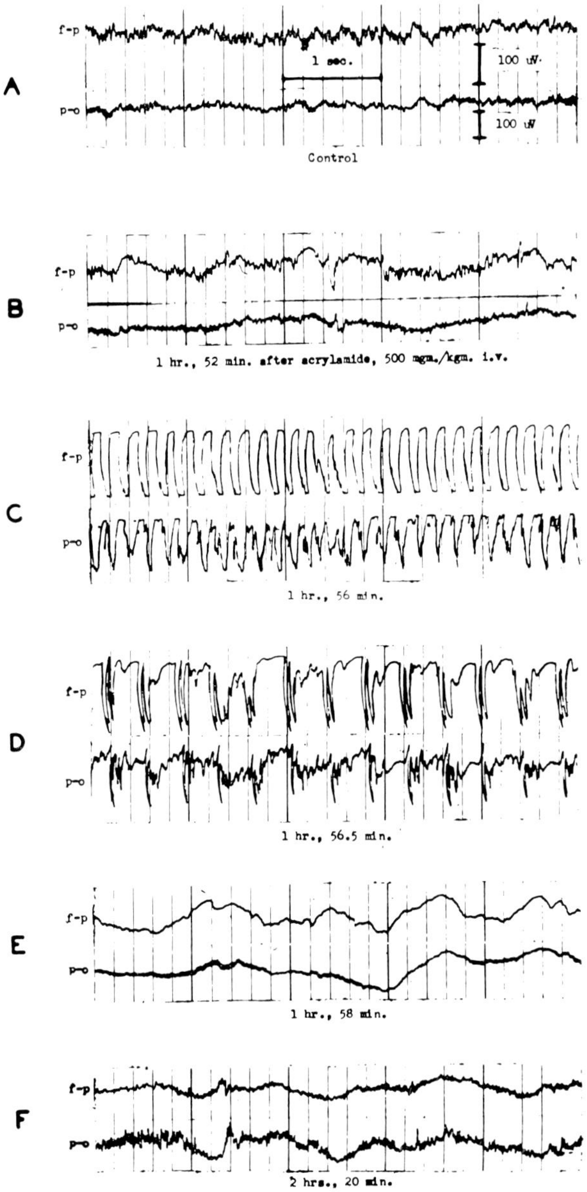

FIG. 5. Effect of convulsive dose of acrylamide on EEG recorded from fronto-parietal (f–p) and parieto-occipital (p–o) regions of scalp.

Postseizure depression shown in E lasted for 20 minutes. Another seizure pattern appeared 23 minutes after tracing F. Cat expired 3 hours and 15 minutes after injection. Scalp electrodes, cat paralyzed with Flaxedil.

In 3 cats poisoned by 25 mgm./kgm. of acrylamide injected daily, the ESG above and below an L1 transection was recorded simultaneously with the EEG. Although the latter underwent the characteristic changes in each case, the ESG above and below the transection remained unaffected.

Influence of convulsive doses on spontaneous electrical activity of the cerebral cortex and spinal cord. Convulsive doses of acrylamide produced high voltage and hypersynchronous electrocortical activity. Two such seizure patterns are shown in figure 5 and other types have been recorded. The production of a variety of seizure

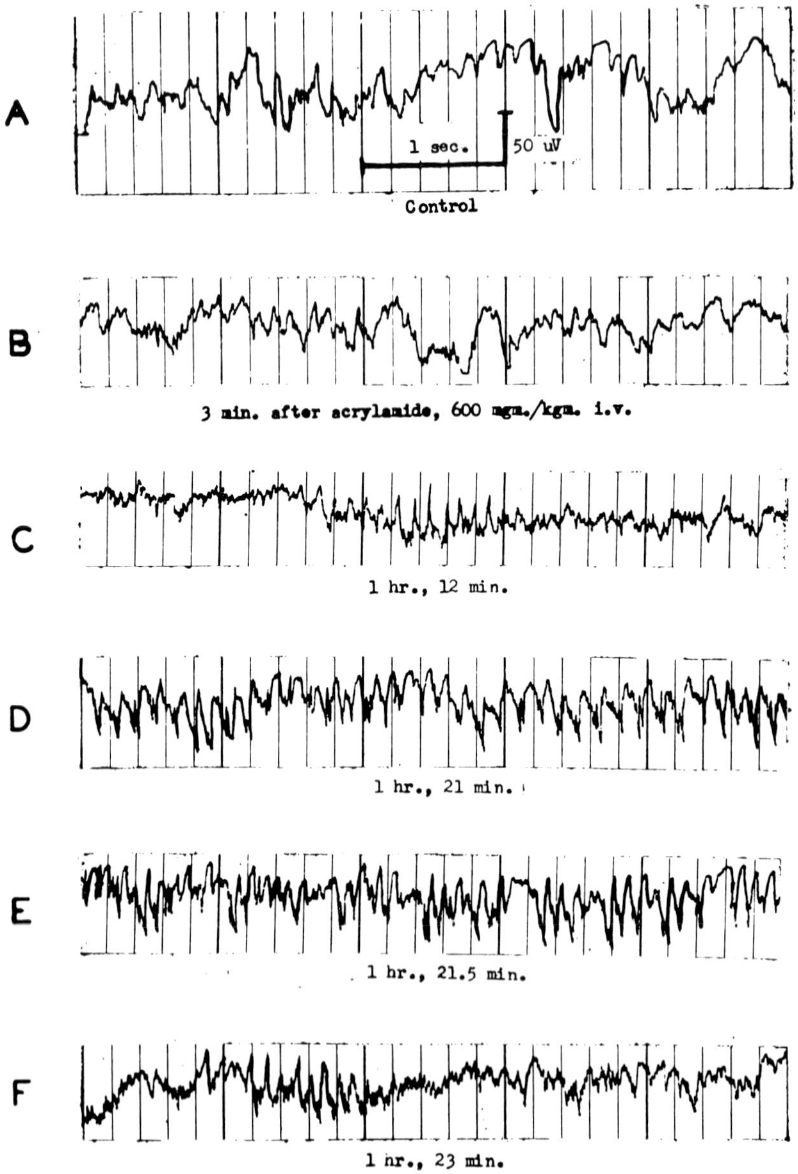

FIG. 6. Effect of convulsive dose of acrylamide on EEG presented by *cerveau isolé* preparation. Drug was administered 3½ hours after operation. Note appearance of spiking in C and seizure patterns in D and E. Postseizure depression was not observed. Cat expired 3 hours and 45 minutes after injection. Recordings taken directly from pial surface.

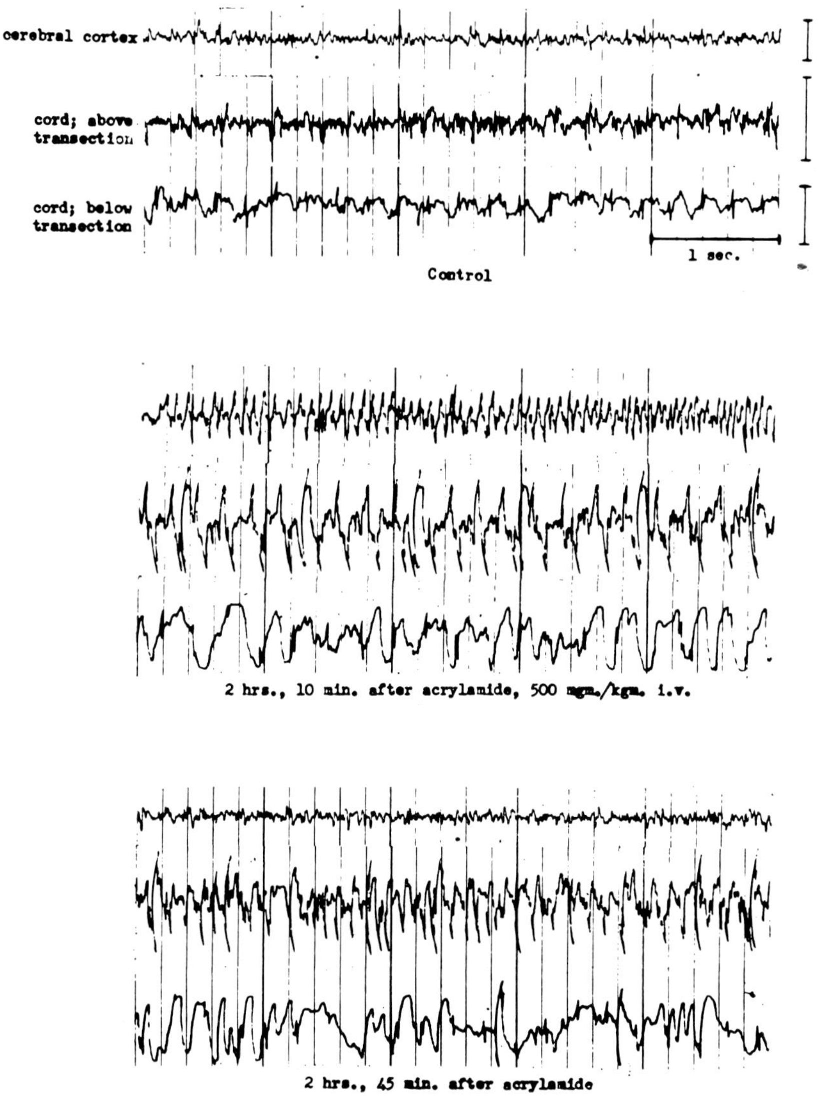

FIG. 7. Effects of convulsive dose of acrylamide on spontaneous electrical activity recorded from cerebral cortex and spinal cord above and below transection at L1.

Spinal section was achieved aseptically 3 days before taking the above tracings. ECG spikes appear occasionally in tracings from severed cord. Note the appearance of marked seizure activity in the intact cord during a period of electrocortical normalcy (bottom tracings). Calibration: 50 microV.

patterns by one convulsive agent is an unusual occurrence. The characteristic curve of action of the electrocortical seizure response is illustrated in figure 5. After a considerable latent period an increase in frequency and spiking developed. Subsequent to a period of this activity a convulsive response was recorded, lasting for 15 to 30 seconds and succeeded by EEG refractoriness. Several more periods of convulsive activity occurred until death. An interim of 20 to 45 minutes separated each seizure pattern and each was followed by an isoelectric phase.

Experiments previously described have indicated that acrylamide convulsions can be initiated from brain stem loci. It has also been noted (figure 4) that a seizure pattern can be recorded from the cortex of a decerebrate cat after the administration of a convulsive dose of acrylamide. The complete curve of this action in a decerebrate cat is shown in figure 6. The electrocortical seizures recorded in this and two other such experiments were brief in duration (10 to 15 seconds), usually lacking in the high voltage hypersynchrony seen in the intact cat and were not followed by isoelectric phases. It is clear then that acrylamide can produce a sustained and intense EEG seizure only in the presence of an intact brain stem. This circumstance is in distinct contrast, however, to the total lack of response of the isolated cerebrum to doses of acrylamide that produce the chronic syndrome of motor incoordination.

Continuous recordings from the spinal cord and cerebral cortex were made in 3 chronic spinal cats paralyzed with Flaxedil and injected with 500 mgm./kgm. of acrylamide. The results of one such experiment are shown in figure 7. Short bursts of cortical seizure activity developed within 1 to 3 hours after injection and hypersynchronous patterns appeared simultaneously in the segment of the spinal cord above the transection. Subsequent convulsive activity was observed in this part of the spinal cord even though the EEG pattern had returned to normality. Meanwhile, the ESG pattern from the severed cord gradually became more synchronous and higher in amplitude. This ESG, however, cannot be considered a true seizure pattern. Accordingly, it should be recalled that this dose of acrylamide did not evoke convulsions in the hind limbs of acute or chronic spinal cats. Therefore, at a time when the EEG appeared normal, convulsive activity above the transection probably descended into the cord from a subcortical focus.

Discussion. It has been shown that small or repeated doses of acrylamide produced a chronic and reversible intoxication which involved no histopathological alterations. The prominent signs of poisoning were ataxia, ataxic tremors and postural tremors. The doses required for development of these effects were sublethal and produced no apparent disturbances other than neurologic ones. A circumscribed locus of action within the central neuraxis was therefore indicated. In contrast, large single doses resulted in diffuse central excitatory actions.

Initial experiments demonstrated that the signs of acrylamide poisoning could not be accounted for by effects on peripheral motor and sensory nerves, neuromuscular junction, voluntary muscle and spinal reflex pathways (Kuperman, 1957). The investigations reported in this paper have suggested the brain stem as the primary locus of action of nonconvulsive doses of acrylamide. The mesencephalon has been particularly implicated. This structurally simple and highly reactive compound, with such a unique pharmacologic specificity, could provide a valuable tool for the elucidation of brain stem function. For this reason, the remainder of the discussion is devoted to an elaboration of this localization concept.

A major obstacle to the validation of a localization hypothesis has been the failure to obtain complete correlation between EEG disturbance and gross signs of poisoning. The absence of the EEG change in 20 per cent of the cats treated with nonconvulsive doses has been especially disconcerting. If, however, the electrocortical effect is actually a result of corticipetal projection from a subcortical focus, the uncertain development of this response may be reasonable. Moreover, the mechanisms which underlie normal electrocortical activity are complex and may confuse any theory that attributes EEG modification to a homogeneous drug effect. Therefore, the experimental evidence presented here is not sufficient to implicate conclusively the midbrain tegmentum as a primary site of action. There are, however, known physiological and anatomical facts which support such an idea and which indicate that further research should be continued along these lines.

Carrea and Mettler (1955) have shown that the anatomical substrate of ataxia in the primate is the rubrospinal tract and the descending limb of the brachium conjunctivum. The descending limb has been well defined in the cat and is known to give off a large number of collaterals into nuclei of the midbrain and pontile tegmentum (Mettler and Zimmerman, 1943). The rubrospinal tract is composed predominantly of axons from the magnocellular portion of the red nucleus, the destruction of which, in conjunction with lesions in the descending limb of the brachium, consistently produced ataxia in the primate (Carrea and Mettler, 1955). Correlating this physiological data obtained from the primate with our present knowledge of the histology of the cat midbrain (Kappers *et al.*, 1936; Crosby and Woodburne, 1943), the cellular locus of ataxia in the cat appears to comprise a large portion of the mesencephalic reticular formation and the red nucleus. In addition to functional resemblances between these cells, many of them are morphologically identical and their axons reach the cord primarily via reticulospinal and rubrospinal pathways. An agent which impairs the activity of these neurons of the midbrain tegmentum would probably produce the type of ataxia seen in chronic acrylamide poisoning.

The postural tremor can also be accounted for by an impairment of function within the midbrain. It has been found that the pathway of destruction for this disturbance in the primate is one which projects from the cerebellum to the thalamus and globus pallidus (Carrea and Mettler, 1955). Approximately half of these ascending neurons synapse with small cells of the red nucleus before proceeding to their more cephalad terminations. These neural pathways are well represented in the cat; therefore, the red nucleus and an extensive surrounding area with similar morphology are implicated as sites of acrylamide action.

The suprasegmental nature of the tremors seen in acrylamide poisoning, in contrast to the predominantly segmental nature of ataxia, was indicated by the failure of the decorticate cats to exhibit tremors after acrylamide treatment. This observation correlates nicely with the well recognized fact that cerebellar tremor in the cat is completely abolished by decortication (Fulton *et al.*, 1932).

It is important to recognize the similarity between the chronic acrylamide EEG pattern and the arousal pattern evoked by stimulation of the brain stem reticular formation (Moruzzi and Magoun, 1949). Both are low amplitude, high frequency, asynchronous and generalized over the entire cortex. The mid-brain reticular formation is a major region of the cat brain stem from which EEG arousal can be induced. The red nucleus and other deep tegmental nuclei involved in signs of cerebellar deficit are components of the ascending reticular activating system or at least possess synaptic connections with it (Starzl *et al.*, 1951a, b). It is possible that acrylamide acts coincidently upon neurons of the reticular activating system, these being different from those whose impairment results in ataxia and tremor.

It is concluded that the signs of chronic acrylamide intoxication may be produced by an effect on phylogenetically, ontogenetically, and in many respects functionally related neurons of the mesencephalic tegmentum. These cells may have certain biochemical similarities which are the basis of their peculiar susceptibility to acrylamide.

SUMMARY

The neurologic effects of acrylamide on the cat have been described and some of the neural loci of the intoxication elucidated. The nature of the syndrome depended upon the dose magnitude, rate of administration and the length of time during which the agent was given. Severe tonic-clonic convulsions and other signs of a diffuse central excitation were produced by lethal doses. The repeated or single administration of sublethal doses gave rise to a chronic and reversible intoxication. This was characterized by an ataxia and tremor which were identical to those of cerebellar asynergia. No other biological effects were apparent at the dose levels required to initiate this syndrome. Histological alterations in neural tissue have not been revealed.

The administration of convulsive doses to cats with specific neural ablations and transections revealed that the excitatory effect was exerted on the entire central neuraxis but with significant quantitative variations. The presence of the cerebral cortex was required for a maximal convulsive effect and the spinal cord was found to be particularly insensitive to the excitatory effects of acrylamide. On the other hand, observations on the same type of surgical preparations suggested that the primary site of action of the nonconvulsive dose was subcortical.

Electroencephalographic studies confirmed the diffuse nature of the excitatory action. The nonconvulsive dose produced a striking but reversible electrocortical response which resembled that invoked by stimulation of the brain stem reticular activating system. Further EEG experiments on *cerveau isolé*, *encephale isolé* and infracollicular decerebrate preparations clearly showed that the focus of this disturbance was subcortical.

On the basis of available anatomical and physiological information and the experimental data reported herein, the mesencephalic tegmentum has been proposed as the primary neural locus of chronic acrylamide intoxication.

ACKNOWLEDGMENT. The author is indebted to Dr. Walter F. Riker, Jr. for his advice throughout the investigation and preparation of the manuscript.

REFERENCES

BLISS, C. I.: Quart. J. Pharmacy & Pharmacol., **11:** 192, 1938.

BREMER, F.: C. R. Soc. Biol. (Paris), **118:** 1235, 1935.

CARREA, R. M. E., AND METTLER, F. A.: J. Comp. Neurol., **87:** 169, 1947.

CARREA, R. M. E., AND METTLER, F. A.: J. Comp. Neurol., **102:** 151, 1955.

CROSBY, E. C., AND WOODBURNE, R. T.: J. Comp. Neurol., **78:** 505, 1943.

FULTON, J. F., LIDDELL, E. G. T., AND RIOCH, D.: Arch. Neurol. & Psychiat., **28:** 542, 1932.

KAPPERS, C. V. A., HUBER, G. C., AND CROSBY, E. C.: The comparative anatomy of the nervous system of vertebrates including man, p. 663, Macmillan Co., New York, 1936.

KUPERMAN, A. S.: Doctoral Thesis, Cornell University, 1957.

LINDSLEY, D. B., BOWDERS, J. W., AND MAGOUN, H. W.: EEG Clin. Neurophysiol., **1:** 475, 1949.

METTLER, F. A., AND ZIMMERMAN, F. T.: J. Comp. Neurol., **78:** 113, 1943.

MORUZZI, G., AND MAGOUN, H. W.: EEG Clin. Neurophysiol., **1:** 455, 1949.

STARZL, T. E., TAYLOR, C. W., AND MAGOUN, H. W.: J. Neurophysiol., **14:** 479, 1951a.

STARZL, T. E., TAYLOR, C. W., AND MAGOUN. H. W.: J. Neurophysiol., **14:** 461, 1951b.

8032

DIFFERENTIAL EFFECTS ON VARIOUS CONDITIONED RESPONSES IN CATS CAUSED BY INTRAVENTRICULAR AND INTRAMUSCULAR INJECTIONS OF RESERPINE AND OTHER SUBSTANCES[1]

E. ROY JOHN, BERNICE M. WENZEL AND R. D. TSCHIRGI

Departments of Physiology and Anatomy, School of Medicine, University of California at Los Angeles

Received for publication February 20, 1958

Along with the recent development of the so-called psychotropic and psychomimetic drugs, there has been increasing application of quantitative methods of behavioral analysis to the problem of evaluation of drug action. In general, workers have used animals trained to make a single conditioned response, or less frequently, groups of animals each conditioned to make a different response, for such purposes.

Each of the animals used in the work to be reported here was trained in a variety of conditioned responses which involved different sensory or motivational systems, in the hope that the observation of differential drug effects on these various behaviors, measured simultaneously in the same animal, might allow a more precise evaluation of the specificity of a centrally active compound.

Further, the work of Feldberg and Sherwood (1954) and Gaddum and Vogt (1956) has demonstrated the utility of the intraventricular (i.v.c.) route of administration of drugs as a method for studying the central effects of pharmacological agents. Since many materials are excluded from the brain entirely or largely by the blood-brain barrier, and also because systemic injections of many materials cause change in noncentral nervous system functions, it is difficult to isolate the interaction of drugs and other materials on the central nervous system *per se*. Understanding of the biochemical mechanisms underlying the action of a drug might thus be aided by the study of the interaction of that drug with other substances when both were injected directly into the brain, bypassing the blood-brain barrier and also minimizing the role of peripheral effects in the phenomena thus elicited. In addition, the effects of central and peripheral administration can be contrasted.

Caution is required in the interpretation of results obtained by this method, in view of the inhomogeneous distribution which results from intraventricular administration.

This paper compares the effects of intraventricular and/or systemic administration of the following drugs on various conditioned responses in cats: reserpine (Serpasil, Ciba Laboratories), 5-hydroxytryptamine (serotonin creatinine sulphate, Abbott Laboratories), iproniazid (Marsilid Phosphate Substance, Hoffman-La Roche Laboratories), epinephrine, norepinephrine, atropine, methamphetamine and eserine.

METHODS. The principal data to be reported were obtained from a group of 8 adult female cats trained to perform at a very high level of proficiency in three different types of apparatus. They lived uncaged in a room 13 ft. by 9½ ft.

Apparatus. 1. This consists of an elevated runway 3½ in. wide with a lucite hurdle, 7 in. high, near the middle. The cat is placed at one end, a piece of raw meat at the other. By traversing the runway, stepping over the hurdle, the cat can obtain the meat, which has been in full view. 2. The second is a walled alley with two parallel compartments at one end, each closed by a door hinged at the top. When the cat is released from the starting box at the opposite end of the alley, it goes down the alley, chooses the correct one of the two compartments, pushes up the door, and finds a piece of raw meat on the platform beyond. The correct compartment is designated by a placard marked with a black circle on a white background, while the incorrect side bears a black square on white. These placards are interchangeable, so that either side can be correct at any time. The cat is not allowed to correct an error.
3. The third testing apparatus is a box divided into two equal compartments by a vertical partition, which extends only part way to the top. The floor is made of parallel brass rods through which current can be applied to the cat's feet. Each compartment is lighted by a 75-watt incandescent bulb. Through a loudspeaker mounted in the cen-

[1] The initial phases of this research were supported by a grant from Ciba Pharmaceutical Products, Inc., and the remainder by a grant No. B-448 from the Public Health Service.

ter of the top, a 1200-cycle tone can be presented. Upon presentation of the tone, or upon darkening of the compartment in which the cat happens to be located, the cat must cross the partition within 5 sec. or it receives intermittent shock until crossing occurs. One wall of the box is one-way vision glass, allowing continuous observation of the animal.

Training. For test #1, the cats were merely familiarized with the routine of the runway by being fed a portion of their food there for many days. Performance was evaluated only loosely in terms of a general tendency to approach the food without urging from the experimenter.

For the second test all cats were trained first in pattern discrimination. They were given 20 trials a day until no more than one error per day occurred for three successive days.

For the third test all cats were trained next in shock avoidance. Four of the group were trained first with the 1200-cycle tone and secondly with the darkened compartment; the other four were trained in reverse order. Twenty trials a day were given with one stimulus until the cat avoided shock on every trial by jumping within 5 sec. of the onset of the stimulus. The same procedure was then followed with the other stimulus. Finally, each cat was presented with a mixed series of 20 trials each day, 10 Tone and 10 Dark in random order, until all responses occurred in 5 sec. These conditioned avoidance responses will subsequently be called the CAR.

Surgery. As soon as training was completed, an intraventricular cannula was implanted in each cat, using the method of Feldberg and Sherwood (1954), modified in cases where the head was so small that their measurements would have placed the cannula in the supraorbital sinus. Postoperatively, all animals were tested for retention and, if necessary, were retrained to return performance to the preoperative level.

Injections. In general, injections were separated by intervals of at least one week, ranging up to as much as eight months. For those experimental sequences to which all animals were subjected, every effort was made to keep the interexperiment intervals identical for all animals.

A standard procedure was followed for all central injections. The injection volume, 0.25 ml. in almost all experiments, was injected into the cannula gradually over a period of one minute. A rinse of the appropriate solvent, 0.05 ml. in volume, followed each injection by about a minute. Control injections consisted of the appropriate volume of whatever solvent had been used. For central injection of reserpine, amounts ranging from 100 to 300 microgm. of reserpine (Serpasil Injectable Solution, Ciba Laboratories) were mixed with placebo (Serpasil Injectable Solution Placebo, Ciba Laboratories) to a final volume of 0.25 ml. For intramuscular injections, amounts of reserpine ranging from 7.5 to 90 microgm./kgm. were prepared in a similar fashion.

To study the interactions of reserpine, serotonin and iproniazid, central injection of 270 microgm. of serotonin base (serotonin creatinine sulphate, Abbott Laboratory) and 135 microgm. of iproniazid (Marsilid Phosphate, Hoffman-La Roche), in a total volume of 0.27 ml. of physiological saline, preceded injection of reserpine by one and one-half to two hours. In a pilot group (see below) the serotonin, with or without accompanying iproniazid, was given centrally as much as 24 hours before reserpine in some experiments, simultaneously with reserpine in some cases, and 4 to 6 hours after reserpine, while the CAR was completely blocked, in some cases.

Pentobarbital sodium was injected in subanesthetic doses of 7.5 to 10 mgm./kgm. in the experiments on the effects of this substance on conditioned behavior.

Details of time and dosage for other experiments are presented in the relevant sections. Injection volumes were 0.25 to 0.50 ml. in all cases.

Behavioral testing. A few minutes before an experiment was planned to start, the cat was tested on all three tasks to make certain that retention was adequate. Testing then occurred at approximate hourly intervals beginning one-half hour after injection, continuing until the peak effect was reached, and spaced irregularly thereafter until preinjection performance returned. After eserine, methamphetamine, atropine and norepinephrine, testing began within 2 to 10 minutes after injection and continued at intervals of about 20 minutes.

In order to detect increased latency of shock avoidance, in the testing situation, the cats were allowed 15 sec. to complete a response before being shocked, rather than 5 sec. as in training. However, for every five test trials of this sort with each stimulus, two trials were given in which shock was delivered in 5 sec. if a response had not been completed. Such trials served to maintain latency at the post-training level in spite of frequent testing with the longer allowance on test trials. Data obtained in these "reminder" trials were not included in the experimental results. If the cat had not completed a response in the time allowed, it was scored as an error and shock was delivered for 1 sec. every 5 sec. until the cat did respond or until 16 sec. had elapsed. In the computation of mean response latencies for a given session an arbitrary value of 15 sec. was assigned as the ceiling for error trials. This was felt to be a conservative procedure since it minimized increases in latency reported after drug injection. Five trials with each stimulus, Tone and Dark, were randomly intermixed in each test run. Intertrial intervals varied from 15 to 60 sec. at random, so that a test run lasted from 7 to 15 min. depending on the severity of increase in latency.

A test of pattern discrimination was sometimes omitted when avoidance was tested, due to the pressure of time or in the interest of maintaining appetite. The number of trials in a test run was most often five, but varied from two to ten. These trials were typically preceded by one trial on the elevated runway. The trials utilizing food approach usually followed each set of avoidance trials by about two minutes.

Other cats (pilot group). In addition to the group just described, a few experiments were done with 5 different cats that were trained to a lower level of proficiency in pattern discrimination and allowed to correct errors. They were also trained to avoid shock within 15 sec. of the onset of a buzzer attached directly to the hurdle box. This group had no experience on the runway. The purpose of the pilot group was to indicate grossly whether these responses were differentially susceptible to drugs and to learn the effects of various dosage levels.

RESULTS. I. *Reserpine.* a. General description of effects: Definite behavioral effects, which will be described in detail in the subsequent sections, can be detected within 30 minutes after intraventricular injection of reserpine, and within one hour after intramuscular injection. The severity of these effects reaches a maximum in 4 to 6 hours and remains pronounced for 12 to 36 hours, with behavioral recovery complete at 48 to 72 hours after injection. Behavioral effects have been observed at low doses with no concomitant autonomic changes. At higher doses, miosis appears well after the onset of behavioral effects, and is followed by an extreme relaxation of the nictitating membrane and ptosis of the eyelids. A severe diarrhea appears frequently at about the same time as ptosis. Sometime later a fine tremor develops which may persist for days, beyond the time at which other changes can no longer be observed. No autonomic change has been observed which is always accompanied by behavioral effects, nor were behavioral effects invariably accompanied by certain autonomic changes.

Control peripheral injections of reserpine placebo caused no detectable effect, control central injections of reserpine placebo were followed by no observed autonomic changes and caused little or no change in CAR latency. However, animals refused to work for food or to eat available food for several hours after such central injections. This was surprising in view of the fact that central reserpine injections, dissolved in the placebo, do not have this effect.

b. Description of reserpine action on the CAR: A brief description of the behavior observed during CAR training is relevant to an evaluation of the action of the drug. During the process of acquisition of the CAR, the following sequence characteristically occurs. Initially, when the conditioned stimulus (CS) is presented, the animal evinces arousal but no overt affective response. When shock is delivered after the CS has been present for 15 seconds, the animal bounds about in an agitated and random fashion, which ultimately leads him by chance to escape into the adjacent compartment. After a number of experiences with shock, this random activity is replaced by a swift, well-directed jump out of the compartment as soon as a single shock is applied, which we term "escape." Some time after the appearance of such directed escape, the animal begins to cringe and growl and move about at the onset of the CS. Spontaneous crossings appear and become more frequent. Then avoidance responses to the presentation of CS alone begin to be elicited, become more and more frequent and of shorter latency, and finally completely replace the escape behavior. These phases are not sharply separated, but coexist during the training period, with their average frequency of incidence changing as learning progresses.

When reserpine is administered, the inverse of this process occurs. Latency of the CAR increases, spontaneous crossings diminish, escape responses appear and become more frequent, and then random agitated behavior appears and dominates the performance. But, as with acquisition, also during the deterioration of conditioned avoidance behavior with reserpine, there is not an abrupt transition from phase to phase, but rather a gradual intermingling and replacement of one phase by the next. Thus, one can observe in one testing session, appropriate avoidance, long latency avoidance, escape, spontaneous crossings, and undirected agitation coexisting side by side, giving the impression that the learned response hangs in a precarious balance. Finally, as the drug effect wears off, the process is reversed, and the animal recapitulates in a matter of hours the pro-

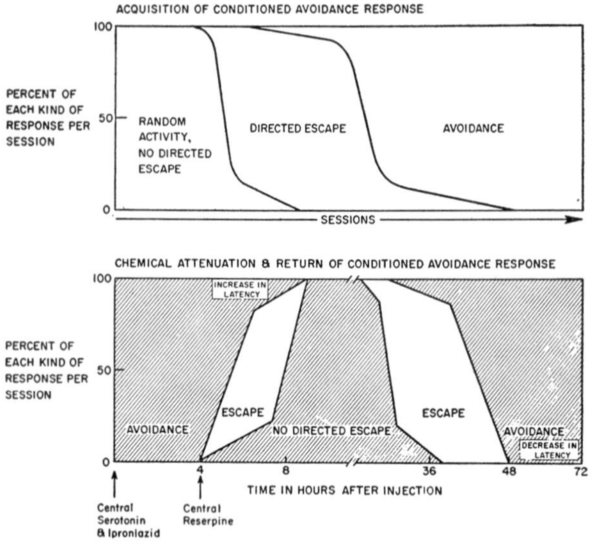

FIG. 1. Acquisition and drug attenuation of the conditioned avoidance response.

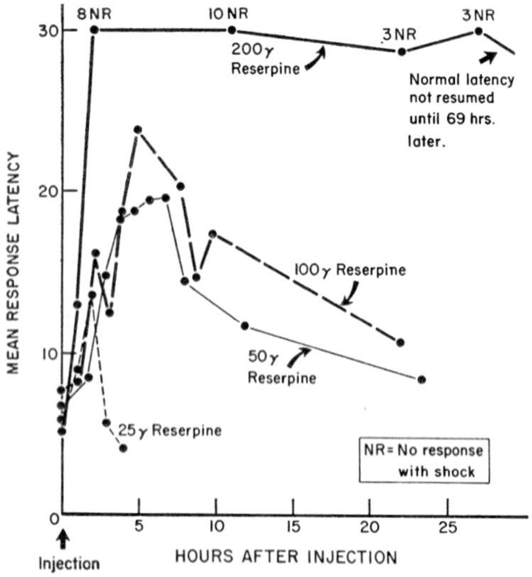

FIG. 2. Graded response curves for reserpine.

gression of changes seen as the response was initially acquired. These observations are diagrammatically presented in figure 1. The data illustrating effects of drug were obtained from a typical experiment on one animal.

A further general observation may be relevant to an attempt to understand the mechanism by which reserpine has its effect. The following sequence has been observed repeatedly. Some period of time after a reserpine injection, the animal is placed in the avoidance situation for testing; on introduction into the apparatus, he is reactive and alert; the nictitating membrane is normal, pupils slightly dilated; on the first few presentations of the CS, fast CAR's are elicited; gradually the latency increases until it becomes necessary to shock the animal; once shock has been delivered, performance abruptly deteriorates, and frequently no further CAR's can be elicited; on removal from the box, the animal is observed to have a relaxed nictitating membrane, constricted pupils and, frequently, a fine tremor. In other words, the behavior of the animal changes rapidly from adaptive to maladaptive during a relatively short period of stress, and the autonomic signs of reserpine simultaneously become more pronounced.

A series of response curves at different intraventricular reserpine doses was obtained in 4 animals of the pilot group, in order to estimate the susceptibility of the CAR to such injections. Data from one animal are presented in figure 2. In the computation of latency for this group of animals, 30 seconds was arbitrarily assigned as the latency for all trials on which avoidance did not occur, including both escape responses and complete failure of response, indicated as NR. The recovery time from a dose which blocks both the avoidance response and the escape response seems disproportionately long when compared to

TABLE 1

Comparison of effects of intramuscular and intraventricular reserpine on the conditioned avoidance response (CAR)

Cat	Intramuscular				Intraventricular			
	Dose*	Interval†	% Avoid-ance	Cutoff‡	Dose	Interval	% Avoid-ance	Cutoff
	microgram				*microgram*			
A	3/300	19 (300)	24	T&D-2 hr.	1/200	First	91	Neither
	4/50	14 (300)	60	T&D-3 hr.	2/300	12 (200)	45	T&D-5 hr.
B	4/25	7 (300)	48	T&D-2½ hr.	1/200	First	87	Neither
					3/300	7 (300)	28	T&D-2 hr.
					5/250	76 (100)	—	T&D<6 hr.
C	1/50	First	99	Neither	3/50	50 (50)	75	Neither
	2/50	7 (50)	48	T&D-12 hr.				
	4/150	26 (50)	—	T&D<6 hr.				
E	3/200	20 (300)	45	T&D-2 hr.	1/200	First	84	D-7 hr. T-not reached
	4/250	285 (200)	—	T&D<6 hr.	2/300	12 (200)	45	T&D-3 hr.
F	2/50	7 (200)	75	T&D-8 hr.	1/200	First	91	Neither
					3/250	190 (50)	—	T&D<5 hr.
G	3/300	19 (200)	29	T&D-2 hr.	1/200	First	53	T&D-28 hr.
					2/200	14 (200)	49	T&D-2 hr.
H	4/25	14 (300)	77	T&D-8 hr.	1/200	First	96	Neither
	5/200	199 (300)	—	T&D<4 hr.	3/300	7 (300)	31	T&D-2 hr.
K	2/50	7 (200)	99	Neither	1/200	First	41	T&D-2 hr.
	3/100	14 (50)	56	T&D-3½ hr.				
L	3/200	8 (300)	31	T&D-1 hr.	1/200	First	90	Neither
	4/25	14 (200)	100	Neither	2/300	11 (200)	39	T&D-3 hr.
	5/200	79 (200)	—	T&D<6 hr.				

* The number before the diagonal refers to the place of the injection in the series of reserpine dosages to which the animal was subjected. Experiments in which the interaction of reserpine with other substances was studied are not included in this comparison. Amounts stated are total doses in micrograms.

† The number before the parentheses represents the number of days elapsed since the last reserpine injection. The number within the parentheses is the total dose in micrograms administered in that previous reserpine injection.

‡ Cutoff is used to denote the time in hours after injection at which no CAR was elicited by one or both of the stimuli throughout a whole testing session. T denotes CAR to the auditory stimulus, D to the visual stimulus.

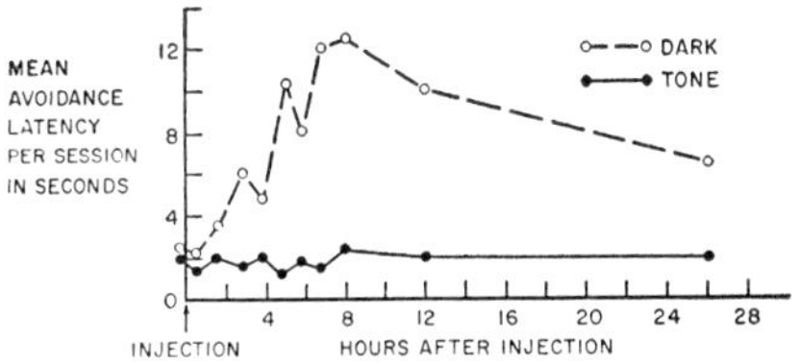

FIG. 3. Differential effects of reserpine on conditioned avoidance response to visual and auditory stimuli.

recovery time for doses which do not depress the behavior to this extent.

c. Comparison of intramuscular and intraventricular reserpine on CAR: The susceptibility of the CAR in cats to central injections of reserpine varies greatly. While some animals are profoundedly affected by doses as low as 25 microgm., most cats require central doses between 200 and 300 microgm. to block the avoidance response completely. In 8 animals for which the central effectiveness of reserpine had been determined, the effects of intramuscular injections of reserpine on the CAR were ascertained. The data obtained after central and peripheral injections are summarized in table 1. In constructing this summary, per cent avoidance was computed by determining the percentage of avoidance responses which occurred from the first set of trials following an injection until latency returned to the preinjection level. Thus 100 per cent avoidance does not necessarily imply that no rise in latency was observed. As described in the METHODS section, trials were run according to a definite schedule. About 100 trials were run in the usual injection experiment. Per cent avoidance has been used instead of the more precise latency measure to facilitate concise presentation of the large amount of data here involved. By "cutoff" in the table is meant that no avoidance responses were elicited throughout an entire session of 10 trials. Blank spaces indicate that data were not gathered at sufficiently short intervals to enable significant calculation. Intervals from 1 to 40 weeks separated the injections, as indicated.

The peripheral dosage required for a stipulated effect on the CAR was frequently markedly less than the central dose. On occasion, peripheral doses as low as 7.8 microgm./kgm. (23 microgm., total dose) had a more drastic effect on the CAR than central injection of 100 microgm./kgm. (300 microgm. T.D.) in the same animal. Previous doses administered were not considered responsible for the increased effectiveness of the peripherally administered reserpine since intraventricular injections separated by comparable intervals showed no comparable enhanced effectiveness.

In comparison with central injections, the effects of peripheral injection of reserpine on the CAR in cats appear to have a slower onset, a greater effect per microgram of reserpine and a greater duration.

d. Differential effects of reserpine on CAR to two different stimuli: After intraventricular reserpine, avoidance responses to the auditory and visual stimuli were affected differentially, with multiple instances in which the CAR could no longer be elicited to the visual stimulus while latency of the CAR to the auditory stimulus was relatively unchanged. This differential was significant at better than the 0.01 level. An example of this differential is illustrated in figure 3. These data are discussed in detail elsewhere (John, Wenzel and Tschirgi, 1958). In subsequent experiments, which will not be discussed here in detail, similar results have been obtained using other visual and auditory stimuli. In general, the larger the dose of reserpine, the less the differential which can be observed.

e. Differential effects of reserpine on approach and avoidance: Reserpine was found to attenuate differentially the CAR and pattern discrimination for food. In each of the 13 cats trained in both responses, at appropriate dose levels the CAR was more markedly (or exclusively) depressed. This differential was sharper after intramuscular injection than after intraventricular injection, perhaps due to the placebo effect mentioned earlier. At higher doses of reserpine, both responses were impaired. For the 8 animals which received intramuscular reserpine, the differential effect on these two responses is summarized in table 2. The two distributions of percentages differ at better than the 0.01 level, according to the sign test (Siegel, 1956).

TABLE 2

*Differential effects of reserpine on conditioned shock avoidance and pattern discrimination for food**

Pattern Discrimination			Shock Avoidance		
Correct	Of total responses made	95%	51%	Of total responses made	Correct
	Of total responses possible	83%	51%	Of total responses possible	
Errors		4%	13%	Escapes	
Approach only to visible food		5%	36%	No response to shock	
Refusal to approach or eat		8%			
Total noncorrect		17%	49%	Total noncorrect	
Control: correct		100%	100%	Control: correct	

* Based upon 730 trials in shock avoidance and 355 trials in pattern discrimination.

From these data, it is clear that the attenuation of the CAR by reserpine is not to be attributed to blocking of the primary sensory pathway.

II. *Pentobarbital sodium.* Subanesthetic doses of pentobarbital administered i.p. differed from reserpine in their effects on conditioned behavior. While motor impairment was more marked following the barbiturate, the attenuation of conditioned behavior was less severe and much less differentiation between the behaviors was observed than was induced by reserpine, although the same relative susceptibility of the conditioned behaviors is displayed to both drugs.

III. *Interaction of reserpine and other substances.* To investigate the mechanism of the action of reserpine on the CAR, studies were initiated of the interaction of intraventricular injections of reserpine and other substances with respect to this conditioned behavior. Although data were gathered on the performance of pattern discrimination throughout these experiments, they are not of utility in studying these interactions, since reserpine has relatively little effect on this approach response. Therefore, only behavioral evidence obtained from the CAR performance is presented in this section.

a. Serotonin and iproniazid: The central route of administration was chosen for serotonin because of the difficulty with which this substance crosses the blood-brain barrier. Iproniazid was injected simultaneously in order to block oxidation of the serotonin by monoamine oxidase. Although slight transient increases in the latency of avoidance responses occurred in several animals after central injection of 270 microgm. of serotonin together with 135 microgm. of iproniazid, no definite prolonged alteration was observed during periods up to 24 hours.

When reserpine (200 to 300 microgm., total dose) was injected intraventricularly 2 to 4 hours after central administration of serotonin and iproniazid, the onset, amplitude and duration of the reserpine effects on the conditioned responses were essentially *identical* with the effects of the same reserpine doses in the corresponding animals, when administered alone. The severe attenuation of the CAR, as in nonserotonin pretreated animals, persisted for 24 hours or more. The effects on CAR latency of an injection of

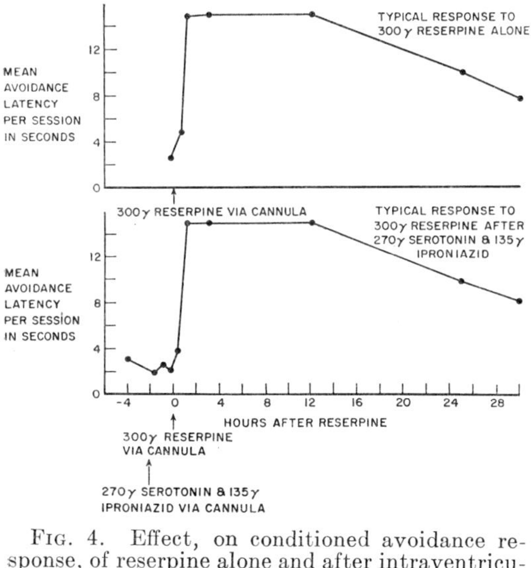

FIG. 4. Effect, on conditioned avoidance response, of reserpine alone and after intraventricular serotonin plus iproniazid.

TABLE 3

*Effects of prior central serotonin plus iproniazid on reserpine action**

Cat	Reserpine Alone (520 trials)		Reserpine After Serotonin and Iproniazid i.v.c. (460 trials)		Serotonin and Iproniazid Alone (240 trials)
	Reserpine dose	% Avoidance	Reserpine dose	% Avoidance	% Avoidance
	microgm.		*microgm.*		
A	300	39	300	39	100
B	300	28	300	23	95
E	300	45	300	42	98
G	200	51	200	42	100
H	300	32	300	42	100
L	300	39	300	49	95
Average.....		39.0		39.5	98.0

* All cats received 270 microgm. of serotonin as the base plus 135 microgm. of iproniazid via intraventricular injection 2 hours before intraventricular injection of the indicated reserpine dosage. Cats E, G and L received "reserpine alone" before "reserpine after serotonin plus iproniazid." The experiments were performed in the reverse order on cats A, B and H. This experiment was not performed on cats C, F and K. "% Avoidance" was computed from the results obtained during 50 hours subsequent to the reserpine injection.

reserpine alone, and after previous central injection of serotonin plus iproniazid are illustrated for one animal in figure 4. The data for 6 animals of the main experimental group are summarized in table 3.

In one experiment in the pilot group, the 300-microgm. dose of reserpine was divided into 3 aliquots and administered over a 12-hour period beginning 24 hours after the serotonin premedication. In this case, the reserpine effects on the CAR were less than those of a single 100-microgm. dose. No cumulative effect, such as would be expected from successive dosage within a short interval, occurred. This experiment must be repeated in order to determine whether the serotonin was involved in this effect.

Finally, in several animals of the pilot group, serotonin and iproniazid were administered both singly and in combination simultaneously with the reserpine injection and, in other experiments, after the onset of the reserpine effects. In no case was the reserpine effect on the conditioned avoidance response blocked nor its duration de-

TABLE 4

Effects of centrally injected norepinephrine before and after reserpine administration

Cat	% Avoidance	
	During 2 hours post-norepinephrine i.v.c. (40 trials)	4 Hours after reserpine subsequent to norepinephrine i.v.c. (10 trials)
3	100	0
8	100	0
H	100	0
L	70*	0
	After reserpine, 15 minutes before norepinephrine i.v.c. (10 trials)	During one hour after norepinephrine i.v.c. (20 trials)
3	0	0*
8	0	0
H	0	0
L	0	0

* Convulsion following injection.

creased. No alteration of the gross effects of reserpine (miosis, ptosis of the eyelids, diarrhea, fine tremor) was observed after serotonin and iproniazid, nor did these materials by themselves mimic the autonomic effects of reserpine.

b. Norepinephrine: The effects of intraventricular injection of 112 microgm. of norepinephrine were studied in 4 animals, both 2 hours before and 4 hours after the central administration of 200 microgm. of reserpine. From the data of Holzbauer and Vogt (1956), this amount of norepinephrine is at least 200 per cent of the total norepinephrine in cat brain.

Norepinephrine alone did not significantly alter the conditioned behavior of these animals, although in one case a brief seizure occurred, nor was the effectiveness of a subsequent dose of reserpine on the CAR diminished. However, the autonomic changes induced by this reserpine dose were attenuated. Diarrhea, hyperthermia and relaxation of the nictitating membrane were reduced. Tremor appeared in all animals and miosis in 3.

Injection of norepinephrine following administration of reserpine did not reverse the blockade of CAR induced by reserpine. In one case, this injection was followed shortly by severe seizures. The data for CAR obtained in these experiments are summarized in table 4.

c. Epinephrine: In 4 animals, amounts of epinephrine ranging from 25 microgm. to 100 microgm. were injected intraventricularly 1 hour before as well as 4 hours after reserpine injection (200 microgm.). When epinephrine injection occurred after the onset of reserpine effects, no diminution of these effects could be observed. However, in 3 out of 7 cases, low doses of epinephrine caused a transient increase in the latency of the conditioned avoidance response, followed by some attenuation of the behavioral effects of subsequent reserpine administration. These slight antagonistic effects could not be demonstrated consistently.

d. Atropine: The data obtained with central or peripheral atropine injection following reserpine are summarized in table 5. In order to test the effect of central injection, 150 microgm. of atropine were injected intraventricularly after complete suppression of the CAR in 4 animals by 200 microgm. of reserpine. Although the miosis so characteristic of reserpine action was replaced by extreme pupillary dilation in 2 of these animals, no marked improvement in the conditioned responses was obtained.

In 4 animals, 5 mgm. of atropine were injected, intraperitoneally, after the complete suppression of the CAR by 200 microgm. of reserpine. A rapid and sustained dilation of the pupils was observed, accompanied by retraction of the nictitating

TABLE 5

Effects of central and peripheral atropine on reserpine action

Cat	% Avoidance	
	After reserpine, 15 minutes before atropine i.p. (10 trials)	10 Minutes after atropine i.p. (10 trials)
3	0	0
3	0	10
8	0	0
C	0	0
E	0	0
	After reserpine, 15 minutes before atropine i.v.c. (10 trials)	10 Minutes after atropine i.v.c. (10 trials)
3	0	0
8	0	0
B	0	0*
F	0	10

* Convulsion following injection.

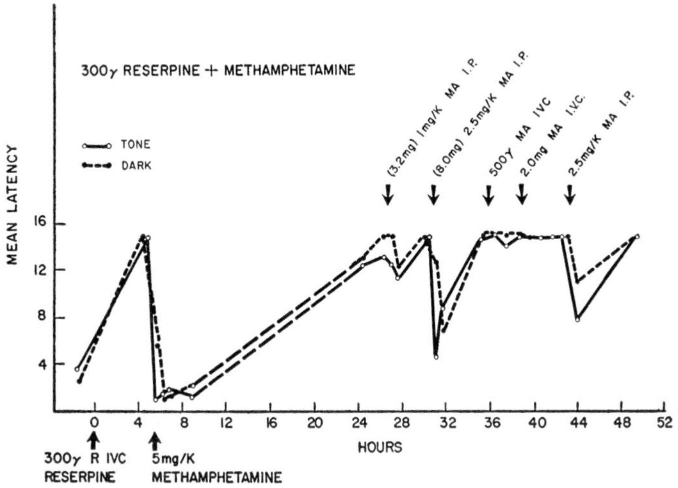

FIG. 5. Reversal of blockade of the conditioned avoidance response after reserpine by peripheral but not by central injection of methamphetamine.

membrane. Conditioned avoidance responses, however, remained blocked. In another animal, 5 mgm./kgm. of atropine i.p., one hour before 150 microgm. of reserpine, did not block the reserpine effect on the CAR, although miosis and relaxation of the nictitating membrane did not occur.

e. Methamphetamine: In 7 cats, methamphetamine was injected repeatedly i.p. in doses ranging from 1 to 5 mgm./kgm. after complete suppression of the CAR by 300 microgm. of reserpine administered intraventricularly. Pupillary dilation and retraction of the nictitating membrane were observed shortly. On each occasion, within a few minutes the CAR was restored. The extent and duration of the restoration of CAR were dependent on the dose of methamphetamine; 5 mgm./kgm. of methamphetamine completely restored the CAR for a period of more than 4 hours; 1 mgm./kgm. of methamphetamine caused a noticeable improvement for somewhat more than an hour; 2.5 mgm./kgm. had a somewhat greater effect than 1 mgm./kgm. and lasted longer. These results are illustrated in figure 5 for one animal.

In one cat, after reversal of the reserpine suppression of the CAR by peripheral administration of methamphetamine, 500 microgm. of methamphetamine were injected centrally (fig. 5). No significant improvement in behavior occurred, although noticeable pupillary dilation occurred and nictitating membrane relaxation lessened. Tremor persisted. Three hours later, 2.0 mgm. of methamphetamine were injected centrally. Hyperventilation, licking and vomiting occurred for six minutes and then subsided. No other differences from the earlier central injection were observed. No marked improvement in conditioned behavior occurred. Subsequent peripheral injection of methamphetamine was still effective in restoring the CAR. In two other animals a definite improvement in CAR was obtained after centrally injected methamphetamine but less than with peripheral injection and of very much shorter duration. In all 3 of these animals, within several minutes of the central injection, the miosis was replaced by marked dilation and the nictitating membrane tone was restored. These data are summarized in table 6.

IV. *Eserine.* Eserine was injected intraventricularly in 5 animals during 9 experiments. Doses ranged from 50 microgm. to 400 microgm. At low doses, salivation and spasmodic twitches of the contralateral trunk were observed. Circling to the side opposite the side of injection was frequently elicited; 400 microgm. was repeatedly found to elicit severe convulsion; 300 microgm. did not do so, nor did two injections of 200 microgm. each, separated by 15 minutes. Thus, it appears that this material is dissipated fairly rapidly, although twitches of the contralateral hind leg may be observed hours later.

The effects of eserine on conditioned avoidance responses were strikingly slight. On repeated occasions, animals twitching rhythmically made perfectly appropriate avoidance responses. Even

TABLE 6

Effects of central and peripheral methamphetamine on reserpine action

Cat	Reserpine Dose	% Avoidance	
		15 Minutes before methamphetamine i.p. (10 trials)	10 Minutes after 5 mgm./kgm. methamphetamine i.p. (10 trials)
	microgm.		
3	250	0	100
B	250	0	100
C	150	0	0*
E	250	0	100
F	250	0	90
H	300	0	100
L	300	0	80
		15 Minutes before methamphetamine i.v.c. (10 trials)	10 Minutes after 2 mgm. methamphetamine i.v.c. (10 trials)
B	250	0	40
F	250	0	20
H	300	0	0

* Grossly excited but no CAR.

in seizure, response was often attempted and created the impression that only the severe motor involvement prevented response, rather than that the animal was not "conscious." A marked increase in spontaneous responses was observed, and response latency decreased somewhat. Approach responses tended to be suppressed immediately after injection, the animals evincing distaste for offered food. After a brief interval, however, approach responses were resumed. The animals showed a slight tendency to make errors when the stimulus was presented on the side opposite the side of injection.

DISCUSSION. The data reported permit a number of inferences. Is it tenable to assert that reserpine interfered with the manifestation of conditioned avoidance behavior by reducing "anxiety"? We think not. That avoidance responses cued by a visual stimulus can be abolished, while simultaneously the same response to an auditory cue remains intact, argues strongly against this interpretation. The retention of visual pattern discrimination clearly demonstrates that the differential blocking of the visually cued avoidance response cannot be attributed to interference with the visual perceptual mechanisms. Likewise, it is obvious that the animals retain the motor capacity for making the response. These facts seem compatible with the conclusion that the effect of reserpine has been at the level of the learned association between an anxiety-evoking stimulus and the appropriate response.

Gross observation of the reserpinized animal at low doses during testing appears to corroborate this proposal. On presentation of the CS, cringing and growling were frequently elicited. On occasion, animals stood up and moved about the compartment, sometimes even attempting to escape. When shock was delivered, animals often ran aimlessly around the compartment, even climbing to the ceiling, but not displaying a directed escape. Anthropomorphically, it seemed that the animals knew something ought to be done, but didn't quite remember what it was.

The rather bizarre sequence of changes during a given experimental session after reserpine generates speculation as to the nature of the factors involved in this deterioration. The abrupt cessation of adaptive behavior after one failure and consequent shock (*cf.* RESULTS), accompanied by enhanced autonomic signs of reserpine action, suggest what we might call a decreased sympathetic resilience, for want of a better term.

The long time necessitated for recovery from a reserpine dose which blocks both avoidance and escape responses is of interest. Since the avoidance response and the escape response are acquired by the animal serially, and since they are clearly different psychologically, it seems reasonable to consider the possibility that they are mediated by two distinct physiological mechanisms. Blockade of one of these mechanisms by reserpine may occur in a different fashion than blockade of the other, and metabolic reversal of such blockade may proceed differently in the two systems. In other words, a reserpine dose which blocks both avoidance and escape behavior may act in a qualitatively different fashion on the two phenomena.

The observation that behavior deteriorates sharply as stress is applied to a reserpinized animal, coupled with the findings of Holzbauer and Vogt (1956) that norepinephrine is depleted in the adrenal medulla and in the hypothalamus after reserpine, suggested that the decrement in performance might result from exhaustion of hypothalamic and/or adrenal norepinephrine. The studies of norepinephrine interaction with reserpine were conducted in order to evaluate this possibility. Central injection of a sufficiently large amount of norepinephrine to prevent the hypothalamic depletion reported by Holzbauer and Vogt did somewhat attenuate the autonomic effects of reserpine, but not the effects on the conditioned behavior. This indicated that hypothalamic norepinephrine depletion may account for some of the peripheral signs of reserpine, but was probably not responsible for the effects of reserpine on the CAR.

On several occasions reserpine injected subsequent to small central doses of epinephrine had a lessened effect on the CAR. Order seemed important, since epinephrine injected after reserpine had no opposing action but appeared to intensify the reserpine effects.

Peripheral epinephrine injections were not used because of the impracticality of establishing a sufficiently lasting rise in peripheral epinephrine in an ambulatory animal to permit time-consuming behavioral measurements.

Central injection of serotonin plus iproniazid, whether injected before, with, or after reserpine, could not be demonstrated to modify the reserpine effects on the CAR or peripheral autonomic signs. Further, the lethargy reported after intraventricular administration of serotonin (Feldberg and Sherwood, 1954; Gaddum and Vogt, 1956) with respect to general reactivity was not observed, nor did serotonin by itself change the latency of the CAR or mimic the effects of reserpine. The difference between the effects of serotonin reported here and those observed by other workers may be due to the fact that more quantitative measures were used in this study or to the fact that our animals were trained in avoidance. In other experiments (Killam and John, unpublished data) we have observed changes in drug action after avoidance conditioning. Since Gaddum and Vogt (1956) have demonstrated that the intraventricular route is adequate for serotonin to exert a pharmacological action which was antagonized by subsequent central injection of LSD, it seems unlikely that the results here reported are due to the site of injection. These findings would seem to argue against the theory that the reserpine action on behavior is mediated by the release of serotonin from binding sites in the brain and its subsequent oxidation by monoamine oxidase (Brodie *et al.*, 1957). However, it is possible that it is the bound serotonin level in the CNS which is important and that intraventricular injection does not alter the amount of bound serotonin. Further experiments should be done to clarify this ambiguity.

The data comparing intramuscular with intraventricular injections of reserpine suggest a greater effectiveness of peripheral injection. Although previous doses would not appear to be responsible for this result, our data do not permit the exclusion of the possibility that the first dose of reserpine has a somewhat different effect than subsequent doses. The present experimental design is not adequate to enable one to rule out the possibility that the initial dose of reserpine somehow "sensitizes" the animal to subsequent doses of reserpine even after that initial dose has been metabolized.

The apparently greater effectiveness of peripheral reserpine may indicate that reserpine action is mediated by a peripheral agent, or that central administration of reserpine is not an efficient route for this substance to reach brain tissue. Relevant to the latter consideration is the fact that the onset of behavioral effects was more rapid after central injection than after peripheral injection of a comparable dose.

Recently, Everett and co-workers (1957) reported reversal of the grossly observable reserpine depression with desoxyephedrine. In order to observe the effects of a long-lasting sympathomimetic substance on the behavioral attenuation caused by reserpine, methamphetamine hydrochloride was injected peripherally and was found to cause a dramatic and reasonably persistent reversal of the reserpine effects on CAR. Central injection of massive doses of methamphetamine, while reversing the miosis and relaxation of the nictitating membrane, as observed with central norepinephrine, caused a lesser improvement in the conditioned behavior. Thus, once more the autonomic signs of reserpine action and the behavioral signs are seen to be affected differentially. Again, the failure of central methamphetamine to reverse CAR blockade by reserpine as effectively as peripheral injection raises the question of a possible peripheral mechanism involved in this aspect of reserpine action.

Since autonomic balance might be upset by either a sympathetic deficiency or a parasympathetic dominance, the effect of parasympatholytic agents was investigated by observing the consequences of both central and peripheral injection of large doses of atropine. Once more, the effects of reserpine on pupillary constriction and nictitating membrane tone were reversed, but the conditioned response remained blocked.

Establishment of a central parasympathetic dominance by central injection of eserine was found to have no effect on the CAR unless seizure was occurring with consequent motor incapacity. (The findings of Feldberg (1955) of catatonic stupor after central eserine injection were not confirmed. It is of interest that the effects of central injections of eserine observed by us are excitatory, in contrast to the sleep or stupor reported after central injections of acetylcholine by Dikshit (1935) and others. The results observed after central injection of eserine are not in agreement with those of Funderburk and Case (1947) and others, on the effects of peripherally administered eserine on conditioned responses.)

Therefore, it appears that the effects of reserpine on pupillary size and nictitating membrane might be attributed to a central sympathetic deficiency, which can be remedied by the central injection of either a sympathomimetic substance or a parasympatholytic agent.

However, the effects of reserpine on the CAR would appear to depend on a different mechanism, perhaps peripherally located, since they can exist independently of the other effects, and since *peripheral* sympathomimetic stimulation seems most effective to reverse them.

One line of evidence is most difficult to reconcile with the suggestion that a peripheral mechanism is involved. Schneider *et al.* (1955) have postulated that reserpine causes an increase of cortical inhibition on diencephalic structures, based on their finding that decerebrate cats in sham rage are quieted by reserpine but the full autonomic effect of reserpine does not appear. Rinaldi and Himwich (1955) asserted that reserpine depresses hypothalamic activity. Recently, Smith *et al.* (1957) investigated the effects of reserpine on normal and brain-operated monkeys. They found that in monkeys with frontal lesions the CAR was suppressed by reserpine as in normals, but that in animals with temporal lesions reserpine did not abolish the CAR. These findings suggest that reserpine activates a temporal region which then exerts an inhibitory effect on the CAR. Studies in our laboratory, reported elsewhere (John, Wenzel and Tschirgi, to be published), have investigated the blocking effect of various other substances on the CAR, and it would be of interest to observe whether comparable effects of temporal lesions on CAR blockade by such substances could be obtained[2].

These results provide specific information about the mode of action of drugs on conditioned responses, but more importantly, demonstrate the desirability of utilizing a number of behavioral measures differing with respect to the sensory modality mediating the conditioned stimulus and the motivational system presumably involved. Exclusive reliance on a single behavioral index may well lead to conclusions about the effects of drug administration which are misleading and which prevent the recognition of alternatives which may generate useful research.

Comparison of our findings with those yielded by previous investigations of the effects of intraventricular injection of drugs (Feldberg and Sherwood, 1954; Gaddum and Vogt, 1956) including some of those used here, which used no conditioned responses as indices, would seem to demonstrate the necessity of quantitative behavioral measurements as an adjunct to such studies. The nature of an optimal battery of measures for use in psychopharmacological research remains to be determined.

SUMMARY

Cats were trained to avoid shock on the presentation of either an auditory or a visual cue, to perform pattern discriminations for food, and to obtain visible food on an elevated runway. The effects of intraventricular and systemic administration of various substances, singly and in

[2] In experiments observing the effects of central injections of cation solutions on these behaviors, reported elsewhere (John, Wenzel and Tschirgi, to be published), it was found that some of the effects herein described as resulting from the injection of various organic molecules could also be obtained with injection of potassium or calcium ions. Potassium effects resembled those of eserine whereas calcium effects were similar to that obtained with reserpine in some respects. In this connection it is of interest to point out that on one occasion potassium injected centrally, which will antagonize the effects of central calcium ion, appreciably lessened the duration of effects of simultaneously injected reserpine. Unfortunately, time has not permitted the repetition of this experiment.

combination, were then studied on these responses.

Reserpine, injected either centrally or peripherally, attenuated avoidance responses while leaving approach responses relatively unaffected with the peripheral route more effective. At sufficiently low doses, it was possible to block visually cued avoidance responses, leaving both avoidance responses to auditory cues and approach responses unaffected. This was interpreted as evidence for a specific action of reserpine on the learned association between the visual stimulus and the evasion response.

The interactions of serotonin, iproniazid, epinephrine, norepinephrine and atropine injected centrally and, in some cases, peripherally, with reserpine were studied. Although some of these substances altered the autonomic effects of reserpine, only epinephrine appeared to attenuate the effects of reserpine on the conditioned behavior.

Methamphetamine consistently completely reversed the effects of reserpine when injected peripherally but central injection of methamphetamine did not reverse the reserpine-induced block of conditioned avoidance responses as effectively, although the autonomic effects of reserpine were reversed.

The implications of these findings are discussed.

REFERENCES

Brodie, B. B., Tomich, E. G., Kuntzman, R., and Shore, P. A.: This Journal, **119:** 461, 1957.
Dikshit, B. B.: J. Physiol., **83:** 42 P., 1935.
Everett, G. M., Toman, J. E. P., and Smith, A. H.: Fed. Proc., **16:** No. 1, Pt. II, 481, 1957.
Feldberg, W., and Sherwood, S. L.: J. Physiol., **123:** No. 1, 148, 1954.
Feldberg, W.: Proc. Roy. Soc. Med., **48:** 853, 1955.
Funderburk, W. H., and Case, T. J.: J. Neurophysiol., **10:** 179, 1947.
Gaddum, J. H., and Vogt, M.: Brit J. Pharmacol. & Chemother. **11:** No. 2, 175, 1956.
Holzbauer, M., and Vogt, M.: J. Neurochem., **1:** 8, 1956.
John, E. R., Wenzel, B., and Tschirgi, R. D.: Science, **127:** 25, 1958.
Rinaldi, F., and Himwich, H.: Ann. New York Acad. Sci., **61:** 27, 1955.
Schneider, J. A., Plummer, A. J., Earl, A. E., and Gaunt, R.: Ann. New York Acad. Sci., **61:** 17, 1955.
Siegel, S.: Non-Parametric Statistics for the Behavioral Sciences, McGraw-Hill, New York, 1956.
Smith, R. P., Wagman, A. I., Wagman, W., Pfeiffer, C. C., and Riopelle, A. J.: This Journal, **119:** 317, 1957.

8033

INDIVIDUAL DIFFERENCES: I. CORRELATION BETWEEN CONTROL LOCOMOTOR ACTIVITY AND SENSITIVITY TO STIMULANT AND DEPRESSANT DRUGS

SAMUEL IRWIN, MARION SLABOK AND GORDON THOMAS

Department of Pharmacology, Schering Corporation, Bloomfield, New Jersey

Received for publication March 14, 1958

This investigation is the first of a series aimed at determining factors which importantly influence the sensitivity or resistance of animals to drugs, *i.e.*, factors which contribute to biological variation. Fritz and Levine (1951) have shown that the vasomotor effects of epinephrine, norepinephrine or acetylcholine are dependent upon the presence of cortisone or its derivatives. Gellhorn and Redgate (1955) and Redgate and Gellhorn (1955) have shown that it is also correlated with the amount of sympathetic outflow from the hypothalamus. The pattern of blood pressure response to epinephrine and methacholine, as an indicator of the sympathetic outflow, has been used by Funkenstein *et al.* (1952) to differentiate psychotic patients and predict their response to treatment.

In the realm of psychology, Wikler and Masserman (1943) have shown a direct correlation between the complexity of a conditioned response and its depression by morphine. They also noted that paradoxical responses to drug could be related to drug-personality interaction. Lasagna, von Felsinger and Beecher (1955) have made similar observations in humans with respect to drug effects on mood. In clinical studies, Luttrell and Morrison (1955) have shown a correlation between the "biological level of activity" of patients and their response to reserpine.

The present paper deals with the influence of drugs on random locomotor activity, and endeavors to show a positive correlation between the locomotor activity level of animals before treatment and their subsequent locomotor response to drugs.

METHODS. The experiments were performed in a semi-soundproof room at 23 to 24°C. The locomotor (running and walking) activity of male or female, nonfasted Carworth rats was measured in 16 revolving activity drums equipped with automatic revolution counters. The blocks of animals employed on any one day were of similar age, weight and sex. The animals were assigned to activity wheels in random order and were returned to their assigned unit for all subsequent experiments.

Routinely, a 2-hour control count of activity was made before treatment. Animals receiving stimulants (pipradrol[1] or methamphetamine hydrochloride) were returned to their activity drums immediately after injection, and animals receiving depressants (chlorpromazine hydrochloride[2], pentobarbital sodium or morphine sulfate) were returned one hour later. This was done so that peak drug effects would coincide with a background of locomotor activity (low and high respectively) that would best emphasize the action of the drug. In contrast to one hour of measurement with depressants, the action of stimulants was observed and summed over four hours. All treatments were given subcutaneously.

On any experimental day, one-half of the animals received saline and the remaining one-half the active drug. The treatments were reversed one week later so that all animals received both drug and placebo. A square root transformation of the activity counts (number of revolutions) was found necessary for the statistical evaluation of the data; the log transformation was unsuitable.

Fearfulness was estimated on the basis of several indices with which it has been shown to be correlated, *e.g.*, constricted spatial movement, increased defecation and urination, and withdrawal behavior when approached. Placidity was estimated from the struggle behavior of an animal when inverted on its back and loosely cupped in the investigator's hand.

RESULTS. *Response to locomotor stimulants.* In figure 1, a comparison is made between the effects of saline and 10 mgm./kgm. of pipradrol. The response to pipradrol (square root) was found to have a slope which did not differ sig-

[1] Generously supplied by William S. Merrell Co.
[2] Generously supplied by Smith, Kline and French Laboratories.

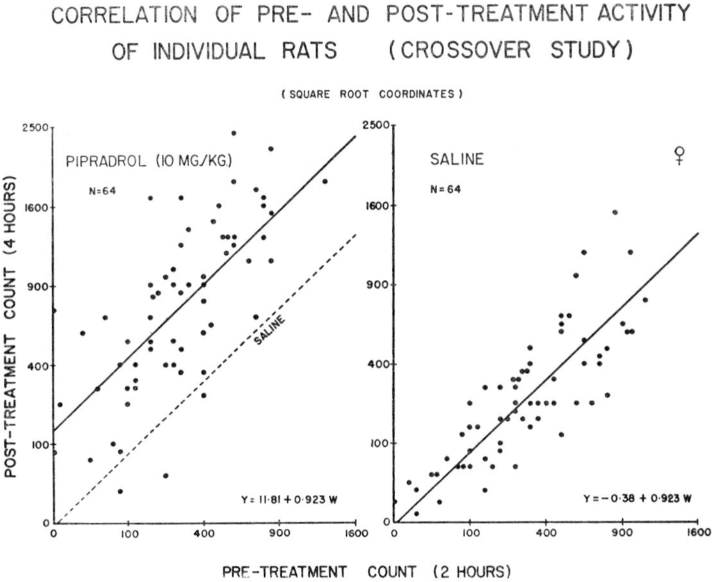

FIG. 1 Correlation of pre- and post-treatment activity counts of individual rats administered saline and pipradrol (10 mgm./kgm.) subcutaneously.

The study was of crossover design, and involved 32 animals receiving each treatment twice.

nificantly from that of saline. An analysis of eighteen separate experiments on six groups of 16 animals each revealed a mean slope difference between saline and pipradrol of only 0.007 ± 0.010.

Animals with high control counts of activity were found to be more sensitive to pipradrol than were animals with low counts. The absolute increase of drum revolutions produced with hyperactive animals was as much as seven times greater than the increase observed with hypoactive (relatively inactive) animals. Several of the hypoactive animals were completely *unresponsive* to drug. No matter how large or small the dose administered, it was impossible to elevate their activity counts.

Doses of pipradrol above 10 mgm./kgm. (16, 20 and 30 mgm./kgm.) tended to produce a disorganization of activity (circling, walking backwards, bizarre prancing of the forelimbs and "searching" head movements) which constricted spatial movement and reduced activity counts. There was no correlation between control activity counts of the animals and their sensitivity to this bizarre, drug-induced behavior, characteristically seen with other central nervous system stimulants and with LSD-25 or bufotenine. The activity counts of hyperactive animals, however, were more strikingly reduced by the disorganizing effects of high dosage of drug than were the counts of less active animals.

The observations made with pipradrol were duplicated in all respects with methamphetamine (2 mgm./kgm.). Hyperactive animals showed a considerably greater locomotor response to methamphetamine than did hypoactive animals. Increase in dosage likewise failed to increase the activity counts of poor drug responders, and produced the bizarre behavior described above. There appeared to be a finite physiological limit of response for each animal which could not be exceeded by adjustment of dosage.

Response to locomotor depressants. As shown in figure 2, relatively large doses of pentobarbital (16 mgm./kgm.) and chlorpromazine (6 mgm./kgm.) were administered to demonstrate a nonparallelism of slope response between saline and depressant drugs. A Youden Square type experiment with several dose levels of chlorpromazine and pentobarbital showed a tendency for the slope to revolve about a common axis toward zero. This is in contrast to a parallelism of slope obtained with increasing dosage of locomotor stimulants.

In these studies, the locomotor activity of the hyperactive animal was depressed, even with the square root transformation, to a considerably greater degree than that of the hypoactive ani-

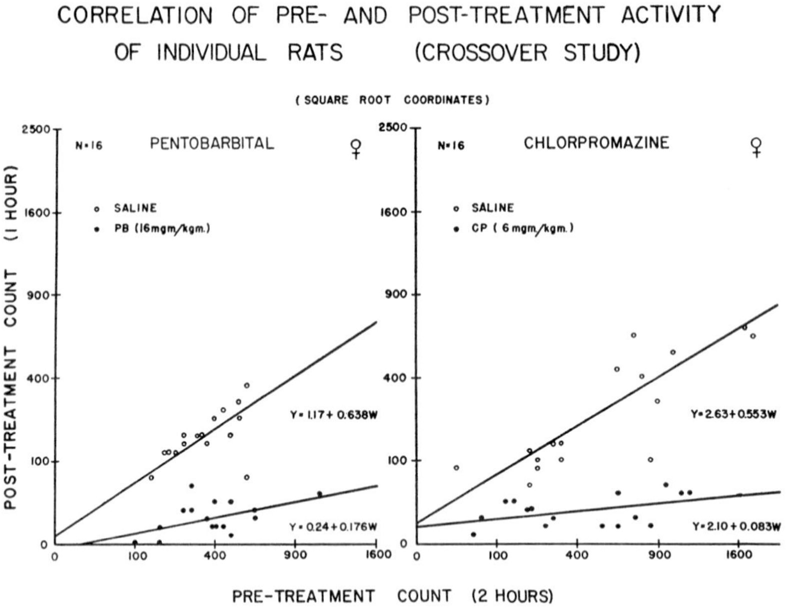

FIG. 2. Correlation of pre- and post-treatment activity counts of individual animals administered saline and pentobarbital (16 mgm./kgm.) in one study, and saline and chlorpromazine (6 mgm./kgm.) in another.

The studies were of crossover design and involved 16 animals on each treatment.

mal. Similar observations were made with various dose levels of morphine. A fundamental difference between pentobarbital and chlorpromazine or morphine in the rat, however, was that it was impossible to obtain significant suppression of locomotor activity with pentobarbital without producing ataxia.

In the experiments with both stimulants and depressants, occasional animals showed reproducible aberrant responses to drug which were poorly correlated with their control or 24-hour activity counts, suggesting still other factors that influence the locomotor response to drug.

Correlation with other drug responses. The locomotor response of the individual animal to stimulant or depressant drugs appeared to be on a relatively selective basis. No correlation was found between the control activity counts of the animals and their affective state (fearfulness, placidity or aggressiveness) or responses to a variety of treatments, such as latency for the tonic extensor component of maximal electroshock seizures, the sensitivity to ataxia, impairment of the righting reflex or anesthesia following pentobarbital, or the bizarre behavior following large doses of pipradrol or methamphetamine (see above). Each effect seemed to be independent of the other.

Correlation of 2- and 24-hour activity. An attempt was made to correlate 2-hour and 24-hour activity of the animals, inasmuch as the experimental situation involved the reactivity of the animals to manipulation (when placed in their drums) as well as to their intrinsic activity drive. For this comparison, a feed bin was attached to the activity drums so that the animals could have access to food. In order to obtain a clear record of 24-hour spontaneous activity, the animals were not disturbed after their 2-hour control count, but were permitted to operate for another 24 hours without interruption. The correlation obtained is presented in figure 3. Although considerable variation was noted about the slope, the 2-hour count of activity appeared to be significantly correlated with the spontaneous activity level of the animals. A summary of the statistical data derived from all treatments is presented in table 1.

Nocturnal activity and response to drugs. The hours selected as being optimal for peak activity were between 10:00 P.M. and 4:00 A.M. However, the animals behaved little differently at night than they did by day, either in terms of their 2-hour control counts (which showed only a small increase) or in their response to pipradrol (10 mgm./kgm.). The experimental situation

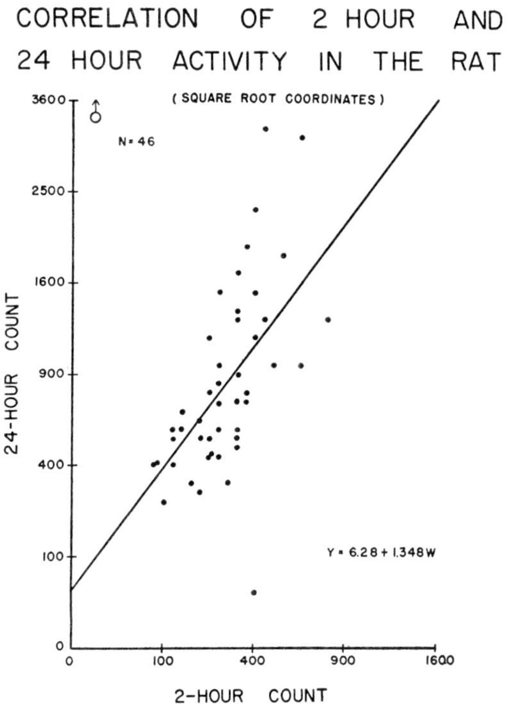

FIG. 3. Correlation of 2-hour and 24-hour activity counts in individual rats.
A total of 46 animals was employed. The animals were permitted access to food in this study.

seemed sufficiently provocative to keep the animals as alert and awake during the day as they normally were at night.

Variation in daily motor activity. The relative stability of 2-hour pretreatment counts of male rats over 3 months of study is shown in figure 4. The points in the upper figure represent the mean activity counts of these separate groups of animals plotted against their age, from approximately 2 to 5 months. The figures in brackets represent the number of animals in each group; the lower figure a composite of the three groups of data. There appeared to be a slight downward trend in activity during this period of observation, but it was not sufficient to be considered significant. The range of daily variation of activity counts of the individual animal was approximately ±4 square root units from its mean. A similar variation was observed in response to treatments.

Occasionally, animals stable at one level of activity were observed to shift abruptly and to stabilize at a higher or lower level of activity. The response to drug also appeared to shift in accordance with the new level. In general, however, the activity of the individual animal tended to remain relatively uniform over a long time course. Shirley (1928) has reported that individual differences in activity also are constant between the 6th and 9th months of a rat's life.

Sex differences. Most of the early studies were carried out in male rats. Female rats as a group exhibited a considerably greater degree and wider range of activity than did male animals. The greater range of activity made it possible to estimate the slopes of drug responses with greater accuracy. Aside from the greater frequency of highly active animals among the female population, there was no significant difference between male and female animals in the slope or intercepts for saline or various drug responses. The two sexes, after due allowance for the differences in their initial activity, appeared to behave as though they were from one population. The greater activity response of female rats as a group to stimulants or depressants, as compared with males, could be accounted for entirely in terms of the difference in their initial levels of locomotor activity.

The high activity level of female rats develops with the onset of estrus, when the animals are approximately two months old. Prior to the onset of estrus, their activity levels do not differ from those of the male (Richter, 1927). It is of interest in this respect that Holck *et al.* (1942) and Moir (1937) have found adult female rats more sensitive to barbiturate effects on "sleeping time" than males, while Moir could find no sex difference in the sensitivity of young rats to drug. Brodie (1956) has attributed this greater response of female rats to a reduced activity of liver enzyme systems (microsome fraction) concerned with the metabolism of the drug. He showed that the enzyme activity could be reduced by estrogen and increased by androgen administration.

It is unlikely however that the differences in drug sensitivity of male and female animals which we have observed can be explained on the basis of differences in the ability to metabolize drugs. The rate of metabolism cannot explain the relative refractoriness of hypoactive male animals to the locomotor actions of stimulant drugs administered over a *wide* range of dosage. Nor can it explain another observation we have made, namely, that although female rats are more sensitive than males to the stimulant or depressant effects of drugs on locomotor activity,

TABLE 1

Correlation of pre- and post-treatment activity counts of individual rats

Summary of data

Group No.	No. Anim.	Sex	Treatment*	Dose	Results			Slope Differences
					a	b	Sd	
				mgm./kgm.				
VII-F$_1$F$_2$	32	F	Saline	—	−0.38	0.923 ± 0.071	±6.2	
			Pipradrol	10	11.81	0.923 ± 0.071	±6.2	N.S.
VII-F$_2$	16	F	Saline	—	2.1	0.672 ± 0.156	±5.3	
			Methamphetamine	2	15.1	0.672 ± 0.156	±5.3	N.S.
VII-F$_1$	16	F	Saline	—	2.63	0.553 ± 0.074	±2.9	
			Chlorpromazine	6	2.10	0.083 ± 0.084	±2.9	$p < 0.001$
VII-F$_2$	16	F	Saline	—	1.17	0.638 ± 0.140	±2.0	
			Pentobarbital	16	−0.24	0.176 ± 0.092	±2.0	$p = 0.01$
VI-A$_1$B$_1$C	46	M	24 hours	—	6.28	1.348 ± 0.340	±8.6	

* Subcutaneous route of administration.

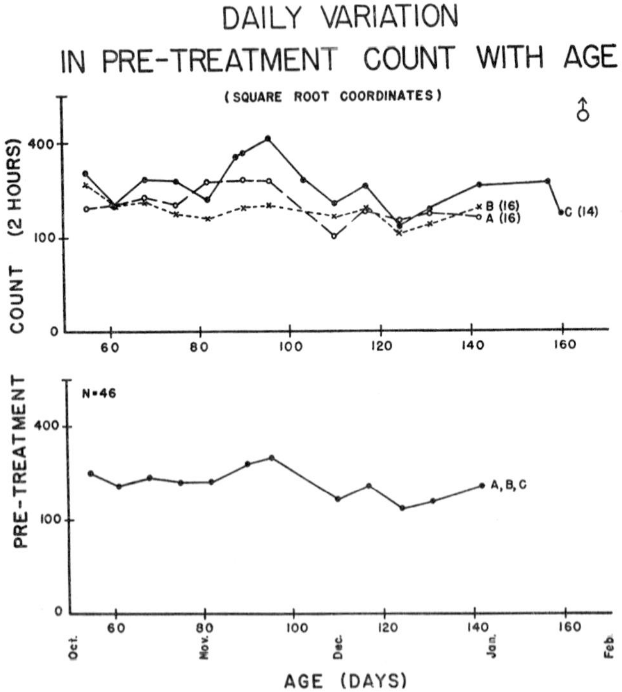

FIG. 4. Variation of 2-hour pretreatment activity counts of 46 male animals.

The upper figure represents the mean activity counts of 3 separate groups of animals plotted in relation to their age, from approximately 2 to 5 months. The figures in brackets represent the number of animals in each group; the lower figure a composite of the 3 groups of data.

they are *less* sensitive than male animals to the depressant effects of the *same* drugs on conditioned avoidance behavior (Irwin, 1958). It would seem, therefore, that the correlation observed by Brodie with respect to barbiturates may be relevant and operative only when very large doses of drug are given, *e.g.*, where the amount of drug administered may exceed the detoxication capacity of the organism.

DISCUSSION. The data presented may establish an experimental corollary to the observed failure of depressive (hypoactive) patients to respond to psychomotor stimulants and the greater efficacy of chlorpromazine and reserpine in the more manic (hyperactive) patient.

From the point of view of screening of drugs with a small number of animals, it would appear possible in behavior studies to draw erroneous conclusions by the fortuitous selection of animals that respond poorly or excessively to the drug. This can be prevented by crossover techniques with a standard compound. In dealing with psychomotor stimulation or depression, a group slope derived from correlations between pre- and post-treatment activity counts of the animals can be used to improve the accuracy and decrease the experimental error of statistical evaluations, for with it one can eliminate the variability between animals as a factor in drug response. It is apparent from our studies that there can be considerable error in direct group comparisons based alone upon mean per cent or absolute mean changes from control data produced by two treatments, and even more error in the comparison of two treatments without benefit of pretreatment data. One might fortuitously select hypoactive animals for one treatment, hyperactive animals for another (as with male and female rats) and draw the conclusion that the treatments differed significantly. If the pre- and post-treatment counts of the individual animals were correlated, on the other hand, one would find a common slope and intercept for response which would reveal that the two treatments did not differ significantly, and that the animals behaved as though they had received a common treatment. In broader terms, we would be in a far better position to make comparisons from the literature if the slopes and intercepts derived from pre- and post-treatment data were given.

SUMMARY

Hyperactive animals were sensitive and hypoactive animals relatively resistant to the changes in locomotor activity produced by various central nervous system stimulants and depressants.

The poor response of hypoactive animals to stimulants could not be improved by adjustment in dosage, suggesting a physiological incapacity to respond.

The locomotor response of the animal to stimulants or depressants was poorly correlated with the intensity of the same animal's response to other qualitative changes produced by the drugs, such as ataxia, bizarre behavior and the like. Each drug action appeared to be affected on an independent basis, suggesting considerable biological variation in the manifold responses of the individual animal to drug, and not just between animals.

Although female animals as a group showed a greater locomotor response to CNS stimulants and depressants than did male animals, this could be accounted for entirely in terms of their higher level of activity prior to therapy. When pre- and post-treatment activity counts were correlated, there were no significant differences between male and female animals in the slope or intercepts for locomotor responses produced by stimulant or depressant drugs.

The locomotor activity counts of male rats and their responses to drugs were found to be relatively stable from the second to fifth month of life.

The implications of these findings in drug comparisons are discussed.

REFERENCES

Brodie, B. B.: J. Pharm. and Pharmacol., **8:** 1, 1956.

Fritz, I., and Levine, R.: Am. J. Physiol., **165:** 456, 1951.

Funkenstein, D. H., Greenblatt, M., and Solomon, H. C.: Psychosom. Med., **14:** 347, 1952.

Gellhorn, E., and Redgate, E. S.: Arch. internat. pharmacodyn., **102:** 162, 1955.

Holck, H. G. O., Mathieson, D. R., Smith, E. L., and Fink, L. D.: J. Am. Pharm. Ass., Sci. Ed., **31:** 116, 1942.

Irwin, S.: Fed. Proc., **17:** 380, 1958.

Lasagna, L., von Felsinger, J. M., and Beecher, H. K.: J.A.M.A., **157:** 1006, 1955.

Luttrell, R. R., and Morrison, A. V.: Ann. New York Acad. Sci., **61:** 183, 1955.

Moir, W. M.: This Journal, **59:** 68, 1937.

Redgate, E. S., and Gellhorn, E.: Arch. internat. pharmacodyn., **102:** 179, 1955.

Richter, C. P.: Quart. Rev. Biol., **2:** 307, 1927.

Shirley, M.: J. Compar. Psychol., **8:** 159, 1928.

Wikler, A., and Masserman, J. H.: Arch. Neurol. and Psychiat., **50:** 401, 1943.

8034

A STUDY OF CENTRAL NERVOUS SYSTEM STIMULANTS

GRAHAM CHEN AND BARBARA BOHNER

Research Laboratories, Parke, Davis & Company, Detroit, Michigan

Received for publication March 17, 1958

The central nervous system stimulants are commonly categorized according to their principal site of action on the spinal cord, the medullary centers, or the cerebral cortex. In our investigation with the various CNS stimulants during the past decade, we have utilized some of their typical neuropharmacological effects for characterization and classification. This approach has been used with two purposes in mind: 1) to investigate the properties of new stimulating agents by comparison with those of reference standards and 2) to examine the neuropharmacological properties of CNS depressants by antagonism.

In this paper, the results obtained with various old and some new CNS stimulants in mice are given; the data are elucidated categorically according to seizure patterns and some other typical pharmacological effects. Studies on CNS depressants will be communicated in a subsequent report.

METHODS. Male albino mice weighing 18 to 22 gm. were used. The effective dose of each stimulant was determined in 10 animals by parenteral administration. Intravenous administration was carried out by slow infusion at the rate of 0.05 ml. per 10 seconds (Orloff, Williams and Pfeiffer, 1949) in the case of the following stimulants: picrotoxin, pentylenetetrazol, caffeine, 10-(2-dimethylaminopropyl)-9-acridone ("Acridone"), 4-methyl-4-ethylglutarimide (Megimide)[1], $\alpha,\alpha,\beta,\beta$-tetramethylsuccinimide (PM 1090) and 1-hydrazinophthalazine (hydralazine, Apresoline). The quantities of the stimulant required for producing the first clonic contracture, for the maximal tonic extension of hind limbs and for respiratory failure were recorded. Since the average body weight of 10 mice was about 20 gm., the amounts of the stimulants used were expressed in mean values of milliliters per 20-gm. mouse. In antagonism experiments where the tonic extensor seizures of some mice were abolished under the influence of a depressant, the results for such a response were given by the fraction of animals so affected.

Cocaine·HCl, desoxyephedrine, α,α-diphenyl-2-piperidinemethanol (pipradrol, Meratran), 2-phenyl-2-piperidine acetic acid methyl ester (methyl phenidate, Ritalin), lysergic acid diethylamide (LSD) and 1,4-dipyrrolidino-2-butyne (Tremorine) were administered intraperitoneally. The signs and symptoms noted were tremors, running movement, pilomotor response, salivation and lacrimation.

For some stimulants, their antiextensor seizure effects were examined by a modified procedure of Toman, Swinyard and Goodman (1946). Three groups of 10 mice each were employed for each dose of the stimulant to determine the three current strengths which would be required to produce tonic extensor seizures in 10 to 90 per cent of the animals. The 50 per cent convulsive threshold of current and standard errors were estimated from a graph relating the percentage of the convulsive animals in probit units to milliamperes of current in logarithms (Miller and Tainter, 1944).

RESULTS AND DISCUSSION. The data are presented under two main divisions on the basis of whether or not intravenous administration of the stimulants will induce tonic extensor seizures in the limbs of mice.

Tonic extensor seizure producing agents. As has been mentioned in a previous report (Chen and Bohner, 1956a), a large number of CNS stimulants can produce clonic and tonic extensor seizures in mice during slow intravenous administration administration. However, under the influence of reserpine and by antagonism with different pharmacological types of anticonvulsant agents, the convulsant properties of these stimulants may be distinctly differentiated. For instance, reserpine will facilitate the tonic extensor seizures of mice induced by pentylenetetrazol or caffeine but it does not affect those induced by strychnine. Dilantin (diphenylhydantoin), on the other hand, is effective in mice in suppressing pentylenetetrazol-induced seizures but not in suppressing strychnine- or caffeine-induced tonic extensor seizures. Under similar experimental conditions ammonium acetate and nikethamide

[1] This compound was investigated by us in 1948 (Benica and Wilson, 1950).

act like strychnine and pentylenetetrazol, respectively. Picrotoxin behaves like pentylenetetrazol against the anticonvulsant effect of Dilantin but behaves like strychnine in the presence of reserpine. A majority of the other compounds available to us for study have convulsant properties similar to those of picrotoxin or pentylenetetrazol. A comparison of four CNS stimulants, which are of current interest, with picrotoxin and pentylenetetrazol is shown by the data in table 1. It may be noticed first from the quantity of the stimulant required to produce tonic extensor seizures that the extensor seizure response of mice to pentylenetetrazol, 4-methyl-4-ethylglutarimide or PM-1090 stimulation was facilitated by reserpine but the response to picrotoxin, hydralazine or "Acridone" was not affected by reserpine. Second, the extensor seizures of the limbs induced by the six convulsants were suppressed or abolished by Dilantin. This influence of Dilantin may be prevented by reserpine. Third, there is an indication that, although phensuximide, mephenesin and barbital were almost equally effective in suppressing the convulsive seizures induced by the six convulsants, their anticonvulsant effects were antagonized by reserpine more efficiently in seizures induced by pentylenetetrazol, 4-methyl-4-ethylglutarimide or PM-1090 than in picrotoxin-, hydralazine- or "Acridone"-induced seizures. Thus, the results appear to indicate that hydralazine and "Acridone" are picrotoxin-like while 4-methyl-4-ethylglutarimide and PM-1090 are pentylenetetrazol-like convulsants.

Excitants. These CNS stimulants are so referred to here simply because they do not produce tonic extensor seizures in mice by intravenous administration. The outstanding signs and symptoms produced by the excitants are tremors, increased body movements, piloerection, salivation or lacrimation. In table 2 are listed eight compounds which may represent the principal types of excitants. The quantities given in column 1 are excitatory doses producing typical symptoms in all 10 mice. Animals receiving diphenhydramine will run or jump intermittently with slight attacks of clonic seizures but without tremors. The typical effect of cocaine is the well-known "circus" movement in which mice circle along the cage rapidly and continuously. At "noncircling" doses of cocaine, slight tremors and ruffling of hair are observable. Desoxyephedrine,

TABLE I

A comparison of the convulsant properties of certain stimulants under the influence of reserpine and different anticonvulsants in mice

Treatment	Route	Time Int.†	Picrotoxin, ml./20‡-gm. (0.15%)			Hydralazine, ml./20-gm. (1.0%)			Acridone, ml./20-gm. (0.05%)			Pentylene-tetrazol, ml./20-gm. (0.5%)			4-Methyl-4-ethyl glutarimide, ml./20-gm. (0.25%)			PM-1090, ml./20-gm. (0.1%)		
			C§	T	L	C	T	L	C	T	L	C	T	L	C	T	L	C	T	L
mgm./kgm.																				
0 (Control)			0.29	0.36	0.39	0.17	0.32	0.37	0.31	0.38	0.43	0.16	0.49	0.55	0.11	0.29	0.34	0.15	0.41	0.48
R* 8	i.p.	5 hr.	0.34	0.37	0.42	0.20	0.29	0.34	0.34	0.39	0.45	0.16	0.17‖	0.17‖	0.10	0.11‖	0.16‖	0.16	0.21‖	0.26‖
Dilantin 10	i.p.	2 hr.	0.28	—¶	0.51	0.17	7/10	0.40	0.37	6/10	0.62	0.15	—	0.87	0.11	2/10	0.49	0.15	2/10	0.64
Dilantin + R			0.36	0.55	0.60	0.20	0.32	0.42	0.37	0.44	0.53	0.19	0.21	0.22	0.11	0.17	0.22	0.16	0.27	0.35
Phensuximide 125	or.	1 hr.	0.36‖	0.53	0.58	0.34‖	0.45	0.51	0.44‖	0.51	0.60	0.20	—	0.82	0.14	0.51	0.62	0.25‖	7/10	0.72
Phensuximide + R			0.49‖	0.71	0.75	0.35‖	0.36	0.51	0.49‖	0.55	0.65	0.33‖	0.42	0.43	0.13	0.20	0.26	0.27‖	0.57	0.68
Mephenesin 125	i.p.	10 min.	0.36‖	—	0.62	0.26‖	0.39	0.44	0.46‖	5/10	0.67	0.19	—	0.97	0.10	5/10	0.52	0.20‖	—	0.82
Mephenesin + R			0.46‖	0.68	0.78	0.29‖	0.46	0.52	0.65‖	0.71	0.85	0.22‖	—	0.75	0.12	2/10	0.52	0.29‖	2/10	0.74
Barbital 100	i.p.	2 hr.	0.38‖	0.55	0.59	0.42‖	0.61	0.65	0.63‖	0.93	0.99	0.33	—	1.00	0.27‖	1.06	1.11	0.28‖	0.88	0.97
Barbital + R			0.52‖	0.78	0.85	0.44‖	0.62	0.67	0.58‖	0.97	1.02	0.44‖	0.96	0.97	0.26‖	1.09	1.14	0.39‖	1.14	1.19

* R = Reserpine.

† Time interval between injection of an antagonist and challenging the mice with a stimulant.

‡ Average quantity of the solution required to produce a typical seizure in a 20-gram mouse calculated from 10 animals.

§ C = clonic seizure, T = tonic extensor seizure; expressed in ml./20-gm. of the stimulant required or in fractions of animals whose tonic extensor seizures were abolished, L = lethal.

¶ Tonic extensor seizures abolished in all animals.

‖ Significantly different from controls at a "P" value of less than 0.01 (Simpson and Roe, 1939).

TABLE 2

The convulsant and antiextensor properties of some excitants in mice

Compound	Motor Activity (Running)	Tremor	Pilo-erection	Salivation	Antiextensor Seizure (CS_{50} ± S.E.)*			
					mgm./kgm.	Route	Time int.†	mA
mgm./kgm., i.p.								
Diphenhydramine, 40	Jerky	No	No	No	50	i.p.	¼ hr.	>200
Cocaine, 40	"Circus"	Slight	Slight	Slight	50	i.p.	½ hr.	>200
Methylphenidate, 20	Increased coordinated	Slight	Very slight	Slight	80	i.p.	½ hr.	71 ±5.8
Pipradrol, 10	Increased coordinated	Slight	Very slight	Slight	40	i.p.	½ hr.	>200
Desoxyephedrine, 5	Increased coordinated	Marked	Slight	Slight	20	i.p.	½ hr.	7.9 ±0.3
Ibogaine, 20	Slightly increased	Slight	No	No	80	i.p.	1 hr.	>200
LSD, 3	"Popcorn"	Very marked	Very marked	Slight	40	i.p.	½ hr.	5.4
Tremorine, 10	Slightly increased	Marked	No	Very marked	20	i.p.	½ hr.	5.5 ±0.2

* CS_{50} ± S.E. of untreated mice = 4.6 ± 0.1 mA.
† Time interval between injection of the drug and electroshock.

TABLE 3

The influence of certain excitants on clonic and tonic extensor seizures induced by strychnine, pentylenetetrazol and caffeine in mice

Compound	Time Int.	Strychnine·NO_3, ml./20-gm. (0.005%)			Pentylenetetrazol, ml./20-gm. (0.5%)			Caffeine, ml./20-gm. (1.0%)		
		C*	T	L	C	T	L	C	T	L
mgm./kgm., i.p.										
0 (Control)		0.27	0.27	0.31	0.31	0.42	0.49	0.23	0.33	0.40
Diphenhydramine 20	15′	0.29	0.29	0.37	0.12	—	0.70	0.30	0.40	0.51
Cocaine 40	15′	0.26	0.26	0.44	0.10	—	0.59	0.20	0.33	0.49
Methylphenidate 120	15′	0.24	0.24	0.31	0.11	—	0.62	0.23	0.36	0.45
Pipradrol 20	15′	0.28	0.28	0.36	0.09	—	0.53	0.24	0.36	0.46
Desoxyephedrine 5	15′	0.23	0.23	0.28	0.13	—	0.55	0.22	0.30	0.39
Ibogaine 80	15′	0.20	0.20	0.25	0.11	—	1.15	0.18	0.31	0.38
LSD 40	30′	0.21	0.21	0.27	0.12	0.32	0.37	0.21	0.32	0.37
Tremorine 20	30′	0.30	0.30	0.48	0.19	0.30	0.35	0.15	0.19	0.36

* Same notations as those used in table 1.

pipradrol and methylphenidate appear to act similarly in mice with piloerection, tremors and coordinated running movements, the pilomotor response and tremors being more marked with desoxyephedrine than with the other two agents. In the case of ibogaine, although the tremor is distinct, running activity and pilomotor reaction are less pronounced. The effects of LSD in mice are most striking in piloerection and intense tremors, without much running, giving rise to so-called "popcorn seizures." Mice given Tremorine exhibit shaking, but still, with profuse salivation and lacrimation. The latter effect of Tremorine distinguishes it from the other excitants.

Interestingly, with the exception of LSD and Tremorine, the other excitants can also suppress and abolish the tonic extensor seizures of mice in response to electrical or pentylenetetrazol stimulation (Swinyard, Jolley and Goodman, 1950;

Tanaka, 1955; Chen and Bohner, 1956b; Schneider and Sigg, 1957). However, in contrast to the effect of anticonvulsants and CNS depressants, the antiextensor seizure effect of the excitants prevails only at highly exciting dose levels. As revealed by our studies of the joint antiextensor effect of Dilantin, phenobarbital and desoxyephedrine in mice, the mode of the antiextensor action of an excitant is apparently different from that of an anticonvulsant drug (Chen, 1957). In the last column of table 2 are given the antiextensor seizure values of these excitants in terms of the current strengths required to produce tonic extensor seizures in 50 per cent of the animals. They were determined with maximal nonlethal doses at the time of their peak effect. The maximal tolerated doses were required instead of the excitatory doses (column 1), in order to obtain a definite antiextensor seizure effect of these compounds.

Their antiextensor seizure activities as determined against pentylenetetrazol-induced convulsions in mice are shown in table 3. Here are presented also data to show that they are ineffective in suppressing strychnine- or caffeine-induced extensor seizures. Therefore, the term "antiextensor" effect of this type of compound as employed by Tanaka and Kawasaki (1957) is applicable only in electrically or pentylenetetrazol-induced convulsions.

Since the electrically induced extensor seizure in animals was introduced by Toman, Swinyard and Goodman in 1946 for the evaluation of anticonvulsant drugs, the question has often been asked but unanswered as to how the extensor seizure is produced neurologically by stimulation with occular or pinnal electrodes. From the drug antagonism studies presented here and elsewhere, it appears to be clear that the neurological mechanism involved in the tonic extension of limbs immediately following electrical stimulation is very much similar to, if not the same as, that by stimulation with pentylenetetrazol. On the other hand, different nervous structures are evidently concerned in the production of tonic extensor seizures in mice by strychnine and caffeine. They probably not only exert their convulsive action on the structures at different levels of the central nervous system, but the convulsive discharges so induced are propagated also along different nervous pathways.

SUMMARY

A number of CNS stimulants have been investigated under two main categories based on whether or not they produce tonic extensor seizures in mice.

Among the tonic extensor seizure producing agents, 10-(2-dimethylaminopropyl)-9-acridone and hydralazine are shown to be picrotoxin-like, while 4-methyl-4-ethylglutarimide and $\alpha,\alpha,\beta,\beta$-tetramethylsuccinimide are pentylenetetrazol-like convulsants.

A comparative study has been carried out with the following excitants: diphenhydramine, cocaine, methylphenidate, pipradrol, desoxyephedrine, ibogaine, lysergic acid diethylamide and 1,4-dipyrrolidino-2-butyne. They are incapable of inducing tonic extensor seizures in mice. The stimulant effects of these compounds differ by the running movements, (disorderly or coordinated), by the intensity of tremors and by the presence or absence of piloerection and salivation.

With the exception of the last two compounds, the other excitants are capable of suppressing electrically or pentylenetetrazol-induced tonic extensor seizures in mice but are ineffective in suppressing strychnine- or caffeine-induced tonic extensor seizures.

Acknowledgment. We are indebted to Dr. G. M. Everett, Dr. J. A. Schneider, the Ciba Pharmaceutical Products Inc., and the Wm. S. Merrell Co. for the supply of Tremorine, ibogaine, Ritalin and Apresoline, and Meratran respectively.

REFERENCES

Benica, W. S., and Wilson, C. O.: J. Am. Pharaceut. Assoc., **39:** 455, 1950.

Chen, G.: Arch. int. Pharmacodyn., **111:** 322, 1957.

Chen, G., and Bohner, B.: This Journal, **117:** 142, 1956a.

Chen, G., and Bohner, B.: Fed. Proc., **15:** 408, 1956b.

Miller, L. C., and Tainter, M. L.: Proc. Soc. Expt. Biol. & Med., **57:** 1261, 1944.

Orloff, J. J., Williams, H. L., and Pfeiffer, C. C.: Proc. Soc. Expt. Biol. & Med., **70:** 254, 1949.

Schneider, J. A., and Sigg, E. B.: Ann. New York Acad. Sci., **66:** 765, 1957.

Simpson, G. G., and Roe, A.: Quantitative Zoology, p. 209, McGraw-Hill, New York, 1939.

Swinyard, E. A., Jolley, J. M., and Goodman, L. S.: Proc. Soc. Expt. Biol. & Med., **75:** 239, 1950.

Tanaka, K.: Proc. Soc. Expt. Biol. & Med., **90:** 192, 1955.

Tanaka, K., and Kawasaki, Y.: Jap. J. of Pharmacol., **6:** 115, 1957.

Toman, J. E. P., Swinyard, E. A., and Goodman, L. S.: J. Neurophysiol., **9:** 231, 1946.

8035

EFFECTS OF MEPROBAMATE, PHENOBARBITAL AND *DEXTRO*-AMPHETAMINE ON REACTION TIME AND LEARNING IN MAN[1]

CONAN KORNETSKY

National Institute of Mental Health, National Institutes of Health, Public Health Service, U. S. Department of Health, Education, and Welfare, Bethesda, Maryland

Received for publication March 1, 1958

Marquis *et al.* (1957) have reported that meprobamate in single doses up to 800 mgm. does not impair the performance of normal subjects on tests of driving skill, steadiness and vision. The present experiment extends the observations of these investigators by using both 800 and 1600 mgm. of meprobamate and by comparing the effects of meprobamate to those of phenobarbital and *dextro*-amphetamine on two tests of reaction time and one of learning.

METHODS. Eight "normal" volunteer subjects, 5 males and 3 females between the ages of 18 and 22, were used for this study. The following drugs were administered to each subject on separate days at the specified doses: meprobamate, 800 and 1600 mgm.; phenobarbital, 60 and 120 mgm.; and *dextro*-amphetamine, 5 and 15 mgm. In addition to the two dose levels of the three drugs, two placebos were administered to all subjects. All treatments were administered according to an 8 x 8 Bugelski Latin square design (Edwards, 1950).

Apparatus. A multiple stimulus-response apparatus was employed that allows the measurement of a variety of types of behavior while always evoking the same motor response on the part of the subject. This apparatus consists of a subject panel of 10 lights and 10 adjacent buttons (see fig. 1). The apparatus is so designed that the experimenter can pair any light to any button and can program the order of stimulus lights in any sequence. In the present study three procedures that measure three levels of behavior were studied.

Procedure A: A simple motor response somewhat analogous to simple reaction time. On the "go" signal from the experimenter the subject would press a neutral button in the center and below the response buttons. This would turn on the first light in the sequence and the subject would as quickly as possible put this light out by pressing the adjacent button. This response would activate the second light, *etc.* Subjects were given 5 trials of this procedure. The score was the mean time per response for the 5 trials of 10 responses each.

Procedure B: A choice visual motor response analogous to choice reaction time. This procedure was similar to procedure "A" except for a random sequence of light stimuli. Subjects were given 10 trials, each on a different random sequence. The score was the mean response time per trial for the 10 trials of 10 responses each.

Procedure C: Simple learning in which the stimulus lights were randomly paired with the response buttons. The task of the subject was to learn what button was paired to wha light. Ten learning trials were given and on each experimental day subjects were required to learn a different program of button-light pairings. The score was the mean time per response for the 10 trials of 10 responses each.

Testing commenced 90 minutes after the drug was administered and lasted from 30 to 45 minutes. The procedures were always administered in the same sequence from A to C.

An analysis of variance (Edwards, 1950) was computed for each procedure. The Dunnett t-test (Dunnett, 1955) was used for comparison between drugs and placebo. On the learning procedure individual trials were compared, as well as overall means.

RESULTS. The results of the analyses of variance on each of the procedures yielded a significant F ratio for drugs and subjects on procedures "A", "B", and "C", and significant day effect on procedures "B" and "C." Although this indicates the presence of practice effects it does not invalidate the comparisons of drug effects since a balanced drug administration order was employed.

Table 1 shows the mean score for each drug on procedures "A", "B" and "C." In all procedures only 1600 mgm. of meprobamate significantly

[1] This study was reported in part at the Fall 1957 meeting of the American Society for Pharmacology and Experimental Therapeutics.

FIG. 1. Subject panel.

TABLE 1

Mean scores and standard errors for all drugs on all procedures in milliseconds

	Procedure "A"	Procedure "B"	Procedure "C"
Placebo	241 ± 10	475 ± 23	1528 ± 265
Meprobamate (800 mgm.)	241 ± 11	480 ± 25	1840 ± 265
Meprobamate (1600 mgm.)	275* ± 17	544* ± 34	2540* ± 307
Phenobarbital (60 mgm.)	242 ± 12	488 ± 28	1484 ± 196
Phenobarbital (120 mgm.)	257 ± 12	494 ± 18	1644 ± 137
d-Amphetamine (5 mgm.)	246 ± 10	477 ± 16	1675 ± 196
d-Amphetamine (15 mgm.)	248 ± 12	482 ± 22	1559 ± 172

* Significantly different than placebo ($P < 0.01$).

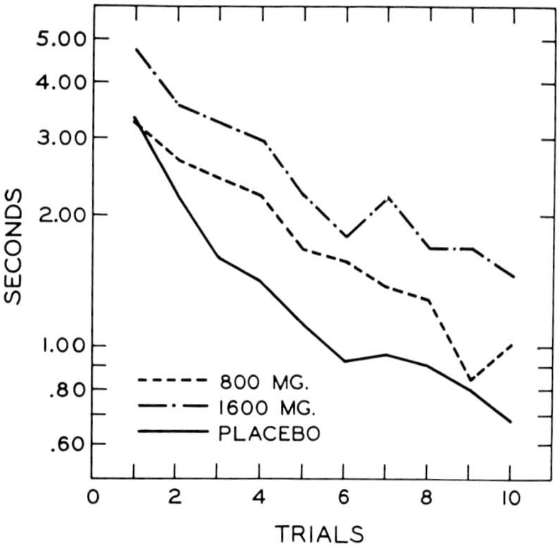

FIG. 2. Comparison of the effects of two doses of meprobamate to a placebo on learning (ordinate in log units).

slowed response time. Fig. 2 shows the effects of both 800 and 1600 mgm. of meprobamate on learning. When the comparisons were made between placebo and 800 mgm. of meprobamate trial by trial this dose of the drug also impaired learning. Significant differences ($p < 0.05$) were found at trial 6, 7 and 8. Fig. 3 and 4 show the learning curve for phenobarbital and *dextro*-amphetamine, respectively. Although these drugs did not cause statistically significant impairment, (the variability of the performance of the subjects after these drugs was considerable) there was a slower mean response time following the low dose of *dextro*-amphetamine and the high dose of phenobarbital.

DISCUSSION. The results obtained after 800 mgm. of meprobamate are in accord with those

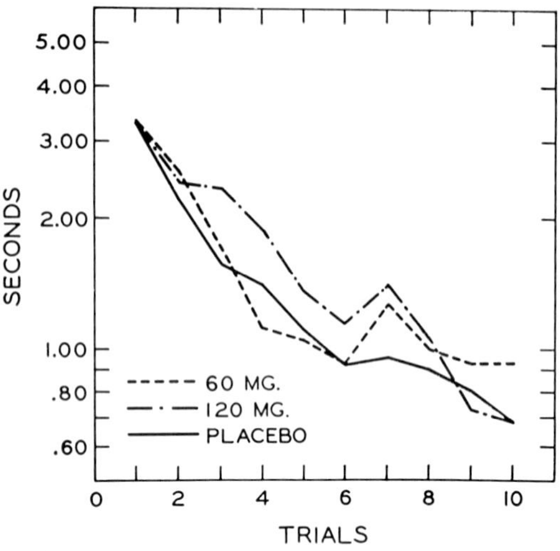

FIG. 3. Comparison of the effects of two doses of phenobarbital to a placebo on learning (ordinate in log units).

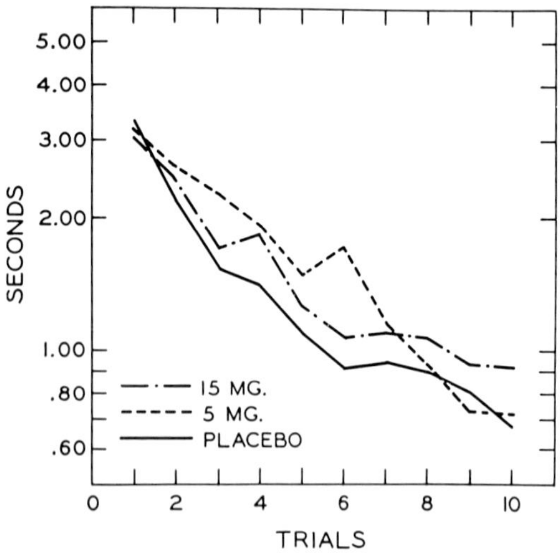

FIG. 4. Comparison of the effects of two doses of *dextro*-amphetamine to a placebo on learning (ordinate in log units).

previously reported (Marquis *et al.*, 1957). These investigators reported no significant impairment in a motor task related to driving skill after this dose of meprobamate. The present experiment shows that meprobamate in doses of 1600 mgm. causes considerable motor impairment. Impairment of learning after 1600 mgm. of meprobamate is also quite apparent. The difference between the curve for 1600 mgm. of meprobamate and that for the placebo cannot be explained as a function of motor impairment alone, for on the last trial after placebo mean time was 0.7 seconds while that for 1600 mgm. of meprobamate is over a second slower. This difference is greater than would be expected if impairment was merely a function of slowed motor response. Also, since 800 mgm. of meprobamate impaired learning it is reasonable to assume that 1600 mgm. would also impair this function.

The evidence for impairment in learning independent of slowed motor response after 800 mgm. of meprobamate is clearer than after 1600 mgm. Eight hundred mgm. of meprobamate caused no significant motor impairment on procedures "A" and "B" and the initial and the final trial on learning were similar to those of the placebo, indicating that any separation of the learning curves between placebo and this dose of meprobamate is the result of a differential rate of learning.

The failure of *dextro*-amphetamine to facilitate performance agrees with the findings of other investigators (Bullock *et al.*, 1952; Hauty and Payne, 1957; Eysenck *et al.*, 1957). Eysenck and collaborators compared the effects of *d*-amphetamine to those of a placebo on a motor task. They found that the relative performance after *dextro*-amphetamine was only facilitated after prolonged continuous testing. This suggests that *dextro*-amphetamine would only facilitate performance when fatigue was present.

Although 120 mgm. of phenobarbital caused a mean decrease in performance level this decrease was not statistically significant. The failure of phenobarbital and *dextro*-amphetamine to have any significant effects might be due to the time of testing after the drug. However, it is unlikely that the effects of these two drugs was dissipated in 120 minutes.

SUMMARY

The effects of 800 and 1600 mgm. of meprobamate, 5 and 15 mgm. of *d*-amphetamine and 60 and 120 mgm. of phenobarbital were studied on the performance of 8 normal subjects on a multiple stimulus-response apparatus. Three procedures were studied: simple motor behavior, choice reaction time and learning. The following conclusions were drawn:

Meprobamate at 1600 mgm. significantly impairs motor coordination and reaction time.

Meprobamate at 800 and 1600 mgm. significantly affects learning rate.

Neither 60 nor 120 mgm. of phenobarbital nor 5 or 15 mgm. of *d*-amphetamine significantly affected motor coordination, reaction time or learning.

REFERENCES

BULLOCK, J. C., LA SAINE, T. A., AND ROBINSON, J. M.: J. Tennessee Acad. Sc., **27:** 296, 1952.

DUNNETT, C. W.: J. Amer. Stat. Assoc., **50:** 1096, 1955.

EDWARDS, A. L.: Experimental design in psychological research, Rinehart & Co., New York, 1950.

EYSENCK, H. J., CASEY, S., AND TROUTON, D. S.: J. Ment. Sci., **103:** 645, 1957.

HAUTY, G. T., AND PAYNE, R. B.: THIS JOURNAL, **120:** 33, 1957.

MARQUIS, D. G., KELLY, E. L., MILLER, J. G., GERARD, R. W., AND RAPOPORT, A.: Ann. New York Acad. Sci., **67:** 701, 1957.

8036

COMPARISON OF THE ANTIPRURITIC EFFECT OF MORPHINE AND PAPAVERINE IN EXPERIMENTAL AND PATHOLOGICAL ITCH IN MAN

SPYROS G. MACRIS, GENE M. SMITH AND HENRY K. BEECHER

Anesthesia Laboratory of the Harvard Medical School at the Massachusetts General Hospital, Boston

Received for publication March 10, 1958

We have two chief purposes in presenting this report: 1) to describe the methods evolved here for studying the effect of drugs on experimentally and pathologically produced itch and 2) to present data to show that papaverine is significantly more effective than a placebo in relieving itch of experimental origin. This is in line with the long-standing interest of this laboratory in quantitative studies of the effects of drugs on subjective responses. Some scattered reports on the effectiveness of papaverine on clinical pruritus, not adequately confirmed by use of this drug in therapeutic practice or by experimental observations, attracted our attention (Wirth, 1947; Corti and Guillot, 1949; Toledo, 1952).

Secondary purposes are: 1) to provide evidence that morphine is effective in relieving itch of pathological origin, 2) to raise some question about the theory that itch and pain sensations are transmitted by the same apparatus (a rather convincing mass of data has been compiled by Bishop (1948) to support the view that itch and pain sensations are transmitted by the same anatomical apparatus), and 3) to examine further our working hypothesis that there are important differences between subjective responses as usually produced experimentally and those which arise in pathology. In regard to the first of these, the statement is commonly made in the clinic that morphine will not relieve pathological itch. It is well-known that opiates often cause itching and they have been used for the experimental production of itch, by intracisternal injection (Méhès, 1938), by intradermal injection (Kenedy, 1936; von Rajka, Korossy and Gozóny, 1956), and by application on scarified skin (Kenedy, 1936), or on skin penetrated by inactivated cowhage trichomes (Broadbent, 1953).

The primary purposes have been achieved. The secondary purposes have been supported, but not conclusively demonstrated.

METHOD. *Experimentally produced itch.* We set out to examine the several points referred to in the introductory section, first by the production and examination of experimentally produced itch and then by study of itch of pathological origin. The production of experimental itch should fulfill certain requirements: it should be harmless to the skin, repeatable without hazard, and should produce after every application on the same subject a response of comparable intensity and duration.

Cowhage, a powder consisting of trichomes collected from the ripe pods of a tropical plant, *Mucuna pruriens*, was used as an itch stimulus and proved satisfactory. Arthur and Shelley (1955) showed that it produces pruritus through the proteolysis caused by an enzyme it contains, mucunaine.

Cowhage was always applied by the same investigator on the upper third of the volar surface of alternate forearms. The area exposed to cowhage was kept constant by the use of adhesive tape with a uniform hole. Two applications were never made on the same spot during the same day. The subjects were ten male volunteer students between 20 and 30 years of age. The first day was used for orientation of the subject and acquaintance with the method of recording itch.

On the first day of the experiment the subject was trained to record the intensity and duration of itch, usually lasting between 3 and 5 minutes after each application of cowhage, by tracing a line on a tape moving with constant velocity. The tape was divided into three equal zones, each representing a different degree of pruritus: *weak* (a mild sensation not producing the scratch reflex), *moderate* (a definite, tolerable itching sensation, with the scratch reflex present but easily controllable), and *severe* (a highly unpleasant sensation, completely attracting the attention of the subject with the scratch reflex controllable only with difficulty). The subject held a pencil against the tape and changed its position from zone to zone as the intensity of the pruritus changed. This record showed the duration of the itching sensation in each intensity zone. After each test the subject was asked to rate it as "the mildest of the day," (see fig. 1) "one of the mildest," "average," "one of the more intense," or "the most intense of the day."

On the second day cowhage was applied six successive times (with 40-minute intervals) without the administration of drugs.

On each of the following experimental days a drug was injected intravenously. An interval of at least two days was maintained between drug administrations. The drugs used were a) placebo (normal saline), b) morphine phosphate, 4 mgm., c) papaverine hydrochloride, 50 mgm., d) pentobarbital sodium, 40 mgm., e) aminophylline, 250 mgm. and f) tripelenamine citrate (Pyribenzamine), 25 mgm. The weights represent the salts. These doses were diluted to 5 ml. and injected intravenously per 70 kgm. of body weight at the rate of 1 ml. per minute. The "double blind" technique was used. The sequence of drug administration was randomized.

Pathological itch. Papaverine, 50 mgm., morphine, 4 mgm., and placebo were given intravenously to six patients with constant pruritus of pathological origin. These patients had "dermatitis, cause unknown" in two cases, and there was one case each of psoriasis, obstructive jaundice, "neuralgia," and drug (penicillin) dermatitis. As far as the symptom of itch is concerned, the patients usually responded alike to the medication, notwithstanding the presumably diverse causes. (This was also the finding as far as the response of the symptom of pain to 10 mgm. morphine was concerned. Observations in our laboratory on postoperative wound pain agree remarkably closely with those of Houde and Wallenstein (1953) on the pain of metastic malignancy, *i.e.*, smooth muscle and periosteal pain (*cf.* Beecher, 1957).) The drugs were diluted and injected as just described for the experimental drug studies. The "double blind" technique was used and the sequence of administration was randomized. The relief was checked by a trained technician 5, 10, 15, 30, 45, 60, 90, 120, 180, 240, 300 and 360 minutes after the administration of the drug. The effect on the pruritus was graded by the patient as "worse than before" or "no relief," called 0; "poor relief," called 1; "good relief," called 2; "complete relief," called 3, according to his estimate of the pruritus after medication.

RESULTS. Of major interest in the part of the work dealing with experimental itch was a comparison of the medications listed above with respect to their effect on duration of itch after drug administration (table 1). It will be remembered that on six occasions after the drug injection, the subject was asked to give a continuous evaluation of the intensity of the itch produced by cowhage. In figure 2 it can be seen that the maximum difference appeared at 35 minutes after medication. The Link-Wallace method of allowances was used to evaluate the effect of the drugs on duration of itch at the 35-minute period. This technique, described by Mosteller and Bush (1954, p. 289) makes possible the simultaneous testing of all possible comparisons among the six

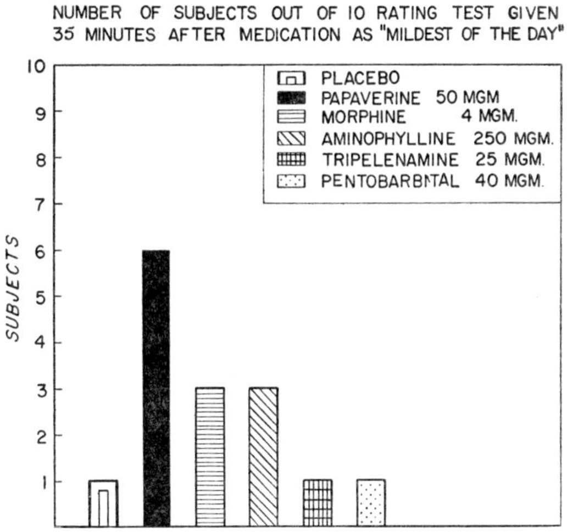

FIG. 1. Mean duration of itch in 10 subjects following medication.

TABLE 1

Duration of experimental itch 35 minutes after the injection of placebo, papaverine, morphine, aminophylline, pentobarbital or tripelenamine

Duration of Itch

Subject	No drug	Placebo	Papaverine	Morphine	Aminophylline	Pentobarbital	Tripelenamine
	sec.	*sec.*	*sec.*	*sec.*	*sec.*	*sec.*	*sec.*
1. RG	174	263	105	199	141	108	141
2. JF	224	213	103	143	168	341	184
3. RS	260	231	145	113	78	159	125
4. SI	255	291	103	225	164	135	227
5. RW	165	168	144	176	127	239	194
6. TS	237	121	94	144	114	136	155
7. GM	191	137	35	87	96	140	121
8. SS	100	102	133	120	222	134	129
9. MU	115	89	83	100	165	185	79
10. OS	189	433	237	173	168	188	317
Average	191.0	204.8	118.2	148.0	144.3	176.5	167.2

medications. With six medications there were 15 medication differences. As Mosteller and Bush point out (1954, p. 304), the use of the "t test" to evaluate the significance of the largest of the observed differences is indefensible, and the analysis of variance "at best . . . (answers) . . . a trivial kind of question." The Link-Wallace analysis indicates that only one of the 15 medication differences reaches the 0.05 level of confidence. This is the papaverine *vs.* placebo difference. None of the other drugs was significantly different from placebo.

In the case of pathological itch morphine appears promising while papaverine does not (table 2). This work with morphine and pathological itch is a secondary issue. We present it as a method of approach which we hope others will use, for persistent itch satisfactory for these studies seems to be rather uncommon: it took two years of attention to accumulate these six patients in a 1000-bed hospital. We hope others will utilize this method and add to the material. Detailed presentation of the grades 0, 1, 2, 3, mentioned under METHOD, is not warranted until more cases are accumulated. Examination of the intensity grades in the data at hand, but not presented, indicates an early morphine effect which diminishes after an hour. This is not true of papaverine.

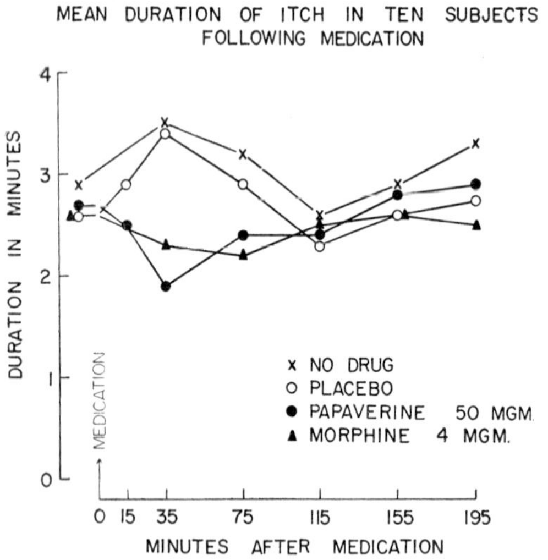

FIG. 2. Number of subjects out of 10 rating test given 35 minutes after medication as "mildest of the day."

TABLE 2

Pathological itch

When morphine or papaverine was better than a placebo in relieving pathological itch it is indicated by +, when the same, by =, and when less than, by −. Four +'s means that four patients got more relief from the active drug than from the placebo.

Minutes after medication	5	15	30	45	60
Morphine phosphate, 4 mgm., i.v.	4+ 1− 1=	4+ 1− 1=	4+ 1− 1=	3+ 2− 1=	3+ 2− 1=
Papaverine hydrochloride, 50 mgm., i.v.	2+ 2− 2=	2+ 0− 4=	3+ 0− 3=	3+ 1− 2=	2+ 3− 1=

In another study in this laboratory the power of papaverine hydrochloride to relieve postoperative wound pain was determined (Macris *et al.*, to be published). The effects of 50 and 100 mgm. of papaverine were compared with that of morphine, 10 mgm., subcutaneously per 70 kgm. of body weight. The weights refer to the salts. The method used for this assay and the evaluation of the data were similar to the procedures described in previous studies in this laboratory (Gravenstein and Beecher, 1957).

It has been shown (Macris *et al.*, to be published) that when the pain level is controlled and correlated data are used, papaverine, 50 and 100 mgm., has the effectiveness regularly found for a placebo, or less. An analysis of variance shows a significant difference in pain relief between morphine and papaverine at all times with either dose. The per cent relief of papaverine in the 50-mgm. dose is that expected from a placebo (25 per cent *vs.* 30 per cent); papaverine, 100 mgm., relieved 14 per cent of the patients in pain. The difference in analgesic power between papaverine, 100 mgm., and morphine, 10 mgm., is constantly greater than the difference between papaverine, 50 mgm., and morphine, 10 mgm. We have also encountered the suggestion of a similar "antianalgesic" effect with the *dextro* rotatory form of isomethadone (Denton and Beecher, 1949).

It can be observed in table 1 that the effectiveness of a placebo in relieving experimental itch is approximately one-half that of papaverine. One can mention that this is comparable to the morphine-placebo situation with respect to pain where placebos also relieved one-half of the pain relievable with a large dose of morphine (Beecher, 1955).

Doubtless itch can be relieved in many ways, just as pain can be (altered attention, drugs, changes in the circulation in some cases, cold, *etc.*), but it is difficult to accept Bishop's view (1948) unreservedly as correct since papaverine does indeed relieve experimental itch but does not relieve pain. If the apparatus and mechanism are the same for both itch and pain production, one might suppose that an agent which would relieve one would relieve the other. The situation is a complex one and many factors remain unknown. We merely record the above as raising some doubt. Acceptance or rejection of Bishop's thesis was not a primary purpose of this report. Support for Bishop's conclusions can be found in the recent careful work of Shelley and Arthur (1957). This report adds further support to the view that itch is mediated only through the C fibers.

SUMMARY

The effect of papaverine, morphine, pentobarbital, aminophylline, tripelenamine and placebo was tested on experimental pruritus induced with cowhage. Only papaverine reduced experimental pruritus to a statistically significant degree.

Since papaverine has been shown in another study in this laboratory not to have analgesic power greater than that associated with placebos, this raises some question about the theory that the same apparatus mediates itch and pain.

ACKNOWLEDGMENTS. This work was supported by a grant from the Medical Research and Development Board of the United States Army (Contract No. DA-49-007-MD-76). We wish to thank Dr. R. P. Arthur and Dr. W. B. Shelley for their suggestions on the use of cowhage, and for providing the cowhage that was used in this study.

REFERENCES

ARTHUR, R. P., AND SHELLEY, W. B.: J. Invest. Dermat., **25:** 341, 1955.
BEECHER, H. K.: J. A. M. A., **159:** 1602, 1955.
BEECHER, H. K.: Pharmacol. Rev., **9:** 59, 1957.
BISHOP, G. H.: J. Invest. Dermat., **11:** 143, 1948.
BROADBENT, J. L.: Brit. J. Pharmacol., **8:** 263, 1953.
CORTI, R. N., AND GUILLOT, C. F.: Prensa méd. argent., **36:** 883, 1949.
DENTON, J. E., AND BEECHER, H. K.: J. A. M. A., **141:** 1146, 1949.
GRAVENSTEIN, J. S., AND BEECHER, H. K.: THIS JOURNAL, **119:** 506, 1957.
HOUDE, R. W., AND WALLENSTEIN, S. L.: Drug Addiction & Narcotics Bull., Appendix F, 660, 1953.
KENEDY, D.: Gior. Ital. di dermat. e sif., **77:** 53, 1936.
MÉHÈS, A. J.: Arch. exper. Path. u. Pharmakol., **188:** 650, 1938.
MOSTELLER, F., AND BUSH, R. R.: Handbook of Social Psychology, Vol. 1, Addison-Wesley Publishing Company, Cambridge, 1954.
SHELLEY, W. B., AND ARTHUR, R. P.: A. M. A. Arch. Dermat., **76:** 296, 1957.
TOLEDO, I. S.: Rev. Fac. cien méd. univ. nac. Córdoba, **10:** 145, 1952.
VON RAJKA, E., KOROSSY, S., AND GÓZONY, M.: Dermatologica, **112:** 81, 1956.
WIRTH, L.: J. Invest. Dermat., **8:** 63, 1947.

8037

RELATIVE HEPATOTOXICITY OF SEVEN HALOGENATED HYDROCARBONS[1, 2]

GABRIEL L. PLAA, ELIZABETH A. EVANS AND CHARLES H. HINE

Department of Pharmacology and Experimental Therapeutics, University of California School of Medicine, San Francisco

Received for publication February 10, 1958

A most interesting phase of toxicology continually posing a problem to the investigator is estimation of the liver-damaging potentiality of a particular agent. Although individual hepatotoxins have been studied extensively, as cited by Drill (1952) and von Oettingen (1955), it is difficult to find reports comparing the compounds in a quantitative manner. One reason for this difficulty is that criteria customarily used for describing liver damage, such as alterations in the results of liver-function tests, are not readily translated into dose-response curves, which are necessary for comparative studies.

In this paper we will describe a simple rapid, screening procedure which we have adapted for the detection of hepatic damage by a study of seven halogenated hydrocarbons of low molecular weight. The method is based on the prolongation of pentobarbital anesthesia which accompanies liver damage, and the data accumulated can be resolved into standard dose-response curves. The duration of anesthesia ("sleeping time") was arbitrarily defined as the period between loss and reappearance of the righting reflex. The correlation of sleeping time with changes in liver function as measured by BSP (bromsulfalein) retention and liver structure as determined by gross and microscopic examination, will be demonstrated.

METHOD. Male albino mice of the Princeton strain, weighing 18 to 25 gm., were used throughout the study.

All of the hydrocarbons except 1,1,1-trichloroethane were fractionally distilled; that fraction coming off within 2°C. of the boiling point of the individual hydrocarbon was used for the experiments. Commercial grade 1,1,1-trichloroethane was used without further purification.

One to three days prior to intoxication with the halogenated compound, the (control) sleeping time of each group was determined, following an intraperitoneal injection of 45 mgm./kgm. of sodium pentobarbital in 0.2 per cent solution. The time when the mouse was able to right himself from a supine position 3 times in one minute was considered to be the end point of his sleeping time. A group of control mice was run with each group of experimental animals. After 270 control observations had been made, the results were pooled to determine the "normal" duration of anesthesia. Thus the animals, though not serving as their individual controls, were members of the group which served as control for the entire study.

The hydrocarbons were injected subcutaneously, diluted with peanut oil in such a manner that the given dose for a 20-gm. mouse would be contained in 0.1 ml. wherever possible. The sleeping time was determined 24 hours later. In one experiment, the hepatotoxic potency of tannic acid, a known liver-damaging agent with no known hypnotic properties, was also determined following subcutaneous administration. The experimental animals were only used once during this study, to circumvent the possibility of an altered response due to the initial exposure to a hepatotoxin.

At selected doses, where sleeping time was significantly prolonged, BSP retention was determined by the method of Casals and Olitsky (1946) 24 hours after administration of the hydrocarbon.

At necropsy, the liver and kidneys were examined for gross pathologic changes. Sections of these organs were then fixed in Bouin's fixative, embedded in paraffin, mounted and stained with hematoxylin and eosin for microscopic study.[3]

[1] A preliminary report has been presented before the American Society for Pharmacology and Experimental Therapeutics, Chicago, April, 1957.

[2] Supported in part by the Raschen Tiedemann Fund, granted through the Committee on Research, University of California School of Medicine, San Francisco, and a grant from E. I. DuPont de Nemours Co., Wilmington, Del.

[3] Histopathologic examinations were made by J. S. Wellington, M.D., Department of Pathology, University of California School of Medicine, San Francisco.

Subsequently, comparisons were made between the various indices of liver damage—gross and microscopic findings, sleeping time and BSP retention.

The dose causing liver damage, as measured by significant prolongation of the sleeping time, in 50 per cent of the animals (ED_{50}), and the LD_{50}, were both estimated by the method of Litchfield and Wilcoxon (1949). The standard errors (SE) of the ED_{50}'s and LD_{50}'s were approximated by dividing the 19/20 confidence limits by 4. This value was then divided by the respective ED_{50} ($SE \cdot ED_{50}/ED_{50}$) or LD_{50} and expressed as a percentage. When determining the LD_{50} of the various agents, the total number of deaths occurring during the 10-day period following the subcutaneous administration of the hydrocarbon was used. The ED_{50} and BSP retention were compared by the Chi-square test (Lacey, 1953).

RESULTS. In 270 control observations (mice that had received no hydrocarbon) the mean pentobarbital sleeping time was 1.5 ± 4.1 minutes. While all of the mice showed visible signs of depression of the central nervous system, primarily ataxia, only 22 per cent actually lost the righting reflex. When the righting reflex was not lost, the sleeping time was rated zero, which accounts for the negative value in the confidence limits. In mice injected with a hydrocarbon, a sleeping time of 10 minutes or longer was considered significant, and indicative of hepatic damage. Only 4.1 per cent of the control animals slept 10 minutes or longer.

The results of the hepatotoxic and lethal dose-response experiments are summarized in tables 1 and 2, respectively. A graphic representation of the hepatotoxic dose-response data is depicted in figure 1. The doses of *sym*-tetrachloroethane that produced hepatotoxicity overlapped those which produced death in 24 hours; consequently, only the survivors could be assayed for sleeping time. The ED_{50} for this compound could only be approximated.

Sleeping time determinations were also carried out 72 hours after intoxication. Only at the highest dose for each compound was significant prolongation observed at this time. In all cases the percentage of animals showing the effect dropped below 40 per cent, in contrast to responses of 70 per cent or better at 24 hours (table 1).

During the course of this study over 400 mice were used, of which 128 were sacrificed after the sleeping time had been determined. Since we were interested in the relative sensitivity of the assay procedure, most of these mice were selected for sacrifice because they exhibited little or no prolongation of sleeping time.

TABLE 1

Summary of dose-response data for hepatotoxicity, based on prolongation of sleeping time

Compound	Dose	Hepatotoxic Ratio*	ED_{50}	Significant Sleeping Time: Mean	Significant Sleeping Time: Range
	mM/kgm.		*mM/kgm.*	*min.*	*min*
Chloroform	4.4	15/20		76	11–240
	3.2	16/24		29	12–115
	1.3	6/10	1.4	13	10–17
	0.63	3/10	(0.92–2.1)	15	10–20
	0.32	7/25		15	12–15
	0.067	0/20		0	0
Carbon tetrachloride	2.6	13/14		115	12–206
	1.6	9/10		121	23–136
	0.78	7/10	0.45	99	35–156
	0.26	4/12	(0.24–0.88)	25	12–64
	0.052	0/10		0	0
1,1,1-Trichloroethane	120	10/10		83	14–172
	100	8/9	84	92	10–160
	78	2/9	(72–99)	19	17–21
	39	0/5		0	0
1,1,2-Trichloroethane	2.6	5/5		179	26–360
	2.4	7/9	2.1	51	10–166
	2.1	6/8	(1.9–2.4)	103	10–304
	1.8	2/10		12	10–13
	1.3	0/5		0	0
sym-Tetrachloroethane	9.5	2/2		169	160–178
	7.2	4/10	7.2†	122	14–162
	4.8	0/10		0	0
	2.4	1/10		11	11
Trichloroethylene	20	13/13		60	27–82
	14	11/13	11	44	13–96
	10	5/10	(8.9–13)	11	10–12
	8.6	1/10		10	10
	5.7	0/10		0	0
Tetrachloroethylene	36	9/13		32	11–85
	29	6/10	27	21	17–23
	24	7/23	(23–33)	19	11–47
	17	4/23		52	17–104
Tannic Acid‡	640	10/10		72	34–97
	320	6/10	245	29	19–47
	160	3/10	(186–322)	33	23–46
	80	0/5		0	0

* Number with significantly prolonged sleeping time/total number tested.

† Approximation only.

‡ Dose and ED_{50} expressed as mgm./kgm.

TABLE 2

Summary of dose-response data for lethality, observed during a ten-day period

Compound	Dose	Mortality Ratio*	Day of Death 1	Day of Death 2	Day of Death 3–10	LD_{50}
	mM/kgm.		*No. Mice*			*mM/kgm.*
Chloroform	13	5/5		4	1	
	9.5	8/10		2	6	5.9
	6.3	5/10		1	4	(4.2–8.2)
	3.2	1/10			1	
Carbon tetrachloride	210	7/10		2	5	
	180	2/15			2	200
	160	1/10			1	(190–220)
1,1,1-Trichloroethane	200	7/10	2	4	1	120
	98	5/10			5	(95–160)
	50	1/10		1		
1,1,2-Trichloroethane	2.9	5/5	5			
	2.0	7/10	3	3	1	1.7
	1.5	8/15	3	3	2	(1.5–1.9)
	1.2	0/10				
sym-Tetrachloroethane	9.2	5/5	3		2	
	6.9	6/10	5	1		6.6
	6.0	4/10	3		1	(6.1–7.0)
	5.5	0/10				
Trichloroethylene	170	7/10	5	1	1	
	120	3/10	3			120
	86	5/10	2	2	1	(67–200)
	57	2/10		2		
	29	0/10				
Tetrachloroethylene	720	5/5	5			
	500	5/10	2	1	2	390
	360	6/10	2		4	(300–510)
	240	2/10			2	
	130	0/10				

* Number that died/total number tested.

The kidneys of most of the animals receiving chloroform and 1,1,2-trichloroethane showed tubular lesions, consisting of broad bands of fibrinoid necrosis within the kidney cortex. These lesions occurred at doses which did not produce evidence of extensive liver derangement (0.32 *mM*/kgm. for chloroform and 1.3 *mM*/kgm. for 1,1,2-trichloroethane), and were not observable grossly.

Grossly, the appearance of the livers ranged from paling to distinct mosaic lobular mottling. Occasional small areas of severe congestion were seen; friable, yellow livers were also observed. The severity of the lesion increased with the dose. No lesion characteristic of any particular compound could be discerned. Microscopically, the livers of most animals in the higher dose ranges of all the compounds except tetrachloroethylene showed varying degrees of central necrosis. In the more severely affected livers, the central veins were dilated and congested, and the adjacent parenchymal cells showed fibrinoid necrosis. At the lower doses, alterations in the staining characteristics of the cells were observed as well as cytoplasmic vacuolation. In general, the peripheral portions of the lobules were spared.

The results of gross and microscopic examination of the livers are compared with the sleeping time in table 3. In the left-hand column are listed the 8 possible combinations of findings. For example, if a mouse had a prolonged sleeping time, gross lesions, plus microscopic evidence of liver damage, he was listed in the first category. In 72 per cent of the observations, all 3 parameters were in agreement. In 85 per cent, the sleeping time was consistent with the microscopic findings, and in 95 per cent it was consistent with either the gross or microscopic findings or both. Mice with a sleeping time greater than 30 minutes uniformly had both gross and microscopic lesions.

There were 99 control observations in the study comparing BSP retention with prolongation of pentobarbital sleeping time (table 4). The mean BSP plasma concentration at 30 minutes was 0.46 ± 0.50 mgm. per cent. A value exceeding 1.5 mgm. per cent, therefore, was considered significant and indicative of hepatic dysfunction in the 113 animals given the hydrocarbon. Only 4.0 per cent of the control plasma concentrations exceeded this value.

At the higher doses of hydrocarbons, it was noted that the mice lost weight within 24 hours. This loss was believed to be a result of cessation of eating and drinking. To test the effect of fasting and dehydration on the pentobarbital sleeping time, 34 mice were assayed before and 24 hours after the removal of feed and water. No difference was found: the prefasting mean sleeping time was 3.3 ± 4.9 minutes; the mean after fasting was 3.5 ± 5.6 minutes.

DISCUSSION. The dose of 45 mgm./kgm. pentobarbital has been found by Pilgrim and De Ome (1955) to be the "anesthetic threshold" in a variety of strains of mice. This dose was considered most suitable for our purposes for several reasons. The duration of action is brief enough to give results in a relatively short period of time.

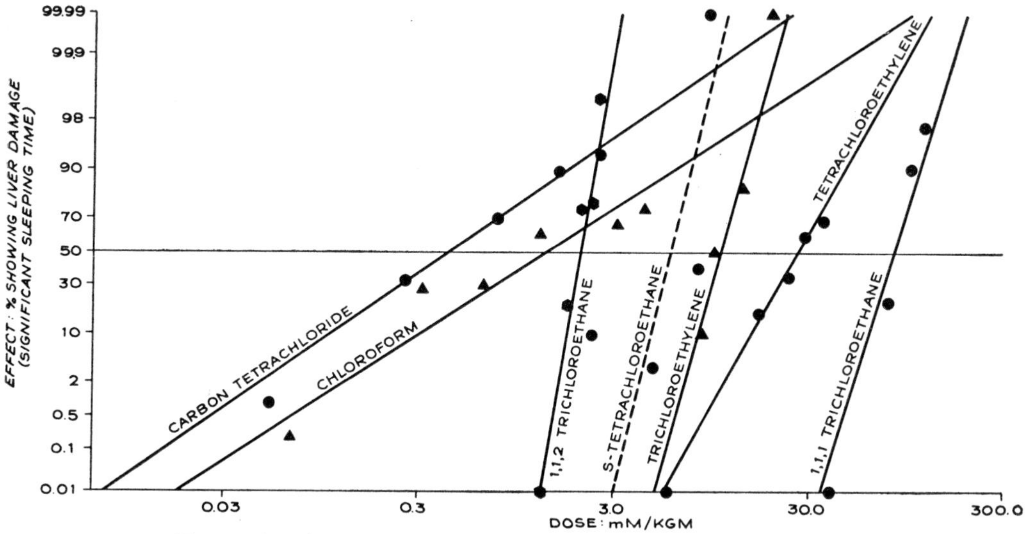

FIG. 1. Graphic representation of hepatotoxic dose-response data.

TABLE 3

Correlation between pentobarbital sleeping time, and gross and microscopic liver damage

Category*†			Number of Mice
ST	G	M	
+	+	+	28
+	+	—	6
+	—	—	5
+	—	+	5
—	—	—	64
—	—	+	7
—	+	+	1
—	+	—	12
Grand Total....................			128

* ST = Sleeping time, G = gross lesions, M = histologic lesions.

† + = Abnormal, — = normal.

TABLE 4

Comparison of the cases of hepatic dysfunction detected by the pentobarbital sleeping time and by the BSP retention method

Compound	Dose	Significant Sleeping Time Ratio	Significant BSP Retention Ratio	Significance* P =
	mM/kgm.			
Chloroform	4.4	15/20	3/19	0.001
Carbon tetrachloride	1.6	9/10	16/20	0.90
	0.26	4/12	0/10	0.20
1,1,1-Trichloroethane	120	10/10	7/18	0.01
	78	2/9	0/10	0.50
1,1,2-Trichloroethane	2.6	5/5	0/9	0.01
sym-Tetrachloroethane	7.2	4/10	0/7	0.20
Trichloroethylene	14	11/13	5/10	0.20
Tetrachloroethylene	36	9/13	1/10	0.02

* Chi-square test.

Further, the variation in sleeping time is less at this "threshold", decreasing the range encompassed by the confidence limits. Therefore, this level offers both convenience and accuracy.

The fact that hepatic damage can significantly prolong anesthesia induced by short-acting barbiturates such as pentobarbital has been well established (Brauer and Root, 1946; Maynert and van Dyke, 1949). That this prolongation occurs even with minimal damage is supported by our data: Firstly, the animals from which the data in table 3 were compiled were selected because they showed little or no prolongation of sleeping time. The correlation was quite good. In 95 per cent, the sleeping time agreed with the gross or microscopic findings, or both. Secondly, while hepatic damage was seen microscopically at low doses, only at the highest doses were distinct centrilobular lesions demonstrable. Thirdly, when attempting to find the best time sequence for the study, it was found that 24 hours after administration of the hydrocarbon was best in most cases, and that at 72 hours the prolongation diminished at low dose levels but persisted at high dose levels. This suggests that at low dose levels sufficient recovery may occur in 72 hours to permit normal metabolism of the anesthetic. Tsuboi and Stowell (1951), studying the histochemical changes following single administrations of carbon tetrachloride, have shown that regeneration can begin during the first day, and that for the next several days regeneration and degeneration proceed concurrently.

We have considered the possibility that, since these hydrocarbons themselves depress the central nervous system to some degree, the amounts remaining after 24 hours might contribute to, or even cause, prolongation of sleeping time. We believe that the following evidence discounts this, however: One compound not included in the series reported here, 1,2-dibromo-3-chloropropane, caused no prolongation of sleeping time within 24 hours, but prolongation did occur after 72 hours. This sequence agreed with the gross findings in the two groups. Secondly, we were able to obtain a dose-response curve for tannic acid, which is a hepatotoxin with no reported depressant action on the central nervous system.

In table 3, one sees that the largest apparent discrepancy between sleeping time and gross lesions occurred when both the sleeping time and the microscopic findings were negative, but gross lesions were recorded. This is understandable, since any change, however slight, was entered as a gross lesion. Gross observations consequently covered the most various and often negligible findings. Yet, in spite of this inclusiveness, the sleeping time was still in agreement with gross lesions in 82 per cent of the mice examined.

When BSP retention was compared with sleeping time, the percentage of positive responses obtained by the former method was consistently lower (table 4). Even with the small numbers of animals used in each group, the differences were significant at the 5 per cent level for 4 of the 7 compounds. The two methods were relatively equal in sensitivity only at the higher dose of carbon tetrachloride. One reason for the different result with carbon tetrachloride might be that this agent produced more extensive damage than the others, as shown by both gross and microscopic observation. Thus, the sleeping-time method of assay appears to be more sensitive than this type of BSP-retention test.

The reliability of the estimate of the ED_{50} is reflected in the ratio $SE \cdot ED_{50}/ED_{50}$ (table 5). Except for chloroform and carbon tetrachloride the ratio was less than 15 per cent. From figure 1, it is quite apparent that the slopes for chloroform and carbon tetrachloride are considerably flatter than the others. Statistically, these two slopes did not deviate significantly from parallelism, and the slopes for the other 5 compounds were mutually parallel.

In terms of hepatotoxicity, and at the ED_{50} only, the relative potency of the compounds is as follows, if we assign to 1,1,1-trichloroethane a potency of 1: tetrachloroethylene, 3; trichloroethylene, 8; *sym*-tetrachloroethane, 12; 1,1,2-trichloroethane, 40; chloroform, 60; and carbon tetrachloride, 190. Similarly, in terms of lethality, the order at the LD_{50} is as follows: tetrachloroethylene, 0.30; carbon tetrachloride, 0.60; 1,1,1-trichloroethane, 1; trichloroethylene, 1; *sym*-tetrachloroethane, 18; chloroform, 20; and 1,1,2-trichloroethane, 71. These relative lethal rankings agree well with those reported for rabbits by Barsoum and Saad (1934). There is a vast difference between the lethality of 1,1,2-trichloroethane, chloroform, and *sym*-tetrachloroethane, and that of the other four agents. It is apparent that there is no necessary correlation between the dose causing liver damage and that causing death.

TABLE 5

Comparison of the hepatotoxic ED_{50} with the LD_{50}

Compound	ED_{50}	$\frac{SE \cdot ED_{50}}{ED_{50}}$	LD_{50}	$\frac{SE \cdot LD_{50}}{LD_{50}}$	$\frac{LD_{50}}{ED_{50}}$
	mM/kgm.	%	*mM/kgm.*	%	
Chloroform	1.4	21	5.9	17	4.2*
Carbon tetrachloride	0.45	36	200	15	450*
1,1,1-Trichloroethane	84	7.9	120	12	14
1,1,2-Trichloroethane	2.1	6.1	1.7	5.8	0.81†
sym-Tetrachloroethane	7.2	—	6.6	3.2	0.92†
Trichloroethylene	11	9.1	120	28	11
Tetrachloroethylene	27	8.7	390	13	14

* ED and LD slopes not parallel.

† Ratio not significant at 5 per cent level.

The hepatotoxic dose of tri- and tetrachloroethylene was about 10 per cent of the lethal dose; the ED of 1,1,1-trichloroethane was about 70 per cent of the LD; and the ED and LD for 1,1,2-trichloroethane and *sym*-tetrachloroethane were indistinguishable. Since the ED and LD slopes for chloroform and carbon tetrachloride were not parallel, one can say only that at the 50 per cent response level the ED of chloroform is about one-fifth of the LD, and the ED of carbon tetrachloride is about one five-hundredth of the LD. Carbon tetrachloride appears to be in an entirely different class from the other compounds.

Unsaturated trichloroethylene and tetrachloroethylene are less toxic and less hepatotoxic than their saturated analogs 1,1,2-trichloroethane and *sym*-tetrachloroethane. It also appears that there are decided differences between the *tri*-substituted chloroethanes; the 1,1,2-grouping is more potent than the 1,1,1-grouping.

It is recognized that another means of comparing the hepatotoxic potencies of these compounds would be to determine the duration and extent of the damage produced. It is felt that the data presented here can not be used thus, since the basic experimental design does not meet the requirements for such a comparison. It is felt, however, that these data will provide a background for future comparisons.

We do not wish to imply that the industrial hazard may be predicted from these data alone. Other factors such as vapor pressure, partition distribution between blood and tissues, and rate and route of absorption must be considered, as well as the nutritional status of the individuals. However, the method of assay described herein is relatively simple, and would appear to be readily applicable for hepatotoxic screening during the course of acute and chronic exposure of small laboratory animals. The initial requirement would be establishment of good control values. It is recommended that the animals to be used in the experimental phases be initially used to establish the control level of significance, as was done in these studies. Once the correlation between sleeping-time prolongation and microscopic hepatic derangement has been established, the same method of assay can be used to estimate the ED_{50} for production of hepatic damage.

SUMMARY

It has been demonstrated that hepatotoxicity can be evaluated simply and practically by the prolongation of pentobarbital sleeping time. The data can be resolved into the standard dose-response curve, thus permitting an estimate of the ED_{50} for production of hepatic damage.

In hepatotoxic potency, the increasing order of toxicity was: 1,1,1-trichloroethane; tetrachloroethylene; trichloroethylene; *sym*-tetrachloroethane; 1,1,2-trichloroethane; chloroform; carbon tetrachloride.

The lethal potency of the compounds increased as follows: tetrachloroethylene; carbon tetrachloride; 1,1,1-trichloroethane; trichloroethylene; *sym*-tetrachloroethane; chloroform; 1,1,2-trichloroethane.

There was a lack of correlation between the dose causing liver damage and the dose causing death.

REFERENCES

Barsoum, G. S., and Saad, K.: Quart. J. Pharm. & Pharmacol., **7**: 205, 1934.
Brauer, R. W., and Root, M. A.: This Journal, **88**: 109, 1946.
Casals, J., and Olitsky, P. K.: Proc. Soc. Exper. Biol. & Med., **63**: 383, 1946.
Drill, V. A.: Pharmacol. Rev., **4**: 1, 1952.
Lacey, O. L.: Statistical methods in experimentation, The Macmillan Co., New York, 1953.
Litchfield, J. T., Jr., and Wilcoxon, F.: This Journal, **96**: 99, 1949.
Maynert, E. W., and van Dyke, H. B.: Pharmacol. Rev., **1**: 217, 1949.
Pilgrim, H. I., and De Ome, K. B.: Exper. Med. & Surg., **13**: 401, 1955.
Tsuboi, K. K., and Stowell, R. E.: Cancer Res., **11**: 221, 1951.
von Oettingen, W. F.: The halogenated hydrocarbons, toxicity and potential dangers, Public Health Service Pub. No. 414, U. S. Govt. Printing Office, Washington, D.C., 1955.

8038

RELATIONSHIP BETWEEN PERIPHERAL CHOLINOLYTIC POTENCY AND TETRAETHYLPYROPHOSPHATE ANTAGONISM OF A SERIES OF ATROPINE SUBSTITUTES

ALEXANDER G. KARCZMAR[1] AND JOHN P. LONG[2]

Pharmacology Section, Sterling-Winthrop Research Institute, Rensselaer, New York

Received for publication March 6, 1958

The protective action afforded by atropine and atropine substitutes against anticholinesterases generally and against organic phosphate anticholinesterases specifically, is well documented-(Langley and Kato, 1915; Bülbring and Burn, 1941; Modell and Krop, 1946; Koppanyi *et al.*, 1947; Wescoe *et al.*, 1948). There is evidence, especially in rodents, that the effectiveness of these compounds is not due to their antagonism of cholinomimetic[3] actions, particularly bronchoconstriction, but to their central blockade (Modell and Krop, 1946; de Candole *et al.*, 1953; Lewis *et al.*, 1955). This was first demonstrated by Langley and Kato (1915).

This paper provides additional evidence for the central site of antagonism between a series of atropine substitutes and tetraethylpyrophosphate (TEPP). Furthermore, it presents data on the peripheral cholinolytic action of atropine substitutes and investigates the question of whether or not this peripheral action is related to the antagonism of TEPP toxicity. If such a relationship could be established, it would support the suggestion that the central action of anticholinesterases is due to their effects on a central cholinergic transmission (Rinaldi and Himwich, 1955; Longo, 1955, 1956), and that the structural characterization suggested for the peripheral acetylcholine-sensitive receptor (*cf.* Lands, 1951; Long *et al.*, 1956) may hold also for the central cholinergic receptor.

METHODS. Peripheral cholinolytic activities were measured by a modification of the mouse mydriasis test described by Pulewka (1932) and Ing *et al.* (1945). Four doses at 0.3-log intervals of the compound tested were given intraperitoneally to albino mice, 18 to 24 gm. body weight, with 10 mice per dose level. The ED_{50} values (the amount of the drug that produces 50 per cent of maximal mydriasis) were estimated from the log dose-probit plot. The ED_{50} values are highly reproducible (*cf.* Long *et al.*, 1956).

The antidotal effect of the compounds tested against anticholinesterase toxicity was assayed in the same strain of mice. The anticholinesterase was tetraethylpyrophosphate (TEPP, Victor Chemical Works, Chicago, Illinois). Stock solutions of TEPP were kept in propylene glycol in which TEPP is stable for at least one month. Solutions of TEPP in water or saline are rapidly hydrolyzed. Earlier data (Grob *et al.*, 1950) suggested that this occurs appreciably only after 6 hours. It was found in the present investigation that the LD_{50} dose of TEPP in saline, concentration of 0.01 per cent, increases by about 45 per cent in 4 hours and that the LD_{99} dose becomes an LD_{50} dose in 3 hours. These data agree with those of Holmstedt (1951) on the hydrolysis of several TEPP analogs. To minimize and to keep the degree of hydrolysis constant, 10- to 15-minute old solutions of TEPP in saline were used exclusively and a fresh solution was prepared for each group of 10 mice. All drugs were administered intraperitoneally. The LD_{50} of TEPP was calculated by the method of Miller and Tainter (1944). In the present experimental series the LD_{50} dose of TEPP was 1.07 ± 0.021 mgm./kgm. (*cf.* Lewis *et al.*, 1955). The cholinolytic drug was given in combination with a constant dose (0.3 mgm./kgm.) of

[1] Present address: Department of Pharmacology, Stritch School of Medicine, University of Loyola, Chicago, Illinois.

[2] Present address: Department of Pharmacology, State University of Iowa, Iowa City, Iowa.

[3] Autonomic pharmacology suffers from excess of terms. In this paper the terms "cholinomimetic" and "cholinolytic" agents and activities will be used in the following sense. All postganglionic parasympathetic (cholinergic) fibers supply a single type of receptor (Lands and Luduena, 1956). This is the site at which the pharmacological activity of acetylcholine appears to be most pronounced. Substances exciting or blocking this receptor are referred to as cholinomimetic and cholinolytic respectively. For many reasons these terms appear to us better and shorter than their older equivalents such as postganglionic parasympathetic depressants or stimulants. In many respects, the terms "cholinomimetic" and "muscarinic" (Hunt, 1918) are synonymous.

Mytolon (benzoquinonium), 15 minutes prior to the administration of the $2LD_{50}$ dose of TEPP. The dose of the cholinolytic agent protecting 50 per cent of the animals treated in the presence of Mytolon was calculated by the log-probit analysis and designated PD_{50M}. For further details of this and related procedures, see Lewis *et al.* (1955). The relationship between anti-TEPP activity and mydriatic potency as expressed respectively by the PD_{50M} and ED_{50} values was analyzed in terms of its regression line and correlation coefficient, as described by Snedecor (1956). In another part of this study, the protective values of the cholinolytics were obtained in the presence of both Mytolon, 0.3 mgm./kgm., and atropine methylnitrate (Eumydrine), 1.26 mgm./kgm. Although Mytolon alone does not affect the LD_{50} dose of TEPP (Lewis *et al.*, 1955), Eumydrine-Mytolon combination increases it by some 30 per cent. The $2LD_{50EM}$ values were therefore used in establishing the PD_{50EM} values.

RESULTS. *The relationship between mydriatic and anti-TEPP potency of 35 cholinolytic agents.* The compounds listed in table 1 are either alkanol substituted amines, substituted acetic acid esters, substituted tropanes, or α- and β-hydroxy acid esters. The table lists their potencies as TEPP antagonists and as mydriatics (PD_{50M} and ED_{50} values, respectively). It should be noted that both of these values were obtained in the same species and by the same route of administration. The correlation of the PD_{50} and ED_{50} with the 95 per cent confidence limits is shown in figure 1. It suggests a close correlation between anti-TEPP activity and peripheral cholinolytic potency with correlation coefficient of 0.868.

The central mechanism of the anti-TEPP action of cholinolytics. Lewis *et al.* (1955) supplied indirect evidence that the effectiveness of atropine and various cholinolytics against TEPP toxicity in mice is not due to the peripheral protection they can afford (*cf.* also Parkes and Sacra, 1954). In this study two additional types of evidence were obtained that support the above hypothesis.

1. The efficacy of Eumydrine protection against TEPP was measured. Eumydrine was used either alone or in the presence of Mytolon, 0.3 mgm./kgm. Eumydrine did not increase the LD_{50} of TEPP until doses in excess of 25 to 30 mgm./kgm. were reached. Even these large doses produced no more than a 30 to 40 per cent increase in the LD_{50} dose. In the presence of Mytolon, Eumydrine afforded limited protection (30 to 40 per cent increase in LD_{50}) with doses of from 1 to 10 mgm./kgm. Larger doses afforded better protection, the optimal increase of about 80 per cent being obtained with doses of 20 to 30 mgm./kgm. of Eumydrine. Similarly, Lewis *et al.* (1955) found that Eumydrine and other quaternary cholinolytics are inactive as evaluated by the PD_{50M} test. The above studies and the present experiments suggest that the protection at the muscarinic site by cholinolytic agents plays an insignificant part in antidoting TEPP toxicity in mice. Quaternary cholinolytics are less able to act on the central sites and, therefore, do not offer protection against TEPP toxicity.

2. It could be hypothesized that the real protective action of the weaker cholinolytics listed in table 1 is obscured because of their poor peripheral activity. If this were true their anti-TEPP effect should be increased considerably by administration of Eumydrine, whereas there should be little difference in the PD_{50M} and PD_{50EM} values of the potent cholinolytics. The regression line shown in figure 1, instead of truly relating two separate parameters, would then primarily measure the peripheral protective effect expressed by the ED_{50} values obtained in the mydriasis assay. To test this possibility, ten compounds were selected because of the wide range in their PD_{50M} and cholinolytic values, and the PD_{50EM} values were then established for these compounds in the presence of both Mytolon (0.3 mgm./kgm.) and Eumydrine (1.26 mgm./kgm.). Table 2 demonstrates that the PD_{50M} and PD_{50EM} values of these compounds do not differ significantly. This shows again that Eumydrine, in a dose expected to effectively block muscarinic effectors, affords little or no protection and indicates the validity of the conclusion reached on the basis of the regression line shown in figure 1.

DISCUSSION. A central component of action of nonquaternary (Koelle and Steiner, 1956) anticholinesterases has been known for a long time (Langley and Kato, 1915; Bülbring and Burn, 1941). More recently, Michaelis *et al.* (1954) demonstrated that a phosphate anticholinesterase causes central accumulation of acetylcholine, thus providing a possible mechanism for the action of cholinesterase inhibitors on the central nervous system. The argument of this DISCUSSION will be that this central component is particularly important in the case of the phosphate toxicity in mice and that the suggestion can be made that

TABLE 1

Anti-TEPP and mydriatic activity of 35 substituted tertiary amines

1. Alkanol substituted amines

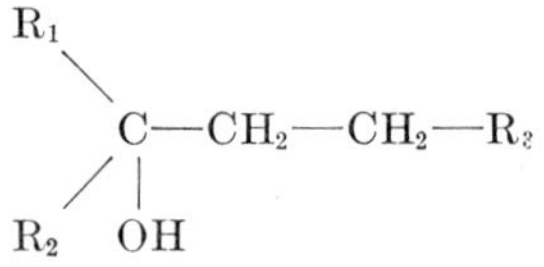

Compound No.	R_1	R_2	R_3	TEPP Antagonism PD_{50M}	Mouse Mydriasis: Per cent atropine sulfate	Mouse Mydriasis: ED_{50}
				mgm./kgm.		*mgm./kgm.*
1	cyclohexyl	cyclohexyl	1′-piperidinyl	13.1	2.4	10.5
2	cyclohexyl	2-thienyl	1′-piperidinyl	4.3	3.3	7.6
3	phenyl	isobutyl	1′-piperidinyl	9.2	3.6	7.0
4	phenyl	cyclopentyl	1′-piperidinyl	7.4	6.1	4.1
5	phenyl	phenyl	$—N(CH_2CH_3)_2$	6.5	2.2	11.4
6	phenyl	cyclohexyl	$—N(CH_2CH_3)_2$	3.1	8.0	3.1

2. Substituted acetic acid esters

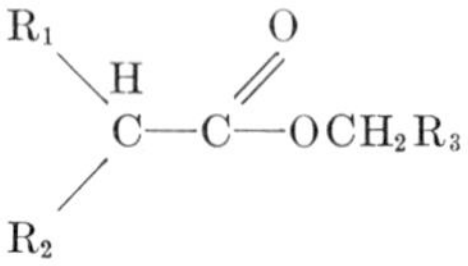

7	phenyl	2-thienyl	3′-N-methylpiperidinyl	18.0	1.3	19.0
8	phenyl	phenyl	3′-N-methylpiperidinyl	8.3	1.8	14.0
9	cyclopentyl	isobutyl	3′-N-methylpiperidinyl	7.4	3.4	7.3

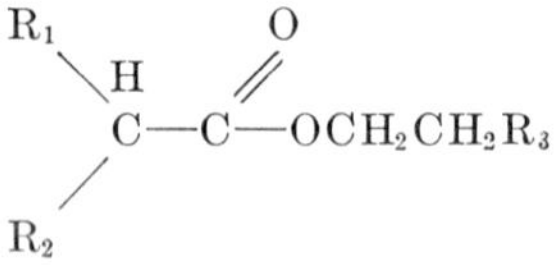

10	cyclopentyl	isobutyl	$N(CH_2CH_3)_2$	17.2	2.0	12.5
11	cyclopentyl	isobutyl	1′piperidinyl	7.3	6.2	4.0

3. Substituted tropanes

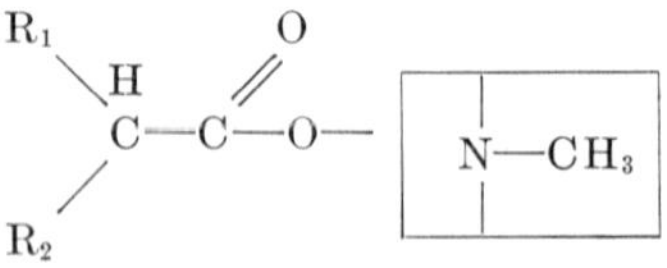

	R_1	R_2			
12	phenyl	phenyl	7.3	3.0	8.2
13	Homatropine·HBr		5.7	4.6	5.5
14	Genoscopolamine·HBr		1.9	83.0	0.3
15	Scopolamine·HBr		0.3	833.0	0.03
16	Atropine sulfate		1.3	100.0	0.25

TABLE 1.—*Continued*

4. Substituted α-hydroxy acid esters

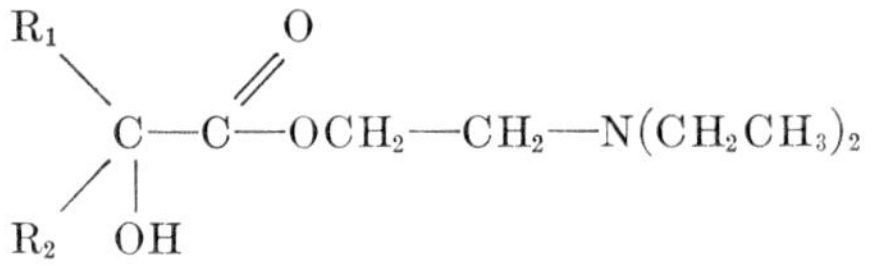

17	2-thienyl	isobutyl	7.0	1.3	19.0
18	phenyl	isobutyl	5.7	10.0	2.5
19 (Suavitil)	phenyl	phenyl	2.6	4.7	5.3
20	2-thienyl	cyclopentyl	0.36	35.7	0.7

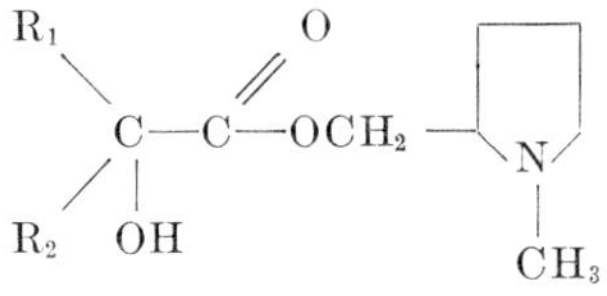

21	phenyl	cyclohexyl	6.1	4.6	5.5
22	phenyl	phenyl	0.7	21.0	1.2

5. β-Hydroxy acid esters

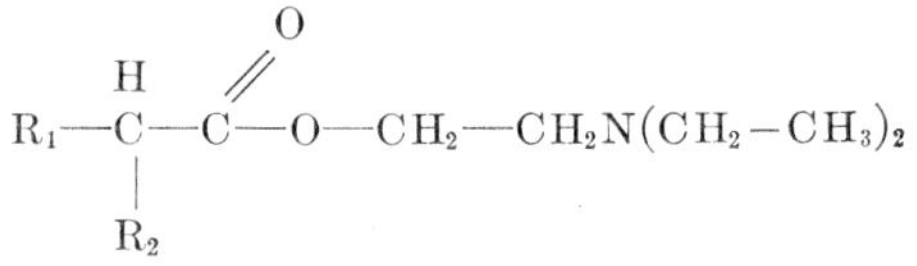

23	cyclohexyl	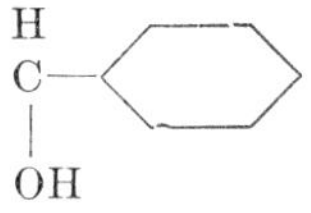	24.1	0.8	30.0
24	1-cyclohexenyl	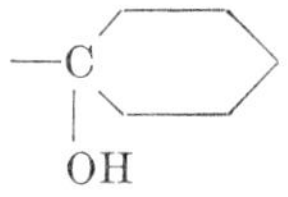	1.8	12.5	2.0
25	2-thienyl	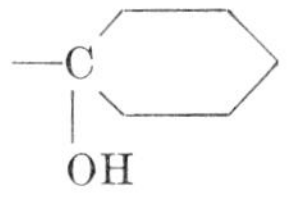	1.8	13.9	1.8
26	phenyl	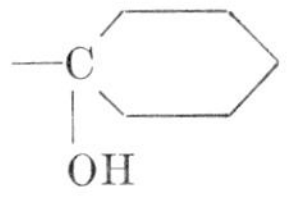	1.3	25.0	1.0
27	2-thienyl	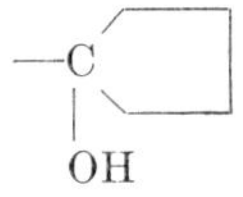	4.6	11.4	2.2
28	cyclohexyl	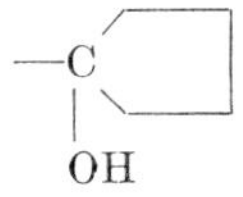	3.6	5.5	4.5
29	phenyl	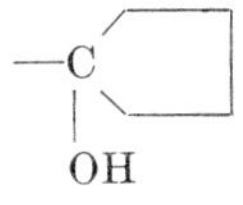	1.1	21.4	1.2

TABLE 1 (*Continued*)

5. β-Hydroxy Acid Esters (*continued*)

30	phenyl	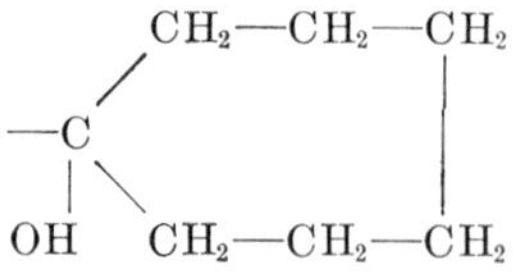	1.4	8.9	2.8
31	phenyl	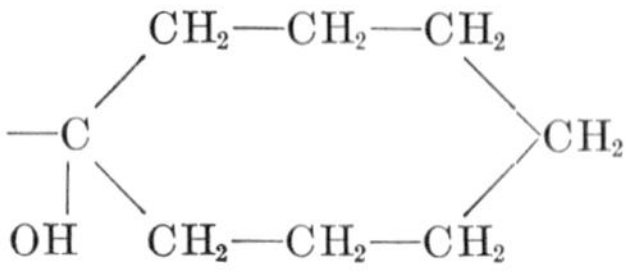	2.8	6.6	3.7
32	cyclohexyl	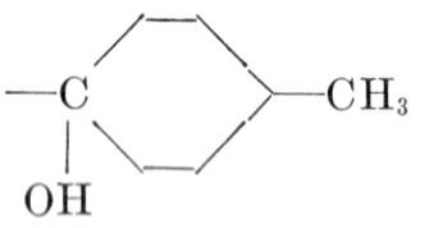	22.5	1.2	21.0
33	phenyl	H—C(OH)—CH_3 (—C(H)(OH)—CH_3)	6.7	3.8	6.5
34	phenyl	—C(OH)—$(CH_3)_2$	5.4	4.9	5.1
35	phenyl	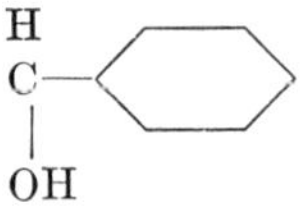	>40.	0.5	>40.0

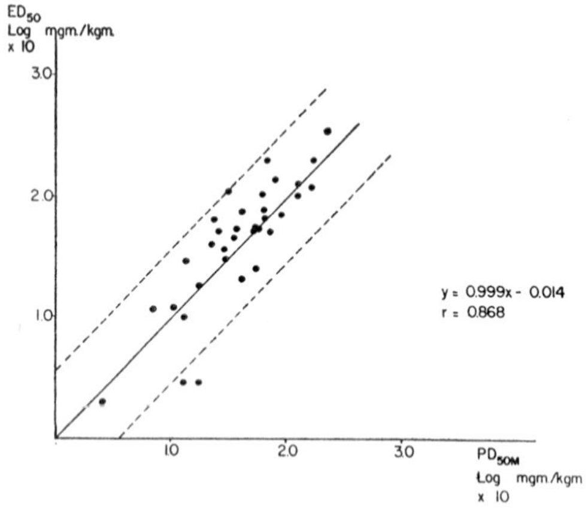

FIG. 1. Relationship between peripheral cholinolytic (mydriatic) activity and TEPP antagonism. Abscissa: PD_{50M}, in log dose, mgm./kgm., × 10. Ordinate: ED_{50}, in log dose, mgm./kgm., × 10. Regression line (y) and correlation coefficient (r) shown in the insert. Dashed lines represent the 95 per cent confidence limits. The points represent the individual compounds shown in table 1. (Compound 35 obviously cannot appear here).

the mechanism involved in the protective action of atropine, scopolamine and their tertiary substitutes is both central and cholinergic in nature.

There seems to be a species difference as to the system responsible for death from phosphate toxicity. In mice, Mytolon does not protect when used alone (Lewis, 1953; Lewis *et al.*, 1955) and protects weakly with any viable dose of Eumydrine. The protective component of action afforded by the bisquaternary Mytolon when used in combination with atropine and atropine-like agents, although not completely known, should be related to its antiacetylcholine action (Luduena and Brown, 1952; Karczmar and Fudema, 1957) exerted at the neuromyal junction (Hoppe 1950; Lewis *et al.*, 1955), thus leading to protection of respiratory musculature. Besides the neuromyal site, the central nervous system is particularly implicated in mice, in the cat and in certain other species (Modell *et al.*, 1946; Krivoy

TABLE 2

Anti-TEPP activity of ten cholinolytic agents in the presence of mytolon or mytolon and eumydrine

Compound No.	Anti-TEPP Toxicity		Peripheral Cholinolytic Activity (per cent Atropine Sulfate)
	$PD_{50}M$	$PD_{50}EM$	
	mgm./kgm.	*mgm./kgm.*	
12	7.3 ± 1.6	5.8 ± 1.1	3.0
19	2.6 ± 0.3	1.3 ± 0.3	4.7
22	0.67 ± 0.1	0.76 ± 0.2	21.0
23	24.1 ± 2.1	>40.0	0.8
30	1.4 ± 0.3	2.1 ± 0.4	8.9
32	22.5 ± 4.7	20.1 ± 5.3	1.5
33	6.7 ± 1.5	5.8 ± 1.3	4.0
35	>40.0	>40.0	0.5
Atropine sulfate	1.3 ± 0.22	1.6 ± 0.4	100.0
Scopolamine·HBr	0.31 ± 0.04	0.28 ± 0.05	833.0

and Marrazzi, 1951; Karczmar and Koppanyi, 1953; Parkes and Sacra, 1954; Karczmar, 1955). The present data are consistent with this concept. In the presence of Mytolon, atropine and the tertiary atropine substitutes were found effective sometimes in doses of only a fraction of a milligram, while measurements of the LD_{50} values in presence of Eumydrine alone or Eumydrine-Mytolon combination showed no protective action of the quaternized atropine (*cf.* also Lewis *et al.*, 1955). Moreover, addition of Eumydrine failed to increase the protection afforded not only by potent peripheral cholinolytics such as atropine and scopolamine, but also by 8 weaker tertiary atropine substitutes (table 2).

These data suggest that the protection at the muscarinic sites must be unimportant in mice, that the tertiary amines must have acted centrally, and that, conversely, the central nervous system was the site of TEPP toxicity. This is in agreement with the more direct evidence for the central component of action of atropine and of scopolamine (Langley and Kato, 1915; Bülbring and Burn, 1941; Longo, 1955, 1956) and with the clinical evidence indicating central action of atropine substitutes leading to therapeutic effects in Parkinsonism or to hallucinations (Pennes *et al.*, 1956). It should be pointed out in this context that among agents found active in the present investigation was benactyzine (Suavitil, compound 19, table 1; *cf.* Jacobson and Sonne, 1955) used as a "tranquilizer" in man.

If we may assume a central site for the protective action of atropine, scopolamine and their tertiary substitutes, can we also suggest a further characterization of this site? The role of acetylcholine in central transmission was recently analyzed by several investigators (Feldberg, 1954; Eccles, 1957). Furthermore, Rinaldi and Himwich (1955) provided evidence for the cholinergic nature of mesodiencephalic activating system which is excited by anticholinesterases and blocked by atropine and scopolamine (Longo, 1955, 1956). However, Longo (1956) concludes that "it is still difficult to decide . . . to what extent the central effects of these alkaloids are connected with the anticholinergic properties which they demonstrate at the level of the vegetative nervous system" and with the antagonism which these and related agents may exhibit towards acetylcholine on a central level. This scepticism is well advised since, for both technical and theoretical reasons there is, as yet, no direct, decisive experimental proof (Eccles, 1957) for chemical transmission, whether cholinergic, adrenergic or other, in any particular central nervous system site.

The present investigation is the first one to our knowledge that attempts to answer this question by testing whether or not there exists a statistically valid correlation between the peripheral cholinolytic activity and presumably central action of a relatively large number of compounds. Moreover, the experimental conditions were devised in order to measure both of these actions in a single species and in a whole animal rather than resorting, for the cholinolytic data, to excised organs. As a result a good relationship with a high correlation coefficient could be demonstrated for 34 compounds including scopolamine and atropine. Moreover several specific structural changes already described (Lands, 1951; Nachod and Lands, 1953; Long *et al.*, 1956, 1957) as improving the peripheral cholinolytic action also improve TEPP antagonism (*cf.* table 1). Such an improvement can be noted following 1) the replacement of one of the hydrogens of the methane by a hydroxyl (compare compounds of group 2 with those of group 4 and 5); 2) the introduction of asymmetric substitutions on the terminal carbon (compare compounds 5 and 6; 1, 2, 4; and 19 and 20); 3) the substitution of the phenyl for the cyclohexyl ring in case of asymmetric compounds (compare compounds 28 and 29); and 4) substitutions on the third carbon that provide the peculiar umbrella-like mass which characterizes the most potent cholinolytic compounds (Pfeiffer, 1948; Lands and Luduena, 1956; compare compounds 33 and 34 with 30 and 31). It also appears, in the case of the central anticholinergic action no less than in that of the peripheral cholinolytic effect, that simple mass is not the only factor which determines the efficacy of the umbrella. In the present study this is illustrated by, for instance, compounds 30 and 32, both with an umbrella of 7 carbons, the former being a powerful cholinolytic agent and a potent TEPP antagonist, while the latter is ineffective.

All this evidence at least suggests that, since the central antagonism between scopolamine, atropine and tertiary atropine-like compounds on one hand and a phosphate anticholinesterase on the other is correlated with and governed by the same structure-activity relationships as peripheral postganglionic cholinergic transmission, the mechanism involved may be cholinergic in nature. Moreover, while a series of structure-activity relationships led Lands and his associated (Lands, 1951; Long *et al.*, 1956; Long and Lands, 1957) to postulate a peripheral cholinergic receptor of a definite shape which contains charges that may serve as points of attraction and binding of the cholinolytic agents, this study indicates that similar suggestions may be made for a central cholinergic receptor, and that not only the postganglionic cholinergic sites but also certain central cholinergic neurones may all be activated by an acetylcholine-sensitive receptor of one single type and of uniform structural and chemical properties.

SUMMARY

Thirty-five alkanol substituted amines, substituted acetic acid esters, substituted tropanes and α- and β-substituted acetic acid esters were tested for their antagonism of tetraethylpyrophosphate (TEPP) toxicity in mice. TEPP antagonism was tested either in the presence of Mytolon or of Mytolon and atropine methylnitrate (Eumydrine). Mouse mydriasis was used to evaluate the peripheral cholinolytic potency of these compounds.

Eumydrine alone or Eumydrine with Mytolon provides only minimal protection against TEPP toxicity. Eumydrine does not increase the protective action of the cholinolytic compounds studied.

The structural changes that increase the peripheral cholinolytic potency also increase the anti-TEPP action of the compounds tested. A close correlation was found between the anti-TEPP and peripheral cholinolytic actions of the 34 compounds tested.

The suggestion is offered that both TEPP toxicity and protection afforded by atropine-like agents is, in mice, central in nature, and that the statistical correlation demonstrated supplies additional evidence for the hypothesis that cholinergic transmission is involved in these phenomena.

ACKNOWLEDGMENT. The authors wish to acknowledge with gratitude the technical assistance provided by Mr. Ken Turner. We want also to thank Dr. A. C. White, Wellcome Research Laboratories, Beckenham, England, for his kindness in supplying us with compound No. 1.

REFERENCES

BÜLBRING, E., AND BURN, J. H.: J. Physiol., **100:** 337, 1941.
DE CANDOLE, C. A., DOUGLAS, W. W., EVANS, C. L., HOLMES, R., SPENCER, K. E. V., TORRANCE, R. W., AND WILSON, K. M.: Brit. J. Pharmacol., **8:** 466, 1953.
ECCLES, J. C.: The Physiology of the Nerve Cells, Johns Hopkins Press, Baltimore, 1957.
FELDBERG, W.: Pharmacol. Rev., **6:** 85, 1954.
GROB, D., GARLICK, W. L., AND HARVEY, A. M.: Bull. Johns Hopkins Hosp., **87:** 106, 1950.
HOLMSTEDT, B.: Acta Physiol. Scand., **25:** Suppl. 90, 1951.
HOPPE, J. O.: THIS JOURNAL, **100:** 333, 1950.
HUNT, C. C.: Am. J. Physiol., **45:** 197, 1918.
ING, H. R., DAWES, G. S., AND WAJDA, I.: THIS JOURNAL, **85:** 85, 1945.
JACOBSEN, E., AND SONNE, E.: Acta Pharmacol. Toxicol., **11:** 135, 1955.
KARCZMAR, A. G., AND KOPPANYI, T.: Arch. exper. Path. u. Pharmakol., **219:** 263, 1953.
KARCZMAR, A. G.: Ann. New York Acad. Sci., **60:** 1108, 1955.
KARCZMAR, A. G., AND FUDEMA, J. J.: Fed. Proc., **16:** 311, 1957.
KOELLE, G. B., AND STEINER, E. C.: THIS JOURNAL, **118:** 420, 1956.
KOPPANYI, T., KARCZMAR, A. G., AND KING, T. O.: Science, **106:** 492, 1947.
KRIVOY, A. W., AND MARRAZZI, A. S.: Fed. Proc., **10:** 316, 1951.
LANDS, A. M.: THIS JOURNAL, **102:** 219, 1951.
LANDS, A. M., AND LUDUENA, F. P.: THIS JOURNAL, **116:** 177, 1956.
LANGLEY, J. N., AND KATO, T.: J. Physiol., **49:** 410, 1915.
LEWIS, J. R.: Chem. Corps Med. Lab., Special Report No. 27, Army Chem. Center, Maryland, August, 1953.
LEWIS, J. R., MCKEON, W. B., AND LANDS, A. M.: Arch. internal. pharmacodyn., **102:** 371, 1955.
LONG, J. P., LUDUENA, F. P., TULLAR, B. F., AND LANDS, A. M.: THIS JOURNAL, **117:** 29, 1956.
LONG, J. P., AND LANDS, A. M.: THIS JOURNAL, **120:** 46, 1957.

LONGO, V. G.: THIS JOURNAL, **116:** 198, 1956.
LONGO, V. G.: Experientia, **11:** 76, 1955.
LUDUENA, F. P., AND BROWN, T. G., JR.: THIS JOURNAL, **105:** 232, 1952.
MICHAELIS, M., FINESINGER, J. E., DE BALBIAN VERSTER, F., AND ERICKSON, R. W.: THIS JOURNAL, **111:** 169, 1954.
MILLER, L. C., AND TAINTER, M. L.: Proc. Soc. Exper. Biol. & Med., **57:** 261, 1944.
MODELL, W., AND KROP, S.: THIS JOURNAL, **88:** 34, 1946.
MODELL, W., KROP, S., HITCHCOCK, P., AND RIKER, W. F.: THIS JOURNAL, **87:** 400, 1946.
NACHOD, F. C., AND LANDS, A. M.: Tr. New York Acad. Sci. Ser. **11**, **16:** 2, 1953.
PARKES, M. W., AND SACRA, P.: Brit J. Pharmacol., **9:** 299, 1954.
PENNES, H. H., AND HOCH, P. H.: Am. J. Psychiat., **113:** 887, 1956.
PFEIFFER, C. C.: Science, **107:** 94, 1948.
PULEWKA, P.: Arch. exper. Path. u. Pharmakol., **168:** 307, 1932.
RINALDI, F., AND HIMWICH, H. E.: A. M. A. Arch. Neruol. & Psychiat., **73:** 387, 1955.
SNEDECOR, G. W.: Statistical Methods Applied to Experiments in Agriculture and Biology, Iowa State College Press, Ames, 1956.
WESCOE, W. C., GREEN, R. E., MCNAMARA, B. P., AND KROP, S.: THIS JOURNAL, **92:** 63, 1948.

8039

FACTORS AFFECTING THE BLOOD PRESSURE RESPONSE OF MAMMALS TO THE GANGLIONIC BLOCKING AGENT, CHLORISONDAMINE CHLORIDE

R. A. MAXWELL, A. J. PLUMMER, S. D. ROSS, A. I. DANIEL AND F. SCHNEIDER

Research Department, CIBA Pharmaceutical Products Inc., Summit, New Jersey

Received for publication March 15, 1958

Laboratory evaluations of the potency and duration of action of hypotensive drugs are often conflicting. This report concerns a study of some of the variables that may be involved in such work[1]. In our experiments we have utilized the antihypertensive drug, chlorisondamine chloride (Plummer *et al.*, 1955). This agent, except for a greater potency and duration of action, is not overtly distinguishable in its pharmacological activity from other ganglionic blocking agents such as hexamethonium and pentapyrrolidinium. We have therefore utilized chlorisondamine as a model compound for this group of agents. Specifically we have observed the effects on the response to chlorisondamine chloride of a) different species of test animals, b) the presence and absence of barbiturate anesthesia and c) the type of experimental hypertension.

METHODS. Adult mongrel dogs were used in this study. All were trained to lie in the supine position and to accept calmly femoral arterial puncture with a 22-gauge needle. Pressures were recorded through the Sanborn electromanometer and polyviso. Several of the dogs were surgically altered as described below.

Adult albino rabbits were restrained in the supine position and femoral arterial punctures were made with a 24-gauge one-half inch needle.

Rhesus monkeys were restrained in a tiltable chair which was lowered to allow femoral puncture with a 24-gauge one-half inch needle.

The systolic arterial pressure of 150 gm. Wistar rats was recorded through the Metro photoelectric tensometer. Anesthetics were administered to rats via the intraperitoneal route and ganglionic blocking agents via the femoral vein. The data concerning the responses of the rats were subjected to statistical treatment by the method of analysis of variance and multiple range tests of Duncan (1955).

RESULTS. *Blood pressure responses of unanesthetized laboratory animals.* Dog: Five unanesthetized normotensive dogs were given 320 microgm./kgm. of chlorisondamine chloride intravenously. This dose of chlorisondamine chloride was sufficient to produce complete relaxation of the nictitating membranes and mydriasis with loss of accommodation. Within one minute there occurred a reduction in systolic pressure. There was no decline in diastolic pressure in any of the five animals tested and in some cases a slight increase was actually observed (fig. 1a). The heart rates increased from approximately 60 to 80/sec. to 130 to 160/sec., this increase lasting for the duration of drug action. Diminution of pulse pressure by approximately one-half was the most striking effect observed. In three unanesthetized dogs the intravenous administration of a very high dose of chlorisondamine chloride (3 mgm./kgm.) produced a transient sharp decline in both systolic and diastolic pressures lasting approximately five minutes, after which diastolic pressure returned to control values, while systolic pressure remained markedly reduced. Sustained tachycardia occurred following drug administration. The effect of the intravenous administration of a high dose of hexamethonium (8 mgm./kgm.) was studied in these same three unanesthetized dogs to determine whether the cardiovascular actions described above would also be produced by another known ganglionic blocking agent. The effects on blood pressure and heart rate produced by 8 mgm./kgm. of hexamethonium were the same as those produced by a 3 mgm./kgm. dose of chlorisondamine.

Rat: Fifteen unanesthetized normotensive rats

[1] Preliminary abstracts of this work were presented by Maxwell, Plummer and Ross (1956a, 1957).

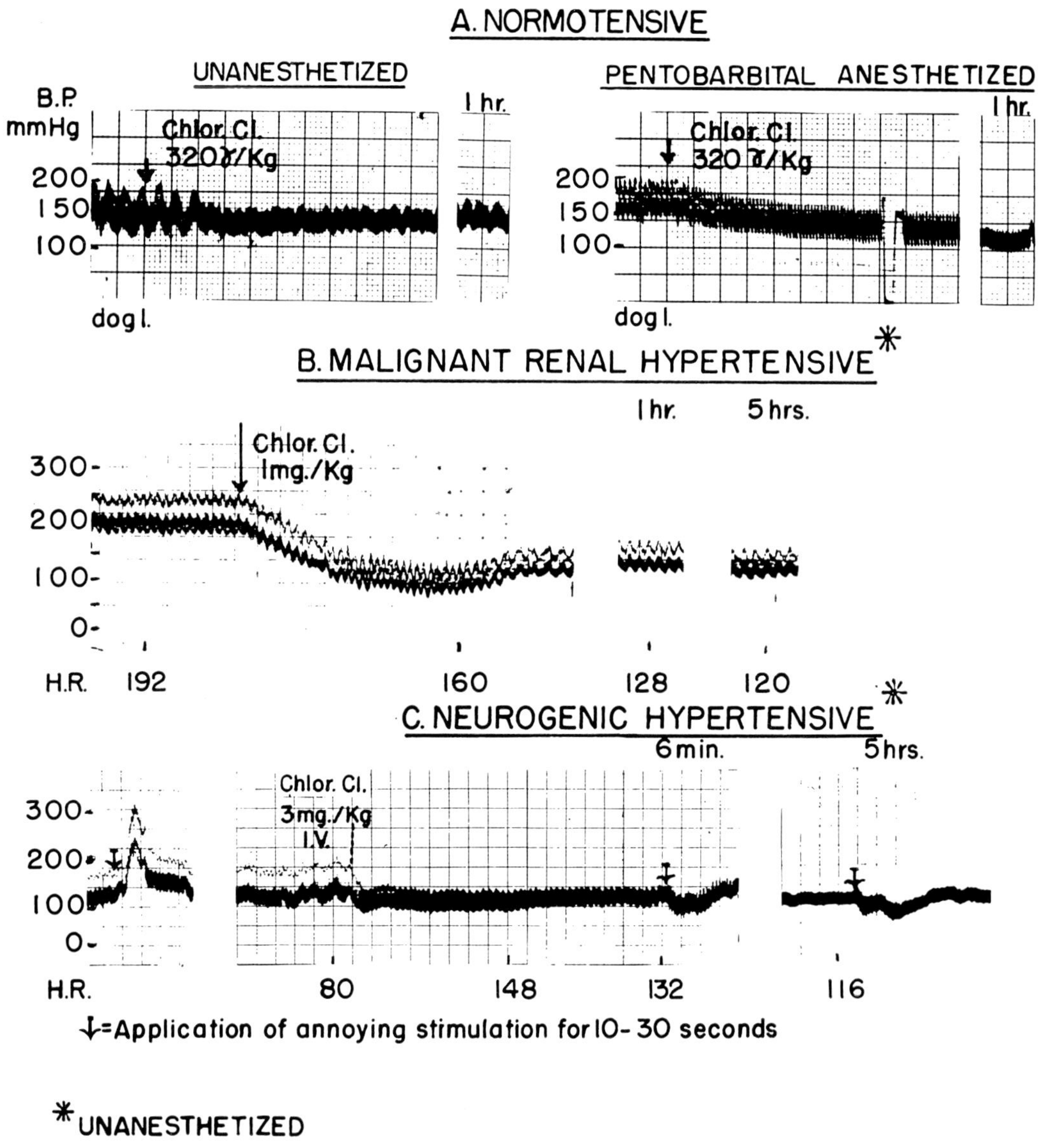

FIG. 1. The effect of intravenous chlorisondamine chloride on the blood pressure of the dog.

were given 1 mgm./kgm. of chlorisondamine chloride intravenously and systolic pressures followed over a one and one-half hour period. No significant differences between control systolic pressures and post-drug systolic pressures were observed (fig. 2). Heart rate was not studied.

Monkey: Two unanesthetized normotensive Rhesus monkeys were given 320 microgm./kgm. and 1 mgm./kgm. intravenously of chlorisonda-damine chloride. These doses produced declines in diastolic pressure of 20 and 30 mm. Hg. A decrease of 50 mm. Hg in systolic pressure occurred in both animals after drug injection with a concomitant decrease in pulse pressure (fig. 3a). Heart rates changed from 136 and 140/min. to 116 and 124/min. respectively.

Rabbit: Five unanesthetized normotensive rabbits were treated with 320 microgm./kgm. of chlorisondamine chloride intravenously. This produced a sharp sustained decline of 30 mm.

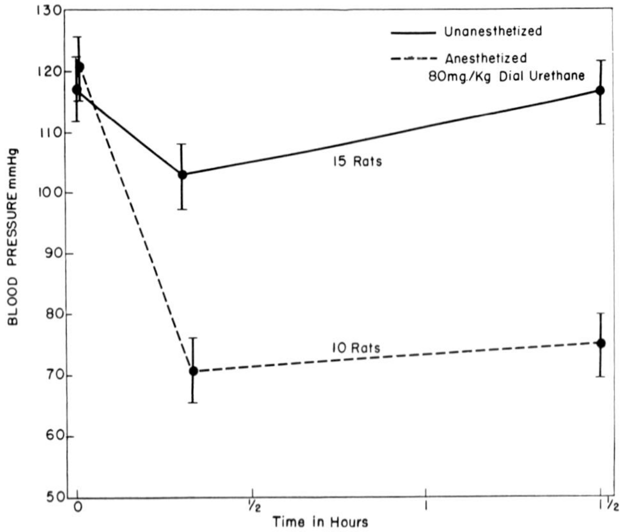

FIG. 2. The effect of Dial-Urethane anesthesia on the systolic pressure response of the rat to 1 mgm./kgm. chlorisondamine chloride intravenously.
The plots indicate that the mean blood pressures ± standard error per unit.

Hg in diastolic pressure and 70 mm. Hg in systolic pressure resulting in a markedly reduced pulse pressure (fig. 3b) in the five animals. Heart rates changed from 200 to 210/min. to 220 to 240/min.

Thus, the blood pressure response of two common laboratory species, the dog and rat, was relatively slight when ganglionic blocking agents were administered in the absence of anesthesia. The normotensive rabbit and monkey, on the other hand, exhibited clear-cut reductions in both diastolic and systolic pressures in the unanesthetized state. Three species exhibited a marked reduction in pulse pressure as a result of administration of ganglionic blocking agents.

Effect of pentobarbital anesthesia on the blood pressure response of the dog. The five dogs reported in the section above were anesthetized with 30 mgm./kgm. of pentobarbital intravenously. The most consistent effect of the anesthesia was to reduce pulse pressure and induce tachycardia. Administration of 320 microgm./kgm. of chlorisondamine to these animals produced clear-cut decline in both systolic and diastolic pressures (fig. 1a) and a relative bradycardia in all five animals which lasted for the duration of drug action.

Effect of Dial-Urethane (diallylbarbituric acid and urethane) on the blood pressure response of the rat. Ten rats were anesthetized with 0.8 ml./kgm. of Dial-Urethane solution. Tracheal cannulae were inserted to insure adequate respiration. One mgm./kgm. of chlorisondamine chloride intravenously produced a marked decline in systolic pressure which was sustained over a one and one-half hour period (fig. 2). The blood pressure levels attained in the anesthetized rats following chlorisondamine chloride administration differed highly significantly at the 0.1 per cent level from the control pressures observed with and without anesthesia and from the pressures attained in the unanesthetized rat subsequent to chlorisondamine chloride injection.

Thus, the dog and rat which did not respond markedly to ganglionic blocking agents in the unanesthetized state responded very dramatically when ganglionic blocking agents were administered during deep barbiturate anesthesia.

Effect of experimental hypertension on the blood pressure response of the dog. Chronic renal hypertension: Three unanesthetized dogs with chronic renal hypertension produced by the method of Goldblatt *et al.* (1933) were treated with 320 microgm./kgm. and 1 mgm./kgm. of chlorisondamine chloride. These animals responded in the same manner as the unanesthetized normotensive dogs, *i.e.*, with a decline in systolic pressure, a narrowing of pulse pressure and tachycardia but not with a marked decline in diastolic pressure.

Malignant renal hypertension: Malignant hypertension was produced in 2 dogs; in one by

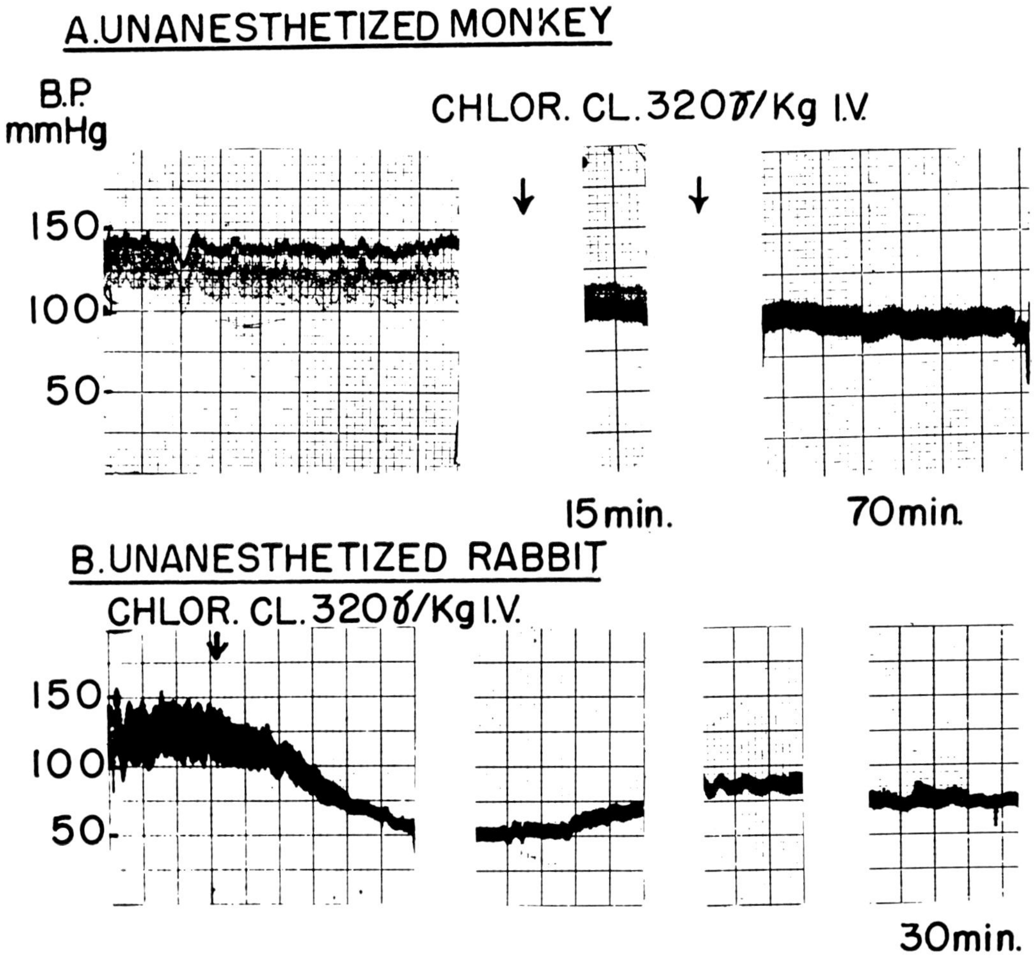

FIG. 3. Effect of chlorisondamine chloride on the blood pressures of the normotensive unanesthetized monkey and rabbit.

the perinephritic method of Page (1939) and in the other by overtightening of Goldblatt clamps. Both animals became ataxic and exhibited anorexia and bloody diarrhea. They responded to 1 mgm./kgm. intravenous chlorisondamine chloride with clearly defined reductions in both systolic and diastolic pressures (fig. 1b). A third animal with overtightened Goldblatt clamps did not exhibit hypertension. However, this animal responded with a decline in both systolic and diastolic pressure following 1 mgm./kgm. of chlorisondamine chloride intravenously.

Neurogenic hypertension: This labile form of hypertension was induced in three dogs by the method of Grimson (1941). With careful and sufficient training to the animal board these dogs did not exhibit markedly elevated blood pressures in the absence of anesthesia. However, slight to moderate shaking of their heads was sufficient to produce marked elevation of their blood pressures (fig. 1c). Chlorisondamine chloride in intravenous doses of 320 microgm./kgm. to 3 mgm./kgm. reduced systolic pressure, narrowed pulse pressure and increased heart rate, but did not produce a sustained fall in diastolic pressure. On the other hand, spikes induced by shaking of the head were antagonized or reversed by administration of chlorisondamine chloride (fig. 1c).

The work presented in this communication demonstrates that 1) barbiturate anesthesia, 2) species differences and 3) type of hypertension within a given species, are factors which influence the blood pressure response produced by the administration of the ganglionic blocking agent chlorisondamine chloride. Of these three factors, the effects of pentobarbital anesthesia on the response of the normotensive dog lends itself most easily to further analysis.

Hemodynamic effect of chlorisondamine in normotensive dogs. The left common carotid arteries of three female boxers (dogs J, T, S) and one male hound (dog W) were exteriorized into a tube of skin. These animals were trained to lie supinely on the board and to accept needle puncture of the exteriorized artery without struggling. Pulse contours were obtained with a Hamilton manometer and an optical recording system. Cardiac outputs (CO) in c.c./sec./m.² body surface were determined by the method of Remington and Hamilton (1947) as amended by Remington (1952). Peripheral resistance was calculated as $PR = \frac{\text{mean blood pressure (mm. Hg)}}{\text{cardiac output (c.c./sec./m.}^2\text{)}}$, where Mean blood pressure (MBP) was taken as diastolic + 0.4 (systolic-diastolic). The use of the 0.4 factor was suggested by Remington (personal communication) on the basis of unpublished data. As can be seen in table 1, the changes in these parameters evoked by chlorisondamine in the unanesthetized dogs were generally the same over the dose range of 0.32 mgm./kgm., 1.0 mgm./kgm. and 3.0 mgm./kgm. The intermediate dose level of 1 mgm./kgm. was also given to the same four animals after they had been anesthetized with 30 mgm./kgm. pentobarbital intraperitoneally.

Fig. 4 illustrates the effect of chlorisondamine on the carotid pulse contour of dog S.

All the data obtained at the 1 mgm./kgm level was subjected to statistical evaluation (see fig. 5 for summary) with the data being analyzed as if the experiment were a 2 × 2 factorial experiment (factor 1 at 2 levels: with anesthesia and without, and factor 2 at 2 levels: chlorisondamine treated and untreated). The analysis of variance and F test (Snedecor, 1956) and the t test, utilizing the

TABLE 1

The effect of chlorisondamine on various aspects of cardiovascular dynamics

Controls					Chlorisondamine chloride i.v.	½ Hr. After Drug					1 Hour After Drug				
Cardiac output	Mean blood pres.	Diastolic blood pres.	Peripheral resistance	Cardiac vol.		Cardiac output	Mean blood pres.	Diastolic blood pres.	Peripheral resistance	Cardiac vol.	Cardiac output	Mean blood pres.	Diastolic blood pres.	Peripheral resistance	Cardiac vol.
c.c./sec./m.²	*mm. Hg*	*mm. Hg*		*c.c./kgm.*	*mgm./kgm.*	*c.c./sec./m.²*	*mm. Hg*	*mm. Hg*		*c.c./kgm.*	*c.c./sec./m.²*	*mm. Hg*	*mm. Hg*		*c.c./kgm.*
Dog J															
59.1	105	84	1.8		0.32	48.4	107	95	2.2		48.6	99	87	2.0	
64.3	124	101	1.9	22.8	1.0	33.3	98	87	2.9	17.5	37.5	101	90	2.7	17.5
72.0	106	81	1.7		3.0	40.0	85	74	2.1		35.8	92	83	2.6	
62.1*	114	100	1.8		1.0	28.8*	63	53	2.2		18.2*	65	53	3.6	
Dog S															
72.1	143	117	2.0		0.32	50.0	143	127	2.9		—	—	—	—	
83.8	133	100	1.6	22.2	1.0	50.0	123	108	2.5	20.2	32.4	124	113	3.8	19.1
59.1	129	107	2.0		3.0	42.5	123	110	2.9		36.6	126	113	3.4	
57.1*	128	114	2.2		1.0	38.7*	99	88	2.6		20.8*	92	86	4.4	
Dog T															
69.6	78	58	1.1		0.32	37.5	95	88	2.5		—	—	—	—	
52.1	102	84	2.0	16.9	1.0	15.9	110	104	6.9	14.2	25.6	102	94	4.0	14.2
56.0	103	82	1.8		3.0	35.0	117	107	3.3		31.1	115	103	3.7	
31.4*	101	92	3.2		1.0	22.4*	67	60	3.0		14.6*	71	65	4.9	
Dog W															
60.8	108	88	1.8		1.0	25.6	92	86	3.6		15.0	87	82	5.8	
33.4*	103	96	3.1		1.0	22.2*	61	55	2.7		20.7*	64	58	3.1	

* Anesthetized with 30 mgm./kgm. of pentobarbital i.p.

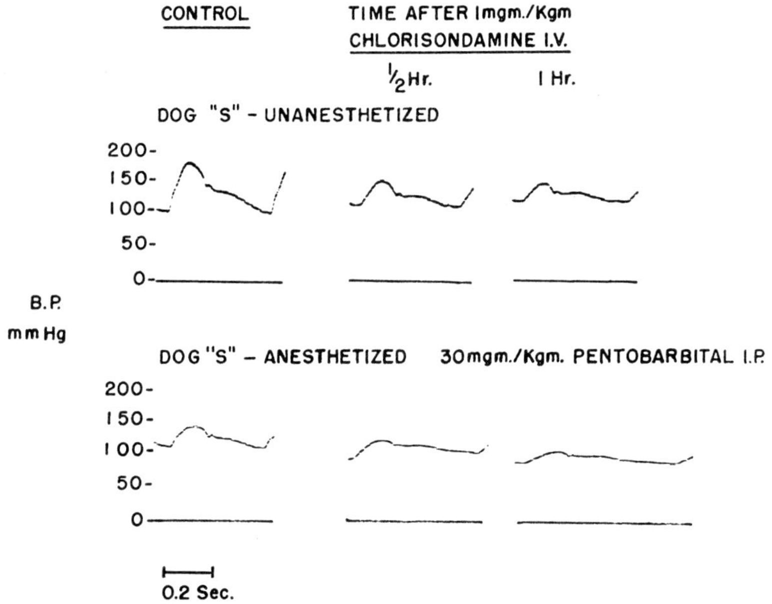

FIG. 4. Effect of chlorisondamine chloride on the carotid pulse contour of the dog.

s estimate based on all groups and derived from the analysis of variance (Bennett and Franklin, 1954), showed:

Cardiac output: In the unanesthetized dog, chlorisondamine administration produced an average decline in output of 52 per cent at the end of one-half hour. At one hour the decrease was 58 per cent. Pentobarbital itself produced an average decline in output of 30 per cent. Superimposition of chlorisondamine chloride produced, at one-half hour, a decline in output of 39 per cent below the control values obtained with anesthesia. At one hour the decline was 60 per cent. All these changes were highly significant at the 0.1 per per cent level (fig. 5).

Mean blood pressure (MBP): Chlorisondamine at one-half hour in the unanesthetized dogs elicited an average decline of 9 per cent in MBP which was not significant, and at one hour an 11 per cent decline which was significant at the 5 per cent level. Pentobarbital *per se* did not affect MBP significantly. Administration of chlorisondamine to the animals under anesthesia produced a decline in MBP of 35 per cent below the control values obtained with anesthesia at one-half hour and at one hour, which were highly significant at the 0.1 per cent level in both cases.

Diastolic blood Pressure (DBP): In the unanesthetized dog DBP was not significantly affected by chlorisondamine at one-half or one hour. Pentobarbital did not affect DBP significantly. The injection of chlorisondamine to the anesthetized animals evoked decreases of 36 per cent and 35 per cent below the control values obtained with anesthesia at one-half and one hour respectively. These decreases were both highly significant at the 0.1 per cent level.

Peripheral resistance: In the unanesthetized dogs chlorisondamine produced, at one-half hour, an average rise in peripheral resistance (PR) of 118 per cent which was highly significant at 0.1 per cent level; at one hour an increase of 123 per cent was obtained which was highly significant at the 0.1 per cent level. Pentobarbital produced an average increase in PR of 41 per cent but this was not significant. Administration of chlorisondamine to these anesthetized dogs produced no significant change at one-half hour and a change of 55 per cent above control values at one hour which was highly significant at the 0.1 per cent level.

Cardiac volume: The effect of 1 mgm./kgm. of intravenous chlorisondamine chloride on the cardiac volume of dogs J, T and S in the unanesthetized state was determined by the X-ray method of Hamilton *et al.* (1950). The data obtained in these experiments are recorded in table 1. There was an average decline in cardiac volume of 16 per cent at one-half hour but this was not significant. At one hour an average decline of 18

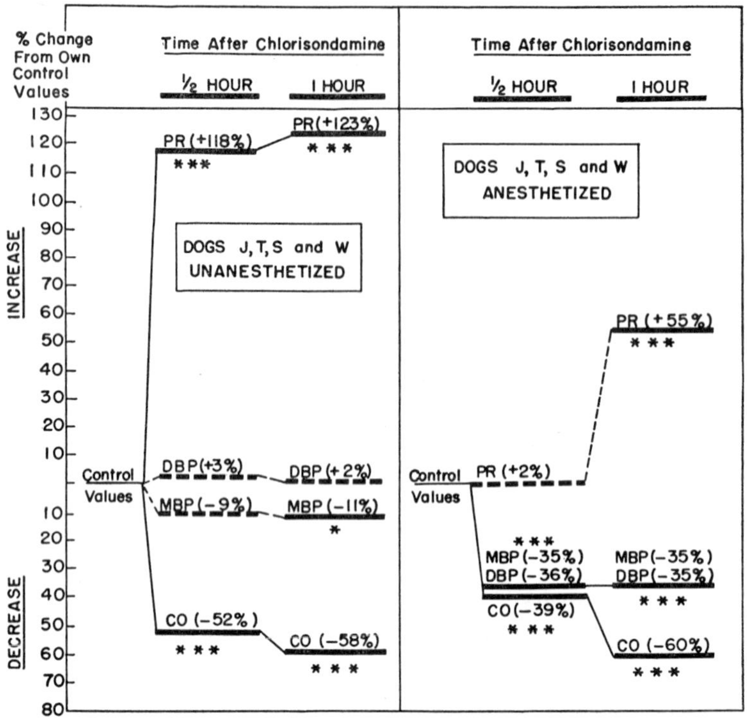

FIG. 5. Effect of pentobarbital on the hemodynamic response of the dog to 1 mgm./kgm. chlorisondamine chloride.

It should be noted that all "unanesthetized values" are in terms of per cent change in each animal from its own unanesthetized controls. Likewise, all "anesthetized values" are in terms of per cent change of each animal from its own anesthetized controls. CO = cardiac output, PR = peripheral resistance, MBP = mean blood pressure, DBP = diastolic blood pressure, * = significantly different from controls at 5 per cent level, *** = highly significantly different from controls at 0.1 per cent level and --- = not significantly different.

per cent occurred. This was significant at the 5 per cent level.

DISCUSSION. The decline in diastolic pressure observed in the normotensive unanesthetized monkey and rabbit following administration of chlorisondamine chloride demonstrates that this ganglionic blocking agent in these species not only produced a hypotensive effect but furthermore acted to prevent compensation by the mechanisms generally operating to restore a reduced pressure in these species.

The failure of ganglionic blocking agents, even in high doses, to produce more than a transient diastolic decline in the unanesthetized normotensive dog and rat, in the unanesthetized benign renal hypertensive dog and in the unanesthetized neurogenic hypertensive dog suggests that the hypotensive effects of ganglionic blocking agents in the absence of anesthesia in the dog and rat are not associated with a pronounced block of the pathways associated with the compensatory mechanisms which serve to sustain diastolic pressure. Freyburger *et al.* (1950), Pardo *et al.* (1950), Cicardo and Dutrey (1954) and Maxwell *et al.* (1956b) have presented evidence that certain efferent sympathetic cardiovascular pathways are not affected by ganglionic blocking agents. The hemodynamic analysis of chlorisondamine action presented here would indicate that the action of chlorisondamine chloride which would tend to lower blood pressure in unanesthetized normotensive dogs is its ability to reduce cardiac output. This reduction in output can possibly be attributed to a decreased venous return which is reflected in our experiments in the reduction of heart size observed after chlorisondamine administration. Cominsky *et al.* (1954) have described "splanchnic pooling" during the hypotensive action of hexamethonium. Burch (1955), Smith and Hoobler (1956) and Trapold (1957) have ascribed part of the cardiovascular action of ganglionic blocking agents to alterations in the venous circulation.

The lack of a marked decline in mean blood pressure and diastolic blood pressure in the unanesthetized dog after chlorisondamine can be accounted for by a markedly increased peripheral resistance. Apparently even in the presence of a high dose of a potent ganglionic blocking agent the unanesthetized normotensive dog is capable of a marked peripheral arteriolar constriction. This would suggest that the blocking effects on the synapses in arteriolar vasoconstrictor pathways of unanesthetized dogs may not be as complete as that blockade which can be demonstrated on the synapses in the superior cervical ganglion of the nerve fibers which innervate the nictitating membrane of the cat (Plummer *et al.*, 1955).

In the malignant phases of renal hypertension compensatory mechanisms are apparently more vulnerable to the action of ganglioplegic agents. Likewise, the fact that full barbiturate anesthesia will permit chlorisondamine to produce a clear and sustained diastolic fall in the normotensive dog and rat would make it seem that the superimposition of the effects of barbiturate anesthesia, *e.g.*, marked decrease in cardiac output (Nash *et al.*, 1956), possible central interference with cardiovascular function (Gellhorn and Redgate, 1955) and great increases in the blood volume of the intestine and spleen (Riecke and Everett, 1957), is sufficient to depress or override the compensatory mechanisms still in operation in these species after the administration of a ganglionic blocking agent. Our hemodynamic analysis supports this view and indicates that pentobarbital anesthesia in the normotensive dog prevents the attainment of a sufficient increase in peripheral resistance to compensate for the marked reduction in cardiac output. In contrast, this necessary compensation is obtainable in the unanesthetized dog following the ganglionic blocking agent chlorisondamine.

Recently Dontas and Nickerson (1957) have presented evidence that the ganglionic blocking agents exhibit central as well as peripheral blocking effects. The fact that these blocking agents have central sites of action renders an interplay between the centrally depressing barbiturates and the so called peripherally acting ganglionic blocking agents quite possible.

SUMMARY

The unanesthetized monkey and rabbit exhibit a well-defined and sustained decline in systolic and diastolic blood pressure following intravenous administration of the ganglionic blocking agent chlorisondamine chloride.

In contrast, the unanesthetized normotensive dog and rat do not respond with a persistent fall in blood pressure following administration of ganglionic blocking agents. The diastolic blood pressure response of the unanesthetized chronic renal hypertensive dog and neurogenic hypertensive dog is likewise not prolonged.

In the malignant phase of renal hypertension the dog responds with a sustained systolic and diastolic decline following chlorisondamine chloride injection.

Normotensive dogs and rats under anesthetic doses of pentobarbital or Dial-Urethane respond with well-defined and sustained falls in both systolic and diastolic pressures following intravenous injection of ganglionic blocking agents. In contrast to unanesthetized dogs, dogs under barbiturate anesthesia exhibit a relative bradycardia following administration of ganglionic blocking agents.

Evidence has been presented which indicates that the barbiturates interfere with compensatory mechanisms which normally function in the normotensive dog and rat during "ganglionic blockade." These compensatory mechanisms appear to be generally less predominant in the monkey and rabbit.

ACKNOWLEDGMENTS. The authors would like to thank Mrs. E. Sullivan and Miss N. Howie for performing the determinations of rat blood pressures. The authors would also like to thank Mrs. H. Sylwestrowicz for the statistical treatment of part of the data presented.

REFERENCES

BENNETT, C. B., AND FRANKLIN, N. L.: Statistical Analysis in Chem. & Chem. Industry, John Wiley & Sons, New York, 1954.
BURCH, R. R.: Circulation, **11:** 271, 1955.
CICARDO, V. H., AND DUTREY, E. D.: Rev. de la Soc. Arg. de Biol., **30:** 132, 1954.
COMINSKY, B., PREEDY, J. R. K., WHEELER, H. O., HAYS, R. M., AND BRADLEY, S. E.: J. Clin. Invest., **33:** 924, 1954.
DONTAS, A. S., AND NICKERSON, M.: THIS JOURNAL, **120:** 147, 1957.
DUNCAN, D. B.: Biometrica, **11:** 1, 1955.
FREYBURGER, W. A., GRUHZIT, C. C., RENNICK,

B. R., and Moe, G. K.: Amer. J. Physiol., **163:** 554, 1950.
Goldblatt, H., Lynch, J., Hanzal, R. F., and Sommerville, W. W.: Amer. J. Path., **9:** 942, 1933.
Gellhorn, E., and Redgate, E. S.: Arch. int. pharmacodyn., **102:** 162, 1955.
Grimson, K. S.: Arch. Surg., **43:** 1, 1941.
Hamilton, W. F., Jr., Dow, P., and Hamilton, W. F.: Amer. J. Physiol., **161:** 466, 1950.
Maxwell, R. A., Plummer, A. J., and Ross, S. D.: Fed. Proc., **15:** 1488, 1956a.
Maxwell, R. A., Plummer, A. J., and Ross, S. D.: This Journal, **119:** 167, 1957.
Maxwell, R. A., Plummer, A. J., Ross, S. D., and Osborne, M. W.: Proc. Soc. Exp. Biol. & Med., **92:** 225, 1956b.
Nash, C. B., Davis, F., and Woodbury, R. A.: Amer. J. Physiol., **188:** 107, 1956.
Page, I. H.: J.A.M.A., **113:** 2046, 1939.
Pardo, E. G., Rennick, B. R., and Moe, G. K.: Amer. J. Physiol., **161:** 245, 1950.
Plummer, A. J., Trapold, J. H., Schneider, J. A., Maxwell, R. A., and Earl, A. E.: This Journal, **115:** 172, 1955.
Remington, J. W.: Fed. Proc., **11:** 750, 1952.
Remington, J. W., and Hamilton, W. F.: Amer. J. Physiol., **148:** 25, 1947.
Riecke, W. O., and Everett, N. B.: Amer. J. Physiol., **188:** 403, 1957.
Smith, J. R., and Hoobler, S. W.: Circulation, **14:** 1061, 1956.
Snedecor, G. W.: Statistical Methods, Iowa St. College Press, Ames, 1956.
Trapold, J. H.: This Journal, **119:** 189, 1957.

8040

REACTIVATION OF DFP-INACTIVATED ACETYLCHOLINESTERASE BY MONOISONITROSOACETONE (MINA) AND DIACETYLMONOXIME (DAM) *IN VIVO*[1]

MANOHAR V. RAJAPURKAR[2] AND GEORGE B. KOELLE

WITH THE TECHNICAL ASSISTANCE OF PRISCILLA SMART

Department of Physiology and Pharmacology, Graduate School of Medicine, University of Pennsylvania, Philadelphia 4

Received for publication April 14, 1958

In the search for more effective means of treating poisoning by the alkylphosphate anticholinesterase (anti-ChE) agents, attention during the past few years has been directed to attempts to reactivate the enzyme. The development of compounds which could accomplish this effectively *in vivo* would represent an important therapeutic advance. Antidotes which are used currently, such as atropine, provide protection against the muscarinic components of anti-ChE poisoning, but are of limited efficacy in combating the central respiratory paralysis, and ineffective with respect to peripheral neuromuscular blockade.

It has been found that several nucleophilic agents, particularly oximes and hydroxamic acids, can reactivate acetylcholinesterase (AChE) following its inactivation by alkylphosphate anti-ChE agents *in vitro* (Wilson and Meislich, 1953; Wilson and Ginsburg, 1955; Childs *et al.*, 1955, Jandorf *et al.*, 1955; Hobbiger, 1955). There is also evidence that the reactivation can take place *in vivo* (Kewitz, 1957; Kewitz and Nachmansohn, 1957; Koelle, 1957a; Hobbiger, 1957; Rutland, 1957). Under the proper experimental conditions, the nucleophilic agents have been shown to protect animals against the lethal action of the alkylphosphate anti-ChE's (Kewitz, Wilson and Nachmansohn, 1956; Askew, 1956), and to reverse their neuromuscular blocking effect (Holmes and Robins, 1955; Wills *et al.*, 1957). However, it has not been established that these pharmacological actions are fully, or even partially, dependent upon reactivation of alkylphosphorylated AChE.

In addition to reactivating the enzyme, the oximes and hydroxamic acids can react directly with the alkylphosphate agents, converting them to inactive products (Hackley *et al.*, 1955; Childs *et al.*, 1955). The apparent reactivation measured *in vitro* can result from a combination of these two actions plus the protection of the active enzyme against the alkylphosphate by the nucleophilic agent (Hobbiger, 1956). Since most of the studies of the antidotal effects of the nucleophilic agents have been conducted by injecting the compounds intraperitoneally prior to or shortly after the subcutaneous injection of the anti-ChE agents, the actions other than AChE-reactivation may have been primarily responsible for the protection afforded. This consideration appears of particular importance in the recent study reported by Askew (1956). Of several agents tested for protection against isopropyl methylphosphonofluoridate (sarin) in rats, among the most effective were monoisonitrosoacetone (MINA) and diacetylmonoxime (DAM):

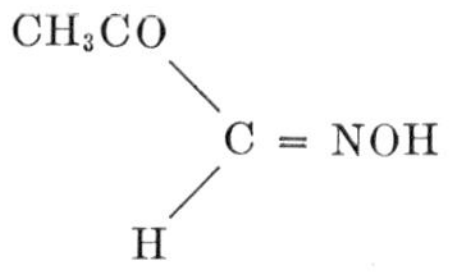

MINA

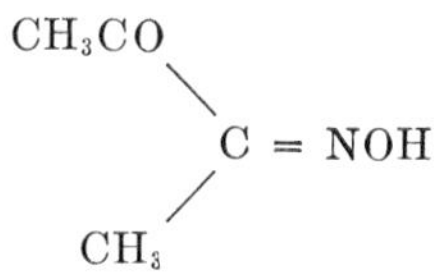

DAM

[1] Taken from a thesis submitted by M. V. Rajapurkar to the Faculty of the Graduate School of Medicine of the University of Pennsylvania, in partial fulfillment of the requirements for the degree of Master of Medical Sciences (M.Sc. (Med.)) in Pharmacology. This investigation was supported by a research grant (B-282 (C 4)) from the National Institute of Neurological Diseases and Blindness, National Institutes of Health, Public Health Service.

[2] On an I.C.A. fellowship of the U. S. Public Health Service, on leave from Nagpur Medical College. Present address: Department of Pharmacology, M. P. Shah, Medical College, Jamnagar, Bombay State, India.

At equimolar doses (0.4 *mM*/kgm.), both compounds, when given prior to sarin, raised the LD_{50} of sarin approximately fivefold. When the same doses of MINA and DAM were given to rats after the onset of signs of intoxication from $2 \times LD_{50}$ ($> LD_{100}$) of sarin, each compound protected equal numbers (9/12) against death. However, signs of anti-ChE poisoning were abolished in the survivors shortly after the administration of MINA, whereas after DAM they persisted for several hours. *In vitro*, MINA inactivates sarin more than five times as rapidly as does DAM (Green and Saville, 1956); the superiority of MINA as a reactivator of the sarin-inactivated enzyme is even greater (Childs *et al.*, 1955). Pyridine-2-aldoxime methiodide (2-PAM), which is a highly effective reactivator of AChE *in vitro* (Wilson and Ginsburg, 1955) provided practically no protection to the sarin-poisoned rats. Thus, the role of AChE-reactivation in the protection afforded by MINA and DAM is questionable.

Recent studies have suggested that normal cholinergic transmission may be dependent upon only the cytologically external or "functional" AChE, which may represent too small a fraction of the total enzyme to be detected by the usual techniques (Koelle and Steiner, 1956; Koelle, 1957b). Histochemically, it has been shown that relatively small doses (0.02 and 0.04 *mM*/kgm., i.v.) of 2-PAM reactivate diisopropylfluorophosphate (DPF)-inactivated AChE of the autonomic ganglia and motor endplates of the cat (Koelle, 1957a). The present investigation was undertaken to determine whether reactivation of DFP-inactivated AChE could be detected by either the histochemical or the Warburg method following MINA or DAM. In addition to elucidating this possible phase of the mechanisms of action of the agents, it was desired to compare the sensitivities of the two methods. Since there is evidence that alkylphosphate-inactivated AChE changes spontaneously from an unstable to a stable form with respect to susceptibility to reactivation (Hobbiger, 1956), the influence of the time-factor was also investigated.[3]

Materials and methods. The procedure followed was in part similar to that reported previously in a histochemical study of the reactivation of DFP-inhibited AChE in the cat by 2-PAM (Koelle, 1957a). In addition, quantitative determinations of AChE-activity of the ganglia and skeletal muscle were conducted with the Warburg apparatus.

Cats of either sex were anesthetized with sodium pentobarbital (30 mgm./kgm., intraperitoneally). Twenty minutes later they were given atropine sulphate (3 mgm./kgm., intraperitoneally), and after 20 minutes the 5 control cats (group A) were sacrificed by the intravenous injection of air. The remaining animals (groups B to F, of 5 cats each) received at this time 20 micromol. (3.68 mgm.)/kgm. of DFP, intravenously. The DFP for injection was always freshly diluted in 0.9 per cent saline solution from a 0.1 *M* stock solution in anhydrous propylene glycol; the stock solution was kept for a period of 2 weeks, during which time it has been found by assay to lose little of its initial AChE-inhibitory potency. The DFP-control cats (group B) were sacrificed 40 minutes after its injection. The remaining groups received the following intravenous doses of reactivator 20 minutes after DFP: groups C and D, 0.04 *mM*/kgm. of MINA and DAM, respectively, and groups E and F, 0.4 *mM*/kgm. of MINA and DAM, respectively. Solutions of MINA and DAM in 0.9 per cent saline solution were prepared from the crystalline material immediately prior to injection. These animals were sacrificed 20 minutes after injection of the reactivator. The sequence of cats used for groups A to D was randomized. Groups E and F were run in pairs, so that one animal of group E was always matched with one of group F, and all procedures were conducted practically simultaneously.

After each cat was sacrificed, the left ciliary ganglion, the left stellate ganglion and a strip of the seventh left intercostal muscle were removed for histochemical examination. Both superior cervical ganglia, the right stellate ganglion, and the entire diaphragm were removed for quantitative determination of AChE-activity. Care was taken to trim the tendinous portion from the diaphragm and the nerve trunks from the ganglia. Whenever possible both the histochemical and Warburg studies were done on the day of the experiment; otherwise, tissues were covered with 0.9 per cent saline solution and stored overnight in the deep-freeze.

Histochemical examination was done according to the established acetylthiocholine method (Koelle and Friedenwald, 1949; Koelle, 1950, 1951, 1955). Ganglia were sectioned on a freezing microtome at 10 micra, muscle at 20 micra. Sections were placed on slides, kept in preincubation solution for 30 minutes, then incubated at 37°C. in acetyl-

[3] We wish to thank Dr. B. J. Jandorf for DFP, and Drs. R. J. Brown and J. H. Wills for MINA and DAM, from the Army Chemical Center, Maryland.

thiocholine medium for 10, 20, 40 or 80 minutes, after which they were developed with $(NH_4)_2S$ solution, gold-toned, dehydrated and mounted. A set of slides incubated for 80 minutes was counterstained with haematoxylin-eosin. Staining was compared in tissues from the 6 groups at each of the incubation periods.

For the Warburg estimations, the right and left superior cervical ganglia were blotted quickly with filter paper, then weighed, and homogenized together in an agate mortar with distilled water (1:200, w/v). The right stellate ganglion was homogenized similarly. The diaphragm was homogenized with 5 parts of distilled water (w/v) in a Waring blendor. The blendor and water were previously chilled in the refrigerator.

All experiments were carried out in the Warburg apparatus at 37°C. with an atmosphere of 5 per cent CO_2—95 per cent N_2. A mixture containing homogenate and final concentrations of 0.03 *M* $NaHCO_3$ and 0.033 *M* $MgCl_2$ was placed in the main wells. Methacholine chloride was tipped in from the side arm to give a final substrate-concentration of 0.03 *M*. The pH after equilibration was 7.6. The total volume of reaction mixture in the microvessels used for the ganglia was 2.0 ml., and in the standard vessels used for muscle was 3.0 ml. Readings for CO_2-liberation were taken at 10, 20, 40 and 70 minutes after the addition of substrate. Figures were corrected for nonenzymatic hydrolysis of the substrate, and CO_2-uptake or production by the homogenate by subtraction of readings from appropriate control vessels. The CO_2-output over the 10 to 70-minute period per unit weight of tissue was then calculated, and expressed as a percentage of the control tissues (group A).

Essentially the same plan was followed for 3 additional groups of two cats each. In this series, the reactivator (MINA or DAM, 0.04 *mM*/kgm.) was injected 60 minutes after DFP, and animals were sacrificed 20 minutes later. The DFP controls were sacrificed 80 minutes after injection of DFP.

RESULTS. Staining for AChE-activity in the tissues taken from control cats was similar to the patterns reported previously (Koelle, 1951, 1955). Staining was intense in the cell membranes and cytoplasm of the cholinergic neurones in the ciliary ganglia. Heavy staining for the enzyme was likewise present in the terminations of the cholinergic preganglionic fibres, which are represented extensively in the stellate ganglion. The adrenergic neurones in the stellate ganglion showed considerably lighter staining. In the intercostal muscle, AChE-activity was concentrated at the motor endplates (fig. 1, column 1).[4]

In the 5 cats treated only with DFP and sacrificed 40 minutes later (group B), there was practically no staining in any of the ganglia after incubation for as long as 80 minutes. The intercostal muscle showed very slight staining of the endplates after 20 minutes' incubation, although it was distinct when incubation was prolonged to 80 minutes (column 2). The same results have been reported in earlier studies (Koelle, 1957a, b).

Administration of the lower dose (0.04 *mM*/kgm., i.v.) of MINA 20 minutes after DFP (0.02 *mM*/kgm., i.v.) resulted in apparent reactivation of AChE in the ganglia of all cats so treated, although the intensity of staining varied considerably in the different animals. In both the ciliary and stellate ganglia, staining was noted at the peripheries and throughout the cytoplasm of cholinergic neurones, and in the fiber tracts and their terminations, represented by the intercellular plexuses. The average intensity of staining of the 20-minute incubated motor endplates of the intercostal muscle fibers in this group was greater than in the DFP-controls (column 3). Tissues from cats which had received the equivalent dose of DAM at the same time-interval showed, in general, less AChE-reactivation (column 4). Both the intensity of staining and the contrast between the degrees of reactivation produced by the two agents were much more marked after the higher dose (0.4 *mM*/kgm.), where the two groups of cats were run as matched pairs. Although there was again some variation in the results obtained with either agent on different days, in every instance the tissues of the MINA-treated cat showed considerably greater AChE-activity than those of the animal treated simultaneously with DAM (columns 5 and 6).

In the two DFP-control cats sacrificed at 80 minutes there was faint staining for AChE in the cytoplasm of the ganglionic neurones, indicating that synthesis of new enzyme had taken place subsequent to inactivation. The ganglia of the two animals which had received 0.04 *mM* of MINA/kgm. 60 minutes after DFP showed slightly greater staining than did those of the controls, whereas the ganglia of the corresponding 60-minute DAM-treated cats were indistinguish-

[4] Photomicrographs were taken by Mr. E. F. Glifort.

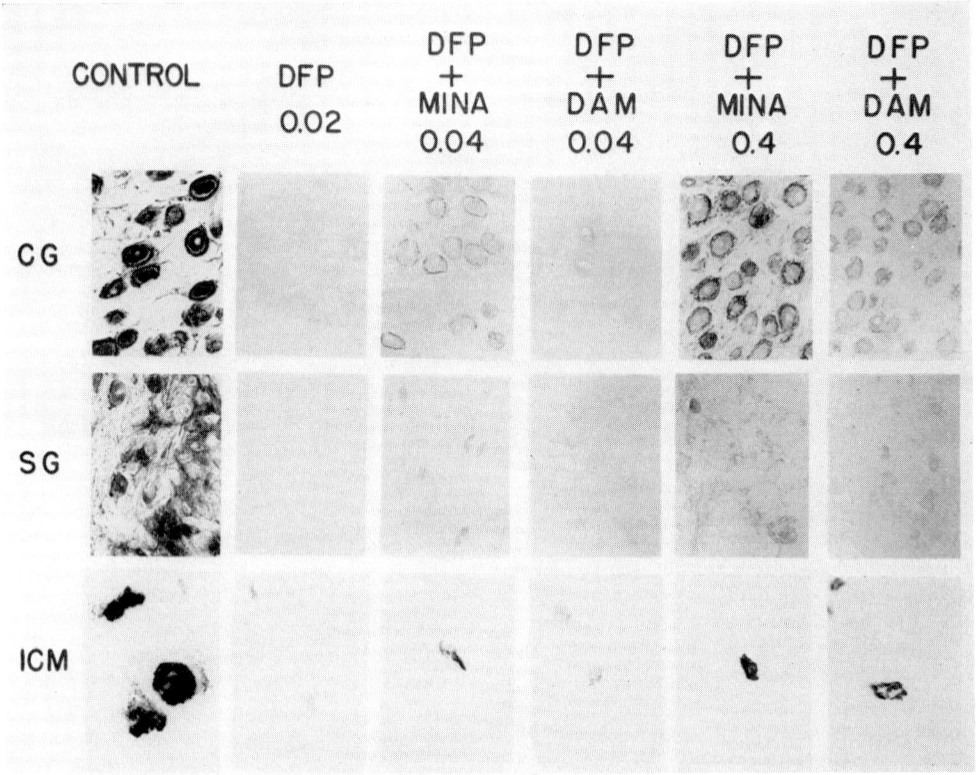

FIG. 1. Sections (10μ) of cat ciliary ganglia (CG) and stellate ganglia (SG) stained for AChE activity by 80 minutes' incubation in AThCh medium; magnification 120 ×.

Intercostal muscle (ICM) sectioned at 20μ, and incubated 20 minutes; magnification 350 ×. All cats excepting controls received 3.68 mgm. (0.02 *mM*) DFP/kgm., i.v., followed in 20 minutes, where indicated, by MINA or DAM, 0.04 or 0.4 *mM*/kgm., i.v., and were sacrificed 40 minutes after DFP.

able from the latter. It was not possible to detect differences between the motor endplates of these three groups.

Quantitative findings. The dose of DFP employed (0.02 *mM*, or 3.68 mgm./kgm., i.v.) is in excess of the LD_{100} in the absence of pretreatment with atropine. In the animals given no reactivator (group B) there was virtually complete inactivation of ganglionic AChE, as detectable by the Warburg technique (table 1). The mean values, and their standard deviations, for the AChE-activities of the superior cervical and stellate ganglia of cats treated with the lower dose (0.04 *mM*/kgm.) of MINA or DAM at 20 minutes indicate that no reactivation occurred. After the higher dose (0.4 *mM*/kgm.) of MINA, there was significant reactivation of AChE in both ganglia, averaging 5 to 8 per cent of the control values. The same dose of DAM produced no detectable AChE-reactivation in the stellate, but possibly slight (one to two per cent) reactivation in the superior cervical ganglia. Although the mean figure for the latter did not differ significantly from that for the DFP controls, the consistency with which activity was detectable, as reflected in the low standard deviation, is suggestive of reactivation.

Acetylcholinesterase-activity was not detectable in the ganglia of the cats treated with the low dose of MINA or DAM at 60 minutes, or in those of the corresponding DFP-controls.

Only one diaphragm-homogenate of the entire series of DFP and reactivator-treated cats showed detectable AChE-activity. This was from an animal which had received the higher dose of MINA, and gave a value of approximately 11 per cent of the mean control figure (1.8 ± 0.2 $mm.^3$ CO_2/10.0 mgm. per hour).

DISCUSSION. The present study has shown that both MINA and DAM are capable of reactivating AChE *in vivo* at ganglionic and neuromuscular sites following its inactivation by DFP. The greater effectiveness noted with MINA is consistent with previous reports of its greater reactivating potency *in vitro*.

Although microscopic histochemical techniques are of limited quantitative significance, the far greater sensitivity of the histochemical procedure than the Warburg method under the conditions of the present investigation is readily apparent. The relative sensitivities and accuracies of microtitrimetric and micromanometric techniques for the same type of study require investigation. The only tissues for which definite evidence of reactivation was obtained by the Warburg method were the ganglia taken from cats which had received the higher (0.4 *mM*/kgm.) dose of MINA 20 minutes after DFP. Yet there was distinct histochemical evidence of AChE-reactivation in the tissues of all MINA- or DAM-treated animals with the exception of the pair which received 0.04 *mM* of DAM/kgm. one hour after DFP. Kewitz (1957) has shown recently that uncombined, $CHCl_3$-extractable DFP may be present in the diaphragms of mice for several hours following its intraperitoneal injection, and may produce further inactivation of residual AChE after homogenization. Although this factor probably contributed to the failure to detect AChE-reactivation in the diaphragmatic tissue by the Warburg method, it is unlikely that it influenced significantly the results obtained with the ganglia, because of the high immediate dilution factor (1 in 200). For the same reason, it can be assumed that no further AChE-reactivation occurred in the ganglionic tissue following homogenization (Hobbiger, 1957).

In a previous histochemical study (Koelle, 1957a), 2-PAM was found to be more effective in reactivating AChE when given one hour after DFP than was MINA under the same conditions in the present investigation, in which DAM was noted to be ineffective. This order of effectiveness is likewise in agreement with the reactivating velocities of the three agents *in vitro*. The decreasing reactivating ability of the nucleophilic agents with the increasing intervals of time of exposure of the enzyme to the alkylphosphates, as noted here, has been studied in detail by Hobbiger (1956), who considers the effect to be due to a progressive transphosphorylation within the enzyme molecule (Wagner-Jauregg and Hackly, 1953; Cohen *et al.*, 1955). The consistently greater intensity of neuronal cytoplasmic staining in the DFP-controls sacrificed at 80 minutes, in comparison with that from the 40 minute cats, has been reported previously (Koelle, 1957a), and attributed to the synthesis of new enzyme, possibly within the endoplasmic reticulum (Porter, 1953; Koelle and Steiner, 1956).

TABLE 1

Acetylcholinesterase activities of cat superior cervical and stellate ganglia after administration of DFP (0.02 mM/kgm., i.v.), followed by MINA or DAM 20 minutes later

Group	Reactivator	Dose, i. v.	Per Cent Control AChE Activity*	
			Superior cervical ganglia	Stellate ganglia
		mM/kgm.		
B	None	—	0†	6.4
	None	—	0	0
	None	—	3.4	0
	None	—	3.7	0
	None	—	0	0
		Mean ± S.D.	*1.4* ± 1.9	*1.3* ± 2.8
C	MINA	0.04	0	0
	MINA	0.04	5.1	1.2
	MINA	0.04	5.2	3.3
	MINA	0.04	0	0
	MINA	0.04	0	0
		Mean ± S.D.	*2.1* ± 2.8	*0.9* ± 1.4
D	DAM	0.04	0	0
	DAM	0.04	0	0
	DAM	0.04	0	0
	DAM	0.04	0	0
	DAM	0.04	0	0
		Mean ± S.D.	*0*	*0*
E	MINA	0.4	1.6	3.1
	MINA	0.4	8.1	13.1
	MINA	0.4	7.4	8.5
	MINA	0.4	4.3	7.1
	MINA	0.4	6.6	7.6
		Mean ± S.D.	*5.6* ± 2.7	*7.9* ± 3.6
F	DAM	0.4	2.2	0
	DAM	0.4	1.3	0
	DAM	0.4	1.6	0
	DAM	0.4	1.8	0
	DAM	0.4	2.0	0
		Mean ± S.D.	*1.8* ± 0.3	*0*

* Mean activities ($mm.^3$ CO_2/10.0 mgm. wet weight per hour) for ganglia of 5 control cats (group A) were: superior cervical, 94 ± 12 and stellate, 67 ± 6.

† Zero activity represents corrected manometric reading of <1.0 mm. over one hour's determination.

Although the ability of a given oxime to reactivate AChE depends upon the alkylphosphate group attached to the enzyme, the species, the time factors involved, and certain other variables, nevertheless the relative reactivating potencies of different oximes and hydroxamic acids under identical conditions remain fairly constant. Therefore the present findings on the reactivation of DFP-inactivated AChE in the cat may be considered to provide a tentative explanation for the results cited above (Askew, 1956), namely, the persistence of signs of intoxication in sarin-poisoned rats following treatment with DAM, in contrast with the rapid reversal of signs noted after an equimolar, equally antilethal dose of MINA. It might be assumed, from the present results, that the same dose (0.4 *mM*/kgm., intraperitoneally) of DAM given in the earlier study reactivated barely enough functional AChE to prevent the accumulation of lethal amounts of ACh at critical synaptic and neuroeffector sites, whereas the equimolar dose of the more effective agent, MINA, reactivated sufficient functional enzyme to abolish all signs of intoxication. It was also noted in the earlier report that with higher doses of DAM, signs of sarin-intoxication could be prevented altogether. Because of its inherent toxicity, MINA could not be tested at higher doses. The previous suggestion (Askew, 1956) that the difference in the responses of sarin-poisoned rats to MINA and DAM might be dependent upon differences in the abilities of the oximes to penetrate to crucial sites is not supported by the present histochemical findings, at least with respect to ganglionic and neuromuscular sites. On the other hand, the failure of the far more potent reactivating agent, 2-PAM, to afford protection under the same conditions of testing may be attributable to its failure to penetrate effectively to the central nervous system (Kewitz, 1957). The importance of the central component in the respiratory failure of poisoning by anti-ChE agents has been stressed by de Candole and associates (1953).

The possibility that actions of MINA and DAM other than reactivation of AChE were also responsible for their ability to prevent death from sarin-poisoning has been discussed (Askew, 1956). Inactivation of the anti-ChE agent prior to its combination with the enzyme seems inadequate to explain the relative degrees of protection reported, since on the basis of their relative activities *in vitro* (Childs *et al.*, 1955), MINA should have been far more effective than the equimolar dose of DAM in raising the LD_{50} of sarin. Other mechanisms to be considered and explored further include protection of the enzyme against the organophosphate (Hobbiger, 1956), and antagonism of ACh, or other direct effects at receptor sites. Reports to date have revealed actions of the latter type only with relatively high doses of MINA or DAM (Holmes and Robins, 1955; Wagley, 1957). However, all these possibilities must be studied for any compound to define the essential mechanisms of the protective action of the nucleophilic agents, as a basis for the development of more effective antidotes.

SUMMARY

A comparison was made of the abilities of monoisonitrosoacetone (MINA) and diacetylmonoxime (DAM) to reactivate diisopropylfluorophosphate (DFP)-inactivated acetylcholinesterase (AChE) of the autonomic ganglia and motor endplates of cats, using both the Warburg and histochemical techniques. By the former method, AChE-reactivation was demonstrated only in ganglionic tissue when the higher dose (0.4 *mM*/kgm., i.v.) of MINA was given 20 minutes after DFP (0.02 *mM*/kgm., i.v.). Reactivation was detected histochemically in ganglia and at the motor endplate after the higher or lower (0.04 *mM*/kgm., i.v.) dose of either agent at the same time interval. Considerably greater reactivation was noted after the higher dose with either agent; at equivalent doses, MINA produced more reactivation than did DAM. When the lower dose of either agent was given one hour after DFP, reactivation was noted at ganglionic sites only after MINA.

Results are discussed in relation to mechanisms other than AChE-reactivation which may contribute to the protection afforded by the nucleophilic agents against alkylphosphate anti-ChE poisoning.

REFERENCES

Askew, B. M.: Brit. J. Pharmacol., **11:** 417, 1956.

Childs, A. F., Davies, D. R., Green, A. L., and Rutland, J. P.: Brit. J. Pharmacol., **10:** 462, 1955.

Cohen, J. A., Oosterbaan, R. A., Warringa, M. G. P. J., and Jansz, H. S.: Faraday Soc. Disc., **20:** 114, 1955.

DE CANDOLE, C. A., DOUGLAS, W. W., EVANS, C. L., HOLMES, R., SPENCER, K. E. V., TORRANCE, R. W., AND WILSON, K. M.: Brit. J. Pharmacol., **8:** 466, 1953.
GREEN, A. L., AND SAVILLE, B.: J. Chem. Soc., 3887, 1956.
HACKLEY, B. E., JR., PLAPINGER, R., STOLBERG, M., AND WAGNER-JAUREGG, T.: J. Am. Chem. Soc., **77:** 3651, 1955.
HOBBIGER, F.: Brit. J. Pharmacol., **10:** 356, 1955.
HOBBIGER, F.: Brit. J. Pharmacol., **11:** 295, 1956.
HOBBIGER, F.: Brit. J. Pharmacol., **12:** 438, 1957.
HOLMES, R., AND ROBINS, E. L.: Brit. J. Pharmacol., **10:** 490, 1955.
JANDORF, B. J., CROWELL, E. A., AND LEVIN, A. P.: Fed. Proc., **14:** 231, 1955.
KEWITZ, H.: Arch. Biochem., **66:** 263, 1957.
KEWITZ, H., AND NACHMANSOHN, D.: Arch. Biochem., **66:** 271, 1957.
KEWITZ, H., WILSON, I. B., AND NACHMANSOHN, D.: Arch. Biochem., **64:** 456, 1956.
KOELLE, G. B.: THIS JOURNAL, **100:** 158, 1950.
KOELLE, G. B.: THIS JOURNAL, **103:** 153, 1951.
KOELLE, G. B.: THIS JOURNAL, **114:** 167, 1955.
KOELLE, G. B.: Science, **125:** 1195, 1957a.
KOELLE, G. B.: THIS JOURNAL, **120:** 488, 1957b.
KOELLE, G. B., AND FRIEDENWALD, J. S.: Proc. Soc. Exper. Biol. & Med., **70:** 617, 1949.
KOELLE, G. B., AND STEINER, E. C.: THIS JOURNAL, **118:** 420, 1956.
PORTER, K. R.: J. Exp. Med., **97:** 727, 1953.
RUTLAND, J. P.: Biochem. J., **66:** 43P, 1957.
WAGLEY, P. F.: Bull. Johns Hopkins Hosp., **100:** 287, 1957.
WAGNER-JAUREGG, J., AND HACKLEY, B. E., JR.: J. Am. Chem. Soc., **75:** 2125, 1953.
WILLS, J. H., KUNKEL, A. M., BROWN, R. V., AND GROBLEWSKI, G. E.: Science, **125:** 743, 1957.
WILSON, I. B., AND GINSBURG, S.: Biochim. et biophys. acta, **18:** 168, 1955.
WILSON, I. B., AND MEISLICH, E. K.: J. Am. Chem. Soc., **75:** 4628, 1953.

8041

THE EXCRETION AND DISTRIBUTION OF MEPROBAMATE AND ITS METABOLITES[1]

SIDNEY S. WALKENSTEIN, CORNELIUS M. KNEBEL, JOYCE A. MACMULLEN AND JOSEPH SEIFTER

Wyeth Institute for Medical Research, Radnor, Pennsylvania

Received for publication May 5, 1958

In earlier studies on the fate of meprobamate (2-methyl-2-n-propyl-1,3-propanediol dicarbamate), Berger (1954) and Agranoff, Bradley and Axelrod (1957) found that about 10 to 12 per cent of the drug was excreted unchanged in the urine along with additional amounts of the drug or its metabolites conjugated with glucuronic acid. The latter investigators found that part of the glucuronide could be hydrolyzed with β-glucuronidase and the remainder with acid or alkali to give meprobamate-like substances. These workers also found fairly uniform distribution of radioactivity in the tissues of rats administered the tritium-labeled drug. Urethane, the only other carbamate whose metabolism has been extensively studied (Bryan, Skipper and White, 1949; Boyland and Rhoden, 1949) was found to be almost completely oxidized to carbon dioxide.

We studied the absorption, sojourn, metabolism and excretion of meprobamate,[2] with the aid of the C^{14}-carbamate labeled drug. Our attention was directed by G. R. Fryers to a report by Bulbrook and Greenwood (unpublished) that meprobamate interfered in the Brown (1955) modification of the Kober test for estriol. This observation suggested possible application of this test to the determination of meprobamate. Other methods proposed are those of Agranoff, Bradley and Axelrod (1957), Ludwig and Hoffman (1957), Ellis, (unpublished), Harris (1958) and Salvesen and Nissen-Meyer (1957), employing respectively, concentrated sulfuric acid, furfural-antimony trichloride, sodium hypochlorite-starch-iodide, nesslerization and the Zimmerman reaction.

MATERIALS AND METHODS. Free meprobamate was determined as follows: 1-ml. aliquots of urine or oxalated plasma were shaken for 1.5 minutes with 5 ml. of ether (Mallinckrodt, anhydrous) in glass-stoppered tubes and then centrifuged. Four ml. of the ether layer were transferred to glass-stoppered tubes containing 400 mgm. of anhydrous potassium carbonate for urine extracts, or 60 mgm. of activated charcoal (Darco G 60) for plasma extracts. The tubes were shaken for 15 seconds and centrifuged. The ether was decanted into other tubes and evaporated in a water bath at 50°C. After addition of 4 ml. of color reagent (prepared by dissolving 2 gm. hydroquinone in a mixture of 85 ml. of concentrated sulfuric acid and 15 ml. of water), the tubes were placed in a boiling water bath and after about one minute glass-stoppered, given a few vigorous shakes, and allowed to remain in the water bath for a total of 25 minutes. The tubes were then cooled to room temperature in cold water. The color, stable for more than 24 hours, was read in a Bausch and Lomb Spectronic 20 colorimeter at 400 mμ. A reagent blank was prepared by subjecting an ether extract of 1 ml. of water to the various steps of the test. Sensitivity of the test could be increased by decreasing the amounts of color reagent added. When the density of the developed color was greater than 0.5, sulfuric acid (85 parts to 15 parts water by volume) was used as a diluent to reduce the reading to below this value. Blanks of dog urine ranged from 0.02 to 0.13 with a mean of 0.08. The range of blank human urines was 0.02 to 0.1 with a mean of 0.05. There was no significant difference between urines of males and females. Plasma blanks from dogs ranged from 0.03 to 0.14 with a mean of 0.1. Reconstituted human plasma gave a reading of 0.1. Meprobamate standards were made up in water at a concentration of 40 microgm. per ml. and run concurrently. Applied to the standard, the urine test gave a density of 0.25 and the plasma test 0.20. When the procedure was simplified by withdrawing the urine layer after ether extraction and adding the potassium carbon-

[1] Presented, in part, at the meetings of the American Society for Pharmacology and Experimental Therapeutics, Baltimore, Maryland, 4–7 September 1957.

[2] Equanil, Wyeth Laboratories.

ate directly to the same tube, the readings were raised about 25 per cent, but the density of the human urine blank also increased to an average of 0.075. When meprobamate was added to plasma and urine Beer's law was found to apply at concentrations between 5 and 60 microgm. per ml., after correction for blank material. Recoveries averaged between 95 and 103 per cent. The method was specific for meprobamate in that the major metabolite, hydroxymeprobamate, and a number of other substances such as urea, various alcohols, lipids and barbiturates did not interfere.

Meprobamate, labeled in both carbamate groups, was prepared by treating the condensation product of C^{14}-phosgene and 2-methyl-2-n-propyl-1,3-propanediol with aqueous ammonia.

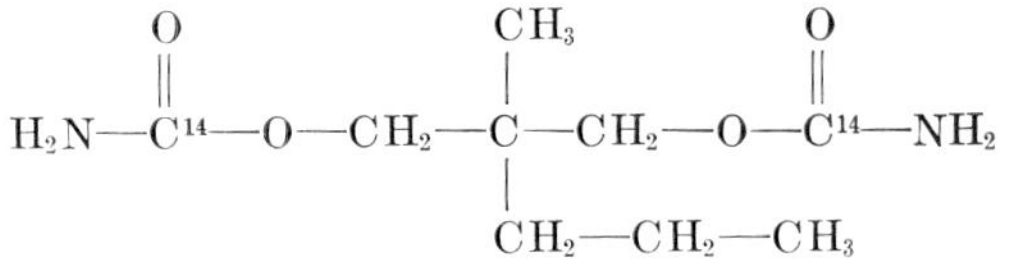

Meprobamate

The product was recrystallized from water and diluted to an activity of 107,000 counts per minute per plate (counted as barium carbonate at infinite thickness in a Nuclear-Chicago flow counter with a micromil window). Radioassay of blood, tissue and excreta was carried out by conversion of samples to barium carbonate and reading at infinite thickness. Nonlabeled meprobamate in blood and urine was determined colorimetrically.

Paper chromatograms of urine and urine extracts on Whatman No. 1 paper were developed in butanol-water (100:15 by volume). Compounds containing the carbamate group were stained by the method of Rydon and Smith (1952). Chromatograms were radio-scanned either manually by passing strips through an improvised adapter on a Tracerlab sample changer, or with a Nuclear-Chicago automatic flow gas counter after sectioning. Radioautographs of the chromatograms were made on Eastman Kodak No-Screen X-ray film.

The results herein reported are based on experiments with 15 dogs, averaging 10 kgm., 20 rats averaging 250 gm., and 9 human subjects.

RESULTS. *Concentrations in plasma.* Although the drug was found to be equally distributed between red cells and plasma, the plasma was used rather than whole blood because of the high blanks given by the latter in the colorimetric test. A comparison of the concentrations of C^{14}-meprobamate (determined colorimetrically) and total metabolites (determined by radioassay) in

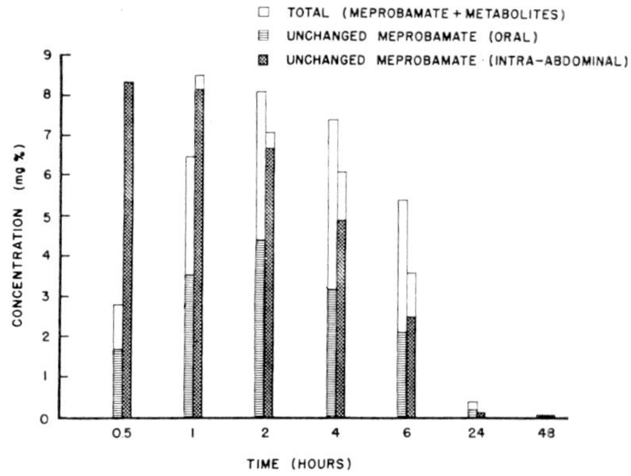

FIG. 1. Levels of meprobamate and metabolites in plasma of dogs.

Total (meprobamate plus metabolites) determined by radioassay, unchanged meprobamate by colorimetry.

the plasma of dogs following oral (5 animals) and intraabdominal (5 animals) administration of 90 mgm. per kgm. of the drug is shown in figure 1. A maximum concentration of 8.5 mgm. per cent of tagged substances was observed between 30 minutes and one hour after intraabdominal injection. After falling 1.4 mgm. per cent between the first and second hours, the plasma level dropped at an average rate of 0.9 mgm. per cent per hour during the next 4 hours. A peak value of 8.1 mgm. per cent was reached 2 hours after the drug was given orally, and the rate of decline averaged 0.7 mgm. per cent per hour from the second to the sixth hour. After an oral dose unchanged meprobamate accounted for only about 50 per cent of the total activity, whereas after intraabdominal injection unchanged meprobamate ranged from 100 per cent 30 minutes after injection to a little less than 70 per cent of the total at the 6th hour.

Excretion. Within one-half hour after either oral or intraabdominal administration of labeled meprobamate to dogs, significant amounts of C^{14} appeared in the urine (figure 2). By the first hour a maximum excretion rate of 11.5 per cent of the dose per hour was reached by the intraabdominal group (4 dogs). This value is about 5 times the rate for the oral group (6 dogs). Between the first and second hours the rate of the former group fell to about 10 per cent per hour, and that of the oral group rose to over 5 per cent per hour. Over the same period the rate for the intraabdominal group fell from 6 per cent to 2.5 per cent per hour. Both groups continued to

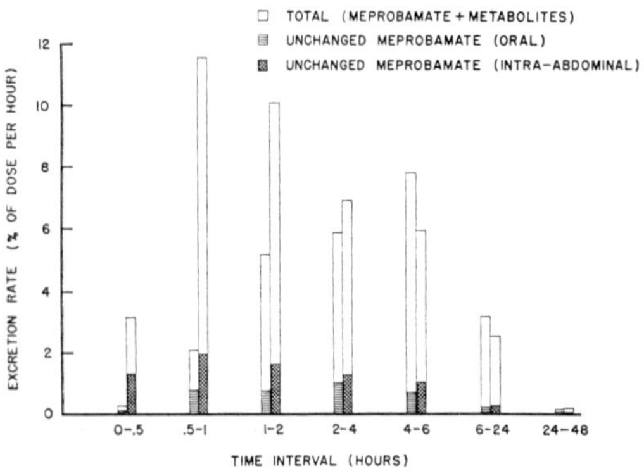

FIG. 2. Levels of meprobamate and metabolites in urine of dogs.

Total (meprobamate plus metabolites) determined by radioassay, unchanged meprobamate by colorimetry.

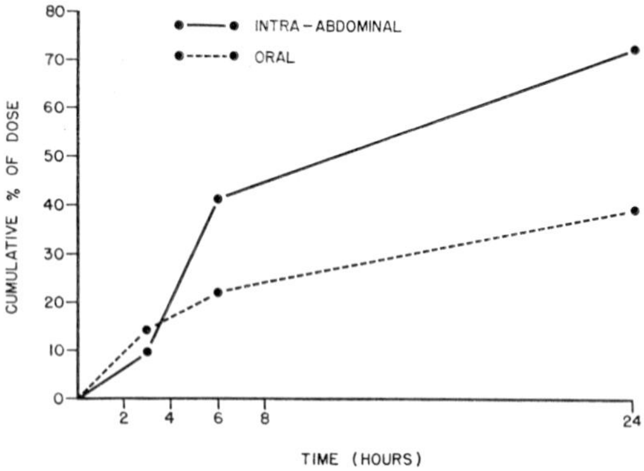

FIG. 3. Content of C^{14} in urine of rats following oral and intraabdominal administration of C^{14}-meprobamate.

excrete detectable amounts of radioactivity (about 3.5 per cent of the dose) over the next 24 hours, although almost 90 per cent of the dose had been excreted within the first 24-hour period.

Although the C^{14} totals excreted by both groups were commensurate with the levels found in plasma, the ratios of unchanged meprobamate in urine were far less. Unchanged meprobamate accounted for about one-half of the total C^{14} excreted by the oral group the first one-half hour. The ratio fell to 10 per cent by the sixth hour. The ratios for the intraabdominal group ranged from about 40 per cent the first one-half hour to about 17 per cent by the sixth hour. As mentioned previously, over the same period, the ratio between unchanged meprobamate and total C^{14} in plasma remained at about 50 per cent for the oral group and ranged from 100 per cent to 70 per cent for the intraabdominal group. The remaining 10 per cent of the dose not appearing in the urine was recovered in the feces.

Rats given oral doses (400 mgm. per kgm.) of tagged meprobamate appear to excrete the labeled carbon at one-half the rate of intra-abdominally injected animals (figure 3) and both groups at a lower rate than the corresponding groups of dogs. By 24 hours only 40 per cent of the orally administered drug was found in the urine, as contrasted with 70 per cent from the intraabdominal group. The lower rate of urinary excretion after an oral dose was neither accounted for by increased elimination through the bowel since feces contained only 7 per cent of the dose, nor was it in the expired air since the activity of the respiratory carbon dioxide amounted to only about one per cent of the administered C^{14}.

TABLE 1

Urinary excretion of unchanged meprobamate by nine human subjects following a single oral dose of one gram

Collection Period	Amount of Dose Excreted
hours	*% ± S.E.*
0–2	0.66 ± 0.21
2–4	1.35 ± 0.10
4–8	2.26 ± 0.41
8–12	2.46 ± 0.38
12–24	2.64 ± 0.70
24–36	1.43 ± 0.35
36–48	0.93 ± 0.18

In a preliminary study 9 human subjects were each given 1 gm. of the unlabeled drug by mouth and the urine collected for the next 48 hours. The amount of unchanged meprobamate excreted during the first 2 hours averaged 0.66 per cent of the dose (table 1). The excretion rate doubled during the next 2 hours to 0.68 per cent per hour and remained at about this level to the twelfth hour. By this time a little less than 7 per cent of the dose was excreted unchanged. An additional 2.64 per cent was excreted between the twelfth and twenty-fourth hours, 1.43 per cent between the twenty-fourth and thirty-sixth hours and an additional 0.93 per cent during the last 12 hours. The excretion rate for the 12-hour period between the thirty-sixth and forty-eighth hours was 0.08 per cent per hour. Altogether, about 11.5 per cent of the administered meprobamate was excreted unchanged during the 48-hour period. One of the subjects excreted as much as 19 per cent of the dose unchanged and another only 8 per cent. These values represent the extremes, however, and the values for the remaining 7 subjects ranged from 9 to 13 per cent.

Distribution. Ten rats were given labeled meprobamate (400 mgm./kgm.) by stomach tube and decapitated in groups of 2 at the time intervals shown in table 2. The persistent high specific activity of the stomach, indicative of a low rate of gastric emptying explains the slow excretion rate observed in this species when the drug was administered orally (figure 3). Even at 24 hours a considerable amount of the dose remained in the stomach. On the other hand, from the rapid decline in activity of intestine and cecum between 30 minutes and one hour after the dose, paralleling the decline in other tissues, it is apparent that the drug was readily absorbed from the intestinal tract. Furthermore, this substantiated the previous observation that this was not a major route of excretion. Brain and fat concentrated less activity than the other tissues during the first hour, but by the third hour the brain manifested the average level of activity. There was no accumulation in adipose tissue as represented by perirenal fat; the 24-hour sample contained no labeled carbon.

In another experiment conducted to determine whether the drug would pass the placental barrier, a group of 6 rats, about two weeks pregnant, were given the labeled drug intraabdominally and decapitated fifteen to thirty minutes later. The placenta, chorion, amnion, amniotic fluid and fetus were all found to contain about the same concentrations of radioactivity as the liver of the parent.

TABLE 2

*Distribution of C^{14} in rat tissue following oral administration of labeled meprobamate**

Tissues Studied	½ Hr.	1 Hr.	3 Hr.	6 Hr.	24 Hr.
Stomach†	1785	1365	662	425	216
Intestine†	131	59	60	82	5
Cecum†	111	19	51	54	21
Lung	230	73	102	48	14
Liver	137	77	55	55	8
Heart	119	62	29	23	3
Spleen	95	72	44	42	15
Kidney	150	51	92	39	9
Brain	19	29	52	31	4
Fat	36	28	19	6	0

* Figures denote specific activity (cpm per gram of tissue).

† Includes contents.

TABLE 3

Urinary excretion products of meprobamate in dogs

Metabolite	R_f	Identity	Per Cent of Dose Excreted
1	0.8	Meprobamate	10–12
2	0.6	Hydroxymeprobamate	60
3	0.3	Unknown	1–1.5
4	0.06	Glucuronide	5–10
5	0.03	Glucuronide	5–10

Metabolism. Failure to locate more than one or two per cent of the labeled carbamate carbon in the respired air indicated that these groups were resistant to hydrolysis. This was not anticipated in view of the urethane studies (Bryan, Skipper and White, 1949; Boyland and Rhoden, 1949) where this compound was found to be almost completely converted to carbon dioxide. However, the fact that the carbamate groups in meprobamate remained intact simplified the task of isolating metabolites. We were able to distinguish 5 distinct metabolites on radioautographs of paper chromatograms of dog and rat urine collected after administration of the labeled drug. R_f values, known or suspected identity, and the mean amounts excreted in dog urine during the 48 hours after administration of the doses are shown in table 3. However, as pointed out in the section on excretion, meprobamate accounts for about one-half of the total amount of metabolites excreted during the first one-half hour. The R_f values indicated are those found in dog urine. The metabolites excreted in rat urine had R_f values identical with those in dog urine except for the glucuronide fraction where the R_f values were 0.07 and 0.15 in the former species, and 0.03 and 0.06 in the latter.

The identity of the material at R_f 0.8 with meprobamate was confirmed by isotope dilution. In the initial attempts to identify the material at R_f 0.6, our attention was focused on the methyl and propyl side chains as the most likely point of attack. Oxidation at the 1- or 3-positions of the propanediol skeleton was ruled out because of the absence of labeled respiratory carbon dioxide which this unstable intermediate should give rise to. The possibility that the methyl group was either removed or displaced was also investigated. However, the demethylated compound 2-n-propyl-1,3-propanediol dicarbamate differed in R_f value from metabolite 2, and when this compound was fed to dogs it failed to give rise to this metabolite. That the propyl group probably remained intact was indicated by failure of 2-allyl-2-methyl-1,3-propanediol dicarbamate to give rise to this metabolite. We had in the meantime isolated a sufficient quantity of metabolite 2 for analysis. The results were consistent with the structure for a hydroxymeprobamate (calculated: C 46.16, H 7.69, N 11.97 per cent; found: C 45.96, H 7.81, N 11.82 per cent). The ceric nitrate test for alcohols was applied and was found to be positive. Infrared analysis was inconclusive since NH absorption occurred in the region where OH would be expected to absorb. The metabolite was compared chromatographically with an authentic sample of 2-hydroxymethyl-2-n-propyl-1,3-propanediol dicarbamate and was found to have the same R_f value. Finally, nonlabeled hydroxymeprobamate was added to urine samples obtained from dogs given labeled meprobamate. The hydroxymeprobamate was extracted and recrystallized to constant specific activity. The results established the identity of the metabolite and indicated that approximately 60 per cent of the dose was excreted in this form. This compound and the corresponding tricarbamate were both tested pharmacologically in dogs and found to lack meprobamate-like activity.

Eluates of metabolites 4 and 5 from paper chromatograms gave positive naphthoresorcinol tests for glucuronides. When these metabolites were incubated (Beer and Gallagher, 1955) separately with β-glucuronidase (Worthington Biochemical Corp.) metabolite 3 appeared to be released from metabolite 5 and metabolite 2, hydroxymeprobamate, from metabolite 4. Metabolite 3 has not been further identified.

SUMMARY

The absorption, excretion, distribution and metabolism of C^{14}-labeled meprobamate, labeled in both carbamate groups, following oral and intraabdominal injection was studied in rats and dogs and of the nonlabeled drug after oral administration to humans. The drug was found to be readily absorbed from the gastrointestinal tract. Significant amounts of C^{14} began to appear in the urine within 30 minutes after an oral or intraabdominal dose and by 24 hours most had been excreted. Feces contained less than 10 per cent of the dose. Blood levels of C^{14} reached a peak two hours after oral administration; 50 per cent of the amount present was unchanged meprobamate. After administration of the drug to rats, lung, kidney and liver were found to have the highest levels of radioactivity.

The major metabolite, accounting for approximately 60 per cent of the dose in dogs, was isolated and identified as hydroxymeprobamate (2 - hydroxymethyl - 2 - n - propyl - 1,3 - propanediol dicarbamate). When this compound or the corresponding tricarbamate was administered to dogs no meprobamate-like activity was observed.

A specific colorimetric method for determination of meprobamate in plasma and urine based on the Brown modification of the Kober reaction was developed and is sensitive to concentrations as low as 5 microgm. per ml.

ACKNOWLEDGMENT. The authors gratefully acknowledge the assistance of Dr. Benjamin L. Hayllar in the clinical portion of these studies, and their indebtedness to Dr. Cathryn Gudmundsen for synthesis of hydroxymeprobamate, to Miss Hazel Kimmel and Mr. James R. King for their technical assistance, and to Dr. B. J. Ludwig of Wallace Laboratories for samples of compounds related to meprobamate.

REFERENCES

AGRANOFF, B. W., BRADLEY, R. M., AND AXELROD, J.: Proc. Soc. Exper. Biol. & Med., **96:** 261, 1957.
BEER, C. T., AND GALLAGHER, T. F.: J. Biol. Chem., **214:** 335, 1955.
BERGER, F. M.: THIS JOURNAL, **112:** 413, 1954.
BOYLAND, E., AND RHODEN, E.: Biochem. J., **44:** 528, 1949.
BROWN, J. B.: Biochem. J., **60:** 185, 1955.
BRYAN, C. E., SKIPPER, H. E., AND WHITE, L.: J. Biol. Chem., **177:** 941, 1949.
HARRIS, E.: Clin. Chem., in press, 1958.
LUDWIG, B. J., AND HOFFMAN, A. J.: Arch. Biochem., **72:** 234, 1957.
RYDON, H. N., AND SMITH, P. W. G.: Nature, **169:** 922, 1952.
SALVESEN, S., AND NISSEN-MEYER, R.: J. Clin. Endocrinol., **17:** 914, 1957.

8042

STUDIES ON THE METABOLISM OF NORNICOTINE IN THE DOG[1, 2, 3]

HOWARD B. HUCKER[4] AND P. S. LARSON

Department of Pharmacology, Medical College of Virginia, Richmond

Received for publication April 3, 1958

In comparison to nicotine[5], nornicotine, the second most important alkaloid in *Nicotiana tabacum*, has received little attention, especially in regard to its metabolism in the mammal. The only reports of this type (Larson and Haag, 1943; Larson, Haag and Finnegan, 1945) compare the over-all rate of disposition (excretion and metabolism) of nicotine and nornicotine in two species. Using the technique of Weatherby (1939), by administration of fractional LD_{50} doses over a period of time to the point of death, it was found that the rabbit disposes of nicotine and nornicotine at comparable rates, whereas the mouse disposes of nicotine much more rapidly than nornicotine. A difference in the acute toxicity for the two species also exists (Larson, Haag and Finnegan, 1945) since nicotine was found to be definitely more toxic than nornicotine to the mouse when administered intravenously, but less toxic than nornicotine to the rabbit.

Larson and Haag (1943) also reported a single observation on the fate of nornicotine in the dog, finding that 6.5 per cent of a dose of nornicotine administered subutaneously was excreted apparently unchanged in the urine. Wada (1956, 1957) has reported the isolation of 3-succinoyl-6-hydroxypyridine and 6-hydroxymyosmine from the degradation of nornicotine by microorganisms isolated from soil.

The relation of the amount of nicotine excreted unchanged to the administered dose has been established for the dog by Finnegan, Larson and Haag (1947). The present report deals with a similar study on nornicotine and, since structurally nicotine and nornicotine differ only in the pyrrolidine nitrogen sustituent, the results illustrate the profound effect that N-demethylation may have on some pharmacological properties of alkaloids of this type.

MATERIALS AND METHODS. Nornicotine was isolated from Maryland Burley tobaccos by percolation of the tobacco with water, followed by extraction of the nicotine and nornicotine from the concentrated alkalinized solution with chloroform. The chloroform was removed *in vacuo* and the mixture distilled. Treatment of the distillate with benzoyl chloride gave a mixture of nicotine and benzoylnornicotine. The nicotine was removed *in vacuo* and the residual benzoylnornicotine hydrolyzed by heating with concentrated hydrochloric acid for 72 hours. The mixture of *l*- and *dl*-nornicotine obtained was treated with perchloric acid (70 per cent), and the crystalline perchlorate salt of the *l*-isomer filtered off and purified according to the procedure of Spath and Zajic (1935). The nornicotine isolated had the following properties: $[\alpha]_D^{25}$, −81.7° (88.8°, Spath and Zajic); dipicrate, m.p. 191–2°C., (191–2°, Spath and Zajic); n_D^{24} 1.5470 (1.5469, Swain *et al.*, 1949).

A procedure similar to that employed by Finnegan *et al.* (1947) was used in the animal experiments. Female dogs under Dial (diallylbarbituric acid) anesthesia were given nornicotine (dissolved in isotonic saline) in dose levels of 3, 6, 9, 12, 15, 18 and 24 mgm./kgm. body weight. Three or more animals were used at each dose level. The solution of the alkaloid was infused over an 8-hour period via a femoral vein at the rate of 1 ml./minute. Carotid blood pressure tracings were made and respiration was recorded by means of a pneumograph.

Dose levels of 9 mgm./kgm. and higher produced respiratory paralysis during the infusion period, the onset of which was judged by the character of the respiratory tracing and the sharp rise of arterial blood pressure. At the onset of failure,

[1] The data herein form a part of the thesis submitted by Howard B. Hucker in partial fulfillment of the requirements for the degree of Doctor of Science, Medical College of Virginia, 1957.

[2] This investigation was supported by a research grant from the American Tobacco Company.

[3] A preliminary report of this investigation was presented to the American Society for Pharmacology and Experimental Therapeutics, French Link, Indiana, October, 1956.

[4] Present address: National Heart Institute, Bethesda, Md.

[5] Throughout this report the terms nicotine and nornicotine will be used to designate the *l*- or (-) isomers.

positive pressure artificial respiration was instituted through a tracheal cannula. This was maintained until the earliest time following completion of the infusion period that the animal could breathe voluntarily, as shown by interrupting the artificial respiration at 15- to 30-minute intervals.

Urine was collected via an indwelling catheter for 24 hours after the start of the infusion and in those experiments where respiratory paralysis ensued, was collected fractionally as follows: that formed prior to respiratory paralysis, that formed during respiratory paralysis, and that formed after respiratory paralysis. In some cases, a 24 to 30 hour sample was also collected.

An aliquot (25 ml.) of the urine, together with 10 ml. of 10 *N* sodium hydroxide, 5 ml. of water,

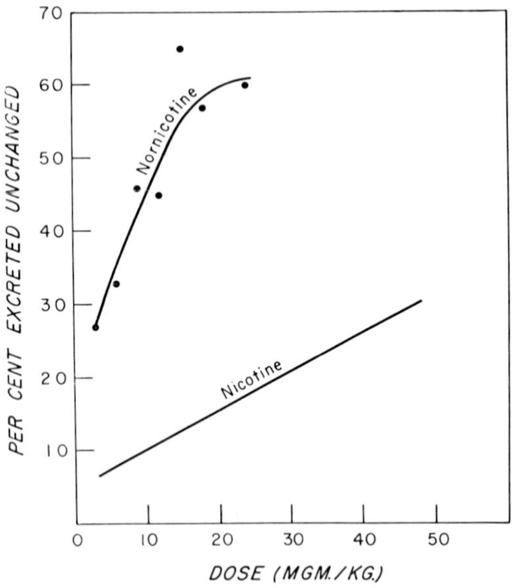

FIG. 1. Relation of nornicotine dosage to per cent excreted unchanged in the urine.
Data for nicotine for comparison is from Finnegan *et al.* (1947).

10 gm. of sodium chloride and an antifoaming agent (Dow-Corning) was distilled until 30 ml. of distillate had collected. Nornicotine was determined colorimetrically by a modification of the method of Larson and Haag (1944). After adjusting the pH of the distillate to 4.1 to 4.2, a suitable aliquot (1.0 to 6.0 ml.) was added to a test tube containing 2.0 ml. of potassium dihydrogen phosphate buffer (1.67 *M*). The final volume was brought to 8.0 ml. by addition of water. After heating in a water bath kept at 80°C. for 5 minutes, the tube was removed for an interval of 15 seconds, during which 2.0 ml. of a 4 per cent solution of cyanogen bromide (Eastman) in water were added, with shaking. Heating was continued for 1 minute and 45 seconds longer, after which the tube was placed in ice-water and allowed to remain for one minute. The per cent transmission at 540 mμ was measured against a control cuvette containing all of the components except the cyanogen bromide. The amount of nornicotine present in the distillate was estimated by reference to a standard curve, prepared by reacting known amounts of nornicotine with cyanogen bromide under identical conditions. The limit of sensitivity of the method is 10 microgm. of nornicotine/ml. of urine.

Since nornicotine could not be quantitatively recovered by distillation from urine, the amount present in the distillate was corrected for recovery. Distillation of standard solutions of nornicotine in normal dog urine gave recoveries of 72 $\pm$ 6 per cent, over the range of 10 to 480 microgm./ml. of urine. This method of correction was shown to be applicable to experimental urine samples in the following manner. Experimental urine samples were distilled, the distillates analyzed as described above, and the nornicotine content (expressed as x mgm.) corrected for 72 per cent recovery. Known amounts of nornicotine (6.0 mgm.) were added to other urine aliquots. Analysis of the distillates, corrected for recovery, showed the presence of 88 to 95 per cent

TABLE 1
*Effect of dosage on rates of metabolism and urinary excretion of nornicotine**

Dose	Ave. Time Onset Respiratory Paralysis	Period of Respiratory Paralysis					
		Average duration	Ave. amount nornicotine injected	Ave. amount of nornicotine excreted	Injected minus excreted	Ave. rate of metabolism	Ave. rate of excretion
mgm./kgm.	*hr.*	*hr.*	*mgm./kgm.*	*mgm./kgm.*	*mgm./kgm.*	*mgm./kgm./hr*	*mgm./kgm./hr*
12	3.19 ± 0.77	8.86 ± 1.03	7.2	3.11 ± 0.3	4.1	0.46	0.35
15	2.44 ± 0.54	10.08 ± 1.30	10.4	6.9 ± 1.4	3.5	0.35	0.68
18	2.63 ± 0.62	12.39 ± 3.07	12.1	7.6 ± 0.4	4.5	0.36	0.61
24	1.18 ± 0.10	17.32 ± 2.45	20.5	13.6 ± 1.9	6.9	0.40	0.78

* The figures are the means of the group and the standard deviations.

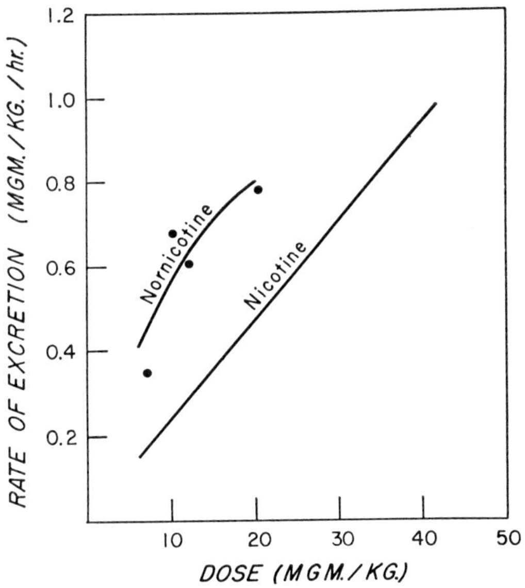

FIG. 2. Rate of urinary excretion of nornicotine in relation to dose.
Data for nicotine for comparison is from Finnegan *et al.* (1947).

point of the mixture was not depressed. The infrared spectrum[6] of the picrate showed no significant variation from that of an authentic sample of nornicotine dipicrate. Carbon-hydrogen analyses[7] of the picrate agreed closely with the calculated values: calculated for $C_{21}H_{17}O_{14}N_8$; C, 41.59; H, 2.99: Found; C, 41.61; H, 2.92.

The urine distillates were also analyzed for nornicotine by the spectrophotometric method of Willitts *et al.* (1950). Satisfactory agreement between the two methods of analysis was obtained with samples in which the nornicotine concentration was greater than 0.15 mgm./ml. but, for lower concentrations, this method was less satisfactory due to high blank readings.

RESULTS. The results of the excretion studies on nornicotine are summarized in figure 1 together with similar data reported for nicotine (Finnegan *et al.* 1947). It is evident that the per cent of nornicotine excreted unchanged in the urine increases much more rapidly with increasing dose than is true for nicotine. The two alkaloids likewise differ in that the per cent of nornicotine

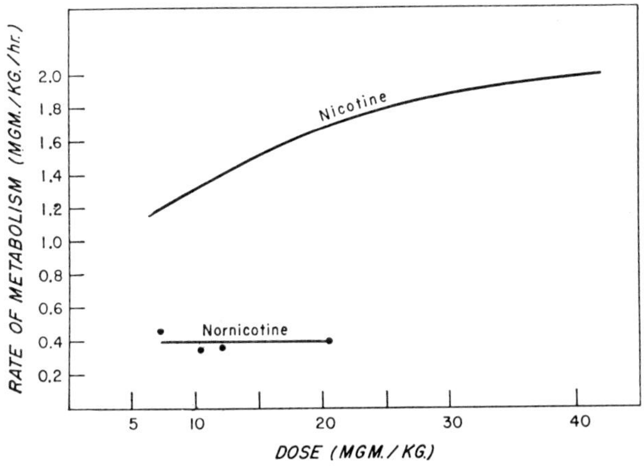

FIG. 3. Rate of metabolism of nornicotine in relation to dose.
Data for nicotine for comparison is from Finnegan *et al.* (1947).

of the amount of nornicotine estimated to be present (x + 6.0 mgm.) by use of the recovery curve.

Further direct evidence that the procedure used for estimation of the nornicotine in the urine was free of significant error was obtained by the isolation of nornicotine (as the dipicrate) from pooled urine distillates in the amount estimated to be present.

The melting point of the picrate obtained from experimental urines was identical with that of authentic nornicotine dipicrate, and the melting

excreted unchanged apparently reaches a maximum (*ca.* 60 per cent) at a dose level of approximately 24 mgm./kgm. whereas the per cent of nicotine excreted unchanged has not reached a maximum value at a dose of 48 mgm./kgm. Excretion of either alkaloid is virtually complete

[6] Kindly determined by Mr. W. B. Wartman of The American Tobacco Company Research Laboratory.
[7] Spang Microanalytical Laboratory, Ann Arbor, Michigan.

within 16 hours following cessation of administration.

The divergent patterns of excretion of the two alkaloids probably result partly from the difference in basicity of the two compounds. Nornicotine, being the stronger base would, at urinary pH, exist to a greater degree in the ionized form and therefore would presumably be less readily reabsorbed by the kidney tubules. The slower rate of metabolism of nornicotine (see below) would also result in more of it being available for excretion.

The rates of excretion and metabolism of nornicotine, for those dose levels that produced respiratory paralysis, are summarized in table 1 and in figures 2 and 3, along with similar data reported for nicotine. The calculations in table 1 are based on the assumption that the body-fluid concentration of nornicotine at resumption of voluntary respiration is essentially the same as that at the onset of respiratory paralysis. This assumption is valid if steady-state conditions prevailed throughout the experiment. Rate of metabolism calculations assume that virtually all unchanged nornicotine like nicotine (Bennett *et al.*, 1954) is excreted in the urine.

In these calculations, the data obtained at the 9 mgm./kgm. dose level were not included since inherent analytical errors are considerably greater because of the relatively brief duration of respiratory paralysis.

The excretion data show that, like nicotine, there is an increased rate of excretion of nornicotine in the urine with increasing dosage (table 1 and figure 2). The rate for nornicotine is seemingly greater and increases more rapidly with increasing dosage than that for nicotine.

Of considerable interest is the discovery that the rate of detoxication for nornicotine is apparently independent of increasing dosage within the range studied (table 1 and figure 3). Particularly in this respect are the two alkaloids strikingly different since the rate of nicotine detoxication increases exponentially with the dose and is decidedly greater than the rate for nornicotine. The metabolism of ethyl alcohol has also been reported to proceed at a rate which is independent of the dosage.

The greater ease of detoxication of nicotine compared to nornicotine is clearly demonstrated also in the times of onset and duration of respiratory paralysis produced by equal doses of the two alkaloids. The onset of respiratory paralysis is more rapid and the duration much longer for nornicotine for any given effective dose, in spite of the fact that nornicotine is being excreted more rapidly.

During the course of this investigation, the intravenous LD_{50} of nornicotine in mongrel dogs of mixed sexes under pentobarbital anesthesia was found to be 4.0 ± 0.2 mgm./kgm., compared to 5.0 mgm./kgm. reported for nicotine (Larson *et al.*, 1949).

SUMMARY

Total per cent excretion of nornicotine in the urine increases with increasing dosage up to a peak of approximately 60 per cent at dose levels of 15 mgm./kgm. and above.

The rate of urinary excretion of nornicotine increases with increasing dosage.

The rate of detoxication of nornicotine appears to be independent of dosage at the levels studied.

Urinary excretion of nornicotine is virtually complete within 16 hours after cessation of administration.

The intravenous LD_{50} of nornicotine in dogs is 4.0 mgm./kgm.

REFERENCES

Bennett, D. R., Tedeschi, R. E., and Larson, P. S.: Arch. int. pharmacodyn., **98:** 221, 1954.
Finnegan, J. K., Larson, P. S., and Haag, H. B.: This Journal, **91:** 357, 1947.
Larson, P. S., and Haag, H. B.: This Journal, **77:** 343, 1943.
Larson, P. S., and Haag, H. B.: Indust. and Eng. Chem. Analyt. Ed., **16:** 86, 1944.
Larson, P. S., Haag, H. B., and Finnegan, J. K.: Proc. Soc. Exper. Biol. & Med., **58:** 231, 1945.
Larson, P. S., Finnegan, J. K., and Haag, H. B.: This Journal, **95:** 506, 1949.
Spath, E., and Zajic, E.: Ber. deutsch. chemisch. Gesellsch., **68B:** 1667, 1935.
Swain, M. L., Eisner, A., Woodward, C. F., and Brice, B. A.: J. Am. Chem. Soc., **71:** 1341, 1949.
Wada, E.: Arch. Biochem., **64:** 244, 1956.
Wada, E.: Arch. Biochem., **72:** 145, 1957.
Weatherby, J. H.: Proc. Soc. Exper. Biol. & Med., **42:** 593, 1939.
Willitts, C. O., Swain, M. L., Connelly, J. A., and Brice, B. A.: Anal. Chem., **22:** 430, 1950.

8043

RELATIONS BETWEEN CALCIUM AND POTASSIUM TRANSFER IN HUMAN ERYTHROCYTES[1]

J. B. KAHN, JR.[2]

Department of Pharmacology, University of Cincinnati College of Medicine, Cincinnati 19, Ohio

Received for publication May 9, 1958

Among the substances which can affect the active transport of potassium into human erythrocytes are cardiac glycosides and their genins (Schatzmann, 1953), other lactones (Kahn, 1957), purines and related compounds (Kahn and Cohen, 1957), rubidium ions (Solomon, 1952), and changes in external sodium concentration (*cf.* Maizels, 1954). Antedating these investigations was the report by Levi (1945) that "... the permeability of red cells to potassium ions *in vitro* is markedly reduced in the presence of increasing amounts of calcium." This finding was not quantified in the original report; it has not been confirmed since, though Solomon and Rees (1953) stated that "... Ca and/or Mg may be implicated in red cell K transport." The statement about "permeability" does not permit one to judge which aspect of transport may be affected—active or passive, influx or efflux. Cold-storage stops the metabolic processes responsible for potassium accumulation, and the cation diffuses out of the cell. Incubation of potassium-depleted cold-stored cells at 37°C. permits the resumption of active potassium accumulation. We have investigated the effects of varying the external calcium ion concentration upon the active re-entry of potassium into incubated cold-stored human red cells.

During these studies red cells were suspended in buffer as well as in plasma. This operation affected the rate of loss of potassium from the suspending medium. We therefore compared the loss of potassium from buffer into cells with that from plasma into cells, and the effects of agents which could affect the rate of transport in the two systems.

The disappearance of radioactive calcium (Ca^{45}) from the plasma of fresh and of cold-stored blood was also examined. Tests were applied to determine whether the loss of Ca^{45} from the plasma of the two kinds of blood fulfilled any criteria of active transport.

MATERIALS AND METHODS. Blood was procured and stored as previously described (Kahn and Acheson, 1955) unless otherwise specified. Potassium concentrations of plasma and whole blood were determined with a Baird flame photometer internally standardized with 10^{-14} lithium.

The buffer used with fresh cells had the following composition: KCl, 5 *mM*/l.; Na_2HPO_4, 6 *mM*/l.; NaH_2PO_4, 2 *mM*/l.; NaCl, 141 *mM*/l.; glucose, 2.5 gm./l. Its pH was 7.35. Blood cold-stored for 6 days has a plasma potassium concentration of 32 *mM*/l. (Kahn and Acheson, 1955); hence, when cold-stored cells were washed or incubated in buffer, the latter was prepared with this KCl concentration. This increase was compensated for by an equivalent decrease in NaCl concentration. When calcium or other divalent cations were added to the buffer an equivalent amount of sodium was withheld.

Two sets of experiments were performed to study the effects of the medium on potassium influx. In the first, cells were cold-stored in plasma, and the blood was divided into three aliquots. The cells of the first were the controls, and were incubated in plasma. The cells of the second were washed twice with buffer and then returned to their plasma for incubation. The cells of the third were both washed and incubated in buffer. In the second series, 4 types of cells were compared: 1) controls, cold-stored and incubated in plasma; 2) cold-stored in plasma, incubated in buffer; 3) cold-stored in buffer, incubated in plasma; and 4) cold-stored and incubated in buffer. Results of both kinds of experiments are expressed as per cent of the potassium influx of the control cells, to avoid the variation between blood from different donors.

The effects of calcium concentration on potassium influx were studied in cold-stored cells incubated in plasma or buffer. High plasma cal-

[1] Supported in part by Grant #H-1506 (C3), National Heart Institute, U.S.P.H.S.

[2] John and Mary R. Markle Scholar in Medical Science, 1954–59.

cium concentrations were achieved by adding $CaCl_2$ to blood just before incubation. Low concentrations of free calcium in plasma were obtained by adding ethylenediaminetetraacetic acid (EDTA) to the blood. No measurements of plasma calcium were made; control levels were assumed to be within the normal limits described by others (2.5 ± 0.25 *mM*/l.) (Elkinton and Danowski, 1955; Albritton, 1951). High or low calcium levels in buffer were obtained by adjusting the amount of $CaCl_2$ used. The latter was made up just before use, as it was found that if the calcium solution was more than about two days old its potency with respect to change of potassium transport was decreased. When other agents were added they were dissolved in 0.9 per cent NaCl in concentrations such that 0.1 ml. of solution was added to 8.0 ml. of blood. Whenever cells were incubated in buffer they were washed twice with it before the incubation was begun.

Two kinds of experiments with Ca^{45} were performed. One set measured the immediate disappearance of Ca^{45} from plasma upon exposure to red cells. Fresh or cold-stored blood was separated into plasma and cells; the plasma was removed and divided into two aliquots. To one was added 5 to 10 mgm./50 ml. of total $CaCl_2$ containing a tracer amount of $Ca^{45}Cl_2$; to the other a tracer amount of I^{131}-labeled human serum albumin. A sample of each plasma was removed for counting. Enough of the rest of each plasma was mixed with packed red cells to give hematocrit values of 0.50. After mixing for less than 30 seconds the blood was centrifuged for less than 2 minutes, and another sample of plasma was counted. Total time of exposure of plasma to cells was 2 to 3 minutes except in one experiment with cold-stored blood in which cells were exposed to plasma for up to 10 minutes. During this procedure cold-stored cells were kept on ice except when they were being centrifuged. The volume of distribution of the I^{131} was taken as representing plasma trapped in the red cell mass. Differences between the volumes of distribution of Ca^{45} and I^{131} were taken as representing immediate loss of Ca^{45} from plasma into or onto cells.

Another series of experiments measured the slower disappearance of Ca^{45} from plasma. $Ca^{45}Cl_2$ was added to fresh or cold-stored blood in amounts of less than 5 mgm. of calcium per 100 ml. of blood. Time was then allowed for the immediate distribution of Ca^{45}, a preincubation sample was withdrawn and centrifuged, and its plasma radioactivity was measured. The remainder of the blood was placed in stoppered flasks on a Dubnoff incubator-shaker, with air as the gas phase. Aliquots were removed 2, 4 and 6 hours after the beginning of incubation, and the radioactivity of the plasma was measured. Incubation was done at 25°C. or 37°C., as indicated.

Calcium[45] radioactivity was determined in either of two ways. With the first method, carrier calcium was added to plasma to a total calcium content of 4 mgm., the calcium was precipitated on filter paper disks as the oxalate, the precipitate was dried, and was then counted in an internal gas-flow counter.[3] The second method was the counting of plasma directly in the well of a scintillation counter. The latter method required the presence of more activity than the former, but was sufficiently sensitive for most of the experiments reported.

RESULTS. A. *Experiments with cells suspended in buffer.* After cold-storage in plasma, cells washed twice with buffer and incubated in plasma gained 88.3 ± 2.1 ($s\bar{x}$) per cent of the potassium gained by unwashed control cells in plasma. Cells both washed and incubated in buffer gained 75.0 ± 3.6 per cent of the potassium gained by control cells. Three such experiments were done. In a second series of two experiments, cells were cold-stored as well as incubated in buffer or plasma. Cells stored in buffer and incubated in plasma regained 80 per cent as much potassium as did control cells stored and incubated in plasma; cells stored in plasma and incubated in buffer gained 81 per cent as much; and cells both stored and incubated in buffer regained only 51 per cent as much potassium as did the control cells.

Since the rate of potassium influx was less in washed cells, we studied the response of their transport system to ouabain and to inosine. In three experiments 5 *mM* inosine was added to cells washed in buffer and suspended in plasma, and to cells washed and incubated in buffer. Under these circumstances the riboside augmented transport to the same degree as it did in control cells (Kahn and Cohen, 1957). Washing or suspending cells in buffer did not alter the concentration-effect curve of ouabain for inhibition of net potassium influx. Less potassium entered buffer-treated cells, but the degree of response to a given concentration of drug was the same as in control cells.

B. *Experiments with varying concentrations of calcium.* Figure 1 shows the effects of added

[3] We wish to express our appreciation to Dr. Richard Goldsmith, V. A. Hospital, Cincinnati, for putting his radioisotope laboratory at our disposal during the counting of Ca^{45} by this method.

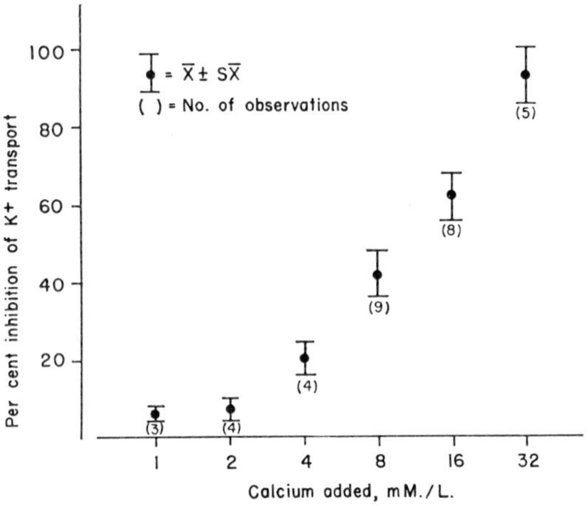

FIG. 1. The effect of added calcium on the transfer of potassium from plasma to cells of incubated cold-stored blood.

Each observation is the mean of duplicate determinations.

calcium, up to 32 *mM* above the normal plasma level, on the net influx of potassium into incubated cold-stored cells. Increasing concentrations produced increasing inhibition of influx. Addition of such amounts of $CaCl_2$ did not appreciably change the blood pH. Similar effects were seen with cells washed and suspended in buffer. When Sr^{++} or Mg^{++} were added (as the chlorides) in concentrations up to 16 *mM*, no effect on the loss of potassium from plasma was seen.

In 6 experiments, inhibitory concentrations of calcium and of ouabain were added to cold-stored blood. In 5 experiments the total inhibition was the sum of the individual effects, while in the sixth it was less. The latter experiment is open to question because the calcium solution was more than 2 days old.

Calcium concentrations in plasma or in buffer which were lower than normal (0 to 2.5 *mM*) did not affect potassium influx. Neither did any of the low calcium concentrations in either medium influence the effect of ouabain on net potassium transfer.

C. *Experiments with* Ca^{45}. Three experiments measured the volume of distribution of Ca^{45} in fresh cells, and one in cold-stored cells. This was compared with the volume of distribution of I^{131}-tagged albumin in plasma. The latter experiment indicated that the packed cells contained 7 per cent of their volume of trapped plasma. (The assumption was made that I^{131}-albumin does not leave the plasma within the 2 to 3 minutes required for the experiment.) The corresponding figure for Ca^{45} loss from fresh or cold-stored plasma was 21.4 ± 0.7 per cent. In cold-stored blood this figure was the same after 10 minutes exposure of the cells to plasma as after 2 minutes.

In fresh blood there was a small but steady loss of Ca^{45} from the plasma over 6 hours, as shown in the lower curve of figure 2. Neither 10^{-6} *M* ouabain nor 5 *mM* inosine affected the results. The loss was the same at 25°C. as at 37°C. in 2 experiments. In another experiment the concentration of calcium in the plasma was increased about fivefold by adding 10 *mM*/l. of $CaCl_2$. The per cent loss of Ca^{45} per hour was the same as that from normal plasma, indicating that calcium was leaving the calcium-enriched plasma 5 times as rapidly as it was the normal plasma.

The loss of calcium from the plasma of cold-stored blood was more rapid, as shown in the upper curve of figure 2. Three experiments were done at 37°C., and another at 25°C. One donor's blood was studied under all 4 conditions—fresh and cold-stored, each at both temperatures. Results from this blood are given in figure 3. The process responsible for the more rapid loss of calcium from cold-stored plasma during the first 2 hours is dependent upon temperature (figure 3). If 2 hours is taken as the time of comparison, the Q_{10} of the process was 2.3. High concentrations

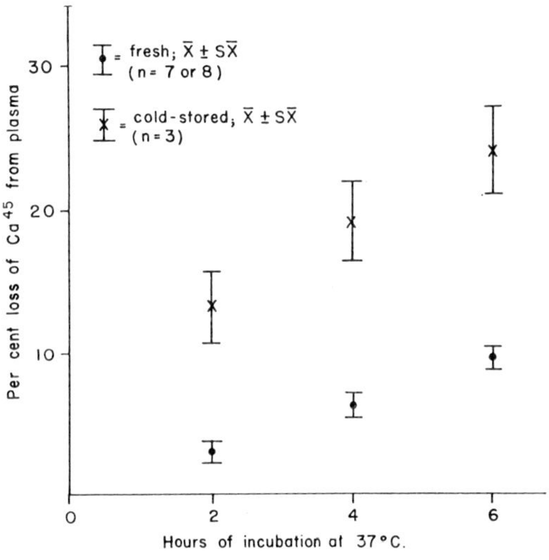

FIG. 2. Comparison of the loss of Ca^{45} from the plasma to the cellular phase of fresh (lower curve) and of cold-stored (upper curve) blood.

Each observation is the mean of duplicate determinations.

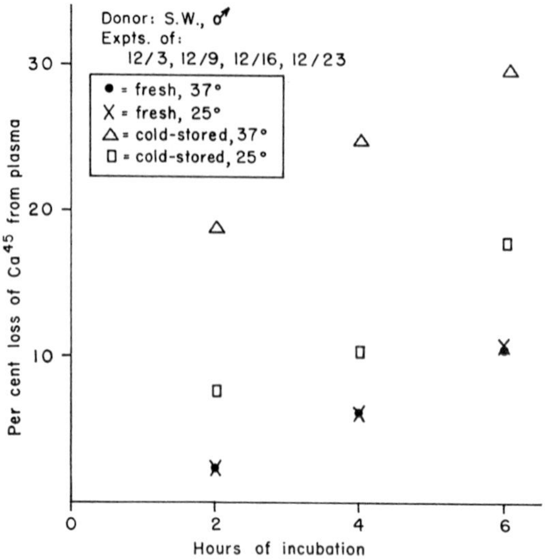

FIG. 3. Comparison of the rate of loss of Ca^{45} from the blood of a single donor under 4 different experimental conditions (fresh and cold-stored at 25°C. and 37°C.).

Each point represents the mean of duplicate determinations from a single experiment.

of ouabain (up to 1.2×10^{-5} *M*) had no detectable effect on the loss of Ca^{45} from the plasma of incubated cold-stored blood.

DISCUSSION. A. When cold-stored cells are exposed to buffer, they transport less potassium actively than do cells exposed just to plasma (RESULTS, part A). The simplest hypothesis is that replacing plasma with buffer removes some substance which is necessary for maximal active potassium transport. If this hypothetical substance does indeed exist, it must not be wholly associated with the plasma, since cells washed in buffer and then incubated in plasma had their potassium influx reduced relative to the control cells. The substance presumed to be involved may be either affixed to the cells loosely enough so that it is easily washed away by buffer deficient in it, or it may be partitioned between cells and plasma, and reach a new equilibrium with each exposure to a medium which lacks it. Solomon and Rees (1953) found that replacing buffer with plasma restored the cells' ability to transfer potassium, and implicated a "plasma factor" in the process. Their data are equally consistent with the concept of some substance being in equilibrium between cells and plasma, as suggested above.

Lovelock (1955) studied the composition of the materials washed off of human red cells under circumstances similar to those reported here. He found that various lipid fractions were removed by successive washings with buffer, the largest removal occurring with the first washing. The loss of lipids from fresh cells was one-half to one-third that from cold-stored cells, in which the first two washings removed about 4 per cent of the cell phospholipid, about 10 per cent of the cholesterol, and about 12 per cent of the lipoprotein. Hemolysis did not occur until over 30 per cent of the "membrane materials" had been washed off. We suggest that although cellular integrity was not sensitive to the loss of the amount of lipid materials removed by two washings, the system responsible for active influx of potassium may be. This implies that some lipid component of the cold-stored red cell is involved in the maintenance of optimal conditions for active potassium influx. Solomon *et al.* (1956) isolated a lipid component of blood which was capable of selectively accumulating potassium ions in organic solvents, and of releasing the potassium into an aqueous medium. Kirschner (1957) found phosphatidylserine to satisfy some requirements of a sodium carrier. Both cases are consistent with the idea that a carrier of monovalent cations may well be lipid in nature. If such a lipid factor is responsible for our results, its presence in normal amounts seems not to be critical for the response of the red cell potassium transfer system to inosine or ouabain. Both of these substances produced their typical response in cells suspended in buffer as well as in plasma.

The net influx of potassium into incubated cold-stored cells was diminished by high external calcium (RESULTS, part B and figure 1), but was not affected by Sr^{++} or Mg^{++}, nor by the reduction of calcium to below its normal level in plasma or buffer. Our results with elevated calcium levels do not agree with those of Lundsgaard-Hansen (1957), who found high calcium concentrations to decrease the exit of potassium from incubated human cold-stored cells, but not to affect the influx. For investigations of potassium influx, he washed the cells 4 times and suspended them in a medium containing potassium, calcium and sodium chloride. For the study of efflux, he incubated the cells in a medium of 97 per cent isosmotic sucrose and 3 per cent "total electrolytes", containing varying mixtures of sodium and calcium chlorides. The differences in suspending media used by him and by us make comparison of results questionable, since the medium can influence cation transfer so markedly. Since our procedures measured only net influx, small changes in passive efflux were not evident. Our results are in accord with those of Levi (1945).

B. The loss of Ca^{45} from plasma may be accounted for by three kinds of processes: 1) a rapid initial distribution, occurring in less than 2 minutes and taking place in fresh and cold-stored cells to the same extent; 2) a slow steady loss, not dependent upon temperature, continuing over at least 6 hours in fresh and cold-stored cells; and 3) a more rapid temperature-dependent loss, seen only in cold-stored cells.

The rapid distribution of Ca^{45} between plasma and cells indicates that a part of the calcium is accumulated on or in the cells within 2 minutes after addition of the isotope (RESULTS, part C). Rothstein (1955) describes the same phenomenon in resting yeast cells. Calcium is known to be concentrated at cell surfaces (*cf.* Danielli, 1950). Most modern views of the red cell membrane state that the outer portion of the surface is lipid (*cf.* Ponder, 1948; Moskowitz and Calvin, 1952). It is likely that the Ca^{45} might rapidly distribute itself in some lipid phase of the red cell surface. Whether this lipid is the same as that which might be important to potassium influx cannot presently be stated. An attractive hypothesis, which the present work does not test, is that the calcium, by its distribution in a lipid phase necessary for at least part of the active potassium entry, might make fewer receptors available for potassium carriage into the cell.

The slow steady loss of Ca^{45} from the plasma of fresh blood (lower curve, figure 2) does not fulfill criteria of an active transport process. The lack of dependence of the process on temperature within the range studied, and its direct dependence upon the external calcium concentration, suggest that it may depend upon diffusion (*cf.* Tosteson, 1955). This is consistent with the normal gradient of calcium concentrations in fresh blood, from plasma (2.5 *mM*/l.) to cells (1 *mM*/l.) (Elkinton and Danowski, 1955; Albritton, 1951). In 3 experiments this movement into fresh cells was 0.048, 0.048 and 0.042 micromol./ml. plasma/hour, or, based on the hematocrit, a mean of 0.056 micromol./ml. of cell phase/hour. The rate of potassium influx into fresh cells (Kahn and Acheson, 1955) is 1.5 micromol./ml. of cell phase/hour. When active influx is stopped with a cardiac glycoside, this rate becomes about 0.07 micromol./ml. of cell phase/hour, a figure not far from that found for calcium entry.

The process responsible for the relatively rapid loss of Ca^{45} from plasma into cold-stored cells is more difficult to classify. The initial influx rate of calcium into the cold-stored cells is at first more rapid than that into fresh cells; during the first 2 hours the average rate is more than 4 times faster. This difference in slope decreases as the duration of incubation increases The initial rapid loss of calcium from the plasma could be the result of an active process, or of some changes in conditions affecting passive entry of calcium. The former cannot be ruled out as it was in the case of the slower entry of Ca^{45}, since the temperature dependence of the more rapid process is consistent with the idea of an active transport. The high Q_{10} could also be consistent with a non-active process, as pointed out by Solomon *et al.* (1956). Cold storage might induce some changes in the cellular membrane which permit calcium to enter passively more rapidly than in fresh cells until a steady state is established, or until the membrane has changed its state so as to reduce the net influx rate. Or it might be that cold-storage reduces calcium efflux, and that this process requires some time to get started again during incubation. In the presence of a constant influx, this could also be responsible for curves such as those of figure 2.

The above discussion has considered possible interactions between calcium and potassium ions, since potassium was the ion being measured. Given the tight coupling between sodium and potassium transport in the erythrocyte (*cf.* Glynn, 1956), the primary action of calcium ions may be on the outwardly-directed sodium transport, and effects on potassium movements may be secondary. The experiments presented here cannot distinguish between these alternatives.

SUMMARY

Cold-stored human erythrocytes exposed to an artificial buffer transport less potassium inward than do control cells exposed only to plasma. The deficit increases with the amount of exposure of the cells to the buffer. It is proposed that some easily-removed lipid component of the red cell membrane is necessary for maximal potassium transport by the erythrocyte. Exposure of cells to buffer does not alter their responses to ouabain or to inosine.

Calcium levels below normal have no effect on potassium influx into cells suspended in plasma or in buffer. Calcium levels higher than normal progressively decrease potassium influx into incubated cold-stored erythrocytes, whether the cells be suspended in plasma or in buffer. Neither strontium nor magnesium ions produced this effect. Inhibition produced by high levels of calcium is additive with that produced by ouabain.

Ca^{45} disappears from plasma exposed to fresh or cold-stored red cells. The disappearance can be accounted for by 3 processes: 1) a rapid distribution, probably onto the surface of fresh or cold-stored cells, which is complete in less than 2 minutes; 2) a slow steady loss, probably diffusion into fresh and cold-stored cells; and 3) a more rapid process which occurs only in incubated cold-stored cells. High concentrations of ouabain did not affect any of these processes.

Calcium ions may block the access of potassium (or sodium) ions to some lipid component of the cell which is important to monovalent cation transport.

REFERENCES

Albritton, E. C. (Ed.): Standard values in blood, USAF Technical Report No. 6039, p. 117, Wright Air Development Center, July, 1951.

Danielli, J. F.: Cell physiology and pharmacology, Elsevier, New York, 1950.

Elkinton, J. R., and Danowski, T. S.: The body fluids, p. 122, Williams and Wilkins, Baltimore, 1955.

Glynn, I. M.: J. Physiol., **134:** 278, 1956.

Kahn, J. B., and Acheson, G. H.: This Journal, **115:** 305, 1955.

Kahn, J. B., and Cohen, S. B.: This Journal, **120:** 9, 1957.

Kahn, J. B.: This Journal, **121:** 234, 1957.

Kirschner, L. B.: Arch. Biochem., **68:** 499, 1957.

Levi, H.: Det Kgl. Danske Videns Selskab., Matem.-Fys. Medd., **23:** 10, 1945.

Lovelock, J. E.: Biochem. J., **60:** 692, 1955.

Lundsgaard-Hansen, P.: Arch. exper. Path. u. Pharmakol., **231:** 577, 1957.

Maizels, M.: in Active transport, S.E.B. Symposia VIII, Academic Press, New York, 1954.

Moskowitz, M., and Calvin, M.: Exp. Cell Res., **3:** 33, 1952.

Ponder, E.: Haemolysis and related phenomena, London, J. Churchill Ltd., 1948.

Rothstein, A.: in Shanes, A. M. (Ed.), Electrolytes in biological systems, American Physiological Soc., Washington, D. C., 1955.

Schatzmann, H. J.: Helv. Physiol. Acta, **11:** 346, 1953.

Solomon, A. K.: J. Gen. Physiol., **36:** 57, 1952.

Solomon, A. K., Gill, T. J., and Gold, G. L.: J. Gen. Physiol., **40:** 327, 1956.

Solomon, A. K., Lionetti, F., and Curran, P.: Nature, **178:** 582, 1956.

Solomon, A. K., and Rees, S. B.: Proc. Internat. Physiol. Cong., **19:** 781, 1953.

Tosteson, D.: in Shanes, A. M. (Ed.), Electrolytes in biological systems, American Physiological Soc., Washington, D. C., 1955.

8044

A STATISTICAL EVALUATION OF THE RELATIONSHIPS AMONG LOCAL ANESTHETIC ACTIVITY, IRRITANCY AND SYSTEMIC TOXICITY[1]

F. P. LUDUENA, JAMES O. HOPPE AND J. K. BORLAND

Pharmacology Section, Sterling-Winthrop Research Institute, Rensselaer, New York

Received for publication March 21, 1958

Although much has been written on the activity and toxicity of local anesthetic drugs, it is difficult to derive any clear understanding of the relationship between these two properties of this class of drug. The relationship between activity and irritancy is even more obscure. It has become increasingly apparent from studies in this laboratory on the activity, irritancy and acute intravenous toxicity of the local anesthetic drugs commonly used in medicine and dentistry and a variety of 2-alkoxybenzoates and thiolbenzoates that activity seems to be directly related to acute toxicity and that activity is related to irritancy only within rather narrow limits (Luduena and Hoppe, 1952, 1956). Because of the importance of these three parameters in the selection of a compound for further study, it became of interest to analyze these data, along with additional observations by both the intradermal and intraspinal methods of determining activity, from a statistical point of view in an effort to establish what correlation exists, if any, among these three parameters. The present communication is a summary of these findings.

METHODS. The compounds studied included the reference compounds: procaine, tetracaine, propoxycaine, cocaine, dibucaine, lidocaine, quinidine and α-fagarine along with 64 2-alkoxybenzoates, 2-alkoxythiolbenzoates and substituted thiazolidones which are identified in tables 1 and 2 of an earlier communication (Luduena and Hoppe, 1956) and in tables 1 and 2 of the present manuscript.

Local anesthesia. Intradermal: The activity of 62 compounds (compounds shown, in table 1 of this paper and compounds I through XL in table 1 in the previously mentioned paper, Luduena and Hoppe, 1956) was determined following intradermal injection in guinea pigs by the method of Bülbring and Wajda (1945). The intradermal TAC_5, the Threshold Anesthetic Concentration expected to produce an average anesthetic score of 5 as estimated from the dose-response curve, was determined for each compound (Luduena and Hoppe, 1956).

Intraspinal: The activity of each of the 25 compounds identified in table 2 was determined by intraspinal injection in rabbits by the method of Bieter *et al.* (1936). Dose-response curves were drawn by plotting duration of spinal anesthesia, in minutes, as determined by abolition of the urethral reflex (Luduena and Hoppe, 1951; Luduena, 1957), against the logarithm of the concentration. Three to five rabbits were injected at three or more dose levels for each drug. The intraspinal TAC_5, the Threshold Anesthetic Concentration expected to produce anesthesia for an average duration of 5 minutes as estimated from the dose-response curve, was determined for each compound. Since the 5-minute duration had been arbitrarily selected as the endpoint, the validity of this decision was investigated by comparing the correlation coefficients for the mouse intravenous LD_{50} and the intraspinal TAC at 2, 8, 15 and 30 minutes in addition to the 5-minute interval.

Irritancy. The degree of local irritation was determined by the trypan blue test (Hoppe, Alexander and Miller, 1950). The TIC_4, Threshold Irritant Concentration equivalent to an irritation score of 4, was estimated graphically by the method previously described (Luduena and Hoppe, 1952).

Toxicity. The acute intravenous $LD_{50} \pm$ s.e. was determined in male, albino, Swiss (Webster) strain mice weighing 20 ± 2 gm. (Luduena and Hoppe, 1952).

Statistical analysis. Correlation coefficients were calculated for a) intradermal local anesthetic activity in the guinea pig *vs.* acute intravenous toxicity in the mouse based on 61[2] of the 62 compounds cited above; b) intraspinal local anesthetic activity in the rabbit *vs.* acute intravenous toxic-

[1] A preliminary report was presented at the XIX International Physiological Congress held at Montreal, Canada, in 1953 (Luduena, Hoppe and Borland, 1953).

[2] Compound IX was not included in this study.

TABLE 1

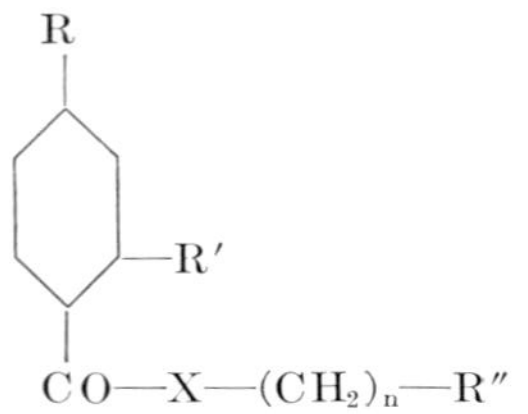

Compound	Structure: R	Structure: R′	Structure: X	Structure: n	Structure: R″	Form used	Toxicity,* i.v. in Mice, LD_{50} ± s.e.	Local Anesthetic Activity* Intra-cut. Wheal Test (Guinea Pigs) TAC_5	Irritancy,* Trypan Blue Method (Rabbits) TIC_4
							mgm./kgm.		*gm./100 ml.*
Procaine	NH_2	H	O	2	$N(CH_2—CH_3)_2$	HCl	52. ± 1.7	0.21	4.2
Propoxy-caine	NH_2	$O—(CH_2)_2—CH_3$	O	2	$N(CH_2—CH_3)_2$	HCl	6.6 ± 0.3	0.023	2.2
Win 3766	NH_2	$O—(CH_2)_2—CH_3$	S	2	$N(CH_2—CH_3)_2$	H_3PO_4	0.53 ± 0.02	0.0028	0.47
Win 3706	NH_2	$O—(CH_2)_3—CH_3$	O	2	$N(CH_2—CH_3)_2$	HCl	3.6 ± 0.3	0.01	1.2
Win 3800	NH_2	$O—(CH_2)_3—CH_3$	S	2	$N(CH_2—CH_3)_2$	HCl	0.53 ± 0.02	0.0028	0.15
Tetracaine.	NH—butyl	H	O	2	$N(CH_3)_2$	HCl	7.3 ± 0.3	0.018	0.33
I	NH_2	$O—(CH_2)_4—CH_3$	O	2	$N—(CH_2—CH_3)_2$	HCl	2.5 ± 0.1	0.0068	—
II	NH_2	$O—(CH_2)_4—CH_5$	S	2	$N—(CH_2—CH_3)_2$	HCl	0.45 ± 0.02	0.0015	—
III	NH-butyl	H	NH	2	$N—(CH_2—CH_3)_2$	2HCl	8.8 ± 0.8	0.028	—
IV	NH_2	$O—(CH_2)_2—CH_3$	NH	2	$N—(CH_2—CH_3)_2$	HCl	9.8 ± 0.5	0.067	—
V	NH_2	$O—(CH_2)_3—CH_3$	NH	2	$N—(CH_2—CH_3)_2$	HCl	4.0 ± 0.2	0.050	—
VI	2-diethylaminoethyl-3-amino-4-propoxybenzoate					HCl	3.0 ± 0.2	0.0066	0.97
VII	2-diethylaminoethyl-3-amino-4-butoxybenzoate					HCl	3.4 ± 0.35	0.0062	0.37
VIII	2-diethylaminoethyl-3-amino-4-butoxythiolbenzoate					HCl	9.5 ± 1.6	0.12	0.054
IX†	2-diethylaminoethyl-4-amino-3-propoxybenzoate					HCl	3.7 ± 0.2	0.011	1.0
Cocaine						HCl	19. ± 1.	0.045	2.4
Dibucaine						HCl	4.7 ± 0.3	0.016	0.19
Lidocaine						Base	20. ± 2.	0.063	1.45
Quinidine						$\frac{1}{2}SO_4H_2—H_2O$	49. ± 3.	0.20	0.34
α-Fagarine						HCl	30.6 ± 1.7	0.26	—

* (All values are expressed in terms of the bases).

† This compound was not included in the activity/toxicity correlation study.

ity in the mouse for 25 compounds and c) intradermal local anesthetic activity in guinea pigs *vs.* intradermal irritancy in the rabbit for 54 of the 62 compounds referred to above.

RESULTS. *Activity vs. toxicity.* Intradermal: The relationship between the log of the intradermal TAC_5 and the log of the intravenous LD_{50} was observed to be linear in nature as shown in fig. 1. The correlation coefficient for these data was $r = 0.74$, indicating that there is less than one chance in a thousand that an observed correlation of this magnitude (with 59 degrees of freedom) would occur by chance alone. About 55 per cent ($r^2 = 0.55$) of the variation in LD_{50} was found to be directly associated with variation in log TAC_5.

The curve in fig. 1 was obtained by computing the regression of toxicity (log $10 \times LD_{50}$) on activity (log $1000 \times TAC_5$): $Y = 0.51 + 0.89X$. Actually two regression lines could be obtained depending upon which set of values was taken as the independent variable. If activity was taken as the independent variable, a line with a somewhat higher slope was obtained ($X = 0.30 + 0.96Y$) with about the same standard error. This way of representing graphically the relationship between toxicity and activity actually understates the degree of correlation because all the variance is attributed to the dependent variable.

A better estimate of the functional relationship between the variables, when both are subject to error in the statistical sense, was obtained by confluence analysis (Lindley, 1947). The line expressing this relationship nearly bisected the two aforementioned regression lines ($Y = 0.39 + 0.98X$).

Intraspinal: The relationship between the log of the intraspinal TAC_5 and the log of the intravenous LD_{50} also was found to be linear in nature but with a considerably smaller scatter (fig. 2) than was observed with intradermal activity *vs.* toxicity (fig. 1). This greater degree of correlation, as might be expected, was confirmed by the finding of a higher correlation coefficient: $r = 0.97$.

The correlation coefficients between the LD_{50} and the concentrations expected to produce average duration of intraspinal anesthesia of 2, 8, 15 and 30 minutes in addition to the r value already mentioned are shown in table 3. The TAC values were estimated from the same dose-response curves from which the TAC_5 values were obtained. Although there was considerable variation in slope among the 25 curves, the differences in the magnitude of the correlation coefficients were not large.

Whether the 2- or the 30-minute duration point in the curve was selected to determine relative activity, a highly significant correlation coefficient was obtained. However, the highest values were obtained at 2 and 5 minutes, after which the significance decreased slowly with each successively higher point in the dose-response (duration) curve selected as the standard anesthetic response. Obviously, the smallest anesthetic concentrations acting, presumably, on the most superficial nerve fibers gave a more accurate measure of anesthetic activity than the highest concentrations.

Activity vs. irritancy. The relationship between intradermal activity in the guinea pig and intradermal irritancy in the rabbit, log-log scale, is shown in fig. 3. As judged from the scatter of the points in fig. 3, the correlation between these two parameters was considerably less than that observed for activity *vs.* toxicity. The correlation coefficient between the intradermal TAC_5 and the TIC_4 was found to be $r = 0.43$ with $P = 0.01$. Less than 20 per cent of the variation in irritancy was found to be associated with activity ($r^2 = 0.19$).

DISCUSSION. On the basis of results obtained with several known local anesthetics Schaumann (1938) concluded that there was a close relationship between conduction anesthesia and systemic toxicity, but not between the latter and topical anesthesia. Beutner and Calesnick (1942) stated that with few exceptions a rough parallelism existed between the corneal anesthetic and the convulsant effects of a series of local anesthetics. In spite of this and the large number of compounds whose toxicity and local anesthetic activity have been studied, the relationship between these two properties has been ignored by most investigators. Reviews as well as pharmacology textbooks have either failed to mention it or taken the position that toxicity does not correlate with activity. This is stated directly (Goodman and Gilman, 1955) or by implication, by emphasizing the value of the "therapeutic index" identified as the activity/toxicity ratio obtained experimentally.

The following reasons may account for this failure to relate the two properties. a) There

TABLE 2

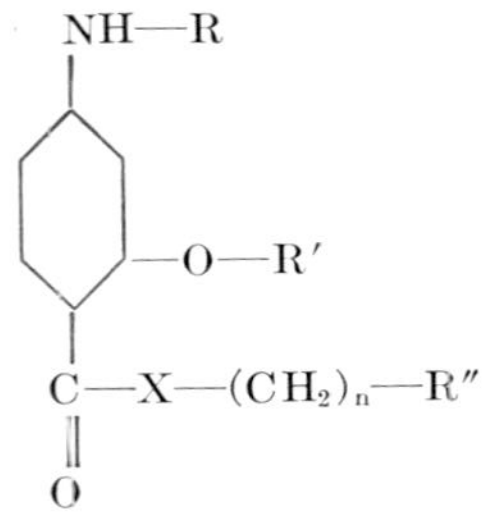

Compound	Structure					Form used	Spinal Anesthetic Activity, TAC_5*	Toxicity in Mice, i.v. $LD_{50} \pm$ s.e.*
	R	R′	X	n	R″			
							mgm./kgm.	*mgm./kgm.*
X	H	H	O	2	$N(Me)_2$	HCl	0.89	58.0 ± 4.
XI	H	Ethyl	O	2	$N(Me)_2$	Base	0.57	37.0 ± 0.7
XII	H	Benzyl	O	2	$N(Me)_2$	H_3PO_3	0.21	20.0 ± 1.5
Propoxycaine	H	Propyl	O	2	$N(Et)_2$	HCl	0.067	6.6 ± 0.3
Win 3706	H	Butyl	O	2	$N(Et)_2$	HCl	0.024	3.6 ± 0.3
XIII	H	Hexyl	O	2	$N(Et)_2$	HCl	0.013	1.8 ± 0.1
XIV	H	Butyl	O	3	$N(Et)_2$	2HCl	0.038	3.0 ± 0.2
Win 3260	H	Methyl	S	2	$N(Et)_2$	H_3PO_4	0.058	5.7 ± 0.4
Win 3766	H	Propyl	S	2	$N(Et)_2$	H_3PO_4	0.0045	0.53 ± 0.02
Win 3800	H	Butyl	S	2	$N(Et)_2$	HCl	0.0022	0.53 ± 0.02
Win 4510	H	Hexyl	S	2	$N(Et)_2$	HCl	0.0015	0.32 ± 0.02
XV	H	Methyl	S	3	$N(Et)_2$	H_3PO_4	0.054	3.6 ± 0.2
XVI	H	Propyl	O	3	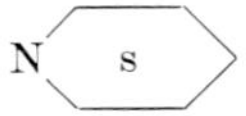	2 HCl	0.054	3.0 ± 0.3
XVII	H	Hexyl	O	3	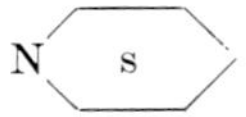	HCl	0.0062	1.3 ± 0.05
XVIII	Bu	Propyl	O	3	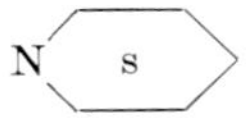	2 HCl	0.034	3.4 ± 0.2

XIX	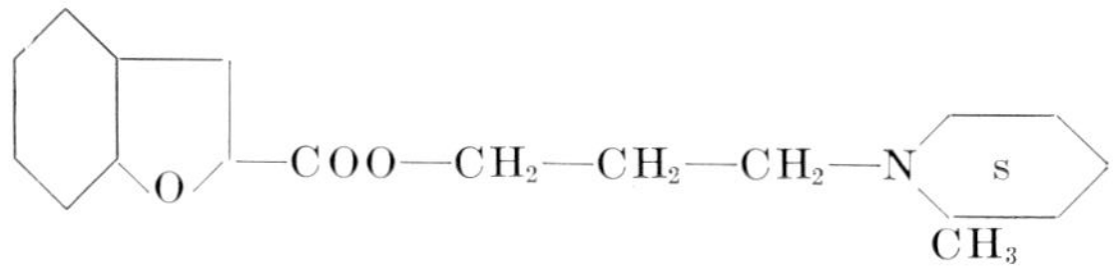	HCl	0.67	33.0 ± 3.0
XX	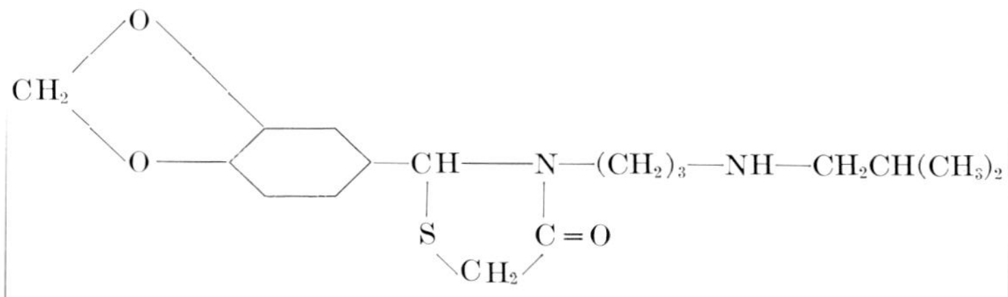	HCl	0.54	36.0 ± 0.9
XXI	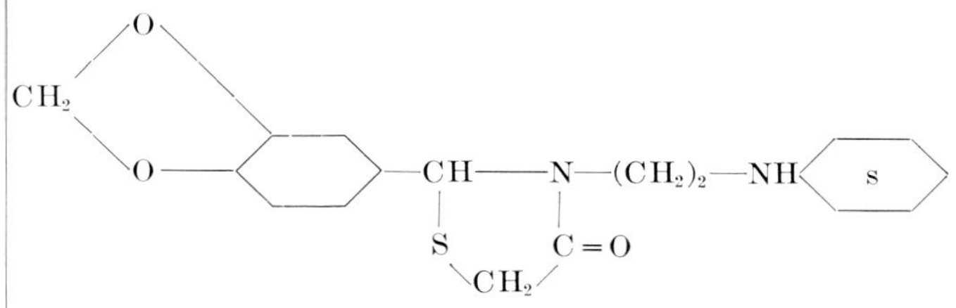	HCl	0.14	27.0 ± 1.0
XXII	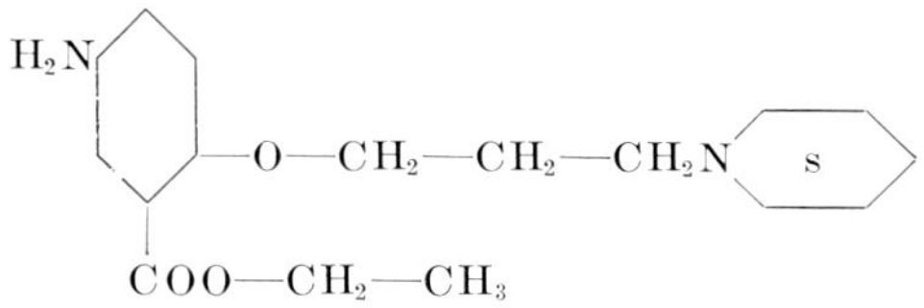	HCl	0.036	3.0 ± 0.2
Procaine (Novocaine)		HCl	0.50	52.0 ± 1.7
Dibucaine (Nupercaine):2-butoxy-N-(2-diethylaminoethyl)cinchoninamide		HCl	0.04	4.7 ± 0.3
Lidocaine (Xylocaine):α-diethylamino-2,6-acetoxylidide		HCl	0.21	20.0 ± 2.0
Piperocaine (Metycaine):3-(2-methyl-1-piperidyl)propyl benzoate		HCl	0.49	21.0 ± 1.0
Cocaine		HCl	0.54	19.0 ± 1.0
Tetracaine		HCl	0.055	7.3 ± 0.3

* In terms of the bases.

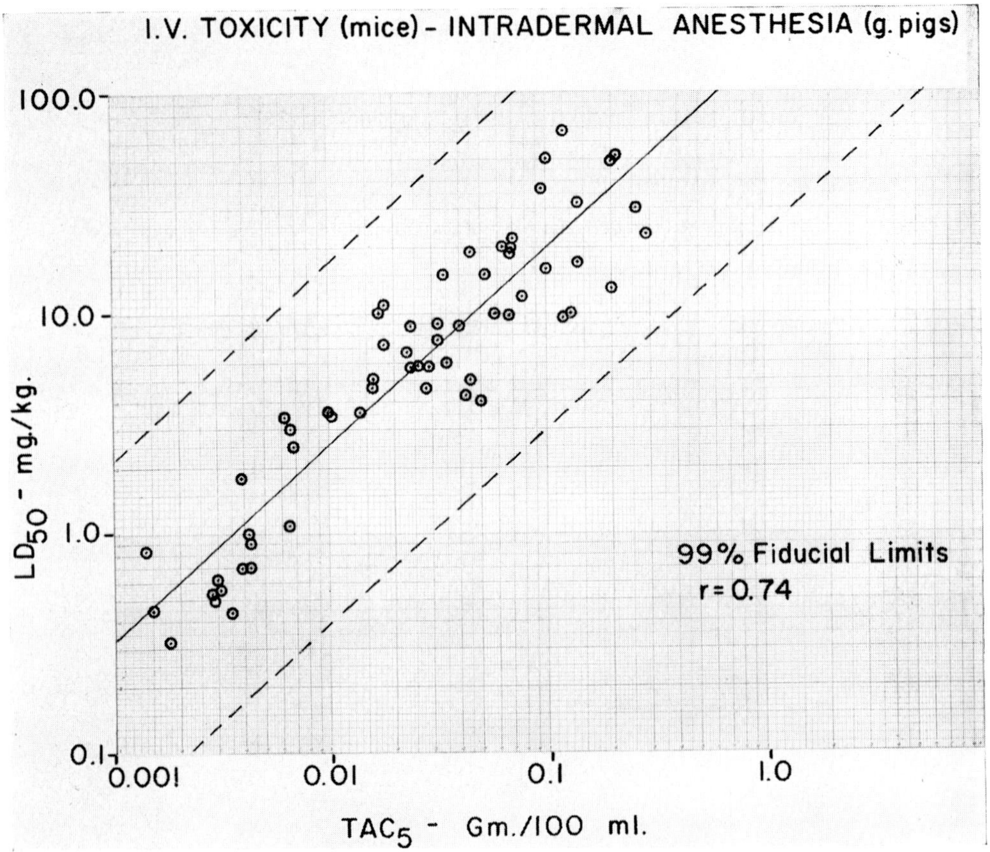

FIG. 1. Regression of toxicity on local anesthetic activity. Abscissae: Threshold Anesthetic Concentration$_5$ (TAC_5).

may have been small difference in the activity range of the compounds tested. If the degrees of activity of the various compounds are spread over a wide range the relationship with toxicity cannot be overlooked even in the presence of large experimental errors. If, on the other hand, the activity range is narrow, experimental error (in a statistical sense) and the other factors enumerated below may hide the relationship between the two properties. b) Inadequate methods may have been used to determine activity and toxicity. c) Large experimental error may have been introduced due to the use of a small number of animals. d) Only a small number of compounds may have been tested.

The results described in this paper show the high degree of correlation between local anesthetic activity as determined by intradermal and intraspinal injection in guinea pigs and rabbits respectively, and systemic toxicity determined by intravenous injection in mice[3].

The results obtained suggest that the mechanism of the lethal and the local anesthetic action of the compounds tested is fundamentally similar. The cause of death in mice is respiratory paralysis preceded by convulsions, but a de-

[3] In experiments with sciatic nerve, with epineurium removed, Skou (1954) has found that tetracaine and dibucaine were 460 and 970 times more active than procaine, respectively. These values are much higher than those reported by several investigators (and those found by us, table 1) and are not correlated with toxicity. Perhaps the explanation lies in the fact that in Skou's experiments the blocking concentration was determined after partition equilibrium had been obtained (after approximately 6 hours in the case of dibucaine). In the experiments described here, the standard responses (anesthesia with the TAC_5 and death) were produced within a few minutes, by concentrations which were constantly changing and therefore without reaching equilibrium at the site of action.

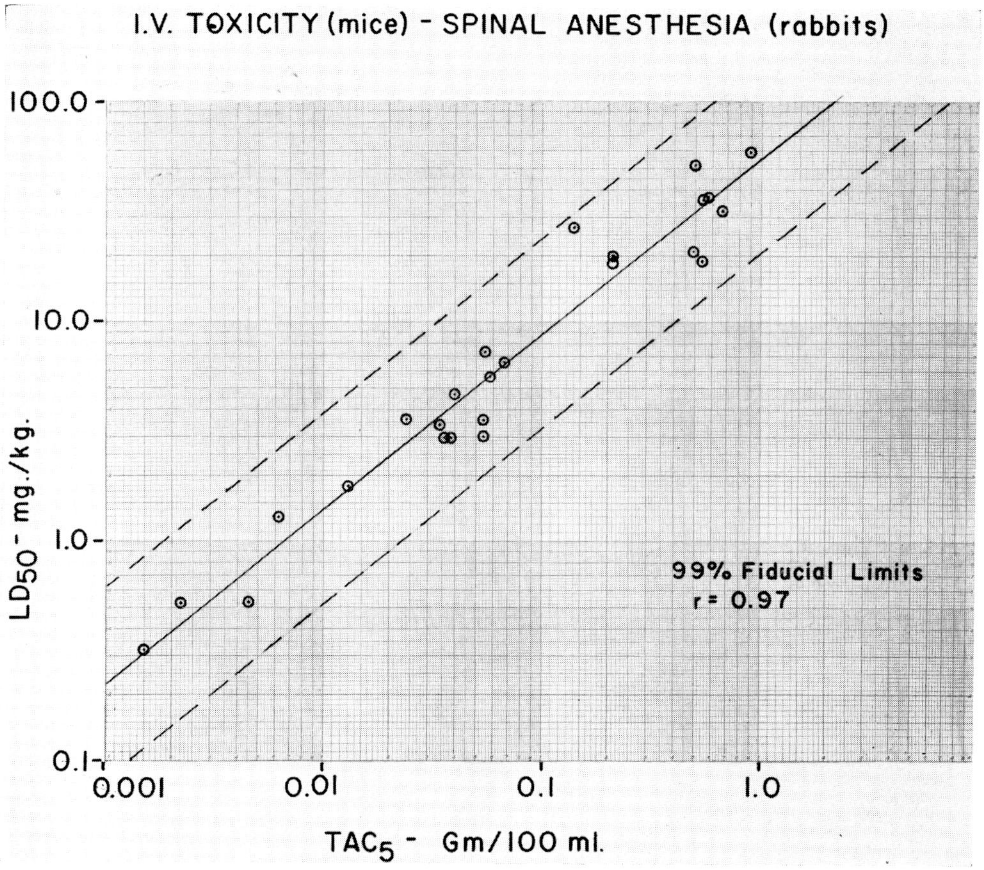

FIG. 2. Regression of toxicity on local anesthetic activity.

pressor effect on the circulation may be a contributory cause. In regard to this point it is interesting to note that a highly significant correlation has been found between local anesthetic activity and the ability to increase the refractory period of the isolated rabbit auricle (Luduena, Howard and Borland, 1956), confirming results obtained by Dawes (1946).

The existence of this correlation implies that there are no important differences in the magnitude of the activity/toxicity ratios of local anesthetics. Differences in other properties may have led to the selection of those compounds that are used clinically. For example, poor diffusibility in the tissues may make a compound less effective clinically for a given local anesthetic procedure than a potentially equitoxic compound. Systemic toxicity may also be affected. For example, the incidence of untoward systemic effects as a result of cumulation would be more likely to occur with those compounds which are not hydrolyzed by pseudocholinesterase. However, these are theoretical considerations. Because we have little information as to the relative toxicity of local anesthetics in man we can only hypothesize that the factors mentioned may have some influence in the clinical effectiveness or the potential toxicity of the compounds.

The relationship between irritancy and activity was not as clear as that between activity and toxicity. A positive correlation was also found between the first two properties, but the correlation coefficient was much lower ($r = 0.43$).

Previous studies carried out in this laboratory with some homologous series have shown that local anesthetic activity, toxicity and irritancy increased with the length of a lipophilic side chain (Luduena and Hoppe, 1952, 1956). Most of the compounds included in this study are members of homologous series in which even the lower members were more active than procaine. The data obtained with those compounds have

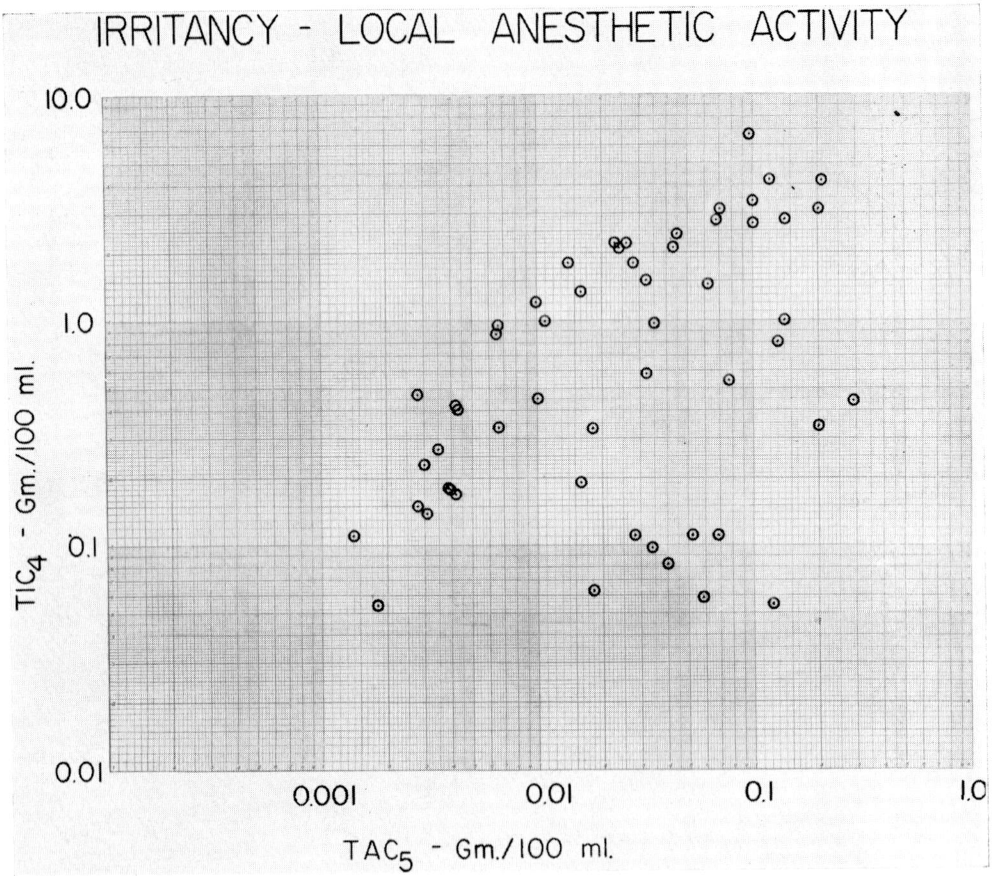

FIG. 3. Relationship between the irritancy and local anesthetic activity of 54 local anesthetics. Ordinate: Threshold Irritant Concentration$_4$ (TIC_4). Abscissae: Threshold Anesthetic Concentration$_5$ (TAC_5).

tended to increase the degree of correlation between local anesthetic activity and irritancy. Examination of the distributions of the points in fig. 3 (TIC_4 plotted against TAC_5 values, on log-log paper) shows that slightly more than two-thirds of the points fall within a fairly narrow diagonal band. For these compounds, activity increases in parallel with irritancy. There are many other compounds with points falling outside, on the right side of the band, whose irritancy is much greater than the activity. On the other hand, there are no points on the upper left side of the chart. This means that starting with what may be called "prototypes" having approximately the same anesthetic activity and very little irritancy, if an increase in activity is obtained by an increase in size in the lipophilic group, the irritancy also grows although the changes are not usually parallel. On the other hand, it is possible to increase the irritancy, by changes in structure which either do not modify the activity or even reduce it. The most outstanding example of this is given by the thiolbenzoate position isomers, Win 3800 and compound VII. Changes in the relative position of

TABLE 3

Spinal anesthesia (rabbits) and intravenous toxicity (mice), correlation between concentrations producing various average durations of anesthesia and LD_{50} values, using the 25 compounds shown in table 2

Ave. duration of anesth. (min.)	2	5	8	15	30
Correlation coefficient	0.975	0.975	0.97	0.96	0.91

the ring substituents in compound VIII decreased the irritancy to less than one-half and increased the activity by more than 40 times. Also the comparison of propoxycaine and Win 3766 with the corresponding N-butyl analogs shows that this substitution greatly increases the irritancy, whereas the activity is not changed or is reduced.

In another study from this laboratory it has been shown that there is a highly significant positive correlation between the irritancy and the surface activity of local anesthetics (Luduena *et al.*, 1955). Changes in structure that lead to an increase in irritancy (and surface activity) *may or may not* lead to an increase in local anesthetic activity. This irritancy of tertiary or secondary amines is most probably similar to that of the cationic surfactants and therefore it has a mechanism of action different from that of local anesthetics, which apparently depends on the presence of the lipid soluble undissociated base. The aforementioned correlation suggests that the mechanism of irritancy is similar whether one deals with the highly active or the poorly active, highly irritant local anesthetics, or with compounds which have practically no local anesthetic activity.

SUMMARY

Correlation studies were carried out between local anesthetic activity and systemic toxicity and between the former and irritancy. A very high correlation coefficient (r = 0.97) was found between the log of the Threshold Anesthetic Concentration$_5$ (TAC_5) of 25 compounds tested by intraspinal injection and the log of their LD_{50}, determined by intravenous injection in mice.

A significant correlation (r = 0.74) was also found between the log of the TAC_5 of 61 compounds tested by intradermal injection in guinea pigs and the log of the LD_{50} determined by intravenous injection in mice.

A much lower correlation coefficient (r = 0.43) was obtained between the log of the Threshold Irritant Concentration$_4$ (TIC_4) of 54 compounds determined by intradermal injection in rabbits (trypan blue method) and the log of the TAC_5 determined by intradermal injection in guinea pigs.

These results suggest that a similar mechanism is responsible for the local anesthetic and the lethal effects of local anesthetics. A different mechanism appears to be responsible for local irritation, although in some cases, activity and irritancy may be modified in the same direction by certain structural changes in local anesthetic compounds.

ACKNOWLEDGMENTS. We are pleased to acknowledge the technical assistance of Miss B. Dertinger, Miss P. Bourgault, Miss K. Kraft and Mr. D. Seppelin.

REFERENCES

BEUTNER, R., AND CALESNICK, B.: Anesthesiol., **3:** 673, 1942.
BIETER, R. N., CUNNINGHAM, R. W., LENZ, O., AND MCNEARNEY, J. J.: THIS JOURNAL, **57:** 221, 1936.
BÜLBRING, W., AND WAJDA, I.: THIS JOURNAL, **85:** 78, 1945.
DAWES, G. S.: Brit. J. Pharmacol., **1:** 90, 1946.
GOODMAN, L. S., AND GILMAN, A.: The Pharmacological Basis of Therapeutics, second ed., p. 355, Macmillan, New York, 1955.
HOPPE, J. O., ALEXANDER, E. B., AND MILLER, L. C.: J. Amer. Pharm. Assoc., **39:** 147, 1950.
LINDLEY, D. V.: J. Roy. Statist. Soc. Suppl., **9:** 218, 1947.
LUDUENA, F. P.: Arch. internat. pharmacodyn., **109:** 143, 1957.
LUDUENA, F. P., AND HOPPE, J. O.: J. Amer. Pharm. Assoc., **40:** 132, 1951.
LUDUENA, F. P., AND HOPPE, J. O.: THIS JOURNAL, **104:** 40, 1952.
LUDUENA, F. P., AND HOPPE, J. O.: THIS JOURNAL, **117:** 89, 1956.
LUDUENA, F. P., HOPPE, J. O., AND BORLAND, J. K.: Abst. of Comm. XIX. Intern. Physiol. Congress, Montreal, page 575, 1953.
LUDUENA, F. P., HOPPE, J. O., NACHOD, F. C., MARTINI, C. M., AND SILVERN, G. M.: Arch. internat. pharmacodyn., **101:** 17, 1955.
LUDUENA, F. P., HOWARD, J. W., AND BORLAND, J. K.: Arch. internat. pharmacodyn., **107:** 335, 1956.
SCHAUMANN, O.: Arch. exper. Path. u. Pharmakol., **190:** 30, 1938.
SKOU, J. C.: Acta pharmacol. et toxicol., **10:** 281, 1954.

8045

THE CARDIOVASCULAR AND RESPIRATORY ACTIONS OF RAUWOLSCINE[1]

BERNARD LEVY AND GEORGE B. KOELLE

Department of Physiology and Pharmacology, Graduate School of Medicine, University of Pennsylvania, Philadelphia 4

Received for publication April 3, 1958

Reports have appeared in the literature indicating that rauwolscine, an alkaloid of *Rauwolfia canescens*, exerts a hypotensive action in laboratory animals. The purpose of the present study was to examine more directly in anesthetized dogs and cats the mechanisms involved in the cardiovascular effects of rauwolscine.

Chakravarti (1942) described rauwolscine as a cardiovascular depressant capable of abolishing the pressor effects of epinephrine. M. D. Mukherjee and Sen (1953) stated that the addition of rauwolscine to the perfusion fluid in a toad-heart preparation caused an immediate decrease in amplitude and frequency of contractions. In mammalian hearts similar results were obtained along with an increase in coronary flow. Mukherjee and Sen (1953a) studied the hypotensive activity of rauwolscine in cats at three levels of blood pressure: hypertensive (produced by the infusion of epinephrine), normotensive, and hypotensive (during infusion of histamine). After suitable doses of rauwolscine the blood pressure was lowered under all three conditions; however, the greatest drop occurred during epinephrine infusion. The simultaneous administration of rauwolscine and epinephrine resulted in a depressor response. Mukherjee (1953) found that at a dose of 1 mgm./kgm., i.v., in the cat, rauwolscine blocked the pressor effect of epinephrine upon blood pressure but it did not counteract the glycogenolytic action of epinephrine. The adrenergic blocking action has been confirmed by a variety of techniques (Kohli *et al.*, 1957). Das *et al.* (1955) stated that rauwolscine caused a marked fall in peripheral resistance in cats and monkeys without significantly affecting cardiac output. The greatest response in monkeys was obtained by intracisternal injection. They concluded therefore that the hemodynamic effects were of predominantly central origin. Miscellaneous actions of rauwolscine which have been found in various species include local anesthesia, stimulation of the central nervous system, respiratory stimulation, penile erection (Kohli and De, 1956), and relaxation of smooth muscle (Mukherjee and Sen, 1953b).

[1] This investigation was supported by a grant from McNeil Laboratories, Inc., Philadelphia, Pennsylvania.

METHODS. A total of 42 mongrel dogs and 16 cats of both sexes was used in the present study. With a few exceptions, experiments were duplicated in both species. In the experiments involving the recording of the pressor response to bilateral carotid occlusion, dogs were anesthetized with *alpha*-choloralose (100 mgm./kgm.) intravenously or intraperitoneally, and cats (80 mgm./kgm., after ether induction) intravenously. In all other experiments both species were usually anesthetized with sodium pentobarbital (36 mgm./kgm., i.p.) or sodium barbital (330 mgm./kgm., i.p.). Blood pressure was recorded from a femoral or carotid artery by means of a Statham P-23-A pressure transducer. Respiratory movements were recorded from a sidearm in the tracheal cannula by means of a Grass pressure transducer. A model III-D Grass EEG. was used as the recording device in all experiments. Blood flow was measured in the femoral arterial bed of dogs and cats by a Soskin "bubble" flowmeter (Soskin *et al.*, 1934) or a Shipley-Wilson rotameter (1951) inserted into the appropriate artery. Heparin was used as the anticoagulant in these animals; following an initial dose of 10 mgm./kgm., i.v., additional doses of 3 mgm./kgm. were given at 60-minute intervals. Contractions of the nictitating membrane were recorded by means of a force displacement transducer. The right superior cervical sympathetic nerve in the cat and the right sympatheticovagus in the dog were stimulated electrically by means of an electrodyne stimulator. Submaximal and maximal stimuli were given (10 cycles/sec., 5 msec. duration, 0.5–1.5 volts). The pressor response to bilateral carotid occlusion was produced by

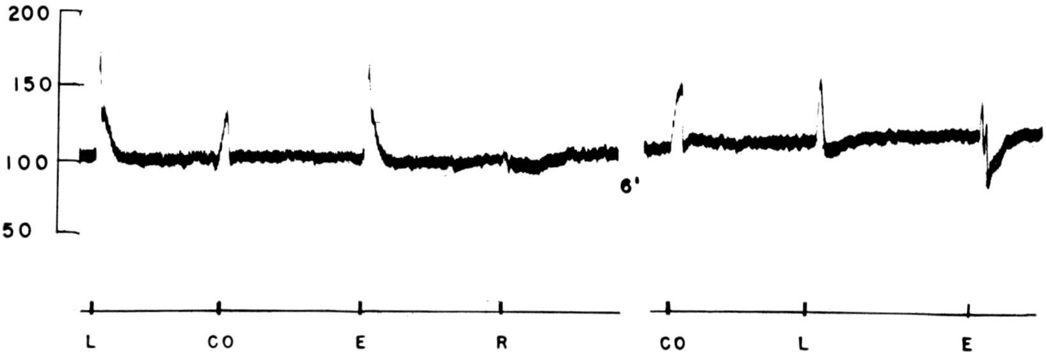

FIG. 1. Effect of rauwolscine (R, 0.3 mgm./kgm., i.v.) on the pressor responses to epinephrine (E, 5.0 microgm./kgm., i.v.), levarterenol (L, 5.0 microgm./kgm., i.v.) and bilateral carotid occlusion (CO, 30 seconds' duration) in the dog.
Six-minute interval at 6′.

clamping gently both carotid arteries between dampened fingertips for 30 seconds. All i.a. injections were made into the outflow side of the flowmeter.

RESULTS. *Arterial pressure.* Rauwolscine produced reversal of the pressor response to epinephrine and reduction of the pressor response to levarterenol in both the dog and cat (fig. 1). The dosage ranges required to produce adrenergic blockade in these two species were quite similar. In both species it was possible to demonstrate inhibition of the epinephrine pressor response with a dose as small as 0.03 mgm./kgm., i.v. The administration of a cumulative dose of 0.3 mgm./kgm. of rauwolscine, i.v., to a total of 11 dogs and 7 cats reversed the pressor response to epinephrine in all dogs and 6 of the 7 cats. In the seventh cat the pressor response to epinephrine was markedly reduced.

In the dog it was possible to produce adrenergic blockade without lowering significantly the resting arterial pressure. Usually with the administration of doses of 0.3 mgm./kgm. or less to the dog the blood pressure dropped briefly but soon returned to its preinjection level, or in some instances to a slightly higher level than before. A dose of approximately 0.5 mgm./kgm. of rauwolscine generally was needed before a significant hypotensive effect could be demonstrated, but even with this dose the blood pressure usually returned to its initial level in less than 30 minutes. In the cat, equivalent doses of rauwolscine exerted a more potent and prolonged hypotensive effect, although the dose of rauwolscine needed to produce adrenergic blockade was approximately the same as in the dog. Despite this difference in the hypotensive activity it was found, by the administration of successively increasing doses, that the hypotensive effect in the cat did not occur before the onset of adrenergic blockade.

The onset of adrenergic blockade in both species occurred within approximately one minute following the administration of rauwolscine. Following rauwolscine a pressor response to epinephrine could be obtained by administering sufficiently large doses of epinephrine (20 to 40 microgm./kgm.). The duration of adrenergic blockade following 0.3 mgm. of rauwolscine/kgm., i.v., in the dog was approximately 2 to 3 hours.

The administration of 0.3 mgm. of rauwolscine/kgm., i.v., to two dogs 15 minutes prior to the administration of Dibenamine (N,N′-dibenzyl-β-chloroethylamine HCl), 10 mgm./kgm., i.v., resulted in the production of adrenergic blockade of a duration similar to that produced by the same dose of rauwolscine alone. Nickerson and Goodman (1948) have shown that following the administration of this dose of Dibenamine, epinephrine, even in massive doses, produces only a depressor response for many hours afterwards. The present results indicate that rauwolscine probably exerts its adrenergic blocking effect at the same sites as Dibenamine, and by the time the rauwolscine effect has worn off, Dibenamine is no longer available to exert an effect. Rauwolscine probably exerts no blocking effect on the inhibitory actions of epinephrine, since the depressor response to isoproterenol was not inhibited following large doses of rauwolscine. The effects of rauwolscine on arterial pressure and on

TABLE 1

Summary of the cardiovascular and respiratory actions of rauwolscine in the dog

Cumulative Dose, i.v.	Control Mean Blood Pressure		Duration of Hypotension		Per Cent Control Value: Mean blood pressure at maximal fall		Per Cent Control Value: Pressure response to carotid occlusion†		Per Cent Control Value: Pressor response to epi. i.v. (5 microgm./kgm.)		Per Cent Control Value: Respiratory rate maximal‡	
	Average	Range	Average	Range	Average	Range	Average	Range	Average	Range	Average	Range
mgm./kgm.	*mm. Hg*	*mm. Hg*	*min.*	*min.*								
0.1	127 (5)*	154	3	4	89	96	109 (3)	114	62	82	206 (4)	440
		105		1		81		103		31		120
0.1–0.3	122 (5)	154	3	4	89	93	141 (3)	273	−32	19	180 (4)	233
		92		1		81		68		−69		150
0.3–0.4	126 (3)	138	4	5	92	93	89 (1)	89	−64	−47	170	235
		105		4		90				−93		100
0.4–0.6	133 (6)	154	4	12	84	92	80 (3)	95	−58	−12	191	240
		105		0		76		62		−105		117
0.6–1.0	126 (7)	138	54	190	69	83	29 (4)	55	−37 (6)	−11	240	444
		105		2		57		0		−47		133
1.0–3.0	128 (6)	157	44	120	64	82	32 (2)	50	−35	−11	407	633
		105		12		52		14		−54		167

* Numbers in brackets in all "Average" columns represent number of animals in which observations were made; unless otherwise indicated, same number of observations as in control column apply to remaining columns.

† Pressor responses to carotid occlusion were determined after the resting arterial pressure had reached a constant level.

‡ Respiratory rate taken at time of maximal change within 1 to 3 minutes after injection of rauwolscine.

the blood pressure responses to epinephrine and levarterenol are summarized in tables 1 and 2.

Carotid sinus pressor reflexes. The effects of rauwolscine on the pressor response to bilateral carotid occlusion were determined in both the dog and cat. In both species, in doses that produced epinephrine-reversal rauwolscine did not significantly inhibit the pressor response to bilateral carotid occlusion (fig. 1). After doses of rauwolscine that resulted in a drop in blood pressure, the pressor response to bilateral carotid occlusion was less than the control response. However, Prochnik *et al.* (1950) have shown that the pressor response to carotid occlusion is directly proportional to the level of the pre-existing mean arterial pressure. In several experiments the injection of rauwolscine produced a vasodepressor response after which the mean arterial pressure returned to a higher level than the pre-injection level. Following this, epinephrine continued to produce a vasodepressor effect but the pressor response to carotid occlusion was increased. As an example of this, following the administration of 0.3 mgm./kgm., i.v., of rauwolscine, one dog showed a pressor response to carotid occlusion that was 173 per cent greater than its control value. Prior to the administration of rauwolscine, carotid occlusion resulted in an increase in blood pressure of only 22 mm. Hg from a resting level of 115 mm. Hg. After the administration of rauwolscine the resting arterial pressure reached a constant level at 140 mm. Hg. Carotid occlusion at this time produced a pressor response of 60 mm. Hg, (table 1). It is therefore likely that the inhibitory effect of moderate doses of rauwolscine on the blood pressure response to carotid occlusion was due chiefly to the drop in blood pressure rather than to a direct effect of the drug itself (tables 1 and 2).

Effects of rauwolscine on contraction of the nictitating membrane. The effect of rauwolscine on the contraction of the nictitating membrane in response to electrical stimulation of the cervical sympathetic trunk was measured in 7 cats and 2 dogs. In both species, much larger doses of rauwolscine were needed to inhibit contraction of the nictitating membrane than to produce epinephrine-reversal of the blood pressure (fig.

TABLE 2

Summary of the cardiovascular actions of rauwolscine in the cat

Cumulative Dose, i.v.	Control Mean Blood Pressure		Duration of Hypotension		Per Cent Control Value					
					Mean blood pressure at maximal fall		Pressor response to carotid occlusion*		Pressor response to epi. i.v. (5 microgm./kgm.)	
	Average	Range	Average	Range	Average	Range	Average	Range	Average	Range
mgm./kgm.	*mm. Hg*	*mm. Hg*	*min.*	*min.*						
0.1	112 (6)†	136	4	13	76	86	113 (1)	113	4	82
		90		0		59				−94
0.1–0.3	135 (6)	168	11	30	70	83	114 (2)	129	6	70
		110		1		40		100		−44
0.3–0.4	122 (3)	134	22 (2)	35	52	59	—	—	−12	45
		105		8		48				−43
0.4–0.6	114 (6)	135	39	60	57	80	87 (2)	174	−25	78
		90		3		30		0		−195
0.6–1.0	117 (5)	134	21 (4)	30	54	67	0 (1)	0	−37 (4)	−12
		90		3		44				−82
1.0–3.0	116 (6)	135	43 (5)	73	47	74	0 (4)	0	−26	78
		90		25		19				−137

* Pressor responses to carotid occlusion were determined after resting arterial pressure had reached a constant level.

† Numbers in brackets in all "Average" columns represent number of animals in which observations were made; unless indicated otherwise, same number of observations as in control column apply to remaining columns.

2). In the first of the two dogs tested, following the administration of a total cumulative dose of 1.4 mgm./kgm., i.v., the contraction of the nictitating membrane in response to supramaximal stimuli was not reduced. In the second dog, a significant reduction occurred after the administration of a total cumulative dose of 3.4 mgm./kgm. of rauwolscine, i.v. In both dogs the pressor response to epinephrine was reversed after a total cumulative dose of 0.3 mgm./kgm., i.v. In the cat, approximately the same dosage relationship was found to exist. In two of the cats, an approximate 50 per cent reduction of the contraction of the nictitating membrane in response to a submaximal stimulus occurred at a dosage range of 0.5 to 0.9 mgm./kgm., i.v. However, 1.8 to 4.8 mgm./kgm. of rauwolscine, i.v., was needed to reduce significantly the contraction in response to supramaximal stimuli. In 3 of the cats, the contraction of the nictitating membrane in response to the i.v. injection of 5 microgm./kgm. of epinephrine, i.v., was reduced by more than 50 per cent by 0.2 to 0.6 mgm. of rauwolscine/kgm., i.v. In all seven cats reduction of the pressor response to epinephrine could be demonstrated after doses of rauwolscine that had no inhibitory effect upon contraction of the nictitating membrane in response to stimulation of the sympathetic trunk. The sum of these observations indicates that the ratio of the adrenolytic activity to the sympatholytic activity of rauwolscine is high, being in the range of approximately eight to one. This is further indicated by the inability of relatively high doses of rauwolscine to inhibit the pressor response to bilateral carotid occlusion.

Effect of rauwolscine on femoral vascular resistance. Rauwolscine, 0.01 mgm./kgm., injected into the femoral artery of the dog, produced an increase in blood flow, no change in systemic pressure, and therefore presumably a marked decrease in vascular resistance, as shown in table 3. Epinephrine, 0.1 to 0.5 microgm./kgm., injected intraarterially prior to rauwolscine, produced a decrease in blood flow, no change in systemic pressure, and therefore a marked increase in vascular resistance. The administration of the same doses of epinephrine intraarterially, after gradually increasing doses of rauwolscine (0.01 to 0.5 mgm./kgm., i.a.) resulted in a gradual inhibition of the vasoconstrictor effect of epinephrine with an eventual unmasking of its vasodilator effect (fig. 3). This sequence was found to

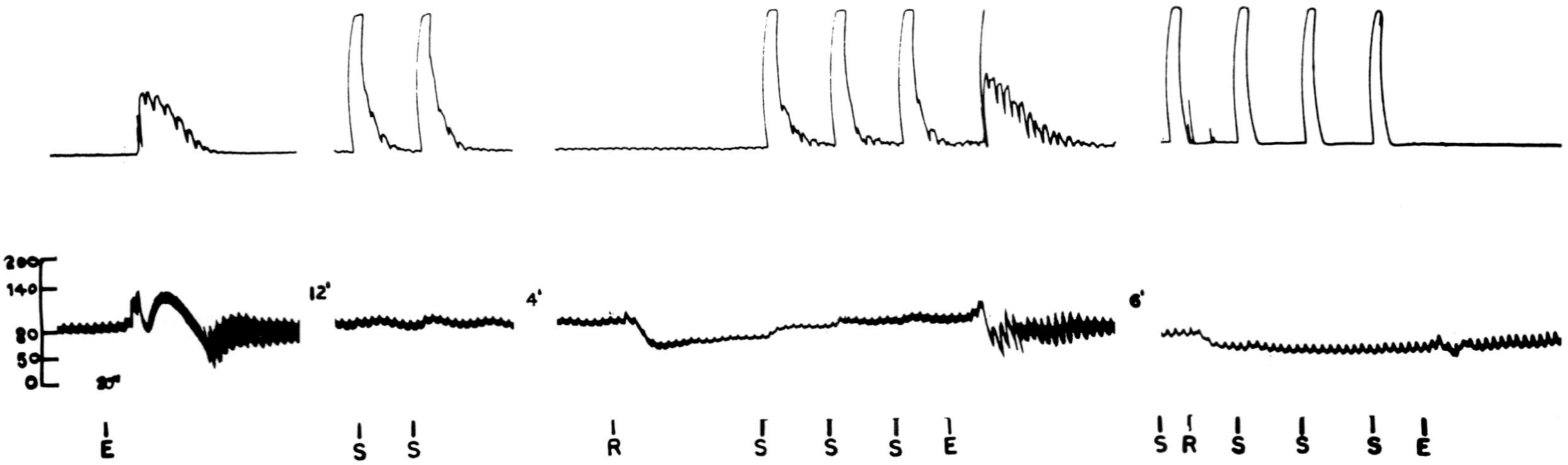

FIG. 2. Modifications of response of the cat's nictitating membrane (upper tracing) to maximal faradic stimulation (1.5 V, 5 msec. duration, 10 cycles/sec., 10-sec. spikes) of cervical sympathetic trunk (S) and epinephrine (E, 5.0 microgm./kgm., i.v.) by rauwolscine (R, 0.3 mgm./kgm., i.v.). Lower tracing is blood pressure. The numerals on the blood pressure scale, from top to bottom, are 200, 140, 80, 50, 0.

TABLE 3

Effects of rauwolscine and epinephrine upon peripheral resistance in the femoral vascular bed of the dog

Dog No.	Dose and Route of Admin. of Rauwolscine	Peripheral Resistance*, Per Cent of Control	Effects of Epinephrine on Peripheral Resistance		
		Rauwolscine alone	Dose of epi., i.a.	Peripheral resistance, per cent of control: Before rauwolscine	Peripheral resistance, per cent of control: After rauwolscine
	mgm./kgm.		*microgm./kgm.*		
1	0.01 i.a.	60	0.5	405	300‡
	0.05 i.a.	52	0.5		84
2	0.03 i.a.	41	0.1	434	157
			0.1 E, 0.03R †		32
3	0.05 i.a.	71	0.5	248	84
4	1.0 i.v.	66	0.5	179	232
5	1.0 i.v.	83	0.2	358	118
6	0.1 i.v.	118	0.2	600	299
	0.3 i.v.	72	0.2		145
	0.5 i.v.	99	0.2		105
	1.0 i.v.	63	0.2		33

* Peripheral resistance (R) = P/F, where P is the mean arterial pressure in mm. Hg and F is the flow in ml./min.

† Epinephrine and rauwolscine were given together intraarterially.

‡ Mean blood pressure rose from a control level of 136 to 147 mm. Hg after rauwolscine. None of the other intraarterial injections of epinephrine or rauwolscine resulted in any change in mean blood pressure.

occur in both the dog and cat. The same type of experiment was repeated using the hind leg of a dog that had been denervated acutely by sectioning the femoral and sciatic nerves. Griffin *et al.* (1954) have shown that this type of denervation abolishes completely responses to stimulation of the sympathetic chain. The results obtained in the denervated preparation were the same as those obtained in the innervated leg. Furthermore, it was possible to demonstrate a vasodilator effect after rauwolscine in a dose (0.5 microgm./kgm., i.a.) that did not modify the effects of epinephrine on blood flow. It is, therefore, probable that rauwolscine exerts a further peripheral vasodilator effect through a peripheral mechanism other than adrenergic blockade. The increased blood flow produced by rauwolscine was not prevented by atropine, hence a parasympathomimetic mechanism is unlikely.

Effects on respiration. The effects of rauwolscine were qualitatively similar in the dog and cat with one striking exception. In the dog, rauwolscine in small doses usually produced a marked increase in the respiratory rate (fig. 4), after either *alpha*-chloralose or sodium pentobarbital. In the cat, rauwolscine was usually without effect upon respiration, although an occasional cat did show a transient increase in the respiratory rate. This effect in the dog was usually prolonged; the respiratory rate did not usually return to normal until all of the other observed effects of the drug had disappeared. The tachypnea produced by rauwolscine in the dog was not affected by vagotomy and bilateral denervation of the carotid sinus area.

In dogs which received morphine sulfate and *alpha*-chloralose, in contrast to those which were anesthetized with *alpha*-chloralose alone or sodium pentobarbital, the tachypneic effect of rauwolscine either did not appear or appeared only late in the experiment. This suggested that the tachypnea produced by rauwolscine was prevented by the morphine. In two dogs that had been anesthetized by 100 mgm./kgm. of *alpha*-chloralose, i.v., alone, the administration of 0.3 mgm./kgm. of rauwolscine, i.v., resulted in the typical tachypnea. After the effects of this single dose of rauwolscine had worn off, morphine sulfate, 0.5 to 2.0 mgm./kgm., i.v., was administered. The administration of the same dose of rauwolscine as previously then produced no significant change in respiratory rate. Several hours later, during which time the effects of both the rauwolscine and morphine had presumably disappeared, another 0.3 mgm./kgm., i.v., dose of rauwolscine was administered. This time rauwolscine again produced a pronounced tachypnea. In two dogs rauwolscine (0.3 mgm./kgm.), pentylenetetrazol (10.0 mgm./kgm.), dimethylphenylpiperazinium iodide (DMPP, 15 microgm./kgm.) and sodium cyanide (1 mgm./kgm.) were all administered by i.v. injection before and after the administration of 2 mgm./kgm. of morphine sulfate, i.m. The dogs had originally been anesthetized by the i.v. injection of 100 mgm./kgm. of *alpha*-chloralose. Prior to the administration of the morphine, DMPP and sodium cyanide produced a transient hyperpnea. Pentylenetetrazol and rauwolscine both produced a prolonged

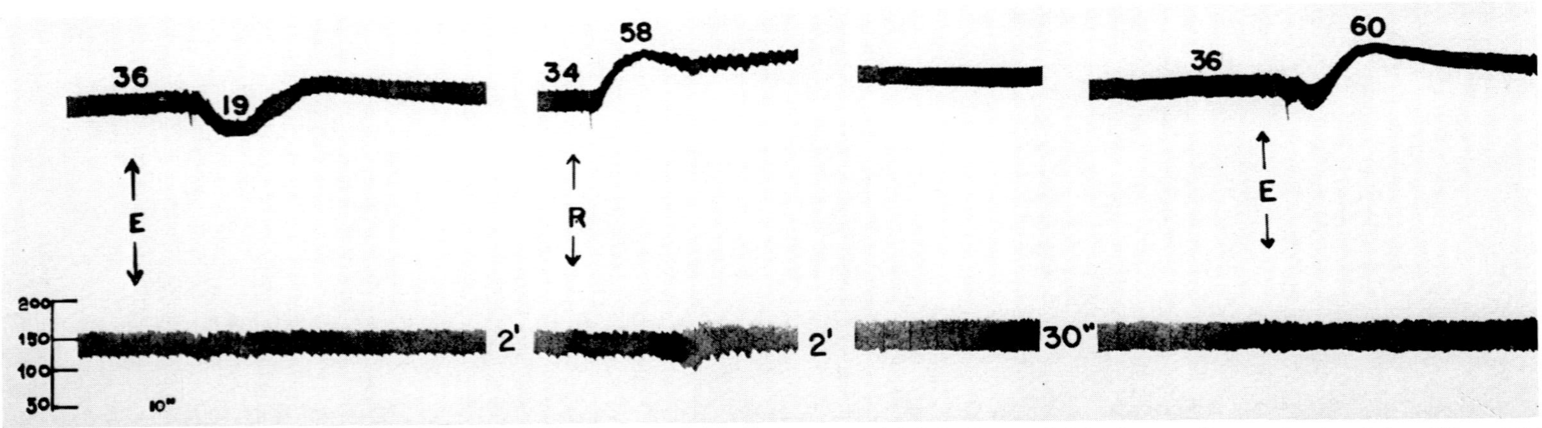

FIG. 3. Blood flow responses in the femoral vascular bed of a dog to intraarterial injections of 0.1 microgm./kgm. of epinephrine (E) and 0.1 mgm./kgm. of rauwolscine (R).

Upper line, blood flow; lower line, arterial pressure. Figures adjacent to upper tracing are rates of flow in ml./min. The numerals on the blood pressure scale, from top to bottom, are 200, 150, 100, 50.

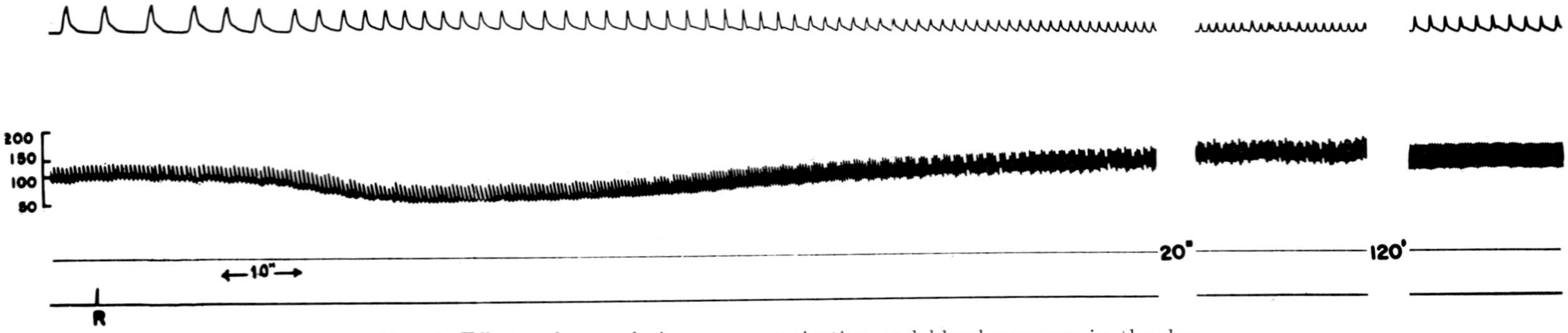

FIG. 4. Effects of rauwolscine upon respiration and blood pressure in the dog.

R indicates intravenous injection of 0.3 mgm./kgm., i.v., of rauwolscine. Upper tracing is respiration. Lower tracing is femoral arterial pressure. The numerals on the blood pressure scale, from top to bottom, are 200, 150, 100, 50.

tachypnea. After morphine, DMPP and sodium cyanide still produced a transient hyperpnea, but the administration of rauwolscine and pentylenetetrazol then resulted in no significant change in respiration. Dimethylphenylpiperazinium iodide, like the cyanide ion, produces hyperpnea by virtue of its ability to stimulate chemoreceptors in the aortic and carotid areas (Heymans, 1951). Pentylenetetrazol, on the other hand, is considered to act centrally. By analogy, it would seem therefore that rauwolscine produces tachypnea through a central mechanism.

Effects on heart rate. The effects of rauwolscine on the heart rate were not striking. In the cat there was usually no significant change in heart rate, even during hypotension. In the dog the most consistent effect was a transient bradycardia, although a number of dogs showed no change or a slight increase in rate. Most of the clinically used adrenergic blocking agents, such as tolazoline, produce tachycardia in accompaniment with hypotension, and the former may be a serious side effect.

DISCUSSION. The present findings indicate that rauwolscine probably exerts its hypotensive effect via mechanisms that are nearly entirely peripheral rather than central. Its peripheral actions include adrenergic blockade and direct vasodilation.

Das *et al.*, (1955) have stated that the cardiovascular effects of rauwolscine are predominantly central in origin. This conclusion was based on the observation that the blood pressure and pulse contour changes in monkeys were essentially the same following the intraperitoneal and intracisternal injection of rauwolscine. However, the doses of rauwolscine (0.5 to 1.0 mgm./kgm., or per animal) by both routes of administration were within the same range. Although the blood-brain barrier may limit the passage of a drug from the circulation to the cerebrospinal fluid, the same compound may pass very rapidly from the cerebrospinal fluid into the systemic circulation (Wallace and Brodie, 1940; Koelle and Steiner, 1956). Thus, the intracisternal injection of a compound might reveal a potential central site of action, but to demonstrate convincingly a primarily central site of action by this technique the effective dose should be considerably smaller than the equivalent dose by a systemic route as has been done with strophanthin-K (Weinberg and Haley, 1955).

The hemodynamic studies demonstrate that rauwolscine is a short acting, reversible adrenergic blocking agent. Doses sufficient to reverse the hypertensive effect of epinephrine and reduce that of levarterenol had little effect on the hypertensive response to carotid occlusion. The latter was reduced significantly only by considerably higher doses of rauwolscine, which produced a distinct fall in resting blood pressure. These observations indicate both the absence of important sites of hypotensive action central to the effector cells, and a relatively high ratio of the sympatholytic to the adrenolytic dose. The latter conclusion is borne out by the studies on the nictitating membrane. In order to inhibit the contraction of the nictitating membrane produced by supramaximal stimulation of the preganglionic trunk, it was necessary to give approximately 8 times the dose required to block the response produced by the intravenous injection of epinephrine.

The blood flow studies demonstrate the ability of rauwolscine to reverse the effects of epinephrine on femoral vascular flow in a manner typical of adrenergic blocking agents. The increased flow produced by rauwolscine in the denervated as well as in the innervated limb suggests an additional direct vasodilator effect not based on adrenergic blockade. This assumption is supported by the demonstration of increased flow after a dose of rauwolscine (0.5 microgm./kgm., i.a.) that did not affect the blood flow response to epinephrine. The direct vasodilatation action was not prevented by atropine, and hence is probably not parasympathomimetic.

Thus, rauwolscine appears to exert hemodynamic effects that are practically identical with those produced by its steroisomer, yohimbine. From the reports on the latter compound found in the literature (Kohli *et al.*, 1957), it appears that the effective dosage ranges of both isomers for the dog and cat are approximately the same.

The production by rauwolscine of tachypnea in the dog, which was not noted in the cat, probably represents a central effect of the drug. This conclusion is based on the experiments which showed that bilateral vagotomy and denervation of the carotid sinus area did not prevent this effect, while small doses of morphine sulfate did. The respiratory responses to pentylenetetrazol were modified similarly by these procedures. The effect of rauwolscine on the respiration in the dog has not been previously reported. This may be due to the fact that most of the previous workers have included morphine in their anesthetic mixture.

SUMMARY

The cardiovascular effects of rauwolscine have been studied in 42 dogs and 16 cats.

Rauwolscine was found to be a short-acting, reversible type of adrenergic blocking agent. The ratio of the sympatholytic to the adrenolytic dose was found to be relatively high (approximately eight to one) as estimated from the doses of rauwolscine needed to inhibit contractions of the nictitating membrane produced by electrical stimulation of the cervical sympathetic trunk and by intravenously administered epinephrine. Furthermore, following doses of rauwolscine which produced "epinephrine-reversal" of the blood pressure, the pressor response to bilateral carotid occlusion was not reduced.

Rauwolscine was shown to exert a peripheral vasodilator effect on both the innervated and denervated hind limb of the dog. The mechanism of the vasodilatation is probably a direct effect, in addition to adrenergic blockade.

Rauwolscine produced tachypnea consistently in the dog but not in the cat. Evidence has been presented to show that the site of the respiratory effect in the dog is central.

The effects of rauwolscine on the heart rate were variable. With hypotensive doses, it usually produced no significant change in the cat and a transient bradycardia in the dog.

REFERENCES

Chakravarti, M. D.: Science and Culture, **7:** 458, 1942.

Das, N. N., Dasgupta, S. P., Mukherjee, K. L., and Werner, G.: Indian J. M. Res., **43:** 101, 1955.

Griffin, P. P., Green, H. D., Youmans, P. L., and Johnson, H. D.: This Journal, **102:** 50, 1954.

Heymans, C.: Acta physiol. scandinav., **22:** 4, 1951.

Koelle, G. B., and Steiner, E. C.: This Journal, **118:** 420, 1956.

Kohli, J. D., and De, N. N.: Nature, **177:** 1182, 1956.

Kohli, J. D., Balwani, J. H., Ray, C., and De, N. N.: Arch. internat. pharmacodyn., **111:** 108, 1957.

Mukherjee, J. N.: Nature, **172:** 867, 1953.

Mukherjee, J. N., and Sen, P. B.: Indian J. Physiol. & App. Sci., **7:** 109, 1953a.

Mukherjee, J. N., and Sen, P. B.: Indian J. Physiol. & App. Sci., **7:** 148, 1953b.

Mukherjee, M. D., and Sen, P. B.: Indian J. Physiol. & App. Sci., **7:** 57, 1953.

Nickerson, M., and Goodman, L. S.: Fed. Proc., **7:** 397, 1948.

Prochnik, G., Maison, G. L., and Stutzman, J. W.: Am. J. Physiol., **162:** 553, 1950.

Shipley, R. E., and Wilson, C.: Proc. Soc. Exper. Biol. & Med., **78:** 724, 1951.

Soskin, S., Priest, W. S., and Schutz, W. J.: Am. J. Physiol., **107:** 427, 1934.

Wallace, G. B., and Brodie, B. B.: This Journal, **68:** 50, 1940.

Weinberg, S. J., and Haley, T. J.: Circ. Res., **3:** 103, 1955.

8046

THE MECHANISM OF THE HYPOTENSIVE ACTION OF NARCOTINE HYDROCHLORIDE[1, 2]

LAWRENCE C. WEAVER, WILLIAM M. ALEXANDER, BENEDICT E. ABREU, ALICE B. RICHARDS, W. RALPH JONES AND ROBERT W. BEGLEY

Research Department, Pitman-Moore Company, Division of Allied Laboratories, Indianapolis 6, Indiana

Received for publication April 3, 1958

The general pharmacology of narcotine has been extensively reviewed by Krueger, Eddy and Sumwalt (1943). It has been suggested that the pharmacologic properties of narcotine are similar to those of papaverine (Goodman and Gilman, 1955). The present study is concerned primarily with a systematic study of the cardiovascular effects of narcotine with some comparison to those of related compounds.

METHODS. Mongrel dogs weighing between 5.9 and 15.7 kgm., unselected as to sex, and anesthetized with sodium pentobarbital, were used for all cardiovascular studies. Mean blood pressures were recorded with a mercury manometer (carotid or femoral artery) or a Sanborn electromanometer. Central pressure pulses were obtained from the carotid artery or the aortic arch with an electromanometer. Electrocardiograms were recorded with a Gilson Electroencephalograph or a Sanborn Viso-Cardiette. Stroke volume was estimated by the pulse contour method of Hamilton and Remington (1947), Remington *et al.* (1949), and Remington (1952); total peripheral resistance was calculated by the method of Wiggers (1944), and left ventricular work by the method of Remington and Hamilton (1947).

A continuous recording rotameter (Shipley and Wilson, 1951) measured the rate of blood flow in the coronary or the femoral artery (Winbury *et al.*, 1950; Winbury and Hambourger, 1953). The circumflex branch of the left coronary artery was supplied by a cannulated carotid or femoral artery; the femoral artery was sectioned, and the rotameter interposed between the central and peripheral ends. Coagulation of blood was prevented by the intravenous (i.v.) injection of 8 mgm./kgm. of heparin[3] followed by a constant infusion at the rate of 4 mgm./kgm./hr. intravenously. Blood lost during the study of coronary blood flow was returned to the dog via i.v. infusion at about the same rate as it was lost. Five-second intra-arterial (i.a.) injections were made into the outflow of the rotameter using the hydrochloride salts in isotonic saline (Winbury *et al.*, 1951); i.v. injections were made into a catheterized femoral vein.

Changes in bronchiolar resistance of dogs were recorded by a modification of the method of Konzett and Rossler (1940). In brief, under constant volume artificial respiration, variations in bronchiolar resistance were indicated by changes in volume of the air in excess of that required for adequate ventilation.

The dose of narcotine hydrochloride[4] that produced 50 per cent lethality (LD_{50}) in dogs following a 15-second i.v. injection was determined. The data were analyzed statistically by the method of Litchfield and Wilcoxon (1949).

RESULTS. *Acute toxicity.* The acute i.v. LD_{50} for narcotine in 23 dogs was 52.0 (46.4 to 58.2) mgm./kgm.; 200 mgm./kgm., administered orally in gelatin capsules, was without effect whereas 500 mgm./kgm. produced the toxic signs observed following injections. The toxic signs observed were those associated with extreme central nervous system stimulation: clonic convulsions with vocalization, opisthotonos and tonic extension of limbs following external stimulus. Other signs included urination, defecation, gasping respiration, slow weak pulse, a flushing of the nonhairy portions of the skin, and slight swelling of ears and lips.

Cardiovascular effects in intact dogs. Narcotine proved to be a relatively potent vasodilator with a duration of action that was usually moderately long. However, individual dogs showed considerable variation. For example, when administered

[1] A preliminary report of this work appeared in Fed. Proc., **16:** 345, 1957.

[2] New generic name is Noscapine.

[3] Heparin sodium was kindly supplied by Dr. R. K. Richards, Abbott Laboratories.

[4] Narcotine HCl was kindly supplied by Dr. Charles Winter, Merck Sharp & Dohme, Inc.

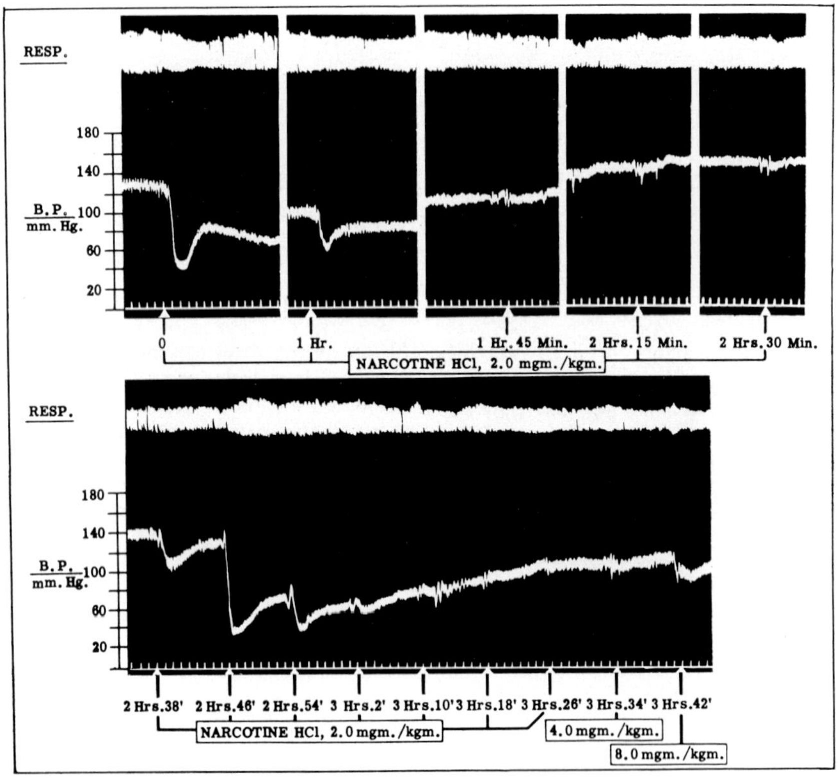

FIG. 1. The development of tachyphylaxis to the vasodepressor effect of intravenous narcotine in a dog anesthetized with pentobarbital.

rapidly intravenously, *one dose per dog*, the percentage decrease (average and range) in systemic blood pressure for various doses, was as follows: 1 mgm./kgm. = 30 (6 to 67, 6 dogs); 2.0 mgm./kgm. = 51 (13 to 91, 4 dogs); and 5.0 mgm./kgm. = 81 (70 to 98, 16 dogs). Similar potency and variability were observed for papaverine: 0.5 mgm./kgm. = 31 (15 to 43, 4 dogs); 1.0 mgm./kgm. = 34 (2 to 83, 6 dogs); and 2.0 mgm./kgm. = 50 (8 to 89, 7 dogs). Slow (30-second) intravenous administration of narcotine produced results not unlike those following rapid administration. The duration of vasodepression was variable. For example, following administration of 5 mgm./kgm., the duration of the decrease in systemic blood pressure ranged from 20 minutes to more than 2 hours.

Tachyphylaxis to the vasodepressive effect of narcotine could be produced following intravenous administration to dogs (figure 1). In studies with this agent, a cumulative effect usually preceded the tachyphylaxis, particularly from injections given at shorter intervals. A greater vasodepressor response was obtained from the second dose than from the first and then the vasodepression decreased until little or no effect was noted. Individual dogs varied in susceptibility to this tachyphylaxis.

Tachyphylaxis to increased femoral arterial blood flow developed similarly. When narcotine was administered (i.a.) in doses adequate for large increases in femoral blood flow but in sufficiently low doses so as to have no effect or an extremely slight and transient effect on systemic blood pressure, tachyphylaxis developed starting with the second dose. Although the increased flow was not always completely eliminated, it became negligible after a few doses.

Tachyphylaxis to the systemic hypotensive action of papaverine hydrochloride, ethaverine hydrochloride or dioxyline phosphate (Paveril[5])

[5] Paveril (dioxyline phosphate) was kindly supplied by Dr. F. G. Henderson, Eli Lilly & Company.

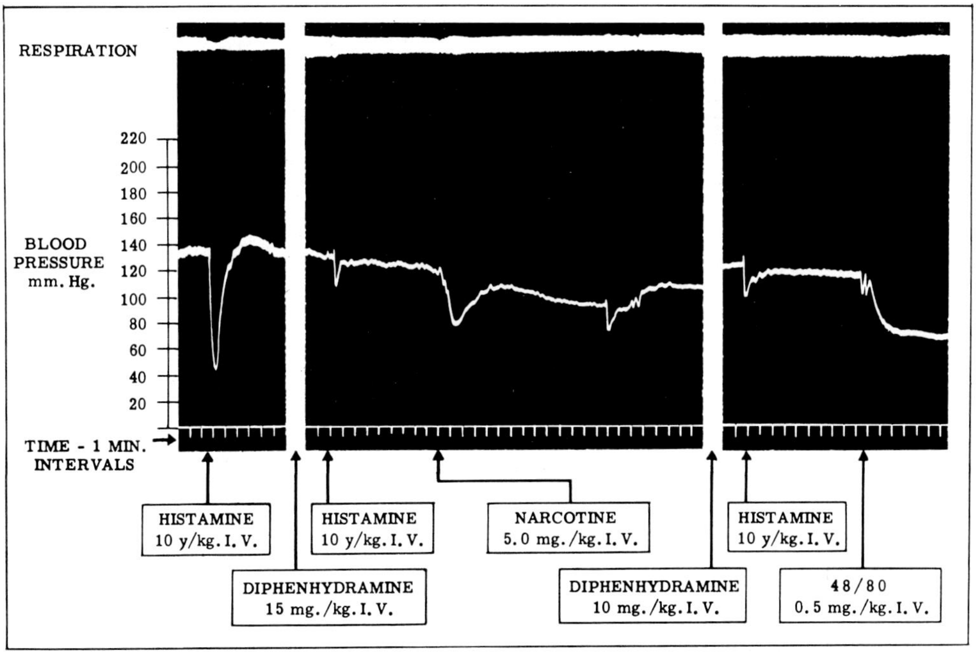

FIG. 2. Effect of diphenhydramine on the vasodepressor responses due to narcotine and 48/80 in a dog anesthetized with pentobarbital.
See figure 6 for the usual vasodepressor response to this dose of narcotine.

did not occur under identical conditions. Neither did cross-tachyphylaxis occur between narcotine and any of these compounds. However, cross-tachyphylaxis between narcotine and 48/80[6] was shown when sufficient narcotine was given to produce a marked decrease in systemic blood pressure.

Tachyphylaxis interfered with the procedures designed to help elucidate the mechanism for this hypotensive effect. Therefore, a dose of 5 mgm./kgm., which produced a consistent effect in 16 dogs, was used in attempts to eliminate the narcotine vasodepression by means of each of the following measures: atropinization (using the vasopressor response to acetylcholine, 1 mgm./kgm., as an indicator); midcervical bilateral vagotomy; carotid sinus and body denervation by careful vessel ligation and adventitial stripping; and the use of the antihistaminic, diphenhydramine hydrochloride. Administration of diphenhydramine was the only measure that significantly altered the narcotine vasodepression (figure 2). The vasodepression produced by 5 mgm./kgm. of narcotine, although never completely eliminated was consistently reduced as was the vasodepression produced by 48/80.

Coronary dilator properties. Coronary blood flow (CBF) studies indicate that both narcotine and papaverine possess significant dilator activity following injection directly into the coronary bed or into the systemic circulation. The actions of 4-microgm./kgm. doses of narcotine and 1-microgm./kgm. doses of papaverine were compared in 5 open-chest dogs (figure 3). Each of these doses produced an immediate increase in CBF. Winbury *et al.* (1950) demonstrated that the increase in CBF was directly related to the size of the dose, but was independent of the mean blood pressure (MBP) or the control flow rate. Their observation was confirmed during these studies. During the period of augmented CBF, there was always a reduction in the coronary resistance $\left(\frac{\text{MBP}}{\text{CBF}}\right)$. The changes in other cardiovascular variables were slight (figure 3), suggesting that increase in CBF is the result of coronary dilatation.

Effects of intravenous injections on CBF. The

[6] 48/80 was kindly supplied by Dr. E. J. deBeer, Wellcome Research Laboratories.

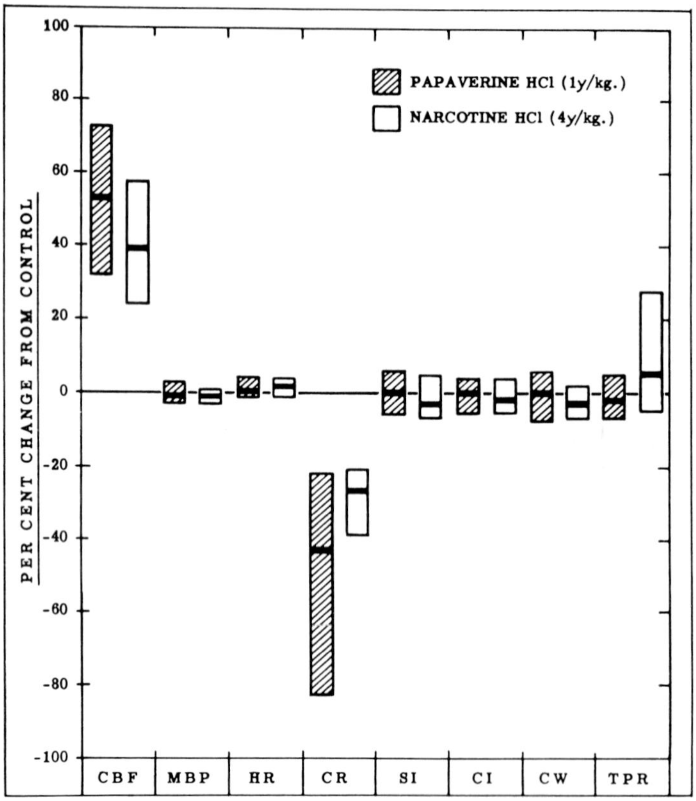

FIG. 3. Simultaneous changes in cardiovascular variables following intracoronary injection of papaverine hydrochloride (1 microgm./kgm.) and of narcotine hydrochloride (4 microgm./kgm.) in 5 paired experiments (5 dogs).

Means are indicated by the solid horizontal bars; range by the limits of the bar. CBF = coronary blood flow (inflow), ml./min., MBP = mean blood pressure, mm. Hg, CR = coronary resistance, MBP/CBF, HR = heart rate, beats/min., SI = stroke index, ml./min./m²., CI = cardiac index, l./min./m²., CW = cardiac work, kgm./min., TPR = total peripheral resistance, absolute units.

effects produced by injections of narcotine and papaverine were studied in 16 dogs. As can be seen from figures 4 and 5, each of these agents, in doses of 0.5 mgm./kgm., caused an increase in CBF, though an initial transient effect was a decline in CBF accompanying a similar fall in MBP lasting about two minutes. While CBF then rose to a point above control level, MBP returned to normal levels more slowly and generally did not exceed the control level. Figures 4 and 5 also illustrate the magnitude of the changes in some of the hemodynamic factors which may be associated with the changes in CBF (Gregg, 1950) following the administration of narcotine and papaverine.

During the period of decreased CBF, stroke index (SI), cardiac index (CI) and coronary resistance (CR) were increased for papaverine but not for narcotine; MBP, total peripheral resistance (TPR), and left ventricular work (CW) were reduced by both drugs. During the period of increased flow, the only consistent directional change was a lowered CR for each drug and an increased CI and CR for papaverine; the average MBP was control or less.

Effects of intravenous injections on cardiac rate. In the intact dog under pentobarbital anesthesia, a dose of 5 mgm./kgm. of narcotine *usually* produced a bradycardia varying from almost 0 to approximately 50 per cent of the control rate. Bilateral midcervical vagotomy prevented the bradycardia but not the vasodepressive effect in 3 of 4 dogs showing that the vasodepressive effects were produced independently of the effects on cardiac rate.

Bronchoconstrictor effects. Narcotine produces a

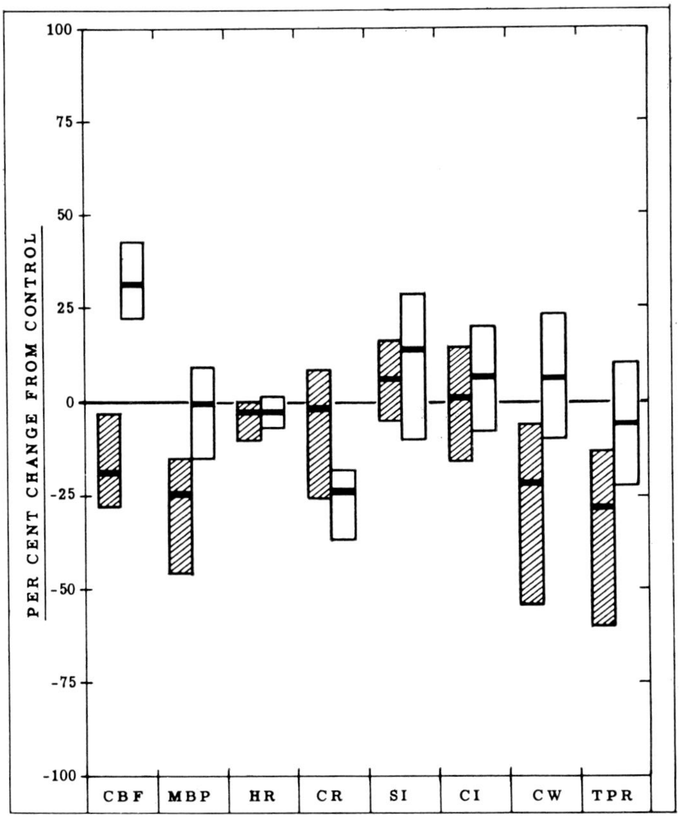

FIG. 4. Simultaneous changes in cardiovascular variables following intravenous injection of narcotine hydrochloride (0.5 mgm./kgm.) in six dogs.
The initial period of decreased CBF is indicated by the filled bars; the subsequent period of increased CBF by the open bars. Means are indicated by the solid black lines, ranges by the limits of the bars. For an explanation of the abbreviations, see figure 3.

profound bronchoconstriction in the dog (figure 6) and, as can be seen, tachyphylaxis to this effect also develops. Similar bronchoconstriction produced by 48/80 is shown in figure 7. Cross-tachyphylaxis between 48/80 and narcotine also is shown to both the bronchoconstrictor and the hypotensive effects. No significant bronchoconstrictor effect could be shown for papaverine, ethaverine or Paveril.

DISCUSSION. Evidence has been presented which suggests the hypothesis that the hypotensive effect of narcotine is, in fact, due to histamine liberation. This evidence may be summarized as follows: 1) tachyphylaxis developed to the systemic vasodepression and to increased femoral blood flow; 2) cross-tachyphylaxis occurred between narcotine and 48/80 (a potent histamine liberator); 3) the vasodepression was considerably reduced by diphenhydramine but was unaffected by atropinization, midcervical bilateral vagotomy and/or carotid sinus and body denervation; 4) peripheral toxic signs occurred in dogs following intravenous administration; and 5) similar bronchoconstrictor effects were produced by narcotine and 48/80. Recently, Slomka[7] completed additional studies which confirm this hypothesis. Dogs under pentobarbital anesthesia were given 5 mgm./kgm. of narcotine hydrochloride. The dogs responding with a marked decrease (71 to 90 per cent) in blood pressure also showed increases in plasma histamine concentration ranging from 0.19 to 0.84 microgm./ml. at maximum depressor response. Plasma histamine concentrations were determined by

[7] The authors are grateful to Dr. M. B. Slomka, Dept. of Pharmacology, Southwestern Medical School, University of Texas for making his results available.

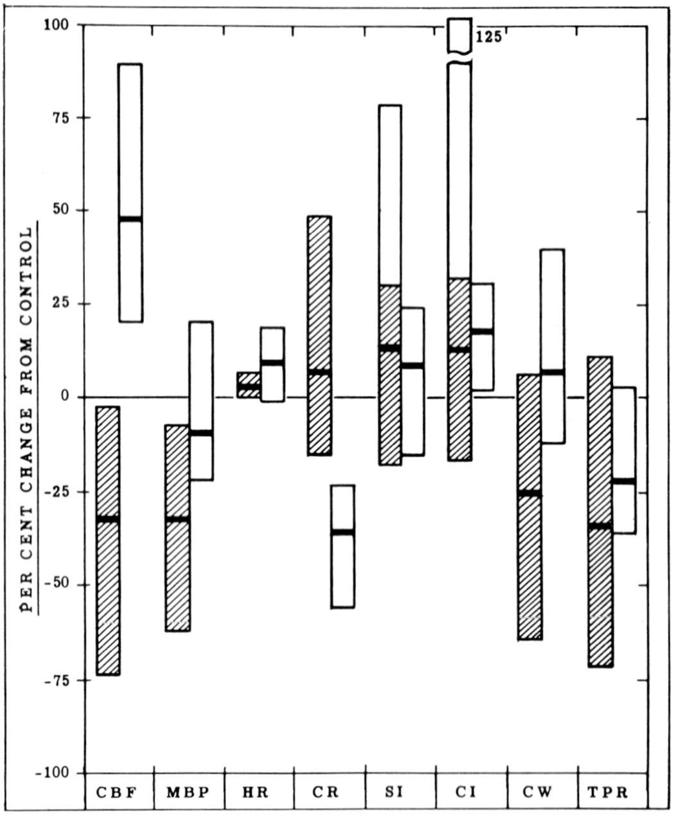

FIG. 5. Simultaneous changes in cardiovascular variables following intravenous injection of papaverine hydrochloride (0.5 mgm./kgm.) in ten dogs.

The initial period of decreased CBF is indicated by the filled bars; the subsequent period of increased CBF by the open bars. The open bars for SI and CI represent the extremes for one dog. Means are indicated by the solid black lines, ranges by the limits of the bars. For an explanation of the abbreviations, see figure 3.

direct assay using atropinized guinea pig ileum. Contractions produced by both histamine-containing plasma and histamine standards were completely inhibited or reduced to less than ten per cent of the original contraction height by diphenhydramine. Furthermore, Slomka observed cross-tachyphylaxis with 48/80 as well as absence of histamine in plasma of dogs when narcotine was administered following tachyphylaxis to narcotine.

Histamine liberation by other opium alkaloids has been reported. The property of histamine liberation was exhibited by morphine, codeine, apomorphine and thebaine, from the phenanthrene group (Feldberg and Paton, 1949, 1951; Nasmyth and Stewart, 1950; Bhattacharya and Lewis, 1956; and others) and, by papaverine from the benzylisoquinoline group (Feldberg and Paton, 1951). Thus, histamine liberation by narcotine might be expected.

The hypotensive effect of narcotine in higher doses in the cat is unlike that observed in the dog. A dose of 5 mgm./kgm. of narcotine, intravenously, in anesthetized cats had no effect whatever on blood pressure, while 10 mgm./kgm. produced a transient fall in blood pressure (Chopra *et al.*, 1930; Winter, personal communication). In doses up to 20 mgm./kgm., we were able to produce a moderate fall in systemic blood pressure in the anesthetized cat. However, control blood pressure was regained usually within ten minutes, and repeated administration failed to show tachyphylaxis (Weaver, unpublished observations). Similar differences exist with regard to bronchoconstriction in the cat. Konzett and Rothlin (1954) studied the effect of narcotine

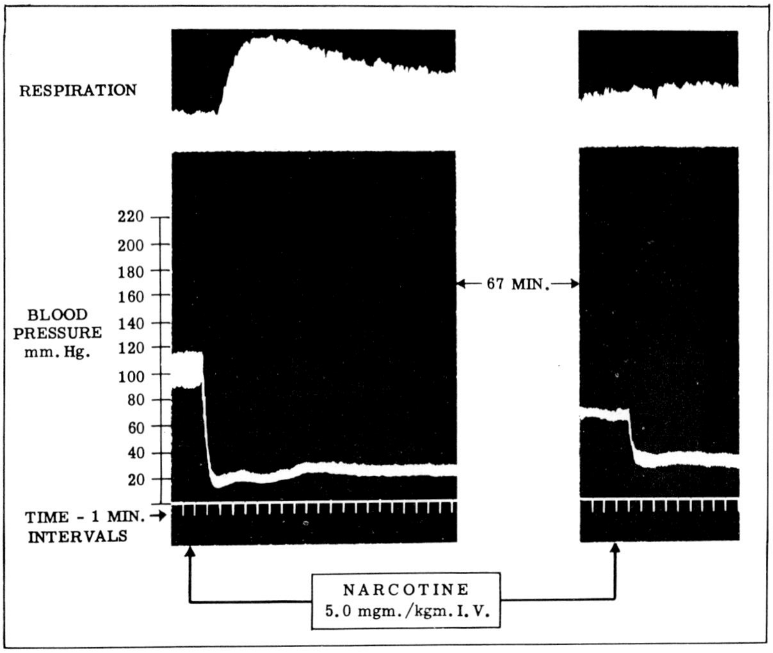

FIG. 6. Effect of narcotine on systemic mean blood pressure and bronchiolar resistance in a dog anesthetized with pentobarbital.

An increase in the width of the respiratory tracing indicates bronchiolar constriction. Tachyphylaxis to the constriction is shown following the second dose of narcotine.

on the bronchial musculature of the cat and observed either no effect or only a slight bronchodilation. Since bronchoconstriction occurs in the dog, it would appear that a species difference exists with regard to the histamine-liberating properties of narcotine.

These data show that narcotine, like papaverine, when injected into the coronary artery produced increased flow without consistent or significant alteration in other cardiovascular variables. That papaverine produces fairly marked coronary vasodilatation has long been known (Essex *et al.*, 1940; Lindner and Katz, 1941; Eckenhoff and Hafkenschiel, 1947; Heidenreich and Schmidt, 1955; and many others). Likewise, coronary relaxation due to narcotine has been reported for the isolated coronary artery of the pig and the coronary vein of the cat (Macht, 1915). Nevertheless, the mechanism whereby CBF is increased for papaverine has not been established unequivocally, and recent evidence for the confirmation of this effect for narcotine is lacking. The experimental results herein confirm and extend the evidence that both alkaloids are potent coronary vasodilators in dogs. However, they do not prove conclusively that increased CBF is in fact due to dilatation. Although the increased CBF was always associated with reduced coronary resistance, this term (CR) is merely a statement of pressure/flow relationship, which can be influenced by several hemodynamic factors other than vasomotor tone (Gregg, 1950). During the period of increased CBF, these other cardiovascular variables (SI, CI, HR and CW) were not consistently or significantly altered. Therefore, the conclusion seems justified that these two alkaloids are capable of increasing CBF by coronary vasodilatation. The patterns of increased flow following i.a. injection (coronary or femoral) were different. With papaverine the increased flow was immediate, reached a peak, and returned to control quickly, whereas, following the administration of narcotine the onset was slower, the peak occurred later, and the duration was very much longer.

The increase in CBF following the intravenous administration of these agents adds little conclusive evidence as to the mechanism for the increased CBF, since it is not known to what extent the changes in other cardiovascular variables may influence this increase. Thus, it would

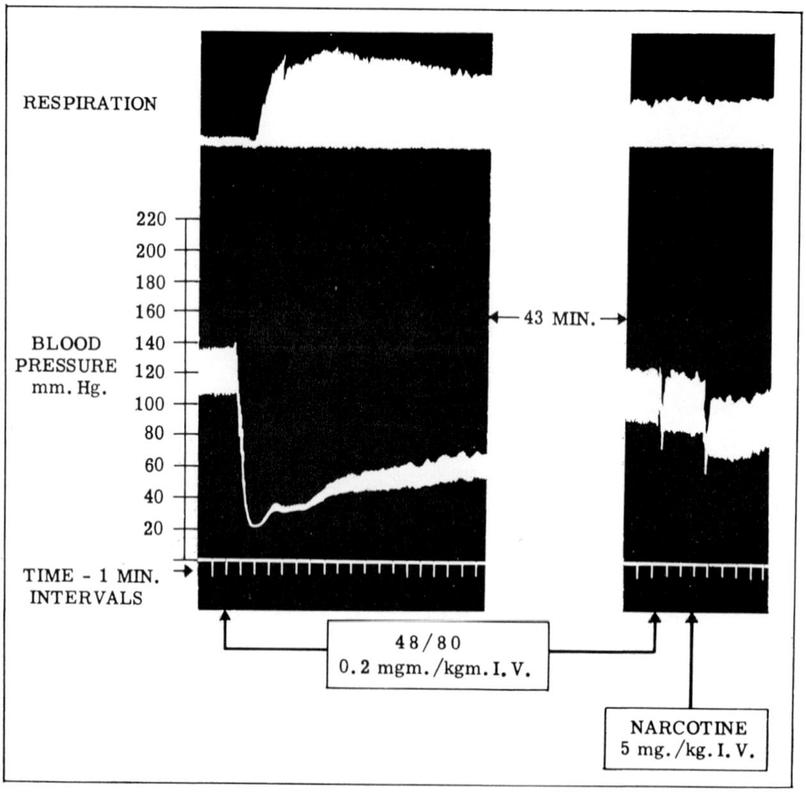

FIG. 7. Effect of 48/80 on systemic mean blood pressure and bronchiolar resistance in a dog anesthetized with pentobarbital.

An increase in the width of the respiratory tracing indicates bronchiolar constriction. Tachyphylaxis to bronchiolar constriction and to the vasodepression is shown following the second dose of 48/80. Cross-tachyphylaxis between 48/80 and narcotine is seen.

seem that the increased coronary blood flow following narcotine might be due to the histamine-liberating properties of this compound, but the corresponding evidence for papaverine failed to show that histamine liberation played a prominent role in the hypotensive action. Nevertheless, it is possible that histamine liberation might be responsible for this increased CBF or, more likely, some other direct depressant action on the smooth muscle of the coronary arterioles.

SUMMARY

Narcotine hydrochloride produces systemic vasodepression which is incompletely blocked by diphenhydramine but is unaffected by atropinization, mid-cervical vagotomy and/or carotid sinus and body denervation.

It also increases coronary blood flow and femoral blood flow. Coronary blood flow is increased without significant effects on the other cardiovascular variables.

Bronchoconstriction is produced in the dog.

Tachyphylaxis develops to the vascular and bronchial effects of this compound. In addition, cross-tachyphylaxis develops between narcotine and 48/80.

It is concluded that the mechanism for these changes is due to histamine liberation.

REFERENCES

BHATTACHARYA, B. K., AND LEWIS, G. P.: Brit. J. Pharmacol., **11:** 202, 1956.
CHOPRA, R. N., MUKHERJEE, B., AND DIKSHIT, B. B.: Indian J. M. Research, **18:** 35, 1930.
ECKENHOFF, J. E., AND HAFKENSCHIEL, J. H.: THIS JOURNAL, **91:** 362, 1947.
ESSEX, H. E., WEGRIA, R., HERRICK, J. F., AND MANN, F. C.: Am. Heart J., **19:** 554, 1940.
FELDBERG, W., AND PATON, W. D. M.: J. Physiol., **111:** 19P, 1950.
FELDBERG, W., AND PATON, W. D. M.: J. Physiol., **114:** 490, 1951.

GOODMAN, L. S., AND GILMAN, A.: The pharmacological basis of therapeutics, 2nd Edition, The MacMillan Company, New York, 1955.
GREGG, D. E.: Coronary circulation in heart and disease, Chapters 5, 6, and 7, Lea and Febiger, Philadelphia, 1950.
HAMILTON, W. F., AND REMINGTON, J. W.: Am. J. Physiol., **148:** 14, 1947.
HEIDENREICH, O., AND SCHMIDT, L.: Arch. exper. Path. u. Pharmakol., **227:** 250, 1955.
KONZETT, H., AND ROSSLER, R.: Arch. exper. Path. u. Pharmakol., **195:** 71, 1940.
KONZETT, H., AND ROTHLIN, E.: Experientia, **10:** 472, 1954.
KRUEGER, H., EDDY, N. B., AND SUMWALT, M.: The pharmacology of the opium alkaloids, Supplement No. 165, part 2, Pub. Health Rep., U. S. Government Printing Office, Washington D. C., 1943.
LINDNER, E., AND KATZ, L. N.: THIS JOURNAL, **72:** 306, 1941.
LITCHFIELD, J. T., JR., AND WILCOXON, F.: THIS JOURNAL, **96:** 99, 1949.
MACHT, D. I.: J. A. M. A., **64:** 1489, 1915.
NASMYTH, P. A., AND STEWART, H. C.: J. Physiol., **111:** 19P, 1950.
REMINGTON, J. W.: Fed. Proc., **11:** 750, 1952.
REMINGTON, J. W., AND HAMILTON, W. F.: Am. J. Physiol., **150:** 292, 1947.
REMINGTON, J. W., HAMILTON, W. F., WHEELER, N. C., AND HAMILTON, W. F., JR.: Am. J. Physiol., **159:** 379, 1949.
SHIPLEY, R. E., AND WILSON, C.: Proc. Soc. Exper. Biol. & Med., **78:** 724, 1951.
WIGGERS, H. C.: Am. J. Physiol., **140:** 519, 1944.
WINBURY, M. M., BEACH, D. A., AND MICHIELS, P. M.: Am. J. Physiol., **165:** 135, 1951.
WINBURY, M. M., AND HAMBOURGER, W. E.: THIS JOURNAL, **108:** 46, 1953.
WINBURY, M. M., MICHIELS, P. M., HAMBOURGER, W. E., STOCKFISH, W. J., AND COOK, D. L.: THIS JOURNAL, **99:** 343, 1950.

8047

SOME PHARMACOLOGICAL ACTIONS OF RYANODINE[1] IN THE MAMMAL[2]

LEONARD PROCITA[3]

Department of Pharmacology, St. Louis University School of Medicine, St. Louis 4, Missouri

Received for publication May 12, 1958

Early pharmacological studies with toxic materials derived from the plant genus *Ryania* were done principally with extracts which were neither pure nor chemically characterized. The toxicity of these materials, termed either "ryanine" or "ryanitine" respectively, was first reported by Nakari and Sano in 1928 and again by these same authors in 1934. According to these investigators frogs, mice, cats, rabbits and dogs, but not fish succumbed to the lethal effect of the above mentioned materials. Death was attributed to "a spasm of the respiratory muscles with subsequent paralysis of the respiratory centers." It was observed also that anesthesia prolonged the survival of the poisoned animals. Merz (1930) reported on observations similar to those of Nakari and Sano. Some studies on the chemistry of materials extracted from the *Ryania* plant, together with some toxicological observations, were reported by Bret (1930) and also by Le Cointe (1930). These early investigations, however, were quite superficial in scope and there was no apparent further interest, to judge by the literature, in the pharmacological properties of the toxic materials extracted from the *Ryania* plant until Kuna and Heal (1948) published some data relative to the acute toxicity of orally administered ryania powder (the ground stem and root of the plant). Nothing, however, was included in this report which contributed to an understanding of the mechanism of action of the toxic principle contained in the powder.

[1] The ryanodine for these experiments was generously supplied by Dr. E. F. Rogers of Merck and Co., Rahway, New Jersey.

[2] This investigation was begun at the Department of Pharmacology, University of Michigan Medical School. It was continued at the Department of Pharmacology, St. Louis University Medical School, supported by a grant from the St. Louis Heart Association.

[3] Present address: Department of Pharmacology, State University of New York College of Medicine, 450 Clarkson Avenue, Brooklyn 3, New York.

Also in 1948, Rogers *et al.* reported the isolation of a chemically pure alkaloid, ryanodine, from the stem and root of the South American plant species *Ryania speciosa Vahl.* Ryanodine was shown to be a crystalline solid with a melting point at 219–220°C. The material is readily soluble in water, alcohol, acetone, ether and chloroform. The ultraviolet absorption spectrum shows a maximum at 268.5 mμ in alcohol solution. The complete molecular structure of ryanodine is not yet known. Kelly *et al.* (1951, 1952) and Kelly (1953) have reported that ryanodine may be hydrolyzed to yield *alpha*-pyrrole carboxylic acid and an alcohol, ryanodol ($C_{20}H_{32}O_8$). The molecular weight is taken as 500.

Since the pure alkaloid became available reports have appeared in the literature concerned with the action of ryanodine on frog skeletal muscle (Edwards *et al.*, 1948; Wills and Murtha, 1948; Edwards and Flinker, 1950; Pick and Tullius, 1951; Pick and Holland, 1951; Jenden and Blum, 1956; Blum *et al.*, 1957). The action of ryanodine on mammalian skeletal muscle (Procita, 1956), cardiac muscle (Furchgott and De Gubareff, 1956; Hillyard and Procita, 1956), and intestinal smooth muscle (Procita and Hillyard, 1957), have also been reported. Other papers have been concerned with the effects of ryanodine on embryonic tissues (Bodenstein, 1950; Cornman, 1951), on respiration of the cockroach (Hasset, 1948), and on cockroach muscle (Becht and Dresden, 1956).

An exhaustive search of the literature revealed that ryanodine had not been subjected to a pharmacological study in the mammal. The present paper is primarily concerned with some aspects of the pharmacology of ryanodine in the cat and dog, and its toxicity in a variety of other mammalian species. Two preliminary reports have already been presented (Procita *et al.*, 1952; Procita and Kuluz, 1956).

METHODS. Aqueous solutions of ryanodine and other drugs were used throughout. It was found, on the basis of acute toxicity tests in various mammalian species, that ryanodine solutions are stable for long periods of time when kept at ordinary room temperatures. To determine the acute toxicity of ryanodine in intact unanesthetized animals it was administered intravenously and orally to dogs; intraperitoneally to cats, guinea pigs, rats, mice, bats and monkeys; and intravenously to rabbits and chickens. An accurate LD_{50} was evaluated only for the mouse by the statistical method of Litchfield and Wilcoxon (1949) and expresses 95 per cent confidence limits.

Dogs, cats and a few rabbits, chosen without regard to sex or weight, were anesthetized with 30 to 35 mgm./kgm. of sodium pentobarbital, administered either intraperitoneally or intravenously. Arterial blood pressure was usually recorded from the carotid artery by means of a mercury manometer. In a number of experiments when using cats, however, the arterial pressure was recorded from the femoral artery or the lower abdominal aorta. Heparin was used as the anticoagulant in the arterial cannula. Injections were made into various veins and arteries as described in the text. Respiratory excursions were recorded by means of an accordion type pneumograph tied about the chest and connected to a Marey tambour. The vagi were sectioned in the neck at the time of tracheal cannulation unless indicated otherwise. Electrocardiograms (lead II) were obtained with a direct writing "Cardiotron" (model *PC-1A*) and with a Beck-Lee "Cardiall." Artificial respiration, when required, was maintained with a Palmer positive pressure pump in dogs, and with a Harvard respirator in cats and rabbits.

Four dog heart-lung preparations were arranged under light pentobarbital anesthesia employing the Krayer-Mendez (1942) modification of the classical Patterson-Starling method. The venous inflow pump and coronary arterial cannula were not employed and the Stolinokov stromuhr was used in place of the Weese type. Continuous recordings of right auricular and arterial pressures were made, in the former instance with a water manometer, and in the latter instance with a mercury manometer. Periodic determinations of systemic cardiac output (left ventricular output minus coronary outflow) were made. Drugs were injected through the cannula leading into the superior vena cava.

The contraction of the lateral rectus muscle, as induced by ryanodine, was studied in 4 dogs. The orbit was approached by reflection of the temporal muscle and removal of the zygomatic arch. All of the extraocular muscles except the lateral rectus were sectioned. A small hook was inserted into the belly of this muscle and connected to a frontal riding lever by a light cotton cord. Artificial respiration was maintained throughout the course of these experiments. Two dogs were curarized with approximately 1 mgm./kgm. of *d*-tubocurarine (Squibb) given intravenously in divided doses over a 15-minute interval.

Results. A.) *Effects in unanesthetized animals.* The directly observable effects resulting when a lethal dose of ryanodine is administered intravenously, intraperitoneally or orally, to a variety of unanesthetized animals does not vary significantly from species to species. Observations are best made, however, when utilizing the larger animals such as the dog, cat or rabbit.

1.) Dog: The rapidity of onset of the ryanodine effect is dependent on the magnitude of the dose and the route of administration. Intravenous injections of 100 microgm./kgm. of ryanodine usually produce death in 20 to 25 minutes. With large doses (500 to 1000 microgm./kgm.) similarly administered, the time interval from injection to death is usually less than 5 minutes.

Ryanodine-induced effects in the dog, following the intravenous administration of 50 microgm./kgm. or more, is first manifested by enophthalmos. Shortly after the ocular signs are noted a spastic rigidity of the hind-limb musculature begins to appear, especially when the animal attempts to walk. During this period salivation may become profuse and vomiting and defecation may occur. A spastic rigidity progressively involves all of the skeletal musculature and the animal succumbs when respiration becomes ineffective and anoxia supervenes. Convulsions, either as a direct action of the drug, or as a result of anoxia, were not seen in the dog. The heart rate becomes very rapid when respiratory embarrassment occurs. When the chest was opened with the animal in the final movements of agonal gasping, ventricular fibrillation was usually observed. In some instances there was cardiac arrest rather than fibrillation, the former situation being observed more often following the intravenous injection of large doses of ryanodine.

Sublethal doses of ryanodine also produced enophthalmos and varying degrees of spastic muscle rigidity. The dog, in addition, became ill and depressed but was fully recovered within 24 hours showing no apparent residual effects of the ryanodine. Equivalent sublethal amounts of the drug on a second or third day produced effects similar to those produced after the initial injection and there did not appear to be any cumulative effect. The salivation, vomiting and defecation, mentioned previously, may occur at all dose levels, but are not seen where muscle rigidity and death supervene quite rapidly following the intravenous administration of large doses of ryanodine.

Dogs receiving ryanodine orally or intraperitoneally reacted to a sublethal or lethal dose in the same manner as those animals receiving the drug by the intravenous route. The time of onset of the usual signs, however, varied somewhat and were considerably delayed. Table 1 presents the acute toxicity data for the dog.

2.) Other species: Tables 1 and 2 present the toxicity data for a variety of species to which ryanodine was administered either intraperitoneally or intravenously. The larger animals for example the cat and rabbit, behaved in general in a manner similar to that already described for the dog. The muscle rigidity in the cat and rabbit was extreme. The behavior of the smaller animals, mouse, rat and guinea pig, cannot be as easily characterized. However, the spastic paralysis of the hind limbs, the difficulty with respiration, with ensuing rigidity and death, were obvious.

TABLE 1

Acute toxicity of ryanodine in dog, cat and rabbit

Species	Route	Dose	Mortality
		microgm./kgm.	
Dog	i.v.	50	0/5
		75	4/7
		90	7/7
		100	6/6
		200	5/5
		400	2/2
		1000	2/2
	oral	100	0/2
		300	1/2
		400	1/1
	i.p.	100	3/4
		150	3/4
Cat	i.p.	50	0/4
		65	2/9
		70	4/10
		75	8/10
		80	9/12
		100	8/8
Rabbit	i.v.	15	0/5
		20	3/15
		25	9/15
		30	10/16
		35	9/12
		50	5/5
		75–1000	17/17

In addition to those species listed in tables 1 and 2, ryanodine was administered intraperitoneally to 4 bats, and intravenously to 6 chickens. The bats succumbed to amounts of ryanodine ranging from 300 to 1500 microgm./kgm., all probably very large doses when considering the toxicity of this drug. The chickens all succumbed to amounts of ryanodine ranging from 100 to 500 microgm./kgm. In both the bat and chicken muscle rigor was extreme.

B.) *Effects in anesthetized animals.* Because death from acute ryanodine poisoning, by any route of administration, was the result of respiratory and/or cardiac arrest in a relatively short but unpredictable period of time, only the effects of this agent on the respiration and the circulation are described.

1.) Respiration: There was no immediate change in the respiratory rhythm of the dog or cat following the rapid i.v. injection of a lethal dose (50 microgm./kgm. or more) of ryanodine. Neither did the respiratory rhythm of the cat immediately change when injections were made into the vertebral artery, the femoral artery, the aorta or, retrograde, into the renal or coeliac arteries. In the anesthetized dog, in contrast to

TABLE 2

Acute toxicity of ryanodine in guinea pig, rat and mouse

Species	Route	Dose	Mortality
		microgm./kgm.	
Guinea pig	i.p.	75	0/5
		100	2/8
		200	2/10
		250	4/7
		300	6/8
		400	7/7
		500	7/8
Rat	i.p.	100	0/5
		200	0/5
		300	1/5
		350	4/4
		400	5/5
		500	10/12
Mouse	i.p.	LD_{50} = 260 ± 17 microgm./kgm.	

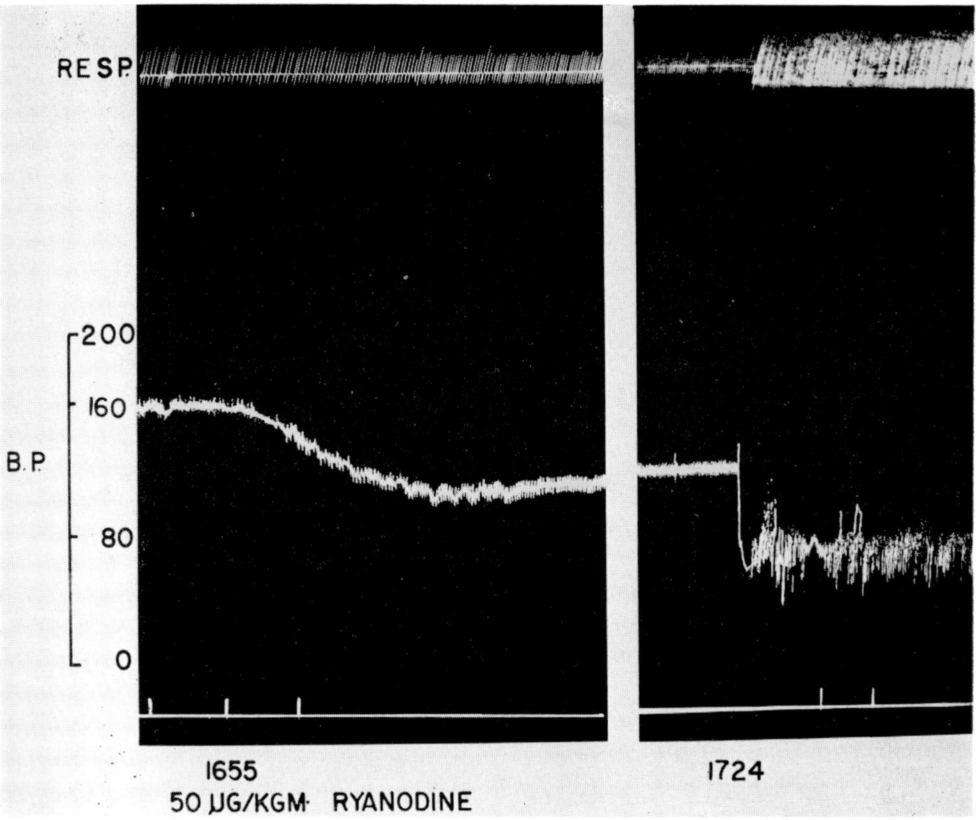

FIG. 1. Effect of ryanodine on the blood pressure and respiration of a dog.
Carotid arterial pressure, scale at left in mm. Hg. I.V. injection of ryanodine at 1655. Artificial respiration instituted in record on the right immediately after precipitous drop in blood pressure. Numerals under tracing represent clock time.

the unanesthetized dog, a single lethal dose of ryanodine usually produced circulatory failure before severe respiratory embarrassment occurred. This is illustrated in figure 1. When, however, sublethal amounts (10 to 25 microgm./kgm.) of ryanodine, insufficient to produce an appreciable, if any, fall of blood pressure, were administered at repeated intervals of from 15 to 30 minutes, there followed a gradual change in the respiratory pattern. This was signified by an increase in the rate of respiration with a concomitant decrease in the depth. This pattern persisted until the dog was unable to respire adequately through its own efforts. Even the prompt institution of artificial respiration, when spontaneous respiration became inadequate, was without a beneficial effect as the cumulative effects of ryanodine led to circulatory failure and death within a period of time which varied from dog to dog.

In the anesthetized cat or rabbit the rapid i.v injection of a single dose of ryanodine, *e.g.* 200 microgm./kgm., insufficient to produce an irreversible hypotension, led to respiratory failure. The same situation also pertained to the cat, when injections were made i.a. (intrafemoral, intravertebral, intraaortic or, retrograde, into the renal or coeliac arteries).[4] Unlike the situation in the anesthetized dog, however, artificial respiration was effective in sustaining the blood pressure of the cat and rabbit when respiratory failure occurred following the administration of ryanodine. The blood puressure of these animals could be sustained for as long as 5 hours. The effect of the ryanodine, even with doses as small as 50 microgm./kgm., on the muscles of respiration was long persisting. Even after 3 to 5 hours of artificial respiration the cat or rabbit was

[4] In subsequent sections i.a. injections refer to these arteries.

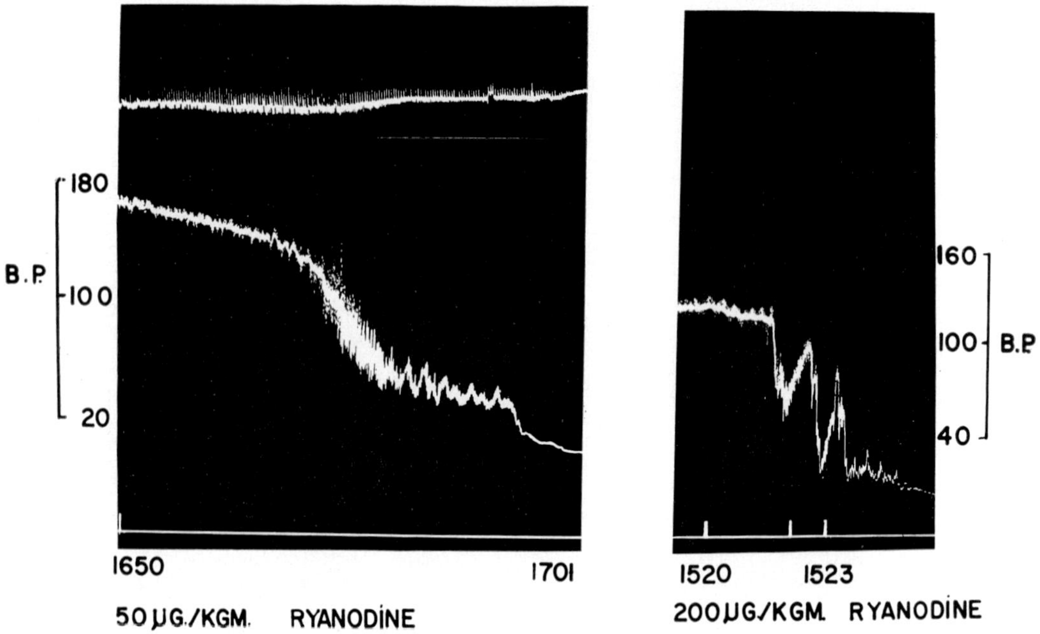

FIG. 2. Effect of ryanodine on blood pressure of two open-chest dogs, artificial respiration. Carotid arterial pressure, scale on left and right in mm. Hg. On the left: ryanodine injected at 1650. Upper line is mechanogram of right diphragmatic leaf electrically stimulated through sectioned phrenic nerve. Note contracture. On the right: ryanodine injected at 1520. Numerals under tracing represent clock time.

unable to respire through its own efforts. It might be pointed out here that with large amounts of ryanodine (usually over 500 microgm./kgm.) death could be brought about rapidly by an irreversible hypotension before respiration was even slightly altered.

2.) Circulation in the dog: The rapid i.v. injection of as little as 50 microgm./kgm. of ryanodine produced a hypotension in this animal. The blood pressure either declined to zero or near zero levels within a few minutes following the injection, and death rapidly supervened (figure 2, left); or, there was an initial decline of blood pressure of an unpredictable and variable magnitude, followed by temporary stabilization at the lowest level. Even in this latter instance, however, circulatory failure supervened in some unpredictable period of time (figure 1).

While it was indicated in the preceding section that the respiratory muscles of the anesthetized dog were affected by ryanodine, most anesthetized dogs succumbed to circulatory failure before there was a severe impairment of respiration. Here, too, artificial respiration was of no value.

3.) Circulation in the cat: The rapid i.v. or i.a. injection of 50 to 100 microgm./kgm. of ryanodine into artificially respired cats produced a rapid fall of blood pressure to levels of 50 mm. Hg or less. Here, too, as in the dog, the magnitude of the hypotensive effect was not predictable for any particular dose of the drug. Unlike the dog, however, recovery of the blood pressure to the preinjection or near preinjection level occurred in most instances following doses of ryanodine within the range mentioned above. However, in open-chest preparations or where a high spinal cord section (C_1-C_2) had been performed, the animal was less able to tolerate the hypotensive phase, and 75 to 100 microgm./kgm. of the drug was enough to insure an irreversible vaso-depression. Figures 3 and 4 illustrate the effect of ryanodine injected into the femoral vein and vertebral artery of 2 cats.

After the blood pressure returned to normal or near normal levels, following a single i.v. or i.a. injection of ryanodine in the anesthetized and artificially respired cat, subsequent injections of the drug, even doses as large as 10 times the initial dose, did not produce an acute depression of the blood pressure. This refractoriness was long

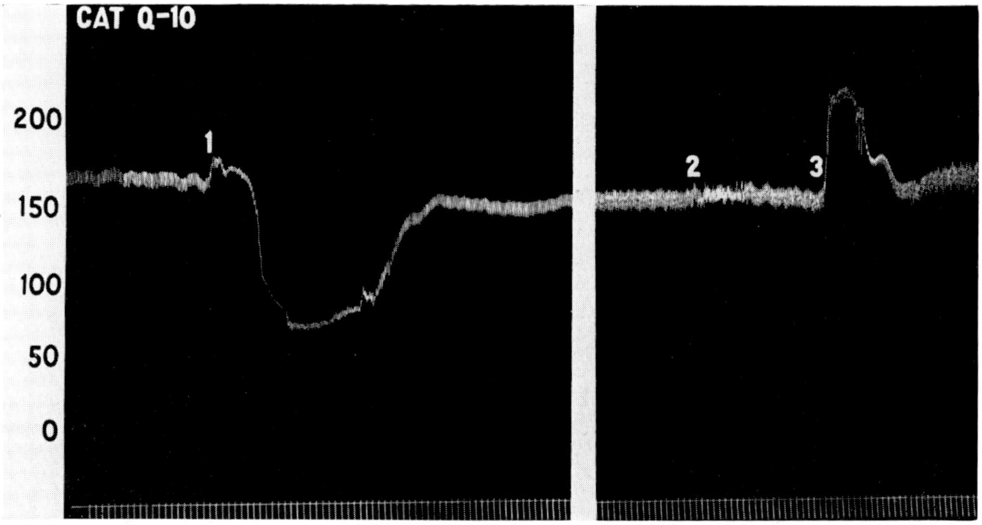

FIG. 3. Effect of ryanodine on blood pressure of artificially respired cat.
Arterial pressure, scale at left in mm. Hg. At 1, 200 microgm./kgm. of ryanodine injected into femoral vein; at 2, 100 microgm./kgm. of ryanodine injected into femoral vein 30 minutes following injection 1; at 3, 50 microgm. of epinephrine i.v. Bottom line, time marker in 10-second intervals.

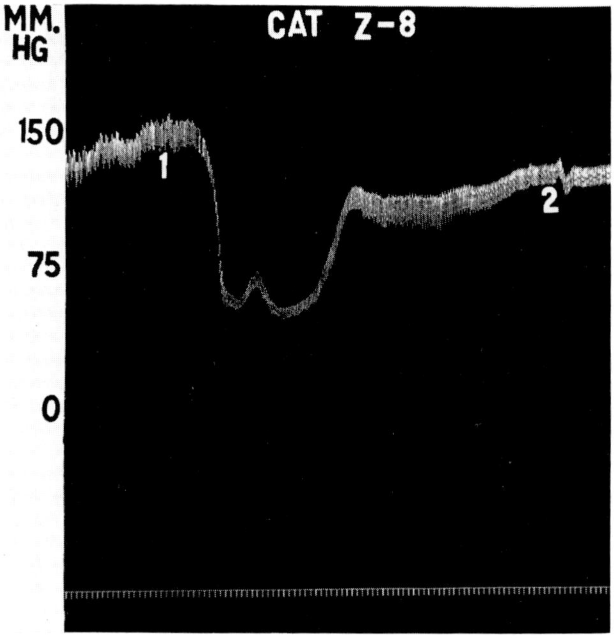

FIG. 4. Effect of ryanodine on blood pressure of artificially respired cat.
Arterial pressure, scale at left in mm. Hg. At 1, 200 microgm./kgm. of ryanodine injected into vertebral artery cephalad; at 2, 200 microgm./kgm. of ryanodine injected into femoral vein 8 minutes after injection 1. Bottom line, time marker in 10-second intervals.

persisting (up to 5 hours), the longest period of time recordings were made in this type of experiment. Figure 3 illustrates the initial vaso-depressor effect of 200 microgm./kgm. of ryanodine injected into the femoral vein with subsequent refractoriness to a second similar dose of ryanodine also injected via the femoral vein. Figures 4 and 5 similarly illustrate the refractoriness of the blood pressure to second doses of ryanodine.

Despite the maintenance of artificial respiration, and the refractoriness of the circulation to additional doses of ryanodine following the administration of the first dose, the blood pressure progressively and irreversibly fell to shock levels within about 2 to 5 hours after the initial injection of ryanodine.

Finally it is worth noting that in a number of experiments carried out on anesthetized rabbits using doses as high as 200 microgm./kgm. of ryanodine, the effects on the circulation were essentially similar to those described for the cat.

4.) Effects of other pharmacologic agents on the ryanodine effects on circulation: In an attempt to assess the possible mechanism by which ryanodine produced its effect on the circulation, a number of pharmacologic agents with known sites of action were used in conjunction with the ryanodine to determine if the effects of these agents could antagonize or modify the effects of the ryanodine.

Since the most obvious result of an i.v. or i.a. injection of ryanodine in the anesthetized animal is a fall of blood pressure, attempts were made to block or modify the hypotension. Vagotomy, or prior administration of atropine (up to 10 mgm./kgm.), had no influence on the ryanodine-induced hypotension. Neither did prior administration of Pyribenzamine (tripelennamine) (4 mgm./kgm.) or Benadryl (diphenhydramine) (10 mgm./kgm.) influence the fall of blood pressure. On the other hand, epinephrine, as shown in figure 3, and levarterenol, continued to produce their respective pressor responses in the presence of ryanodine. Similarly, the pressor response to carotid clamping (figure 5) and asphyxia also persisted.

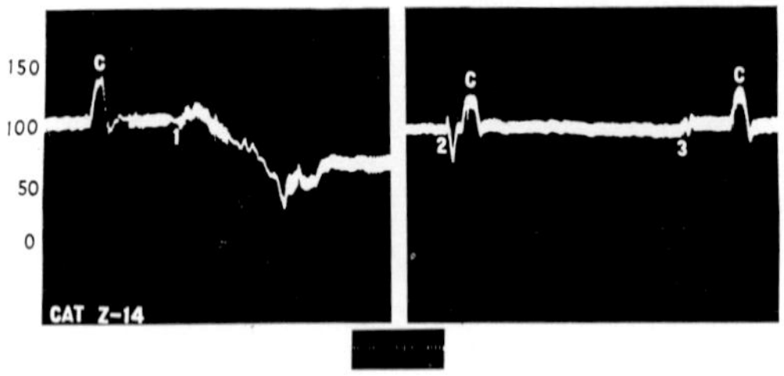

FIG. 5. Effect of bilateral carotid clamping in artificially respired cat following the administration of ryanodine.

Reading from left: arterial pressure scale in mm. Hg.; at C carotid clamp; at 1 and 2, 50 microgm./kgm. of ryanodine injected into femoral vein; at 3, 500 microgm./kgm. of ryanodine injected into femoral vein 10 minutes after injection 1. Bottom segment, time marker in 10-second intervals.

In two cats ryanodine was administered in the presence of a ganglionic blockade produced by 4 to 5 mgm./kgm. of tetraethylammonium chloride (TEA). The i.v. injection of 200 microgm./kgm. of ryanodine during the period of maximal hypotension produced by TEA resulted in a further decrease of the blood pressure from which there was no recovery.

Attempts to protect the dogs and cats with the cardiac glycosides, ouabain and digoxin, from the deleterious effect or effects of ryanodine on the circulation, with particular reference to the heart itself, were unsuccessful. These agents neither prevented, by prior administration, nor reversed the circulatory failure which usually ensued following the administration of ryanodine.

5.) Effect of ryanodine on electrocardiogram of dog and cat: Immediately following the rapid i.v. administration of ryanodine there was no particular change in the pattern of the electrocardiogram of the anesthetized dog. The initial hypotension with stabilization as observed in figure 1 on the left, is not associated with any slowing of the heart rate, whereas the precipitous and irreversible fall of blood pressure shown on the right of figure 1 is associated with a sinus tachycardia followed by ventricular fibrillation or simply cardiac arrest.

In the anesthetized and self-respiring cat, the most common and significant alteration of the electrocardiogram occurred following respiratory arrest produced by ryanodine whether the drug be rapidly administered intravenously or intra-arterially or, administered slowly by intravenous infusion. The cardiogram usually observed is illustrated in figure 6. In this particular experiment, 450 microgm. of ryanodine were infused into a 3.1-kgm. cat over a period of 48 minutes when respiratory difficulties became pronounced and the animal was unable to respire through its own efforts 9 minutes later. See legend for detail and it will be immediately clear that the arrhythmia was reverted to a fairly normal rhythm by the institution of artificial respiration. Cessation of artificial respiration resulted in the reappearance of the ventricular arrhythmia.

6.) Effect on the lateral rectus muscle of the dog: Since an enophthalmos was consistently observed in the unanesthetized animal, particularly in the dog and cat, following the administration of ryanodine by any route, four experiments were performed in which the movement

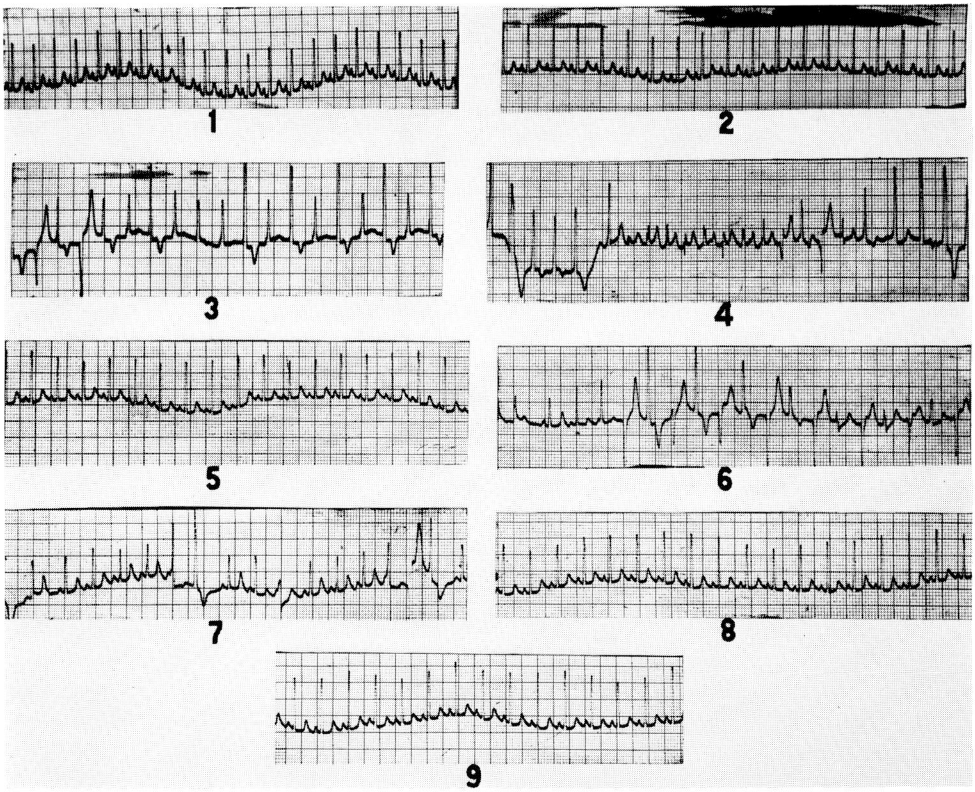

FIG. 6. Electrocardiogram of cat during and following an intravenous infusion of 450 microgm. of ryanodine.

1 Control recording; 2 during infusion; 3 arrhythmia after respiration becomes affected; between 3 and 4 artificial respiration instituted; between 5 and 6, artificial respiration discontinued; between 7 and 8 artificial respiration reinstituted.

of the lateral rectus muscle of the eye was recorded. In both noncurarized and heavily curarized (1 mgm./kgm., *d*-tubocurarine) animals, a gradual contraction of the lateral rectus muscle was produced following the i.v. injection of 100 microgm./kgm. of ryanodine.

C.) *Effect on dog heart-lung preparation.* The administration of 25 to 500 microgm. of ryanodine into the circuit of 4 heart-lung preparations produced myocardial decompensation and failure within 20 to 30 minutes. The usual therapeutic doses of ouabain were of no benefit, either when failure had ensued or when administered prior to the injection of ryanodine. On the other hand, the positive chronotropic and inotropic effects of epinephrine were clearly demonstrable in the ryanodine-failed heart-lung preparations. The failure was reversed only briefly, however.

DISCUSSION. The high toxicity of ryanodine for a variety of mammalian species has been unquestionably demonstrated. It is not the high toxicity *per se*, however, which makes this an agent of great interest, but rather its unique property of producing an irreversible contracture of skeletal muscle. This occurs very noticeably in all of the visible skeletal musculature of the unanesthetized animal, while in the anesthetized animal the the effect on the skeletal musculature is confined primarily to those muscles concerned with respiration. In either case, however, where the administered dose of ryanodine does not produce a death of cardiovascular origin, death ensues from paralysis of the muscles of respiration.

The rapidity with which rigor occurs in unanesthetized animals following the i.v. injection of large amounts of ryanodine raises the possibility that the action on the muscle is indirectly mediated through an enhanced activity of the central nervous system. In the rabbit, the initial effect of a large i.v. dose is a tonic-like spasm resembling in some respects what one might observe when a large amount of strychnine is similarly administered. In the dog and the cat, an LD_{50} or a somewhat lesser amount of the drug, administered by any route, causes vomiting which is most likely central in origin. In the dog, however, large amounts of ryanodine administered i.v. produce rigor and death so rapidly that observations with reference to the central nervous system are precluded.

The absence of any noteworthy effect of ryanodine on the muscles of the anesthetized animal, excluding those of respiration and the extraocular muscles, presumptively suggests that the action of ryanodine is in some manner dependent on a certain degree of activity or inherent tone in the muscle itself. A previous publication (Procita, 1956) clearly indicated that in a quick twitch muscle, such as the tibialis anticus of the cat, ryanodine produced an irreversible contracture of both the directly and indirectly electrically driven muscle *in situ*, but not in the resting muscle. This could be brought about with as little as 50 microgm. of the drug administered i.a. into the operated leg. It was also indicated that the ryanodine-induced contracture could be either prevented or arrested by agents which directly or indirectly diminish the activity of skeletal muscle; and conversely, the contracture could be accelerated by agents which directly or indirectly increase the activity of skeletal muscle. Thus it is reasonable to assume that in the anesthetized animal, skeletal muscle activity or tone (excluding muscles of respiration) is so reduced that the action of ryanodine on the circulation may come into prominence before its effect on skeletal muscle becomes significant.

The effect of ryanodine on the circulation of the anesthetized animal is of considerable interest but as yet difficult to analyze. The prominent action of ryanodine in producing a pronounced fall of blood pressure in the anesthetized animal raises the question of whether a similar phenomenon occurs in the unanesthetized animal with death ensuing as a consequence of an irreversible hypotension. This again is a difficult situation to assess, just as are the possibilities of a central nervous action, as has been previously indicated when large amounts are administered i.v. and muscle rigidity ensues very quickly. A not unreasonable argument against a primary cardiovascular collapse occurring in unanesthetized animals is that when pharmacologic agents (*e.g.* cocaine, nitrites, mercurials or histamine) capable of producing acute cardiovascular collapse are administered to unanesthetized animals, muscle flaccidity and not rigidity is what one observes.

In the anesthetized animal, present evidence would suggest that the hypotension and eventual circulatory failure are a reflection of the action of ryanodine on the heart. Anoxia, which ensues in the self-respiring animal, does not appear to be a major factor since if it were, the prompt institution of artificial respiration would save the situation, but this has not as yet been the case. In addition, artificial respiration maintained throughout the course of the experiment does not prevent the circulatory collapse.

While in the open chest preparation a definite diminution in the strength of the cardiac contraction can be visualized, the decompensation and failure produced by ryanodine in the dog-heart-lung preparation strengthens the possibility of a direct action on the heart. Additional evidence supporting a direct action of ryanodine on cardiac muscle is derived from experiments with isolated mammalian auricle preparations. Hillyard and Procita (1956), utilizing spontaneously beating auricles of kittens, as well as rabbits and rats, and Furchgott and De Gubareff (1956), using electrically driven left auricles of the guinea pig, have shown that ryanodine in final concentrations as low as $10^{-8}M$ produces an irreversible failure of atrial muscle. The latter investigators also indicated, in their work, that the failure was not associated with any significant decrease in the levels of either creatine-phosphate or adenosine-triphosphate. In this connection, however, none of the reported investigations to date with ryanodine (Roeder, 1948; Pick and Tullius, 1951; Procita, 1956; Blum *et al.*, 1957) have shown it to be a metabolic inhibitor.

One of the interesting but more obscure effects of ryanodine on the circulation is the failure of all doses, subsequent to the first dose, even when the magnitude of these later doses may be 10 times greater than the former, to produce an acute hypotension in the cat and rabbit. While a rapid diminution in the pressor response is observed with some sympathomimetic amines and in the depressor response with nitrites, immediate refractoriness following a single injection does not appear to be a common property of pharmacologic agents producing either a pressor or depressor response. A possible exception would be the histamine-release agents. It is unwarranted, however, to consider ryanodine in this category as the depressor response is not only not blocked by Pyribenzamine or Benadryl, but a depressor response is produced in the rabbit, an animal in which histamine usually produces a pressor response.

SUMMARY

Some toxicological and pharmacological properties of ryanodine, a purified alkaloid derived from the South American plant *Ryania speciosa Vahl*, have been investigated in the cat, dog and a variety of other mammalian species.

Ryanodine has been shown to be a highly toxic compound to all species studied.

In the unanesthetized animal ryanodine produces an irreversible contracture of striated skeletal muscle and death may be attributed to a paralysis of the muscles of respiration.

In the anesthetized dog, however, ryanodine produces a hypotension and circulatory failure before the respiration is too severely embarrassed. Artificial respiration is of no value. On the other hand, in the anesthetized cat ryanodine usually produces a paralysis of the muscles of respiration before the circulation is irreversibly affected. In this animal artificial respiration will sustain the circulation for up to 5 hours, but failure will gradually ensue.

The origin of the hypotension produced in the cat and dog by ryanodine has not been exactly determined, but the experimental data existing to date suggest that both the hypotension and circulatory failure result from a direct effect of ryanodine on the cardiac muscle.

REFERENCES

Becht, G., and Dresden, D.: Nature, **177:** 835, 1956.
Blum, J. J., Creese, R., Jenden, D. J., and Scholes, N. W.: This Journal, **121:** 477, 1957.
Bodenstein, D.: J. Exptl. Zool., **113:** 601, 1950.
Bret, G.: Bol. esc. Chim. Ind. (Belem), **1:** 48, 1930.
Cornman, I.: Exptl. Cell Res., **2:** 256, 1951.
Edwards, G. L., Weiant, E. A., Slocombe, A. G., and Roeder, K. D.: Science, **108:** 330, 1948.
Edwards, L. E., and Flinker, M. L.: Proc. Soc. Exper. Biol. & Med., **75:** 93, 1950.
Furchgott, R. F., and De Gubareff, T.: Fed. Proc., **15:** 425, 1956.
Hassett, C. C.: Science, **108:** 138, 1948.
Hillyard, I. W., and Procita, L.: Fed. Proc., **15:** 438, 1956.
Jenden, D. J., and Blum, J. J.: This Journal, **116:** 32, 1956.
Kelly, R. B., Whittingham, D. J., and Weisner, K.: Canadian J. Chem., **29:** 905, 1951.
Kelly, R. B., Whittingham, D. J., and Weisner, K.: Chemistry and Industry, p. 857, 1952.
Kelly, R. B.: Ph.D. Thesis, University of New Brunswick, 1953.
Krayer, O., and Mendez, R.: This Journal, **74:** 350, 1942.
Kuna, S., and Heal, R. E.: This Journal, **93:** 407, 1948.
Le Cointe, T.: Bol. Esc. Chim. ind. (Belem), **1:** 43, 1930.
Litchfield, J. T., Jr., and Wilcoxon, F.: This Journal, **95:** 99, 1949.
Merz, K. W.: Arch. Pharm., **268:** 593, 1930.
Nakari, S., and Sano, T.: J. Pharm. Soc. Japan, **48:** 1102, 1928.
Nakari, S., and Sano, T.: Arch. Pharm., **272:** 1, 1934.
Pick, E. P., and Tullius, E. J.: Arch. internat. pharmacodyn., **86:** 121, 1951.
Pick, E. P., and Holland, H. L.: Arch. internat. pharmacodyn., **87:** 377, 1951.
Procita, L., Shideman, F. E., and Rathbun, R.: This Journal, **106:** 411, 1952.
Procita, L., and Kuluz, M.: Fed. Proc., **15:** 469, 1956.
Procita, L.: This Journal, **117:** 363, 1956.
Procita, L., and Hillyard, I. W.: This Journal, **119:** 178, 1957.
Roeder, K. D.: Chemical Corps Contract Progress Report No. 15, Sept. 30, 1948.
Rogers, E. F., Konivszy, F. R., Shavel, J., Jr., and Folkers, K.: J. Amer. Chem. Soc., **70:** 3086, 1948.
Wills, J. H., and Murtha, E. F.: Am. J. Physiol., **155:** 478, 1948.

PERPHENAZINE, A POTENT AND EFFECTIVE ANTIEMETIC[1, 2]

S. C. WANG

Department of Pharmacology, College of Physicians and Surgeons, Columbia University, New York City

Received for publication May 12, 1958

Many drugs are used clinically to prevent emesis under a variety of disease conditions and chlorpromazine has been reported to be by far the most potent and effective agent (Friend and Cummins, 1954). Experimentally, the drug effectively prevented vomiting induced by apomorphine (Courvoisier *et al.*, 1953; Boyd *et al.*, 1954) and by morphine and Hydergine (Brand *et al.*, 1954; Glaviano and Wang, 1955).

In the past few years, a number of phenothiazine compounds on the market have been shown to possess antiemetic properties. Among these perphenazine[3] was found to be most potent (Rosenkilde and Govier, 1957). This investigation was undertaken: a) to establish quantitatively the degree of protection afforded by certain doses of perphenazine against relatively large doses of apomorphine; b) to establish the relative effectiveness of perphenazine and chlorpromazine against apomorphine and other emetic agents, such as morphine, Hydergine and lanatoside C; and c) to elucidate the mechanism and the site of the antiemetic action of perphenazine.

METHODS. The antiemetic potency of perphenazine was determined in a group of 80 healthy mongrel dogs weighing from 6 to 13 kgm. The dogs were given food first, and 30 minutes later, varying intravenous doses of perphenazine. After another 10 to 15 minutes, they were challenged by one of the emetic agents; apomorphine hydrochloride, 0.1 mgm. or 0.5 mgm. per kgm.; morphine sulfate, 1.0 mgm. per kgm.; Hydergine, 0.09 mgm. per kgm.; and lanatoside C[4], 0.1 mgm. per kgm. These dosage levels were chosen because they are 100 per cent effective doses or above.[5] All drugs were administered intravenously except morphine which was given intramuscularly (Wang and Glaviano, 1954). Perphenazine was given in doses 0.025 mgm., 0.035 mgm., 0.05 mgm., 0.075 mgm. and 0.1 mgm. per kgm. For purposes of comparison, the antiemetic potency of chlorpromazine[6] was determined in an identical manner, using doses of 0.5 mgm., 0.75 mgm., 0.85 mgm., 1.0 mgm., and 2.0 mgm. per kgm. The procedure used in the analysis of the data was the method of probits as described by Finney (1952), and the potency of perphenazine relative to that of chlorpromazine[7] was computed separately for the two sets of data (apomorphine at 0.1 mgm. per kgm. and at 0.5 mgm. per kgm.). The number of animals showing a positive vomiting response at each dosage level of the drug was converted to a percentage of the total number observed. The percentage vomiting at each dose was converted to probits. Two cycles of probit calculations, based on a provisional graphical analysis, were then performed to secure adequate convergence. The potency computations, ED_{50}'s and their respective 95 per cent confidence limits were estimated in the usual manner. In all of these computations a

[1] A preliminary report of this work was presented to the American Society for Pharmacology and Experimental Therapeutics during the Federation meetings at Philadelphia in April, 1958, and was published in Fed. Proc., **17:** 417, 1958.

[2] This investigation was supported by a grant from the National Institute of Neurological Diseases and Blindness, B31(C), and also by a grant from the Schering Corporation, Bloomfield, N. J.

[3] Perphenazine was originally developed as Sch 3940 by the Schering Corporation, and is now marketed under the trade name Trilafon. The author wishes to thank Dr. J. Black of the Schering Corporation for his interest in this investigation and for the generous supply of the drug.

[4] Deslanoside C, U.S.P.

[5] Doses of the emetic agents which have been found to produce vomiting in all animals tested, in previous studies, are: apomorphine HCl, 0.02 mgm. per kgm. (Wang and Borison, 1952); morphine SO_4, 1.0 mgm. per kgm. (Wang and Glaviano, 1954); Hydergine, 0.03 mgm. per kgm., lanatoside C, 0.08 mgm. per kgm. (Borison and Wang, 1951).

[6] Chlorpromazine is marketed under the trade name, Thorazine. The author wishes to thank Mr. D. B. Cheetham of the Smith, Kline and French Laboratories for the generous supply of the drug.

[7] The author wishes to acknowledge the valuable contribution of Mr. Gordon Thomas of the Schering Corporation in providing the statistical treatment of the data.

joint estimate of the slope was used. The analysis of Chi square shown in table 2B shows that the four slopes did not differ significantly and that therefore the use of average slope is justified in the potency calculations.

The effect of perphenazine on the emesis provoked by intragastric copper sulfate was also investigated. For this test, the animals were fasted for at least 18 hours. The threshold in response to copper sulfate was first determined (usually 40 mgm., see Wang and Borison, 1951), and only animals which responded to 40 mgm. were subsequently chosen to be tested again with the same dose of copper sulfate but with pretreatment by an intravenous dose of perphenazine (0.1 mgm. per kgm.).

In all tests dogs were observed for one hour after they had received the emetic agents; if vomiting occurred during this time, the period of latency was noted. None of the dogs was tested more than once every five days.

RESULTS. While the dogs did not appear to be sedated by 0.1 mgm. per kgm. of perphenazine given intravenously, they were generally amenable to venipuncture. The large majority of them showed no emesis to as large a dose as 0.5 mgm. per kgm. of apomorphine hydrochloride (an amount which is approximately 25 to 50 times the average threshold dose for vomiting), but they exhibited the usual signs of excitation, pacing and defecating movements. From table 1, it is evident that the 50 per cent effective dose of perphenazine to prevent emesis induced by 0.1 mgm. per kgm. of apomorphine is around 0.035 mgm. per kgm., and that against 0.5 mgm. per kgm. of apomorphine, it is around 0.075 mgm. per kgm. On the other hand, 2 mgm. per kgm. of chlorpromazine is quite ineffective against 0.5 mgm. per kgm. of apomorphine, providing protection in only 17 per cent of animals. Larger doses of chlorpromazine were not used because of its spreading depression to the central vomiting mechanism (Glaviano and Wang, 1955). Table 2A shows the calculated ED_{50}. At the level of 0.1 mgm. per kgm. of apomorphine HCl, perphenazine is 16.6 times more potent than chlorpromazine, and 12.1 to 22.1 times more potent at 95 per cent limits. At the level of 0.5 mgm. per kgm. of apomorphine HCl, perphenazine became even more potent, *i.e.*, 47.8 times, and 30.2 to 90.7 times at 95 per cent limits. From these data, it is apparent that perphenazine gains in relative effectiveness as the apomorphine doses are increased.

Against emesis provoked by 1.0 mgm. per kgm.

TABLE 1

Relative antiemetic effectiveness of perphenazine and chlorpromazine against varying doses of intravenously administered apomorphine in dogs

Apomorphine·HCl	Antiemetic Agents	No. Dogs Tested	No. Dogs Vomited	Latency Average	Latency Range	% Protection
mgm./kgm.	*mgm./kgm.* *Perphenazine*					
0.1	0.025	12	12	1.7	1–3	0
0.1	0.035	12	5	3.0	2–5	58
0.1	0.05	12	5	2.6	1–4	58
0.1	0.1	12	1	3.0		93
0.5	0.05	12	8	2.2	2–3	66
0.5	0.075	12	7	5.2	2–17	42
0.5	0.1	12	2	5.0	5–5	83
	Chlorpromazine					
0.1	0.5	12	9	1.5	1–2	25
0.1	0.75	12	6	2.2	2–3	50
0.1	0.85	12	5	2.8	2–3	58
0.1	1.0	12	2	3.5	3–4	83
0.5	1.0	12	12	2.1	2–3	0
0.5	2.0	12	10	1.8	1–6	17

TABLE 2

A. *Calculated ED_{50} of perphenazine and chlorpromazine against varying doses of intravenously administered apomorphine in dogs*

Apomorphine·HCl	Antiemetic Agents	ED_{50}	95% Limits
mgm./kgm.		*mgm./kgm.*	*mgm./kgm.*
0.1	perphenazine	0.043	0.035–0.054
0.1	chlorpromazine	0.71	0.58–0.86
0.5	perphenazine	0.07	0.06–0.09
0.5	chlorpromazine	3.31	1.78–4.75

B. *Analysis of Chi Square*

Nature of Variation	df	SS	
Common slope	1	31.600	Very highly significant
Nonparallelism	3	0.109	Not significant
Residual	5	9.919	Not significant
Slope b = 41.4116			

TABLE 3

Antiemetic effectiveness of perphenazine against various emetic agents: morphine, Hydergine, lanatoside C and copper sulfate

Emetic Agents, Dose and Route	Perphenazine	No. Dogs Tested	No. Dogs Vomited	Latency		% Protection
				Average	Range	
mgm./kgm.	*mgm./kgm.*			*min.*	*min.*	
Morphine SO_4						
1.0 i.m.	0.05	12	6	11.5	5–22	50
1.0 i.m.	0.1	12	5	10.4	4–15	58
Hydergine						
0.09 i.v.	0.05	12	8	21.0	10–43	33
0.09 i.v.	0.1	12	0			100
Lanatoside C						
0.1 i.v.	0.05	12	11	9.6	2–28	7
0.1 i.v.	0.1	12	4	14.5	11–22	67
Copper SO_4						
40 mgm./dog, i.g.	0.1	15	11	24.8	14–40	27

of morphine sulfate given intramuscularly, perphenazine appeared to be equally effective in doses of 0.05 mgm. or 0.1 mgm. per kgm. (table 3). On the other hand, against 0.09 mgm. per kgm. of Hydergine, there was considerable increase in the degree of protection when perphenazine was given in the dose of 0.1 mgm. instead of 0.05 mgm. per kgm. In contrast to the total ineffectiveness of chlorpromazine (Glaviano and Wang, 1955), perphenazine was also useful in combating emesis induced by lanatoside C. In the dose of 0.1 mgm. per kgm. perphenazine gave 27 per cent protection against intragastric copper sulfate emesis, indicating a moderate degree of depression of the vomiting center comparable to that afforded by an intravenous administration of 2.0 mgm. per kgm. of chlorpromazine.

Discussion. Rosenkilde and Govier (1957) reported that perphenazine was about 24 times more potent than chlorpromazine in blocking the emetic action of the ED_{95} of apomorphine (22.5 microgm.). From our experiments, the calculated potency of perphenazine was 16.6 times greater than chlorpromazine when tested against 0.1 mgm. per kgm. of apomorphine. However, a higher potency rating by itself means merely that a smaller dose is required for a particular therapeutic effect. It becomes highly significant and useful only if the potent therapeutic agent is not accompanied by numerous side effects at equieffective doses, or if it is effective in a large variety of disease conditions. Perphenazine has been put to clinical use only recently, so it is difficult to evaluate the drug as to undesirable side effects. Ayd (1957) reported no cases of dermatitis, photosensitivity, seizures, jaundice, agranulocytosis, hyperthermia or hypotension. According to this investigator, the only troublesome complication encountered among patients treated with perphenazine was Parkinsonism.

Our data suggest that as an antiemetic agent perphenazine is far more effective than chlorpromazine against large doses of apomorphine. Protection afforded by 2 mgm. per kgm. of chlorpromazine against 0.5 mgm. per kgm. of apomorphine is only 17 per cent, while that provided by 0.075 mgm. per kgm. of perphenazine is 42 per cent. When the dosage of perphenazine is increased to 0.1 mgm. per kgm., its effectiveness is increased to 83 per cent. Indeed, nearly all animals that vomited in the last two groups showed delayed responses to this latter dose of apomorphine (averages, 5.2 min. and 5.0 min. as against an average latency of approximately 1.5 min. in the normal untreated dogs). Furthermore, perphenazine appears to be more effective against emesis provoked by morphine, Hydergine and especially lanatoside C. For ready comparison, the protective effects of chlorpromazine against these three emetic agents are summarized in table 4. The most striking difference is that whereas chlorpromazine was totally ineffective against emesis induced by digitalis, perphenazine in the dose of 0.1 mgm. per kgm. prevented vomiting in 67 per cent of such cases. While it is generally true that emesis in digitalis therapy signals an overdosage, nausea and vomiting with doses far below toxicity do occur in occasional patients. Therefore, it is our opinion that perphenazine is a highly potent and versatile antiemetic agent, and should be tried in cases of emesis not amenable to other therapeutic remedies. Indeed, perphenazine is reported to be effective in therapeutic trials for vomiting of pregnancy (Birnberg, personal communication), postoperative vomiting (Moore *et al.*, 1958), radiation sickness (Dickson, 1958), and vomiting from miscellaneous causes (Preisig and Landman, 1958; Weiss *et al.*, 1958).

In 1952, Wang and Borison reported evidence to indicate the existence of a chemoceptive emetic trigger zone located in the area postrema, the site of action of many so-called central emetic agents, such as apomorphine (Wang and Borison, 1950), cardiac glycosides (Borison and Wang, 1951), morphine (Wang and Glaviano, 1954), and Hydergine (Wang and Glaviano, 1954). Animals deprived of the trigger zone bilaterally do not vomit in response to these emetic agents, although their emetic center is intact. On the other hand, their threshold of emetic response to orally administered copper sulfate is unaltered (see diagram, Wang and Borison, 1952). The fact that an antiemetic agent prevents apomorphine-induced vomiting does not warrant the conclusion that the agent acts on the trigger mechanism. There remains the possibility that it depresses the vomiting center in the reticular formation. In the latter instance, both apomorphine and intragastric copper sulfate thresholds for emesis are elevated (Wang and Borison, 1951). For this reason, *the alteration of intragastric copper sulfate threshold under the influence of an antiemetic agent is crucial in determining whether its site of action is the chemoceptive emetic trigger zone, the vomiting center, or both.*

In a previous communication Glaviano and Wang (1955) reported that chlorpromazine in doses of 2.0 mgm. per kgm. raised the apomorphine threshold approximately tenfold and yet only moderately altered the response to intragastric copper sulfate. This was interpreted to suggest that at this dosage level chlorpromazine prevents vomiting primarily by acting on the receptors located in the chemoceptive trigger zone. Our present experiments indicate that in dogs receiving threshold doses of intragastric copper, perphenazine in the dose of 0.1 mgm. per kgm. afforded 27 per cent protection (table 3), which is comparable to that afforded by 2 mgm. per kgm. of chlorpromazine (table 4). This fact is interpreted to mean that both perphenazine and chlorpromazine at these dosage levels depress the medullary emetic center only moderately, and that the site of antiemetic action is largely confined to the chemoceptive emetic trigger zone. We should like further to suggest that the increased potency and versatility of perphenazine as an antiemetic agent is related to its greater affinity to and its tighter binding with the receptors in the trigger zone.

We (Wang and Glaviano, 1954) have previously reported that chlorpromazine is slightly effective against emesis induced by morphine, but not effective against that caused by digitalis glycosides (see also Brand *et al.*, 1954). Brand *et al.* suggested that there may be more than one type of chemoreceptor in the trigger zone and that the receptors sensitive to lanatoside C are different from those sensitive to apomorphine. Only the latter is blocked by chlorpromazine. If this were the case, these two types of receptors must be scattered in the area postrema and intermingled with one another in this region, for none of the more than 100 dogs with surgical ablation of the chemoceptive trigger zone showed an increase of threshold limited to only one group of "central" emetic agents. Indeed, the existence of various specific receptors is not substantiated by the histologic evidence presented by Brizzee and Neal (1954).

We have previously suggested that the protective property of chlorpromazine depends upon its relative ability to compete with receptors at the chemoceptive trigger zone. Lanatoside C is notoriously known to provoke repeated bouts of vomiting lasting 3 or 4 hours. This long duration of emetic action indicates to us that the binding between the receptor substance and such emetic agents as morphine and lanatoside C might be so great that chlorpromazine is unable to displace these agents. If this interpretation is correct, we should like to suggest that the increased potency and versatility of perphenazine as an

TABLE 4

Antiemetic effectiveness of chlorpromazine against various emetic agents: morphine, Hydergine, lanatoside C and copper sulfate

Emetic Agents, Dose and Route	Chlorpromazine	No. Dogs Tested	No. Dogs Vomited	Latency: Average	Latency: Range	% Protection
mgm./kgm.	*mgm./kgm.*			*min.*	*min.*	
Morphine SO_4						
1.0 i.m.	2.0 s.c.	13	9	3.4	2–6	31
1.0 i.m.	6.0 i.v.	8	4	5.2	4–7	50
Hydergine						
0.09 i.v.	1.0 i.v.	9	2	5.5	5–6	78
0.09 i.v.	4.0 i.v.	10	1		15	90
Lanatoside C						
0.07–0.1 i.v.	2.0 s.c.	8	8	13.2	10–24	0
0.07–0.1 i.v.	4.0 i.v.	8	8	11.5	7–21	0
Copper SO_4						
40 mgm./dog, i.g.	2.0 i.v.	13	9	24.3	6–33	31

antiemetic agent is related to its greater affinity to the receptors in the trigger zone.

SUMMARY AND CONCLUSIONS

The antiemetic effectiveness of two phenothiazine derivatives, perphenazine and chlorpromazine, has been compared. Against 0.1 mgm. per kgm. of apomorphine hydrochloride, perphenazine was found to be 16.6 times more potent than chlorpromazine. When the doses of apomorphine were increased to 0.5 mgm. per kgm., the potency ratio was raised to 47.8 times. Perphenazine appears to gain in relative efficacy as the emetic stimulus is increased. Perphenazine was also highly effective against vomiting induced by morphine, Hydergine and especially lanatoside C. Therefore, perphenazine is not only a potent, but also a highly versatile antiemetic agent.

As has been suggested in the DISCUSSION, the high potency of perphenazine as an antiemetic agent may presumably be due to its greater affinity for the receptors in the trigger zone.

REFERENCES

AYD, F. J., JR.: Dis. Nerv. System, **18:** 394, 1957.

BORISON, H. L., AND WANG, S. C.: Proc. Soc. Exper. Biol. & Med., **76:** 335, 1951.

BOYD, E. M., BOYD, C. E., AND CASSELL, W. A.: Canad. M. A. J., **70:** 276, 1954.

BRAND, E. D., HARRIS, T. D., BORISON, H. L., AND GOODMAN, L. S.: THIS JOURNAL, **110:** 86, 1954.

BRIZZEE, K. R., AND NEAL, L. M.: J. Comp. Neurol., **100:** 41, 1954.

COURVOISIER, S., FOURNEL, J., DUCROT, R., KOLSKY, M., AND KOETSCHET, P.: Arch. internat. pharmacodyn., **92:** 305, 1953.

DICKSON, R. J.: Radiol., **70:** 259, 1958.

FINNEY, D. J.: Statistical methods in biological assay, p. 468, Hafner Publishing Co., New York, 1952.

FRIEND, D. G., AND CUMMINS, J. F.: New England J. Med., **250:** 997, 1954.

GLAVIANO, V. V., AND WANG, S. C.: THIS JOURNAL, **114:** 358, 1955.

MOORE, D. C., BRIDENBAUGH, L. D., VAN ACKEREN, E. G., AND COLE, M. D.: Anesthesiol., **19:** 72, 1958.

PREISIG, R., AND LANDMAN, M. E.: Am. Pract. & Digest. Treat., **9:** 740, 1958.

ROSENKILDE, H., AND GOVIER, W. M.: THIS JOURNAL, **120:** 375, 1957.

WANG, S. C., AND BORISON, H. L.: Arch. Neurol. and Psychiat., **63:** 928, 1950.

WANG, S. C., AND BORISON, H. L.: Am. J. Physiol., **166:** 712, 1951.

WANG, S. C., AND BORISON, H. L.: Gastroenterol., **22:** 1, 1952.

WANG, S. C., AND GLAVIANO, V. V.: THIS JOURNAL, **111:** 329, 1954.

WEISS, S., WEISS, J., AND WEISS, B.: Am. J. Gastroenterol., **29:** 173, 1958.

8049

CARBONIC ANHYDRASE INHIBITION. IX. AUGMENTATION OF THE RENAL EFFECT OF MERALLURIDE BY ACETAZOLAMIDE[1]

THOMAS H. MAREN[2]

Experimental Therapeutics Section, Research Division, American Cyanamid Company, Stamford, Connecticut

Received for publication March 17, 1958

Increase of the renal effects of mercurial diuretics by metabolic acidosis has been recognized for over thirty years (Keith and Whelan, 1926). The acidosis was generally brought about by administration of salts whose cation was destroyed (as NH_4Cl) or unabsorbed (as $CaCl_2$) *in vivo*, leaving Cl^- to match available H^+. The phenomenon has been shown to be true potentiation, *i.e.*, the response to the mercurial and to the acidifying agent given in combination exceeded the sum of the responses to the individual agents (Ethridge, Myers and Fulton, 1936). The basis of the potentiation has been controversial; in the case of NH_4Cl it has been suggested that it is due to hyperchloremia (Axelrod and Pitts, 1952), but this view has recently been disputed (Levy, Weiner and Mudge, 1957).

Continuous carbonic anhydrase inhibition also causes metabolic acidosis, due to initial urinary loss of HCO_3^- which is not replenished as long as the inhibitor is given (Maren *et al.*, 1954). In the present study, the effects of a mercurial diuretic were tested in dogs made acidotic by *prior* administration of a carbonic anhydrase inhibitor. As expected in this situation, the mercurial produced a greater excretion of Na^+ and Cl^- than in the nonacidotic, normal dog. A number of combinations of acetazolamide and meralluride were explored. It was found that the most effective scheme for (48-hour) renal loss of Na^+ was alternation of these agents.

These experiments also suggest that the potentiation of mercurials by prior acetazolamide is due to metabolic acidosis *per se*, rather than to hyperchloremia.

METHODS AND MATERIALS. These have been described (Maren *et al.*, 1954). The following additions are relevant. Meralluride sodium solution was given intramuscularly. This substance is said to contain 39 mgm. of Hg as N-(β-hydroxymercuri-2-methoxy) propyl-N′-succinylurea, and 48 mgm. of theophylline per ml.[3] Because the substance is a mixture, we have used the convention of ml./kgm. in expressing the dose. At the doses of meralluride used, approximately 4 mgm./kgm. of theophylline were injected as part of the dose. This is substantially less theophylline than required for chloruresis in the dog. We obtained no effect at 20 mgm./kgm. intramuscularly (given as aminophylline), and Fulton *et al.* (1932) obtained no effect with about 10 mgm./kgm. intravenously.

Acetazolamide is 2-acetylamino-1,3,4-thiadiazole-5-sulfonamide.[4] This drug was administered orally by capsule.

Animals were female beagles; they were fed at 9 A. M. each test day and ate well during and prior to the test. The composition of the diet, including electrolytes, is given in the publication from this laboratory cited above.

RESULTS. I. *Potentiation of response to meralluride during metabolic acidosis due to acetazolamide.* Meralluride (0.08 ml./kgm.) was tested in the experimental situation in which acetazolamide at 10 mgm./kgm. orally had been given at 9 a.m. and 9 p.m. of the previous day (figure 1). This schedule of acetazolamide treatment caused a moderate acidosis, due to HCO_3^- depletion, 24 hours after the first dose (table 1). However, virtually no acetazolamide is present in plasma at this time (Maren *et al.*, 1954). The mercurial was used on day 2, therefore, under conditions of

[1] Presented in part at the San Francisco meeting of the American Society for Pharmacology and Experimental Therapeutics, April, 1955 (Fed. Proc., **14:** 366, 1955).

[2] Present address: Department of Pharmacology and Therapeutics, University of Florida College of Medicine, Gainesville, Florida.

[3] From U.S.P. XV. The registered trade-mark of Lakeside Laboratories for this product is Mercuhydrin.

[4] The registered trade-mark of the American Cyanamid Company for acetazolamide is Diamox. It was formerly known as Cl 6063.

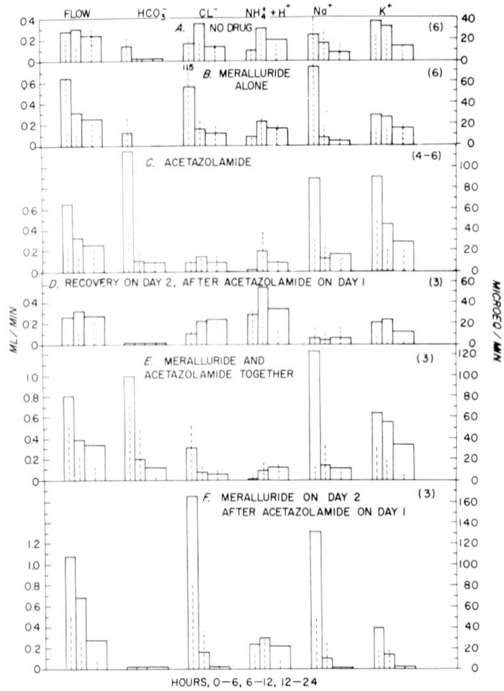

FIG. 1. Excretion rates of urine and ions following meralluride and acetazolamide administration, singly and in combination.

Meralluride, intramuscular, 0.08 ml./kgm. at 0 time; acetazolamide by capsule 10 mgm./kgm. at 0 time and 12 hours. Dogs fed 9 a.m. each day, just prior to 0 time. Each group of 3 columns represents 24 hours, divided into 0 to 6, 6 to 12 and 12 to 24 hour periods. Averages given by column height; magnitude of range given by dotted line within column; value in parenthesis is number of experiments. Example: In first 6-hour column at upper left, average flow is 0.28 ml./min. with range of 0.20 ml./min., *i.e.* in the 6 experiments flow varied between 0.18 and 0.38 ml./min.

metabolic acidosis, but without the complication of simultaneous carbonic anhydrase inhibition.

To gauge the effects of meralluride in this situation, comparison was made with renal excretion patterns of untreated dogs, of dogs that received meralluride or acetazolamide alone, of dogs that received acetazolamide on day 1 and nothing on day 2, and of dogs that received simultaneous meralluride and acetazolamide. Figure 1 shows the excretion *rates* over a 24-hour period. Table 1 includes blood electrolytes and gives 48-hour *totals* of urinary excretion for these and some additional schedules (discussed in part II below).

Effect of meralluride alone (B in figure 1): This follows the expected pattern of urinary Na^+ and Cl^- loss, in roughly equimolar proportions. There is a wider range of Cl^- excretion following meralluride than there is of HCO_3^- excretion following acetazolamide. The renal effect of meralluride in promoting Cl^- and Na^+ output lasts 4 to 6 hours, following which there is some retention of Cl^- and N^+; on this dose there is often no net 24-hour loss of Cl^- or Na^+. The dose of meralluride selected (0.08 ml./ kgm., i.m.) gave moderate renal effects in two of the dogs, and striking effects in the third dog, on each of the 2 tests performed in each animal. Meralluride at 0.15 ml./kgm. gave essentially maximal effects (no greater response at 0.3 ml./ kgm.) for the intramuscular route in all of 4 dogs tested, based on samples collected 2 or 4 hours after the dose.

Effects of acetazolamide alone, (C of figure 1) and of recovery from acetazolamide (D in figure 1): These have been discussed previously (Maren *et al.*, 1954). The magnitude of the acetazolamide effect on acid-base balance at 24 hours is estimated by urinary base depletion,[5] and averages 4.6 mEq./kgm. There was plasma acidosis, net loss of Na^+ and K^+, and slight Cl^- retention, but little or no hyperchloremia. If no acetazolamide is given on the following day, the metabolic acidosis is largely corrected through extra excretion of H^+ and NH_4^+, and retention of Na^+.

Effects of simultaneous meralluride and acetazolamide (E in figure 1): This schedule may be compared with that of either drug alone. The following conclusions may be drawn from this comparison. When the drugs are given at the same time, the following conditions apply.

A) $HCO_3^- - (NH_4^+ + H^+)$ output is the same as that following acetazolamide alone. B) K^+ output is slightly less than that with acetazolamide alone. This difference alone is not significant, but when the two drugs are used together the urinary Na^+/K^+ ratio is invariably higher than following acetazolamide. C) Na^+ output is more than after either drug alone but less than the sum of the individual effects (6 hours). The 24-hour value is no greater than with acetazolamide alone. D) Cl^- output is about one-half that observed following meralluride alone.

These data suggest that there is no practical

[5] From table 1. From the control 24-hour value of $(NH_4^+ + H^+ - HCO_3^-)$ in row 1 minus that following acetazolamide, row 2. Specifically, $+21 - (-40) = 61$ mEq. The average weight of these dogs was 13 kgm. This is discussed more fully by Maren *et al.* (1954).

TABLE 1

*Forty-eight hour urinary excretion patterns, and blood acid-base balance, following various combinations of meralluride and acetazolamide**

Schedule and Number of Tests (tests in parentheses)	Blood pH	Plasma		Urinary Excretion				
		HCO_3^-	Cl^-	$(NH_4^+ + H^+) - HCO_3^-$	Cl^-	Na^+	K^+	Total
		mEq./l.	*mEq./l.*	*mEq.*	*mEq.*	*mEq.*	*mEq.*	*ml.*
1. No drug (6): 48-hr. totals	7.39	21.1	101	+42	64	40	68	772
2. Acetazolamide day 1 (7)	7.23	16.3	103	−40	14	51	73	556
+ nothing day 2 (3)	7.27	20.0	101	+55	29	8	25	409
				+15	43	59	98	965
3. Acetazolamide day 1 (7)	7.23	16.3	103	−40	14	51	73	556
+ acetazolamide day 2 (1)	7.26	15.0	115	+12	6	9	34	245
				−28	20	60	107	801
4. Meralluride day 1 (6)	7.38	22.9	99	+22	33	30	30	500
+ meralluride day 2 (1)	7.36	24.9	98	+23	13	13	12	526
				+45	46	43	42	1026
5. Meralluride + acetazolamide day 1 (3)	7.26	16.4	105	−49	18	57	68	677
+ nothing day 2 (1)	7.39	21.1	106	+60	26	1	24	554
				+11	44	58	92	1231
6. Meralluride + acetazolamide day 1 (3)	7.26	16.4	105	−49	18	57	68	677
+ meralluride day 2 (1)	7.28	19.0	93	+28	30	19	14	667
				−21	48	76	82	1344
7. Meralluride + acetazolamide day 1 (3)	7.26	16.4	105	−49	18	57	68	677
+ acetazolamide day 2, 9 a.m. only (1)	7.29	18.9	102	+37	21	7	33	282
				−12	39	64	101	959
8. Acetazolamide day 1 (7)	7.23	16.3	103	−40	14	51	73	556
+ meralluride day 2 (3)	7.27	19.7	96	+36	66	50	20	820
				− 4	80	101	90	1376
9. Meralluride day 1 (6)	7.38	22.9	99	+22	33	30	30	500
+ acetazolamide day 2 (2)	7.27	16.7	99	−33	19	68	82	718
				−11	52	98	112	1218

* Na^+ intake 20 mEq./day; K^+ intake 30 mEq./day. Plasma values are those for the end of each 24-hour period. Urine values are averages recorded for each 24-hour period, and for the 48-hour total. Acetazolamide given orally 10 mgm./kgm. at 9 a.m. and 9 p.m.; meralluride given i.m., 0.08 ml./kgm., at 9 a.m. Collection period started at 9 a.m. each day.

advantage to the simultaneous treatment schedule, and a probable disadvantage, since acetazolamide appears to repress the chloruretic action of meralluride.

Effect of meralluride on day 2 after acetazolamide on day 1 (F of figure 1): In the setting of metabolic acidosis due to acetazolamide, 6-hour Cl^- excretion due to meralluride is tripled and Na^+ output doubled, when compared with the effect of meralluride in the normal non-acidotic dog. In the acidotic setting, the variability is also diminished. In contrast to meralluride alone, there is a reproducible net 24-hour Cl^- and Na^+ loss. Recovery from plasma acidosis due to acetazolamide was not appreciably altered by meralluride.

The practical result of giving acetazolamide on day 1 and meralluride on day 2 is that net loss of sodium may be observed on *both* days of the 48-hour period. In the data of table 1 the 2-day figure for net Na^+ loss is 61 mEq. (Na^+ output in row 8 minus that of two control days, row 1). Advantage is taken of the fact that acetazolamide is itself natriuretic, and at the same time it prepares the animal for an augmented response to mercury. Both acetazolamide alone (row 3) and meralluride alone (row 4) cause substantial retention of Na^+ on the second day of treatment in dogs.

II. *Trials of various combinations of meralluride and acetazolamide: 48-hour effects.* Table 1 is a summary of our experience with various combinations of these two drugs, given over a 48-hour period. Some of these data are based on single tests; however, the dogs used were of the same strain, and various studies over a 4-year period have not shown marked individual differences in response. They are presented as a general guide to types of response that may be elicited, and, as such, form a reasonably coherent pattern.

Since Na^+ excretion is the property common to acetazolamide and meralluride, it is of particular interest to examine this aspect of the data. It may be seen at once that the only cases in which the Na^+ outputs on day 1 *and* day 2 both exceeded those of the controls are the two schedules (rows 8 and 9) in which the drugs are alternated. Actually, negative balance was achieved through at least 3 days in the experiment of row 9, table 1 (meralluride day 1 and acetazolamide day 2). Meralluride on day 3 (not shown in the table) elicited a loss of 32 mEq. of Na^+ and 39 mEq. of Cl^-, which are still somewhat above the control values. At the same time excess secretion of H^+ and NH_4^+ on that day resulted in partial restoration of the base deficit which had been elicited by acetazolamide on day 2.

In the alternating schedule (row 8 in table 1) Na^+ and Cl^- removal in 48 hours are roughly in their physiological proportions. On this schedule also, these ions reach their highest concentration in urine. Since removal of edema fluid, which presumably approaches isotonicity, is the goal of diuretic therapy, schedule 8 would appear the best of those studied here.

III. *Basis for potentiation of meralluride by prior acetazolamide.* The principal effect of acetazolamide 24 hours after the start of treatment is a metabolic acidosis. We believe that this alteration itself is responsible for the enhancement of mercurial effect, although we cannot say in what manner this comes about. At the time when meralluride is producing its maximal effect (0 to 6 hr., F in figure 1) there is excess urinary acidification and NH_4^+ output, which suggests acidosis of renal cells. When there is renal output of HCO_3^-, *i.e.* renal alkalosis, (0 to 6 hr., E in figure 1) the chloruretic effect of meralluride is repressed.

There was no correlation between plasma Cl^- concentration and enhancement or repression of the meralluride effect. In the 3 experiments of row 8, table 1, in which meralluride was given following acetazolamide, plasma Cl^- at that time was 109, 102 and 99 mEq./l. The enhanced effect was seen in every case, with no relation between Cl^- concentration and Cl^- output. In the 3 experiments of row 5 in which the two drugs were given simultaneously and Cl^- output was repressed, plasma Cl^- was initially normal and rose through the experiment. Average figures were 101 mEq./l. at 0 time, 103 mEq./l. at 6 hours, and 105 mEq./l. at 24 hours.

Discussion. Two main points emerge from this study. 1. Prior administration of acetazolamide enhances the chloruretic and natriuretic effect of meralluride. 2. This does not appear to be due to hyperchloremia, and is probably due to renal acidosis, that is the state of the kidney as it is responding to metabolic acidosis.

The first point may bear on the treatment of congestive heart failure. It would be of interest to test the alternating plan in edematous patients on the basis both of their 2-day response and of several months of clinical observation. Moyer and Hughes (1955) did study simultaneous treatment of congestive heart failure with 250 mgm. acetazolamide twice a day and 20 mgm. mercury as chlormerodrin four times a day. As would be expected from the present work, such a system was no more effective than either drug alone.

The second point bears on the argument regarding the mechanism of mercurial enhancement. Retention of chloride or hyperchloremia appears not to be a necessary factor in the augmentation of mercurial diuresis by metabolic acidosis. This agrees with the finding by Ethridge, Myers and Fulton (1936) that acidifying salts other than NH_4Cl (*i.e.* NH_4NO_3) would produce the effect. A main argument of Axelrod and Pitts (1952) in favor of the role of chloride in augmentation of mercurial diuresis was the fact that augmentation was not observed in respiratory acidosis with normal plasma Cl^-. But there are several other significant differences between metabolic and respiratory acidosis. The renal response to respiratory acidosis (*i.e.*, acidification and NH_4^+ output) is small compared to that of metabolic acidosis (Longson and Mills, 1953). The renal response to acetazolamide (HCO_3^- output) is blocked by metabolic acidosis (Maren, 1956) but not by respiratory acidosis (Nadell, 1953). In general, all of these differences are apparent at about the same blood pH, suggesting that other elements in the acid-base equilibrium of the body are more significant in determining renal reactivity.

The common factor responsible for the *increased* effect of mercurials following addition of acid (as NH_4Cl) or loss of base (due to acetazolamide) may be intracellular acidosis. This is in harmony with the work of Mudge and Hardin (1956), who found that the diuretic action of mercurials is normal or increased in the extracellular alkalosis of K^+ depletion, presumably due to concomitant intracellular acidity of renal cells. It has recently been suggested that acidosis produces its effect by increasing the dissociation of organically bound mercury, since chloruresis following $HgCl_2$ is not potentiated by acidosis or repressed by alkalosis (Levy *et al.*, 1957). The effect of $HgCl_2$ in acetazolamide-induced acidosis would be of interest in this connection.

The *decreased* chloruretic effect of meralluride observed in the immediate period following simultaneous administration with acetazolamide may be due to renal intracellular alkalosis. Such an alkalosis could result from a diminished rate of hydration of CO_2 in renal cells during carbonic anhydrase inhibition, and would be expected to decrease the effect of the mercurial diuretic (Ethridge *et al.*, 1936; Mudge and Hardin, 1956).

SUMMARY

After administration of the carbonic anhydrase inhibitor, acetazolamide, at 0 time and at 12 hr., there is augmentation of the effect of a mercurial diuretic, meralluride, when given at 24 hr., in promoting renal excretion of Na^+, Cl^- and H_2O. This augmentation appears to be due to prior excretion of HCO_3^- following acetazolamide, and the ensuing metabolic acidosis which is probably reflected in acidosis of renal cells. This may occur in the presence of normal plasma Cl^- concentration.

When meralluride and acetazolamide are given at the same time, and depending on the time intervals studied, chloride excretion may be less than that following meralluride alone. It is suggested that this repression is due to metabolic alkalosis of renal cells during carbonic anhydrase inhibition, at the time that the mercurial is acting. For maximal chloruretic effects, it is inadvisable to give the two agents together.

Of a number of sequences studied, the most effective for 48-hour net sodium and chloride removal is acetazolamide on day 1 and meralluride on day 2.

ACKNOWLEDGMENT. We wish to thank Mrs. Lena B. Vidone and Miss Clara Pellicci for their careful and devoted work throughout these studies. We are grateful to Dr. Douglas Riggs for his critical evaluation of the manuscript.

REFERENCES

AXELROD, D. R., AND PITTS, R. F.: J. Clin. Invest., **31:** 171, 1952.
ETHRIDGE, C. B., MYERS, D. W., AND FULTON, M. N.: Arch. Int. Med., **57:** 714, 1936.
KEITH, N. M., AND WHELAN, M.: J. Clin. Invest., **3:** 149, 1926.
LEVY, R. I., WEINER, I. M., AND MUDGE, G. H.: Fed. Proc., **16:** 317, 1957.
LONGSON, D., AND MILLS, J. N.: J. Physiol., **122:** 81, 1953.
MAREN, T. H., WADSWORTH, B. C., YALE, E. K., AND ALONSO, L.: Bull. Johns Hopkins Hosp., **95:** 277, 1954.
MAREN, T. H.: Bull. Johns Hopkins Hosp., **98:** 159, 1956.
MOYER, J. H., AND HUGHES, W. M.: J. Chronic Dis., **2:** 678, 1955.
MUDGE, G. H., AND HARDIN, B.: J. Clin. Invest., **35:** 155, 1956.
NADELL, J.: J. Clin. Invest., **32:** 622, 1953.

ABSORPTION
aniline 8017
dissociation constant 8017
drug concentration 8017
foreign compounds 8017
lipoid barrier 8017
membrane solubility 8017
organic acids 8017
organic bases 8017
pH 8017
pKa values 8017
quaternary ammonium compounds 8017
salicylic acid 8017
small intestine 8017
ACETALDEHYDE
alcohol administration 8016
blood level 8016
charcoal pretreatment 8016
charcoal treatment 8016
cyanamide pretreatment 8016
disulfiram pretreatment 8016
ACETAZOLAMIDE
blood acid-base balance 8049
carbonic anhydrase 8018
8049
diuretic action 8018
electrolyte excretion 8018
electrolyte reabsorption 8018
meralluride 8049
metabolic acidosis 8049
natriuretic action 8049
sequence administration 8049
urinary excretion patterns 8049
ACETYLCHOLINESTERASE
ambenonium analogs 8023
DFP-inactivation 8040
diacetylmonoxime(DAM) 8040
histochemical examination 8040
intercostal muscle 8040
monoisonitrosoacetone(MINA) 8040
quantitative activity determinations 8040
reactivation *in vivo* 8040
stellate ganglion 8040
superior cervical ganglion 8040
tissue homogenates 8040
ACID-BASE
acetazolamide 8049
chloride excretion 8049
mercurial diuresis 8049
metabolic acidosis 8049
plasma chloride concentration 8049
renal intracellular acidosis 8049
ACRYLAMIDE
acute poisoning 8031
ataxia 8031
behavioral disturbances 8031
blood pressure 8031
brain stem effects 8031
central excitation 8031
chronic poisoning syndrome 8031
EEG patterns 8031
electrospinograms(ESP) 8031
mass sympathetic discharge 8031
neurologic deficit 8031
tonic-clonic convulsions 8031
tremors 8031
ACTH
adrenal ascorbic acid depletion 8010
chlorpromazine pretreatment 8010
reserpine pretreatment 8010
ADRENALECTOMY
anesthetized rabbit 8006
blood pressure 8006
histamine response 8006
ADRENERGIC BLOCKADE
adrenalectomy 8006
blood pressure 8006
DHE 8006
epinephrine response 8006
histamine response 8006
phentolamine 8006
ADRENERGIC BLOCKING AGENTS
dibenamine 8045
rauwolscine 8045
ALCOHOL
blood level 8016
charcoal pretreatment 8016
charcoal treatment 8016
human subjects 8016
oral administration 8016
2-ALKOXYBENZOATES
irritancy 8044
local anesthetic activity 8044
systemic toxicity 8044
2-ALKOXYTHIOLBENZOATES
irritancy 8044
local anesthetic activity 8044
systemic toxicity 8044

AMBENONIUM ANALOGS
anticholinesterase activity 8023
skeletal muscle 8023
structure action correlations 8023
toxicity 8023
AMINE OXIDASE
imidazole-acylcholine esters 8019
2-AMINO-5-CHLOROBENZOXAZOLE (FLEXIN)
spinal segmental reflexes 8029
AMINOPHYLLINE
antipruritic activity 8036
human subjects 8036
AMPHETAMINE
blood pressure 8007
methylphenidate 8007
nictitating membrane 8007
d-AMPHETAMINE
human subjects 8035
learning rate 8035
reaction time 8035
ANALGESICS
demethylating enzyme receptors 8030
3-hydroxy-N-allylmorphinan inhibition 8030
3-hydroxyl group etherification 8030
liver microsome system 8030
morphinan-type 8030
morphinan-type isomers 8030
morphine analogs 8030
narcotic action receptors 8030
N-demethylation 8030
O-demethylation 8030
ANESTHESIA,GENERAL
anesthetized rabbit 8006
blood pressure 8006
histamine response 8006
ANESTHETICS,LOCAL
activity 8044
correlation studies 8044
intradermal injection 8044
intraspinal injection 8044
irritancy 8044
statistical evaluation 8044
systemic toxicity 8044
threshold anesthetic concentration 8044
threshold irritant concentration 8044
ANTICHOLINESTERASES
ambenonium analogs 8023
atropine-like protective agents 8038
central respiratory control 8022
halopyruvic acids 8012
morphine 8022
neuromuscular transmission 8022
phospholine 8022
phospholine analog (217-AO) 8022
TEPP toxicity 8038
ANTICONVULSANTS
CNS stimulants 8034
reserpine influence 8034
ANTIEMETIC AGENTS
chlorpromazine 8048
perphenazine 8048
ANTIRHEUMATIC AGENTS
phenylbutazone metabolites 8014
ARTHRITIS,ACUTE GOUTY
phenylbutazone metabolites 8014
ASCORBIC ACID
acute stress 8010
adrenal gland depletion 8010
chlorpromazine 8010
reserpine 8010
ATROPINE
antagonistic action 8022
central nervous system 8022
cholinesterase activity 8022
conditioned avoidance responses 8032
phospholine analog (217-AO) 8022
reserpine 8032
ATROPINE METHYLNITRATE (EUMYDRINE)
atropine substitutes 8038
mytolon 8038
protective action 8038
TEPP toxicity 8038
ATROPINE SUBSTITUTES
anti-TEPP activity 8038
CNS activity 8038
peripheral cholinolytic potency 8038
AUTONOMIC GANGLIA
acetylcholinesterase activity 8040
DFP pretreatment 8040
diacetylmonoxime(DAM) 8040
monoisonitrosoacetone(MINA) 8040

AUTONOMIC NERVOUS SYSTEM, CENTRAL
acrylamide poisoning 8031
atropine 8032
conditioned avoidance responses 8032
epinephrine 8032
eserine 8032
levarterenol 8032
mass sympathetic discharge 8031
methamphetamine 8032
reserpine 8032

BARBITAL
anticonvulsant activity 8034
blood-brain barrier 8015
lipid solubility 8015
reserpine influence 8034
BARBITURATES
brain concentration 8015
brain penetration 8015
hypnotic effects 8015
lipid solubility 8015
plasma concentration 8015
BENZOQUINONIUM (MYTOLON)
atropine substitutes 8038
eumydrine 8038
protective action 8038
TEPP toxicity 8038
N,N'-BIS(DIETHYLAMINOETHYL)-OXAMIDE-BIS-BENZALDEHYDE
anticholinesterase activity 8023
motor facilitation 8023
muscle relaxation 8023
neostigmine potentiation 8023
quaternary salts 8023
structure action correlations 8023
TEPP antagonism 8023
toxicity 8023
BLOOD FLOW
atropine 8045
epinephrine 8045
femoral vascular bed 8045 8046
narcotine 8046
rauwolscine 8045
tachyphylaxis 8046

BLOOD PRESSURE
acetylcholine 8019
amphetamine 8024
amphetamine hypertension 8007
anesthetized rabbit 8006
antihistamines 8046 8047
arterial pressure 8047
atropinization 8046 8047
BITU 8004
carotid body denervation 8046
carotid sinus denervation 8046
chlorisondamine 8004 8039
cholinesterase activity 8022
C-O pressor response 8007 8045 8047
DMPP 8004 8019
epinephrine 8006 8019
epinephrine pressor response 8047
epinephrine reversal 8045
hydroxy-1-azepine-propionamidoxime 8024
hexamethonium 8004
histamine 8006 8019
hypertensive dogs 8024
imidazole-acylcholine esters 8019
isoproterenol depressor response 8045
levarterenol 8004 8024
levarterenol pressor response 8045 8047
malignant renal hypertension 8039
methylphenidate 8007
narcotine hypotension 8046
neurogenic hypertension 8039
papaverine 8046
pentobarbital anesthesia 8039
phentolamine pretreatment 8022
phospholine 8022
phospholine analog (217-AO) 8022
rauwolscine 8045
renal hypertension 8007
right atrial pressure 8047

ryanodine hypotension 8047
serotonin 8019
tachyphylaxis 8046
TEA 8047
unanesthetized mammals 8039
vagotomy 8046
8047
BRAIN
lipid solubility 8015
oxybarbiturate penetration 8015
thiobarbiturate penetration 8015
BRAIN STEM
acrylamide action 8031
chronic poisoning 8031

CAFFEINE
anticonvulsants 8034
clonic seizures 8034
CNS antiextensor excitants 8034
reserpine 8034
rigidity 8008
salamander 8008
spinal cord transection 8008
tonic extensor seizures 8034
tonic seizures 8008
CALCIUM
Ca^{45} distribution 8043
erythrocyte transport 8043
human erythrocytes 8043
ouabain 8043
potassium transport 8043
CARBON TETRACHLORIDE
hepatotoxicity 8037
lethal potency 8037
CARBONIC ANHYDRASE
acetazolamide inhibition 8018
8049
chlorothiazide inhibition 8018
meralluride diuresis 8049
CARDIAC GLYCOSIDES
environmental temperature 8028
myocardial response 8028
ouabain 8028
CARDIOVASCULAR SYSTEM
antihypertensive activity 8007
bis-isothiourea (BITU) 8004
circulatory failure 8047
DMPP 8004
ECG 8046
hemodynamic responses 8046
hexahydro-1-azepine-propionamidoxime (Su-4029) 8024
levarterenol 8004
methylphenidate 8007
narcotine 8046
papaverine 8046
rauwolscine 8045
ryanodine 8047
CENTRAL NERVOUS SYSTEM
acrylamide poisoning 8031
action localization 8031
anticonvulsants 8034
antiextensor excitants 8034
atropine-like antidotes 8038
autonomic changes 8032
behavior 8008
8032 8033
biological variation 8033
cholinesterase activity 8022
comparative study 8034
conditioned avoidance responses 8032
convulsant drugs 8008
8034
crossover techniques 8033
depressant drug sensitivity 8033
electrical activity 8008
locomotor activity 8033
methamphetamine reversal 8032
narcotine convulsions 8046
phospholine 8022
phospholine analog (217-AO) 8022
post-treatment activity counts 8033
pretreatment activity counts 8033
reserpine 8032
8034
respiratory control 8022
salamander 8008
statistical evaluations 8033
stimulant drug sensitivity 8033
TEPP toxicity 8038
tonic extensor seizures 8034
CHARCOAL,ANIMAL
adsorbent agents 8016
alcohol administration 8016
alcohol metabolism 8016
alcohol sensitivity 8016
alcoholic patients 8016
blood acetaldehyde levels 8016
blood alcohol levels 8016

chemical analysis 8016
disulfiram-like action 8016
extraction studies 8016
oral administration 8016
toxicity 8016
vegetable charcoals 8016
CHEMOTHERAPY,VIRUS
purines 8013
CHLORIDE EXCRETION
acetazolamide 8049
mercurial diuresis 8049
metabolic acidosis 8049
plasma chloride concentration 8049
renal intracellular acidosis 8049
CHLORISONDAMINE
cardiac output 8039
cardiac volume 8039
diastolic blood pressure 8039
ganglionic blocking action 8039
heart rate 8039
hexamethonium 8039
mean blood pressure 8039
pentobarbital anesthesia 8039
peripheral resistance 8039
unanesthetized dogs 8039
CHLORMERODRIN
diuretic action 8018
electrolyte excretion 8018
electrolyte reabsorption 8018
CHLOROFORM
hepatotoxicity 8037
lethal potency 8037
CHLOROTHIAZIDE
carbonic anhydrase 8018
diuretic action 8018
electrolyte excretion 8018
electrolyte reabsorption 8018
CHLORPROMAZINE
acute stress 8010
adrenal ascorbic acid 8010
antiemetic activity 8048
exogenous ACTH 8010
locomotor responses 8033
MET 8009
perphenazine 8048
pituitary adreno-corticotrophic activity 8010
post-treatment counts 8033
pretreatment counts 8033
spontaneous motor activity 8009
CHOLINE ESTERS
brain homogenates 8019
comparative actions 8019
dihydromurexine 8019
hydrolysis 8019
imidazoleacetylcholine 8019
murexine 8019
CHOLINESTERASES
esterolytic activity 8021
halopyruvic acids 8012
human blood serum 8021
imidazoleacetylcholine 8020
imidazole-acycholine esters 8019
inhibition 8012
metal ion influence 8021
n-fatty acid esters 8021
pyridylacetylcholine 8020
spectrophotometric method 8021
substrate variation 8021
CHOLINOLYTIC AGENTS
anti-TEPP activity 8038
mydriatic activity 8038
peripheral potency 8038
substituted tertiary amines 8038
COCAINE
antiextensor seizure activity 8034
CNS stimulants 8034
CONDITIONED REFLEXES
approach responses 8032
avoidance responses 8032
methamphetamine reversal 8032
reserpine suppression 8032
CONVULSANTS
behavior 8008
CNS 8008
electrical activity 8008
muscular system 8008
neurological tests 8008
salamander 8008
sensory-motor side effects 8008
COPPER SULFATE
chlorpromazine 8048
emetic action 8048
intragastric threshold 8048
perphenazine 8048
CORONARY BLOOD FLOW
coronary resistance 8046
narcotine 8046
papaverine 8046

CYANAMIDE
alcohol administration 8016
alcohol sensitivity 8016
blood acetaldehyde levels 8016
oral administration 8016

DEMETHYLATION
dealkylation 8030
liver microsome system 8030
3-methylcholanthrene 8030
3-methyl-MAB 8030
morphinan-type analgesics 8030
morphine analogs 8030
pH optima 8030
SKF 525-A 8030
DESOXYEPHEDRINE
antiextensor seizure activity 8034
CNS stimulants 8034
DIACETYLMONOXIME
DFP-inactivated acetylcholinesterase 8040
reactivating action *in vivo* 8040
10-(2-DIMETHYLAMINOPROPYL)-9-ACRIDONE (ACRIDONE)
anticonvulsants 8034
clonic seizures 8034
CNS antiextensor excitants 8034
reserpine 8034
tonic extensor seizures 8034
1,1-DIMETHYL-4-PHENYLPIPERAZINIUM (DMPP)
arterial pressure 8004
BITU potentiation 8004
methylphenidate 8007
pressor response 8007
DIPHENHYDRAMINE
antiextensor seizure activity 8034
CNS stimulants 8034
narcotic vasodepression 8046
DIPHENYLHYDANTOIN
anticonvulsant activity 8034
reserpine influence 8034
1,4-DIPYRROLIDINO-2-BUTYNE (TREMORINE)
antiextensor seizure activity 8034
CNS stimulants 8034
DISULFIRAM
alcohol administration 8016
alcohol sensitivity 8016
alcoholic patients 8016
blood acetaldehyde levels 8016
blood alcohol levels 8016
oral administration 8016
DIURETICS
acetazolamide 8018
action mechanism 8018
chlormerodrin 8018
chlorothiazide 8018
glomerular filtration rate 8018

ELECTROCARDIOGRAM
ryanodine 8047
ELECTROENCEPHALOGRAM
chronic acrylamide poisoning 8031
ELECTROLYTES
diuretics 8018
phenylbutazone metabolites 8014
renal excretion 8018
renal reabsorption 8018
sodium-retaining effect 8014
ELECTROLYTES,ORGANIC
intestinal absorption 8017
lipid-solubility 8017
pKa values 8017
unionized form 8017
ELECTROSHOCK
MET 8009
phenothiazines 8009
EMESIS,DRUG INDUCED
apomorphine-induced 8048
chemoceptive trigger zone 8048
chlorpromazine treatment 8048
emetic agents 8048
perphenazine treatment 8048
ENZYMES
human blood serum 8021
hydrolysis 8021
m-hydroxybenzoic acid esters 8021
EPINEPHRINE
anesthetized rabbit 8006
blood pressure 8045
cardiac effects 8005
cardiac stimulation 8047
conditioned avoidance responses 8032
heart content 8027
heart-lung preparation 8027
heart rate 8027

histamine antagonism 8006
nictitating membrane 8045
peripheral vascular resistance 8045
plasma content 8027
pressor effect 8006
rat lung content 8027
rauwolscine 8045
reserpine 8032
reserpine pretreatment 8027
ryanodine cardiac depression 8047

ERYTHROCYTES
buffer suspension 8043
calcium transport 8043
cold stored blood 8043
fresh blood 8043
membrane lipid factor 8043
plasma suspension 8043
potassium transport 8043

ESERINE
conditioned avoidance responses 8032
reserpine 8032

ESTERASES
esterolytic activity 8021
human blood serum 8021
m-hydroxybenzoic acid esters 8021
metal ion influence 8021
n-acyl carbon atoms 8021
physostigmine 8021
serum cholinesterase 8021

GANGLIONIC BLOCKADE
adrenalectomy 8006
blood pressure 8006 8039
chlorisondamine 8039
compensatory mechanisms 8039
epinephrine response 8006
hexamethonium 8006
histamine response 8006
pendiomide 8006
pentobarbital anesthesia 8039

HEART
absolute refractory period 8005
action potential 8005
arrhythmia 8005 8047
A-V conduction time 8005
BITU 8004
cardiac arrest 8047
cardiac output 8004 8039 8047
cardiac volume 8039
chlorisondamine 8039
heart-lung prepartion 8004
irritability 8005
pentobarbital 8039
rate 8047
right atrial pressure 8004
ryanodine depression 8047
stimulation threshold 8005
vasopressor agents 8005

HEART ARRHYTHMIA
ryanodine 8047
ventricular fibrillation 8047

HEART, ISOLATED
cardiac rate 8027
heart-lung preparation 8027
hexahydro-1-azepine-propionamidoxime 8024
levarterenol release 8027
pentobarbital failure 8027
reserpine 8027
veratramine 8027

HEART MUSCLE
digoxin 8047
ouabain 8047
ryanodine depression 8047

HEART RATE
A-V rhythm 8026
blood pressure 8039
chlorisondamine 8039
l-epinephrine 8026
heart-lung preparation 8026 8027
5-hydroxytryptamine 8027
narcotine 8046
pentobarbital anesthesia 8039
rauwolscine 8045
reserpine pretreatment 8027
reserpine response 8026 8027
S-A rhythm 8026

HEART RHYTHM
vasopressor agents 8005

HEART VENTRICLE
contractile force 8028
frequency 8028

isolated strips 8028
ouabain 8028
temperature 8028
HEXAHYDRO-1-AZEPINEPROPIONAMID-
OXIME (SU-4029)
amphetamine 8024
"annoying" stimulation 8024
antihypertensive effects 8024
blood pressure 8024
central nervous activity 8024
chemical structure
specificity 8024
chlorisondamine 8024
C-O pressor response 8024
cumulative effect 8024
DMPP 8024
ECG 8024
ephedrine 8024
epinephrine 8024
ganglionic blocking agents 8024
high cord transection 8024
hypertensive dogs 8024
levarterenol 8024
morphine 8024
nictitating membrane 8024
oral activity 8024
phentolamine 8024
reserpine 8024
serotonin 8024
side effects 8024
smooth muscle 8024
toxicity 8024
HISTAMINE
adrenalectomy 8006
adrenergic blockade 8006
anesthetized rabbit 8006
epinephrine antagonism 8006
ganglionic blockade 8006
general anesthesia 8006
narcotine vasodepression 8046
pressor effect 8006
HISTAMINE LIBERATION
compound 48/80 8046
narcotine 8046
HYDERGINE
chlorpromazine 8048
emetic action 8048
perphenazine 8048
1-HYDRAZINOPHTHALAZINE
anticonvulsants 8034
clonic seizures 8034
CNS antiextensor excitants 8034
reserpine 8034
tonic extensor seizures 8034
HYDROCARBONS,HALOGENATED
dose-responses 8037
lethal potency 8037
liver damage 8037
pentobarbital sleeping time 8037
HYPERTENSION
amphetamine-induced 8024
ephedrine-induced 8024
hexahydro-1-azepinepropion-
amidoxime treatment 8024
naphazoline 8024
neurogenic 8024
renal 8024
renin 8024
HYPERTENSION,EXPERIMENTAL
chlorisondamine 8039
ganglionic blockade 8039

IBOGAINE
antiextensor seizure activity 8034
CNS stimulants 8034
IMIDAZOLEACETYLCHOLINE
comparative actions 8019
imidazole-acylcholine esters 8019
neuromuscular function 8020
IMIDAZOLEACRYLCHOLINE
pharmacologic actions 8019
IMIDAZOLE-ACYLCHOLINE ESTERS
acute toxicity 8019
amine oxidase 8019
atropine 8019
autonomic ganglia 8019
blood pressure 8019
cholinesterases 8019
edrophonium 8019
eserine 8019
hexamethonium 8019
histamine 8019
hydrolysis 8019
neuromuscular function 8019
nictitating membrane 8019
peripheral cholinergic
neuroeffectors 8019
respiration 8019
smooth muscle 8019
d-tubocurarine 8019

IMIDAZOLEPROPIONYLCHOLINE
pharmacologic actions 8019

LANATOSIDE C
chlorpromazine 8048
emetic action 8048
perphenazine 8048
LEARNING RATE
d-amphetamine 8035
human subjects 8035
meprobamate 8035
phenobarbital 8035
reaction time 8035
LEVARTERENOL
arterial pressure 8004
BITU potentiation 8004
cardiac effects 8005
conditioned avoidance responses 8032
heart content 8027
heart-lung preparation 8027
heart rate 8027
methylphenidate 8007
plasma content 8027
pressor response 8007
rat lung content 8027
reserpine 8032
reserpine pretreatment 8027
LIVER
methylated aminoazo dyes 8030
microsome system 8030
narcotic compounds 8030
N-demethylation 8030
O-demethylation 8030
species differences 8030
LIVER DAMAGE
BSP retention 8037
halogenated hydrocarbons 8037
pathological changes 8037
pentobarbital sleeping time 8037
LYSERGIC ACID DIETHYLAMIDE
antiextensor seizure activity 8034
CNS stimulants 8034

MEPAZINE
MET 8009
spontaneous motor activity 8009
MEPHENESIN
anticonvulsant activity 8034
reserpine influence 8034
MEPHENTERMINE
cardiac effects 8005
MEPROBAMATE
C^{14}-carbamate labeled 8041
distribution 8041
glucuronide 8041
human subjects 8035 8041
hydroxymeprobamate 8041
learning rate 8035
metabolites 8041
motor coordination 8035
plasma levels 8041
reaction time 8035
urinary excretion products 8041
MERALLURIDE
acetazolamide pretreatment 8049
blood acid-base balance 8049
chloruretic action 8049
metabolic acidosis 8049
natriuretic action 8049
plasma chloride concentration 8049
sequence administration 8049
urinary excretion patterns 8049
MERCURIAL DIURETICS
acetazolamide 8049
blood acid-base balance 8049
meralluride 8049
urinary excretion patterns 8049
METHAMPHETAMINE
conditioned avoidance responses 8032
locomotor responses 8033
post-treatment counts 8033
pretreatment counts 8033
reserpine 8032
METHOXAMINE
cardiac effects 8005
4-METHYL-4-ETHYL-GLUTARIMIDE (MEGIMIDE)
anticonvulsants 8034
clonic seizures 8034
CNS antiextensor excitants 8034
reserpine 8034
tonic extensor seizures 8034
METHYLPHENIDATE
amphetamine 8007
antiextensor seizure activity 8034
baroreceptor function 8007

blood pressure 8007
cardiovascular actions 8007
carotid sinus infiltration 8007
CNS stimulants 8034
C-O pressor response 8007
DMPP 8007
efferent sympathetic transmission 8007
epinephrine 8007
levarterenol 8007
nictitating membrane 8007
phentolamine 8007
preganglionic sympathetic faradization 8007
renin 8007
spinal dog 8007

MONOISONITROSOACETONE
DFP-inactivated acetylcholinesterase 8040
reactivating action in vivo 8040

MORPHINE
analogs 8030
antipruritic activity 8036
chlorpromazine 8048
cholinesterase activity 8022
emetic action 8048
human subjects 8036
liver microsome system 8030
morphinan compounds 8030
N-demethylation 8030
O-demethylation 8030
perphenazine 8048
phospholine 8022
phospholine analog antagonism 8022
rauwolscine tachypnea 8045
respiratory arrest 8022

MUSCLE,SKELETAL
ambenonium analogs 8023
circulatory failure 8047
motor facilitation 8023
paralysis 8023
respiratory depression 8047
ryanodine contracture 8047

MUSCLE,SMOOTH
acetylcholine 8024
bronchiolar resistance 8046
compound 48/80 8046
environmental temperature 8025
epinephrine 8024
hexahydro-1-azepinepropionamidoxime 8024
histamine 8019 8024
imidazole-acylcholine esters 8019
levarterenol 8024
longitudinal muscle tonus 8025
narcotine 8046
rabbit duodenal strips 8025
rhythmical activity 8025
ryanodine-induced contracture 8025
spontaneous activity 8025
tachyphylaxis 8046
tracheal chain 8019

NARCOTINE
action mechanism 8046
acute toxicity 8046
blood pressure 8046
cardiovascular system 8046
compound 48/80 8046
coronary blood flow 8046
diphenhydramine 8046
femoral blood flow 8046
histamine 8046
histamine liberation 8046
hypotensive action 8046
papaverine 8046
respiration 8046
smooth muscle 8046
species differences 8046
tachyphylaxis 8046

NEUROMUSCULAR FUNCTION
choline esters 8019

NEUROMUSCULAR JUNCTION
acetylcholinesterase activity 8040
cholinesterase activity 8022
DFP pretreatment 8040
diacetylmonoxime (DAM) 8040
monoisonitrosoacetone (MINA) 8040
phospholine analog (217-AO) 8022
phospholine blockade 8022

NICOTINE
clonic seizures 8008
localized tremors 8008
salamander 8008
spinal cord transection 8008

NICTITATING MEMBRANE
cervical sympathetic stimulation 8045
epinephrine injection 8045
rauwolscine 8045
NIKETHAMIDE
athetoid movements 8008
salamander 8008
spinal cord transection 8008
tonic seizures 8008
NORNICOTINE
detoxication 8042
dosage effect 8042
intravenous toxicity 8042
metabolism 8042
urinary excretion 8042

OUABAIN
human erythrocytes 8043
positive inotropic action 8028
potassium transport 8043
temperature 8028
ventricle strips 8028
2,2'-OXYBIS(p-PHENYLMETHYLENE) BISISOTHIOUREA (BITU)
arterial pressure 8004
cardiovascular actions 8004
DMPP 8004
hexamethonium 8004
levarterenol 8004
nictitating membrane 8004
plasma histamine levels 8004
potentiating action 8004
vascular resistance 8004
vasomotor reactions 8004

PAPAVERINE
antipruritic activity 8036
coronary blood flow 8046
hemodynamic responses 8046
human subjects 8036
narcotine 8046
PENTOBARBITAL
blood-brain barrier 8015
conditioned avoidance responses 8032
halogenated hydrocarbons 8037
lipid solubility 8015
liver damage estimation 8037
locomotor activity 8033
post-treatment counts 8033
pretreatment counts 8033
reserpine 8032
sleeping time 8037
PENTYLENETETRAZOLE
anticonvulsants 8034
clonic seizures 8008
8034
CNS antiextensor excitants 8034
reserpine 8034
salamander 8008
spinal cord transection 8008
tonic extensor seizures 8034
tonic seizures 8008
PERPHENAZINE
antiemetic activity 8048
apomorphine-induced emesis 8048
chlorpromazine 8048
emetic agents 8048
PHENOBARBITAL
blood-brain barrier 8015
human subjects 8035
learning rate 8035
lipid solubility 8015
reaction time 8035
PHENOTHIAZINES
depressant effect 8009
minimal electroshock seizure threshold 8009
spontaneous motor activity 8009
PHENSUXIMIDE
anticonvulsant activity 8034
reserpine influence 8034
PHENTOLAMINE
blood pressure 8022
central respiratory control 8022
cholinesterase activity 8022
phospholine analog (217-AO) 8022
PHENYLBUTAZONE METABOLITES
acute gouty arthritis 8014
antirheumatic action 8014
chloride clearance 8014
electrolyte excretion 8014
inulin clearance 8014
phenylbutazone 8014
phenylbutazone hydroxylation 8014
physiological disposition 8014
plasma levels 8014
plasma protein binding 8014
side reactions 8014
sodium clearance 8014

sodium-retaining effect 8014
urate clearance 8014
uricosuric effect 8014
water excretion 8014
PHOSPHOLINE
anticholinesterase activity 8022
blood-brain barrier 8022
morphine 8022
neuromuscular transmission 8022
respiration 8022
tertiary analog (217-AO) 8022
PHOSPHOLINE ANALOG (217-AO)
antagonistic action 8022
anticholinesterase activity 8022
central respiratory control 8022
lipoid solubility 8022
morphine respiratory arrest 8022
neuromuscular transmission 8022
PICROTOXIN
anticonvulsants 8034
clonic seizures 8008
8034
CNS antiextensor excitants 8034
reserpine 8034
salamander 8008
spinal cord transection 8008
tonic extensor seizures 8034
tonic seizures 8008
PIPRADOL
antiextensor seizure activity 8034
CNS stimulants 8034
locomotor responses 8033
post-treatment counts 8033
pretreatment counts 8033
PITUITARY-ADRENAL SYSTEM
acute stress 8010
adrenal ascorbic acid 8010
adrenocorticotrophic activity 8010
chlorpromazine pretreatment 8010
exogenous ACTH 8010
reserpine pretreatment 8010
POTASSIUM
calcium 8043
erythrocyte transpost 8043
human erythrocytes 8043
inosine response 8043
magnesium 8043
ouabain response 8043
strontium 8043
PROCHLORPERAZINE
MET 8009
spontaneous motor activity 8009
PROMAZINE
MET 8009
spontaneous motor activity 8009
PROMETHAZINE
MET 8009
spontaneous motor activity 8009
PROTEIN,PLASMA
albumin 8011
curarization level 8011
electrophoretic fractions 8011
gamma-globulin 8011
refractory subjects 8011
d-tubocurarine binding properties 8011
PRURITUS
experimental origin 8036
human subjects 8036
morphine treatment 8036
papaverine treatment 8036
pathological origin 8036
PURINES
benzimidazoles 8013
competitive metabolite reversal 8013
pyrazolo-(3,4d)pyrimidines 8013
quinoxalines 8013
virus inhibition 8013
virus tissue culture 8013
PYRIDYLACETYLCHOLINE
acetylcholine 8020
blood pressure 8020
cholinesterases 8020
edrophonium 8020
enzyme studies 8020
ganglionic transmission 8020
hexamethonium 8020
hydrolysis 8020
imidazoleacetylcholine 8020
neuromuscular transmission 8020
nictitating membrane 8020
respiration 8020
succinyldicholine 8020
d-tubocurarine 8020
PYRUVIC ACIDS, Beta-HALOGENATED
alpha-ketoglutarate oxidation 8012
analgesia 8012

atropine pretreatment 8012
cholinesterase inhibition 8012
cholinomimetic actions 8012
homogenate systems 8012
lacrimation 8012
malate oxidation 8012
pyruvate oxidation 8012
salivation 8012
substrate oxidation 8012
toxic signs 8012

QUATERNARY AMMONIUM COMPOUNDS
dissociation constant 8017
intestinal absorption 8017
mucosal permeability 8017

RAUWOLSCINE
adrenergic blocking action 8045
blood pressure 8045
cardiovascular system 8045
epinephrine 8045
heart rate 8045
hypotensive action 8045
morphine 8045
nictitating membrane 8045
peripheral blood flow 8045
respiration 8045
REACTION TIME
d-amphetamine 8035
human subjects 8035
learning rate 8035
meprobamate 8035
phenobarbital 8035
REFLEXES
dorsal root stimulation 8029
peroneal nerve stimulation 8029
spinal segmental distribution 8029
ventral root discharges 8029
zoxazolamine (flexin) 8029
RENAL FUNCTION
chloride 8014
clearance studies 8014
inulin 8014
phenylbutazone metabolites 8014
sodium 8014
urate 8014
RESERPINE
acute stress 8010
adrenal ascorbic acid
anticonvulsants 8034
approach responses 8032
auditory stimuli 8032
autonomic nervous system 8032
A-V rhythm 8026
avoidance latency 8032
CAR blockade 8032
cardiac output 8026
cardiovascular effect 8026
8027
CNS stimulants 8034
conditioned avoidance
responses (CAR) 8032
escape response 8032
exogenous ACTH 8010
heart-lung preparation 8026
8027
intraventricular injection 8032
levarterenol release 8027
mammalian heart 8027
methamphetamine reversal 8032
pattern discrimination 8032
pentobarbital failure 8027
pituitary adreno-
corticotrophic activity 8010
positive inotropic effect 8027
rate-decreasing effect 8026
S-A rhythm 8026
systemic administration 8032
veratramine 8027
visual stimuli 8032
RESPIRATION
anesthesia 8047
artificial respiration 8047
atropine pretreatment 8022
central control 8022
cholinesterase activity 8022
cyanide 8045
diaphragmatic contractions 8022
DMPP 8045
imidazole-acylcholine esters 8019
morphine influence 8045
morphine-induced arrest 8022
nornicotine metabolism 8042
pentylenetetrazole 8045
phentolamine pretreatment 8022
phospholine 8022
phospholine analog (217-AO) 8022
phrenic nerve action
potentials 8022
rauwolscine 8045

ryanodine 8047
spastic arrest 8047
tachypnea 8045
RYANODINE
acute toxicity 8047
ATP 8025
atropine 8025
blood pressure 8047
caffeine 8025
calcium concentration 8025
cardiac decompensation 8047
cardiac glycosides 8047
circulatory failure 8047
contracture 8025
creatine phosphate 8025
cyanide 8025
dinitrophenol 8025
epinephrine 8025
8047
heart-lung preparation 8047
hypotension 8047
irreversibility 8025
magnesium concentration 8025
mammalian species 8047
papaverine 8025
pharmacological actions 8047
procyclidine 8025
pyrilamine 8025
rabbit duodenal strips 8025
respiration 8047
skeletal muscle contracture 8047
muscle smooth 8025
sodium pyrophosphate 8025
spastic muscle rigidity 8047
vasopressor agents 8047

SALAMANDER
behavior 8008
convulsant drugs 8008
electrical activity 8008
neurological tests 8008
neuromuscular system 8008
SEROTONIN
conditioned avoidance responses 8032
iproniazid 8032
reserpine 8032
SPINAL CORD
motoneurone activity 8029
segmental reflexes 8029
spinal cats 8029
zoxazolamine (flexin) 8029
STATISTICAL EVALUATION
CNS depressants 8033
CNS stimulants 8033
crossover techniques 8033
individual animal differences 8033
locomotor responses 8033
STRESS
adrenal ascorbic acid 8010
chlorpromazine 8010
pituitary adreno-corticotrophic activity 8010
reserpine 8010
STRYCHNINE
anticonvulsants 8034
clonic seizures 8008
8034
CNS antiextensor excitants 8034
reflex arcs 8008
reserpine 8034
salamander 8008
spinal cord transection 8008
tonic extensor seizures 8034
SYMPATHOMIMETIC AMINES
ephedrine accelerator action 8026
l-epinephrine accelerator action 8026
heart-lung preparation 8026
heart rate 8026
reserpine antiaccelerator action 8026

TANNIC ACID
hepatotoxicity 8037
pentobarbital sleeping time 8037
TEMPERATURE
ouabain 8028
positive inotropic action 8028
ventricle strips 8028
sym-TETRACHLOROETHANE
hepatotoxicity 8037
lethal potency 8037
TETRACHLOROETHYLENE
hepatotoxicity 8037
lethal potency 8037
TETRAETHYLAMMONIUM 8047
ryanodine hypotension 8047

TETRAETHYLPYROPHOSPHATE
ambenonium analogs 8023
antidotal pretreatment 8023
atropine-like antidotes 8038
toxicity 8038
TETRAMETHYLSUCCINIMIDE (PM1090)
anticonvulsants 8034
clonic seizures 8034
CNS antiextensor excitants 8034
reserpine 8034
tonic extensor seizures 8034
THIAZOLIDONE DERIVATIVES
irritancy 8044
local anesthetic activity 8044
systemic toxicity 8044
THIOBARBITAL
blood-brain barrier 8015
lipid solubility 8015
THIOBARBITURATES
brain concentration 8015
brain penetration 8015
hypnotic effects 8015
lipid solubility 8015
plasma concentration 8015
THIOPENTAL
blood-brain barrier 8015
lipid solubility 8015
THIOPHENOBARBITAL
blood-brain barrier 8015
lipid solubility 8015
TISSUE CULTURE,VIRUS
adenine reversal 8013
adenovirus 8013
chemical inhibition 8013
cytopathogenic effects 8013
folic acid reversal 8013
growth curves 8013
guanine reversal 8013
influenza A 8013
inoculation mortality 8013
poliomyelitis 8013
purines 8013
TRANSMISSION,GANGLIONIC
pyridylacetylcholine 8020
TRANSMISSION,NEUROMUSCULAR
atropine pretreatment 8022
cholinesterase activity 8022
phospholine 8022
phospholine analog (217-AO) 8022
pyridylacetylcholine 8020
1,1,1-TRICHLOROETHANE
hepatotoxicity 8037
lethal potency 8037
1,1,2-TRICHLOROETHANE
hepatotoxicity 8037
lethal potency 8037
TRICHLOROETHYLENE
hepatotoxicity 8037
lethal potency 8037
TRIFLUOPERAZINE
MET 8009
spontaneous motor activity 8009
TRIPELENAMINE
antipruritic activity 8036
human subjects 8036
d-TUBOCURARINE
curarization level 8011
plasma levels 8011
plasma protein fractions 8011
protein binding 8011
refractory subjects 8011

URICOSURIC AGENTS
phenylbutazone metabolites 8014

VASOMOTOR SYSTEM
BITU 8004
hexamethonium 8004
VASOPRESSOR AGENTS
absolute refractory period 8005
A-V conduction 8005
blood pressure 8005
cardiac arrhythmia 8005
cardiac effects 8005
diastolic threshold 8005
tachyphylaxis 8005
VASOPRESSOR RESPONSES
anesthetized rabbit 8006
epinephrine 8006
histamine 8006

ZOXAZOLAMINE
blood pressure 8029
polysynaptic pathways 8029
spinal segmental reflexes 8029
ventral root discharges 8029

AUTHOR INDEX

Abreu B E 8046
Aladjemoff L 8011
Alexander W M 8046
Arnold A 8023

Banda E 8006
Beecher H K 8036
Begley R W 8046
Benigni J P 8009
Bertino J R 8029
Bohner B 8034
Borland J K 8044
Brand L 8015
Brodie B B 8014 8015 8017
Brooks C McC 8005
Burns J J 8014 8015
Busch H 8012

Campomanes C I 8015
Cervoni P 8029
Chen G 8034
Clark W C 8016

Daniel A I 8007 8039
Dikstein S 8011

Eckhardt E T 8019
Elder C J 8009
Evans E A 8037
Ezz E A 8010

Flanigan J V 8009
Frank M 8012
Fuentes J 8026

Geiger L E 8029
Gilbert J L 8005
Govier W M 8019 8020
Gutman A B 8014

Heidenreich O P A 8018
Hendershot L C 8004
Hillyard I W 8025
Hine C H 8037
Hofstee B H J 8021
Hogben C A M 8017
Hollinshead A C 8013
Hoppe J O 8023 8044
Hucker H B 8042
Hulpieu H R 8016

Irwin S 8033

Job C 8022
John E R 8032
Jones W R 8046

Kahn J B Jr 8043
Karczmar A G 8038
Kessler R H 8018
Kirchner F K 8023
Knebel C M 8041
Koelle G B 8040 8045
Kornetsky C 8035
Krayer O 8026 8027
Kruck F 8018
Kuperman A S 8031

Lands A M 8023
Lange G 8005
Larson P S 8042
Levy B 8045
Long J P 8038
Lozano R 8018
Luduena F P 8044

Macmullen J A 8041
Macris S G 8036
Mahfouz M 8010
Mannering G J 8030
Maren T H 8049
Mark L C 8015
Martin W R 8012
Maxwell R A 8007 8024 8039
Mershon J 8019 8020
Monteleone F 8029

Nair P V 8012
Naranjo P 8006

Paasonen M K 8027
Papper E M 8015
Paton B C 8014
Peters J J 8008
Pitts R F 8018
Plaa G L 8037
Plummer A J 8007 8024 8039
Polevoy I 8005
Powers T H 8008
Procita L 8025 8047

Rajapurkar M V 8040
Richards A B 8046
Ross S D 8007 8024 8039
Roth F E 8019
Rubin A A 8019 8020

Sanyal P N 8028
Saunders P R 8028
Schanker L S 8017
Schaumann W 8022
Schneider F 8039
Seifter J 8041
Shafrir E 8011
Slabok M 8033
Smith G M 8036
Smith P K 8013

Tabachnick I I A 8019 8020
Takemori A E 8030
Taylor D W 8018
Tedeschi D H 8009
Thomas G 8033
Tocco D J 8017
Trousof N 8015
Tschirgi R D 8032

Vonderahe A R 8008

Walkenstein S S 8041
Wang S C 8048
Weaver L C 8046
Wenzel B M 8032

Yeager J C 8009
Yü T F 8014